CONTENTS

D0181918

Frommer's®

Las Vegas

2011

by Rick Garman

Wiley Publishing, Inc.

Published by:
Wiley Publishing, Inc.
111 River St.
Hoboken, NJ 07030-5774

ISBN 978-0-470-63866-8 (paper); ISBN 978-0-470-87720-3 (paper); ISBN 978-0-470-94577-3 (ebk); ISBN 978-0-470-94583-4 (ebk); ISBN 978-0-470-94584-1 (ebk)

Editor: Naomi P. Kraus
Production Editor: Heather Wilcox
Cartographer: Elizabeth Puhl
Photo Editors: Richard Fox, Alden Gewirtz
Cover Photo Editor: Richard Fox
Design and Layout by Vertigo Design
Graphics and Prepress by Wiley Indianapolis Composition Services

Front cover photo: Neon sign on the exterior of the Golden Gate Casino ©Alan Schein Photography / Corbis

Back cover photo: *Left*: A roulette wheel ©Comstock Images / Getty Images. *Middle*: A woman hiking in Valley of Fire State Park ©Brad Wrobleski / Masterfile. *Right*: The fountains of the Bellagio, with Paris Las Vegas in the background ©Marla Holden / Alamy Images.

For information on our other products and services or to obtain technical support, please contact our Customer Care Department within the U.S. at 877/762-2974, outside the U.S. at 317/572-3993 or fax 317/572-4002.

Wiley also publishes its books in a variety of electronic formats. Some content that appears in print may not be available in electronic formats.
Manufactured in the United States of America

5 4 3 2 1

LIST OF MAPS

ABOUT THE AUTHOR

Rick Garman began visiting Las Vegas as soon as he was not barred from doing so by pesky things like laws. He started writing about the city in 1997 when he and his best friend Mary Herczog were invited to write *Frommer's Las Vegas*. He went on to create *Vegas4Visitors.com*, one of the most respected Las Vegas travel resources on the Web and has appeared in various outlets as a self-proclaimed Vegas expert, although most of that expertise has been gained sitting at a slot machine with a glazed look in his eye while mumbling incoherently to himself. When not gambling away his life savings, Rick lives in Los Angeles and works in the entertainment industry.

A NOTE FROM THE AUTHOR

Mary Herczog wrote this book starting with the 1998 edition that we co-authored, our first collaboration as professionals but certainly not our first as best friends. It was not long after that book hit the shelves that Mary was first diagnosed with breast cancer. Over the next dozen years, Mary faced her illness with a kind of aplomb that most people found either inspiring or confounding, as she chose to focus less on whatever treatment she was undergoing and more on what fantastic meal she was going to get to eat on her next trip to Vegas. She wrote about what she called her "tribulations" in a series of articles for the *Los Angeles Times* and later on her website *CancerChick.com* as a way of demystifying the process, hoping that it might make it a little less scary for anyone else that might be going through the same thing. Through it all, she continued to write her guide books to Vegas and New Orleans and other destinations, which she loved doing partly out of her adoration of travel in general and partly out of her incredible knack for being able to tell people what to do and usually be right.

Mary Herczog died on February 16, 2010, surrounded by her family, her friends, and her dogs, exactly as she wanted it to be . . . if it had to be at all. About a week earlier, she'd asked me to take over this book and I am both humbled and honored to do so. Even though my name is on the title page, this is and always will be her book. Viva Las Vegas, Mary . . . the city will not be the same without you.

HOW TO CONTACT US

In researching this book, we discovered many wonderful places—hotels, restaurants, shops, and more. We're sure you'll find others. Please tell us about them, so we can share the information with your fellow travelers in upcoming editions. If you were disappointed with a recommendation, we'd love to know that, too. Please write to:

Frommer's Las Vegas 2011
Wiley Publishing, Inc. • 111 River St. • Hoboken, NJ 07030-5774
frommersfeedback@wiley.com

AN ADDITIONAL NOTE

Please be advised that travel information is subject to change at any time—and this is especially true of prices. We therefore suggest that you write or call ahead for confirmation when making your travel plans. The authors, editors, and publisher cannot be held responsible for the experiences of readers while traveling. Your safety is important to us, however, so we encourage you to stay alert and be aware of your surroundings. Keep a close eye on cameras, purses, and wallets, all favorite targets of thieves and pickpockets.

FROMMER'S STAR RATINGS, ICONS & ABBREVIATIONS

Every hotel, restaurant, and attraction listing in this guide has been ranked for quality, value, service, amenities, and special features using a **star-rating system.** In country, state, and regional guides, we also rate towns and regions to help you narrow down your choices and budget your time accordingly. Hotels and restaurants are rated on a scale of zero (recommended) to three stars (exceptional). Attractions, shopping, nightlife, towns, and regions are rated according to the following scale: zero stars (recommended), one star (highly recommended), two stars (very highly recommended), and three stars (must-see).

In addition to the star-rating system, we also use **seven feature icons** that point you to the great deals, in-the-know advice, and unique experiences that separate travelers from tourists. Throughout the book, look for:

Special finds—those places only insiders know about

Fun facts—details that make travelers more informed and their trips more fun

Kids—best bets for kids and advice for the whole family

Special moments—those experiences that memories are made of

Overrated—places or experiences not worth your time or money

Insider tips—great ways to save time and money

Great values—where to get the best deals

The following abbreviations are used for credit cards:

| **AE** | American Express | **DISC** | Discover | **V** | Visa |
| **DC** | Diners Club | **MC** | MasterCard | | |

TRAVEL RESOURCES AT FROMMERS.COM

Frommer's travel resources don't end with this guide. Frommer's website, **www.frommers.com,** has travel information on more than 4,000 destinations. We update features regularly, giving you access to the most current trip-planning information and the best airfare, lodging, and car-rental bargains. You can also listen to podcasts, connect with other Frommers.com members through our active-reader forums, share your travel photos, read blogs from guidebook editors and fellow travelers, and much more.

THE BEST OF
LAS VEGAS

1

The point about [Las Vegas], which both its critics and its admirers overlook, is that it's wonderful and awful simultaneously. So one loves it and detests it at the same time.
—David Spanier, WELCOME TO THE PLEASUREDOME: INSIDE LAS VEGAS

A s often as you might have seen it on TV or in a movie, nothing can prepare you for your first sight of Las Vegas. The skyline is hyper-reality, a mélange of the Statue of Liberty, giant lions, a pyramid, and a sphinx, and preternaturally glittering buildings. At night, it's so bright, you can actually get disoriented—and suffer from a sensory overload that can reduce you to hapless tears or fits of giggles. And that's without setting foot inside a casino, where the shouts from the craps tables, computer-generated noise from the slots, and the general roar combine into either the greatest adrenaline rush of your life or the ninth pit of hell.

Las Vegas is a true original; there is nothing else like it in the world. In other cities, hotels are built near the major attractions. Here, the hotels *are* the major attractions. What other city has a skyline made up of buildings from other cities' skylines?

PREVIOUS PAGE: **Fountain of the Gods at Caesars Palace.** ABOVE: **The Bellagio fountain show at night.**

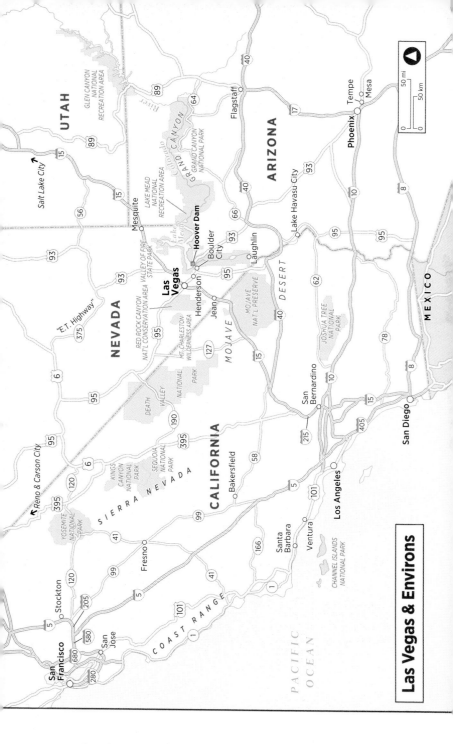

Las Vegas & Environs

Once you get to Vegas, you'll want to come back again, if only to make sure you didn't dream it all. It's not just the casinos with their nonstop action and sound, the almost-blinding lights, or the buildings that seek to replicate some other reality (Paris, Venice, New York, ancient Egypt). It's not the mountains of shrimp at the buffets, the wedding chapels that will gladly unite two total strangers in holy wedlock, or the promise of free money. It's the whole package. It's Frank and Dino and Sammy. It's Elvis—the Fat Years. It's Britney and Paris behaving scandalously at nightclubs. It's volcanoes and magic shows and cocktail waitresses dressed in short-short Roman togas. It's cheesy, sleazy, and artificial and wholly, completely unique. It's wonderful. It's awful. It's wonderfully awful and awfully wonderful.

Las Vegas can be whatever a visitor wants, and for a few days, a visitor can be whatever he or she wants. Just be prepared to leave all touchstones with reality behind. Here, you will rise at noon and gorge on endless amounts of rich food at 3am. You will watch your money grow or (more likely) shrink. You will watch fountains dance and pirates fight sexy showgirls. This is not a cultural vacation, okay? Save the thoughts of museums and historical sights for the real New York, Egypt, Paris, and Venice. Vegas is about fun. Go have some. Go have too much. It won't be hard.

The Vegas of the Rat Pack years does not exist anymore. Even as ancient civilizations are replicated, "old," in Vegas terms, is anything over a decade. Indeed, thanks to teardowns and renovations, there is virtually nothing original left on the Strip. In a way, that is both admirable and ghastly, and it's also part of what makes Vegas so *Vegas*. What other city can completely shed its skin in such a short amount of time? But as much as one might mourn the loss of such landmarks as the Sands, one has to admit that time marches on, and Vegas has to keep pace. Nostalgia for the vanished does not mean you can't enjoy what turns up in its place. Even as you might sneer at the gaudy tastelessness of it all, you have to admit that what's out there is remarkable.

And when it's all lit up at night . . . well, even those who have lived here for years agree there is nothing like the sight of the Strip in all its evening glory. Everything is in lights in Vegas: hotels, casinos, 7-Elevens, the airport's parking garage. Stand still long enough and they'll probably cover *you* in neon.

Oh, the gambling? Yep, there's plenty of that. Let's not kid ourselves: Gambling is the main attraction of Vegas. The rest—the celebrity-chef restaurants, the shows, the cartoonish buildings—is so much window dressing to lure you and your money to the city. But even a nongambler can have a perfectly fine time in Vegas, though the lure of countless slot machines has tempted even the most puritanical of souls in their day.

The days of an inexpensive Las Vegas vacation are mostly a memory, although it's amazing what a global economic meltdown can do to hotel rates. The cheap buffets and meal deals still exist, and rooms are certainly cheaper (as a general rule) than they were a few years ago, but it is shockingly easy to drain your bank account without even stepping foot inside a casino.

However, free drinks are still handed to anyone lurking near a slot, and even if show tickets aren't in your budget, you won't lack for entertainment. Free lounges, some with singers or go-go dancers, abound, and the people-watching opportunities never disappoint. From the Armani-clad high rollers in the baccarat rooms to the polyester-sporting couples at the nickel slots, Vegas attracts a cross section of humanity.

Hang out with dolphins at the Mirage's Dolphin Habitat.

Yes, it's noisy and chaotic. Yes, it's really just Disneyland for adults. Yes, it's a shrine to greed and the love of filthy lucre. Yes, there is little ambience and even less "culture." Yes, someone lacking self-discipline can come to great grief. But in its own way, Vegas is every bit as amazing as the nearby Grand Canyon, and every bit as much a must see. It's one of the Seven Wonders of the Artificial World. And everyone should experience it at least once.

FROMMER'S favorite LAS VEGAS EXPERIENCES

- **Strolling on the Strip After Dark:** You haven't really seen Las Vegas until you've seen it at night. This neon wonderland is the world's greatest sound-and-light show. Begin at Luxor and work your way past the incredible hotels and their attractions. You'll pass the gotta-see-it-to-believe-it New York–New York on your way, and if your strength holds out, you will end at Circus Circus, where live acrobatic acts take place overhead while you gamble. Make plenty of stops en route to take in the *Sirens* show at Treasure Island, see The Mirage volcano erupt, take a photo of the full moon over the Eiffel Tower, and marvel at the choreographed water-fountain ballet at Bellagio.

- **Casino Hopping on the Strip:** The interior of each lavish hotel-casino is more outrageous and giggle inducing than the last. Just when you think they can't possibly top themselves, they do. From Venice to Paris, from New York City to the Manhattan-style chic of CityCenter, it is all, completely and uniquely, Las Vegas.

- **Spending an Evening in Glitter Gulch:** Set aside an evening to tour the Downtown hotels and take in the overhead light show of the **Fremont Street Experience** (p. 217). Unlike the lengthy and exhausting Strip, here you can hit a dozen casinos in about 5 minutes.

- **Bingeing at Buffets:** Many are no longer the very best of bargains, but there is something about the endless mounds of food that just scream "Vegas" to us. Our choices for the best in town are listed in "Best Dining Bets," later in this chapter.

- **Taking a Creative Adventures Tour:** Char Cruze, of **Creative Adventures** (*©* **702/893-2051;** www.creativeadventuresltd.net), provides personalized tours unlike anything offered by a commercial tour company, full of riveting stories and incredible facts about both natural and artificial local wonders. See p. 242.

- **Visiting the Dolphins at The Mirage:** This is a most un-Vegas experience. Watch these gorgeous mammals frolic in their cool blue pool. If you're really lucky, they'll play ball with you. See p. 221.

- **Playing Penny Slots:** Even the most budget-conscious traveler can gamble for hours. Penny slots used to be as rare as a non-silicone-enhanced show-girl, but now they're in all the major casinos. See chapter 8.

- **Shopping the Big-Three Casino Arcades:** Take what Napoleon called "the greatest drawing room in Europe," replicate it, add shops, and you've got the **Grand Canal Shoppes at The Venetian** (p. 290)—it's St. Mark's Square, complete with canals and working gondolas. It's now connected to its sister property, **The Palazzo,** where it is not themed, but is still quite impressive, with envy-inducing designer stores. Then there are **The Forum Shops at Caesars Palace** (p. 287), which replicate an ancient Roman streetscape, with classical piazzas and opulent fountains. Don't miss the scary audio-animatronic statues as they come to glorious, cheesy life. And while **Miracle Mile at Planet Hollywood** (p. 289) is now sort of a glitzy generic mall, the variety of shops makes it one of the better hotel shopping experiences.

- **Being Amazed by Cirque du Soleil's O, KÀ, and Mystère:** You haven't really seen Cirque du Soleil until you've seen it performed in a showroom equipped with state-of-the-art sound and lighting systems and a seemingly infinite budget for sets, costumes, and high-tech special effects. It's an enchantment. See chapter 10.

- **Seeing Your Favorite Headliners:** As soon as you arrive in town, pick up a show guide and see who's playing during your stay. For the top showrooms, see chapter 10.

Glide on a gondola through the Grand Canal Shoppes at The Venetian.

Elephant Rock, Valley of Fire State Park.

o **Finding the Worst Lounge Shows:** Some feel this is the ultimate Vegas experience. Be sure to watch out for **Mr. Cook E. Jarr.** See chapter 10 for some ideas.

o **Red Rock Canyon and Valley of Fire State Park:** No money-grubbing businessperson caused these awe-inspiring desert rock formations to be built, and they will be standing long after Vegas. See p. 352.

best **HOTEL BETS**

o **Best for Conventioneers/Business Travelers:** The **Las Vegas Hilton,** 3000 Paradise Rd. (© **888/732-7117;** www.lvhilton.com), adjacent to the Las Vegas Convention Center and the setting for many conventions, offers extensive facilities that include a full business center. It's also a stop on the monorail, making access to the Strip easier than ever. See p. 134.

o **Best Luxury Resorts:** A visit to **Encore Las Vegas,** 3131 Las Vegas Blvd. S. (© **888/320-7125;** www.encorelasvegas.com), may alter your definition of a boutique luxury hotel. Certainly it's too big to be truly "boutique," but it feels intimate, ready to pamper your every whim, and without a doubt luxurious. You might, however, want something a little more familiar, and for that, you must go to the **Four Seasons,** 3960 Las Vegas Blvd. S. (© **877/632-5000;** www.fourseasons.com), because experience running luxury resorts around the world makes them the only true claimant to the throne within Vegas. See p. 82.

o **Best Resort for the Indecisive:** So you want a proper resort getaway, but you don't want to be too far from Vegas action. **Red Rock Resort,** 11011 W. Charleston Rd. (© **866/767-7773;** www.redrocklasvegas.com), is a smashing facility that has it all: luxe rooms, an excellent pool area, good and relatively inexpensive food, fab decor, and a breathtaking view of the red rocks of the canyon. Many a well-heeled celeb has kept a low profile by the pool. See p. 137.

o **Best Archetypically Las Vegas Hotel:** To be honest, these days there aren't any. Las Vegas hotels are one and all doing such massive face-lifts that the archetype is mostly a memory. Still, despite some major changes, **Caesars Palace,** 3570 Las Vegas Blvd. S. (✆ 877/427-7243; www.caesarspalace. com), will probably continue to embody the excess, the romance and, well, downright silliness that used to characterize Vegas—and to a certain extent still does. See p. 204.

o **Best Non-Vegas Vegas Hotel:** New to Vegas in 2009, the **Mandarin Oriental,** 3752 Las Vegas Blvd. S. (✆ 888/881-9578; www.mandarinoriental. com), is a virtual oasis in a sea of Sin City insanity. From the breathtaking 23rd floor Sky Lobby to the elegantly appointed rooms to the world-class service, this is a hotel that sits apart, and in many ways above, the din. But if you want the din, it's just a few feet away outside the front door. See p. 83.

o **Best Swimming Pools:** There are acres of water park fun at **Mandalay Bay,** 3950 Las Vegas Blvd. S. (✆ 877/632-7800; www.mandalaybay. com)—wave pool, lazy river, beach, regular swimming pools, even its own open-air casino . . . no wonder they check IDs carefully to make sure only official guests enter. Everyone wants to swim and splash here. See p. 88. If you can't, you won't be disappointed by the amorphously shaped pools, with water fountains and slides, plus a rather festive atmosphere, at **The Mirage,** 3400 Las Vegas Blvd. S. (✆ 800/627-6667; www.mirage.com). See p. 112. But if you've ever longed to swim at Hearst Castle, **Bellagio,** 3600 Las Vegas Blvd. S. (✆ 888/987-6667; www.bellagio.com), with six swimming pools in a neoclassical Italian garden setting (and a more hushed, chic ambience), is for you. See p. 101. Then again, the pool at

One of several pools at Mandalay Bay.

Lobby of Caesars Palace.

Green Valley Ranch Resort, 2300 Paseo Verde Pkwy. (at I-215), Henderson (© **866/782-9487;** www.greenvalleyranchresort.com), with its foliage, beach, and everything else, may have them both beat. But its distant location (in Henderson) takes it out of the running. But only just. See p. 137.

o **Best Spas/Health Clubs:** We only wish our own gym were as handsomely equipped as the one at the Canyon Ranch Spa in **The Venetian,** 3355 Las Vegas Blvd. S. (© **888/283-6423;** www.venetian.com), which also has a number of other high-priced amenities on which you can blow your blackjack winnings. See p. 107. We are also partial to the full complement of machines at the health club at **Bellagio,** 3600 Las Vegas Blvd. S. (© **888/987-6667;** www.bellagio.com), probably the best-equipped club of all. Attentive attendants, a well-stocked locker room, and comfortable lounges in which to rest up after your workout are other pluses. For a straight spa experience, the **Spa at Encore,** 3121 Las Vegas Blvd. S. (© **888/320-7125;** www.encorelasvegas.com), is a 70,000-square-foot oasis for the mind, body, and spirit, from its gorgeous Moroccan-infused design themes to its full menu of pampering delights. See p. 121.

o **Best Hotel Dining:** Foodies can't miss the chance to eat French food from the hands of a true master at **Joël Robuchon at the Mansion,** in the MGM Grand (© **702/891-7358**)—if, of course, you don't mind taking out a small bank loan to fund that gastronomic venture. Also in the MGM Grand is **L'Atelier de Joël Robuchon** (© **702/891-7925**), a more casual and somewhat cheaper experience, but just as lauded. Otherwise, you can work up a good case of gout trying all the haute-cuisine options at Bellagio or Aria, both of which have restaurants by Todd English (**Olives,** © **866/259-7111;** and **Todd English P.U.B.,** © **702/489-8080**) and Julian Serrano (**Picasso,** © **866/259-7111;** and **Julian Serrano,** © **877/230-2742**). Between them, the two hotels have eight James Beard Foundation Award–winning chefs on staff. Wynn Las Vegas has brought in a number of name-brand chefs, including Alex Strada (**Alex,** © **888/352-3463**) and Paul

Bartolotta (**Bartolotta Ristorante di Mare,** © 888/352-3463). The Venetian isn't too far behind, with restaurants from Emeril Lagasse (**Delmonico Steakhouse,** © 702/414-3737), Joachim Splichal (**Pinot Brasserie,** © 702/414-8888), Mario Batali (**B&B Ristorante,** © 702/266-9977), and a version of Thomas Keller's bistro **Bouchon** (© 702/414-6200). See chapter 6.

○ **Best for 20-Somethings to Baby Boomers: Palms Casino Resort,** 4321 W. Flamingo Rd. (© 866/942-7777; www.palms.com), is the single most happening hotel for the hip and hip-hop sets. See p. 113. The **Hard Rock Hotel & Casino,** 4455 Paradise Rd. (© 800/473-7625; www.hardrockhotel.com), bills itself as the world's "first rock-'n'-roll hotel and casino" and "Vegas for a new generation." See p. 130.

The Venetian's Canyon Ranch Spa.

○ **Best Interiors:** *Texture* is the watchword of interior design these days and nowhere in Vegas does it as dramatically or as elegantly as **Aria Las Vegas,** 3730 Las Vegas Blvd. S. (© 866/359-7757; www.arialasvegas.com). Stone, wood, glass, fabric, metal, and surprising natural and artificial light combine with art from masters such as Maya Lin to turn the inside spaces into a visual feast.

○ **Best for Families:** The classic choice is **Circus Circus Hotel & Casino,** 2880 Las Vegas Blvd. S. (© 877/434-9175; www.circuscircus.com), with ongoing circus acts, a vast video-game arcade, a carnival midway, and a full amusement park. See p. 127. Less aged, and less hectic, **Mandalay Bay,** 3950 Las Vegas Blvd. S. (© 877/632-7800; www.mandalaybay.com), is a more modern choice, right for families because you can gain access to both the guest rooms and the pool area (itself fun for kids, with a beach, a wave pool, and a lazy river) without trotting through the casino. See p. 88.

○ **Best Rooms off the Strip:** Again, we love **Red Rock Resort,** 11011 W. Charleston Rd. (© 866/767-7773; www.redrocklasvegas.com), where the smashing rooms include lush bathrooms and beds that are like sleeping in a bowl of whipped cream—both offering places to relax while watching big flatscreen TVs. See p. 137.

○ **Best Rooms on the Strip:** We need to break this down. If one is talking actual suites, then **THEhotel,** 3950 Las Vegas Blvd. S. (© 877/632-7800; www.thehotelatmandalaybay.com), wins the day, with its one-bedroom, could-be-a-great-apartment-in-Manhattan sophisticated wonders. See p.

93. Best "suites" (because no matter how the hotel bills them, these accommodations are really just one big room) are clearly the 700-square-foot extravaganzas at **The Venetian,** 3355 Las Vegas Blvd. S. (© 888/283-6423; www.venetian.com), and **The Palazzo,** 3325 Las Vegas Blvd. S. (© 877/883-6423; www.palazzolasvegas.com), with separate sitting and bedroom areas, full of all sorts of special details. See p. 105. Best "room" goes to the **Wynn Las Vegas,** 3131 Las Vegas Blvd. S. (© 888/320-9966; www.wynnlasvegas.com), and its sister hotel **Encore,** 3121 Las Vegas Blvd. S. (© 888/320-7125; www.encorelasvegas.com), where the rooms are quite big, the bathrooms are not far behind, the beds are plush, the TVs (plural!) are flatscreen, and the tubs are deep. See p. 121. The upgraded "Go" rooms at the **Flamingo,** 3555 Las Vegas Blvd S. (© 800/732-2111; www.flamingolasvegas.com), pay homage to its venerable past with vintage photos and hot pink accents—plus various luxuries and other style touches that make them ring-a-ding! See p. 109.

o **Best Rooms Downtown:** The rooms at the **Golden Nugget,** 129 E. Fremont St. (© 800/846-5336; www.goldennugget.com), have gotten some much-needed love that have returned them to the top of the heap, especially those in the newer Rush Tower (p. 140), but don't forget about the lovely **Main Street Station,** 200 N. Main St. (© 800/465-0711; www.main streetcasino.com), with lots to offer both in the rooms and beyond. It has done a terrific job of renovating an older space, boasting solidly good restaurants and surprisingly nice rooms for an inexpensive price. See p. 144.

o **Best Bathrooms:** This honor goes to **THEhotel,** 3950 Las Vegas Blvd. S. (© 877/632-7800; www.thehotelatmandalaybay.com), where each good-size marble bathroom features a large glass shower, a separate water closet, a flatscreen TV, and a soaking tub so deep that the water comes up to your

The living area in a suite at THEhotel.

11

chin. It's a wonder anyone ever leaves to go to the casino. See p. 93. Not far behind is **Wynn Las Vegas,** 3131 Las Vegas Blvd. S. (𝄢 **888/320-9966;** www.wynnlasvegas.com), which offers a similar layout, including a plasma TV and deep, long tub, plus lemongrass-scented amenities and silky robes to cradle you afterward. See p. 123.

Dining room at L'Atelier de Joël Robuchon.

o **Best Noncasino Hotel: Four Seasons,** 3960 Las Vegas Blvd. S. (𝄢 **877/632-5000;** www.fourseasons.com; p. 82), used to win this category, but now it's a tie with **THEhotel,** 3950 Las Vegas Blvd. S. (𝄢 **877/632-7800;** www.thehotelatmandalaybay.com; p. 93). It can't be a coincidence that both are found around Mandalay Bay. Once you've experienced the Four Seasons' quiet good taste, superior service and pampering, and the serenity of their noncasino property, or the sophistication and elegance of THEhotel, it's hard to go back to traditional Vegas hotels. But should you want the best of both worlds, you need only pass through one door to have access to Mandalay Bay and all its traditional Vegas hotel accouterments, including that missing casino. Coming in a close second is the **Mandarin Oriental,** 3752 Las Vegas Blvd. S. (𝄢 **888/881-9578;** www.mandarinoriental.com), the first Vegas entry from the luxury Asian hotelier. They spared no expense in bringing the luxe to the desert, and it shows in details both big (check out those floor-to-ceiling window views) to small (we love how everyone bows toward you!).

o **Best Casinos:** Our favorite places to gamble are anywhere we might win. But we also like the casinos in **Caesars Palace** (as close to "classic Vegas" as you're going to find on the Strip, while refreshingly up-to-date; p. 104), **New York–New York** (some of the Gotham detail has gone away, but it's still silly in a good way—it almost makes losing fun; p. 92); and **Planet Hollywood** (probably the liveliest, most modern gambling space in town; p. 114).

o **Best Views:** The top floor rooms of **Aria Las Vegas,** 3730 Las Vegas Blvd. S. (𝄢 **866/359-7757;** www.arialasvegas.com; p. 84 rise above the others on the Strip and, unsurprisingly, offer up the best views of the glittery surroundings, while the top floors in the **Wynn Las Vegas,** 3131 Las Vegas Blvd. S. (𝄢 **888/320-9966;** www.wynnlasvegas.com), and **The Palazzo,** 3325 Las Vegas Blvd. S. (𝄢 **866/263-3001;** www.palazzolasvegas.

com), come mighty darn close to reaching Aria's heights. See p. 105. If you are lucky, your room at **Red Rock Resort,** 11011 W. Charleston Rd. (© **866/767-7773;** www.redrocklasvegas.com), will overlook those very same red rocks, though at some distance. See p. 137.

best **DINING BETS**

A number of celebrity chefs are cooking in Vegas, awakening us to the opinion that Vegas's rep for lackluster restaurants is no longer deserved.

○ **Best Restaurant to Blow Your Money On:** You could lighten your wallet at the craps table—and why not?—or you could spend that same amount, and take a lot longer doing so, exalting in the culinary work being done at **Joël Robuchon at the Mansion** (© **702/891-7925;** p. 156), in the MGM Grand, where you will have a once-in-a-lifetime meal. Somewhat less in the stratosphere, but still plenty costly, are **Alex** (© **888/352-3463;** p. 180) and **Paul Bartolotta's** (© **888/352-3463;** p. 181) eponymous places in Wynn Las Vegas, not to mention **L'Atelier de Joël Robuchon** (© **702/891-7925;** p. 157), the master chef's less-formal venue at MGM Grand that won the James Beard Foundation Award for Best New Restaurant 2007. Meals come dear at all five places, but each is turning out works of edible art, from four different inspired sources of creation. To us, this is what Vegas indulgence is all about, and the memories make us much happier than our losses at the table.

○ **Best All-Around Restaurant:** Given our druthers, we are hard-pressed to choose between **Sinatra,** in Encore Las Vegas (© **702/770-3463;** p. 182), which transcends its subtle Chairman of the Board theme with

The bistro dishes at Bouchon are exquisitely prepared.

The "wine goddesses" of Aureole fetch bottles from the restaurant's giant wine tower.

some of the freshest, liveliest food on the Strip; and **Rosemary's Restaurant**, 8125 W. Sahara Ave. (✆ **702/869-2251;** p. 192), a 20-minute drive off the Strip—and worth twice as much effort—for some Southern-influenced cooking. Each of these may well put the work of those many high-profile chefs, so prominently featured all over town, to shame. Speaking of high-profile chefs, we have just sworn allegiance to Thomas Keller's **Bouchon** (✆ **702/414-6200;** p. 172), in Venezia, at The Venetian. Keller may be the best chef in America, and while this is simply his take on classic bistro food, you should never underestimate the joys of simple food precisely prepared. We also never ever turn down a chance to eat what Julian Serrano is making over at **Picasso** (✆ **866/259-7111;** p. 170), at Bellagio.

o **Best Inexpensive Meal: Capriotti's,** 322 W. Sahara Ave. (✆ **702/474-0229;** p. 185), serves monster submarine sandwiches. It roasts beef and turkey on the premises and assembles it (or cold cuts, or even vegetables) into delicious well-stuffed sandwiches, ranging in size from 9 to 20 inches, and most of them are under $10. We never leave town without one or two.

o **Best Buffet:** On the Strip, it's **Le Village Buffet** (in Paris Las Vegas, ✆ **888/266-5687;** p. 203), where the stations break from standard form by adhering to regional French food specialties (from places such as Provence, Alsace, and Burgundy), and the results are much better than average. Though not cheap, this is a reasonable substitute for an even more costly fancy meal. If you want a little more traditional buffet—as in, one not devoted to one particular cuisine—**Wynn Las Vegas** (in Wynn Las Vegas; ✆ **702/770-3463**) is terrific all the way, even through the usual buffet weakness, dessert. See p. 205. Downtown, the **Main Street Station Garden Court** (in Main Street Station; ✆ **702/387-1896**) has an incredible buffet, with all live-action stations (where the food is made in front of you, sometimes to order): wood-fired brick-oven pizzas; fresh, lovely salsas and guacamole in the Mexican section; and better-than-average desserts. See p. 207.

o **Best Group Budget Meal Deal: Capriotti's,** 322 W. Sahara Ave. (✆ **702/474-0229;** p. 185), again—a large sandwich can feed two with leftovers, for about $5 each.

o **Best Bistro:** We ate nearly the entire menu at Thomas Keller's **Bouchon,** in The Venetian (✆ **702/414-6200;** p. 172), and didn't find a misstep, just what you might expect from one of the most critically lauded chefs in the country. But don't overlook **Mon Ami Gabi** (✆ **702/944-4224**), in Paris Las Vegas. Offering lovely, reasonably priced bistro fare (steak and *pommes frites,* onion soup), it's also a charming spot. See p. 177.

o **Best Restaurant/Nightclub Interiors:** The designers ran amok in the restaurants of **Mandalay Bay.** At **Aureole** (✆ **877/632-1766**), a four-story wine tower requires that a pretty young thing be hauled up in a harness to fetch your chosen vintage. See p. 154. The cheeky, peek-a-boo stripper/brothel look of **Strip House** (✆ **702/737-5200;** p. 171) is a fun change of pace to the usually staid steakhouse genre. Speaking of change, that's what happens to the walls and decor of **Switch** (✆ **702/248-3463;** p. 182), with a different atmosphere every 20 minutes. And then there is the futuristic fantasy of **Mix** (✆ **702/632-9500**), on top of THEhotel, where stunning views of the Strip compete with a giant beaded curtain made of hand-blown glass balls, to say nothing of silver pods in lieu of booths. See p. 157.

o **Best Spot for a Romantic Dinner:** **Alizé** (✆ **702/951-7000**), at the top of the Palms, has windows on three sides of the dining room, with no other buildings around for many blocks. You get an unobstructed view of all of Vegas, the desert, and the mountains from every part of the restaurant. Aren't you in the mood already? See p. 165.

o **Best Spot for a Celebration:** Let's face it, no one parties like the Red Party, so head to **Red Square** (✆ **702/632-7407**) in Mandalay Bay, where you can have caviar and vodka in the ultimate capitalist revenge. See p. 158.

o **Best Free Show at Dinner:** At Wynn Las Vegas, **Daniel Boulud Brasserie** (✆ **888/352-3463**) provides front-and-center seating for the strange-yet-compelling Lake of Dreams show. And then there is the vista offered by the restaurants in Bellagio— **Picasso** (✆ **866/259-7111**), **Le Cirque** (✆ **866/259-7111**), **Olives**

Alizé mixes fine cuisine with top-notch views of the Strip.

(© 866/259-7111), and **Circo** (© 702/693-8150)—which are grouped to take advantage of the view of the dancing water fountains. See chapter 6.

○ **Best Wine List:** It's a competitive market in Vegas for such a title, and with sommeliers switching around, it's hard to guarantee that any wine list will retain its quality. Still, you can't go wrong at Mandalay Bay's **Aureole** (© 877/632-1766), which has the largest collection of Austrian wines outside of that country, among other surprises. See p. 154.

○ **Best Beer List: Rosemary's Restaurant,** 8125 W. Sahara Ave. (© 702/869-2251), offers "beer pairing" suggestions with most of its menu options, and includes some curious and fun brands, including fruity Belgian numbers. See p. 192.

○ **Best Views: Mix** (© 877/632-1766; p. 157), on top of THEhotel, and **Alizé** (© 702/951-7000; p. 165), at the top of the Palms,

The traditional Vegas showgirl is disappearing but still makes waves at *Jubilee!*

win with their floor-to-ceiling window views, but there is something to be said for seeing all of Vegas from the revolving **Top of the World** (© 702/380-7711), 106 stories off the ground in the Stratosphere Casino Hotel & Tower. See p. 171.

○ **Best Italian:** You won't find anything more authentic outside of Italy than at **Bartolotta Ristorante di Mare** (© 888/352-3463), at Wynn Las Vegas. Given that the chef has his fish flown in daily from the Mediterranean, this also wins "Best Seafood." See p. 181.

○ **Best Deli:** Wars are fought over less, so all you New Yorkers can square off on behalf of **Carnegie Deli,** in The Mirage (© 702/791-7310), while Los Angeles residents fight for the branch of their beloved **Canter's Deli** (© 702/894-7111), in Treasure Island. The rest of us will find our mouths too packed with pastrami to weigh in. See p. 180.

○ **Best New Orleans Cuisine:** Emeril's **Delmonico Steakhouse** (© 702/414-3737), in The Venetian, brings the celebrity chef's "Bam!" cuisine to the other side of the Mississippi, and we are glad. See p. 166.

○ **Best Red Meat: Lawry's The Prime Rib,** 4043 Howard Hughes Pkwy. (© 702/893-2223; p. 186), has such good prime rib, it's hard to imagine ever having any better. If you want cuts other than prime rib, **Strip House** (© 702/737-5200; p. 171) has some of the best steaks in town, though the more budget-conscious might want to either split the enormous cuts or try the justly popular **Austin's Steakhouse,** in Texas Station, 2101 Texas Star Lane (© **702/631-1033;** p. 192).

best OF VEGAS AFTER DARK

○ **Best Production Show:** It's a total deadlock between **Cirque du Soleil's KÀ** and **O** (© **866/774-7117** for KÀ; © **888/488-7111** for O; p. 304 and 305). The latter is more "traditional"—if you can call a human circus that uses a giant tank of water as a stage "traditional"—in that it has only a loose semblance of narrative, whereas KÀ actually has a plot. Both are dazzling and, given the extremely high production values, seem worth the extremely high ticket prices.

○ **Best Old-Time Vegas Production:** You know: big, huge stage sets, pointless production numbers, showgirls, nipples on parade, Bob Mackie headdresses. Ah, *Jubilee!* (© **800/237-7469**), this world would be dreary without you. See p. 310.

○ **Best Smart Show:** This town isn't good enough for either **Blue Man Group** (© **866/641-7469;** p. 303) or **Penn & Teller** © **888/746-7784;** p. 313).

○ **Best Local Hang:** Hard-core types (including punks; off-duty strippers; off-duty waitstaff; and, on certain nights, Blue Man men, sans makeup, doing weird percussion things) gather way after hours at the **Double Down Saloon,** 4640 Paradise Rd. (© **702/791-5775**). See p. 320.

○ **Best Night Club:** If by "best" you mean "most popular," and by "most popular" you mean "people are willing to start standing in line hours before they open and pay $30 a pop, and that's before alcohol, just to get a foot in the

The Red Room at PURE.

Treasures.

door," then **PURE,** in Caesars Palace (℡ **702/731-7110**), beats out the competition by a long shot. See p. 331. But if substance over style is more your bag, head toward **XS,** at Encore Las Vegas (℡ **702/770-0097**), where the lines are just as long and the covers are just as high but the reward is a high-class indoor/outdoor club experience that truly lives up to its excessive moniker.

o **Best Ultralounge:** That's just Vegas-speak for "fancy-pants hotel bar," but most of them are pretty nice, if trying too hard to be all that. Still, we like the vibe at **Tryst** at Wynn Las Vegas (℡ **702/770-3375**). See p. 333.

o **Best Reason to Wait in Line:** We never think there is a good enough reason, but **ghostbar,** in the Palms (℡ **702/942-6832;** p. 321), is a fantastic hotel bar, especially because of its outstanding view, perched high above the Strip. Meanwhile, there's a good reason **Rain Nightclub,** 4321 W. Flamingo Rd. (℡ **702/942-6832;** p. 332), keeps packing them in—it's *plus ne ultra* for dance clubs.

o **Best Strip Club:** You know you want to know. We give the honors to **Treasures,** 2801 Westwood Dr. (℡ **702/257-3030**), because we think all strip joints should insist on production numbers with stage effects and look like old-fashioned English brothels. See p. 338.

2

LAS VEGAS IN DEPTH

There has rarely been a time in Vegas's post-Bugsy history when the city wasn't booming, but lately the boom, while not quite a "bust," has certainly been less sonic. Proving that no corner of the globe was immune to the global recession, Las Vegas of late has struggled with the same kind of debt-to-asset imbalances that people everywhere have, only on a scale measured in billions. While new development is still happening, its pace has slowed to a crawl and the entire city seems to be poised for yet another reinvention. It wouldn't be the first time.

A LOOK AT THE PAST
The Eighth Wonder of the World

For many years after its creation, Las Vegas was a mere whistle-stop town. That all changed in 1928 when Congress authorized the building of nearby Boulder Dam (later renamed Hoover Dam), bringing thousands of workers to the area. In 1931, gambling once again became legal in Nevada, and Fremont Street's gaming emporiums and speakeasies attracted dam workers. Upon the dam's completion, the Las Vegas Chamber of Commerce worked hard to lure the hordes of tourists who came to see the engineering marvel (it was called "the Eighth Wonder of the World") to its casinos. But it wasn't until the early years of World War II that visionary entrepreneurs began to plan for the city's glittering future.

Las Vegas Goes South

Contrary to popular lore, developer Bugsy Siegel didn't actually stake a claim in the middle of nowhere—he just built a few blocks south of already-existing properties.

And in 1941, El Rancho Vegas, ultraluxurious for its time, was built on the same remote stretch of highway (across the street from where the Sahara now stands). Scores of Hollywood stars were invited to the grand opening, and El Rancho Vegas soon became the hotel of choice for visiting film stars.

Beginning a trend that continues today, each new property tried to outdo existing hotels in luxurious amenities

PREVIOUS PAGE: **Elvis Presley, arguably the greatest headliner in Vegas history.** ABOVE: **The Flamingo Las Vegas, when it was a "real class joint."**

and thematic splendor. Las Vegas was on its way to becoming the entertainment capital of the world.

Las Vegas promoted itself in the 1940s as a town that combined Wild West frontier friendliness with glamour and excitement. As chamber of commerce president Maxwell Kelch put it in a 1947 speech, "Las Vegas has the impact of a Wild West show, the friendliness of a country store, and the sophistication of Monte Carlo." Throughout the decade, the city was Hollywood's celebrity playground. The Hollywood connection gave the town glamour in the public's mind. So did the mob connection (something Las Vegas has spent decades trying to live down), which became clear when notorious underworld gangster Bugsy Siegel built the fabulous Flamingo, a tropical paradise and "a real class joint."

A steady stream of name entertainers came to Las Vegas. In 1947, Jimmy Durante opened the showroom at the Flamingo. Other headliners of the 1940s included Dean Martin and Jerry Lewis, tap-dancing legend Bill "Bojangles" Robinson, the Mills Brothers, skater Sonja Henie, and Frankie Laine. Future Las Vegas legend Sammy Davis, Jr., debuted at El Rancho Vegas in 1945.

While the Strip was expanding, Downtown kept pace with new hotels such as the El Cortez and the Golden Nugget. By the end of the decade, Fremont Street was known as "Glitter Gulch," its profusion of neon signs proclaiming round-the-clock gaming and entertainment.

The 1950s: Building Booms & A-Bombs

Las Vegas entered the new decade as a city (no longer a frontier town), with a population of about 50,000. Hotel growth was phenomenal. The Desert Inn, which opened in 1950 with headliners Edgar Bergen and Charlie McCarthy, brought country-club elegance (including an 18-hole golf course and tennis courts) to the Strip.

In 1951, the Eldorado Club Downtown became Benny Binion's Horseshoe Club, which would gain fame as the home of the annual World Series of Poker. In 1954, the Showboat sailed into a new area east of Downtown. The Showboat not only introduced buffet meals, but it also offered round-the-clock bingo and a bowling alley (106 lanes to date).

In 1955, the Côte d'Azur–themed Riviera became the ninth big hotel to open on the Strip. Breaking the ranch-style mode, it was, at nine stories, the Strip's first high-rise. Liberace, one of the hottest names in show business, was paid the unprecedented sum of $50,000 a week to dazzle audiences in the Riviera's posh Clover Room.

Elvis appeared at the New Frontier in 1956 but wasn't a huge success; his fans were too young to fit the Las Vegas tourist mold. In 1958, the $10 million,

Tests of the atomic bomb just outside Vegas were a major tourist attraction in the 1950s.

1,065-room Stardust upped the spectacular stakes by importing the famed *Lido de Paris* spectacle from the French capital. It became one of the longest-running shows ever to play Las Vegas.

Throughout the 1950s, most of the Vegas hotels competed for performers whose followers spent freely in the casinos. The advent of big-name Strip entertainment tolled a death knell for glamorous nightclubs in America; owners simply could not compete with the astronomical salaries paid to Las Vegas headliners. Two performers whose names have been linked to Las Vegas ever since—Frank Sinatra and Wayne Newton—made their debuts there. Mae West not only performed in Las Vegas, but also cleverly bought up a half mile of desolate Strip frontage between the Dunes and the Tropicana.

The Rat Pack's famous "Summit Meeting" at the Sands.

Competition for the tourist dollar also brought nationally televised sporting events such as the PGA's Tournament of Champions. In the 1950s, the wedding industry helped make Las Vegas one of the nation's most popular venues for "goin' to the chapel." Celebrity weddings of the 1950s that sparked the trend included singer Dick Haymes and Rita Hayworth, Joan Crawford and Pepsi chairman Alfred Steele, Carol Channing and TV exec Charles Lowe, and Paul Newman and Joanne Woodward.

On a grimmer note, the '50s also heralded the atomic age in Nevada, with nuclear testing taking place just 65 miles northwest of Las Vegas. A chilling 1951 photograph shows a mushroom-shaped cloud from an atomic bomb test visible over the Fremont Street horizon. Throughout the decade, about one bomb a month was detonated in the nearby desert (an event, interestingly enough, that often attracted loads of tourists).

The 1960s: The Rat Pack & a Circus

The very first month of the new decade made entertainment history when the Sands hosted a 3-week "Summit Meeting" in the Copa Room that was presided over by "Chairman of the Board" Frank Sinatra, with Rat Pack cronies Dean Martin; Sammy Davis, Jr.; Peter Lawford; and Joey Bishop (all of whom happened to be in town filming *Ocean's Eleven*).

The building boom of the '50s took a brief respite. Most of the Strip's first property, the El Rancho Vegas, burned down in 1960. And the first new hotel of the decade, the first to be built in 9 years, was the exotic Aladdin, in 1966.

Las Vegas became a family destination in 1968, when Circus Circus burst onto the scene with the world's largest permanent circus and a "junior casino,"

THE mob IN LAS VEGAS

The role of the mafia in the creation of Las Vegas is little more than a footnote these days, but it isn't too bold of a statement to suggest that without organized crime the city would not have developed in the ways that it did and its past would have certainly been less colorful.

Meyer Lansky was a big name in the New York crime syndicate in the 1930s, and it was largely his decision to send Benjamin "Bugsy" Siegel (pictured below) west to expand their empire. Although the Strip had already begun to form with the opening of El Rancho in 1941 and The Frontier in 1942, it was Bugsy's sparkling Flamingo of 1946 that began a mafia-influenced building boom and era of control that would last for decades. Famous marquees, such as the Desert Inn, the Riviera, and the Stardust, were all built, either in part or in whole, from funding sources that were less than reputable.

During the '60s, negative attention focused on mob influence in Las Vegas. Of the 11 major casino hotels that had opened in the previous decade, 10 were believed to have been financed with mob money. Then, like a knight in shining armor, Howard Hughes rode into town and embarked on a $300-million hotel- and property-buying spree, which included the Desert Inn itself (in 1967). Hughes was as "Bugsy" as Benjamin Siegel any day, but his pristine reputation helped bring respectability to the desert city and lessen its gangland stigma.

During the 1970s and 1980s, the government got involved, embarking on a series of criminal prosecutions across the country to try to break the back of the mafia. Although not completely successful, it did manage to wrest major control of Las Vegas away from organized crime through its efforts, aided by new legislation that allowed corporations to own casinos. By the time Steve Wynn built The Mirage in 1989, the

mafia's role was reduced to the point where the most it could control were the city's innumerous strip clubs.

These days strict regulation and billions of dollars of corporate money keep things on the up and up, but the mob's influence can still be felt even at the highest levels of Las Vegas government. Mayor Oscar B. Goodman, first elected mayor in 1999, was a lawyer for the mafia in the 1960s and 1970s, defending such famed gangsters as Meyer Lanksy and Anthony "Tony the Ant" Spilotro. The popular and colorful Goodman cheerfully refers to his mafia-related past often, joking about his desire to settle conflicts in the desert at night with a baseball bat like "in the good old days." Goodman is also championing a mob museum in Las Vegas, which would be built in a former courthouse in the Downtown area that was the site of a number of mafia prosecutions.

featuring dozens of carnival midway games on its mezzanine level. In 1969, Elvis made a triumphant return to Las Vegas at the International's showroom and went on to become one of the city's all-time legendary performers. His fans had come of age.

Hoping to establish Las Vegas as "the Broadway of the West," the Thunderbird Hotel presented Rodgers and Hammerstein's *Flower Drum Song*. It was a smash hit. Soon the Riviera picked up *Bye, Bye, Birdie*, and, as the decade progressed, *Mame* and *The Odd Couple* played at Caesars Palace. While Broadway played the Strip, production shows, such as the Dunes' *Casino de Paris*, became ever more lavish, expensive, and technically innovative.

The 1970s: Merv & Magic

In 1971, the 500-room Union Plaza opened at the head of Fremont Street, on the site of the old Union Pacific Station. It had what was, at the time, the world's largest casino, and its showroom specialized in Broadway productions. The same year, talk-show host Merv Griffin began taping at Caesars Palace, taking advantage of a ready supply of local headliner guests. He helped popularize Las Vegas even more by bringing it into America's living rooms every afternoon.

The year 1973 was eventful: Over at the Tropicana, illusionists extraordinaire Siegfried & Roy began turning women into tigers and themselves into legends in the *Folies Bergere*.

Two major disasters hit Las Vegas in the 1970s. First, a flash flood devastated the Strip, causing more than $1 million in damage. Second, gambling was legalized in Atlantic City. Las Vegas's hotel business slumped as fickle tourists decided to check out the new East Coast gambling mecca.

As the decade drew to a close, an international arrivals building opened at McCarran International Airport, and dollar slot machines caused a sensation in the casinos.

The 1980s: The City Erupts

As the '80s began, Las Vegas was booming once again. McCarran Airport began a 20-year, $785-million expansion program.

Siegfried & Roy were no longer just the star segment of various stage spectaculars. Their own show, *Beyond Belief*, ran for 6 years at The Frontier, playing a record-breaking 3,538 performances to sellout audiences every night. It became the most successful attraction in the city's history.

The Mirage's lush tropical atrium.

The Excalibur—a monument to the Vegas theme era and the city's failed attempt to seduce families.

In 1989, Steve Wynn made Las Vegas sit up and take notice. His gleaming white-and-gold Mirage was fronted by five-story waterfalls, lagoons, and lush tropical foliage—not to mention a 50-foot volcano that dramatically erupted regularly! Wynn gave world-renowned illusionists Siegfried & Roy carte blanche (and more than $30 million) to create the most spellbinding show Las Vegas had ever seen.

The 1990s: King Arthur Meets King Tut

The 1990s began with a blare of trumpets heralding the rise of a turreted medieval castle, fronted by a moated drawbridge and staffed by jousting knights and fair damsels. Excalibur reflected the '90s marketing trend to promote Las Vegas as a family-vacation destination.

More sensational megahotels followed on the Strip, including the *new* MGM Grand hotel, backed by a full theme park (it ended Excalibur's brief reign as the world's largest resort), Luxor Las Vegas, and Steve Wynn's Treasure Island.

In 1993, a unique pink-domed 5-acre indoor amusement park, Grand Slam Canyon, became part of the Circus Circus hotel. In 1995, the Fremont Street Experience was completed, revitalizing Downtown Las Vegas. Closer to the Strip, rock restaurant magnate Peter Morton opened the Hard Rock Hotel, billed as "the world's first rock-'n'-roll hotel and casino." The year 1996 saw the advent of the French Riviera–themed Monte Carlo and the Stratosphere Casino Hotel & Tower, its 1,149-foot tower the highest building west of the Mississippi. The unbelievable New York–New York arrived in 1997.

But it all paled compared with 1998–99. As Vegas hastily repositioned itself from "family destination" to "luxury resort," several new hotels, once again eclipsing anything that had come before, opened. Bellagio was the latest from Vegas visionary Steve Wynn, an attempt to bring grand European style to the desert, while at the far southern end of the Strip, Mandalay Bay charmed. As if this weren't enough, The Venetian's ambitiously detailed re-creation of everyone's favorite Italian city came along in May 1999, and was followed in short order by the opening of Paris Las Vegas in the fall of 1999.

Colorful artwork in the lobby of Wynn Las Vegas, the resort that launched the Las Vegas luxe era.

The 2000s: The Lap of Luxury

The 21st century opened up with a bang as the Aladdin blew itself up and gave itself a from-the-ground-up makeover (which in turn only lasted for a handful of years before Planet Hollywood took it over and changed it entirely), while Steve Wynn blew up the Desert Inn and built a new showstopper named for himself. Along the way, everyone expanded, and then expanded some more, ultimately adding thousands of new rooms. Caesars produced two new towers, plus a multistory addition to its Forum Shops. Bellagio and The Venetian followed suit with their own additional towers. Mandalay Bay upped the ante by making their new tower an entirely separate establishment, THEhotel, which sent the signal that the priorities in this latest incarnation of Vegas had shifted. There is no casino in THEhotel (though guests have adequate access to the one in Mandalay Bay), while rooms are all one-bedroom suites, permanently breaking with the convention that no one comes to Vegas to spend time in their room. Other hotels followed with similar plush digs. The watchword became "luxury," with a secondary emphasis on "adult." Little by little, wacky, eye-catching themes were phased out (as much as one can when one's hotel looks like a castle) and generic sophistication took its place. Gaming is still number one, but the newer hotels are trying to top each other in terms of other recreations—celebrity chef–backed restaurants, decadent nightclubs, fancy spas, and superstar shows.

"More is more" seems to be the motto, and so The Venetian's new annex, The Palazzo, is taller than Encore, the new extension of the Wynn. Even bigger hotels are currently under construction or well into the planning stages. Eclipsing all of it—for the moment, anyway—is the massive CityCenter, perhaps the most ambitious project in the city yet. Comprised of a 4,000-room megaresort, two 400-room boutique hotels, condos, shopping, dining, clubs, and more, it covers 60 acres and, as such, is a city-within-the-city. Clearly, no one can rest on their laurels in Vegas, for this is not only a town that never sleeps, but also one in which progress never stops moving, even for a heartbeat.

LAS VEGAS TODAY

No major city in America has reinvented itself as many times, especially in such a short period, as Las Vegas. Just look at the recent decades. In the '80s, it was a discount afterthought. In the '90s, it was family and theme heaven. The new millennium brought in ultraluxury and sky-high prices on everything from rooms to shampoo in the sundry stores.

Today, Vegas may be on the cusp of yet another reinvention.

For the better part of the last 10 years, the watchword has been "expensive." The average room rate soared to over $200 a night, significantly higher than visitors, lulled by lower double-digit bargains, were used to paying. It was not unusual for the high-end hotels to be charging $400 or even $500 for a standard room, and even the formerly "bargain" hotels were asking for two to three times what they had been getting just a few years before.

And why not? The crowds kept coming. Occupancy rates in Vegas were well over 90%, nearly 50% higher than the national average. Flush with big returns on their stock investments, equity in their home, or simply easy-flowing credit, those who could afford it flocked to the city in record numbers, generating record profit for the casinos. Vegas became hip, drawing a younger, more-affluent demographic that lined up to pay for the fancy hotel rooms, the exclusive nightclubs, the celebrity-chef restaurants, and the high-limit gaming tables.

The "Average Joe," on the other hand, got priced right out of town. For a lot of people—the people whose money helped build those massive hotels and casinos—the idea of a Vegas vacation became cost prohibitive. In the '90s, you could easily get a room on the Strip for a weekend, eat at buffets or even some of the better restaurants, see a show, and more for under $500. In the 2000s, that $500 might pay for your room for the weekend. Maybe.

But then came the global economic meltdown, and Vegas has been hit hard. The number of visitors coming to the city has dropped dramatically and those who are coming are spending a lot less money in the casinos. The average room rate has plunged to the lowest level in nearly a decade and more rooms are going empty, with occupancy rates in the low 80% range—still good when compared to the national average but scary low for a city that depends upon filling those rooms to keep its economy going. The well-heeled crowd disappeared from Vegas faster than their stock profits, and suddenly hotels are left with expensive rooms, expensive shows, expensive nightclubs, and expensive restaurants that they can't fill.

Granted, Las Vegas is not a ghost town these days. When you're talking about the difference between, say, 200,000 people and 150,000 people on the Strip, it's a big percentage

Ultramodern CityCenter.

difference—but 150,000 people is still a heck of a lot of people. You may head to Vegas and think it is just as busy as it always has been, but trust us when we tell you it's not.

Many gaming companies have fallen into bankruptcy, and while their casinos have remained open, their bank accounts have slammed shut. New development has mostly ground to a halt, and the ongoing renovations that were a fixture at major hotels are mostly nonexistent these days. Just like many Americans who ran up too much credit card debt, the gaming companies are operating under obligations that run into the billions, and they are having a hard time paying the bills.

So does this mean that the new decade will signal yet another reinvention for Vegas? It's possible. There is already talk that future development, when it happens, will be aimed at the midmarket, "Average Joe" kind of tourist. For the foreseeable future, getting a room in Vegas should cost you a lot less than it has recently; and, while things will certainly go up when the economy improves, the hotel companies are skittish about the idea of returning them to their sky-high levels, because they are worried that the national mood of extravagant spending has changed.

Let's reconvene in 2020 and see how things turned out, shall we?

Tourists vs. Natives

So where have the "Average Joes" gone? In many instances, they just stayed home. But a lot of them were still able to find the kind of rates they could afford in Vegas, just not on the Strip.

Las Vegas Boulevard is the epicenter of the tourism industry in the city, drawing tens of millions of people each year to roughly a 4-mile stretch of road. However, most of the people who actually live and work in Las Vegas never go to the Strip unless they are employed by one of the hotels there. But this doesn't mean that they don't go gamble, eat at the hotel restaurants, and drink in the casino lounges. Scattered around town are dozens of big and small properties that are known as locals' casinos. The larger hotels offer just about everything the Strip hotels do—casinos, multiple restaurants, bars and clubs, movie theaters, bowling alleys, and more—often for a fraction of the cost. Consequently, that's where the smart folks who inhabit the city spend most of their time.

It's also where the smart, budget-conscious tourist can spend a lot of time. You will need a rental car to get to and fro, but, even with that added expenditure, you can save a significant amount of money by choosing to stay somewhere other than the Strip.

Bumper-to-bumper traffic on the Strip.

There's even better news in terms of the friendliness factor. As prices went up on the Strip, so did the snootiness, to the point where it's hard to get even a smile out of check-in agents or blackjack table dealers. Locals' hotels are an entirely different animal altogether, in that you can often find the kind of familial service that can make a huge difference in how much you enjoy your stay. Save money and get a smile? Hard to beat that.

Adapting to Las Vegas

Las Vegas is, for the most part, a very casual town. Although there are a few restaurants that have a restrictive dress code, most of them—and all of the showrooms, casinos, and attractions—are pretty much come as you are. Some people still choose to dress up for their night on the town, resulting in a strange dichotomy where you might see a couple in a suit and evening gown sitting next to a couple in shorts and sandals at a show or in a nice restaurant.

Generally speaking, nice casual (slacks or nice jeans, button up shirts or blouses, a simple skirt or dress) is the best way to go in terms of what to wear, allowing you to be comfortable in just about any situation. Go too far to one extreme or the other and you're bound to feel out of place somewhere.

The only exception to this rule is the nightclubs, which often have very strict policies on what you can and cannot wear. They vary from club to club, but, as a general rule, sandals or flip-flips, shorts, and baseball caps are frowned upon. A nice pair of jeans, a clean T-shirt, and a simple pair of sneakers will get you in the door, while fancier clothes (jackets, cocktail dresses) may get you past the velvet rope a little faster.

Yes, it does get hot in Las Vegas, so you really should factor that in when you're planning your wardrobe for your trip. It's important to note that every enclosed space (casino, showroom, restaurant, nightclub, and so on) is heavily air-conditioned, so it can actually get a bit chilly once you get inside. Think light layers and you should be okay.

Las Vegas is a 24-hour town, so you can find something to eat or drink all the time; but many of the nicer restaurants open only for dinner, with 5 or 6pm to 10 or 11pm the standard operating hours. Nightclubs usually open around 10pm and go until dawn, with the bulk of the crowds not showing up until midnight at the earliest. There are a few afternoon shows, but most are in the evenings and often run two shows a night with start times that range from 7pm until 10:30pm. Casinos and most regular bars are open 24 hours a day.

BOOKS & MOVIES

- Brinkley, Christina. *Winner Takes All: Steve Wynn, Kirk Kerkorian, Gary Loveman, and the Race to Own Las Vegas* (Hyperion, 2008). The explosion that is today's Las Vegas didn't just happen; it was largely the work of these three competing tycoons, who come together in a crush of money, ambition, and vision.

- Castleman, Deke. *Whale Hunt in the Desert: Secrets of a Vegas Superhost* (Huntington Press, 2009). A fascinating look at one of the city's leading casino hosts and the process by which Vegas lures in high rollers.

- Cooper, Marc. *The Last Honest Place in America* (Nation Books, 2004). Long fascinated by Sin City, the reporter-author investigates its evolution into its current corporation-driven status.

ANTHONY ZUIKER'S TOP SEVEN
LAS VEGAS movies

A graduate of the University of Nevada at Las Vegas who's lived in Vegas for 35 years, Anthony Zuiker worked for The Mirage as a graveyard-shift tram driver, bell-boy, and ad writer before he was inspired to create *CSI*, once the number-one-rated TV show in the country. Here are Zuiker's seven favorite Las Vegas flicks and what he thinks about them.

- *Ocean's Eleven* **(the remake)** It's our modern-day Rat Pack actors. Who can deny George Clooney and Brad Pitt (pictured below)?

- *Fear and Loathing in Las Vegas* It epitomizes the surreal journey of coming to Las Vegas, and it captures the hyper-reality very well.

- *Indecent Proposal* I remember seeing Demi Moore shooting the film at the Hilton, and Bruce Willis was playing blackjack at the tables while the filming was going on. She would run over to him and kiss him, and then go back and shoot the scene. That was my first taste of Hollywood glory long before I was in the business.

- *Ocean's Eleven* **(the original)** It's timeless actors and classic Vegas, platinum swagger that can never be replicated. I watch it, remembering that Sinatra would do just one take and that was it. Being in the business now, I marvel at that. He was always dressed so amazingly in those sweaters, he always had a cocktail, and he was just so cool.

- *Viva Las Vegas* To me, this was the first movie to put Las Vegas on the map, with the King of Rock 'n' Roll, no less, exemplifying what Vegas was all about, in its true glory days. Back then, times were good, it was all about the gambler, and it was amazing.

- *Casino* I actually grew up in town during this era, so I remember these characters very well. It was one of the first movies that took us inside the world of the casino, not just on the floor, but also behind the scenes. It was the look of the mob era in Vegas, how it really was; and because I knew of those men, I could see both how accurate it was and where creative license was taken.

- *Leaving Las Vegas* It's one of my top-five films of all time. The concept of an alcoholic going to Vegas because they never close the bars was a genius dramatic idea. And the way that director Mike Figgis shot Nick Cage, with Luxor in the background, with the red lights of Bally's blinking, the seedy hotel, it all just felt like the dark, surreal side of Vegas that we are used to as locals on a much more gut and emotional level. A wonderful movie.

- Denton, Sally. *The Money and the Power: The Making of Las Vegas and Its Hold on America* (Vintage, 2002). An exhaustive, often behind-the-scenes investigative history of Vegas.

- Fischer, Steve. *When the Mob Ran Vegas: Stories of Murder, Mayhem and Money* (Berkline Press, 2005). Ah, the good old days.

- Hess, Alan. *Viva Las Vegas: After Hours Architecture* (Chronicle Books, 1993). Vegas doesn't have architecture as much as set design, and here you can learn all about how its bizarre skyline is really an icon of model American urban culture.

- Martinez, Andrez. *24/7 Living It Up and Doubling Down in the New Las Vegas* (Villard, 1999). The author chronicles his efforts to spend his $50,000 book advance in a wild Vegas spree.

- McCracken, Robert. *Las Vegas: The Great American Playground* (University of Nevada Press, 1997). A comprehensive history of Vegas up to the last decade.

- McManus, James. *Positively Fifth Street* (Picador, 2004). The author came to write about the 2000 World Series of Poker and stayed to play, with surprising results that only demonstrate the seductive and strange lure of the city.

- Mezrich, Ben. *Bringing Down the House: The Inside Story of Six MIT Students Who Took Vegas for Millions* (Free Press, 2002). The title says it all. Recently the basis for the movie *21*.

- O'Brien, John. *Leaving Las Vegas* (Grove, 1995). The basis for the critically acclaimed movie, this novel demonstrates that not everything that happens in Vegas is fun and games, as the protagonist comes to town to drink himself to death.

- Puzo, Mario. *Inside Las Vegas* (Grossett & Dunlap, 1972). Though out of print, it's not that hard to find, and well worth reading to get the take on the man who invented the Corleones in the city invented by the mob.

- Spanier, David. *Welcome to the Pleasure Dome: Inside Las Vegas* (University of Nevada Press, 1992). First-person history and analysis of the Las Vegas phenomenon.

- Thompson, Hunter S. *Fear and Loathing in Las Vegas* (Random House, 1971). The gonzo journalist and his Samoan lawyer head to Sin City for the all-time binge. An instant classic, made into a movie starring Johnny Depp.

- Tronnes, Mike, ed. *Literary Las Vegas* (Henry Holt, 1995). A terrific collection of essays and excerpts from books about Vegas.

3

PLANNING YOUR TRIP TO LAS VEGAS

Whether you are visiting Las Vegas for the first time or the 50th, planning a trip here can be an overwhelming experience—as overwhelming as the city itself. With more than 150,000 hotel rooms, nearly as many slot machines, thousands of restaurants, and dozens of shows and attractions, there are seemingly endless ways to lose or waste your money. This chapter is designed to help you navigate the practical details of designing a Vegas experience that is tailored to your needs, from getting to and around the city to advice on the best times to visit and more.

Lots of people, both from the U.S. and abroad, believe that Las Vegas is the way it is portrayed in movies and television. For the most part, it isn't. Well, okay, you are more likely to run into a random showgirl or Elvis impersonator here than you are in say, Wichita, but they aren't in the background of every photo opportunity. International visitors, especially, should pay close attention to the material that follows in order to prepare for the most common nonshowgirl issues you may encounter in Las Vegas or on your way here. We also suggest that you check out chapter 10, "Las Vegas After Dark," before you leave home. If you want to see the most popular shows, it's a good idea to call ahead and order tickets well in advance to avoid disappointment. Ditto if you want to dine in one of the city's top restaurants: Head to chapter 6, "Where to Dine," for reviews and contact information.

For additional help in planning your trip and for more on-the-ground resources in Las Vegas, please turn to "Fast Facts," on p. 362.

WHEN TO GO

Most of a Las Vegas vacation is usually spent indoors, so you can have a good time here year-round. The most pleasant seasons are spring and fall, especially if you want to experience the great outdoors.

Weekdays are slightly less crowded than weekends. Holidays are always a mob scene and come accompanied by high hotel prices. Hotel prices also skyrocket when big conventions and special events are taking place. The slowest times of year are June and July, the week before Christmas, and the week after New Year's.

If a major convention is to be held during your trip, you might want to change your date. Check the box on p. 36 for convention dates, and contact the **Las Vegas Convention and Visitors Authority** (© 877/847-4858 or 702/892-7575; www.visitlasvegas.com), as convention schedules often change.

FACING PAGE: **The city's iconic neon sign greets visitors at the southern end of the Strip.**

The Weather

First of all, Vegas isn't always hot, but when it is, it's *really* hot. One thing you'll hear again and again is that even though Las Vegas gets very hot, the dry desert heat is not unbearable. We know this is true because we spent a couple of days there in 104°F (39°C) weather and lived to say, "It wasn't all that bad, not really." The humidity averages a low 22%, and even on very hot days, there's apt to be a breeze. Having said that, once the temperature gets into triple digits, it is wise to limit the amount of time you spend outdoors and to make sure you are drinking

wild WEATHER

Las Vegas rests in the middle of a desert, so how wacky can the weather possibly get? A lot crazier than you think. Although Las Vegas's location results in broiling-hot temperatures in the summer, many people tend to forget that deserts get cold and rainy, while wind is also a potential hazard.

Winter temperatures in Las Vegas have been known to dip below 30°F (–1°C), and when you toss in 40-mile-an-hour winds, that adds up to a very chilly stroll on the Strip. And snow is not an unheard-of occurrence. Most years see a flurry or two falling on Las Vegas, and since 1949, a total of 12 "storms" have resulted in accumulations of 2 inches or greater, with the largest storm dropping 9 inches onto the Strip in January 1949. In December 2003, parts of Las Vegas got 6 inches of the white stuff and although it didn't stick around too long on the Strip, the sight of the famous "Welcome to Fabulous Las Vegas" sign in the middle of a driving blizzard was quite a spectacle. And more recently (the winter of 2008–09), Vegas received nearly 3 inches of snow on the Strip itself, with nearly 10 inches accumulating in other areas of town. Locals usually find the snow a charming addition to the city (and the stuff melts completely in a day or two, so they don't have to shovel it—lucky them).

But although snow is a novel quirk that many Vegas residents and visitors welcome, rain isn't always as well received. The soil in Las Vegas is parched most of the year, making it difficult for the land to absorb large amounts of water coming down in a short time. Between June and August, when most of the area's rainfall takes place due to the Southwest's monsoon season, there is a good possibility of flash flooding.

At times, the skies just open up, resulting in flooding that wreaks havoc on Sin City. On July 9, 1999, Mother Nature unleashed more than 3 inches of rain *in just a few hours* on a city that averages about 4 inches of rain a year. The deluge killed two people, swamped hundreds of cars, and destroyed millions of dollars in property. As the Strip turned into a raging river, tourists took refuge in the hotels, but at least one resort—Caesars Palace—had to close its casino and shopping arcade because of flooding.

The topography of the Las Vegas region also makes it prone to high, often damaging winds. Situated at the bottom of a bowl ringed by mountains, 15 to 20 mph steady winds are not uncommon and gusts of 70 to 80 mph have been recorded. In 1994, a brief windstorm knocked down the massive sign at the Las Vegas Hilton and in 2010 a storm tore apart the Cloud 9 balloon, billed as the largest tethered helium balloon in the world.

plenty of water even while you are inside enjoying the blessed air-conditioning (which is omnipresent). Dehydration and heatstroke are two of the most common ailments that affect tourists—don't be a victim of one of them. Also, except on the hottest summer days, there's relief at night, when temperatures often drop by as much as 20°.

Las Vegas's Average Temperatures (°F & °C) & Rainfall

	JAN	FEB	MAR	APR	MAY	JUNE	JULY	AUG	SEPT	OCT	NOV	DEC
TEMP. (°F)	47	52	58	66	75	86	91	89	81	69	55	47
TEMP. (°C)	8	11	14	19	24	30	33	32	27	21	13	8
HIGH TEMP. (°F)	57	63	69	78	88	99	104	102	94	81	66	57
HIGH TEMP. (°C)	14	17	21	26	31	37	40	39	34	27	19	14
LOW TEMP. (°F)	37	41	47	54	63	72	78	77	69	57	44	37
LOW TEMP. (°C)	3	5	8	12	17	22	26	25	21	14	7	3
RAINFALL (IN.)	0.59	0.69	0.59	0.15	0.24	0.08	0.44	0.45	0.31	0.24	0.31	0.40

But this is the desert, and it's not hot year-round. It can get quite cold, especially in the winter, when at night it can drop to 30°F (−1°C) and lower. Although rare, it does snow occasionally in Las Vegas. The winter of 2008–2009 dropped

WHAT TO pack

Most Las Vegas hotel rooms are fully stocked with basics—shampoo, conditioner, hand lotion, mouthwash, and in some cases things like sewing kits and cotton swabs. If you don't have allergy or skin sensitivity issues to contend with, you may want to consider leaving those types of sundry items at home to free up some room in your suitcase. The same goes for your travel iron as most rooms have a full-size iron and ironing board or they are available by request through housekeeping.

Comfortable walking shoes are a must for Las Vegas as you'll be doing a lot of it. Yes, your Jimmy Choo's will look fabulous for your night out at the party spots but do you really want to navigate the crowds across a 100,000-square-foot casino in them?

Checking the weather forecast before your trip can provide you with guidance on what types of clothes to bring, but packing a light sweater or jacket even during the summer months is not a bad idea. It gets windy in Las Vegas and there can be a chill in the evenings, plus many of the casinos and showrooms set the air-conditioning on

"Siberia," so light layers that you can peel off when you go back outside into the heat are recommended.

If you are bringing your computer or other mobile devices, don't forget to bring your power cords, chargers, and other imperatives like an Ethernet cord. Most hotels offer Wi-Fi service but if you can't connect and need to use their cords, you could get charged extra for it.

Lastly, consider safety when packing by tossing in a small flashlight. During an emergency, this could become invaluable in helping you navigate your way out of a 4,000-room hotel.

nearly 3 inches of snow on the Strip. There's nothing quite like the sight of Luxor's Sphinx covered in snow. The breeze can also become a cold, biting wind of up to 40 mph and more. And so there are entire portions of the year when you won't be using that hotel pool at all (even if you want to; most of the hotels close huge chunks of those pool areas for "the season," which can be as long as the period from Labor Day to Memorial Day). If you aren't traveling in the height of summer, bring a jacket. Also, remember sunscreen and a hat—even if it's not all that hot, you can burn very easily and very fast.

MAJOR convention DATES FOR 2011

Listed below are Las Vegas's major annual conventions, with projected attendance figures for 2011; believe us, unless you're coming for one of them, you probably want to avoid the biggies. Because convention schedules frequently change, contact the **Las Vegas Convention and Visitors Authority** (✆ **877/847-4858** or 702/892-7575; www.visitlasvegas.com) to double-check the latest info before you commit to your travel dates.

Event Attendance	Dates	Expected
Consumer Electronics Show	Jan 6–9	120,000
Adult Entertainment Expo	Jan 6–9	37,000
Shooting, Hunting, and Outdoor Trade Show	Jan 18–21	45,000
World of Concrete	Jan 18–21	65,000
Winter Las Vegas Market (Design)	Jan 24–28	50,000
International Air-Conditioning Exposition	Jan 31–Feb 2	40,000
Photo Marketing Association Show	Feb 1–3	35,000
International Pizza Expo	Mar 1–3	10,000
International Hospitality Week	Mar 8–10	30,000
Kitchen/Bath Industry Show	Apr 26–28	55,000
RECon 2011	May 22–24	30,000
Int'l Esthetics, Cosmetics & Spa Conference	Jun 18–20	32,000
Associated Surplus Dealers	July 31–Aug 3	41,000
Pack Expo Las Vega	Sept 26–29	25,000
American Dental Association 2011	Oct 10–13	45,000
National Business Aviation Association	Oct 10–12	35,000
Automotive Aftermarket Industry Week	Nov 1–4	106,000
International Association of Amusement Parks	Nov 15–18	30,000

Las Vegas Calendar of Events

You may be surprised that Las Vegas does not offer as many annual events as most other tourist cities. The reason is Las Vegas's very raison d'être: the gaming industry. This town wants its visitors spending their money in the casinos, not at Renaissance fairs and parades.

When in town, check the local paper and contact the **Las Vegas Convention and Visitors Authority** (✆ **877/847-4858** or 702/892-7575; www.visitlasvegas.com) or the **Las Vegas Chamber of Commerce** (✆ **702/735-1616;** www.lvchamber.com) to find out about other events scheduled during your visit.

Note that two big events, June's CineVegas Film Festival and November's The Comedy Festival, were canceled for 2010 but may return in 2011.

For an exhaustive list of events beyond those listed here, check **http://events.frommers.com**, where you'll find a searchable, up-to-the-minute roster of what's happening in cities all over the world.

MARCH

NASCAR/Winston Cup. The **Las Vegas Motor Speedway,** 7000 Las Vegas Blvd. N. (✆ **800/644-4444;** www.lvms.com), has become one of the premier facilities in the country, attracting races and racers of all stripes and colors. The biggest races of the year are the Sam's Town 300 and the UAW-DaimlerChrysler 400, held in early March.

JUNE

World Series of Poker. When Harrah's Entertainment bought the legendary Binion's Horseshoe, in Downtown Vegas, out of bankruptcy, it quickly turned around and sold the hotel but kept the hosting rights to this famed event and moved its location and place on the calendar. Now held at the **Rio All-Suite Hotel and Casino,** 3700 W. Flamingo Rd. (✆ **800/752-9746**), in June and July (with

the final table held in November for some incomprehensible reason) the event features high-stakes gamblers and showbiz personalities competing for six-figure purses. There are daily events, with entry stakes ranging from $125 to $5,000. To enter the World Championship Event (purse: $1 million), players must pony up $10,000. It costs nothing to crowd around the tables and watch the action, but if you want to avoid the throngs, you can catch a lot of it on TV. For more information, visit **www.worldseriesofpoker.com**.

OCTOBER

Oktoberfest. This boisterous autumn holiday is celebrated from the first of October through the end of the month at the **Mount Charleston Resort** (✆ **800/955-1314** or 702/872-5408; www.mtcharlestonlodge.com), about a 35-minute drive

northwest of Las Vegas, with music, folk dancers, singalongs around a fire, special decorations, and Bavarian cookouts.

Justin Timberlake Shriners Hospitals for Children Open. This PGA Tour event is played at TPC Summerlin. For details, call ✆ **702/873-1010.**

DECEMBER

National Finals Rodeo. This is the Super Bowl of rodeos, attended by about 200,000 people each year and offering nearly $5 million in prize money. Male rodeo stars compete in calf roping, steer wrestling, bull riding, team roping, saddle bronco riding, and bareback riding. Women compete in barrel racing. An all-around Cowboy of the Year is chosen. In connection with this event, hotels book country stars into their showrooms, and a cowboy shopping spree—the **NFR Cowboy Christmas Gift**

Show, a trade show for Western gear—is held at Cashman Field. The NFR runs for 10 days, during the first 2 weeks of December, at the 17,000-seat Thomas & Mack Center of the University of Nevada, Las Vegas (UNLV). Order tickets as far in advance as possible (© **866/388-3267**). For more information, see **www.nfrexperience.com**.

MAACO Bowl Las Vegas Week. A championship college football event in mid-December pits the winners of the Mountain West Conference against the fourth or fifth selection of the Pac-10 Conference. The action takes place at the 32,000-seat Sam Boyd Stadium. Call © **702/732-3912,** or visit **www.lvbowl.com** for ticket information.

New Year's Eve. Between 300,000 and 400,000 people descend on Las Vegas to ring in the New Year, making it one of the largest gatherings for the holiday outside of New York's Times Square. Fireworks are the dominant entertainment, with pyrotechnics launched from the roofs of many hotels on the Strip and under the canopy at Fremont Street in Downtown Las Vegas. The Strip is closed to vehicles for the night, and so traffic and parking are a nightmare, as is booking a room, which should be done well in advance (and expect to pay a hefty premium if you get one).

ENTRY REQUIREMENTS

Passports

Virtually every air traveler entering the U.S. is required to show a passport. All persons, including U.S. citizens, traveling by air between the United States and Canada, Mexico, Central and South America, the Caribbean, and Bermuda are required to present a valid passport. **Note:** U.S. and Canadian citizens entering the U.S. at land and sea ports of entry from within the Western Hemisphere must now also present a passport or other documents compliant with the Western Hemisphere Travel Initiative (see www.getyouhome.gov for details). Children 15 and under may continue entering with only a U.S. birth certificate, or other proof of U.S. citizenship.

Visas

For information on obtaining a Visa, please see "Fast Facts," on p. 365.

The U.S. State Department has a **Visa Waiver Program (VWP)** allowing citizens of the following countries to enter the United States without a visa for stays of up to 90 days: Andorra, Australia, Austria, Belgium, Brunei, Czech Republic, Denmark, Estonia, Finland, France, Germany, Hungary, Iceland, Ireland, Italy, Japan, Latvia, Liechtenstein, Lithuania, Luxembourg, Malta, Monaco, the Netherlands, New Zealand, Norway, Portugal, San Marino, Singapore, Slovakia, Slovenia, South Korea, Spain, Sweden, Switzerland, and the United Kingdom. (**Note:** This list was accurate at press time; for the most up-to-date list of countries in the VWP, consult www.travel.state.gov/visa.) Even though a visa isn't necessary, in an effort to help U.S. officials check travelers against terror watch lists before they arrive at U.S. borders, visitors from VWP countries must register online through the Electronic System for Travel Authorization (ESTA) before boarding a plane or a boat to the U.S. Travelers must complete an electronic application providing basic personal and travel eligibility information. The Department of Homeland Security recommends filling out the form at least 3 days before traveling. Authorizations are valid for up to 2 years or until the traveler's passport expires, whichever comes first. Currently, there is no fee for the online application. *Note:* Any passport issued on or after October 26, 2006, by a VWP country must be an **e-Passport** for VWP travelers to be eligible to enter the U.S. without a visa. Citizens of these nations also need to present a round-trip air or cruise ticket upon arrival. E-Passports contain computer chips capable of storing biometric information, such as the required digital photograph of the holder. If your passport doesn't have this feature, you can still travel without a visa if the valid passport was issued before October 26, 2005, and includes a machine-readable zone; or if the valid passport was issued between October 26, 2005, and October 25, 2006, and includes a digital photograph. For more information, go to **www.travel.state.gov/visa**. Canadian citizens may enter the United States without visas, but will need to show passports and proof of residence.

Citizens of all other countries must have (1) a valid passport that expires at least 6 months later than the scheduled end of their visit to the U.S.; and (2) a tourist visa.

Customs

WHAT YOU CAN BRING INTO THE U.S.

Every visitor 21 years of age or older may bring in, free of duty, the following: (1) 1 U.S. quart of alcohol; (2) 200 cigarettes, 50 cigars (but not from Cuba), or 3 pounds of smoking tobacco; and (3) $100 worth of gifts. These exemptions are offered to travelers who spend at least 72 hours in the United States and who have not claimed them within the preceding 6 months. It is forbidden to bring into the country almost any meat products (including canned, fresh, and dried meat products such as bouillon, soup mixes, and so forth). Generally, condiments, including vinegars, oils, pickled goods, spices, coffee, tea, and some cheeses and baked goods, are permitted. Avoid rice products, as rice can often harbor insects. Bringing fruits and vegetables is prohibited since they may harbor pests or disease. International visitors may carry in or out up to $10,000 in U.S. or foreign currency with no formalities; larger sums must be declared to U.S. Customs on entering or leaving, which includes filing form CM 4790. For details regarding U.S. Customs and Border Protection, consult your nearest U.S. embassy or consulate, or **U.S. Customs** (www.customs.gov).

WHAT YOU CAN TAKE HOME FROM LAS VEGAS

For information on what you're allowed to take home, contact one of the following agencies:

CANADIAN CITIZENS Canada Border Services Agency, Ottawa, Ontario, K1A 0L8 (✆ **800/461-9999** in Canada, or 204/983-3500; www.cbsa-asfc.gc.ca).

U.K. CITIZENS HM Customs & Excise, Crownhill Court, Tailyour Road, Plymouth, PL6 5BZ (✆ **0845/010-9000** or 020/8929-0152 from outside the U.K.; www.hmce.gov.uk).

AUSTRALIAN CITIZENS Australian Customs Service, Customs House, 5 Constitution Ave., Canberra City, ACT 2601 (✆ **1300/363-263** or 612/6275-6666 from outside Australia; www.customs.gov.au).

NEW ZEALAND CITIZENS New Zealand Customs, The Customhouse, 17–21 Whitmore St., Box 2218, Wellington, 6140 (✆ **04/473-6099** or 0800/428-786; www.customs.govt.nz).

Medical Requirements

Unless you're arriving from an area known to be suffering from an epidemic (particularly cholera or yellow fever), inoculations or vaccinations are not required for entry into the United States.

GETTING THERE & GETTING AROUND

Getting to Las Vegas

BY PLANE

Las Vegas is served by **McCarran International Airport,** 5757 Wayne Newton Blvd. (© **702/261-5211,** TTY 702/261-3111; www.mccarran.com), just a few minutes' drive from the southern end of the Strip, where the bulk of casinos and hotels are concentrated. The airport is known online by the code **LAS.** For a list of airline websites see "Fast Facts," p. 365.

Getting into Town from the Airport

Getting to your hotel from the airport is a cinch. **Bell Transportation** (© **800/274-7433** or 702/739-7990; www.bell-trans.com) runs 20-passenger minibuses daily (7:45am–midnight) between the airport and all major Las Vegas hotels and motels. The cost is $6.50 per person each way to hotels on the Strip or around the Convention Center and $8 to Downtown or other off-Strip properties (north of the Sahara Hotel and west of I-15). Several other companies run similar ventures—just look for the signs for the shuttle bus queues, located just outside of the baggage claim area. Buses from the airport leave every few minutes. When you want to check out of your hotel and head back to the airport, call at least 2 hours in advance to be safe (though often you can just flag down one of the buses outside any major hotel).

Even less expensive are **Citizens Area Transit (CAT)** buses (© **702/CAT-RIDE** (228-7433); www.rtcsnv.com/transit). The no. 109 bus goes from the airport to the South Strip Transfer Terminal at Gilespie Street and Sunset Road, where you can transfer to the Gold Line that runs along the Strip. Alternately, the no. 108 bus departs from the airport and takes you to the Stratosphere, where you can transfer to the Deuce Line, which stops close to most Strip- and Convention Center–area hotels. The fares for buses on Strip routes are $3 for adults, $1.50 for seniors and children 6 to 17, and free for children 5 and under. **Note:** You might have a long walk from the bus stop to the hotel entrance, even if the bus stop is right in front of your hotel. Vans are able to get right up to the entrance, so choose a van if you're lugging lots of baggage.

If you have a large group with you, you might also try one of the limos that wait curbside at the airport, and charge $45 to $65 for a trip to the Strip. The price may go up with additional passengers, so ask about the fee very carefully. The aforementioned Bell Transportation is one reputable company that operates limousines in addition to their fleet of shuttle buses (call in advance).

BY CAR

The main highway connecting Las Vegas with the rest of the country is **I-15;** it links Montana, Idaho, and Utah with Southern California. The drive from Los Angeles is quite popular and, thanks to the narrow two-lane highway, can get very crowded on Friday and Sunday afternoons with hopeful weekend gamblers making their way to and from Las Vegas. An expansion project has widened most of that stretch of road to three lanes in each direction, which is helping the situation a lot. (By the way, as soon as you cross the state line, there are three casinos ready to handle your immediate gambling needs, with two more about 12 min. up the road, 30 miles before you get to Las Vegas.)

From the east, take I-70 or I-80 west to Kingman, Arizona, and then U.S. 93 north to Downtown Las Vegas (Fremont St.). From the south, take I-10 west to Phoenix, and then U.S. 93 north to Las Vegas. From San Francisco, take I-80 east to Reno, and then U.S. 95 south to Las Vegas.

Vegas is 286 miles from Phoenix, 759 miles from Denver, 421 miles from Salt Lake City, 269 miles from Los Angeles, and 586 miles from San Francisco.

See "Renting a Car" below for a list of rental-car agencies.

International visitors should note that insurance and taxes are almost never included in quoted rental-car rates in the U.S. Be sure to ask your rental agency about these. They can add a significant cost to your car rental.

BY TRAIN

Amtrak (© **800/872-7245;** www.amtrak.com) does not currently offer direct rail service, although plans have been in the works to restore the rails between Los Angeles and Las Vegas for years. We've been hearing these reports for so long now, they just make us roll our eyes.

In the meantime, you can take the train to Los Angeles or Barstow, and Amtrak will get you to Las Vegas by bus, which takes 5 to 6 hours depending on traffic.

BY BUS

Bus travel is often the most economical form of public transit for short hops between U.S. cities, but it's certainly not an option for everyone. Though getting to Vegas this way is cheaper, especially if you book in advance, it's also time-consuming (a 1-hr. flight from L.A. becomes a 5- to 8-hr. trek by bus) and usually not as comfortable. So you need to figure out how much time and comfort mean to you. **Greyhound** (© **800/231-2222;** www.greyhound.com) is the sole nationwide bus line. International visitors are eligible for the **Greyhound North American Discovery Pass.** The pass can be obtained from foreign travel agents or directly from Greyhound (www.discoverypass.com), for unlimited travel and stopovers in the U.S. and Canada.

The main Greyhound terminal in Las Vegas is located Downtown next to the Plaza hotel, 200 S. Main St. (© **702/383-9792**), and is open 24 hours. Although it's just a block from the Fremont Street Experience, it's several miles from the Strip in both location and atmosphere (why can't they put bus stations in nice neighborhoods?). Cabs are usually available right out front to whisk you to more scenic areas, but guard your valuables on arrival.

Getting Around

It isn't too hard to navigate your way around Vegas. But remember, between huge hotel acreage, increased and very slow traffic, and lots and lots of people—like you—trying to explore, getting around takes a lot longer than you might think. Heck, it can take 15 to 20 minutes to get from your room to another part of your hotel! Always allow for plenty of time to get from point A to point B.

BY CAR

If you plan to confine yourself to one part of the Strip (or one cruise down to it) or to Downtown, your feet will suffice. Otherwise, we highly recommend that visitors rent a car. The Strip is too spread out for walking (and Las Vegas is often too hot or too cold to make strolls pleasant); Downtown is too far away for a cheap cab ride, and public transportation is often ineffective in getting you where you want to go. Plus, return visits call for exploration in more remote parts of the city, and a car brings freedom, especially if you want to do any side trips at your own pace.

You should note that places with addresses some 60 blocks east or west of the Strip are actually less than a 10-minute drive—provided there is no traffic.

Having advocated renting a car, we should warn you that traffic is getting worse, and it's harder and harder to get around town with any certain swiftness. A general rule of thumb is to avoid driving on the Strip whenever you can, and avoid driving at all during peak hours (8–9:30am and 4:30–6pm), especially if you have to make a show curtain.

Parking is usually a pleasure because all casino hotels offer free valet service. That means that for a mere $1 to $2 tip, you can park right at the door, though the valet usually fills up on busy nights. In those cases, you can use the gigantic self-parking lots (free on the Strip, nominal fees Downtown) that all hotels have.

If you're visiting from abroad and plan to rent a car in the United States, keep in mind that foreign driver's licenses are usually recognized in the U.S., but you may want to consider obtaining an international driver's license. Also, international visitors should note that insurance and taxes are almost never included in quoted rental-car rates in the U.S. Be sure to ask your rental agency about these. They can add a significant cost to your car rental.

Renting a Car

If there is one bit of advice we can give you about visiting Las Vegas that we stress above most others, it is this: Rent a car! Not only will it allow you greater freedom and flexibility in what you can see and do, but it can also save you money in the long run. If you are planning on getting off the Strip at all, cabs will cost you more than a small rental and if you are truly budget minded, you can get a cheaper hotel elsewhere in town that will more than make up for the money you spend on a vehicle. Parking is abundant and usually free and so the only real downside is the traffic, which can be a nightmare at peak times (see p. 46 for some helpful tips on how to get around the worst of it).

Major companies with outlets in Las Vegas include **Advantage** (© 800/777-5500; www.advantagerentacar.com), **Alamo** (© 877/227-8367; www.alamo.com), **Avis** (© 800/230-4898; www.avis.com), **Budget** (© 800/527-0700; www.budget.com), **Dollar** (© 800/800-3665; www.dollar.com), **Enterprise** (© 800/261-7331; www.enterprise.com), **Hertz** (© 800/654-3131; www.hertz.com), **National** (© 800/227-7368; www.nationalcar.com), **Payless** (© 800/729-5377; www.paylesscarrental.com), and **Thrifty** (© 800/847-4389; www.thrifty.com).

Rental policies vary from company to company, but generally speaking you must be at least 25 years of age with a major credit or debit card to rent a vehicle in Las Vegas. Some companies will rent to those over 21 but will usually charge extra ($20–$30 per day) and will require proof of insurance and a major credit card and may restrict the type of vehicle you are allowed to rent (forget those zippy convertibles).

All of the major car rental companies are located at a consolidated facility at 7135 Gilespie St., just a block off Las Vegas Boulevard near Warm Springs Road and about 2½ miles from the airport. When you arrive, look for the signs for BUSES AND SHUTTLES in the baggage claim area and follow them outside where you'll find blue-and-white buses marked MCCARRAN RENT-A-CAR CENTER. It takes about 10 minutes to make the trip, although it's worth noting that the lines for buses and at the car rental counters can be long—budget some extra time if you have somewhere to be right after you get to town.

The rental-car facility is modern and easily navigable and just in case you resisted while at the airport, there are slot machines next to the car rental counters as well. Welcome to Vegas!

When exiting the facility, take three right turns and you are on the Strip, about 2 miles south of Mandalay Bay.

Car rental rates vary even more than airline fares. The price you pay depends on the size of the car, where and when you pick it up and drop it off, the length of the rental period, where and how far you drive it, whether you purchase insurance, and a host of other factors. A few key questions could save you hundreds of dollars.

- Are weekend rates lower than weekday rates? In Vegas this is usually true, although holiday or special events weekends can be more costly. Ask if the rate is the same for pickup Friday morning, for instance, as it is for Thursday night.

- Is a weekly rate cheaper than the daily rate? Even if you need the car for only 4 days, it may be cheaper to keep it for 5.

- Does the agency assess a drop-off charge if you don't return the car to the same location where you picked it up? Is it cheaper to pick up the car at the airport than at a Downtown location?

- Are special promotional rates available? If you see an advertised price in your local newspaper, be sure to ask for that specific rate; otherwise, you may be charged the standard cost. Terms change constantly, and reservations agents are notorious for not mentioning available discounts unless you ask.

- Are discounts available for members of AARP, AAA, frequent-flier programs, or trade unions? If you belong to any of these organizations, you may be eligible for discounts of up to 30%.

- In Las Vegas, expect to add about 35% to 40% on top of the rental fee, including a $1.35 per day vehicle license fee, a $3.25 per day facility fee, a 10% airport concession fee, and 20% sales tax. Ouch.

- What is the cost of adding an additional driver's name to the contract?

- How many free miles are included in the price? Free mileage is often negotiable, depending on the length of the rental.

Some companies offer "refueling packages," in which you pay for an entire tank of gas up front. The price is usually fairly competitive with local gas prices, but you don't get credit for any gas remaining in the tank and because it is virtually impossible to use up every last bit of fuel before you return it, you will usually wind up paying more overall than you would if you just filled it up yourself. There are several gas stations within a few blocks radius of the car rental center, including three at the intersection of Las Vegas Boulevard and Warm Springs Road. You may pay a few extra pennies at them than you would at stations elsewhere in town, but in the long run it's still a better deal.

Many available packages include airfare, accommodations, and a rental car with unlimited mileage. Compare these prices with the cost of booking airline tickets and renting a car separately to see if such offers are good deals. Internet resources can make comparison shopping easier.

Surfing for Rental Cars

For booking rental cars online, the best deals are usually found at rental-car company websites, although all the major online travel agencies also offer rental-car reservations services. **Priceline** (www.priceline.com) and **Hotwire** (www.hotwire.com) work well for rental cars; the only "mystery" is which major rental company you get, and for most travelers, the difference between Hertz, Avis, and Budget is negligible. Also check out **Breezenet.com,** which offers domestic rental-car discounts with some of the most competitive rates around.

Demystifying Rental-Car Insurance

Before you drive off in a rental car, be sure you're insured. Hasty assumptions about your personal auto insurance or a rental agency's additional coverage could end up costing you tens of thousands of dollars—even if you are involved in an accident that was clearly the fault of another driver.

If you already hold a **private auto insurance** policy in the United States, you are most likely covered for loss of or damage to a rental car, and liability in case of injury to any other party involved in an accident. Be sure to find out whether you are covered in Vegas, whether your policy extends to all persons who will be driving the rental car, how much liability is covered in case an outside party is injured in an accident, and whether the type of vehicle you are renting is included under your contract. (Rental trucks, sport utility vehicles, and luxury vehicles may not be covered.)

Most **major credit cards** provide some degree of coverage as well—provided they were used to pay for the rental. Terms vary widely, however, so be sure to call your credit card company directly before you rent. If you don't have a private auto insurance policy, the credit card you use to rent a car may provide primary coverage if you decline the rental agency's insurance. This means that the credit card company will cover damage or theft of a rental car for the full cost of the vehicle. If you do have a private auto insurance policy, your credit card may provide secondary coverage—which basically covers your deductible. *Credit cards do not cover liability* or the cost of injury to an outside party and/or damage to an outside party's vehicle. If you do not hold an insurance policy, you may want to seriously consider purchasing additional liability insurance from your rental company. Be sure to check the terms, however: Some rental agencies cover liability only if the renter is not at fault; even then, the rental company's obligation varies from state to state. Bear in mind that each credit card company has its own peculiarities; call your own credit card company for details before relying on a card for coverage. Speaking of cards, members of AAA should be sure to carry their membership ID card with them, which provides some of the benefits touted by the rental-car agencies at no additional cost.

The basic insurance coverage offered by most rental-car companies, known as the **Loss/Damage Waiver (LDW)** or **Collision Damage Waiver (CDW),** can cost $20 per day or more. The former should cover everything, including the

DRIVE IN style

If the idea of tooling around Las Vegas in a pedestrian rent-a-box just doesn't sound appealing, you can always indulge your fantasies by going with something more exotic.

Several companies in Las Vegas specialize in rentals of high-end, luxury vehicles—the kinds of rides that are normally reserved for the rich and famous. **Rent-a-Vette Exotic Car Rentals** (© **800/372-1981** or 702/736-2592; www.exoticcarrentalslasvegas.com) has a fleet from makers such as Lamborghini, Bentley, Ferrari, and Porsche, plus a stable of their namesake Chevrolet Corvettes. They even feature an Aston Martin Vantage, if you want to work out your inner James Bond while buzzing between casinos. Rates start at about $400 per day and go up from there—sometimes, way up. The Lamborghini Gallardo Spyder will set you back a cool $1,445 per day, or roughly what you'll pay for 5 nights in a room at Bellagio or Wynn Las Vegas. **Las Vegas Exotic Car Rentals** (© **866/871-1893;** www.vegasexotic rentals.com) offers a similar lineup plus some big-guy toys such as Hummer H2s and Cadillac Escalades. And if you prefer Elvis over James Bond, they even have some classics, such as a 1970 Cadillac Deville Convertible. You will need to supply your own *Viva Las Vegas* soundtrack.

loss of income to the rental agency, should you get in an accident (normally not covered by your own insurance policy). It usually covers the full value of the vehicle, with no deductible, if an outside party causes an accident or other damage to the rental car. You will probably be covered in case of theft as well. Liability coverage varies, but the minimum is usually at least $15,000. If you are at fault in an accident, you will be covered for the full replacement value of the car—but not for liability. In Nevada, you can buy additional liability coverage for such cases. Most rental companies require a police report in order to process any claims you file, but your private insurer will not be notified of the accident. Check your own policies and credit cards before you shell out money on this extra insurance because you may already be covered.

It's worth noting that rental-car companies seem to be pushing the extra coverage especially hard these days. Doing your research on what types of coverage you do and do not need will allow you to smile politely and decline if it is appropriate. Don't let them pressure or scare you into spending extra money for items you don't need.

BY TAXI

Because cabs line up in front of all major hotels, an easy way to get around town is by taxi. Cabs charge $3.30 at the meter drop and 20¢ for each additional $\frac{1}{12}$ mile, plus an additional $1.80 fee for being picked up at the airport and time-based penalties if you get stuck in a traffic jam. A taxi from the airport to the Strip will run you $15 to $23, from the airport to Downtown $18 to $25, and between the Strip and Downtown about $12 to $18. You can often save money by sharing a cab with someone going to the same destination (up to five people can ride

CHOPPER TOM'S traffic tips

"Chopper" Tom Hawley has watched Las Vegas grow since he was a little kid catching lizards in the desert, back in the '60s. A self-described "traffic geek," Tom reports from a helicopter and from a studio most mornings and afternoons in Las Vegas, on KVBC-TV/Channel 3. For further information on the following projects, traffic tips, and much more, stop by Channel 3's website at **www.kvbc.com** and click on "Traffic."

○ **Monorail Mania:** This 4-mile system is a larger, faster, and more modern version of the Disney hand-me-down that used to run between the MGM and Bally's. The Las Vegas Monorail has seven stations sprinkled from the MGM to the Sahara, with a one-way fare running $5 per person. (Discounts are available for multiple trips.) You may have heard about some less-than-glorious months for the system, but we're happy to report that as of this writing, things seem to be in fine working order. The bad news is that the whole thing went bankrupt in 2009 and although it's still running, plans for extensions to the airport or Downtown are probably nothing more than dreams.

○ **People Movers Galore:** Las Vegas has a greater variety of independent people-mover systems than any other city in the world, and they're a great way to get around without having to get into your car. In addition to the people movers at McCarran Airport, a variety of trains will take you from hotel to hotel. The Mandalay Bay Train whisks you from the Tropicana

walkways to the Excalibur, Luxor, and Mandalay Bay hotels. Smaller shuttles operate between The Mirage and Treasure Island and between the Circus Circus Big Top and East Tower. The newest monorail connects the Monte Carlo and Bellagio with CityCenter.

○ **Spaghetti Bowl:** The "Spaghetti Bowl" is what locals call the mess where I-15 intersects U.S. 95. The entire thing was reconstructed in 2000, but some studies indicate that it's carrying more traffic than it was designed for, so don't expect a congestion-free ride.

○ **U.S. 95 Widening:** A 7-year project to widen the west leg of U.S. 95 (connecting to the busy northwest valley) is now complete. Though still busy in weekday rush hours, this freeway hasn't moved better in 20 years.

○ **Keep Your Feet off the Streets:** Local engineers have been trying to improve traffic on the Strip by separating the cars from the pedestrians. The first overhead pedestrian walkways opened at Tropicana Avenue, in

for the same fare). All this implies that you have gotten a driver who is honest; many cabbies take you the long way around, which sometimes means the shortest physical distance between two points—right down the Strip—but longest time on the clock and, thus, on the meter. Either way, you could end up paying a fare that . . . let's just say a new pair of shoes would have been a much more fun way to spend that jackpot. Your only recourse is to write down the cab number and call the company and complain. They may not respond, but you can try.

1995; similar bridges were completed at Flamingo Avenue in 2000, Spring Mountain in 2003, and Harmon Avenue in 2009.

- **Do D.I. Direct:** Most visitors seem to get a lot of mileage out of the Strip and I-15. But, if you're checking out the local scene, you can bypass both of those, using Desert Inn Road, which is now one of the longest streets running from one side of the valley to the other. Plus, the 2-mile "Superarterial" section between Valley View and Paradise zips you nonstop over the interstate and under the Strip.

- **Grin and Bear It:** Yes, there are ways to avoid traffic jams on the Strip. But at least these traffic jams are entertaining! If you have the time and patience, go ahead and take a ride along the Strip from Hacienda to Sahara. The 4-mile drive might take an hour, but while you're grinding along, you'll see a Sphinx, an active volcano, a water ballet, and some uniquely Vegas architecture.

- **Rat Pack Back Doors:** Frank Sinatra Drive is a bypass road that runs parallel to the Strip from Russell Road north to Industrial. It's a great way to avoid the traffic jams and sneak in the back of hotels such as Mandalay Bay, Luxor, and Monte Carlo. On the other side of I-15, a bunch of high-end

condo developers talked the city into rechristening a big portion of Industrial Road as Dean Martin Drive. It's still called Industrial from near Downtown to Twain, and it lets you in the back entrances to Circus Circus, Treasure Island, and others. It's a terrific bypass to the Strip and I-15 congestion.

- **Beltway Bypass:** The 53-mile 215 Beltway was completed in 2003, wrapping three quarters of the way around the valley, allowing easy access to the outskirts while bypassing the Resort Corridor. While the initial beltway is done, some portions still need to be built out from half-beltway and frontage road systems to a full freeway—a process that will take until 2013 at least.

- **That Dam Bridge:** In 2002, work began on a magnificent bridge over the Colorado River to handle traffic between Arizona and Nevada. It was supposed to be done in 2008, but a construction mishap pushed completion to late 2010, meaning it should be operating by the time you read this. Of course that doesn't mean that traffic to the Hoover Dam will be eliminated all together. The best advice is to start your trip by 8am, and especially to avoid midday on Saturday and Sunday.

If you just can't find a taxi to hail and want to call one, try the following companies: **Desert Cab Company** (© 702/386-9102), **Whittlesea Blue Cab** (© 702/384-6111), or **Yellow/Checker Cab/Star Company** (© 702/873-2000).

BY MONORAIL

The first leg of a high-tech monorail opened in 2004, offering riders their first and best shot of getting from one end of the Strip to the other with a minimum of frustration and expense. The 4-mile route runs from the MGM Grand, at the southern end of the Strip, to the Sahara, at the northern end, with stops at Paris/Bally's, the Flamingo, Harrah's, the Las Vegas Convention Center, and the Las Vegas Hilton along the way. Note that some of the actual physical stops are not particularly close to their namesakes, so there can be an unexpected—and sometimes time-consuming—additional walk from the monorail stop to wherever you intended to go. Factor in this time accordingly.

These trains can accommodate more than 200 passengers (standing and sitting) and make the end-to-end run in about 15 minutes. They operate Monday through Thursday from 7am until 2am and Friday through Sunday from 7am until 3am. Fares are $5 for a one-way ride (whether you ride from one end to the other or just to the next station); discounts are available for round-trips and multiride/multiday passes.

A variety of behind-the-scenes issues, mostly having to do with money and bankruptcy, may change the way it's run, extend the route, or even shut it down altogether, although the latter seems highly unlikely. None of this will happen before 2011, and even if it does change, it may not be in such a way that you will notice.

BY PUBLIC TRANSPORTATION

The Deuce and Gold-Line buses operated by the **Regional Transportation Commission** (**RTC;** ✆ **702/CAT-RIDE** [228-7433]; www.rtcsouthernnevada. com) are the primary public transportation on the Strip. The double-decker Deuce and double-carriage Gold-Line run a route between the Downtown Transportation Center (at Casino Center Blvd. and Stewart Ave.) and a few miles beyond the southern end of the Strip. The fare is $5 for adults for 2 hours, $2 for seniors 60 and older and children 6 to 17, and free for children 5 and under. An all-day pass is $7 ($3.50 for seniors or children), and a 3-day pass is $20 ($10 for seniors and children). CAT buses run 24 hours a day and are wheelchair accessible. Exact change is required.

Although they are certainly economical transportation choices, they are not the most efficient as it relates to time or convenience. They run often but are usually very crowded and are not immune to the mind-numbing traffic that clogs the Strip at peak times. Patience is required.

Is That The Mirage or Just a Mirage?

Maybe it's the desert that makes distances here so deceiving, or the fact that the buildings are so darned big that it makes them seem closer than they really are. But getting from point A to point B always seems to take much longer in Las Vegas than you think it will. We can't count the number of times we've said, "Here we are at The Mirage/Treasure Island/Bellagio and we have dinner/business/show tickets for Caesars/The Mirage/the Monte Carlo next door. We'll leave about 15 minutes before we need to be there." Thirty-five minutes later, after negotiating the casino crowds at our hotel, trekking through to the exit, using the moving sidewalk, tram, or our feet to get to the next stop, finding the entrance, negotiating the crowds there, and getting lost . . . we finally arrive. Barely. The moral of the story is to always give yourself extra time, even if you are just going next door.

There are also a number of **free transportation services,** courtesy of the casinos. A free monorail connects Mandalay Bay with Luxor and Excalibur; another connects Monte Carlo, Bellagio, and CityCenter; and a free tram shuttles between The Mirage and Treasure Island. Given how far apart even neighboring hotels can be, thanks to their size, and how they seem even farther apart on really hot (and cold and windy) days, these are blessed additions.

MONEY & COSTS

The Value of the Dollar vs. Other Popular Currencies

US$	CAN$	UK£	EURO €	AUS$	NZ$
$1	C$1	£0.62	€0.71	A$1	NZ$1.29

Frommer's lists exact prices in the local currency. The currency conversions quoted above were correct at press time. However, rates fluctuate, so before departing consult a currency exchange website such as **www.oanda.com/convert/classic** to check up-to-the-minute rates.

Because Las Vegas is a town built on the concept of separating you from your money, it should come as no surprise that gaining access to money is very easy—sometimes too easy. There are ATMs (also known as "cash machines" or "cashpoints") conveniently located about every 4 feet (okay, an exaggeration, but not by a lot); and check cashing, credit card–advance systems, and traveler's-check services are omnipresent.

And while Vegas visitors used to require a great deal of change in order to play the slots and other gaming machines, few, if any, still accept coins. Gone are the once-prevalent change carts. All machines now take bills in most denominations, and you get "change" in the form of a credit slip that appears when you cash out. You then take this slip to the nearest cashier's cage to exchange for actual money.

So getting to your money isn't a problem. Keeping it may be.

Las Vegas has grown progressively more expensive, with the concept of a cheap Sin City vacation a distant memory. The average room rate is over $200 a night, those formerly cheap buffets have been replaced by $30-a-person lavish spreads, and top-show tickets easily surpass $100 a head. And then, of course, there are the casinos, a money-losing proposition for the traveler if there ever was one.

But there are Las Vegas vacations available for just about any budget, so pay (no pun intended) close attention to chapter 5, "Where to Stay," and chapter 6, "Where to Dine," which break down your choices by cost.

Beware of hidden credit card fees while traveling. Check with your credit or debit card issuer to see what fees, if any, will be charged for overseas transactions. Recent reform legislation in the U.S., for example, has curbed some exploitative lending practices. But many banks have responded by increasing fees in other areas, including fees for customers who use credit and debit cards while out of the country—even if the charges are made in U.S. dollars. Fees can amount to 3% or more of the purchase price. Check with your bank before departing to avoid any surprise charges on your statement.

WHAT THINGS COST IN LAS VEGAS	US$
Taxi from the airport to the Strip	15.00–23.00
Taxi from the airport to Downtown Las Vegas	18.00–25.00
One-way Las Vegas monorail ticket	5.00
All-day Deuce bus pass	7.00
Standard room at Bellagio, Fri–Sat	275.00–400.00
Standard room at MGM Grand, Fri–Sat	200.00–300.00
Standard room at Bally's, Fri–Sat	100.00–200.00
Dinner for two at Picasso, prix fixe	230.00
Dinner for two at Austin's Steakhouse	75.00
Wynn Las Vegas buffet, weekend champagne brunch	39.00
Main Street Station Garden Court buffet champagne brunch	11.00
Ticket to Cirque du Soleil's *Viva Elvis*	99.00–175.00
Ticket to Mac King (comedy magic show)	25.00
Domestic beer at Haze	8.00
Domestic beer at the Double Down Saloon	4.00

STAYING HEALTHY

By and large, Las Vegas is like most other major American cities in that the water is relatively clean, the air is relatively clear, and illness-bearing insects and animals are rare. However, in a city with this many people coming and going from all over the world, there are a couple of specific concerns worth noting.

Regional Health Concerns

FOOD POISONING Food preparation guidelines in Las Vegas are among the strictest in the world, but when you're dealing with the sheer volume that this city is, you're bound to run into trouble every now and then. All restaurants are required by law to display a health certificate and letter grade (A, B, or C) that indicate how well they did on their last Health Department inspection. An A grade doesn't mean you won't get food poisoning, but it does mean the staff does a better-than-average job in the kitchen.

NOROVIRUS Over the past few years, there have been a few outbreaks of norovirus at Las Vegas hotels. This virus, most commonly associated with cruise ships, is rarely serious but can turn your vacation into a very unpleasant experience of intestinal illness. Because it is spread by contact, you can protect yourself by washing your hands often, especially after touching all of those slot machines.

SUN EXPOSURE In case you weren't paying attention in geography, Las Vegas is located in the middle of a desert and so it should come as no surprise that the sun shines particularly bright here. Heat and sunstroke are dangers that all visitors should be concerned about, especially if you are considering spending any amount of time outdoors. Sunscreen (stick to a minimum SPF 30) is a must even if you are just traveling from one hotel to another and you should always carry a bottle of

water with you to stay hydrated even when temperatures are moderate. The low desert humidity means that your body has to work harder to replenish moisture, so help it along with something other than a free cocktail in the casino. The good news: Low humidity means it's hard to have a bad hair day.

If You Get Sick

The closest full-service hospital to the Strip is **Sunrise Hospital,** 3186 Maryland Pkwy. (© **702/731-8080**), but for lesser emergencies, the **Harmon Medical Urgent Care,** 105 E. Harmon (© **702/796-1116**), offers 24-hour treatment. Additionally, most major hotels in Las Vegas can provide assistance in finding physicians and/or pharmacies that are well suited to your needs.

We list additional **emergency numbers** in "Fast Facts," p. 362.

CRIME & SAFETY

CSI: Crime Scene Investigation, one of the nation's top-rated TV shows, may turn up new corpses each week, but the crime rate in real-life Vegas isn't higher than in any other major metropolis of its size.

With all that cash floating around town, pickpockets and thieves are predictably active. At gaming tables and slot machines, men should keep wallets well concealed and out of the reach of pickpockets, and women should keep handbags in plain sight (on laps). If you win a big jackpot, ask the pit boss or slot attendant to cut you a check rather than give you cash—the cash may look nice, but flashing it can attract the wrong kind of attention. Outside casinos, popular spots for pickpockets and thieves are restaurants and outdoor shows, such as the volcano at The Mirage or the fountains at Bellagio. Stay alert. Unless your hotel room has an in-room safe, check your valuables into a safe-deposit box at the front desk.

When in your room, be sure to lock and bolt the door at all times and only open it to hotel employees that you are expecting (such as room service).

A special safety concern for women (and even men occasionally) centers on behavior at nightclubs. Do not ever accept a drink from a stranger no matter how handsome he is and keep your cocktail in your hand at all times, even on the dance floor. Instances of people getting something slipped into their drink are rare but they have happened, so best to take precautions.

SPECIALIZED TRAVEL RESOURCES

In addition to the destination-specific resources listed below, please visit Frommers.com for other specialized travel resources.

LGBT Travelers

For such a licentious, permissive town, Las Vegas has its conservative side, and it is not the most gay-friendly city. This does not manifest itself in any signs of outrage toward open displays of gay affection, but it does mean that the local gay community is largely confined to the bar scene. This may be changing, with local gay-pride parades and other activities gathering steam each year. See listings for gay bars, in chapter 10. For gay and lesbian travel resources, visit **Frommers.com.**

Travelers with Disabilities

On the one hand, Las Vegas is fairly well equipped for travelers with disabilities, with virtually every hotel having wheelchair-accessible rooms and ramps and other requirements. On the other hand, the distance between hotels (particularly on the Strip) makes a vehicle of some sort virtually mandatory for most people with disabilities, and it may be extremely strenuous and time-consuming to get from place to place (even within a single hotel, because of the crowds). Even if you don't intend to gamble, you still may have to go through the casino, and casinos can be quite difficult to maneuver in, particularly for a guest in a wheelchair. Casinos are usually crowded, and the machines and tables are often arranged close together, with chairs, people, and such blocking easy access. You should also consider that it is often a long trek through larger hotels between the entrance and the room elevators (or, for that matter, anywhere in the hotel), and then add a crowded casino to the equation.

For more on organizations that offer resources to travelers with limited mobility, go to **Frommers.com.**

Family Travel

Family travel can be immensely rewarding, giving you new ways of seeing the world through smaller pairs of eyes. That said, Vegas is hardly an ideal place to bring the kids. For one thing, they're not allowed in casinos at all. Because most hotels are laid out so that you frequently have to walk through their casinos to get to where you are going, you can see how this becomes a headache. Some casino hotels do not allow the children of nonguests on the premises after 6pm—and this policy is seriously enforced.

Note also that the Strip is often peppered with people distributing fliers and other information about decidedly adult entertainment options in the city. Sex is everywhere. Just walking down the Strip might give your kids an eyeful of items that you might prefer they avoid. (They don't call it "Sin City" for nothing!)

On top of everything else, there is a curfew law in Vegas: Kids younger than 18 are not permitted on the Strip without a parent after 9pm on weekends and holidays. In the rest of the county, minors can't be out without parents after 10pm on school nights and midnight on the weekends.

Although still an option at most smaller chain hotels and motels, the major casino-hotels on the Strip offer no discount for children staying in your room, so you may have to pay an additional fee ($10–$40 per person per night) to have them bunk with you. You'll definitely want to book a place with a pool. Some hotels also have enormous video arcades and other diversions.

To locate accommodations, restaurants, and attractions that are particularly kid friendly, look for the "Kids" icon throughout this guide.

Women Travelers

Thanks to the crowds, Las Vegas is as safe as any other big city for a woman traveling alone. A woman on her own should, of course, take the usual precautions and should be wary of hustlers and drunken businessmen who may mistake her for a "working girl." (Alas, million-dollar proposals à la Robert Redford are a rarity.) Many of the big hotels have security guards stationed at the elevators at night to prevent anyone other than guests from going up to the room floors. If you're anxious, ask a security guard to escort you to your room. *Always* double lock your door *and* deadbolt it to prevent intruders from entering.

For general travel resources for women, go to www.frommers.com/planning.

Senior Travelers

One of the benefits of age is that travel to most destinations often costs less—but that's rarely true in Las Vegas. Discounts at hotels, shows, restaurants, recreation, and just about anything else you want to do are rare. About the only discounts offered to seniors are at some of the local attractions, which will give a few bucks off to those over 62 or 65 (see chapter 7).

Members of **AARP,** 601 E St. NW, Washington, DC 20049 (© **888/687-2277;** www.aarp.org), get discounts on hotels, airfares, and car rentals. AARP offers members a wide range of benefits, including *AARP The Magazine* and a monthly newsletter. Anyone over 50 can join.

The U.S. National Park Service (NPS) offers an **America the Beautiful—National Park and Federal Recreational Lands Pass—Senior Pass** (formerly the **Golden Age Passport**). You'll find it useful for some of the side trips covered in chapter 11. The pass gives seniors 62 years or older lifetime entrance to all properties administered by the National Park Service—national parks, monuments, historic sites, recreation areas, and national wildlife refuges—for a one-time processing fee of $10. The pass must be purchased in person at any NPS facility that charges an entrance fee. Besides free entry, the America the Beautiful Senior Pass also offers a 50% discount on some federal-use fees charged for such facilities as camping, swimming, parking, boat launching, and tours. For more information, go to www.nps.gov/fees_passes.htm or call the **United States Geological Survey (USGS),** which issues the passes, at © **888/275-8747.**

RESPONSIBLE TOURISM

Las Vegas is a city that was built on the concept of mass consumption—overconsumption, really—of just about everything. Water, electricity, food, alcohol—you name it and probably too much of it is used here. The fact that all of this consumption happens in the middle of a desert where such resources are scarce only amplifies the problem.

Drought is a major concern here, with water levels at the major lakes and reservoirs in the area falling to dangerously low levels. You can do your part by limiting the amount of water your vacation consumes in a couple of simple yet effective ways. First, although that soaking tub looks tempting, perhaps a short shower will do the trick. Second, reuse your towels whenever possible so they don't have to be run through the laundry every day. Most housekeeping staff will only launder towels left on the floor and will leave those on racks alone.

Many newer hotels (CityCenter and The Palazzo, to name a couple) have been built with sustainable practices that limit the amount of energy you use while visiting. Some have automatic shutdown systems that turn off all the lights when you leave the room and then restore your settings when you return, but if yours doesn't, there is always the light switch. Use it.

For transportation, the greenest (and most scenic) way of getting around is your own two feet. Vegas, especially on the Strip, is very pedestrian friendly provided you follow the marked crosswalks and signals. But if you need wheels, most major rental-car companies in town have hybrids or electric vehicles in their fleet. We don't recommend trying to use a bicycle around the Strip—it's just too difficult to navigate the crowds and the traffic—but if you really want to, your hotel's concierge can direct you to the nearest local bike rental company. And if you're staying at Aria Las Vegas, they'll even valet your two-wheeler for you!

STAYING CONNECTED

Mobile Phones

Just because your mobile phone works at home doesn't mean it'll work everywhere in the U.S. (thanks to our nation's fragmented mobile phone system). Whether or not you'll get a signal depends on your carrier and where you happen to be standing when you are trying to make a call. Hotel rooms and casinos are notoriously bad places to be if you want to chat with someone back home on your cell phone, but step outside and things will usually improve dramatically. Note that if you *can* get a signal in a casino, don't try to use your phone while sitting at a gaming table—that's a big no-no.

Once you leave Las Vegas proper, you are in the wilds of the Nevada desert and so unless you are near a major byway (like I-15), expect to get very few, if any, bars on your phone.

If you're not from the U.S., you'll be appalled at the poor reach of the **GSM (Global System for Mobile Communications) wireless network,** which is used by much of the rest of the world. Your phone will probably work in Las Vegas but it probably won't once you get into more rural areas. To see where GSM phones work in the U.S., check out www.t-mobile.com/coverage. And you may or may not be able to send SMS (text messaging) home.

Internet & E-mail

Most resort hotels in Vegas offer wireless access, but for a hefty daily fee (usually starting around $14). Some chain hotels offer free Wi-Fi in public areas, while others still offer high-speed access. In Las Vegas, you can find free Wi-Fi at most stand-alone McDonald's, Starbucks, and in the Fashion Show Mall. To find additional public Wi-Fi hot spots, go to **www.jiwire.com**; its Wi-Fi Finder holds the world's largest directory of public wireless hot spots.

For dial-up access, most business-class hotels in the U.S. offer dataports for laptop modems.

Wherever you go, bring a **connection kit** of the right power and phone adapters, a spare phone cord, and a spare Ethernet network cable—or find out whether your hotel supplies them to guests.

For information on electrical currency conversions, see "Electricity," in "Fast Facts" (p. 361).

Some Vegas hotels still offer Internet service through the television, with a wireless keyboard (provided). Figure, on average, that you'll pay about $15 a day for the privilege.

There are usually no easily accessible cybercafes in Vegas, and even those that open tend to close without warning. To check for possibilities, try **www.cybercaptive.com** and **www.cybercafe.com**.

Most major airports have **Internet kiosks** that provide basic Web access for a per-minute fee that's usually higher than cybercafe prices. Check out copy shops, such as **FedEx Office,** which offer computer stations with fully loaded software (as well as Wi-Fi). A list of convenient locations is in "Fast Facts" on p. 361.

Newspapers & Magazines

The *Las Vegas Review-Journal* is the major daily periodical in the city, which is now partnered with the *Las Vegas Sun,* its former newspaper rival. Both offer the latest news, weather, and information and can be valuable resources for coupons and up-to-the-minute show listings.

What's On Las Vegas is a local magazine listing shows, restaurants, happenings, and more, and it often features discount offers to attractions that could save you some dough.

Telephones

Generally, Vegas hotel surcharges on long-distance and local calls are astronomical. You are often charged even for making a toll-free or phone-card call. You're better off using your **cellphone** or a **public pay telephone.** Some hotels are now adding on an additional "resort fee" to the cost of the room, which is supposed to cover local calls (as well as using the pool and other elements that ought to be givens). The fee can range from $1 (Motel 6) to $15 per day.

Many convenience groceries and packaging services sell **prepaid calling cards** in denominations up to $50. Many public pay phones at airports now accept American Express, MasterCard, and Visa. **Local calls** made from most pay phones cost either 25¢ or 35¢. Most long-distance and international calls can be dialed directly from any phone. **To make calls within the United States and to Canada,** dial 1 followed by the area code and the seven-digit number. **For other international calls,** dial 011 followed by the country code, city code, and the number you are calling.

Calls to area codes **800, 888, 877,** and **866** are toll free. However, calls to area codes **700** and **900** (chat lines, bulletin boards, "dating" services, and so on) can be expensive—charges of 95¢ to $3 or more per minute. Some numbers have minimum charges that can run $15 or more.

For **reversed-charge or collect calls,** and for person-to-person calls, dial the number 0 then the area code and number; an operator will come on the line, and you should specify whether you are calling collect, person-to-person, or both. If you are making an international call, ask for the overseas operator.

For **directory assistance** ("Information"), dial 411 for local numbers and national numbers in the U.S. and Canada. For dedicated long-distance information, dial 1, then the appropriate area code plus 555-1212.

SUGGESTED LAS VEGAS ITINERARIES

W hen you visit Las Vegas, you certainly won't be lacking in things to do. But the sheer enormity of the city and its laundry list of sights, attractions, restaurants, shows, recreation, and other activities could leave even the most intrepid traveler feeling a little overwhelmed.

The itineraries in this chapter are designed to help narrow the big list down a little while maximizing your time. This way you can spend less energy planning and more simply having fun. Each has a theme, but you can always mix and match to create your perfect Las Vegas getaway.

Instead of a step-by-step tour, the itineraries are broken down by morning, afternoon, and nighttime activities with multiple suggestions for each, again allowing you to customize your vacation in a way that makes sense for you. If you prefer something a bit more structured, see the day-by-day itineraries on p. 209.

ORIENTATION

Located in the southernmost precincts of a wide, pancake-flat valley, Las Vegas is the biggest city in the state of Nevada. Treeless mountains form a scenic backdrop to hotels awash in neon glitter. Although it is one of the fastest-growing cities in America, for tourism purposes, the city is quite compact.

Visitor Information

All major Las Vegas hotels provide comprehensive tourist information at their reception and/or sightseeing and show desks.

Other good information sources are the **Las Vegas Convention and Visitors Authority,** 3150 Paradise Rd., Las Vegas, NV 89109 (© **877/847-4858** or 702/892-7575; www.visitlasvegas.com), open daily 8am to 5pm; the **Las Vegas Chamber of Commerce,** 6671 Las Vegas Blvd. S., Ste. 300, Las Vegas, NV 89119 (© **702/735-1616;** www.lvchamber.com), open Monday through Friday 8am to 5pm; and, for information on all of Nevada, including Las Vegas, the **Nevada Commission on Tourism** (© **800/638-2328;** www.travelnevada.com), open 24 hours.

Help for Troubled Travelers

The **Travelers Aid Society** is a social-service organization geared to helping travelers in difficult straits. Its services include reuniting families separated while traveling, feeding people stranded without cash, and even providing emotional counseling. If you're in trouble, seek them out. In Las Vegas, services are provided by **Help of Southern Nevada,** 1640 E. Flamingo Rd., Ste. 100, near Maryland Parkway (© **702/369-4357;** www.helpsonv.org). Hours are Monday through Thursday 7am to 5pm.

PREVIOUS PAGE: The Double Down Saloon.

The North Strip is home to several resorts, the iconic Stratosphere, and the Fashion Show Mall.

City Layout

There are two main areas of Las Vegas: the **Strip** and **Downtown.** For many people, that's all there is to Las Vegas. But there is actually more to the town than that: Although maybe not as glitzy and glamorous as the Strip and Downtown—okay, definitely not—Paradise Road and east Las Vegas are home to quite a bit of casino action; Maryland Parkway boasts mainstream and some alternative-culture shopping; and there are different restaurant options all over the city. Many of the "locals hotels" (pretty much anything with "Station" in the name, for starters), most of which are off the regular tourist track, offer cheaper gambling limits plus budget food and entertainment options. Confining yourself to the Strip and Downtown is fine for the first-time visitor, but repeat customers (and you will be) should get out there and explore. Las Vegas Boulevard South (the Strip) is the starting point for addresses; any street that crosses it starts with 1 East and 1 West at its intersection with the Strip (and goes up from there).

THE STRIP

The Strip is probably the most famous 4-mile stretch of highway in the nation. Officially called Las Vegas Boulevard South, it contains most of the top hotels in town and offers almost all the major showroom entertainment. First-time visitors will, and probably should, spend the bulk of their time on the Strip. If mobility is a problem, we suggest basing yourself in a South or Mid-Strip location.

For the purposes of organizing this book, we've divided the Strip into three sections. The **South Strip** can be roughly defined as the portion of the Strip south of Harmon Avenue, including the MGM Grand, Mandalay Bay, the Monte Carlo, New York–New York, Luxor, CityCenter, and many more hotels and casinos.

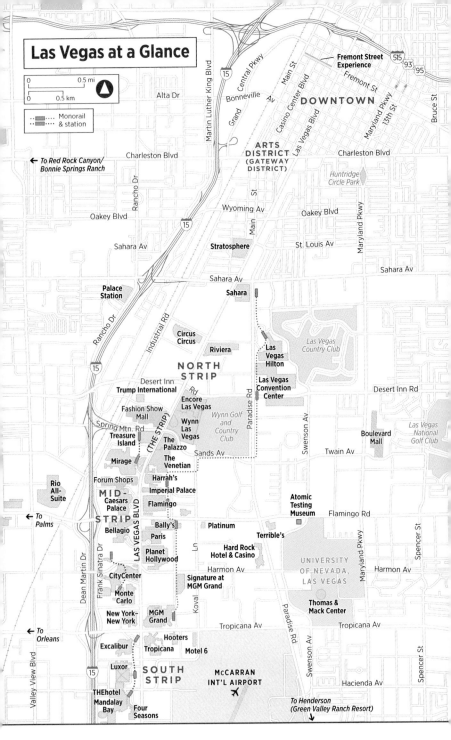

Las Vegas at a Glance

0   0.5 mi
0   0.5 km

Monorail & station

← To Red Rock Canyon/
Bonnie Springs Ranch

Alta Dr

Bonneville Av

Grand Av

Central Pkwy

Martin Luther King Blvd

15

Main St

Casino Center Blvd

Las Vegas Blvd

DOWNTOWN

Fremont Street
Experience

Fremont St

515
93
95

Maryland Pkwy

13th St

Bruce St

Charleston Blvd

ARTS DISTRICT (GATEWAY DISTRICT)

Charleston Blvd

Huntridge Circle Park

Wyoming Av

Main St

Oakey Blvd

Maryland Pkwy

Oakey Blvd

Rancho Dr

Sahara Av

15

St. Louis Av

Sahara Av

Stratosphere

Sahara Av

Sahara

Sahara Av

Palace Station

Industrial Rd

Rancho Dr

Las Vegas Country Club

Circus Circus

Riviera

Las Vegas Hilton

NORTH STRIP

Paradise Rd

Las Vegas Convention Center

Desert Inn Rd

Desert Inn Rd

Trump International

Fashion Show Mall

Spring Mtn. Rd

Treasure Island

Mirage

(THE STRIP)

Encore Las Vegas

Wynn Las Vegas

The Palazzo

The Venetian

Wynn Golf and Country Club

Sands Av

Swenson Av

Boulevard Mall

Las Vegas National Golf Club

Twain Av

Rio All-Suite

Forum Shops

MID-STRIP

Caesars Palace

Harrah's

Imperial Palace

Flamingo

Las Vegas Blvd

Atomic Testing Museum

← To Palms

Bellagio

Bally's

Paris

Platinum

Flamingo Rd

Planet Hollywood

Koval Ln

Terrible's

Hard Rock Hotel & Casino

Spencer St

Dean Martin Dr

Frank Sinatra Dr

CityCenter

Monte Carlo

Harmon Av

Signature at MGM Grand

UNIVERSITY OF NEVADA, LAS VEGAS

Maryland Pkwy

Harmon Av

← To Orleans

New York-New York

MGM Grand

Thomas & Mack Center

Tropicana Av

Hooters

Excalibur

Tropicana

Motel 6

Tropicana Av

Swenson Av

Spencer St

SOUTH STRIP

Luxor

15

McCARRAN INT'L AIRPORT

Hacienda Av

Valley View Blvd

THEhotel

Mandalay Bay

Four Seasons

To Henderson
(Green Valley Ranch Resort)

Mid-Strip is a long stretch of the street between Harmon Avenue and Spring Mountain Road, including Bellagio, Caesars, The Mirage, Treasure Island, Bally's, Paris Las Vegas, the Flamingo Las Vegas, and Harrah's, among other hotels and casinos.

The North Strip stretches north from Spring Mountain Road all the way to the Stratosphere Casino Hotel & Tower and includes Wynn Las Vegas, Encore, Sahara, the Riviera, and Circus Circus, to name a few of the accommodations and attractions.

EAST OF THE STRIP/CONVENTION CENTER

This area has grown up around the Las Vegas Convention Center. Las Vegas is one of the nation's top convention cities, attracting around 3 million conventioneers each year. The major hotel in this section is the Las Vegas Hilton, but Marriott has a big presence here and the Hard Rock Hotel is a major draw. You'll find many smaller chain/name brand hotels and motels southward, along Paradise Road. All these hotels offer proximity to the Strip.

"Sassy Sally" is one of several old-style neon signs overlooking Downtown Las Vegas.

BETWEEN THE STRIP & DOWNTOWN

The area between the Strip and Downtown is a seedy stretch dotted with tacky wedding chapels, bail-bond operations, pawnshops, and cheap motels. However, the area known as the Gateway District (roughly north and south of Charleston Blvd. to the west of Las Vegas Blvd. S.) keeps trying to make a name for itself as an artists' colony. Studios, small cafes, and other signs of life continue to spring up.

DOWNTOWN

Also known as "Glitter Gulch" (narrower streets make the neon seem brighter), Downtown Las Vegas, which is centered on Fremont Street, between Main and 9th streets, was the first section of the city to develop hotels and casinos. With the exception of the Golden Nugget, which looks like it belongs in Monte Carlo, this area has traditionally been more casual than the Strip. But between the Fremont Street Experience (p. 217) and other ongoing improvements, Downtown offers a more affordable alternative to the Strip. With prices on the Strip running amok, there is more reason than ever to focus your tourist attention and dollars down here. The area is clean, the crowds are low-key and friendly, there is a collection of great bars just east of the Experience, and the light show itself is as ostentatious as anything on the Strip. Sure, by comparison with the overblown Strip, it feels more like a small town than even old-time "Vegas," but don't let that allow you to overlook this area. Las Vegas Boulevard runs all the way into Fremont Street Downtown.

Orientation

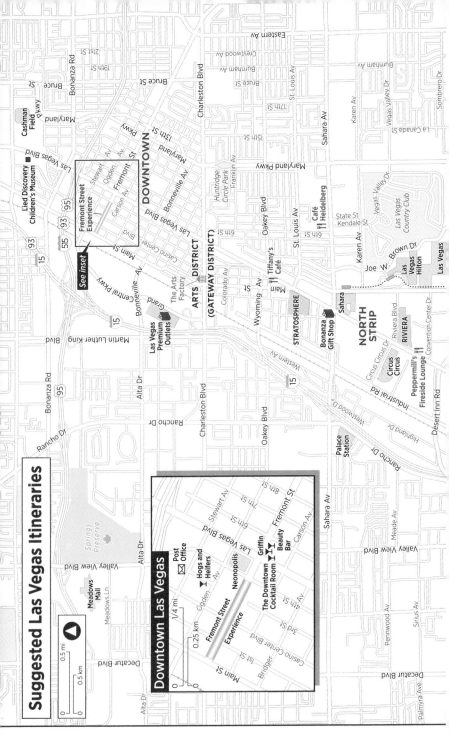

Suggested Las Vegas Itineraries

Lied Discovery Children's Museum

Cashman Field

Fremont Street Experience

See inset

DOWNTOWN

ARTS DISTRICT (GATEWAY DISTRICT)

The Arts Factory

Las Vegas Premium Outlets

Huntridge Circle Park

Café Heidelberg

Tiffany's Café

State St
Kendale St

Las Vegas Country Club

Las Vegas Hilton

Las Vegas

Joe W.

Brown Dr

STRATOSPHERE

Bonanza Gift Shop

NORTH STRIP

Circus Circus

RIVIERA

Peppermill's Fireside Lounge

Palace Station

Meadows Mall

Springs Preserve

Downtown Las Vegas

Post Office

Hogs and Heifers

Neonopolis

Fremont Street Experience

Griffin

Beauty Bar

The Downtown Cocktail Room

1/4 mi

0.25 km

0   0.5 mi

0   0.5 km

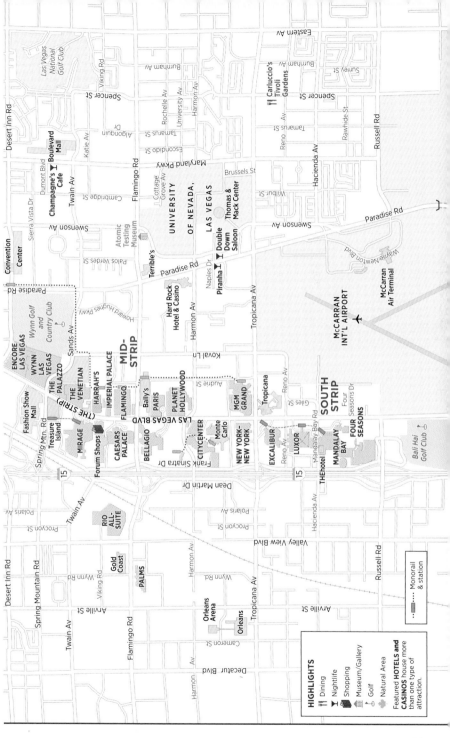

HIGHLIGHTS

🍴 Dining
🍸 Nightlife
🛍 Shopping
🏛 Museum/Gallery
⛳ Golf
✳ Natural Area

Featured **HOTELS and CASINOS** house more than one type of attraction.

······· Monorail & station

OVER-THE-TOP LAS VEGAS

Las Vegas was built on the idea that "average" and "normal" were adjectives that should never be used to describe the city. They don't just build hotels here; they build the biggest hotels in the world. And then they throw a roller coaster or a volcano or a $500-per-person golf course or a $400-per-meal restaurant into the mix. Vegas is all about extravagance, so this itinerary will help you find the biggest of the big, the wildest of the wild, and the most outrageous, over-the-top experiences the city has to offer.

Mornings

You're going to have a busy day of excess so it's important to start out with a hearty breakfast to keep your energy level high. Room service is always an option—there's nothing quite as extravagant as having people bring you food without ever getting out of bed—but if you feel like getting out and about, try the sumptuous **brunch buffets at Wynn Las Vegas or Bellagio.** Both offer an almost mind-boggling amount of food, all of which is a cut above your standard buffet. Handmade omelets and crepes, freshly baked breads, and heaping mounds of bacon, sausage, and even steak will go well with your unlimited mimosas. At more than $30 per person, the price will remind you that this is no pedestrian all-you-can-eat experience.

The a.m. hours are the best time to schedule your outdoor activities. Not only are crowds often lighter, as a lot of people sleep in (it is a vacation after all), but temperatures are also more moderate, especially in the summer when an afternoon stroll down the Strip can emulate a trek across the desert. So use this time to catch some rays poolside or, if you are recreationally minded, work up a moderate sweat with a round of golf.

To fit with this over-the-top theme, consider staying at hotels where the experience of sunbathing is taken to a different level, such as **The Four Seasons,** where they provide chilled towels and have people walking around spritzing you with Evian water (at your request of course). Or, if you are a guest of **Wynn Las Vegas** or **Encore,** you can play the links at the **Wynn Las Vegas Golf Club** for a princely sum of $500 per person.

End your morning with a visit to a spa for some pampering and luxuriating. The **Qua Baths & Spa at Caesars Palace** offers virtually every massage, aromatherapy, skin-care treatment, and relaxation technique known to man—some of which will cost you more for 30 minutes than you are paying for your hotel room. Soak in the Jacuzzi or sit in the unique ice room before heading out for the rest of the day.

One of the many tempting offerings at the Wynn Las Vegas Buffet.

Afternoons

If you worked off your breakfast with all that massaging and lying around by the pool, you'll need to find a good lunch spot to refuel. Belly up

Qua Bath & Spa's luxurious Roman Baths.

to the **Burger Bar** in Mandalay Place and order the Kobe beef patty topped with black truffles, and voila! You have spent $45 on a burger. Congratulations!

Then it's off to the shopping malls where the true excess can really begin. The **Forum Shops at Caesars Palace, the Grand Canal Shoppes at The Venetian, Crystals at CityCenter,** and the **Miracle Mile at Planet Hollywood** are all filled with high-end retailers that are designed to drain your checking account and max out your credit cards. Pick up a little bauble at **Harry Winston Jewelers** or a pair of those *Sex in the City*–endorsed Manolo Blahnik shoes. Or if you're feeling that a $100,000 diamond tiara just isn't "over the top" enough, then head to the **Ferrari-Maserati dealership,** at Wynn Las Vegas, to get something to park in your driveway that will make the neighbors really jealous.

If those are a little out of your price range, consider going the completely opposite direction at the **Bonanza Gift and Souvenir Shop.** Billed as the largest souvenir shop in the world, this is the place where you can find pretty much anything—from tacky to, well, more tacky—emblazoned with the words "Las Vegas" on it. The kitsch factor here is off the charts.

Finally, experience some of the quintessential, only-in-Vegas attractions, such as riding a gondola through a shopping mall at **The Venetian,** or watching the **Fountains of Bellagio** put on a water ballet.

Nights

Start your evening with a meal at **Joël Robuchon,** the multi-Michelin-star-winning darling of the foodie world—and with good reason. It'll only cost you a mere $300 a person (and that's before wine) to find out why.

Next you'll want to see a show, and you should focus on those that can only be seen here. If **Garth Brooks** is in town, you should seize the opportunity to catch one of his concerts at Encore or Caesars Palace respectively, because they aren't playing anywhere else. Or check out any of the Cirque du Soleil productions that are Vegas-only experiences, the best of which are **O,** at Bellagio, and **KÀ,** at MGM Grand. Each is set in its own multimillion-dollar theater, with stage sets—a giant pool and an enormous revolving platform, respectively—unlike anything you are likely to have seen before.

Nighttime is the best time for getting the true Strip experience, so how about renting a limousine (maybe one of those superstretch Hummers, if you are feeling really crazy) and instruct the driver to just cruise Las Vegas Boulevard. Hanging out of the sunroof with a cocktail in your hand is discouraged, but people do it anyway.

Most of the Vegas club scene starts late (11pm or midnight), so have your driver take you to one of the hip hot spots, such as **XS,** at Encore, or **Tao,** at The Venetian. These are see-and-be-seen places, so dress to impress and be on the lookout for a celebrity or three hanging out in the VIP areas. You can drop a grand easily if you want to sit at a table with bottle service.

If it's more of the classic Las Vegas vibe you're looking for, try **Peppermills,** with its retro-'70s/'80s interior. So cheesy, it's hip again.

Your final destination should be in the spot that makes Vegas tick, the casino. Yes, there are casinos all over the country now, but there's nothing quite like tossing the dice at a craps table at **Caesars Palace** or spinning the reels in the high-limit lounge at **Wynn Las Vegas.**

GUYS' GETAWAY

Not every trip to Vegas with the guys needs to get as crazy as the movie *The Hangover,* but if you're looking for a real man's man experience, no other city does it quite like this one. Whether it's a bachelor blowout weekend or just an excuse to blow off steam without your significant other giving you disapproving glances, this itinerary is designed to explain why they call this place "Sin City."

Mornings

You were probably out late the night before and there may have been alcohol involved so start your morning with a hearty guy's breakfast at **Hash House a Go Go.** Its huge portions of twisted farm food are chest-poundingly substantial, and there is even a specialty called "O'Hare of the Dog that Bit You"—a Budweiser served in a paper bag with a side of bacon.

To get your body in shape for the day ahead, spend the morning taking advantage of the various sports and recreation options available around town. Nearly every hotel has a fitness center and some, such as Bally's and the Flamingo, offer full tennis courts. If you're a fan of the fairway, head over to **Bali Hai golf course,** located conveniently on the Strip, for 18 holes and some wheeling around in their GPS-enabled golf carts. Or, if you need something more extreme, visit the **Adventure Spa,** at Red Rock Resort, where you can arrange everything from rock climbing to horseback riding to river rafting.

If you're serious about your gambling, then late mornings are a great time to hit the casinos as well. The crowds are thinner, so you'll usually be able to find a table or a slot easily, while the blackjack limits are often lower so you can save money for your big day ahead.

Afternoons

The name **Dick's Last Resort** isn't meant to be descriptive—but it is the place where obnoxious and unruly behavior rules the day. Waiters are abusive, portions are large (the food is usually fried and served in buckets), and the atmosphere is party hearty.

Bali Hai offers 18 lush holes smack in the middle of the desert.

Daytime is playtime in Las Vegas where the newest trend is to have night-club-worthy experiences during the afternoon at some of the hotel pools. **Bare Pool Club** at The Mirage, **Tao Beach** at The Venetian, and **Wet Republic** at the MGM Grand are all open to the general public (for a cover charge) and include everything from live DJs to fully stocked bars and certainly a bevy of bikini-wearing partiers (hopefully female, but you never know—it is Vegas after all).

Next, head back to the casino for a little sports book action. You can place a wager on just about any type of sporting event in existence (Cricket, anyone?), and, depending on the season and the day of the week, you might be able to catch a game in action. The **sports books** at The Mirage and Caesars Palace are always good options for their huge screens and high energy, but you may want to consider the M Resort, The Venetian, or The Palazzo, which have the only sports books in the city currently offering in-running betting. Popular in the U.K., this means that you can not only wager on the outcome of the game but also place bets during the action as well.

And if you need to get your adrenaline flowing, consider one of the serious thrill rides in town, such as the **Manhattan Express Roller Coaster** at New York–New York, or, to prove how much of a man you really are, the extreme rides atop the 1,000-foot **Stratosphere Tower,** at the Stratosphere Hotel. You can play a little game and make whichever of your friends who screams the loudest while on **Insanity: The Ride** or **Sky Jump** buy the first round of drinks later that night.

Nights

We know. We already sent you to some sports books, but you should go back to the only one that is a real restaurant. The 45,000-square-foot **Lagasse's Stadium** is a sports bar on steroids, with 100 flatscreen TVs and a menu crammed with highlights from Emeril's American and Creole cuisine.

The Pussycat Dolls gambling pit, Caesars Palace.

Now for some nighttime entertainment. If you want class, try the choreographed erotic stylings of **Crazy Horse Paris,** at the MGM Grand, where the girls actually strip and tease and get pretty naked. If you want crass, go for **Crazy Girls,** at the Riviera, where taste is not on the menu. But if you want it "just right," go for the peek-a-boo fairy tale **Peepshow,** at Planet Hollywood, which usually has a rotating cast of comely C-List celebrities—such as *The Girls Next Door* star Holly Madison or former Spice Girl Mel B—in the partially clad cast.

Time to hit the dance floor. The **Playboy Club** at the Palms is an obvious place to start, but **Tao,** at The Venetian, is where the action really is. The party gets started late in Vegas, so you might want to start at a bar or two, such as **Coyote Ugly,** at New York–New York (just like the movie only you pay more), or **Hogs and Heifers,** in Downtown Las Vegas.

What's that? You haven't had enough gambling? Well, while you're at the Playboy Club, you can play some games of chance in the boutique gaming salon, or you could head over to Caesars Palace to the **Pussycat Dolls gambling pit,** complete with lingerie-clad dealers at the blackjack tables and go-go girls in cages.

And if you want more girly action, there are **strip clubs** a-plenty. We have reviewed them in chapter 10. You're a guy; you'll know which one appeals to you most.

GIRLS' GETAWAY

With the plethora of strip clubs and showgirls in this town, you'd think that Vegas is a man's world. Not so! There are plenty of activities and attractions for the ladies, from wild weekend, bachelorette-style craziness to relaxing, leave-your-cares-at-home style getaways. Here are just a few suggestions.

Mornings

If you dream of going to Paris, skip the hotel of the same name and go more or less across the street to Caesars Palace and **Payard Patisserie & Bistro** for breakfast. The chef is from the city of lights, and you'll know it when you taste his croissants. The food is not cheap, but it is high quality, generously portioned, and just plain delightful. (It's also worth an evening stop for the amazing desserts.)

Vegas is retail heaven, and you could spend your whole day going to branches of pretty much every designer name you can think of in the major hotel malls (**Crystals** at CityCenter, **The Forum Shops** at Caesars Palace, **Grand Canal Shoppes** at Venetian/Palazzo, **Miracle Mile** at Planet Hollywood, Bellagio, Wynn Las Vegas). In particular, it is worth noting the branch of NYC's fashion apex **Barney's** department store and a **Christian Louboutin** at The Palazzo, **Tiffany & Co.** at Bellagio and Crystals, **Hermes Paris** at Crystals, **Agent Provocateur** at The Forum Shops, and an **H&M** in the Miracle Mile. Bargain shoppers will want to check out the **Las Vegas Premium Outlets** near Downtown. Truth be told, there are not a lot of bargains there, but it's an outlet, so something will turn up.

Afternoons

You can have a fabulous girly lunch at the pink and orange **Serendipity 3,** a branch of the beloved New York establishment. The hot dogs are authentic, but, more to the point, it's got the frozen hot chocolate!

Okay, it's time for some serious pampering. You could just stretch out by the pool (didn't you just buy a new bikini this morning?), but it's hot outside. So make your way to the spas at **Encore, Bellagio,** or **The Venetian** (which is a branch of the Canyon Ranch), for a full menu of massages, facials, weird treatments imported from countries you've never heard of, and lots more—all designed to make you feel as relaxed and limp as an al dente noodle.

Nights

If your girls'-getaway weekend is of the rowdy bachelorette variety, have dinner at **Tacos and Tequila,** at Luxor. Not only is the food fun and frivolous, the margaritas are also among the best in town. DJs only add to the atmosphere, so you can get as loud as you want. If it's a more laid-back experience you need,

High-end boutiques dominate the offerings at The Shoppes at the Palazzo.

Serendipity 3's legendary frozen hot chocolate is worth every calorie.

then fly to the moon at **Sinatra,** in Encore Las Vegas. The restaurant interior, which is surprisingly light on all things Frank, is really quite striking, and the food matches—so bursting with freshness that it seems as though it was harvested mere moments before it hit your table.

Hey, speaking of getting rowdy, not to mention all those signs with scantily clad women all over the place, equal time can be attained at such shows as the male-stripper review **Chippendales,** at the Rio. Or get your performance art on at the **Blue Man Group,** at The Venetian—they are weird and wonderful, and they make the audience go berserk.

The **Petrossian** bar at Bellagio is a calm, sophisticated place to have a tipple to gear up for the rest of your evening. Plus, the bartenders generally are trained mixologists who really know how to prepare a classic drink, not to mention pour a mean glass of champagne. A somewhat more gearing-up-for-the-clubs atmosphere is across the way at **Caramel,** where the drinks tend to be such things as chocolate- and apple-tinis.

Finally, strap on that pair of Christian Louboutin's you bought earlier today (lucky you), because it's time to go dancing. If you're single and looking to mingle (or whatever, we don't judge), the scenes at **PURE** at Caesars Palace, **XS** at Encore Las Vegas, and **ghostbar** at the Palms are such that people will stand in line for hours (and pay outrageous cover charges) just to get inside. We have to admit they are awfully fun.

Wanna just go dance? Consider going to gay clubs, such as **Krave Las Vegas,** at Planet Hollywood, or **Piranha,** just off the Strip. They welcome women, but remember that you aren't going to be the priority here.

UNLIKELY LAS VEGAS

It's really hard to overlook the Strip—after all, a number of people have spent billions and billions of dollars to ensure that you don't—but there are still some surprisingly unusual and captivating sights to see in and around Las Vegas. This itinerary is designed to help you discover them. You will need a car to do this tour.

Mornings

Those pricey buffets at the casinos may offer you truckloads of food but even the ones at the out-of-the-way hotels are the very definition of "discovered." Instead, go to the edge of Downtown Las Vegas for a true coffee-shop experience at **Tiffany's.** The lunch counter, nearly last of an iconic and dying breed, inside a pharmacy, serves up healthy portions of stick-to-your-ribs food at a price all the cheaper when you compare it to breakfast at your hotel.

Walk off that breakfast by exploring the nearby **Gateway District,** home to a number of art galleries and studios, bravely taking

Desert flowers in the gardens at Springs Preserve.

The Double Down Saloon.

a stance against prefab, soulless Vegas. You might take special note of **The Arts Factory,** a collection of art spaces. If it's the first Friday of the month, you could come back and stroll here in the evening, as that's when the galleries open their new exhibits.

Springs Preserve is a remarkable destination, literally living with nature and ecological concerns. The interpretive center examines the history of the region as related to water consumption, which sounds "dry" but really isn't. Need proof? Try the so-real-you-are-there flash-flood exhibit or the 3-D movie theater that puts you atop the Hoover Dam as it is being built. Outside are trails through the wetlands, animal habitats, and other exhibition halls dealing with the environment and recycling. The place is informative, entertaining, and absolutely vital in this day and age, and you can't believe that something of this quality and social significance is anywhere near Vegas.

Afternoons

We have a soft spot for old school, or should we say in this case, *alte Schule,* and **Cafe Heidelberg** is just that sort of place. We're talking schnitzel. We're talking red booths. We're talking German beer. We are not talking $45 hamburgers with Kobe beef and truffles. Get the picture?

From there, we're recommending a duo of only-in–Las Vegas museums. Begin with **The Atomic Testing Museum.** It's about more than just the 5 minutes when the bomb was awesome (apparently people really thought that—they have photos that you won't believe; check out the one of Miss Atomic Bomb), instead tracing the history of the atomic age and focusing specifically on the aboveground nuclear testing that occurred just outside of Las Vegas. It's a fascinating and sobering experience.

If you want to take a drive, the **Clark County Heritage Museum** is a bit out of the way, but it's a sweet look back at Vegas before, you know, all the neon. This place really was interesting before it got *really* interesting, and this institution, with both indoor and outdoor exhibitions, showcases it in its own low-key but still engaging way.

If you want to skip the latter, consider taking in the afternoon show by **Mac King** at Harrah's Las Vegas, considered one of the best shows in Vegas and a good value for the money. King is an illusionist and comedian of great personal charm, who still practices magic that doesn't require computer technology. You can often get discounted (or even 2-for-1) tickets in local magazines or at the players' club desk at Harrah's.

Nights

Now we'll send you far west to a place only foodies tend to know about: **Rosemary's Restaurant.** The chefs/owners spent a lot of time cooking in New Orleans and working with celebrity chef Emeril, and their clever southern-inspired dishes show that off. It's one of the best restaurants in town. Or you could go east for a true Vegas experience at **Carluccio's Tivoli Gardens.** Once owned by Liberace, it serves classic Italian-American food in a room that still screams Liberace.

For postdinner drinks, you can join local punks and alt-rockers at the beer-soaked **Double Down Saloon.** If that skews too young, join the old and the old-at-heart at the delightfully seedy **Champagnes Cafe.** Both are Vegas institutions.

If that's a little too sleazy for you, there is a burgeoning bar scene right next to Downtown with the newish **Griffin, Beauty Bar,** and **The Downtown Cocktail Lounge** all within steps of each other. Each has its own vibe and is mostly populated by locals, so try them on for style and see which one fits.

VEGAS BY air

Most people are satisfied with the views of Las Vegas from terra firma. Walking or driving up the Strip, especially at night, is a requirement for the first-time Vegas visitor.

But, for some, there is no better way to see Sin City in all its neon glamour than from the air. If you are one of these intrepid souls, then a helicopter tour of Las Vegas is what you're looking for.

There are more than a dozen competing companies offering tours of the city and surrounding areas, and most offer the same type of services at very similar prices. We're including a few of the more well-known companies below, but comparison shopping and checking out safety records are highly encouraged. **Maverick Helicopters** (② 702/261-0007; www.maverickhelicopter.com) is one of the most well-known tour operators in Las Vegas. Its large fleet of ECO-Star helicopters has one of the

best safety records in the business, and a variety of packages is available, including twilight and night flights over the Strip. If you want to venture farther, Hoover Dam and Grand Canyon packages are available. Rates start at around $99 per person and go up from there, depending on the length and distance of the tour you choose. Most include transportation to and from your hotel.

VegasTours.com (② 866/218-6877; www.vegastours.com) features a similar list of air adventures, including a nighttime flight over Vegas and several to the Grand Canyon; while **Papillon Tours** (② 888/635-7272; www.papillon.com) not only offers helicopter tours, but also airplane and ground excursions as well.

WHERE TO STAY

f there's one thing Vegas has, it's hotels. Big hotels. And lots of them. You'll find 9 of the 10 largest hotels in the United States—8 of the top 10 in the world—right here. And you'll find a whole lot of rooms: 150,000 rooms, give or take, as of this writing.

It used to be that whenever a convention, a fight, or some other big event is happening darn near all of those 150,000 rooms would be sold out. And while it is still true that over the course of a regular year, the occupancy rate for hotel rooms in Las Vegas is significantly higher than the nationwide average, tourism has declined just about everywhere including Vegas. Getting a room these days is easier than it used to be and often cheaper. But you should still plan in advance so that you can have your choice: Ancient Egypt (kinda) or Ancient Rome (kinda)? New York or New Orleans? Strip or Downtown? Luxury or economy? Vegas has all that and way too much more.

The bottom line is that with a few, mostly subtle differences, a hotel room is a hotel room is a hotel room. After you factor in location and price, there isn't that much difference between rooms, except for perhaps size and the quality of their surprisingly similar furnishings.

Hotel prices in Vegas are anything but fixed, so you will notice wild price ranges. The same room can routinely go for anywhere from $60 to $250, depending on demand. So use our price categories with a grain of salt, and don't rule out a hotel just because it's listed as "Very Expensive"—on any given day, you might get a great deal on a room in a pricey hotel. On the negative side, some hotels start with their most typical lowest rate, adding "and up." Don't be surprised if "up" turns out to be way up. Just look online or call and ask.

Yes, if you pay more, you'll probably (but not certainly) get a "nicer" establishment and clientele to match (perhaps not so many loud drunks in the elevators). On the other hand, if a convention is in town, the drunks will be there no matter how upscale the hotel—they'll just be wearing business suits and/or funny hats. And frankly, the big hotels, no matter how fine, have mass-produced rooms; at 3,000 rooms or more, they are the equivalent of '60s tract housing. Consequently, even in the nicest hotels, you can (and probably will) encounter plumbing noises, notice scratch marks on the walls or furniture, overhear conversations from other rooms, or be woken by the maids as they knock on the doors next to yours that don't have the DO NOT DISTURB sign up.

COMING ATTRACTIONS

Part of the reason that we patiently tell people they haven't really been to Vegas, even if they have, is because if they haven't been by in the last, oh, week—okay,

PREVIOUS PAGE: **A Renaissance Suite at The Venetian.**

let's say 2 or 3 years—they might find several surprises awaiting them on the Strip. And if it's been more than a decade, well, forget it. All the classic old hotels are either gone (Sands, Hacienda, The Frontier, and Stardust) or renovated virtually beyond recognition (Caesars, the Flamingo). In their place rise bigger and better and trendier resort hotels, changing the landscape and altering the welcome that Vegas visitors receive.

The new era of Vegas hotels was ushered in by The Mirage, and since then, everyone has been trying to up the ante. The year 1997 began with the opening of New York–New York, which set yet another level of stupendous excess that remained unmatched for at least 18 months.

The fall of 1998 saw the official beginning of the new era of Vegas luxury resorts (many with themes), with the opening of the opulent Bellagio, followed by Mandalay Bay and Four Seasons. And then these took a backseat (sort of) to The Venetian, which combines the jaw-dropping detail and extravagance of New York–New York (complete with canals and gondolas) with the luxury of Bellagio. Could anything top it? Possibly—hot on its heels was Paris, themed as you can imagine, and just a few months later, the new and improved Aladdin, with its desert-fantasy decor.

The first half of this decade was less about new stuff and more about old stuff getting bigger and/or better. Sure, Caesars opened its Roman Coliseum replica, built just to house Céline Dion's new show. One old hotel, The Maxim, was reborn as a business-swank Westin, complete with its trademark Heavenly Beds. The rest of the action was all about expansions: The Venetian added 1,000 rooms, a new pool, a fancy restaurant, and more, in the new Venezia Tower; Mandalay Bay added more than 1,000 rooms and other goodies, in a facility they call THEhotel; Bellagio joined the fray with more than 900 new rooms and a swank new spa in a new tower; and Caesars Palace added a new 700-room tower to its empire.

The year 2005 kicked off what is an unprecedented wave of development, with the arrival of Wynn Las Vegas, the latest hotel concept from Steve Wynn, the man behind Mirage Corp., at a mere cost of $2.7 billion. (As you will see, that formerly record-breaking total is peanuts compared with what's coming up.) In 2006, we saw the addition of Red Rock Resort, designed to lure tourists away from the busy Strip, and two top-to-bottom overhauls, with the creaky old San Remo going pneumatic as the Hooters Casino Hotel (no, really) and the relatively new Aladdin getting an extreme makeover to become Planet Hollywood Resort & Casino (no, really, again).

The year 2007 saw the debut of yet another expansion to The Venetian, a 3,000-room resort and casino called The Palazzo, seeking to continue the parent hotel's Italian aesthetic. And 2008 brought an inaugural foray for The Donald in Vegas, with Trump International. Things really ratcheted up with the late-2008 birth of Wynn's second baby, Encore, a more than $1.7-billion, 2,000-room hotel and casino aimed at the ultraluxury market. Before the housing market imploded like an old Sin City hotel, condos seemed to be the property development trend, so if you haven't been to Vegas in awhile, and you wonder what that, and that over there, and also that really big tall tower is, it's more than likely a condo building. Whether or not anyone lives there is a completely different question.

But the biggest of the big new developments, which opened in late 2009, is **CityCenter,** a $9-billion (yes, you read that right) complex of hotels, condos, casinos, shopping, and entertainment spread across 66 acres just north of the Monte Carlo.

reservations SERVICE

The **Las Vegas Convention and Visitors Authority** runs a room-reservations hot line (✆ **877/847-4858** or 702/892-0711; www.visitlasvegas.com) that can be helpful. The operators can apprise you of room availability, quote rates, contact a hotel for you, and tell you when major conventions will be in town.

A couple words of warning: Make sure they don't try to book you into a hotel you've never heard of. Try to stick with the hotels listed in this book. Always get your information in writing, and then make some phone calls just to confirm that you really have the reservations that they say they've made for you.

The economic turbulence of the last few years has hit Vegas hard and development has effectively stopped, or at least slowed to a crawl.

The next major hotels to hit the Strip should be **The Cosmopolitan of Las Vegas,** a 3,000-room resort and casino between CityCenter and Bellagio due to open by the time you read this book; and **Fontainebleau,** a 4,000-room casino hotel on the north end of the Strip near the Riviera that should open sometime this decade. Both have had major financial difficulties during their development and are years behind schedule, but it seems that for the Cosmopolitan, at least, things might be back on track.

The same may not be true for another pair of massive developments. **Echelon,** a multibillion-dollar development that is replacing the Stardust, and **Plaza Las Vegas,** a $5-billion version of the famed New York landmark, have both been put on hold indefinitely. The former is partially built but dormant and the latter is nothing but a dusty lot where The Frontier used to be. Whether or not these happen is dependent upon whether the companies behind them can raise the cash to move forward. Anybody got a billion dollars to loan a poor hotelier? Regardless, even if they get a windfall soon, it will be years before they are up and running.

Obviously, the big story for Vegas of late—just as it has been for the rest of the globe—is the recession. Vegas was hit hard by the economic downturn. The number of visitors to the city plunged as people found better things to do with their discretionary income, resulting in lower occupancy rates, lower room rates, and more than one major casino company declaring bankruptcy, with several others on the verge.

The unthinkable has happened with the closure of some truly terrific properties, including The Ritz-Carlton Lake Las Vegas, which was shuttered in May 2010. As of this writing, Binion's has closed all of its hotel rooms, the Sahara has shut down many of theirs, and the new towers at Caesars Palace and CityCenter have been built but not opened and may not be until 2011 at the earliest.

As with everything about the recession, it's hard to predict Vegas's future; but it is possible that when you read this, there will be all kinds of massive deals available. It's also possible that Vegas will have another run of luck, and high prices will once again rule the day. But put a very large asterisk next to anything that isn't open yet and, in fact, next to some things that already are.

THREE QUESTIONS TO ASK
BEFORE YOU BOOK A ROOM

Where Should I Stay?

Your two main choices for location are the Strip and Downtown. The Strip, home to many of the most dazzling hotels and casinos in Vegas, is undeniably the winner—especially for first-timers—if only because of the sheer, overwhelming force of its "Vegas-ness." On the other hand, it is expensive, crowded, confining, and strangely claustrophobic. We say "strangely claustrophobic" because the hotels only *look* close together: In reality, they are situated on large properties, and it's a long (and often very hot or very cold) walk from one place to the next.

Contrast that with Downtown, which is nowhere near as striking but is more easily navigated on foot. Within 5 minutes, you can reach more than a dozen different casinos. The Fremont Street upgrade has turned a declining area into a very pleasant place to be, and the crowds reflect that: They seem nicer and more relaxed, and a calmer atmosphere pervades. Hotels certainly aren't state-of-the-art down there, but the rooms at many are not just clean and acceptable but rather pleasant. The establishments' smaller sizes often mean friendlier, faster service than at the big 'uns uptown, and you often can't beat the rates. There are also several other development plans afoot that might add even more aesthetic and entertainment appeal to the area. Because it's only a 5-minute ride by car between Downtown and Strip hotels (the Convention Center is more or less in between), there's no such thing as a bad location, if you have access to a car. Main Street Station even provides a free shuttle to the Strip.

For those of you without a car and who don't want to spend the $10 to $15 on a cab ride between Downtown and the Strip: Although the bus ride between Downtown and the Strip is short in distance, it can be long in time, if you get stuck in traffic. You should also be aware that the buses become quite crowded once they reach the Strip and may bypass a bus stop if no one signals to get out and the driver does not want to take on more passengers. Without a car, your ease of movement between different areas of town is limited.

Frankly, for first-timers, there probably isn't any point to staying anywhere but the Strip—you're going to spend most (if not all) of your time there anyway. For future visits, however, we'd strongly advise you to consider Downtown.

But the Strip vs. Downtown location isn't the end of the debate; there is also the issue of where to stay on the Strip. Staying on the **South Strip** end means an easy trip (sometimes in the air-conditioned comfort of covered walkways or monorail) to CityCenter, Mandalay Bay, MGM Grand, New York–New York, Tropicana, Luxor, and Excalibur—all virtually on one corner. **Mid-Strip** has Caesars, The Mirage, Bellagio, Treasure Island, Paris, The Venetian, The Palazzo, Bally's, the Flamingo, Harrah's, and so forth. The **North Strip** gets you Wynn Las Vegas, Encore, the Riviera, Sahara, and Circus Circus, though with a bit more of a walk between them. For this reason, if mobility is a problem and you want to see more than just your own hotel casino, the South and Mid-Strip locations are probably the best bets.

What Am I Looking for in a Hotel?

If gambling is not your priority, what are you doing in Vegas? Just kidding. But not 100% kidding. Vegas's current identity as a luxury, and very adult, resort destination means there are several hotels that promise to offer you all sorts of alternatives to gambling—lush pool areas, fabulous spas, incredible restaurants, lavish shopping. But if you look closely, much of this is Vegas bait-and-switch; the pools are often chilly (and often partially closed during nonsummer months), and it will be years before there is more foliage than concrete in these newly landscaped environments. The spas cost extra (sometimes a whole lot extra), the best restaurants can require a small bank loan, and the stores are often the kinds of places where average mortals can't even afford the oxygen. So what does that leave you with? Why, that's right—gambling.

The other problem with these self-proclaimed luxury hotels is their size. True luxury hotels do not have 3,000 rooms—they have a couple of hundred, at best, because you simply can't provide first-class service and Egyptian-cotton sheets in mass quantity. But while Wynn, Encore, Bellagio, The Venetian, The Palazzo and, to a lesser extent, Mandalay Bay have done their best to offer sterling service and to make their rooms more attractive and luxurious than those at other Vegas hotels, there's only so much that any place that big can do. Don't get us wrong—these places are absolutely several steps up in quality from other large hotels, and compared to them, even the better older hotels really look shabby. But they are still sprawling, frequently noisy complexes.

Having said that, there is an additional trend in Vegas; many of the big hotels have put up new towers or additions that function as virtually separate hotels. This began with the Four Seasons, which occupies the top floors of Mandalay Bay and has its own separate entrance. Mandalay Bay has the sterling THEhotel, while The Venetian and Bellagio have separate towers. And The Venetian added The Palazzo, which is more or less The Venetian without the overt Venice elements. Each has its own check-in area and functions like a separate hotel entity. You gain some quiet (with the exception of The Palazzo, there are no casinos in these venues); in the case of THEhotel, considerable style; and, overall, at least the illusion of better service (and probably some reality of it, too, as there are fewer rooms under the special monikers). Classier grown-ups, or well-heeled families, should make these new additions first on their list.

Sadly, it's relatively easy for both you and us to make a mistake about a hotel; either of us may experience a particular room or two in a 1,000-plus-room hotel and, from there, conclude that a place is nicer than it is or more of a dump than it is. Maintenance, even in the best of hotels, can sometimes be running a bit behind, so if there is something wrong with your room, don't hesitate to ask for another. Of course, if it's one of those busy weekends, there may not be another

Who Kept the Kids Out?

Some hotels—notably Bellagio, which started the practice, and Wynn Las Vegas—ban children who are not staying on-site from stepping foot on the hotel premises and ban strollers even if you are staying there. Child-free adults love the bans, but families who travel to Vegas (can we say yet again that this is not a family destination?) may be seriously inconvenienced by it. The policy doesn't appear to be uniformly enforced (hotels don't want to offend parents who have plenty of dough to gamble, after all), but we've seen families and teenagers get turned away from a hotel because they couldn't produce a room key. If you're traveling with your kids, or want to be free of someone else's, your best bet is to call your chosen hotel and ask what its policy is.

room to be had, but at least this way you've registered a complaint, perhaps letting a busy hotel know that a certain room needs attention. And who knows? If you are gracious and persistent enough, you may be rewarded with a deal for some future stay.

If you want a true luxury-resort hotel, there are only two options: the Four Seasons and the Mandarin Oriental. In addition to that same service and level of comfort only found at a smaller hotel, both offer those extra goodies that pile on the hidden charges at other hotels—health club, poolside cabanas, and so on—as part of the total package, meaning that their slightly higher prices may be more of a bargain than you'd think. Actually, there is a third option: The Red Rock Resort is attracting well-heeled and high-profile tabloid types, who, presumably, know luxury. However, Red Rock charges for all the extras you get as a regular part of your stay at the Four Seasons and the Mandarin.

Still, if you want peace and quiet and aren't in the tax bracket that Four Seasons/Mandarin caters to, there are other, less high-profile hotels without casinos. Make certain the hotel has a pool, however, especially if you need some recreation. There is nothing as boring as a noncasino, nonpool Vegas hotel—particularly if you have kids. For a more detailed analysis of these types of hotels, we refer you to *Frommer's Portable Las Vegas for Non-Gamblers.*

Casino hotels, by the way, are not always a nice place for children. It used to be that the casino was a separate section in the hotel, and children were not allowed inside. (We have fond memories of standing just outside the casino line, watching Dad put quarters in a slot machine "for us.") But in almost all the new hotels, you have to walk through the casino to get anywhere—the lobby, the restaurants, the outside world. This makes sense from the hotel's point of view; it gives you many opportunities to stop and drop $1 or $10 into a slot. But this often long, crowded trek gets wearying for adults—and it's far worse for kids. The rule is that kids can walk through the casinos, but they can't stop, even to gawk for a second at someone hitting a jackpot nearby. The casino officials who will immediately hustle the child away are just doing their job, but, boy, it's annoying.

So, take this (and what a hotel offers that kids might like) into consideration when booking a room. Again, please note that those gorgeous hotel pools are often cold (and again, sometimes closed altogether) and not very deep. They look like places you would want to linger, but often (from a kid's point of view) they are not. Plus, the pools close early. Hotels want you inside gambling, not outside swimming.

Finally, the thing that bothers us the most about this latest Vegas phase—it used to be that we could differentiate between rooms, but that's becoming harder and harder. Nearly every major hotel has changed to more or less the same effect; gone is any thematic detailing and in its place is a series of disappointingly similar (if handsome and appealing) looks. Expect clean-lined wood furniture, plump white beds, and monochromes everywhere you go. All that may distinguish one from another would be size of the room or quality of furnishings.

Ultimately, though, if it's a busy time, you'll have to nab any room you can, especially if you get a price you like. How much time are you going to spend in the room anyway?

What Will I Have to Pay?

The rack rate is the maximum rate that a hotel charges for a room. It's the rate you'd get if you walked in off the street and asked for a room for the night. Hardly anybody pays these prices, however, especially in Vegas, where prices fluctuate wildly with demand and there are many ways around rack rates. Here are some tips for landing a low rate.

- **Don't be afraid to bargain.** Get in the habit of asking for a lower price than the first one quoted. Always ask politely whether a less-expensive room is available than the first one mentioned or whether any special rates apply to you. If you belong to the players' club at the hotel casino, you may be able to secure a better deal on a hotel room there. Of course, you will also be expected to spend a certain amount of time, and money, gambling there. See below for more details on players' clubs.

- **Rely on a qualified professional.** Certain hotels give travel agents discounts in exchange for steering business their way, so if you're shy about bargaining, an agent may be better equipped to negotiate discounts for you.

- **Dial direct.** When booking a room in a chain hotel (Courtyard by Marriott, for example), call the hotel's local line, as well as the toll-free number, and see where you get the best deal. A hotel makes nothing on a room that stays empty. The clerk who runs the place is more likely to know about vacancies and will often grant deep discounts in order to fill up. *Beware:* Many Vegas hotels are now charging a fee if you book via phone, preferring you use the Internet instead.

- **Remember the law of supply and demand.** Las Vegas hotels are most crowded and therefore most expensive on weekends. So the best deals are offered midweek, when prices can drop dramatically. If possible, go then. You can also call the **Las Vegas Convention and Visitors Authority** (✆ **877/847-4858**) to find out whether an important convention is scheduled at the time of your planned visit; if so, you might want to change your date. Some of the most popular conventions are listed under "When to Go," in chapter 3. Remember also that planning to take your vacation just a week before or after official peak season can mean big savings.

- **Look into group or long-stay discounts.** If you come as part of a large group, you should be able to negotiate a bargain, because the hotel can then guarantee occupancy in a number of rooms. Likewise, when you're planning a long stay in town (usually from 5 days to a week), you'll usually qualify for a discount.

- **Avoid excess phone charges.** We can't stress this enough. Virtually every hotel in Vegas charges like crazy for phone calls. At best, it will be $1 for a local call, and sky-high prices for long distance (a 7-min. call to California set us back $35). At worst, it's all that plus an additional charge—as much as 30¢ a minute—for all local calls lasting more than 30 minutes.

- **Beware of hidden extras.** Almost all the major hotels (Four Seasons is one notable exception) charge extra for things that are always free in other destinations, such as health-club privileges. Expect to pay anywhere from $15 to $35 to use almost any hotel spa/health club. Wi-Fi also doesn't come free; usually there is a $12 to $15 charge per 24-hour period. (We've noted when there is a fee in the listings that follow so that you won't be taken by surprise.)

o **Beware of not-so-hidden extras.** Room rates have dropped dramatically in the last couple of years, but many Vegas hotels have found ways to add to their bottom line through the addition of the infamous "resort fee." These fees range anywhere from $5 to $25 per night and although the specifics vary from property to property, they often cover amenities like Internet service, health club access, newspapers, printing of boarding passes, maybe a bottle of water or two, and the like. So what if you're not going to use any of that? Too bad—you still have to pay it. Many hotels include this in their totals when you book your room, but a few wait and sock it to you at check-out, so be sure to ask ahead. In the listings below we included the ones that we knew of at press time, but be aware that the situation is changing often, with hotels adding, dropping, and adjusting the fees on an almost weekly basis while they try to figure out what formula is going to cause the least amount of complaints.

o **Watch for coupons and advertised discounts.** Scan ads in your local Sunday travel section, an excellent source for up-to-the-minute hotel deals. *The Fun Book,* available from the Las Vegas Convention and Visitors Authority (see above), offers some discounts on lodging.

o **Consider a suite.** If you are traveling with your family or another couple, you can pack more people into a suite (which usually comes with a sofa bed) and thereby reduce your per-person rate. Remember that some places charge for extra guests and some don't.

o **Investigate reservations services.** These outfits usually work as consolidators, buying up or reserving rooms in bulk and then dealing them out to customers at a profit. Most of them offer online reservations services as well.

As far as room prices go, keep in mind that our price categories are rough guidelines, at best. If you see a hotel that appeals to you, even if it seems out of your price range, give them a call anyway. They might be having a special, a slow week, or some kind of promotion, or they may just like the sound of your voice (we have no other explanation for it). You could end up with a hotel in the "expensive" category offering you a room for $60 a night. It's a toll-free call, so it's worth a try.

Consider also, even if you think from the outset that this is your one and only trip to Vegas, joining a hotel's players' club—or possibly every hotel's players' club. This costs you nothing, and players/members often get nifty offers in the mail for heavily discounted, and occasionally even free, rooms (plus meals, shows, and so on). Players' clubs reward you with freebies and discounts when you play in their casinos, regardless of whether you win. Recently, ridiculous bargains were showing up in e-mail boxes—such as the Bellagio for $59 a night. How much you have to play to get these deals varies, but if you are going to gamble anyway, why not make it work more to your advantage? You can sign up online, which will get you e-mail-only offers. You can do this on almost every hotel's website, and it's worth it, though it does mean scheduling your Vegas vacation to take advantage of the times the offers are valid.

We've classified all our hotel recommendations based on the average rack rate that you can expect to be quoted for a double room on an average night (not when the Consumer Electronics Show is in town, and not on New Year's Eve). Expect to pay a little less than this if you stay only Sunday to Thursday, and a little more than this if you stay Friday and Saturday. And on any given night when business is slow, you might be able to stay at a "very expensive" hotel for a "moderate" price. For that matter, if the economy continues to slow, prices are very likely to fall considerably.

Note: All the casinos for the major hotels on the Strip and Downtown (and a few other ones) are reviewed in chapter 8.

SOUTH STRIP
Very Expensive

Four Seasons Hotel Las Vegas ★★★ ☺ Various mammoth Vegas hotels attempt to position themselves as luxury resorts, insisting that service and fine cotton sheets can be done on a mass scale. But there is only one true luxury resort—in some people's eyes, *the* luxury resort—in town (see "Henderson," later in this chapter for two more luxury options), located on the top five floors of Mandalay Bay, though in many ways, the Four Seasons is light-years away from the vibe of Mandalay. A separate driveway and portico entrance, plus an entire registration area, set you up immediately. This is one fancy hotel in town where you are not greeted, even at a distance, with the clash and clang of slots and the general hubbub that is the soundtrack of Vegas.

Inside the hotel, all is calm and quiet. But it's really the best of both worlds—all you have to do is walk through a door, and instantly you are in Mandalay Bay, with access to a casino, nightlife, and, yes, general hubbub. The difference is quite shocking, and frankly, once you've experienced Vegas this way, it's kind of hard to go back to the constant sensory overload. So let's scurry quickly back to the womblike comfort of Four Seasons.

The rooms don't look like much at first—slightly bland but in good taste—but when you sink down into the furniture, you appreciate the fine quality. Here at last is a Vegas hotel where they really don't care if you ever leave your room, so the beds have feather pillows and down comforters, robes are plush, and amenities (such as pricey L'Occitane products in the lush bathrooms) are really, really nice.

Pool at the Four Seasons Hotel Las Vegas.

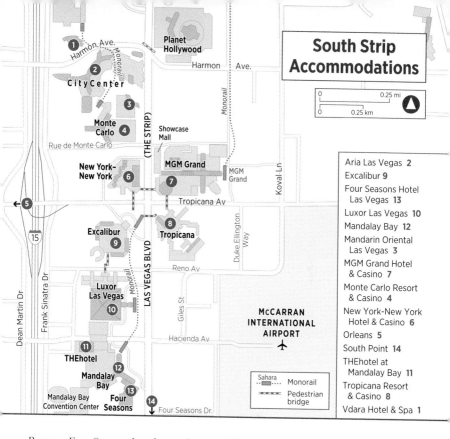

Because Four Seasons has the southernmost location on the Strip, its Strip-view rooms (the most expensive units) give you the whole incredible panorama.

Service is superb (if they say 20 min. for room service, you can expect your food in 19½ min.). Your needs are anticipated so quickly that you're tempted to sink to the floor in the lobby because you know someone will have a chair under your rear before you land. Children are encouraged and welcomed with gifts of toys and goodies, rooms are childproofed in advance, and the list of comforts available for the asking is a yard long. Once you factor in all the freebies (gym/spa access and various other amenities), not to mention the service and the blessed peace, the difference in price between Four Seasons and Bellagio (with all its hidden charges) is nothing.

3960 Las Vegas Blvd. S., Las Vegas, NV 89119. ✆ **877/632-5000** or 702/632-5000. Fax 702/632-5195. www.fourseasons.com. 424 units. $450 and up double; $630 and up suite. Extra person $30. Children 17 and under stay free in parent's room. AE, DC, DISC, MC, V. Valet parking $19; no self-parking. Pets under 25 lb. accepted. **Amenities:** 2 restaurants; concierge; executive-level rooms; elegant health club (free to guests); heated outdoor pool; room service; spa. *In room:* A/C, TV/DVD w/pay movies, fridge (on request), hair dryer, minibar, Wi-Fi (for a fee).

Mandarin Oriental ★★★ With the much-lamented closure of the Ritz-Carlton at Lake Las Vegas in 2010, a window has opened up for another hotel to slip in and battle for the crown of "Most Luxurious" in Vegas. The Mandarin Oriental seems more than up for the fight. The Asian hotelier chain is better

Spa Orchid Room at the Mandarin Oriental.

known in Europe and the Far East but this is actually the sixth property in the U.S. It is a bold statement of true boutique luxury in a city that likes to pretend that a 3,000-room hotel can be either of those things.

This property has just under 400 hotel rooms and another 200 residential units—small by Vegas standards—allowing for a level of service and amenities that simply can't be replicated at a larger hotel. The accommodations are not huge, but are still comfortable and roomy; all with a subtle Asian decor scheme, so-comfortable-you-could-faint-into-them beds, plush robes and towels, and even a valet closet so the "help" doesn't need to come into the room to pick up your laundry or drop off a newspaper. Classy.

But you don't need to wait to get to your room—the playground of the rich vibe greets you as soon as you walk in the door. The top hat–wearing doorman will greet you and attendants will guide you to an elevator that whisks you to the 23rd floor Sky Lobby. With floor-to-ceiling windows facing the Strip, it is without a doubt the most dramatic lobby in town. A tearoom, bar, and a French restaurant from world-renowned chef Pierre Gagnaire, complete this floor all with similar stunning views.

The pool and spa area are on the seventh and eighth floors with still more windows, including in the treatment rooms and whirlpool areas. Have a soak while sipping vitamin-infused water and gazing out at the city lights? Why yes, thank you.

There are a couple of other restaurants, including a delightful patisserie on street level, but that's it inside the building. Luckily the very deep catalog of restaurants, nightclubs, bars, shopping, casinos, and entertainment options at the other properties within CityCenter are just a short walk away.

3752 Las Vegas Blvd. S., Las Vegas, NV 89109. ✆ 888/881-9578 or 702/590-8881. Fax 702/590-8880. www.mandarinoriental.com. 392 units. $299 and up double; $499 and up suite. Extra person $35. No discount for children. AE, DC, DISC, MC, V. Free self- and valet parking. **Amenities:** 3 restaurants; concierge; executive-level rooms; health club; heated pool; room service; spa. *In room:* A/C, TV w/pay movies, fridge (on request), hair dryer, minibar, Wi-Fi (for a fee).

Expensive

Aria Las Vegas ★★★ Sitting at the virtual center of the massive CityCenter complex, Aria Las Vegas seems to elicit the classic "love it or hate it" reaction from visitors. To be sure, it is unlike any Vegas megaresort that has come before it—all

A deluxe queen room at Aria Las Vegas.

gleaming, glass skyscraper and contemporary interior design instead of the themed wackiness or faux old-school luxury of its predecessors. It feels almost out of place here, like someone picked up a big chunk of some ultra-cosmopolitan city (which Vegas most certainly is not, no matter how much it wants to be) and dropped it down in the middle of the Strip. It is dramatic and unexpected, modern without being cold or sterile, and for the record we are firmly in the "love it" camp.

The sinuous glass and steel exterior of the building gives way to a gorgeously appointed series of public spaces, each filled with the kind of attention to design detail that evokes reactions from "cool!" to "wow!" There is no such thing as a blank wall here—everything has a texture or pattern, using wood, stone, glass, fabric, metal, and other natural elements to create a richness that is lacking in other Vegas hotels. Throw in a lot of natural light and some exciting artworks (yes, that is a sculpture by Maya Lin hanging behind the check-in desk) and you have a unique and endlessly gawkable space.

More than 4,000 rooms come in all shapes and sizes, with standard rooms continuing the warm modern theme. Deep hues in the woods and fabrics would lend a cavelike air in other places, but the full wall of floor-to-ceiling windows fixes that nicely here. Standard amenities are plentiful and virtually everything (drapes, temperature, entertainment systems, lights) is controlled by an integrated touch-screen device that will even warn you if you've left the door unlocked. Bathrooms are generously sized with abundant frosted glass and marble, and one seriously odd design element: Although the shower and tub are separate, they are in one enclosure so you have to pass through the former to get to the latter. Space saving but strange.

Back downstairs you'll find more than a dozen restaurants, including tapas from **Julian Serrano** (p. 159) and upscale Italian at **Sirio** (p. 159). And if that's not enough, there are nearly a dozen more restaurants at the neighboring mall and hotels in CityCenter. There is also the requisite high-energy dance club **Haze** (p. 330), several other bars and lounges, the latest Cirque du Soleil production **Viva Elvis** (p. 306) featuring the music of, appropriately enough, Elvis Presley (would've been weird if it were Led Zeppelin, huh?), and a gorgeous spa, salon, workout facility, and lushly landscaped pool area.

Oh, and there's the casino, lest we forget. With more than 150,000 square feet it is one of the largest in Vegas and features all the regular table games, a sports book, two high-limit lounges, and thousands of slot machines, many of which are server based, meaning you can switch the theme or denomination at will.

Downsides are the size (which is leviathan and feels it), parking (both self-parking and the valet pickup are miles from where you want to be), and the crowds—which at least at the beginning seem to be indicating that more people are in the love it camp than the hate it one.

3730 Las Vegas Blvd. S., Las Vegas, NV 89109. ☎ **866/359-7757** or 702/590-7757. Fax 702/531-3887. www.arialasvegas.com. 4,004 units. $159 and up double; $359 and up suite. Extra person $35. No discount for children. AE, DC, DISC, MC, V. Free self- and valet parking. **Amenities:** 17 restaurants; casino; concierge; executive-level rooms; health club; heated outdoor pools; room service; spa; showroom. *In room:* A/C, TV w/pay movies, hair dryer, Internet (for a fee), minibar.

locals' HOTELS

Most residents of Las Vegas—the locals—never go anywhere near The Strip. They prefer to play, eat, be entertained, and occasionally stay at hotel-casinos in their own neighborhoods partly because of convenience, but mostly because it will usually cost a lot less money.

All of the following hotels are admittedly located away from the main tourist areas, but if you have a car at your disposal, you can save yourself some dough by being flexible with your location. Several offer free shuttles to other sister properties.

Just west of the Strip is one of the best options, the **Palace Station** ★, 2411 W. Sahara Ave. (© **800/634-3101** or 702/367-2411; www.palacestation.com). It's plain, but comfortable and unexpectedly nice with recently refurnished rooms (love the huge flatscreen TVs and in-room coffeemakers), a rambling low-limit casino, lots of bargain eats, and friendly service—usually for well under $100 per night.

About 5 miles west of the Strip along Boulder Highway are four local hotel options. **Boulder Station** ★, 4111 Boulder Hwy. (© **800/683-7777** or 702/432-7777; www.boulderstation. com), has more than 300 guest rooms, a 75,000-square-foot casino, movie theaters, restaurants, bars, and a concert venue. Rates usually run from $75 to $125 a night, but rooms can be had for as little as $49 per night. **Sam's Town Hotel & Gambling Hall** ★, 5111 Boulder Hwy. © 800/897-8696 or 702/456-7777; www.samstownlv.com), is a Western-themed property that offers free shuttles to the Strip and Downtown to help you with any feelings of isolation. It has more than 600 rooms, an 18-screen movie theater, a 56-lane bowling alley, a child-care center that provides diversions for the kids, and a 150,000-square-foot casino that provides diversions for you. A multitude of restaurants, nightclubs, pools, and even a laser and water show with animatronic figures (pictured right) are bonuses. **Arizona Charlie's East** ★, 4575 Boulder Hwy. (© **888/236-9066** or 702/951-5900; www.arizonacharlies.com) features 300 minisuites, a 37,000-square-foot casino, several restaurants, and a casino lounge. It's only a step or two above budget accommodations but still very well maintained and usually priced like the former. New to this area (as of 2008) is the **Eastside Cannery** ★, 5255 Boulder Hwy. (© **866/999-4899**; www.eastsidecannery.com). It has relatively upscale accommodations (sleek furnishings, flatscreens, nice bathrooms) without the upscale costs (we've seen them as low as $49 a night). There is a full array of restaurants, nightclubs, recreation, and a casino with both modern and "classic" slots (ones that take and dispense actual coins!).

In addition to the fantastic **Green Valley Ranch** (p. 145) and **M Resort** (p. 146) in Henderson, you'll find a couple of local favorites. The rooms at **Sunset Station** ★★, 1301 W. Sunset Rd., Henderson (© **888/786-7389** or 702/547-7777; www.sunsetstation. com) are simple but have all the basic amenities covered. On-site you'll find more than a dozen restaurants, a bowling alley, movie theaters, entertainment, and a huge casino with much lower gaming limits than the Strip ($5 blackjack tables abound!). Prices are usually below $100 a night. Just down the street a bit is the southwestern-themed **Fiesta Henderson** ★, 777 W. Lake Mead Dr., Henderson (© **888/899-7770** or

702/558-7000; www.fiestacasino.com). It has equally basic yet comfortable lodgings, plus plenty of gaming options, restaurants, bars, movie theaters, and more. Things are even cheaper here, with rooms going for as low as $30 a night during the week.

On the north and west sides of town are several smaller properties popular with locals. **Texas Station** ★, 2101 Texas Star Lane (© **800/654-8888** or 702/631-1000; www.texasstation.com), has a 91,000-square-foot casino, 200 rooms, movie theaters, a bowling alley, concert venues, bars, and a number of very fine restaurants, including the recommended and justly popular Austin's Steakhouse (p. 192). You can often get rooms for as low as $40 a night here. Right across the street is **Fiesta Rancho** ★, 2400 N. Rancho Rd. (© **888/899-7770** or 702/631-7000; www. fiestacasino.com), similar in concept and execution to its sister property mentioned above. In addition to the 100 rooms, there is a big casino and a regulation-size ice-skating rink, complete with equipment rentals and lessons. Prices go as low as $40 a night. Continue north on Rancho Road, and you'll run into **Santa Fe Station** ★★, 4949 N. Rancho Rd. (© **866/767-7771**

or 702/658-4900; www.santafestation lasvegas.com). It has a spiffy casino, rooms with stylish furnishings and plenty of amenities, lots of restaurants and bars, a bowling alley, movie theaters, and more. All this for rates as low as $35 a night and rarely over $100. And if you continue north—about as far north as you can go without running into a mountain—you'll find **Aliante Station** ★★, 7300 Aliante Pkwy., North Las Vegas (© **877/477-7627** or 702/692-7777; www.aliantecasino hotel.com), a beautifully done resort with smallish rooms that are gorgeously decorated with all of the latest amenities. The facility boasts several restaurants, bars and lounges, a Strip-worthy pool, and a big casino all wrapped up in warm design elements. It's a solid 25-minute drive from the Strip without traffic, but with prices as low as $49 a night for rooms this nice, it might just be worth it.

Also on the north side of town is **The Cannery** ★, 2121 E. Craig Rd. (© **866/999-4899** or 702/507-5700; www.cannerycasinos.com), a '40s patriotic World War II–themed hotel and casino, with a couple hundred fine and very inexpensive rooms (usually under $100 a night), a fun casino, a terrific buffet restaurants, movie theaters, and more.

Lastly, don't think that locals' hotels are always budget affairs in terms of price or amenities. The **JW Marriott** ★, 221 N. Rampart (© **877/869-8777** or 702/869-7777; www.jwlasvegasresort. com) is a handsome Spanish Mission–style building with fabulously landscaped grounds and tricked-out rooms; this is much more of a true resort property than any Strip destination. But then again, what you gain there, you lose in location—with traffic, it could take 30 minutes to get to the Strip.

Mandalay Bay ★★ ☺ Mandalay Bay is one of our favorite hotels. Why? Well, we love that the lobby (impossibly high ceilings; calm, gleaming with marble; and housing a large aquarium), and the other public areas really do make this seem more like an actual resort hotel than just a Vegas version of one. You don't have to walk through the casino to get to any of these public areas or the guest-room elevators, the pool area is spiffy, and the entire complex is marginally less confusing and certainly less overwhelming than some of the neighboring behemoths.

We wouldn't say it really evokes colonial Southeast Asia—oh, maybe around the edges, if you squint, thanks to the odd bit of foliage or Balinese carving. This may well keep out the gawkers, who are looking for bigger visual thrills, but we find a place whose theme doesn't bop you over the head refreshing.

The spacious rooms are among the most desirable on the Strip. There is no tropical influence; they've gone with geometrics, like everyone else, though theirs are very handsome indeed. The bathrooms are the crowning glory: downright large with impressive, slightly sunken tubs, glassed-in showers, double sinks, and separate water closets, plus lots of fab amenities. Rooms on higher floors have some of the best Strip views in town, but usually cost an additional fee.

Service overall is pretty good, and those pool-area employees are the tops in Vegas, though there were no security guards at the guest elevators. A monorail system connects the hotel with Luxor and Excalibur, which are located in the heart of the Strip action, and this should more than help you get over any feelings of isolation.

The restaurants in Mandalay Bay feature some of the most innovative interiors in Vegas, each one more whimsical and imaginative than the next. Even if you don't eat at the hotel, drop in and poke around the restaurants: **Aureole,** a highly rated branch of Charlie Palmer's renowned New York City restaurant; **Border Grill, Red Square,** and the **Bayside Buffet** are reviewed in chapter 6. And then there's **rumjungle,** which features a dramatically skewered all-you-can-eat multicourse Brazilian feast, which you'll enjoy while listening to world-beat drums, surrounded by walls of fire and water and other striking visual features. More casual food can be found at **House of Blues,** whose Southern delicacies are often quite palate pleasing; HOB is probably the best place in town to see rock bands. Mandalay Bay has a showroom, where Disney's *The Lion*

📎 Understanding CityCenter

Much has been written about CityCenter, the $9-billion (yes, you read that right) development in the heart of the Las Vegas Strip that opened in late 2009. What is confusing, however, is that CityCenter is not a hotel, specifically, but rather a collection of them and other facilities. Aria Las Vegas (the only one with a casino), Mandarin Oriental, and Vdara are the hotels, each listed separately in this chapter; the Crystals mall is reviewed in chapter 9. Another hotel, The Harmon, is due to open in 2011.

The complex features its own monorail, connecting Monte Carlo to the south and Bellagio to the north and has multiple parking garages and valets. Although considered to be the largest privately funded construction project in history, the developers went out of their way to remain as green as possible, with heavy reuse of material (93% of the construction waste was recycled), energy-saving devices (radiant cooling, sunshades over the windows), and even the world's first fleet of natural gas–powered limousines.

The lobby of Mandalay Bay.

King launched a new run in 2009 and a separate arena that was inaugurated by none other than the late Luciano Pavarotti. See chapter 10 for details on the hotel's major nightlife offerings. There's also a big, comfortable casino, airier and less claustrophobic than most, plus three bars, often featuring live music at night.

There are no fewer than four pools (entering this area is like going to a water park, thanks to upgraded security—*all* guests, regardless of age, must show a room key), including the touted wave pool, which is, unfortunately, a classic example of Vegas bait-and-switch. It can't handle waves of any serious size, but bobbing in the miniwaves is delightful, as is floating happily in the lazy river (tubes are available for rental—we say save some bucks and share a tube with friends, taking turns using it). Though it was already the finest pool area in town, recent overhauls have given it even more style, adding in a poolside casino, restaurant, and bar. All in all, this area alone makes this resort a top choice for families (except, perhaps, the topless swimming area). The downside of creating such an alluring pool package is that it lures lots and lots of people to its sandy shores—so many that at times it becomes more of a pain than a pleasure. If a quiet poolside retreat is what you are looking for, you may want to go elsewhere.

The health club is sufficiently stocked to give you a good workout (it should be, as there is a daily charge of $30 to use it—$20 for the gym only, at THEhotel's facility). The spa area proper—featuring hot and warm pools, plus a cold plunge pool—is exotically designed, as close to those found in the Turkish spas in Eastern Europe as we've come across, though without the weathered decay of decades or centuries, which can be a good thing. Load up on that rich moisturizer when dressing—it costs $17 a bottle in the store outside the door.

See the separate listing on p. 93 for Mandalay Bay's THEhotel addition.

3950 Las Vegas Blvd. S. (at Hacienda Ave.), Las Vegas, NV 89119. © **877/632-7800** or 702/632-7108. Fax 702/632-7228. www.mandalaybay.com. 3,309 units (excluding THEhotel). $99 and up double; $149 and up suite; $149 and up House of Blues Signature rooms. Extra person $30. Children 14 and under free in parent's room. AE, DC, DISC, MC, V. Free self- and valet parking. **Amenities:** 22 restaurants; aquarium; casino; concierge; 12,000-seat events center; executive-level rooms; health club; Jacuzzi; 1,700-seat performing-arts theater; 4 outdoor pools w/lazy river and wave pool; room service; sauna; spa; watersports equipment/rentals. *In room:* A/C, TV w/pay movies, hair dryer, Wi-Fi (for a fee).

MGM Grand Hotel & Casino ★★ ☺ Vegas goes back and forth on its position on whether size matters, and the MGM Grand is a perfect example of that. The hotel management now downplays the once-touted "hugeness," trying to pretend that the really big casino is actually several medium-big casinos. Whatever.

Despite plenty of signage, it is still a lengthy, confusing schlep from anywhere to anywhere. The 80 or so 42-inch TV monitors (apprising registering guests of hotel happenings) in the vast white-marble lobby only add to the chaotic confusion a guest might feel—all the worse if you are toting kids. At least the lobby is now immediately accessible from the outside world.

Having said all of that, we've grown very fond of this hotel, and we have to admit that it's gone to some efforts to make the ridiculous size work to its—and, thus, your—advantage. Although the original standard rooms in the main tower with 1930s-era Hollywood glam styling have been replaced by somewhat more blandly upscale decor (there are still black-and-white movie star photos and some Deco-inspired curves to some of the furniture), there's nothing wrong, really, with blandly upscale. They are generously proportioned and equipped with pretty much everything you might need, and while they may not be as large or as opulent as some of the superluxe hotels in town, they are also not as expensive (usually). A second section of the tower is called the West Wing, and it is here that you'll find the memorable accommodations. With a kicky contemporary style, these rooms are smaller (a rather tiny 350 sq. ft.) but full of the trendy touches we are complete suckers for. There is no counter space in the open bathroom plan, but frosted green glass doors preserve privacy. Rooms include DVD and CD players, TVs in the bathroom mirrors, and fluffy bedding, plus there's liberal use of electronic "gee whiz" moments, such as lamps that turn on and off if you touch them, while all lights in the rooms are controlled by the insertion of your room key. Each has a king-size bed and a shower-only bathroom. Overall, guests report that the staff couldn't be more friendly and helpful.

MGM houses a prestigious assemblage of dining rooms, among them **Joël Robuchon**'s two sterling entries and **Emeril's New Orleans Fish House.** These, along with buffet offerings, are reviewed in chapter 6.

A mammoth bronze lion guards the entrance to the MGM Grand Hotel & Casino.

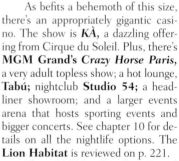

As befits a behemoth of this size, there's an appropriately gigantic casino. The show is **KÀ,** a dazzling offering from Cirque du Soleil. Plus, there's **MGM Grand's** *Crazy Horse Paris,* a very adult topless show; a hot lounge, **Tabú;** nightclub **Studio 54;** a headliner showroom; and a larger events arena that hosts sporting events and bigger concerts. See chapter 10 for details on all the nightlife options. The **Lion Habitat** is reviewed on p. 221.

The MGM Grand's **Grand Spa** ★★ is a Zen-Asian minimalist wonder, all natural stone and aged wood. The services offered are quite marvelous, with everything from standard massages to 2-hour "rituals" in a private room for over $300. The state-of-the-art health club is larger than most, with some serious machines, including ones equipped with fancy computer video monitors. It'll cost you $25 to work up a sweat here most of the day, but you can use the gym facilities only, without the whirlpools and other amenities of the spa, for $15.

The swimming pool area is a rousing success. The 6½ acres of landscaped grounds feature five pools, including the longest lazy river in town (though we wish portions of it weren't closed off for nonsummer months). The "pool club"— sort of like a nightclub, but during the day—called Wet Republic only further pushes kids out of the picture.

Note that the MGM Grand has its own separate, noncasino, all-suite addition called **The Signature.** Prices are a bit high for what you get, but if money is not an issue, and a more grown-up atmosphere is, you might want to inquire.

3799 Las Vegas Blvd. S. (at Tropicana Ave.), Las Vegas, NV 89109. ℭ**800/929-1111** or 702/891-7777. Fax 702/891-1030. www.mgmgrand.com. 5,034 units. $99 and up double; $159 and up suite. Extra person $35. Children 12 and under stay free in parent's room. AE, DC, DISC, MC, V. Free self- and valet parking. **Amenities:** 15 restaurants; nightclub; cabaret theater; casino; concierge; events arena; executive-level rooms; large health club; Jacuzzi; Lion Habitat; 5 outdoor pools w/lazy river; room service; salon; shopping arcade; spa; 2 wedding chapels. *In room:* A/C, TV w/pay movies, hair dryer, Internet (for a fee).

Monte Carlo Resort & Casino ★ When it was built, the massive Monte Carlo was the world's seventh-largest hotel. It's now considerably overshadowed by its high-profile, all the more luxe-intensive brethren. Entering it is still nice, as it comes off as a European casino hotel alternative, replete with Corinthian colonnades, triumphal arches, and big and busy statuary, with an entranceway opening onto a bustling casino that got a substantial 2009 makeover, turning a bland white space into a slightly less-bland, but much nicer, space. A separate entrance in the rear of the hotel leads to a splendid marble-floored, crystal-chandeliered lobby evocative of a European grand hotel. We love that the guest rooms are accessible without going through the casino, but we don't really love the rooms themselves, as they are smaller than what we've grown accustomed to, especially in terms of bathroom square footage. The pool area, once the very last word in local pool fun, is now put to shame by better versions (including superior lazy rivers) at Mandalay Bay and the MGM Grand. It does have a number of child-/family-/budget-friendly restaurants.

The top level has been completely redone and made into an independently operated mini–boutique hotel called Hotel 32. A free limo ride whisks you to a greeter who puts you in your private elevator straight to the top and checks you into your handsome and masculine room or suite, which comes with some pretty swish details. Don't miss the club room with the free snacks. You're going to pay five times as much for these perks, but it might work out to be a better deal for luxury than the Four Seasons, so comparison shop.

Diablo's Cantina and the **Monte Carlo Buffet** are described in chapter 6. In addition, the bad news that the original classic Downtown French restaurant **Andre's** has closed was somewhat leavened by the fact that the branch here is still serving (p. 154). Monte Carlo's health club and spa are nothing special and at $23 a day, not cheap.

3770 Las Vegas Blvd. S. (btw. Flamingo Rd. and Tropicana Ave.), Las Vegas, NV 89109. ℭ**800/311-8999** or 702/730-7777. www.montecarlo.com. 3,002 units. $99 and up double; $145 and up suite. Extra person $25. No discount for children. Daily resort fee $13, includes use of fitness center, local calls, Internet, and newspaper. AE, DC, DISC, MC, V. Free parking. **Amenities:** 7 restaurants; food court; casino; concierge; executive-level rooms; fitness center; Jacuzzi; outdoor

A suite in the Monte Carlo's top-level Hotel 32.

pool w/wave pool and lazy river; room service; showroom; spa; watersports equipment/rentals; wedding chapel. *In room:* A/C, TV w/pay movies, hair dryer, Internet.

New York–New York Hotel & Casino ★★ ☺ Isn't this exactly the kind of hotel you think about—or dream about or fear—when you think "Las Vegas?" There it is, a jumbled pile mock-up of the venerable Manhattan skyline—the Empire State Building, the Chrysler Building, the Public Library—all crammed together, along with the 150-foot Statue of Liberty and Ellis Island, all built to approximately one-third scale. And as if that weren't enough, they threw in a roller coaster running around the outside and into the hotel and casino itself.

Inside is a different story these days. Once as highly themed as the outside, the main casino space has gotten a makeover that has removed much of the New York detail. Gone are the Big Apple Bar and Central Park–themed gaming areas, replaced by a sleekly modern decor that while pretty, is nowhere near as entertaining. The replica of Greenwich Village, down to the cobblestones, the manhole covers, the tenement-style buildings, and the graffiti, remains (Yes, they even re-created that!), and you'll still find enough of the Gotham silliness elsewhere to probably evoke a smile or three, but dizzy laughter over the sheer spectacle is a thing of the past.

Upstairs is the arcade, which is Coney Island–themed (naturally), and just as crowded as the real thing. Kids play boardwalk games in the hopes of winning tickets redeemable for cheap prizes. (You're never too young to start learning about gambling.) The line for the roller coaster starts here. There are many restaurants, all housed in buildings that fit the theme of whatever New York neighborhood is represented in that particular part of the hotel.

Rooms are housed in different towers, each with a New York–inspired name. The place is so massive and mazelike that finding your way to your room can take a while. There are 64 different layouts for the rooms, which have moved them ever farther from the original Deco-inspired decor to something bland, albeit comfortable, and though the bathrooms are small, they are pleasantly decorated. There can be a loooonnnggg walk from the elevators, so if you have ambulatory issues, you had best mention this while booking. Rooms in the single digits seem to be in the Empire Tower, if that helps give you a clue to location. Light sleepers should request a room away from the roller coaster. The health club and spa are

New York—New York replicates the Manhattan skyline.

nice but nothing to write home about and the mediocre pool is right next to the parking structure.

In addition to a particularly good food court and a number of more-than-decent restaurants, including reliable Italian chain Il Fornaio, there are several festive and beautifully decorated bars throughout the property. **Coyote Ugly** is a party-hearty bar, where dancing on furniture is encouraged and the female bartenders are hired just to be sassy. At **The Bar at Times Square,** dueling pianos set the mood for a lively neighborhood bar conviviality. This is home to the topless and adults-only Cirque du Soleil production **Zumanity,** which we think is improving but not the best that Cirque has to offer. Chapter 10 offers more on the hotel's nightlife.

3790 Las Vegas Blvd. S. (at Tropicana Ave.), Las Vegas, NV 89109. © **800/693-6763** or 702/740-6969. Fax 702/740-6920. www.nynyhotelcasino.com. 2,024 units. $79 and up double. Extra person $30. No discount for children. Daily resort fee $12, includes use of fitness center, local calls, Internet, and newspaper. AE, DC, DISC, MC, V. Free self- and valet parking. **Amenities:** 7 restaurants; food court; casino; executive-level rooms; fitness center; Jacuzzi; outdoor pool; room service; showrooms; spa. *In room:* A/C, TV w/pay movies, hair dryer, Internet.

THEhotel at Mandalay Bay ★★★ The rather silly nomenclature of this utterly fabulous Vegas accommodation reminds us of our previous consideration regarding the Four Seasons' relationship with Mandalay Bay (located on the top floors but operated as a separate entity)—it's part *of* the hotel, but not precisely *the* hotel. In this case, this really is *THE*hotel, in all senses, not the least of which is that even though we were quite fond of Mandalay Bay prior to the opening of this conjoined twin of a property, we now think of it as the frowzy sister from the sticks who looks tawdry and rumpled next to its sleek *Vogue*-magazine-editor sibling. (Actually, we still like Mandalay Bay a great deal.) Yes, if Prada were a hotel, it would look something like THEhotel. Certainly, if there are Prada wearers in town, we bet they are going to be staying here.

The new trend in Vegas hotels seems to be hotels that allow you, if you so choose, to forget you are in Vegas. Never mind that psychology. What that translates to here is an entirely separate entrance and an entirely different atmosphere. This is not a casino hotel—though it is connected to one by a long hallway—but a world of sleek towering walls of lighting, ambiguous modern art, and both

FAMILY-FRIENDLY hotels

We've said it before, and we'll say it again: Vegas is simply not a good place to bring your kids. Most of the major hotels have backed away from being perceived as places for families, no longer offering babysitting, much less exciting children's activities. Further, fewer hotels offer discounts for children staying in a parent's room, and many others have lowered the age for children who can stay for free.

In addition to the suggestions below, you might consider choosing a noncasino hotel, particularly a reliable chain, and a place with kitchenettes.

- **Circus Circus Hotel & Casino** (p. 127) Centrally located on the Strip, this is our first choice if you're traveling with the kids. The hotel's mezzanine level offers ongoing circus acts daily from 11am to midnight, dozens of carnival games, and an arcade. And behind the hotel is a full amusement park.

- **Excalibur** (p. 97) Though the sword-and-sorcery theme has been considerably toned down, Excalibur features an entire floor of midway games, a large video-game arcade, and more. It also has some child-oriented eateries and shows. It also now has a heavily promoted male-stripper show, though, so it's not perfect.

- **Four Seasons** (p. 82) For free goodies, service, and general child pampering, the costly Four Seasons is probably worth the dough. Your kids will be spoiled!

- **Mandalay Bay** (p. 88) Mandalay Bay certainly looks grown-up, but it has a number of factors that make it family friendly: good-size rooms, to start, which you do not have to cross a casino to access; a variety of restaurants; a family-appropriate show; a big ol' shark attraction; and,

best of all, the swimming area—wave pool, sandy beach, lazy river, lots of other pools—fun in the Vegas sun!

- **MGM Grand** (p. 89) While decidedly no longer targeted toward families—its high-profile nudie show *Crazy Horse Paris!* should be your tip-off—MGM Grand is still frequented by families, thanks to an excellent swimming pool area, a decent arcade, and other goodies.

- **New York–New York** (p. 92) Over-stimulating and hectic, for sure, but between the roller coaster and the Coney Island–style midway, not to mention just looking around, this has options for children (though going almost anywhere requires walking through the casino).

- **The Orleans** (p. 138) Considered a "local" hotel, its proximity to the Strip makes it a viable alternative, especially for families seeking to take advantage of its plus-size pool area, kid's activity area, bowling, and movie theaters.

- **Stratosphere Las Vegas Hotel & Casino** (p. 126) For families looking for reasonably priced, if not particularly exciting, digs, this is a good choice. Plus, it's not in the middle of the Strip action, so you and your kids can avoid that. Thus far, it's not moving in the "adult entertainment" direction, and it has thrill rides at the top.

guests and employees in head-to-toe black. Like any good Vegas hotel, it wows you from the start, but not in the usual Vegas marble-gilt-and-chandelier screaming "look-how-you-can-live-if-only-you-hit-that-jackpot-over-there" way, but in a way that coolly says, "You probably already live like this, don't you?" while handing you a nicely chilled Cosmopolitan. In other words, this isn't Donald Trump's version of the best, but rather that of Mr. Big from *Sex and the City.* Don't get us wrong, everything here is still out-of-proportion large, but it's sophisticated and chic, all blacks, tans, woods, and midcentury modern sharp lines. We fell for it instantly, and that's before we went to our room.

Ah, the rooms: Every one is a genuine suite (not just separated living room and bedroom, but even a wet bar and second water closet), done in more black, tans, and gleaming woods, like your professionally decorated Manhattan dream apartment. There are plasma-screen TVs in every room, including the enormous marble bathroom, where the tub is so deep, the water comes up to your chin when you sit down. Bathroom amenities are posh, the comforters are down, and the sheets—well, remember our complaints about how you just can't get good sheets in big hotels? Feel the soft heft of these. *That's* what we want. Two complaints might be the excess of mirrors (the wall-length double closet and TV cabinet are covered in them, as is another wall) and the overall lack of good lighting. But seriously, you won't care. For once, a hotel room in Vegas designed to make you want to stay put. Not that you have to; as stated, all the amenities of Mandalay Bay (their incredible pool area, a number of terrific restaurants) are just down a long hall, though the instant you step from this grown-up world into the world of, well, noisy grown-up pursuits, which isn't the same thing at all, you might well want to turn right back around.

Having raved about it all, we do have some complaints. The staff is hardly cuddly, and service reflects that. Costs at the sleek cafes are higher than even the usual elevated hotel restaurant prices. Then again, you can use just the workout

Bathhouse Spa at THEhotel.

Lobby bar at Vdara.

facilities at the **Bathhouse Spa ★★**, the rather unfortunately named but gorgeous health club and spa, for only $20 (cheap compared to other comparable hotels, though it's $30 if you also want to use the saunas and the like). This is the place we would splash out on (and certainly would leap on any specials offered), but with the understanding that it's still, despite appearances, a Vegas hotel, though very likely the best there is.

3950 Las Vegas Blvd. S., Las Vegas, NV 89119. ℂ **877/632-7800** or 702/632-7777. Fax 702/632-9215. www.thehotelatmandalaybay.com. 1,120 units. $160 and up suite. Extra person $30. Children 13 and under stay free in parent's room. AE, DC, DISC, MC, V. Free self- and valet parking. **Amenities:** 2 restaurants; bar; access to Mandalay Bay restaurants/pool/casino; health club; room service; spa. *In room:* A/C, 3 TVs, CD/DVD player, hair dryer, minibar, Wi-Fi (for a fee).

Vdara ★ Although a part of CityCenter, Vdara seems to be a world away both physically and spiritually from the rest of the eye-popping visual splendor that makes up the complex. Saying that it is located at the far northwest corner of the property doesn't seem like much until you know that we're talking 66 acres and with a road and a wide circular drive in between it and everything else, it definitely sits apart. But beyond that it is sedate and reserved where everything else is dramatic and statement worthy.

This is understandable, perhaps, considering that Vdara is a condominium-hotel, designed to be a residential facility first and a tourist accommodation second. Each of the units is owned by someone who then puts it into a rental pool when they are not in residence, allowing Average Joes like us the opportunity to see how folks who can afford places like this live.

Most of the units are studios with a very small kitchenette and dining table and a combo living room/bedroom. The design scheme is sleekly modern; muted brown and gray with a few splashes of color, and all distinctly grown-up. Bathrooms are big, bright white affairs with all the comforts of home. One and two bedroom units are also available with full kitchens and separate living spaces if you need more room to stretch out.

On-site there is one restaurant and a lobby bar plus a pool and spa, but there is nary a slot machine, showroom, or white tiger in sight. Luckily the hotel is connected via a very long walkway to Bellagio next door and the CityCenter monorail will take you to the heart of the development if you get bored. And quite frankly, you just might. Don't get us wrong, it's all very nice and some people may appreciate the anti-Vegas feeling (and it's certainly a good place for families), but if you're looking for Vegas-style excitement you may want to look elsewhere.

2600 W. Harmon Ave., Las Vegas, NV 89109. ℰ **866/745-7767** or 702/590-2767. Fax 702/669-6233. www.vdara.com. 1,500 units. $159 and up double; $299 and up suite. Extra person $35. No discount for children. AE, DC, DISC, MC, V. Free valet parking; no self-parking. **Amenities:** Restaurant; concierge; executive-level rooms; health club; heated outdoor pool; room service; spa. *In room:* A/C, TV w/pay movies, hair dryer, kitchen or kitchenette, minibar, Wi-Fi (for a fee).

Moderate

Excalibur ★ ☺ One of the largest resort hotels in the world, Excalibur (also known as the Realm) is a gleaming white, turreted castle complete with moat, drawbridge, battlements, and lofty towers. And it's huger than huge. To heck with quiet good taste; kitsch is cool. And it's becoming harder and harder to find in a town that once wore tacky proudly. If your soul is secretly thrilled by overblown fantasy locations—or if you just want a pretty good budget option on the Strip—the Excalibur is still here for you. And yet, we just know that any minute now, the Lords of Taste will bring an end to its sword and sorcery imagery. Actually, the decorating fairies have already made some quiet changes (the deep reds in the public areas have been switched to creams), and there are some ominous rumblings in keeping with the rest of Vegas's careening away from the "family-friendly" image—gone is the animatronic dragon and wizard show out front although the carnival-style midway and the SpongeBob SquarePants–themed virtual reality ride remain. It's really too bad because, without the excess, this is just another hotel—a mighty big and chaotic hotel, thanks to a sprawling casino full of families and small-time gamblers, which is located smack-dab in the middle of everything, including, naturally, the path between you and the elevators to your room. Parents should be warned that on the way to the SpongeBob ride you may see posters for the male-stripper act, *Thunder from Down Under* also in residence at the hotel.

Newer "widescreen" rooms only slightly reflect the Olde English theme and feature the brown suede headboards that are all the rage, flatscreen TVs, spiffed-up bathrooms with new marble fixtures, and nice wallpaper. Older "standard" rooms are about as motel basic as they come. Guests who have stayed in Tower 2 have complained about the noise from the roller coaster across the street at New York–New York (it runs till 11pm, so early birds should probably ask to be put in a different part of the hotel). Frankly, we prefer stopping in for a visit rather than actually settling here, but we know single-minded others (read: Vegas is for gambling, and so is the majority of the vacation budget) who wouldn't consider staying anywhere else.

Medieval architecture rules the realm at Excalibur.

The second floor holds the Medieval Village, where Excalibur's restaurants and shops are peppered along winding streets and alleyways, a sort of permanent Renaissance Faire, which could be reason enough to stay away (or to come). Up here you can access the enclosed, air-conditioned, moving sidewalk that connects with the Luxor. The pool area got a face-lift to add in better landscaping, fancy cabanas, and the like. There are plenty of restaurants, including the **Roundtable Buffet** (p. 202), and a pretty good prime rib joint. **Dick's Last Resort** and the buffet are reviewed in chapter 6. Excalibur won our hearts forever by installing a branch of Krispy Kreme Doughnuts on the second level, on the way to the Luxor walkway. The **Tournament of Kings** (p. 315) is a medieval-style dinner show, and there's a very loud, claustrophobic casino.

3850 Las Vegas Blvd. S. (at Tropicana Ave.), Las Vegas, NV 89109. ℂ **800/937-7777** or 702/597-7700. Fax 702/597-7163. www.excalibur.com. 4,008 units. $59 and up double. Extra person $20. Children 12 and under stay free in parent's room. Daily resort fee $10, includes local calls, Internet, and newspaper. AE, DC, DISC, MC, V. Free self- and valet parking. **Amenities:** 5 restaurants; food court; casino; concierge; outdoor pools; room service; showrooms; wedding chapel. *In room:* A/C, TV w/pay movies, hair dryer, Internet.

Luxor Las Vegas ★★ Kitsch worshipers were dealt a blow when the people behind this hotel came to the inexplicable decision to eliminate anything Egypt from the inside of it, casting aside identity in favor of generic luxury. Obviously, they can't get rid of certain elements—the main hotel is, after all, a 30-story onyx-hued pyramid, complete with a really tall 315,000-watt light beam at the top. (Luxor says that's because the Egyptians believed their souls would travel up to heaven in a beam of light. We think it's really because it gives them something to brag about: "The most powerful beam on Earth!") Replicas of Cleopatra's Needle and the Sphinx still dominate the exterior and touches of Egypt remain in the lobby and main entrance (you figure out what to do with those three-story high statues of Ramses). But other than that, virtually every other trace of the land of the

The Luxor atrium is the largest of its kind in the world.

Pharaohs is gone. And some magic is now gone from Vegas. Now guests will be attracted only by the generally good prices, not by the giddy fun the theme produced. That is, unless said price rises in accordance with the place's lofty ambitions.

But they can't take away fundamentals and so staying in the pyramid part means you get to ride the 39-degree high-speed inclinators—that's what an elevator is when it works inside a pyramid. Really, they are part conveyance, part thrill ride—check out that jolt when they come to a halt. Rooms in the pyramid open onto the vast center that

South Point's Equestrian Center hosts the annual National Rodeo Finals in December.

contains the casino—indeed, ground-level rooms open more or less right into the action (though many of these have been turned into offices), so if you want only a short drunken stumble back to your room, these are for you. Otherwise, ask for a room higher up. Marvelous views are offered through the slanted windows (the higher up, the better, of course), but the bathrooms are shower only, no tubs. Bathrooms are better in the Tower rooms, including deep tubs.

MORE, The Buffet at Luxor (p. 202), offers a cool archaeological-dig atmosphere. **Criss Angel: *Believe*** pairs the popular exotic magician with the spectacle of Cirque du Soleil (p. 307). Comedian Carrot Top is also in residency. Enormous nightclub LAX is state of the art, and attracting a fashionable crowd. Two notable attractions here are **Titanic: The Exhibition** (p. 228) and **Bodies . . . The Exhibition** (p. 214).

3900 Las Vegas Blvd. S. (btw. Reno and Hacienda aves.), Las Vegas, NV 81119. (C) **888/777-0188** or 702/262-4000. Fax 702/262-4478. www.luxor.com. 4,400 units. $69 and up double; $150 and up whirlpool suite; $249–$800 other suites. Extra person $30. Children 11 and under stay free in parent's room. AE, DC, DISC, MC, V. Free self- and valet parking. **Amenities:** 7 restaurants; food court; nightclub; casino; concierge; executive-level rooms; health club; 5 outdoor pools; room service; showrooms; spa. *In room:* A/C, TV w/pay movies, hair dryer, Wi-Fi (for a fee).

South Point ★★ 🔪 Including the South Point in the South Strip category stretches the definition almost to the breaking point. Located about 6 miles south of Mandalay Bay, it is still on Las Vegas Boulevard but certainly not within walking distance of anything else of interest except for maybe a convenience store. Still, this hotel is a worthwhile addition both to the city and to this category, offering an "expensive" level of accommodations at a "moderate" price.

South Point follows the same formula established by its ancestors: nice rooms at reasonable prices; plenty of low-priced food outlets; tons of entertainment options, including movie theaters, a bowling alley, and more; and a massive casino with lower-than-average limits on everything from slots to craps tables. There's also a giant Equestrian Center out back, large enough for just about any rodeo, complete with air-conditioned horse stalls and a pen for thousands of head of cattle. A unique offering to be sure, but we'd recommend you choose a non-event time to stay here, if possible, because no matter how much odor-absorbing wood chips you throw at them, 2,000 head of cattle emit a less-than-pleasant odor that may make an afternoon by the pool rather unenjoyable.

The overall scheme is Southern California modern, with plenty of sunny paint schemes and airy architectural details. Think Santa Barbara instead of Hollywood, and you're probably in the ballpark. Rooms are large and aesthetically pleasing, each over 500 square feet and crammed full with expensive and luxurious furnishings, 42-inch plasma televisions, and all the other pampering amenities one would expect in a room three times the price. Seriously, a weekend rate check had rooms here at less than $100 per night, while Bellagio and Wynn were well over $250. Although we wouldn't put these rooms on quite the same level as the ones at those two ultraluxe establishments, we have a hard time coming up with a $150 amount of difference. Venerable local restaurant Michael's relocated here, along with a number of other restaurants.

9777 Las Vegas Blvd. S., Las Vegas, NV 89183. *C* **866/796-7111** or 702/796-7111. Fax 702/365-7505. www.southpointcasino.com. 2,100 units. $79 and up double. Extra person $20. Children 16 and under stay free in parent's room. AE, DC, DISC, MC, V. Free self- and valet parking. **Amenities:** 8 restaurants; 70-lane bowling center; casino; concierge; 4,400-seat equestrian and events center; 16-screen movie theater; outdoor pool; room service; spa. *In room:* A/C, TV w/pay movies, hair dryer, Wi-Fi (for a fee).

Tropicana Resort & Casino For years we've been telling you about major potential changes at the Tropicana and for years we have been made to look the fools when absolutely nothing changed. But now everything has changed and we mean that almost literally. New owners took the place out of bankruptcy and immediately dumped more than $100 million into the property, revamping rooms, the casino, restaurants, the showroom, the exterior, the pool area, the convention center, and more. Just about the only thing not getting a makeover is the parking structure.

Gone is the faded and dusty Caribbean/tropical theme, replaced with a bright, white and orange South Beach/tropical theme. New carpets, marble, gaming tables, and slots liven up the casino by about a million percent with a sunny vibe (think white marble and plantation shutter clad support columns). And that continues upstairs where all the rooms were basically stripped to the cement and redone with sandy rattan and bamboo furnishings, crisp white linens, bright orange chaise lounges or sofas, white plantation shutters on the windows, and even a white-framed 42-inch TV. Bathrooms were similarly updated and although they couldn't make them any bigger, they certainly are more modern and comfortable.

Note: Construction on all of this was supposed to be done by the end of 2010, but there may be some lingering issues, including the pool area, which is getting a Miami Beach makeover as well and is set to debut in the spring of 2011.

3801 Las Vegas Blvd. S. (at Tropicana Ave.), Las Vegas, NV 89109. *C* **888/826-8767** or 702/739-2222. Fax 702/739-2469. www.tropicanalv.com. 1,658 units. $99 and up double. Extra person $25. Children 11 and under stay free in parent's room. AE, DC, DISC, MC, V. Free self- and valet parking. **Amenities:** 6 restaurants; casino; executive-level rooms; health club; 3 outdoor pools; showroom; wedding chapel. *In room:* A/C, TV w/pay movies, hair dryer, minibar, Wi-Fi (for a fee).

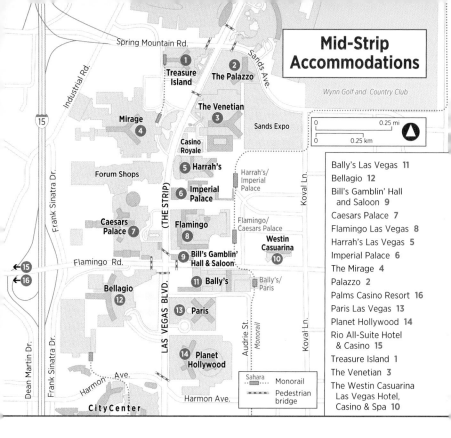

Mid-Strip Accommodations

Wynn Golf and Country Club

Bally's Las Vegas **11**

Bellagio **12**

Bill's Gamblin' Hall
and Saloon **9**

Caesars Palace **7**

Flamingo Las Vegas **8**

Harrah's Las Vegas **5**

Imperial Palace **6**

The Mirage **4**

Palazzo **2**

Palms Casino Resort **16**

Paris Las Vegas **13**

Planet Hollywood **14**

Rio All-Suite Hotel
& Casino **15**

Treasure Island **1**

The Venetian **3**

The Westin Casuarina
Las Vegas Hotel,
Casino & Spa **10**

MID-STRIP
Very Expensive

Bellagio ★★ This is the luxury resort that ushered in the new post-Vegas-is-for-families elegance epoch, and it was so successful that many of its attributes can now be found, in varying forms, in every hotel built since. An 8-acre Lake Como stand-in out front, complete with a dazzling choreographed water-ballet extravaganza, sets this place apart along with a representation of an Italian lakeside village.

But does it work as a luxury hotel? Sort of. It certainly is much closer to a European casino hotel than a Vegas one. Fabulous touches abound, including a lobby that's unlike any other in Vegas. It's not just grand, with marble and an eye-popping Dale Chihuly blown-glass flower sculpture on the ceiling (the largest of its kind in the world), but it's also brave with plants, natural lighting, and actual seating. There's also a downright lovely conservatory, complete with brightly colored flowers and plants, preposterously (and delightfully) changed every few months to go with the season (yellows and whites for Easter, for example, though we could have done without the ginormous animatronic bald eagle chicks as part of the extremely gaudy July 4th decor)—it's one of the sweetest spots in all of Vegas.

On the downside, you still can't avoid a walk through the casino to get just about anywhere (with the inevitable ruckus shattering your blissful state every time you exit the elevators from your room). At least the casino is laid out in an easy-to-navigate grid with wide aisles. Another downside is that there are hidden charges galore, such as a pricey fee for the spa, another one for poolside cabanas. The rooms are quite nice, showing off a cosmopolitan look with handsome sage greens and dark woods, but given the relatively puny size, it may still not be enough for the price. Having said that, you can find deals on Bellagio's website, depending on day of week and time of year. Furnishings are plush (good, cushy beds with quality linens, comfy chairs), the roomy bathrooms even more so (marble and glass, plus good-smelling soap and hair dryers—it works every time), but compared to the more recently upgraded rooms at other hotels, these feel a little out-of-date (tube televisions instead of flatscreens? How 2002!). Strip-side rooms, while featuring a much-desired view of the hotel's dancing water fountains (see below), don't quite muffle the booms the fountains make as they explode (although we didn't find it annoying). Rooms in the newer Spa Tower are more desirable if you want a shorter walk to the pool and the gym and spa areas (guests in the original building will have a long jog around the casino perimeter instead), but only a "partial" (read: a bit set back with a parking lot in the foreground) view of the fountains. Still, service is top-notch, despite the size of the place; the staff is eager to please and nonpatronizing.

Meanwhile, many of the better restaurants are found in Bellagio. Full reviews of **Picasso, Le Cirque, Circo, Michael Mina, Fix, Sensi,** and **Olives** are found in chapter 6, as is a review of the **Bellagio Buffet.** And the man who brought us a free pirate show and a volcano explosion now brings us a **water ballet ★★★**, courtesy of a dancing fountain with jets timed to a rotating list of songs (everything from pop to Sinatra to Broadway to opera). This sounds cheesy, but it absolutely is not. It's really quite delightful and even witty (no, really) and is the best free show in Vegas (p. 224). **Note:** A channel on the TV will play the songs as the fountains dance because you can't quite hear the music from your room.

Bellagio also features an upscale casino and **O** (p. 305), one of the most incredible shows yet from Cirque du Soleil. Bellagio is also home to **Petrossian** (p. 322), a bar, and **The Bank** (p. 328), a high-end nightclub.

The hotel's pool area has skidded to the top of our favorites list; it boasts six swimming pools (two heated year-round and two with fountains) geometrically set in a neoclassical Roman garden, with flowered, trellised archways and Italian opera piped in over the sound system. The Grand Patio could have come right off a movie set

Dale Chihuly's *Fioro di Como* glass sculpture adorns the ceiling of Bellagio's lobby.

The neoclassical pool area at Bellagio was inspired by the one at Hearst Castle in San Simeon, California.

(pillars, domes, you get the idea). A more sophisticated environment than the tropical party over at The Mirage (our other favorite), it is surely the sort of place where thonged model types hang out with moneyed jetsetters—it comes off as *that* chic.

The **health club** is marvelous, large, and well stocked with top-of-the-line machines, with natural light coming in through windows to the outside world, but at $25 a pop, it's pretty pricey if all you want is a simple session on a treadmill (though with your fee, you are allowed to return throughout the day for additional soakings/steamings/workouts). Attendants ply you with iced towels and drinks. The **spa ★★** is not quite as pretty as some others around town, but it does offer a full range of pricey treatments and has a serene soaking area, with plunge pools ranging in temperature from icy to boiling. In addition to drinks and snacks, smoothies are sometimes offered—take one.

The shopping area, called **Via Bellagio,** features all the stores that advertise in color in glossy magazines: Tiffany, Armani, Gucci, Prada, Hermès, and the like. There's also an **art gallery** (p. 287) that boasts enough highly regarded works to draw some million visitors a year.

What does all this add up to? As good as a casino-hotel can provide and perform the duties of a luxury resort experience, certainly. If it doesn't quite work, that's probably more the fault of the initial concept than the hotel itself.

3600 Las Vegas Blvd. S. (at the corner of Flamingo Rd.), Las Vegas, NV 89109. © **888/987-6667** or 702/693-7111. Fax 702/693-8546. www.bellagio.com. 3,933 units. $169 and up double; $450 and up suite. Extra person $35. No discount for children. AE, DC, DISC, MC, V. Free self- and valet parking. **Amenities:** 14 restaurants; nightclub; casino; concierge; executive-level rooms; large health club; 6 outdoor pools; room service; showrooms; spa; wedding chapel. *In room:* A/C, TV w/pay movies, hair dryer, Internet (for a fee).

Caesars Palace ★★ Since 1966, Caesars has stood simultaneously as the ultimate in Vegas luxury and the nadir (or pinnacle, depending on your values) of Las Vegas cheese. It's the most Vegas-style hotel you'll find, covering all the bases, from the tacky fabulous schmaltz of the recent past to the current trend in high-end luxury.

When Caesars was originally built to reflect Roman decadence, its designers probably had no idea how guffaw-inducing this would be some years later. It's the level of kitsch all should aspire to: Roman colonnades, Roman pillars, gigantic faux-marble Roman statues, staff attired in gladiator outfits—it's splendidly ridiculous. It's what Vegas ought to be.

But all things change, and Caesars was outshined over the years by more modern glamour. And frankly, its facade was looking dated 2 decades ago. Never one to rest on any kind of laurels, Roman or otherwise, Caesars gave itself a massive face-lift and keeps on building and expanding. Never fear, the Roman statues remain, as do the toga-clad models wandering around posing for pictures, and so does the Caesars giggle factor (it's still pretty campy). Past or future, Caesars remains spectacular. The haphazard layout has become ever more confusing and hard to negotiate, and it takes forever to get anywhere—especially out to the Strip. Sometimes you feel like just surrendering and staying in, which isn't necessarily a bad thing, especially because Caesars is also known for its service.

Accommodations occupy five towers (a sixth is under construction but has been delayed until at least late 2010), and there are too many decorating schemes to describe here. Rooms in the newer Augustus tower are done in the sleek, unfussy neutrals that are all the rage, plus whirlpool tubs, marble and wood sinks, and little flatscreen TVs in the bathrooms. If you like elbow room, it's worth it. If you are looking for old-time Caesars romance, ask for rooms with a Greco-Roman theme (some have classical sculptures in niches); furnishings

Reproductions of classical Roman statues are situated throughout Caesars Palace.

The Atlantis Fountain Show in The Forum Shops at Caesars Palace.

tend to neoclassic styles; Roman columns, pilasters, and pediments are common. Some newer rooms have floor-to-ceiling windows that offer a hypnotizing panoramic view and, better still, older ones have lavish tubs in the middle of the room (which can be uncomfortable, if you wish to shower and don't want your shower to be a spectator sport).

Caesars has a well-deserved reputation for superior in-house restaurants. There are quite a few in the hotel, plus dining facilities in The Forum shopping area. All are highly recommended. The hotel's sushi restaurant, **Hyakumi,** its Southwestern-themed **Mesa Grill,** and a replica of New York's famous **Rao's** are described in chapter 6, as are the hotel's food court and buffets. Restaurants in The Forum Shops arcade include **Spago** and **The Palm**—both are discussed in chapter 6. In the newer Atlantis section is a Cheesecake Factory. For a review of the nightclubs **PURE** and **Cleopatra's Barge,** see p. 331 and 329, respectively.

Having spent over $160 million renovating its **Garden of the Gods,** Caesars has created a tasteful, undeniably Caesaresque masterpiece. With eight pools on three levels there is plenty of space for frolicking in the hot sun. Each has the classic granite columns and intricately carved sculptures that you'd expect from an area that names each of its pools after Roman deities or words that lend context to its unique mission (Fortuna has swim-up blackjack, Bacchus is for VIP guests only, and Apollo gets the most sun of any of them). To feel even more regal, snatch one of the shaded cabanas that offer a phone, TV, and air-conditioning; they start at $150 a day (reserve early). Several amenities are also available by the pool area, including massage, four whirlpools, the Neptune Bar, swim-up blackjack, and food service.

Qua spa is a knockout. Stone-and-water themed Roman baths with infinity pools, an ice room with shaved ice exfoliation, rain showers, and best of all, heated tile lounge chairs. Add in a tea lounge with drinks, and you've got the perfect place for postparty detox. If you have the energy, the fitness room is large, with plush padded equipment and plenty of windows. Go work off some of that Caesars indulgence and then get a little pampered.

The Forum Shops ★★★ (p. 287) are in the grandest mall you can imagine (think of the *La Dolce Vita* walk on the Via Veneto), with stores ranging from the pedestrian (Gap) to the exclusive (Dolce & Gabbana). Not content to stop paying contractors, Caesars also added the 4,000-seat Coliseum, a replica of the original building in Rome. This was built for one purpose only—to give diva **Céline Dion** a place to play. No kidding. After a 5-year absence, Céline is coming back in 2011. If the tickets cost too much, opt for one of two free animatronics shows that are just the sort of bizarre spectacles you'd expect in Las Vegas.

3570 Las Vegas Blvd. S. (just north of Flamingo Rd.), Las Vegas, NV 89109. ☎ **877/427-7243** or 702/731-7110. Fax 702/697-5706. www.caesarspalace.com. 3,348 units. $129 and up double; $549 and up suite. Extra person $30. No discount for children. AE, DC, DISC, MC, V. Free self- and valet parking. **Amenities:** 25 restaurants; nightclub; casino; concierge; executive-level rooms; health club; 8 outdoor pools; room service; spa; 4 wedding chapels. *In room:* A/C, TV w/pay movies, hair dryer, Wi-Fi (for fee).

The Palazzo ★★ The Palazzo is an expansion of the impressive Venetian, but one that functions as a separate hotel, with its own massive grand lobby, own restaurants, and own rates. It's even more expensive, for roughly the same experience, so choosing this one over the other isn't a must-do. Though, if we had to say it, the rooms are a wee bit nicer, which is saying a lot, because The Venetian has some of the nicest rooms in town. Like its sister property, The Palazzo's rooms

Guest room at the Palazzo.

are "suites"—a bedroom plus a sunken living room, with a sectional couch perfect for crashing and channel surfing. Three flatscreen TVs (two quite big, one smaller one badly positioned in the bathroom), a particularly squishy white bed with superior linens and pillows, remote control curtain and shades, and a deep bathtub in a generously sized, gleaming bathroom add up to the kind of accommodations that are hard to leave. Stay here only if what you mostly wanted to see in the city is your fabulous hotel room.

Should you leave, there are 14 restaurants, including **Table 10** (p. 178), an eatery by celebrity chef Emeril; Carnevino, a steakhouse from Mario Batali; and Grand Lux Café, a moderately priced alternative to the mostly higher-end offerings. The high-end shopping area (covered in chapter 9) is anchored by Barneys New York. The excellent Canyon Ranch spa and health club will set you back an additional $35 a day.

3325 Las Vegas Blvd. S., Las Vegas, NV 89109. © **877/883-6423** or 702/414-4100. Fax 702/414-4805. www.palazzolasvegas.com. 4,027 units. $199 and up double; $229 and up suite. Extra person $35. Children 12 and under stay free in parent's room. AE, DC, DISC, MC, V. Free self- and valet parking. **Amenities:** 15 restaurants; casino; concierge; executive-level rooms; health club & spa shared w/Venetian; 7 outdoor pools shared w/Venetian; room service; showroom. *In room:* A/C, TV w/pay movies, fax, fridge (on request), hair dryer, Wi-Fi (for a fee).

Paris Las Vegas Casino Resort ★ *Sacre bleu!* The City of Light comes to Sin City in this, one of the few theme-run-amok hotels left to its giddy devices. Stay here if you came to Vegas for the silly fantasy. The outside reproduces various Parisian landmarks (amusing anyone familiar with Paris, as the Hotel de Ville is crammed on top of the Louvre), complete with a half-scale perfect replica of the Eiffel Tower. The interior puts you in the middle of a dollhouse version of the city. You can stroll down a mini Rue de la Paix, ride an elevator to the top of the Eiffel Tower, stop at an overpriced bakery for a baguette, and have your photo taken near several very nice fountains.

You'll find signage employing the kind of dubious use of the French language that makes genuine Frenchmen really cross ("le car rental" and so forth), while all the employees are forced to dust off their high school French ("Bonjour, Madame! Merci beaucoup!") when dealing with the public. Don't worry, it's not quite enough to make you sick to "le stomach."

Quel dommage, this attention to detail does not extend to the rooms, which are nice enough but uninteresting, with furniture that only hints at mock French Regency. Bathrooms are small but pretty, with deep tubs. If you don't mind the upgraded price, go for the newer Red rooms on the upper floors, done in a modern French bordello theme complete with suede sofas that look like puckered lips. Try to get a Strip-facing room so that you can see Bellagio's fountains across the street; note also that north-facing rooms give you nice Peeping-Tom views right into neighboring Bally's. The monorail has a stop out back, which adds to the convenience factor. Overall, not a bad place to stay, but a great place to visit—*quel hoot!*

The hotel has eight more-or-less French-themed restaurants, including the highly lauded **Le Village Buffet,** the **Eiffel Tower Restaurant** (located guess where), and bistro **Mon Ami Gabi,** all of which are covered in chapter 6. The bread for all these restaurants is made fresh on-site at the bakery. You can buy delicious, if pricey, loaves of it at the bakery, and we have to admit, that's kinda fun. There are also five lounges. For entertainment (as if it wasn't entertaining enough already), the **Eiffel Tower** attraction is covered on p. 215 and **Barry Manilow** has taken up residence in the hotel's Parisian opera house–themed showroom (p. 303).

3655 Las Vegas Blvd. S., Las Vegas, NV 89109. ✆ **888/266-5687** or 702/946-7000. www.parislv.com. 2,916 units. $119 and up double; $350 and up suite. Extra person $30. No discount for children. AE, DC, DISC, MC. V. Free self- and valet parking. **Amenities:** 12 restaurants; casino; concierge; executive-level rooms; health club; outdoor pool; room service; showrooms; spa; 2 wedding chapels. *In room:* A/C, TV w/pay movies, hair dryer, Wi-Fi (for a fee).

The Venetian ★★ One of the most elaborate hotel spectacles in town, The Venetian falls squarely between an outright adult Disneyland experience and the luxury resort experience currently dominating the Vegas landscape. The big draw here is the rooms, all suites, and all successful examples of that same luxury

Paris Las Vegas features re-creations of various Parisian landmarks.

resort mindset, though the commitment to theme in the Grand Canal Shoppes is certainly appealing.

The hotel's exterior, which re-creates most of the top landmarks of Venice (the Campanile, a portion of St. Mark's Square, part of the Doge's Palace, a canal or two), ranks right up there with New York–New York as a must see, and because you can wander freely through the "sights," it even has a slight edge over New York–New York. As stern as we get about re-creations *not* being a substitute for the real thing, we have to admit that the attention to detail here is impressive indeed. Stone is aged, for that weathered look, statues and tiles are exact copies of their Italian counterparts, security guards wear Venetian police uniforms—all that's missing is the smell from the canals, but we are happy to let that one slide.

Inside, it's more of the same, particularly in the lobby area and the entrance to the extraordinary shops, as ceilings are covered with hand-painted re-creations of Venetian art. With plenty of marble, soaring ceilings, and impressive pillars and archways, it's less kitschy than Caesars but more theme park than Bellagio.

A room makeover has pared down the previously over-the-top fussy decor, which is a good thing, but then again, apart from the size it's not as dreamily romantic on the eye. Now the suites have the same sleek new look as The Palazzo, though the beds lack The Palazzo's fluffy comforters. The marbled bathrooms rocketed virtually to the top of our list of favorites, in a tie for second place with those at Bellagio. (Mandalay Bay's THEhotel are the best.)

And all this is even before the **Venezia Tower,** with over 1,000 more rooms, with the same large and lush footprint and style as the originals. The tower has its own check-in and gestalt—somehow it comes off even more lush than the original hotel, which is pretty frilly to start. Many celebrity chefs and high-profile restaurants are in residence at The Venetian. Reviews of **Bouchon** (by Thomas Keller, perhaps America's top chef), **Delmonico Steakhouse, Canaletto, Valentino,** Mario Batali's **B&B Ristorante,** and **Pinot Brasserie** can be found in chapter 6. Nightlife options include the **Blue Man Group** and a special production of the long-running *Phantom* (both reviewed in chapter 10). And, of course, there is an elegant but confusingly laid-out casino.

The Venetian has five pools and whirlpools, but its pool area is disappointingly sterile and bland. Pools are neoclassical (think rectangles with the corners lopped off), and the fourth-floor location probably means that more dense foliage is not going to be forthcoming. The Venezia Tower has a courtyard pool area that is amusing, but the water space is tiny.

The **Canyon Ranch SpaClub** ★★★ is run by a branch of arguably the finest getaway spa in America. This is an unbelievably lavish facility, certainly the finest hotel spa in town. From the Bed Head and Bumble & Bumble products on sale in the shop to the nutritionists, physical therapists, and acupuncturists on staff to the vibrating massage chairs that you rest in during pedicures—geez, what more could you want? Well, we want our own home gym to be as nice as the one here, with ample equipment, racks of big TVs, and a staff eager to help you with advice and bring you bottled water. The $35-a-day fee is high, but it does include a full day's worth of classes, ranging from regular aerobics to yoga, Pilates, and dance. Did we mention the rock-climbing wall, which, because this is Vegas, costs extra?

The **Grand Canal Shoppes** ★★ (p. 290) rank with the Caesars Palace shops as an absolute must see. Like Caesars, the area is a mock Italian village with a blue, cloud-studded, painted sky overhead. But down the middle runs a canal,

Elaborate frescoes decorate the soaring ceilings of The Venetian.

The lovely Wildlife Habitat at The Flamingo is home to a number of the resort's namesake birds.

complete with singing gondoliers. (The 10-min. ride costs about $15, which seems steep, but trust us, it's a *lot* more in the real Venice.) The entire thing finishes up at a small re-creation of St. Mark's Square, which features glass blowers, traveling musicians, flower sellers, and the like. Expect to run into famous Venetians, such as a flirty Casanova and a travel-weary Marco Polo. It's ambitious and a big step up from animatronic figures. Oh, and the stores are also probably worth a look—a decent mixture of high-end fashion and more affordable shops.

3355 Las Vegas Blvd. S., Las Vegas, NV 89109. © **888/283-6423** or 702/414-1000. Fax 702/414-4805. www.venetian.com. 4,027 units. $169 and up double. Extra person $35, $50 in executive level. Children 12 and under stay free in parent's room. AE, DC, DISC, MC, V. Free self- and valet parking. **Amenities:** 18 restaurants; casino; concierge; executive-level rooms; health club; 6 outdoor pools; 24-hr. room service; extensive shopping arcade; showroom; spa; wedding chapels. *In room:* A/C, TV w/pay movies, fax, fridge (on request), hair dryer, Wi-Fi (for a fee).

Expensive

Flamingo Las Vegas ★ The Flamingo is the Strip's senior citizen, boasting a colorful history. It's changed a great deal since Bugsy Siegel opened his 105-room oasis "in the middle of nowhere" in 1946. It was so luxurious for its time that even the janitors wore tuxedos. (Hey, new Vegas? That's class.) Renovations and expansions over the years aren't going to make Siegel's "real class joint" cause you to forget about, say, the rooms at The Palazzo, but they have freshened the joint up.

By Vegas standards, the old girl is Paleozoic, but not only is it hanging in there; some of the changes have made us reconsider it entirely. Rushing headlong into the Dean Martin/Rat Pack retro vibe, the GO rooms are kicky candy modern, with hot pink (the signature Flamingo color!) accent walls, hot pink lights in the bathroom where you can also find TV screens embedded in the mirror, candy-striped wallpaper, black-and-white photos of the Flamingo from its early

It isn't flashy, but Harrah's has a friendly and fun vibe.

days, squishy white beds with chocolate accents and vinyl padded headboards, huge flatscreens with HDTV, iPod docking stations, and more. Two-bedroom suites scream classic playboy bachelor pad. It's ring-a-ding fun, and Dino would surely have approved—well worth the extra $50 currently charged for the upgraded rooms. Standard rooms are, well, standard but certainly nothing to sneeze at with spare, modern furnishings and cushy beds.

The **Paradise Garden Buffet** (p. 204) is a decent choice. There are also several bars, plus a huge casino. And the monorail has a stop out back.

For those planning some leisure time outside the casino, the Flamingo's exceptional pool area, spa, and tennis courts are big draws. Five gorgeous swimming pools, two whirlpools, and water slides are located in a 15-acre Caribbean landscape amid lagoons, meandering streams, fountains, waterfalls, a rose garden, and islands of live flamingos. Ponds have ducks, swans, and koi, and a grove of 2,000 palms graces an expanse of lawn. Although the water can be a little chilly, kids should be able to spend hours in the pool area.

A health club ($10 per day for machines only; $20 for spa and health club) offers a variety of weight machines, treadmills, stair machines, free weights, a sauna, a steam room, a TV lounge, and hot and cold whirlpools. Spa services include massages, facials, salt glows, and body wraps.

3555 Las Vegas Blvd. S. (btw. Sands Ave. and Flamingo Rd.), Las Vegas, NV 89109. ℂ**800/732-2111** or 702/733-3111. Fax 702/733-3353. www.flamingolv.com. 3,517 units. $85 and up double; $350 and up suite. Extra person $30. Timeshare suites available. AE, DC, DISC, MC, V. Free self- and valet parking. **Amenities:** 8 restaurants; casino; executive-level rooms; health club; 5 outdoor pools; room service; showrooms; spa; 3 night-lit tennis courts; wedding chapels. *In room:* A/C, TV w/pay movies, hair dryer, Wi-Fi (for a fee).

Harrah's Las Vegas ★ Here's another property that is doing its best to keep up with the pace in Vegas, to mixed success. Though parts of Harrah's benefited from a reworking of the place a few years ago, the rest of it evokes Old Las Vegas in the way the Riviera does—as in, dark, dated, and claustrophobic. Still, there is much to like here, and occasional quite good rates might make the so-so bits worth overlooking. Certainly, it wants to be the fun and convivial place we wish more of Vegas were (instead of pretty much catering to high rollers and simply tolerating the rest of us with normal budgets). The monorail stop is a draw, too, because it is now easier to get to and from here.

The rooms have undergone some cosmetic fluffing to the tune of good new mattresses and those white bed covers that are now more or less standard in most local hotels. The rooms aren't flashy, but they are reliable for what is ultimately a gamblers' hotel and provide guests with most of the necessary amenities.

The Range steakhouse is one of the few hotel restaurants that overlooks the Strip. Other restaurant options include a Toby Keith–themed joint, featuring down-home cooking and nightly entertainment, a buffet, and a food court for quick bites to eat. The casino has a fun, festive atmosphere. There's a showroom (that used to be home to Sammy Davis, Jr., back in the day), a comedy club, **Mac King**'s wonderful comedy/magic act (p. 312), and other amusing entertainment diversions.

Carnaval Court (p. 288) is a festive, palm-fringed shopping plaza where strolling entertainers perform. It's notable because it's right on the Strip but entirely outdoors; similar ventures at other hotels are inside artificial environments. Note that lounge singer legend **Cook E. Jarr** (p. 299) often plays here late on varying nights.

Harrah's has an Olympic-size swimming pool and sundeck area with a waterfall, trellised gardens, and a whirlpool. It's a pretty underwhelming pool by Vegas standards.

The hotel's health club is small but offers a full-range spa and a gym with Lifecycles, treadmills, stair machines, rowing machines, lots of Universal

SO YOUR TRIP GOES swimmingly . . .

Part of the delight of the Vegas resort complexes is the gorgeous pools—what could be better for beating the summer heat? But there are pools and there are *pools,* so you'll need to keep several things in mind when searching for the right one for you.

During the winter, it's often too cold or windy to do much lounging, and even if the weather is amenable, the hotels often close part of their pool areas during winter and early spring. The pools also are not heated for the most part, but in fairness, they largely don't need to be.

Most hotel pools are shallow, chest-high at best, only about 3-feet deep in many spots (the hotels want you gambling, not swimming). Diving is impossible—not that a single pool allows it anyway.

And finally, during those hot days, be warned that sitting by pools next to heavily windowed buildings such as The Mirage and Treasure Island allows you to experience the same thing a bug does under a magnifying glass with a sun ray directed on it. Regardless of time of year, be sure to slather on the sunscreen; there's a reason you see so many unhappy lobster-red people roaming the streets. Many pool areas don't offer much in the way of shade. On the other hand, if your tan line is important to you, head for Caesars, Mandalay Bay, Wynn Las Vegas, or Stratosphere (to name a few), all of which have topless sunbathing areas where you can toast even more flesh than at the other hotels.

At any of the pools, you can rent a cabana (which often includes a TV, special lounge chairs, and even better poolside service), but these should be reserved as far in advance as possible, and, with the exception of the Four Seasons's complimentary shaded lounging area, most cost a hefty fee. If you are staying at a chain hotel, you will most likely find an average pool, but if you want to spend some time at a better one, be aware that most of the casino-hotel pool attendants will ask to see your room key. If they are busy, you might be able to sneak in, or at least blend in with a group ahead of you.

equipment, and free weights. Its $20-a-day access charge is more reasonable than the fees at other hotels.

3475 Las Vegas Blvd. S. (btw. Flamingo and Spring Mountain roads.), Las Vegas, NV 89109. ✆ **800/427-7247** or 702/369-5000. Fax 702/369-5283. www.harrahslasvegas.com. 2,526 units. $79 and up double; $199 and up suite. Extra person $30. No discount for children. AE, DC, DISC, MC, V. Free self- and valet parking. **Amenities:** 9 restaurants; casino; concierge; executive-level rooms; health club; outdoor pool; room service; showrooms; spa. *In room:* A/C, TV w/pay movies, hair dryer, Internet (for a fee).

The Mirage ★★ Imagine the levels of frustration of the Las Vegas hotel-casino. There you are, once the hottest thing on the Strip, and then everyone copies you and takes it to the next level of luxury, or theme, or lunacy, depending on what this year's trend is; and there you are, the former front-runner, now years behind the ever-evolving curve. Desperate fashion crazes call for desperate measures, and so, if you are The Mirage, you dump nearly all your tropical theme in favor of that sleek, sophisticated, dark-wood look that is currently all the rage. It was a good choice. The Asian elegance produces unexpected sharp design touches— just peer in at the bar of Stack Steakhouse, full of sensuous wood curves. The place is looking sharp, stylish, and grown-up, instead of tired. Even though it has become somewhat eclipsed by the very hotels whose presence it made possible, we still really like this place. From the moment you walk in and breathe the tropically perfumed air and enter the lush rainforest, it's just a different experience from most Vegas hotels.

Occupying 102 acres, The Mirage is fronted by more than a city block of cascading waterfalls and tropical foliage centering on a "volcano," which, after dark, erupts every 15 minutes, spewing fire 100 feet above the lagoons below. (That volcano cost $30 million, which is equal to the entire original construction

A sculpture of Siegfried, Roy, and one of the duo's famous white tigers in front of The Mirage.

The Playboy Club at the very hip Palms Casino Resort.

cost for Caesars next-door.) The lobby is dominated by a 53-foot, 20,000-gallon simulated coral-reef aquarium stocked with more than 1,000 colorful tropical fish. This gives you something to look at while waiting (never for long) for check-in.

Next, you'll walk through the rainforest, which occupies a 90-foot domed atrium—a path meanders through palms, banana trees, waterfalls, and serene pools. If we must find a complaint with The Mirage, it's with the next bit, because you have to negotiate 8 miles (or so it seems) of casino mayhem to get to your room, the pool, food, or the outside world. It gets old, fast. On the other hand, the sundries shop is located right next to the guest-room elevators, so if you forgot toothpaste, you don't have to travel miles to get more.

Fresh room renovations have turned the lodgings into that white bed/bold, solid colors/70s-inspired look that everyone is sporting a variation of these days. Admittedly it does fit the current mod look of the hotel. Plus, a pillow-top mattress and 42-inch LCD TVs do wonders for overcoming any decor concerns. The bathrooms remain small—though they have been given a solid makeover as well—which won't bother you unless you have space issues and/or have seen the bigger ones elsewhere on the Strip. The **Mirage Cravings Buffet** is detailed in chapter 6. The Cirque production *Love* is reviewed in chapter 10, as is a show starring Terry Fator, winner of *America's Got Talent*. The Mirage has one of our favorite casinos and some excellent nightclubs and bars. We miss the so-Vegas-it's-bad lounge but have to admit that the **Zen Japonais Lounge** is more appealing in every way, with its fluttering spalike curtains and proximity to the rainforest. It's an odd bit of serenity right off the casino bustle.

Out back is the pool, one of the nicest in Vegas, with a quarter-mile shoreline, a tropical paradise of waterfalls and trees, water slides, and so forth. It looks inviting, but truth be told, it's sometimes on the chilly side and isn't very deep. But it's so pretty you'll hardly care. There is also Bare, a "European-style pool" offering a more adult aquatic experience. Free swimming lessons and water-aerobics classes take place daily at the pool. Behind the pool are the **Dolphin Habitat** and Siegfried & Roy's **Secret Garden** (p. 221). **The Mirage Day Spa ★** teems with friendly staff anxious to pamper you, bringing you iced towels to cool you during your workout, and refreshing juices and smoothies afterward. The gym is one of the largest and best stocked on the Strip.

3400 Las Vegas Blvd. S. (btw. Flamingo and Spring Mountain roads), Las Vegas, NV 89109. © **800/627-6667** or 702/791-7111. Fax 702/791-7446. www.mirage.com. 3,044 units. $109 and up double; $275 and up suite. Extra person $30. No discount for children. AE, DC, DISC, MC, V. Free self- and valet parking. **Amenities:** 11 restaurants; casino; concierge; executive-level rooms; health club; beautiful outdoor pool; room service; showrooms; spa. *In room:* A/C, TV w/pay movies, hair dryer, Wi-Fi (for a fee).

Palms Casino Resort ★★ The Palms was Britney Spears's base for her (first) wedding debacle and is still the retreat of choice for tabloid staples. In keeping with the tropical-foliage name, it's more or less Miami themed (but without the pastels), with a strange aversion to straight lines (really, check out all those curves). Inside a bland building is a pretty nice complex with some downright family-friendly touches—which we say only because it's a puzzle that the place is such a hot spot. That's mostly due to the nightlife options—**ghostbar, Playboy Club,** and the nightclubs **Rain** and **Moon** have lines of people every night the facilities are open, offering to sell their firstborn sons for a chance to go inside. Why did those two places catch on so? Quite possibly MTV's *The Real World: Las Vegas,* which featured seven strangers picked to live in the Palms and have their lives taped . . . oh, never mind . . . what you need to know is that the entrances to the clubs stand right by the elevators to your hotel room, which means on a busy weekend night, there can be upwards of 4,000 gorgeous and antsy (if not angry) people standing between you and access to your hotel room. If you are a Hilton sister, or wish to see whether one will date you, this could be heaven, but if encountering the beautifully dressed and coifed, with 0% body fat and sullen expressions of entitlement, and the 19-year-olds who seek to become all that (and usually affect a thuggish demeanor) makes you, like us, itch, this might not be the most comfortable place to stay. And yet there is an excellent child-care facility, **Kid's Quest,** plus movie theaters, and a family-ready food court (with a McDonald's, Panda Express, pizza, and subs). So it's both totally wrong for kids and rather right at the same time.

The Palms has perhaps some of the most comfortable beds in Vegas, thanks to fluffy pillows and duvets that make one reluctant to rise, plus big TVs and huge bathrooms. The workout room is decent size, but the spa is underwhelming, especially for a $25 daily admission fee, though it does offer yoga and Pilates classes. The pool areas got party-spot makeovers, turning what were kind of bland "stand and pose" watering holes into the kind of trendy must-visit beach areas this kind of crowd loves. Also on the property is the gorgeous and romantic **Alizé** (p. 165), one of the best restaurants in town.

4321 W. Flamingo Rd. (just west of I-15), Las Vegas, NV 89103. ℂ **866/942-7777** or 702/942-7777. Fax 702/942-6859. www.palms.com. 703 units. $99 and up double. Extra person $30. No discount for children. AE, DC, DISC, MC, V. Free self- and valet parking. **Amenities:** 7 restaurants; food court; casino; concierge; executive-level rooms; health club; movie theater; nightclub/showroom; outdoor pool; room service; spa. *In room:* A/C, TV w/pay movies, hair dryer, Wi-Fi (for a fee).

Planet Hollywood Resort & Casino ★★ We were sad when the once fairy-tale fantastic Aladdin was purchased by Planet Hollywood—it was the end of yet another era. Sure, today's Aladdin wasn't the same building where Elvis married 'Scilla, but even so. But thanks to that same Planet Hollywood and its memorabilia gimmick, the rooms are currently the most distinctive in town.

The reconstructed Strip entrance, heavy on the LED screens (it's supposed to evoke the visual mania of Times Square), certainly makes the interior easier to access than the last incarnation of Aladdin. Inside, those looking for the pop kitsch sensibility of the Planet Hollywood restaurants will be disappointed; it's actually kind of classy and design intensive. But you are going to come here for the rooms. Each has a movie or entertainment theme, such as *Pulp Fiction,* which might have John Travolta's suit in a glass case and a glass coffee table filled with more original memorabilia from the film. Although more than one room may share the same movie theme, no two rooms will have the same objects. The vibe of the room can vary radically depending on if the theme is Judy Garland in some charming musical or Wesley Snipes in *Blade,* so ask when booking. As gimmicks go, it's a catchy one, and a good use for all that junk the company's accumulated over the years.

A 2010 addition tacked on a couple of thousand new rooms in the PH Tower, a timeshare/hotel concept that offers the typical sleek design and decor of

Hollywood Hip room, Planet Hollywood Resort & Casino.

modern Vegas hotels but throws in a Hollywood twist through art and amenities. Studios through four-bedroom suites each have kitchens (from wee to wow), projector televisions that use the blackout shades for truly gigantic screen viewing, and whirlpool tubs. They are definitely nicer than those in the main tower, albeit with a little less personality.

The whole shebang was purchased in 2010 by Harrah's and is now a sister to places like Caesars Palace and next-door-neighbor Paris Las Vegas. What this means to you is a heavier emphasis on customer service, which Harrah's been paying attention to of late, and points in their Total Rewards players' club when you gamble in the stylish and sexy casino.

Note: The parking lot is all the way on the other side of the Miracle Mile shopping area, thus requiring guests to drag their suitcases all the way through the mall and a good chunk of the hotel before getting to registration. It's a very, very long and unpleasant schlep. Do not self-park here if you have mobility issues of any kind. Instead, follow the signs for casino (as opposed to mall) valet parking (free, except for the tip), which is right outside the front desk. Or better yet, choose the PH Tower, which has its own, much-less busy valet (also free), and direct access to the parking garage.

Restaurants include the massively popular 24-hour coffee shop Planet Daily, Sammy Hagar's **Cabo Wabo Cantina** (p. 175), P.F. Chang's, **Strip House** (a New York steakhouse with a bordello theme; p. 171), and the **Earl of Sandwich** (p. 179), from the very same noble family that lent its name to the food that the cafe is serving.

And then there is the **Miracle Mile** shopping area (p. 289), winding its way in a giant horseshoe shape around the property, another one to rival the capitalist ventures over at Caesars and The Venetian. This also has a new owner (separate from Planet Hollywood), and while we resent its makeover from the aesthetically delightful Casbah theme to a much more generic upscale mall, as a shopping and dining option, it's still tops. The hotel also has its own arena, the **Center for the Performing Arts,** which is attracting big names back to Vegas. Finally, there is the **Mandara spa ★★★**, which aesthetically might be our hands-down local favorite. The designers went to Morocco for ideas, and it shows in this Medina-flavored facility; just looking at it is pampering, and that's before one of the attentive staff puts you in a wrap and "dry float" (a womblike water bed–style cradle).

Rio All-Suite Hotel & Casino.

3667 Las Vegas Blvd. S., Las Vegas, NV 89109. ℰ **877/333-9474** or 702/785-5555. Fax 702/785-5558. www.planethollywoodresort.com. 2,400 units. $99 and up double. Extra person $30. No discount for children. AE, DC, DISC, MC, V. Free self- and valet parking. **Amenities:** 19 restaurants; 7 bars/lounges; casino; concierge; executive-level rooms; health club; 2 Jacuzzis; performing-arts center; 2 outdoor pools; room service; showroom; spa; wedding chapel. *In room:* A/C, TV w/pay movies, hair dryer, Wi-Fi (for a fee).

Rio All-Suite Hotel & Casino ★ Rio bills itself as a "carnival" atmosphere hotel, which means hectic, crowded, and noisy, and an apparent edict requiring the Most Scantily Clad Waitresses in Town to burst into song and dance in between delivering beers. The Masquerade Village is actually pretty pleasant, with a very high ceiling, but the older section's low ceilings seem to accentuate only how crowded the area is in both the number of people and the amount of stuff (slot machines, gaming tables, and so on). This party atmosphere, by the way, is strictly for adults; the hotel actively discourages guests from bringing children.

The hotel touts its room size. Every one is a "suite," which does not mean two separate rooms, but rather one large room with a sectional, corner sofa, and coffee table at one end. The dressing areas are certainly larger than average and feature a number of extra amenities, such as fridges (unusual for a Vegas hotel room) and small snacks. Windows, running the entire length of the room, are floor to ceiling, with a pretty impressive view of the Strip, Vegas, or the mountains (depending on which way you're facing). The furniture doesn't feel like hotel-room standard, but otherwise the decor is fairly bland.

The hotel's first-rate **Carnival World Buffet** is described in chapter 6. You might consider checking out the **Wine Cellar Tasting Room,** which bills itself as "the world's largest and most extensive collection of fine wines," and, hyperbole aside, it's certainly impressive and a must do for any wine aficionado.

Penn & Teller, the smartest show in town, is reviewed in chapter 10, as is the **VooDoo Lounge** and other clubs. The casino, alas, is dark and claustrophobic. The party/carnival theme gets a distinct R rating, with the newly reconceived **Show in the Sky,** the Rio's free entertainment spectacle. Sort of an homage to Rio Carnival, courtesy of floats that move on grids set in the ceiling above the casino, it now includes sets, such as spas and 17-foot-long beds, with "performers of seduction" gyrating to the Pussycat Dolls. Performed Thursday through Sunday in the evening.

Out back is a pool with a sandy beach, and two others in imaginative fish and shell shapes that seem inviting until you get up close and see how small they are. It could be especially disappointing after you have braved the long, cluttered walk to get there. Three whirlpool spas nestle amid rocks and foliage, there are two sand-volleyball courts, and blue-and-white-striped cabanas (equipped with rafts and misting coolers) can be rented for $250 to $500 per day. The 18-hole championship **Rio Secco golf course,** located on the south side of town (transportation included), was designed by Rees Jones.

3700 W. Flamingo Rd. (just west of I-15), Las Vegas, NV 89103. ✆ **888/752-9746** or 702/777-7777. Fax 702/777-7611. www.riolasvegas.com. 2,582 units. $99 and up suite. Extra person $30. No discount for children. AE, DC, MC, V. Free self- and valet parking. **Amenities:** 12 restaurants; sports book dining; casino; concierge; executive-level rooms; golf course; health club; 4 outdoor pools; room service; showrooms; spa. *In room:* A/C, TV w/pay movies, fridge, hair dryer, Wi-Fi (for a fee).

Treasure Island ★★ Huh? What happened to Treasure Island? What happened to the pirates? Why, Vegas grew up, that's what. Or, rather, it wants the kids it once actively tried to court to grow up, or at least, not come around until they are able to drink and gamble properly.

Originally the most modern family-friendly hotel, Treasure Island (commonly referred to as "TI" by most folks) was a blown-up version of Disneyland's *Pirates of the Caribbean.* But that's all behind them now, and the slight name change is there to make sure you understand that this is a grown-up, sophisticated resort. There might still be the odd pirate element here and there, but only because someone absentmindedly missed it in a ruthless purging of the last remnants. One victim is the pirate stunt show out front; it's been revamped so that the pirates (and you have no idea how much we wish we were making this up) now "battle" scantily clad strippers . . . er, "sirens."

And now, a new captain has taken over the ship. Former Frontier owner Phil Ruffin threw several hundred million dollars at MGM Resorts International in 2009, and TI is no longer part of that family of hotels. Ruffin has promised business as usual, at least for now, but it could mean some changes down the road.

To be fair, none of this matters a whit, unless, like us, you got a kick out of the skulls and crossbones and treasure chests bursting with jewels and gold that originally decorated the place. What remains, after they stripped the pirate gilt, is such a nice place to stay that in some ways, it even outranks its older sister, The Mirage. The good-size rooms are getting redone, and while they aren't breaking

Treasure Island stages a free pirate "battle" outside its doors every night.

from the mold of geometric neutrals, they are more striking than some. Good bathrooms feature large soaking tubs—a bather's delight. Best of all, Strip-side rooms have a view of the pirate battle—views are best from the sixth floor on up. You know, so you can see right down the sirens' dresses.

The hotel offers half a dozen restaurants, including **Isla** (p. 177); **Dishes, The Buffet at TI** (p. 204); a branch of Los Angeles's **Canter's Deli** (p. 180); and a return of the country-western favorite **Gilley's** (p. 176). Treasure Island is home to Cirque du Soleil's *Mystère* (p. 304), one of the best shows in town.

There's a full-service spa and health club with a complement of machines, plus sauna, steam, whirlpool, massage, on-site trainers, TVs and stereos with headsets, and anything else you might need (including a full line of Sebastian grooming products in the women's locker room).

The pool is not that memorable, with none of the massive foliage and other details that make the one at The Mirage stand out. So blah is it that the staff didn't even bother to check room keys when last we swam here. It's a large, free-form swimming pool with a 230-foot loop slide and a nicely landscaped sun-deck area. It's often crawling with kids, so if that's a turnoff, go elsewhere.

A free tram connects the TI with The Mirage.

3300 Las Vegas Blvd. S. (at Spring Mountain Rd.), Las Vegas, NV 89109. © **800/944-7444** or 702/894-7111. www.treasureisland.com. 2,885 units. $89 and up double; $140 and up suite. Extra person $30. No discount for children. Inquire about packages. Daily resort fee $20 includes Internet, gym access, newspaper, and other discounts. AE, DC, DISC, MC, V. Free self- and valet parking. **Amenities:** 6 restaurants; casino; concierge; executive-level rooms; health club; outdoor pool; room service; showrooms; spa; wedding chapels. *In room:* A/C, TV w/pay movies, fax, hair dryer, Wi-Fi (for a fee).

The Westin Casuarina Las Vegas Hotel, Casino & Spa ★★

When the ever-more-seedy Maxim was more or less stripped to its bones and turned into a Westin, we were thrilled. What Vegas needs, we kept saying, was a true kicky boutique hotel, one that puts real service and real style ahead of slot machines. This Westin won't fill that bill—coming a lot closer would be THEhotel at Mandalay Bay—but business travelers who want a little style, and don't mind if said style is just a tad generic and sterile, will be pleased with this hotel.

There is nothing wrong with the rooms—they are in excellent taste, done in eye-pleasing sages and wheats, complete with The Westin's self-congratulatory trademarked Heavenly Bed, which caused one occupant to dream she was sleeping on clouds (and the other to note it has a whole lot of polyester in its makeup). The bathrooms are gleaming, if small—but they pale compared to some of the (admittedly occasionally lurid) fantasies around town. For the price, especially if you were looking for something Vegas-riffic, you might be disappointed. It doesn't help that the cool exec-style lobby/check-in area melds into a casino area that seems to have been missed in the renovations; it's weirdly dated. It also doesn't help that the staff says, "No, that's not something we do or offer" more often than, "Yes, we can do that," though they say it nicely enough. There is an adequate (and free!) gym, reached by walking right by all the business meeting areas and a decent pool. And this is the only hotel in Las Vegas that bans smoking in all rooms and public areas (except for the casino, where folks can still puff away). Ultimately, it's too good a property not to give a relatively high rating, but you need to understand that, by Vegas standards—which means different things to different people—it's boring.

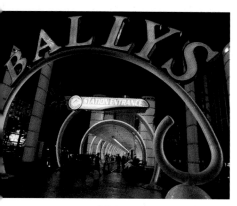

FROM LEFT: Bally's Las Vegas; stained glass inside Bill's Gamblin' Hall and Saloon.

160 E. Flamingo Rd., Las Vegas, NV 89109. ✆ **866/837-4215** or 702/836-5900. Fax 702/836-5996. www.westin.com/lasvegas. 825 units. $139 and up double. Extra person $30. Children 17 and under stay free in parent's room. AE, DC, DISC, MC, V. Free self- and valet parking. Pets accepted, $35 fee and a deposit. **Amenities:** Restaurant; bar; coffee shop; casino; concierge; health club; outdoor heated pool; room service. *In room:* A/C, TV, hair dryer, minibar, Wi-Fi (for a fee).

Moderate

Bally's Las Vegas ★ With all the fancy-pants new hotels in town, it's hard to keep up with the Joneses, or the Wynns, as the case may be. And here's poor Bally's, with a perfect location, and it's got no big fountain or Eiffel Tower or anything to make a passerby think "Gotta go gamble there," much less a tourist booking long distance to think "Gotta stay there." And we aren't really going to make you change your mind, though we might give you a reason to consider it. After all, you can get a room for a ridiculously low rate these days (not reflected in the official rack rates below, but give them a try), and those rooms, which are larger than average, have some swell touches, including modern curvy couches, big TVs, and marble this and that. The public areas still feel a little dated, but the hotel is connected to its sister property, Paris Las Vegas, which is swanky and modern enough. Also, it's a stop on the monorail system, so you'll be able to go just about everywhere by foot or by swift train, and, thanks to those nice rooms, you've got someplace pleasant to return to.

Bally's has the usual range of dining choices with many more next door at sister hotel Paris Las Vegas The casino is large, well lit, and colorful, and there's also a headliner showroom and the splashy *Jubilee!* revue (p. 310).

3645 Las Vegas Blvd. S. (at Flamingo Rd.), Las Vegas, NV 89109. ✆ **800/634-3434** or 702/739-4111. Fax 702/967-3890. www.ballyslv.com. 2,814 units. $99 and up double; $300 and up suite. Extra person $30. No discount for children. AE, DC, MC, V. Free self- and valet parking. **Amenities:** 13 restaurants; casino; concierge; health club; outdoor pool; room service; showrooms; spa; 8 night-lit tennis courts. *In room:* A/C, TV w/pay movies, hair dryer, Internet (for a fee).

Bill's Gamblin' Hall and Saloon You can't fault the location of this hotel. It's right on the busiest corner of the Strip, smack in the middle of the action. With all the hotel business (the itty-bitty reception desk and tiny sundries/gift-shop counter) set on the fringes of the small, dark, cluttered casino, this is very old Vegas, which is sort of a good thing; but unfortunately, it's becoming harder to wrap one's mind around it in these days of megacasino complexes.

Each room has an extra corner of space for a couple of chairs or a couch alongside the very cramped bathroom. ***Beware:*** The very loud intersection outside can make rooms noisy.

3595 Las Vegas Blvd. S. (at Flamingo Rd.), Las Vegas, NV 89109. © **866/245-5745** or 702/737-2100. Fax 702/894-9954. www.billslasvegas.com. 200 units. $60 and up double. Extra person $19. No discount for children. AE, DC, DISC, MC, V. Free self- and valet parking. **Amenities:** 2 restaurants; casino; room service. *In room:* A/C, TV w/pay movies, hair dryer, Wi-Fi (for a fee).

Inexpensive

Imperial Palace What? The Imperial Palace is still around? Why, yes it is, despite repeated attempts to make it go away. When Harrah's bought the hotel in 2005, they made no secret about their desire to tear the place down and replace it with something bigger, better, and more modern. They even started closing restaurants and moving shows to make room for the wrecking ball (though, for the record, they never said that was the reason). But while the plans for the IP's demise may have been drawn up, they were never executed and the place soldiers on as one of the few affordable (read: cheap) casino-hotels on the Strip.

There have been a few attempts at spiffing the place up, especially in the much lighter but still cramped casino, but for the most part the IP is exactly how it always has been: basic. If you're used to the spic-and-span comforts of more modern hotels, stepping out of the elevators into the hotel's almost industrial lobbies can be a bit disconcerting. Ditto the simple rooms with motel-style furnishings and tiny bathrooms. But everything is clean and relatively well kept. Many of the rooms have balconies; all have air-conditioning, a bed, a shower, and towels. And, really, what else do you need? This is the kind of place where you check in, dump your bags, and use all the money you have saved to go somewhere else to party until dawn, and then come back and crash for a few hours when you absolutely won't care that there aren't 300-thread-count linens on the beds.

If you feel like staying on-site for entertainment, there is a casino with relatively low limits; a few shows, bars, and restaurants, including the delightful **Hash House a Go Go** (p. 176); and a pretty basic pool. But really all of that is just window dressing for the real reason you'd bunk here: the cost. Although you may long for a few more creature comforts while you are staying here, getting the bill at the end, which will be a fraction of what you would've paid at just about any other major hotel on the Strip, will make you forget you ever wanted anything else.

3535 Las Vegas Blvd. S., Las Vegas, NV 89109. © **800/351-7400** or 702/731-3311. Fax 702/735-8328. www.imperialpalace.com. 2,640 units. $99 and up double; $159 and up suite. Extra person $30. Children 7 and under stay free in parent's room. AE, DC, DISC, MC, V. Free self- and valet parking. **Amenities:** 8 restaurants; concierge; executive-level rooms; health club; heated outdoor pool; room service; spa; showrooms; salon; museums; wedding chapel; casino. *In room:* A/C, TV, Wi-Fi (for a fee).

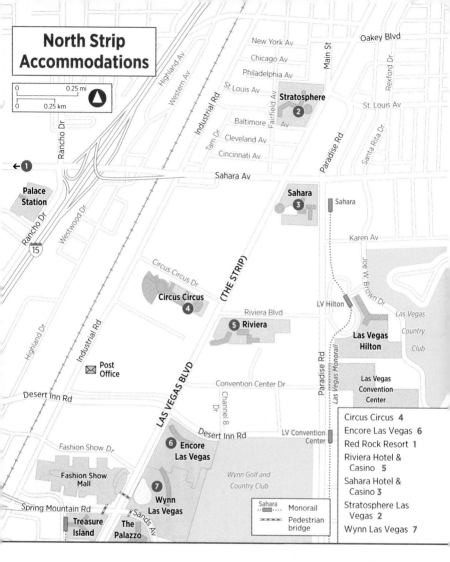

North Strip Accommodations

Circus Circus	4
Encore Las Vegas	6
Red Rock Resort	1
Riviera Hotel & Casino	5
Sahara Hotel & Casino	3
Stratosphere Las Vegas	2
Wynn Las Vegas	7

Sahara ··· ■■··· Monorail
━━━ Pedestrian bridge

NORTH STRIP

Very Expensive

Encore Las Vegas ★★ What do you do after you have built a casino empire, sold it all, and then reentered the fray by creating an all-new paradigm for modern Vegas luxury? Well, you have an encore, of course.

The thusly named Encore is the second act for Vegas impresario Steve Wynn and his eponymous Wynn Las Vegas. Located just north of that hotel and sharing its gracefully curved bronze exterior look, the baby sister of the family is intended to be at once more luxurious (no, really!) and more whimsical, with a design scheme that is heavy on the springtime cues (think butterflies) with Greek and Moroccan touches liberally applied everywhere you look. Oh, and red.

Lots of red. It shouldn't work, really, and yet it does, turning the model of what a Las Vegas casino-hotel should be on its head once again.

Enter from the Strip or via the store-lined walkway from Wynn Las Vegas and you are deposited (naturally) into the casino, smaller than most Strip gambling spaces to start with and made seemingly even more so by the use of plantation shutters and heavy drapes that break up the room into cozy salon-type areas. Natural light imbues the area from a wall of windows facing the main pool and a soaring atrium filled with trees and plants fronts a second one. Gamble during the day and it will take a moment to get used to, sitting at a blackjack table bathed in sunlight.

While they follow a similar aesthetic, the rooms at Encore are grander than those at Wynn both in terms of size and amenities. Most are "suites" with a sleeping area separated from a living room space by a partial wall (and a giant flatscreen TV). Furnishings are modern but with an elegant panache, and high tech, thus allowing you to operate everything from the lights to the TVs to the drapes to the air-conditioning from a single remote that remembers your preferences. Bathrooms are massive and packed with plush towels and robes, high-quality bath amenities, and enough marble to build your own Colosseum.

The main pool area in the center of the property is yet another winner, done as a European garden with more of the springtime touches and Greek statuary. New as of 2010 is the Encore Beach Club, a 60,000-square-foot pool/nightclub/restaurant concept with luxury cabanas, an indoor/outdoor dance club, and restaurant. The 70,000-square-foot **Spa at Encore** is gorgeous.

Five restaurants serve up high-end cuisine, including a shrine to the Chairman of the Board at **Sinatra** (p. 182), the gimmicky but effective French-inspired steakhouse **Switch** (p. 182), and the 24-hour **Society Café** among others. And, of course, the restaurants at Wynn are just a short walk away.

As with its big sister, prices here are not for the faint of heart. While the recession may have knocked down the overall bill during its inaugural run, room rates will almost always be more expensive here than just about anywhere else on the Strip. Ditto restaurant prices, table game limits, and the cost of a bottle of water in the sundry store.

3121 Las Vegas Blvd. S. (near Spring Mountain Rd.), Las Vegas, NV 89109. ☎ **888/320-7125** or 702/770-7171. Fax 702/770-1571. www.encorelas vegas.com. 2,034 units. $159 and up double. Extra person $50. No discount for children. AE, DC, DISC, MC, V. Free self- and valet parking. **Amenities:** 5 restaurants; casino; concierge; executive-level

You'll find butterfly motifs throughout Encore Las Vegas.

Whimsical lanterns overlook the viewing area for the Lake of Dreams at Wynn Las Vegas.

rooms; health club; 2 outdoor pools; room service; spa; casino. *In room:* A/C, TVs w/pay movies, CD/DVD player, fax, hair dryer, Wi-Fi (for a fee).

Wynn Las Vegas ★★ Because Steve Wynn is a modern-day Vegas legend, because this town almost entirely owes its present-day look and outlook to him, because this hotel (built on the site of the old Desert Inn and opened on the same day, Apr 28, that grand old dame was originally opened) came with a $2.7-billion price tag, and because there was a great deal of hype that used words and phrases such as "like nothing you've ever seen before," there was a corresponding amount of anticipation surrounding the opening of this, one of Vegas's newest and perhaps most-trumpeted resorts. The result? Something that is at once pretty "wow" and a whole lot "It looks like Bellagio."

The hotel feels a little bit cramped when you first enter—we are used to swooping Vegas lobby displays—and the reception area is impractically proportioned, resulting in some check-in waits. The suspicion is that all this makes the place seem less behemoth and more resort size. The hotel has no discernible theme (apart from that tendency to prompt constant comparisons to Bellagio), which may be disappointing for those looking for theme-aganza. The interior has some superior moments, including considerable use of natural light (via various skylights and atriums), unusual in this town and most welcome; a floral motif reflected in eye-catching, brightly hued floor mosaics; artistic fresh-flower arrangements throughout; and, best of all, the atrium that runs down the center and, like its predecessor at Bellagio, features frequently changed displays. There are also some of the most garish lighting fixtures in a town not known for its subtlety in chandeliers. The layout is devoted to old-school Vegas floor planning, which forces guests to maneuver around and through the casino to get anywhere.

As with all other Wynn hotels, there is an installation in front of the building, a 150-foot-tall man-made mountain covered in trees (many mature trees taken from the old Desert Inn golf course) and waterfalls, and, like the others, this comes with a "free show." The quotation marks are because said show is not viewable from the street—neither, in fact, is the mountain itself. The latter can be glimpsed only in bits and pieces, though there is a decent shot at a portion of it as you enter from the Strip across from the pedestrian walkway; the former can be viewed only when either dining at the SW Steakhouse or Daniel Boulud Brasserie, or having a drink at a couple of bars, where you will be required to purchase two drinks per person, starting at $12 a glass. There is one truly free viewing platform, but it is tiny.

These complaints notwithstanding, there's nothing really wrong with the place; we just nitpick because the hype invites it. In fact, there is much to like here. The rooms are hands down the best on the Strip (at least, that aren't suites, such as at The Venetian or THEhotel, or those at sister Encore). They're particularly large (and have kind of ruined us for even the more spacious of other rooms), with much-appreciated floor-to-ceiling views (west side shows off the mountain and waterfalls, east side the golf course; both are choice); deeply comfortable beds, with high-thread-count sheets and feather beds atop good-quality mattresses, plus down comforters; flatscreen TVs; and excellent up-to-the-minute bathrooms, complete with quite long and deep tubs, their own flatscreen TVs, and lemony amenities. Take note of the silky-satiny robes (the best we've ever had in a hotel) and plush velour slippers. All the rooms are done in shades that happily break the recent trend toward bland parchment tones, but at least one of the palettes is a strange hybrid of salmon and terra cotta, so while we appreciate the effort, the result can be disconcerting. Love the Warhol flower prints, though.

The gym is excellent, stuffed with up-to-the-minute equipment, most with individual TV screens, though we could do without the windows looking onto an interior hallway that make our workout visible to all passersby. The spa area is serene and particularly pretty, with an atrium emitting natural light into the bathing areas. The pool area has four oval-shaped numbers connected by some stretches long enough for laps, plus a "European sun-bathing" (read: topless) area that includes outdoor blackjack tables.

Dining options are superb (though generally exceptionally pricey), including **Alex, Bartolotta, Daniel Boulud Brasserie, Red 8,** and the **Wynn Las Vegas Buffet,** all reviewed in chapter 6. A shopping street features high-end choices—Chanel, Cartier, Manolo Blahnik, Gaultier—but still seems a bit more lower economic (that's relative, mind you) than a similar one at Bellagio. Make special note of the apothecary-style shop next to the sundries shop; it stocks all sorts of fine lotions and potions, including, remarkably, the centuries-old, coveted (and still difficult-to-find) monk-produced line from the Santa Maria Novella Pharmacy in Florence. Monk-made products in Vegas? Well, why not? There's also a Ferrari dealership—no, really; and, what's more, it's so popular that it actually charges admission to gawk for a while.

In the end, this is a very adult hotel, in the best sense—classy and mature. But still, so was the old Desert Inn, which hit all the right resort notes even in its last days, only to be replaced by the bigger-is-better ethos.

3131 Las Vegas Blvd. S. (corner of Spring Mountain Rd.), Las Vegas, NV 89109. ℂ **888/320-9966** or 702/770-7100. Fax 702/770-1571. www.wynnlasvegas.com. 2,716 units. $199 and up double. Extra person $50. No discount for children. AE, DC, DISC, MC, V. Free self- and valet parking. **Amenities:** 22 restaurants; casino; concierge; executive-level rooms; health club; 4 outdoor pools; room service; showrooms; spa; 3 wedding chapels. *In room:* A/C, TVs w/pay movies, CD/DVD player, fax, hair dryer, Wi-Fi (for a fee).

Expensive

Riviera Hotel & Casino  Its best days long past, this former Strip star is looking awfully dumpy these days. Between that and its promotion as an "alternative for grown-ups" and an "adult-oriented hotel," you should probably stay here only if you can get a deal and simply must be on the Strip. You certainly shouldn't bring the kids, who are actively discouraged as guests.

Opened in 1955 (Liberace cut the ribbon, and Joan Crawford was the official hostess of opening ceremonies), the Riviera was the first "high-rise" on the Strip, at nine stories. Today it tries to evoke the Vegas

Old school signage marks the exterior of the Riviera Hotel & Casino.

of the good old days—"come drink, gamble, and see a show"—and while it is appropriately dark and glitzy, it's also very crowded and has a confusing layout. Don't miss your chance to have your photo taken with the bronze memorial to the Crazy Girls (their premier, largely nekkid, show), and their butts, outside on the Strip. There is a pool here, but it's very dull.

Some rooms received makeovers, bringing in modern furnishings, the ubiquitous white comforters, flatscreen TVs, and the like. Be sure to ask for one of these. There is the predictable assortment of dining options—though an excellent choice for families, ironically, is the **Mardi Gras Food Court,** which, unlike most of its genre, is extremely attractive. White-canvas umbrella tables and Toulouse-Lautrec–style murals create a comfortable, French-cafe ambience. Food choices are wide ranging, including burgers, pizza, gyros, falafel, and Chinese fare. The Riviera's enormous casino is a rambling, equally dingy affair; see chapter 10 for reviews of its production show **Crazy Girls** (sexy Las Vegas–style revue).

2901 Las Vegas Blvd. S. (at Riviera Blvd.), Las Vegas, NV 89109. ☎ **800/634-6753** or 702/734-5110. Fax 702/794-9451. www.rivierahotel.com. 2,074 units. $79 and up double; $155 and up suite. Extra person $20. No discount for children. AE, DC, MC, V. Free self- and valet parking. **Amenities:** 5 restaurants; food court; casino; executive-level rooms; health club; outdoor pool; room service; showrooms; spa; wedding chapel. *In room:* A/C, TV w/pay movies, Wi-Fi (for fee).

Moderate

Sahara Hotel & Casino One of the few venerable old casino hotels still standing in Vegas (it's come a long way since it opened in 1952 on the site of the old Club Bingo), how you now view the Sahara may simply depend on which direction the sun is shining. It's been a few years since a spiffy renovation really pulled in some solid Moroccan details (an arched neon dome with Moroccan detailing, plenty of marble and chandeliers, plus small tiles and other Arabian Nights decorations) and caused the loss of the landmark sign, once the tallest in Vegas. Then they added a roller coaster around the outside (quite a good ride, enthusiasts assure us), you know, just because.

Rooms are a bit too motel-room bland (though the windows open, which is unusual for Vegas). Again, this may simply be in comparison to the gleaming new kids in town, a comparison suffered by most of the older hotels. If you are looking for four walls and a mattress, this isn't a bad choice at all. It should be noted that the Sahara feels that it is not as well equipped as other hotels for children and discourages you from bringing yours—and yet, it added a roller coaster. Go figure.

The hotel includes the Sahara Buffet. The casino is a pretty pleasant one to gamble in, and there's a showroom as well. There is one pool.

2535 Las Vegas Blvd. S. (at E. Sahara Ave.), Las Vegas, NV 89109. ✆ **888/696-2121** or 702/737-2654. Fax 702/791-2027. www.saharavegas.com. 1,720 units. $45 and up double. Extra person $20. No discount for children. AE, DC, DISC, MC, V. Free self- and valet parking. **Amenities:** 5 restaurants; casino; executive-level rooms; outdoor pool; room service; showroom and lounge w/ free entertainment; spa. *In room:* A/C, TV w/pay movies, fridge (on request), hair dryer, Internet (for a fee).

Stratosphere Las Vegas Hotel & Casino ★ ☺ A really neat idea, in that Vegas way, in a really bad location. At 1,149 feet, it's the tallest building west of the Mississippi. In theory, this should have provided yet another attraction for visitors: Climb (okay, elevator) to the top and gaze at the stunning view. But despite being on the Strip, it's a healthy walk from anywhere—the nearest casino is the Sahara, which is 5 very long blocks away. This, and possibly the hefty price charged for the privilege of going up to the top of the tower, may have conspired to keep the crowds away.

And although the crowds might have been justified before, you might reconsider, especially if you are looking for a friendly place to hang your hat, but nothing more. The smaller rooms here are basically motel rooms—really nice motel rooms, but with that level of comfort and style. Then again, you can often get such a room for around $49 a night. And do join the casino's players' club—they

The Sahara's pool is a friendly place to chill out on a hot Vegas day.

tend to offer free rooms with more or less minimal play. Perfect if you are coming to Vegas with no plans to spend time in your room except to sleep (if even that).

That isn't to say there aren't other elements to like, including the afore-mentioned casino, a midway area with kiddie-oriented rides, a pool with a view, and some of the friendliest, most accommodating staff in town. You can still ride the following incredible thrill rides (provided the wind isn't blow-ing too hard that day) on top of the tower: the **Big Shot,** a fabulous free-fall ride that thrusts passengers up and down the tower at speeds of up to 45 mph; **X-Scream,** a giant teeter-totter device that gives you the sensation of falling off the side of the building; and **Insanity: the Ride,** a whirligig con-traption that spins you around more than 900 feet above terra firma; and **SkyJump,** which allows you to literally

The Stratosphere Las Vegas Hotel & Casino tower is a Strip landmark and marks its northern boundary.

jump off the top of the tower in a controlled descent—although whether you can control yourself during the experience is an entirely different question (see p. 228 for reviews of all of these adrenaline pumpers). Indoor and outdoor observa-tion decks offer the most stunning city views you will ever see, especially at night. For the price, this might be the right place for you. Just remember that you need a rental car or a lot of cash for cabs to get to the true thrills down the Strip.

In addition to the casino, the hotel sports two production shows: *American Superstars* (an impression-filled show, reviewed on p. 302) and *BITE.*

2000 Las Vegas Blvd. S. (btw. St. Louis and Baltimore aves.), Las Vegas, NV 89104. © **800/998-6937** or 702/380-7777. Fax 702/383-5334. www.stratospherehotel.com. 2,444 units. $49 and up double; $109 and up suite. Extra person $15. Children 12 and under stay free in parent's room. AE, DC, DISC, MC, V. Free self- and valet parking. **Amenities:** 9 restaurants; several fast-food outlets; casino; children's rides and games; concierge; executive-level rooms; large pool area w/great views of the Strip; room service; showrooms; wedding chapel. *In room:* A/C, TV w/pay movies, hair dryer, Wi-Fi (for a fee).

Inexpensive

Circus Circus Hotel & Casino ★ ☺ This is the last bastion of family-friendly Las Vegas—indeed, for years, the only hotel with such an open mind, which is also not to say that you should confuse this with a theme-park hotel. All the circus fun is still built around a busy casino. The midway level features dozens of carnival games, a large arcade (more than 300 video and pinball games), trick mirrors, and ongoing circus acts under the big top from 11am to midnight daily. The world's largest permanent circus, it features renowned trapeze artists, stunt cyclists, jugglers, magicians, acrobats, and high-wire daredevils. Spectators can view the action from much of the midway or get up close and comfy on benches

Midway arcade at Circus Circus Hotel & Casino.

in the performance arena. There's a "be-a-clown" booth, where kids can be made up with clown makeup (easily washed off!) and red foam-rubber noses. They can grab a bite to eat in McDonald's (also on this level), and because the mezzanine overlooks the casino action, they can also look down and wave to Mom and Dad—or, more to the point, Mom and Dad can look up and wave to the kids without having to stray too far from the blackjack table. Circus clowns wander the midway, creating balloon animals and cutting up in various ways.

The thousands of rooms here occupy sufficient acreage to warrant a free Disney World–style aerial shuttle (another kid pleaser) connecting its many components. Tower rooms have newish, just slightly better-than-average furnishings. The Manor section comprises five white, three-story buildings out back, fronted by rows of cypresses. Manor guests can park at their doors; and a gate to the complex that can be opened only with a room key ensures security. These rooms are usually among the least expensive in town, but we've said it before and we'll say it again: You get what you pay for. A renovation of these rooms added a coat of paint and some new photos on the wall but not much else. All sections of this vast property have their own swimming pools, additional casinos serve the main tower and sky-rise buildings, and both towers provide covered parking garages.

Adjacent to the hotel is **Circusland RV Park,** which is KOA run, with 399 full-utility spaces and up to 50-amp hookups. It has its own 24-hour convenience store, swimming pools, saunas, whirlpools, kiddie playground, fenced pet runs, video-game arcade, community room, and Wi-Fi. The rate is $55 and up, with peak rates around $100. For gorging, there's always the **Circus Circus Buffet** (p. 205), and, for a classic steakhouse experience, try the appropriately, if unimaginatively, named **The Steakhouse** (p. 184).

In addition to the ongoing circus acts, there's also the upgraded **Adventuredome** (p. 239) indoor theme park out back. There are three full-size casinos, all crowded and noisy, where you can gamble, while trapeze acts take place overhead.

2880 Las Vegas Blvd. S. (btw. Circus Circus and Convention Center drives), Las Vegas, NV 89109. ℂ **877/434-9175** or 702/734-0410. Fax 702/734-5897. www.circuscircus.com. 3,774 units. $59 and up double. Extra person $15. Children 17 and under stay free in parent's room. AE, DC, DISC,

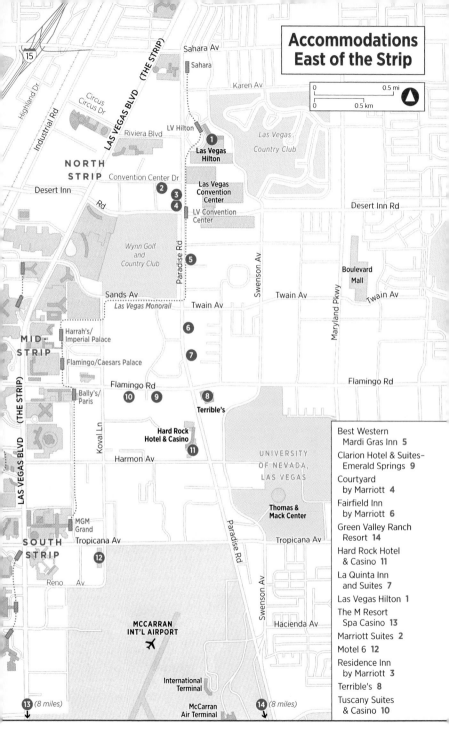

Accommodations East of the Strip

0   0.5 mi
0   0.5 km

Sahara Av

Karen Av

Las Vegas
Country Club

Desert Inn Rd

Boulevard
Mall

Twain Av

Flamingo Rd

Tropicana Av

Hacienda Av

UNIVERSITY
OF NEVADA,
LAS VEGAS

Thomas &
Mack Center

MCCARRAN
INT'L AIRPORT

International
Terminal

McCarran
Air Terminal

Sahara

LV Hilton

Las Vegas
Hilton

Riviera Blvd

**NORTH
STRIP** Convention Center Dr

Las Vegas
Convention
Center

LV Convention
Center

Desert Inn

Rd

Wynn Golf
and
Country Club

Paradise Rd

Swenson Av

Maryland Pkwy

Sands Av

Las Vegas Monorail

Twain Av

**MID-
STRIP**

Harrah's/
Imperial Palace

Flamingo/Caesars Palace

Bally's/
Paris

Flamingo Rd

Terrible's

Koval Ln

Hard Rock
Hotel & Casino

Harmon Av

MGM
Grand

**SOUTH
STRIP** Tropicana Av

Reno   Av

LAS VEGAS BLVD (THE STRIP)

LAS VEGAS BLVD (THE STRIP)

Highland Dr

Industrial Rd

Circus
Circus Dr

15

① Las Vegas Hilton
② ③ ④
⑤
⑥
⑦
⑧ Terrible's
⑨ ⑩
⑪
⑫
⑬ (8 miles)
⑭ (8 miles)

Best Western
  Mardi Gras Inn **5**

Clarion Hotel & Suites–
  Emerald Springs **9**

Courtyard
  by Marriott **4**

Fairfield Inn
  by Marriott **6**

Green Valley Ranch
  Resort **14**

Hard Rock Hotel
  & Casino **11**

La Quinta Inn
  and Suites **7**

Las Vegas Hilton **1**

The M Resort
  Spa Casino **13**

Marriott Suites **2**

Motel 6 **12**

Residence Inn
  by Marriott **3**

Terrible's **8**

Tuscany Suites
  & Casino **10**

MC, V. Free self- and valet parking. **Amenities:** 7 restaurants; several fast-food outlets; casino; circus acts and midway-style carnival games; executive-level rooms; 2 outdoor pools; room service; wedding chapel. *In room:* A/C, TV w/pay movies, hair dryer, Wi-Fi (for a fee).

EAST OF THE STRIP

In this section, we cover hotels near the Convention Center, along with those farther south on Paradise Road, Flamingo Road, and Tropicana Avenue. Note that in the area around Paradise, there are more than a dozen chain-style hotels—various Marriotts (Courtyard, Residence Inn), a Budget Suites, and many others—any one of which is going to provide comfortable, reliable, utterly undistinguished lodging, and all of which often go for more money than they ought to. We've singled out a few here, but they are really quite interchangeable. Do some searching around online, and don't hesitate to try to play them off each other in an attempt to get a deal.

Very Expensive

Hard Rock Hotel & Casino ★★ A 2009 expansion project more than doubled the size of just about everything at the Hard Rock. Additions included two new hotel towers, a second pool area, more casino space, more restaurants and nightclubs, and more of everything that makes this particular hotel "rock."

As soon as you check out the Hard Rock clientele, you'll know you are in a Vegas hotel that's like no other. The body-fat percentage (and median age) plummets; the percentage of black clothing skyrockets. Yep, the hip—including Hollywood and the music industry, among others—still flock to the Hard Rock,

Rock music memorabilia at the Hard Rock Hotel & Casino.

drawn by the cool 'n' rockin' ambience and the goodies offered by a boutique hotel (only in Vegas could 657 rooms be considered a "boutique hotel"). Our problem is that we are not famous pop stars and we do not look enough like Pamela Anderson to warrant the kind of attention that the staff seems to reserve for those types.

It's that Boomer-meets-Gen-X sensibility that finds tacky chic so very hip. Original rooms are spacious and almost painfully self-aware in how cool they are trying to be, with mod furnishings and funky amenities. Balconies are a nice touch here. The newer Paradise Tower has a touch more sophistication with a black and gray design scheme, contemporary furnishings, and bathrooms that are sleek enough to be in a nightclub (note they only have showers, no tubs). The HRH Tower is the pinnacle in terms of amenities—and cost. The gleaming white suites are plush and feature multiple TVs and an entertainment system that allows you to plug your MP3 player into the wall and create your own playlist or listen to one of theirs.

The main casino is a cramped, circular affair dominated by gaming tables (rare for Vegas) while the 2009 addition in the space once occupied by The Joint nightclub has more machines and tables and a bit more breathing room. On the perimeter is a collection of rock memorabilia, ranging from sad (a Kurt Cobain tribute) to cool (various guitars and outfits) to useless (various other guitars and outfits). The Hard Rock now has a permanent, if unwelcome, bit of rock trivia for its collection: John Entwistle, bassist for The Who, died in one of its rooms on the eve of the start of a tour with the band.

There are several fine restaurants, including **Nobu,** a branch of highly famed Chef Nobu Matsuhisa's wildly popular Japanese restaurant, and **AGO,** a restaurant co-owned by Robert DeNiro. Kicky and funky Mexican food can be had at lunch, and dinner is served in the folk-art-filled **Pink Taco** (p. 191); and **Mr. Lucky's 24/7** (p. 167) is the hotel's 'round-the-clock coffee shop, displaying rock memorabilia and old Las Vegas hotel signs. The **Hard Rock Cafe** (p. 163) is adjacent to the hotel. **The Joint** (p. 316) is a major showroom that often hosts big-name rock musicians.

If you've ever dreamed of being in a beach-party movie, or on the set of one of those MTV summer beach-house shows, the pool at the Hard Rock is for you. Multiple pools are joined by a lazy river and fringed in spots by actual sand beaches. You won't get much swimming done—the water is largely so shallow that it won't hit your knees—but there is swim-up blackjack (they give you little plastic pouches to hold your money), and a stage that features live music in the summer and is fronted by a sandy area, so you can make like Frankie, Annette, and Erik Von Zipper and do the Watusi. Or just pose in a thong bikini and new breasts. Whichever. On warm days and nights, this is *the* hangout scene.

A new spa facility mixes Moroccan details with stripper poles. Oh but that we were making that up. There is actually a room in the spa where you can practice your, um, technique under the disguise of exercise. Whatever makes you happy.

Plus there's a tattoo shop, so yeah, it's still that kind of place (or trying to be).

4455 Paradise Rd. (at Harmon Ave.), Las Vegas, NV 89109. ☏ **800/473-7625** or 702/693-5000. Fax 702/693-5588. www.hardrockhotel.com. 1,500 units. $109 and up double; $250 and up suite. Extra person $75. Children 12 and under stay free in parent's room. AE, DC, MC, V. Free self- and valet parking. **Amenities:** 6 restaurants; casino; concierge; small health club; executive-level rooms; 2 outdoor pools w/lazy river and sandy-beach bottom; room service; showroom; spa. *In room:* A/C, TV w/pay movies, hair dryer, Wi-Fi (for a fee).

Expensive

Courtyard by Marriott ★ A complex of three-story buildings in an attractively landscaped setting of trees, shrubbery, and flower beds, the Courtyard is a welcome link in the Marriott chain. Although the services are limited, don't picture a no-frills establishment. This is a good-looking hotel (in a chain-establishment kind of way), with a pleasant, plant-filled lobby and very nice rooms indeed. Public areas and rooms still look brand-spanking new. Most rooms have king-size beds, and all have balconies or patios. It's also right across the street from a monorail station. Still, it's probably not worth the price, given the location and in comparison to what you can get at a comparably priced Strip hotel.

3275 Paradise Rd. (btw. Convention Center Dr. and Desert Inn Rd.), Las Vegas, NV 89109. ✆ **800/321-2211** or 702/791-3600. Fax 702/796-7981. www.courtyard.com. 149 units. $149 and up double (up to 4 people); $189 and up suite (up to 4 people). No charge for extra person. AE, DC, DISC, MC, V. Free parking at your room door. **Amenities:** Restaurant; free computer and Wi-Fi in lobby; executive-level rooms; small exercise room; Jacuzzi; outdoor pool; room service. *In room:* A/C, TV w/pay movies, hair dryer, Internet.

La Quinta Inn and Suites ★ This is a tranquil and visually appealing alternative (within the limited range of chains) to the Strip's hubbub, featuring courtyards, rustic benches, attractive pools, barbecue grills, and picnic tables. The staff is friendly and incredibly helpful. The rooms are immaculate and attractive. Spend the extra money for an executive room, which features a queen-size bed, a small fridge, a wet bar, and a microwave oven. Double queens are larger but have no kitchen facilities. And two-bedroom suites are not just spacious, they are really full apartments, with large living rooms (some with sofa beds), dining areas, and full kitchens. Ground-floor accommodations have patios, and all accommodations feature bathrooms with oversize whirlpool tubs.

3970 Paradise Rd. (btw. Twain Ave. and Flamingo Rd.), Las Vegas, NV 89109. ✆ **800/531-5900** or 702/796-9000. Fax 702/796-3537. www.laquinta.com. 251 units. $89 and up double; $99 and up executive queen; $119 and up suite. Rates include continental breakfast. AE, DC, DISC, MC, V. Up to 2 pets, free with security deposit. Free self-parking. **Amenities:** Free airport/Strip shuttle; Jacuzzi; outdoor pool. *In room:* A/C, TV w/pay movies, hair dryer, kitchen (in executives and suites), Wi-Fi.

Marriott Suites ★ Oh, sure, you don't lack for Marriotts in Las Vegas, but it is a reliable chain (if a tad overpriced), and you can't fault the location of this one. It's just 3 blocks off the Strip (and not much farther from the Convention Center)—a 10-minute walk at most, though in 100°F (38°C) heat, that may be too far. This is a solid choice for business travelers, but families might also like the lack of casino and accompanying mayhem, not to mention the extra-large, quite comfortable rooms. Each suite has a sitting area separated from the bedroom by French doors. And there are gorgeous prints on the walls—far, far better than you would expect in a hotel, much less in one of the chain variety.

325 Convention Center Dr., Las Vegas, NV 89109. ✆ **800/228-9290** or 702/650-2000. Fax 702/650-9466. www.marriott.com. 278 units. $159 and up suite (up to 4 people). AE, DC, DISC, MC, V. Free parking. **Amenities:** Restaurant; executive-level rooms; small exercise room; Jacuzzi; outdoor pool; free Wi-Fi in business center. *In room:* A/C, TV w/pay movies, fridge, hair dryer, Wi-Fi (for a fee).

Residence Inn by Marriott ★ Staying here is like having your own apartment in Las Vegas. The property occupies 7 acres of perfectly manicured lawns with tropical foliage, neat flowerbeds, and a big pool area. It's a great choice for families and business travelers.

Accommodations, most with working fireplaces, are housed in condolike, two-story wood-and-stucco buildings fronted by little gardens. Studios have adjoining sitting rooms with sofas and armchairs, dressing areas, and fully equipped eat-in kitchens complete with dishwashers. Every guest receives a welcome basket of microwave popcorn and coffee. All rooms have balconies or patios. Duplex penthouses, some with cathedral ceilings, add an upstairs bedroom (with its own bathroom, phone, TV, and radio) and a full dining room. A monorail station is just across the street.

3225 Paradise Rd. (btw. Desert Inn Rd. and Convention Center Dr.), Las Vegas, NV 89109. ✆ **800/677-8328** or 702/796-9300. www.marriott.com. 192 units. $159 and up studio; $179 and up penthouse. Rates include breakfast buffet. AE, DC, DISC, MC, V. Free self-parking. Pets accepted with $100 nonrefundable fee. **Amenities:** Guest access to small exercise room next door at the Courtyard by Marriott; Jacuzzi; outdoor pool; free Wi-Fi in public areas. *In room:* A/C, TV w/pay movies, hair dryer, kitchenette, Internet.

Moderate

Best Western Mardi Gras Inn 🍴 This well-run little casino-hotel has a lot to offer and is apparently popular with budget-minded Europeans (which can sometimes result in some risqué Continental-style sunbathing around the pool). A block from the Convention Center and close to major properties, its three-story building sits on nicely landscaped grounds. There's a gazebo out back where guests can enjoy a picnic lunch.

Accommodations are all spacious: queen-size-bedded minisuites with sofa-bedded living-room areas and eat-in kitchens, the latter equipped with wet bars, refrigerators, and coffeemakers. All are what you'd expect from a midlevel motel, but the furnishings are well tended, if not exactly luxurious. Staying here is like having your own little Las Vegas apartment. A pleasant restaurant/bar off the lobby, open from 6:30am to 11pm daily, serves typical coffee-shop fare.

3500 Paradise Rd. (btw. Sands Ave. and Desert Inn Rd.), Las Vegas, NV 89109. ✆ **800/634-6501** or 702/731-2020. Fax 702/731-4005. www.mardigrasinn.com. 314 units. $59 and up double (up to 4 people per room). AE, DC, DISC, MC, V. Free parking at your room door. **Amenities:** Restaurant; free airport shuttle; small casino; Jacuzzi; outdoor pool; room service. *In room:* A/C, TV w/pay movies, hair dryer, kitchenette, Wi-Fi.

Clarion Hotel & Suites—Emerald Springs ★ 🍴 Housed in three peach-stucco buildings, the Emerald Springs offers a friendly, low-key alternative to the usual glitz and glitter of Vegas accommodations. You'll enter via a charming marble-floored lobby with a waterfall fountain and lush, faux tropical plants under a domed skylight. There's a small lounge area with a television and comfortable couches off the main lobby. Although your surroundings here are serene, you're only 3 blocks from the heart of the Strip.

Public areas and rooms here are notably clean and spiffy. Pristine hallways are hung with nice abstract paintings and have small seating areas on every level, and rooms are nicely decorated with bleached-oak furnishings. Even the smallest accommodations (studios) offer small sofas, desks, and armchairs with hassocks.

Shimmer Cabaret, Las Vegas Hilton.

325 E. Flamingo Rd. (btw. Koval Lane and Paradise Rd.), Las Vegas, NV 89109. ℂ **800/732-7889** or 702/732-9100. Fax 702/731-9784. www.clarionlasvegas.com. 150 units. $99 and up studio; $119 and up whirlpool suite; $159 and up hospitality suite. Extra person $20. Children 17 and under stay free in parent's room. AE, DC, DISC, MC, V. Free self-parking. **Amenities:** Restaurant; free limo to airport/Strip; concierge; executive-level rooms; small exercise room; Jacuzzi; outdoor pool. *In room:* A/C, TV w/pay movies and Nintendo, hair dryer, kitchenette or minibar and fridge, Wi-Fi.

Fairfield Inn by Marriott 🍸 This pristine property is a pleasant place to stay. It has a comfortable lobby with sofas and armchairs, where coffee, tea, and hot chocolate are provided free all day. Rooms are cheerful. Units with king-size beds have convertible sofas, and all accommodations offer well-lit work areas with desks; TVs have free movie channels as well as pay-movie options. Local calls and high-speed Internet access are free. Breakfast pastries, fresh fruit, juice, and yogurt are served free in the lobby each morning, and many restaurants are within easy walking distance.

3850 Paradise Rd. (btw. Twain Ave. and Flamingo Rd.), Las Vegas, NV 89109. ℂ **800/228-2800** or 702/791-0899. Fax 702/791-2705. www.fairfieldinn.com. 129 units. $62 and up double (up to 5 people). Rates include continental breakfast. AE, DC, DISC, MC, V. Free self-parking. **Amenities:** Free airport shuttle; small exercise room; Jacuzzi; outdoor pool; free Wi-Fi in lobby and breakfast areas. *In room:* A/C, TV w/pay movies, hair dryer, Internet.

Las Vegas Hilton ★★ It's easy for us to overlook this dinosaur—look, we even called it a dinosaur. Totally unfair. It's one of the last of the dying breed of old Vegas hotels, but unlike many of its peers, it's still offering fine accommodations and even a bit more than that. A good place for adults looking for Vegas fun. The overall vibe is still old-school Vegas, with an old-fashioned glitzy casino that is small enough to navigate without a GPS device. Consider it even if you aren't an old-timer, and don't be put off by the distance from the Strip; the monorail stops here, making access easier than ever. When you consider that on nights when you can't touch a room on the Strip for less than $175, the Hilton will put you in a nice room with plenty of marble and clean, well-maintained furnishings for a decent price, it seems silly not to make the Hilton a top choice. There are quite a few solidly good restaurants, too. Those very same facilities, however, mean that even a small convention can sometimes drive the prices up at odd times—then again, because conventions are often booked for weekdays, an atypical drop in price can occur on weekends. Just call or look at the website. The recently renovated, generously sized rooms look fresh and include very good pillow-top mattresses and excellent amenities. Bathrooms are smallish but do have nifty oval tubs. Upgrading to club level gets some complimentary food and beverages served in a grown-up lounge.

The Hilton has a strong showing of restaurants, including **TJ's Steakhouse, Benihana,** and a **buffet** (p. 205). The **Shimmer Cabaret,** a first-rate casino lounge/nightclub, has live entertainment and ongoing shows nightly. It's a great place to hang out in the evening, when it features regular sets by local cover bands. One of Elvis's sequined jumpsuits is enshrined in a glass case in the front, near the entrance to the lobby/casino (he played 837 sold-out shows here, and Colonel Tom Parker's memorial service was held here in the hotel). There's also a major **showroom** (see chapter 10), featuring guest performers.

The third-floor roof comprises a well-landscaped 8-acre recreation deck with a large swimming pool, a 24-seat whirlpool spa, six Har-Tru tennis courts lit for night play, and more. Also on this level is a luxurious 17,000-square-foot state-of-the-art health club offering Nautilus equipment, Lifecycles, treadmills, rowing machines, three whirlpool spas, a steam room, a sauna, massage, and tanning beds. There's a $20-per-day fee to use the facilities, but guests are totally pampered: All toiletries are provided; there are comfortable TV lounges; complimentary bottled waters and juices are served in the canteen; and treatments include facials and oxygen pep-ups. Discounts on health club fees are available for multiday use.

INEXPENSIVE HOTEL alternatives

If you're determined to come to Vegas during a particularly busy season and you find yourself shut out of the prominent hotels, here's a list of moderate to very inexpensive alternatives.

ON OR NEAR THE STRIP
Budget Suites of America, 4205 W. Tropicana Ave.; ✆ **702/889-1700**
Budget Suites of America, 3655 W. Tropicana Ave.; ✆ **702/739-1000**
Travelodge, 3735 Las Vegas Blvd. S.; ✆ **800/578-7878**

PARADISE ROAD & VICINITY
AmeriSuites, 4250 Paradise Rd.; ✆ **800/833-1516**
Candlewood Suites, 4034 Paradise Rd.; ✆ **877/226-3539**

DOWNTOWN & VICINITY
Econo Lodge, 1150 Las Vegas Blvd. S.; ✆ **877/424-6423**

EAST LAS VEGAS & VICINITY
Super 8 Motel, 5288 Boulder Hwy.; ✆ **800/800-8000**

WEST LAS VEGAS & VICINITY
Motel 6, 5085 Dean Martin Dr.; ✆ **800/466-8356**

3000 Paradise Rd. (at Riviera Blvd.), Las Vegas, NV 89109. ℂ **888/732-7117** or 702/732-5111. Fax 702/732-5805. www.lvhilton.com. 3,174 units. $49 and up double. Extra person $35. Children 17 and under stay free in parent's room. AE, DC, DISC, MC, V. Free self- and valet parking. **Amenities:** 13 restaurants; food courts; casino; executive-level rooms; health club; outdoor pool; room service; showrooms; spa; 6 night-lit tennis courts. *In room:* A/C, TV w/pay movies, fridge (in some), hair dryer, Wi-Fi (for a fee).

Tuscany Suites & Casino ★ This may be the right kind of hybrid between chain hotel and fancy resort—not as lush as the latter but not anywhere near as expensive, either, with far more personal detail and indulgent touches than you can find at chains. It's another all-suite hotel, and another where "suite" really means "very big room." The rooms aren't memorable, just like the chain rooms, but they are smart enough that you won't get depressed like you might when you see some of the rooms in similarly priced hotels. The large complex (27 acres, complete with a winding pool) isn't so much Italian as it is vaguely evocative of the idea of Italian architecture, but it, too, is more stylish than most of the chains in town. And, unlike those other chains, this one comes with a large casino, roped off in such a way that this is still an appropriate place for families who want the best of all worlds (price, looks, family-friendly atmosphere, and gambling), especially as each room has a separate dining area, a kitchenette, and large TVs, plus convertible couches, on request. While the kids play, there is a large soaking tub for their folks to relax in. There's a good Italian restaurant on the premises, plus a lounge.

255 E. Flamingo Rd., Las Vegas, NV 89169. ℂ **877/887-2261** or 702/893-8933. Fax 702/947-5994. www.tuscanylasvegas.com. 700 units. $79 and up suite. Extra person $20. Children 12 and under stay free in parent's room. AE, DISC, MC, V. **Amenities:** Restaurant; lounge; casino; concierge; fitness center; outdoor pool; room service. *In room:* A/C, TV w/Nintendo, fridge, hair dryer, Wi-Fi (for a fee).

Inexpensive

Motel 6 ✦ Fronted by a big neon sign, this Motel 6 is the largest in the country, and it happens to be a great budget choice. Most Motel 6 properties are a little out of the way, but this one is quite close to major Strip casino hotels (the MGM is nearby). It has a big, pleasant lobby, and the rooms, in two-story, cream-stucco buildings, are clean and attractively decorated. Some rooms have showers only; others have tub/shower combo bathrooms. Local calls are free. And the Wi-Fi fee is the lowest in town!

195 E. Tropicana Ave. (at Koval Lane), Las Vegas, NV 89109. ℂ **800/466-8356** or 702/798-0728. Fax 702/798-5657. www.motel6.com. 607 units. $45 and up single. Extra person $6. Children 17 and under stay free in parent's room. AE, DC, DISC, MC, V. Free parking at your room door. Small pets accepted. **Amenities:** 2 outdoor pools. *In room:* A/C, TV w/pay movies, Wi-Fi (for a fee).

Terrible's ★ 🎁 First of all, this place isn't terrible at all. (The hotel was created by Ed "Terrible" Herbst, who operates a chain of convenience stores and gas stations.) Second, it isn't a bit like the hotel it took over, the rattrap known as the Continental. The Continental is gone and good riddance. In its place is an unexpected bargain, a hotel frequently offering ridiculously low prices. Try this on for size: $39 a night! Near the Strip! Near a bunch of really good restaurants! Hot diggity! So what do you get?

Well, don't expect much in the way of memorable rooms; they are as basic as can be (despite some sweet attempts with artwork depicting European idylls), and some have views of a wall (though even those get plenty of natural light).

Some, however, are considerably larger than others, so ask. The newer hotel tower has both suites and standard rooms, with new furnishings and flatscreen TVs, plus high-speed Internet. The pool area is a surprise; it looks like what you might find in a nice apartment complex (which, actually, is what Terrible's resembles on the outside), with plenty of palms and other foliage. There's a small but thoroughly stocked casino (not to mention penny slots, continuing the budget theme), plus a very good 24-hour coffee shop. How could you want for anything more? Did we mention the price and location? Plus a free airport shuttle? Okay, so we wish they had used a bit more imagination with the rooms.

The parent company of this property sank into bankruptcy in 2009, so new owners could make some changes by the time you read this.

4100 Paradise Rd. (at Flamingo Rd.), Las Vegas, NV 89109. © **800/640-9777** or 702/733-7000. Fax 702/765-5109. www.terribleherbst.com. 330 units. $39 and up double. Extra person $12. Children 17 and under stay free in parent's room. AE, DC, DISC, MC, V. Free self-parking. **Amenities:** 2 restaurants; outdoor pool; room service. *In room:* A/C, TV w/pay movies and Nintendo (for a fee), hair dryer, Internet (in some, for a fee).

WEST OF THE STRIP
Very Expensive

Red Rock Resort ★★★ The same people who brought you the fantastic Green Valley Ranch Resort trumped themselves by opening the swank Red Rock Resort in 2006, a hotel and casino complex that pretty much outdoes every other non-Strip hotel and most of the Strip hotels, also.

Guest room with a view of the mountains at Red Rock Resort.

Built at a cost of nearly a billion dollars (an outrageous sum for an 800-room hotel not located on Las Vegas Blvd.), the hotel is named for its perch right on the edge of the **Red Rock Canyon National Conservation Area** (see chapter 11), a stunning natural wonderland of red-hued rock formations and desert landscape. It's a toss-up, really, which view you should choose—to the west, you get the beautiful natural vistas, and to the east, you get an unimpeded view of the Strip and Downtown Las Vegas, about 11 miles away.

Yes, it is a bit of a trek out here, but people seeking a luxury resort experience with the added bonus of a casino, restaurants, and more will find it worth the drive. Start with that casino, an 80,000-square-foot monster that is one of the most appealing in town, meandering through the building wrapped in natural woods, stonework, glass sculptures, and stunning amber-hued chandeliers. Ten restaurants serve up a wide variety of food selections, among them a buffet and a food court that knocks it up a notch with a **Capriotti's** outlet, offering some of the best submarine sandwiches we've ever tasted. Throw in a 16-screen movie theater; a day-care center; nightclubs and bars; a sumptuous spa and health club; and a 3-acre circular "backyard" area with a sandy beach, swimming and wading pools (eagle-eyed sunbathers caught a pre-second-pregnancy-announcement Britney Spears wandering around here after a spousal tiff, so you know this is an instant celeb hot spot and getaway), Jacuzzis, private cabanas, and a stage where big-name entertainers perform, and you've got a terrific recipe for success.

The rooms are impressive, modern wonders with high-end furnishings and linens, 42-inch high-def plasma TVs, iPod sound systems, giant bathrooms, and more, all wrapped up in clean, sleek lines and vibrant earth tones. Once ensconced in one, we were hard-pressed to leave.

One negative feature is a mandatory $25-per-night "amenities" charge that is tacked on to the room rate. This fee covers unlimited entry to the merely average health club and spa (services extra), nightly turndown service, and an airport shuttle, among other miscellanea. While it's a good deal if you plan to actually use any of that stuff, most people probably won't, so it's just another thing to jack up the room rates. Turndown, after all, should be automatically included. Then again, you can get rooms as low as $95 if you book online, which is a bargain for a hotel this good.

11011 W. Charleston Rd., Las Vegas, NV 89135. ℂ **866/767-7773** or 702/797-7777. Fax 702/797-7053. www.redrocklasvegas.com. 816 units. $160 and up (up to 4 people). Amenities fee $25 per night. Extra person $35. Children 15 and under stay free in parent's room. AE, DC, DISC, MC, V. **Amenities:** 10 restaurants; food court; bars, lounges, and nightclub; casino; concierge; day-care center; health club; 16-screen movie theater; outdoor pools and beach area; room service; spa. *In room:* A/C, TV w/pay movies, hair dryer, minibar, Wi-Fi (for a fee).

Inexpensive

The Orleans ★ ☺ ✎ The Orleans is a little out of the way, and there is virtually nothing around it, but with an 18-screen movie complex, complete with a food court and day-care center, a bowling alley (that keeps ridiculously late hours; we know of more than one recent guest who found a 3am game just the right way to wind down after a hectic clubbing night), and a 9,000-seat arena for a minor-league hockey team (but also available for concerts and the like), this is a reasonable alternative to staying on the hectic Strip. Plus, there is a shuttle that runs continuously to the Gold Coast, Sam's Town, and Suncoast. The facade is aggressively fake New Orleans, more reminiscent of Disneyland than the actual Big Easy. Inside, it's much the same.

The Orleans.

As long as prices hold true (as always, they can vary), this hotel is one of the best bargains in town, despite the location and a staff that can be rotten, which can seriously sour a bargain experience (on the other hand, room service seems fine). The rooms are nice enough and have a definite New Orleans–French feel. Each is L-shaped, with a seating alcove by the windows and comes complete with an old-fashioned, overstuffed chair and sofa. The beds have brass headboards, the lamps (including some funky iron floor lamps) look antique, and lace curtains flutter at the windows. The one drawback is that all these furnishings, and the busy floral decorating theme, make the rooms seem crowded (particularly down by the seating area in front of the bathrooms). Still, it's meant to evoke a cozy, warm Victorian parlor, which traditionally is very overcrowded, so maybe it's successful after all. The hotel has your basic Vegas-type places to eat. Worth noting are **Big Al's Oyster Bar,** a not-unauthentic Creole/Cajun-themed restaurant, and **Don Miguel's,** a basic but satisfying Mexican restaurant that makes its own tortillas while you watch. There are several bars, including one with live music at night. **The Orleans Showroom** is an 827-seat theater, featuring live entertainment; **The Orleans Arena** is a large facility for concerts and sporting events; and, of course, there's a casino.

4500 W. Tropicana Ave. (west of the Strip and I-15), Las Vegas, NV 89103. © **800/675-3267** or 702/365-7111. Fax 702/365-7505. www.orleanscasino.com. 1,886 units. $59 and up double; $185 and up suite. Extra person $15. Children 15 and under stay free in parent's room. AE, DC, DISC, MC, V. Free parking. **Amenities:** 12 restaurants; 9,000-seat arena; 70-lane bowling center; casino; children's center offering amusements and day care for kids 3–12; concierge; executive-level rooms; health club; 18-screen movie theater; 2 outdoor pools; room service; showroom; spa. *In room:* A/C, TV w/pay movies, hair dryer, Wi-Fi (for a fee).

DOWNTOWN

Expensive

Golden Nugget ★★ Always the standout hotel in the Downtown area, a recent face-lift and expansion has made it more appealing than ever. Everything feels brighter, lighter, and more spacious. The redo is a good complement of the best of old and new Vegas; new enough not to be dated, but still user-friendly.

The Golden Nugget opened in 1946 as the first building in Las Vegas constructed specifically for casino gambling. Steve Wynn, who is basically responsible for the "new" Vegas hotel look, took over the Golden Nugget as his first major project in Vegas in 1973. He gradually transformed the Old West/Victorian interiors (typical for Downtown) into something more high rent and genuinely luxurious. The sunny interior spaces are a welcome change from the Las Vegas tradition of dim artificial lighting. Don't forget their mascot (well, it ought to be): the world's largest gold nugget. The *Hand of Faith* nugget weighs in at 61 pounds, 11 ounces and is on display for all to see.

Standard rooms are attractive and comfortable but do splurge a bit (maybe an extra $25 per night) for the newer Rush Tower rooms. Opened in 2009, the rooms here are stunning—rough-hewn wood accents, leather furnishings, and an enormous wall of built-ins that features everything from a minibar to a DVD player for the flatscreen TV. You don't have to walk through the casino to get to your room, but you do have to walk a distance to get to the newly redone pool, a chic and snazzy highlight, complete with a water slide that goes right through a glass tunnel in the shark tank. The Rush Tower has its own adults only (not topless, just no kids) heated infinity pool with cabanas and a bar. The presence of the pool, and general overall quality, makes this the best hotel Downtown for

Hand of Faith, Golden Nugget.

View of the Fremont Street Experience from the balcony at Fitzgeralds Casino & Hotel.

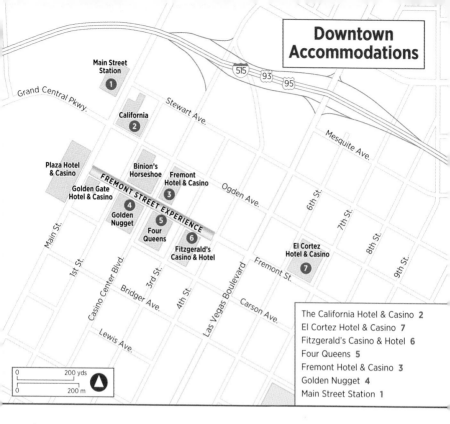

Downtown Accommodations

Main Street Station **1**

Grand Central Pkwy.

California **2**

Stewart Ave.

Mesquite Ave.

Plaza Hotel & Casino

Binion's Horseshoe

Fremont Hotel & Casino

Ogden Ave.

Golden Gate Hotel & Casino **4**

FREMONT STREET EXPERIENCE

Golden Nugget

Four Queens **5**

Fremont Hotel & Casino **3**

Fitzgerald's Casino & Hotel **6**

El Cortez Hotel & Casino **7**

Fremont St.

515 93 95

6th St.

7th St.

8th St.

9th St.

Main St.

1st St.

Casino Center Blvd.

3rd St.

4th St.

Bridger Ave.

Lewis Ave.

Las Vegas Boulevard

Carson Ave.

0 200 yds

0 200 m

The California Hotel & Casino **2**
El Cortez Hotel & Casino **7**
Fitzgerald's Casino & Hotel **6**
Four Queens **5**
Fremont Hotel & Casino **3**
Golden Nugget **4**
Main Street Station **1**

families; the other Downtowners seem geared toward the much older set and/or the single-minded-gambler set.

The **Golden Nugget Buffet,** which is home to a fine Sunday brunch, is described in chapter 6. Oh, and yes, there is a casino. Don't think they'd forget that!

The Nugget's top-rated health club ($20 per day) offers a full line of Universal equipment, Lifecycles, stair machines, treadmills, rowing machines, free weights, a steam sauna, and massages. Salon treatments include everything from leg waxing to seaweed-mask facials. Free Sebastian products are available for sprucing up afterward. The spa's opulent Palladian-mirrored foyer is modeled after a room in New York's Frick Museum.

129 E. Fremont St. (at Casino Center Blvd.), Las Vegas, NV 89101. ☎ **800/846-5336** or 702/385-7111. Fax 702/386-8362. www.goldennugget.com. 2,425 units. $69 and up double; $275 and up suite. Extra person $20. No discount for children. AE, DC, DISC, MC, V. Free self- and valet parking. **Amenities:** 5 restaurants; casino; executive-level rooms; health club; outdoor pool; room service; showroom; spa. *In room:* A/C, TV w/pay movies, hair dryer, Wi-Fi (for a fee).

Moderate

Fitzgeralds Casino & Hotel ★ A few years ago, Fitzgeralds got a new owner, the first African American to own a Vegas casino, an interesting bit of history. Positive changes have come in his wake, with total overhauls of the public areas and rooms. Largely gone is the luck-o'-the-Irish theme, which makes us sad when we think about Mr. O'Lucky, the hotel's longtime mascot, but not so much when it comes to all the rest of the leprechauns and shamrocks and other bits of Blarney nonsense. The casino has been brightened up, so it's now one of the nicer places to gamble Downtown; the hallways and check-in area have been redone, and a new outdoor pool opened. Right now, you can expect a sort of Irish country-village walkway, complete with giant fake trees, leading to the room elevators. Fitzgeralds has the only balcony in Downtown from which you can watch the Fremont Street Experience. You can also sit in its McDonald's and gawk at the light show through the atrium windows.

The rooms are clean and comfortable, featuring standard hotel-room decor you will forget the moment you walk into the hallway. Because this is the tallest building Downtown (34 stories), you get excellent views: snowcapped mountains, Downtown lights, or the Strip. Whirlpool-tub rooms are slightly larger, offering wraparound windows.

301 Fremont St. (at 3rd St.), Las Vegas, NV 89101. ✆ **800/274-5825** or 702/388-2400. Fax 702/388-2181. www.fitzgeralds.com/vegas. 638 units. $59 and up double. Extra person $20. Children 11 and under stay free in parent's room. AE, DC, DISC, MC, V. Free self- and valet parking. **Amenities:** 5 restaurants; lounge; casino; concierge; Internet in business center (for a fee); unheated outdoor pool; room service. *In room:* A/C, TV w/pay movies.

Four Queens ★ Opened in 1966 with a mere 120 rooms, the Four Queens (named for the owner's four daughters) has evolved over the decades into a major Downtown property, occupying an entire city block. One of the last bastions of original Vegas glamour that still exists, if this isn't the luxurious place it once was, there is still plenty to like here, including sometimes very low rates. As the staff says, this is the place to stay if you just want to gamble—or if you want a genuine retro experience. A remodel has given the place a bit of a lift. Newly redone rooms come in a bright color palate, which is jarring given the monochromes that otherwise rule local decor. They can be rather wee, but the ones in the South Tower are a shade larger than the others, though we wouldn't hold any multiperson slumber parties in either. In most cases, rooms in the North Tower offer views of the Fremont Street Experience. The restaurant, **Hugo's Cellar** (p. 197), has a cozy lounge with a working fireplace; the inexpensive yet satisfying **Magnolia's Veranda** (p. 200) is open 24 hours a day; and two bars serve the casino.

202 Fremont St. (at Casino Center Blvd.), Las Vegas, NV 89101. ✆ **800/634-6045** or 702/385-4011. Fax 702/387-5122. www.fourqueens.com. 690 units. $49 and up double; $119 and up suite. Extra person $15. Children 11 and under stay free in parent's room. AE, DC, DISC, MC, V. Free self- and valet parking. **Amenities:** 3 restaurants; 2 bars; casino; room service. *In room:* A/C, TV w/pay movies, hair dryer, Wi-Fi (for a fee).

Inexpensive

California Hotel & Casino This is a hotel with a unique personality. California themed, it markets itself mostly in Hawaii, and because 85% of its guests are from the Aloha State, it offers Hawaiian entrees in several of its restaurants and even has an on-premises store specializing in Hawaiian foodstuffs. You'll also notice that dealers are wearing colorful Hawaiian shirts. The rooms, however, reflect neither California nor Hawaii; they have mahogany furnishings and attractive marble bathrooms.

12 Ogden Ave. (at 1st St.), Las Vegas, NV 89101. ✆ **800/634-6255** or 702/385-1222. Fax 702/388-2660. www.thecal.com. 781 units. $40 and up double. Extra person $10. Children 12 and under stay free in parent's room. AE, DC, DISC, MC, V. Free self- and valet parking. **Amenities:** 4 restaurants; casino; small rooftop pool. *In room:* A/C, TV w/pay movies, hair dryer.

A palm tree–studded courtyard leads into the surprisingly modern interiors of the El Cortez Hotel & Casino.

El Cortez Hotel & Casino ★★

Finally, a much-needed (as opposed to just done because everyone else is doing it) and well-conceived renovation has given an old-timer an unexpected new shot of life. The public areas are totally refreshed: Check out those cherrywood and oxidized metal panel sheets on the walls—you just don't see something that contemporary and design intensive all that often in Downtown. By daringly removing half the slot machines, the casino floor has been opened up and aired out. The new entrance exterior, with its stonework, planters, hitching posts, and stone driveway, makes this feel like an entirely new hotel. Even more exciting, a proper plaza, with trees, fountains, and the like, which seems totally alien to the concept of Vegas, has been added. Rooms in the main hotel (some quite large) have gotten new traditional furnishings; admittedly, nothing stands out, but with such amenities as flatscreen TVs, nice new (if small) bathrooms, armoires with actual minifridges, and Wi-Fi (for a fee), they are right behind Main Street Station for recommendable, affordable Downtown lodgings.

Most notable here are the Cabana Suites. Formerly the rattrap Ogden House across the street, the building was remodeled into a modern/retro wonder complete with mod decor, Swarovski crystal chandeliers, custom furnishings, a small gym, and a funky lobby with a fireplace and concierge service. They took 102 rooms and turned them into 64 bigger rooms, all with updated appointments, modern bathrooms, and a full host of amenities. These rooms could compete with many on the Strip for significantly less money.

There are a couple of dependable restaurants including a steakhouse on-site, and future renovations will include a pool. Many of the employees have been here well over a dozen years, which says a lot. Local legend Jackie Gaughan still lives in the penthouse and wanders through the property. Forget the manufactured versions—this is the real thing, updated but without losing its identity, and for at least half the price.

600 Fremont St. (btw. 6th and 7th sts.), Las Vegas, NV 89101. ☎ **800/634-6703** or 702/385-5200. Fax 702/474-3626. www.elcortezhotelcasino.com. 428 units. $35 and up double; $55 and up suite. Extra person $10. No discount for children. AE, DISC, MC, V. Free self- and valet parking. **Amenities:** 3 restaurants; small food court; casino. *In room:* A/C, TV, Wi-Fi (for a fee).

Fremont Hotel & Casino When it opened in 1956, the Fremont was the first high-rise in Downtown Las Vegas. Wayne Newton got his start here, singing in the now-defunct Carousel Showroom. Step just outside the front door, and there you are, in the **Fremont Street Experience** (p. 217). Rooms are larger (the bathrooms, however, are the opposite of "large") and more comfortable than you might expect. (Though, up until midnight, you can hear, sometimes all too well, music and noise from the Fremont Street Experience show. But then again, if you are in bed before midnight in Vegas, it's your own fault.) The staff is shockingly friendly, partly because you actually can have personal service with hotels this size (another advantage of staying Downtown), partly because they just are. The hotel encourages environmental awareness by changing linens only every other day; upon request, it can be more often, but why not help out the planet a bit? For that matter, why not help out your wallet a bit and stay here?

The Fremont boasts an Art Deco restaurant, called the **Second Street Grill** (p. 198), along with the **Paradise Buffet** (p. 206). Guests can use the swimming pool at the nearby California Hotel, another Sam Boyd enterprise.

200 E. Fremont St. (btw. Casino Center Blvd. and 3rd St.), Las Vegas, NV 89101. © **800/634-6182** or 702/385-3232. Fax 702/385-6229. www.fremontcasino.com. 447 units. $40 and up double. Extra person $10. No discount for children. AE, DC, DISC, MC, V. Free valet parking; no self-parking. **Amenities:** 5 restaurants; casino; access to outdoor pool at nearby California Hotel. *In room:* A/C, TV w/pay movies, DVD players (on request), fridge, hair dryer.

Main Street Station ★★ 👜 Though not actually on Fremont Street, Main Street Station is just 2 short blocks away, barely a 3-minute walk. Considering how terrific it is, this is hardly an inconvenience. Having taken over an abandoned hotel space, Main Street Station, in our opinion, remains one of the nicest hotels in Downtown and one of the best bargains in the city.

The overall look here, typical of Downtown, is early-20th-century San Francisco. However, unlike everywhere else, the details here are outstanding, resulting in a beautiful hotel by any measure. Outside, gas lamps flicker on wrought-iron railings and stained-glass windows. Inside, you'll find hammered-tin ceilings, ornate antique-style chandeliers, and lazy ceiling fans. The small lobby is filled with wood panels, long wooden benches, and a front desk straight

Second Street Grill, Fremont Hotel & Casino.

out of the Old West, with an old-time key cabinet with beveled-glass windows. Check out the painting of a Victorian gambling scene to the left of the front desk. Even the cashier cages look like antique brass bank tellers' cages. They are proud of their special antiques, such as stained glass from the Lillian Russell mansion and doors from the Pullman mansion. It's all very appealing and just plain pretty. An enclosed bridge connects the hotel with the California Hotel across the street, where you will find shopping and a kids' arcade.

Period details help create a warm atmosphere at the Main Street Station.

The long and narrow rooms are possibly the largest in Downtown, though the ornate decorating downstairs does not extend up here, but the rooms are plenty nice enough. The bathrooms are small but well appointed. Rooms on the north side overlook the freeway, and the railroad track is nearby. The soundproofing seems quite strong—we couldn't hear anything when inside, but then again, we're from L.A. A few people have complained about noise in these rooms, but the majority of guests haven't had any problems. If you're concerned, request a room on the south side.

The Pullman Grille is a steak-and-seafood place and is much more reasonably priced than similar (and considerably less pretty) places in town. The stylish **Triple 7 Brew Pub** is described in detail in chapter 10. The excellent buffet, **Main Street Station Garden Court,** is described in chapter 6. And the casino, thanks to some high ceilings, is one of the most smoke free around.

200 N. Main St. (btw. Fremont St. and I-95), Las Vegas, NV 89101. ✆ **800/465-0711** or 702/387-1896. Fax 702/386-4466. www.mainstreetcasino.com. 406 units. $59 and up double. Extra person $10. No discount for children. AE, DC, DISC, MC, V. Free self- and valet parking. **Amenities:** 3 restaurants; casino; access to outdoor pool at nearby California Hotel; free shuttle to Strip and sister properties; free Wi-Fi in lobby. *In room:* A/C, TV w/pay movies and games.

HENDERSON
Expensive

Green Valley Ranch Resort, Spa and Casino ★★ This flat-out fabulous resort makes up for its somewhat far-flung local with earnest efforts and slightly lower prices than comparable accommodations on the Strip. It seems that Green Valley's designers took careful notes on places like the now-closed Ritz-Carlton when coming up with their design—the interiors, rooms, and public spaces feel completely influenced by the same, while the exterior pool area borrowed much from hip hotel concepts such as the Standard and the W. This sounds like a potentially risky combination, but it works smashingly. You can stay here with your parents or your kids, and every age group should be happy.

Drop Bar in Green Valley Ranch Resort, Spa & Casino.

Inside, all is posh and stately—a dignified, classy lobby; large rooms with the most comfortable beds in town (high-thread-count linens, feather beds, plump down comforters); and luxe marble bathrooms.

Outside is the hippest pool area this side of the Hard Rock: part lagoon, part geometric, with shallow places for reading and canoodling, and your choice of poolside lounging equipment, ranging from teak lounge chairs to thick mattresses strewn with pillows, plus drinks served from the trendy Green Valley Beach. There is also a secluded topless bathing area for daring adults. The tiny health club is free, and the spa is also modern and hip.

At night, you can hang out at **Drop Bar** (p. 320); or you can head over to the entirely separate casino area, which offers a disappointingly old-school gambling area, plus a variety of restaurants and a multiscreen movie theater. A shopping area, the District, conveniently located next door, features a simulated street scene, where you'll find your usual mall and catalog favorites (Williams-Sonoma, Pottery Barn), plus still more restaurants. This addition does help alleviate the resort's somewhat isolated nature.

2300 Paseo Verde Pkwy. (at I-215), Henderson, NV 89052. ℂ **866/782-9487** or 702/617-7777. Fax 702/617-7778. www.greenvalleyranchresort.com. 490 units. $129 and up double. Extra person $35. Children 17 and under stay free in parent's room. AE, DC, DISC, MC, V. Free self- and valet parking. **Amenities:** 10 restaurants; food court; free shuttle service to the airport and the Strip; casino; concierge; executive-level rooms; health club; lounge; movie theater; outdoor pool; room service; spa. *In room:* A/C, TV w/pay movies, hair dryer, Wi-Fi (for a fee).

Moderate

M Resort ★★ Red Rock Resort is one of our favorite hotels in the entire city. We bring this up here because in many ways, M Resort is a lot like Red Rock: beautifully designed, lots to do, great value (in comparison), and roughly 9 bazillion miles from anything you're going to want to do in Las Vegas. Okay, that's an exaggeration, but when you're sitting in the inevitable traffic on the roughly

10-mile slog north on I-15 to the southern end of the Strip, it will seem like 9 bazillion miles. But that's really the only downside here. The hotel is stunning, with abundant use of natural elements (wood, stone, crystal, mother of pearl ceilings) and huge windows that flood the entire property with light. The designers wanted to bring the outside in and they succeeded, creating one of the most airy and light spaces in town.

Rooms are large at about 550 square feet, many with great views of the city off in the distance (9 bazillion miles, remember), which you can even see while soaking in the tubs—there are windows from the bathroom into the bedroom. Glossy streamlined furnishings give them a mod feeling and everything is the highest of high tech. To power up the room you have to insert your key into a holder next to the door. Remove it and everything shuts off, maintaining your settings for when you return.

On-site you'll find a 95,000-square-foot casino with all the latest bells and whistles, seven restaurants and the interactive Studio B Buffet (complete with its own television studio), several bars and lounges, a spa/salon/gym facility, a very nicely landscaped pool area, and the hotel's very own wine cellar. And should you need a refill, there is even an on-site pharmacy where you can use points earned on your players' club card to pay for your prescriptions. Welcome to Vegas!

With prices, on average, about half of what you would pay for similar digs on the Strip, it almost makes that 9-bazillion-mile trek worth considering.

12300 Las Vegas Blvd. S. (at St. Rose Pkwy.), Henderson, NV 89044. © **877/673-7678** or 702/797-1000. Fax 702/797-3010. www.themresort.com. 390 units. $129 and up double. Extra person $30. Children 17 and under stay free in parent's room. AE, DC, DISC, MC, V. Free self- and valet parking. **Amenities:** 6 restaurants; shuttle service to the Strip; casino; concierge; executive-level rooms; health club; spa & salon; heated outdoor pool; room service; pharmacy. *In room:* A/C, TV w/pay movies, hair dryer, minibar, Wi-Fi (for a fee).

Pool area of the M Resort.

6

WHERE TO DINE

Among the images that come to mind when people think of Las Vegas are food bargains so good the food is practically free. They think of the buffets—all a small country can eat—for only $3.99!

While minor hotels still seek to attract guests with meal deals, eating in Las Vegas is no longer something you don't have to worry about budgeting for. The buffets are certainly there—no good hotel would be without one—as are the cheap meal deals, but you get what you pay for. Some of the cheaper buffets, and even some of the more moderately priced ones, are mediocre at best, ghastly and inedible at worst.

Meanwhile, the Vegas food scene has seen an enormous change. Virtually overnight, there was an explosion of new restaurants, most the creations of the so-called celebrity chef phenomenon. Look at this partial list: Celebrity chefs Wolfgang Puck and Emeril Lagasse have over a dozen restaurants in town between them; multi-Michelin-starred chef Joël Robuchon opened two restaurants in the MGM Grand; master Italian chef Mario Batali has two; deservedly famed chef Julian Serrano reigns at Bellagio's **Picasso** and his eponymously named tapas eatery at Aria; Thomas Keller, the brains behind Napa Valley's French Laundry—considered by many to be the best restaurant in the United States—has a branch of his **Bouchon** bistro; legendary chef Alain Ducasse is behind **Mix** at THEhotel; and branches of L.A., New York, San Francisco, and Boston high-profile names such as **Pinot Brasserie, Le Cirque, Aureole, Olives, Border Grill, Nobu,** and others have all rolled into town.

For awhile, this boom affected only the very highest end of the price category. In other words, boy, can you eat well, as long as you have a trust fund. While those restaurants still thrive and multiply, it seems, there has been a recent move toward more moderately priced restaurants that manage to provide excellent dining experiences without breaking the bank. Having said that, the truly great restaurants in town will still cost you an arm and a leg (and perhaps a kidney).

If you get off the Strip, you can find some cheaper, more interesting alternatives, which we have listed below. Getting outside those enormous hotel resorts is a major proposition (and don't think that's not on purpose), which is why visitors often settle for what the hotel has to offer. Walking to another hotel—on the Strip, a major investment of time—means probably encountering much of the same thing. But not always: Take some time to explore and you may just find something worth your time and your money.

Our Best Las Vegas Restaurant Advice

GETTING IN There are tricks to surviving dining in Vegas. If you can, make reservations in advance, particularly for the better restaurants. (You might get to town, planning to check out some of the better spots, only to find that they

FACING PAGE: **Gorging on sweet treats at a buffet is an integral Vegas experience.**

SHHHHHH . . . half-price meals, **ON THE STRIP & OFF**

Here's the latest in restaurant discounting: Cut-price meals, at some of the city's top eateries, are being sold by Tix4Tonight, the same people who peddle theater tickets. Either stop by a booth, call ☎ **800/269-8499,** or visit www.tix4dinner.com. Request a reservation from their list of partner restaurants, and when you get your bill at the end of the evening, you'll have saved either 50% or 33% off the cost of entrees or 35% off the entire bill, including drinks (the type of discount varies by restaurant). If you make your reservation by phone, you still have to go to a Tix4Tonight booth to pick up a coupon to present to your waiter when you order. Occasionally, it's difficult to get the reservation time you want, but usually the process is hassle free.

Booths can be found at the following locations:

- In the Fashion Show Mall (across from the Wynn)

- In the Hawaiian Marketplace (near Harmon St.)

- Just south of the Riviera Hotel (across from Circus Circus)

- In Bill's Casino (at the corner of Flamingo Blvd.)

- In the Showcase Mall (at the base of the giant Coca-Cola bottle)

- In The Four Queens Casino (Downtown, on Fremont St.)

- In the Casino Royale (across from The Mirage)

- At the Town Square shopping center (across from Claim Jumper)

are totally booked throughout your stay.) Eat during off-hours when you can. Know that noon to, say, 1:30 or 2pm is prime time for lunch, and 5:30 to 8:30pm (and just after the early shows get out) is prime time for dinner. Speaking of time, give yourself plenty of it, particularly if you have to catch a show. We once tried to grab a quick bite in the Riviera before running up to *La Cage.* The only choice was the food court, where long lines in front of all the stands (fast-food chains only) left us with about 5 minutes to gobble something decidedly unhealthy.

SAVING MONEY So you want to sample the creations of a celebrity chef, but you took a beating at the craps table? Check our listings to see which of the high-profile restaurants are open for lunch. Sure, sometimes the more interesting and exotic items are found at dinner, but the midday meal is usually no slouch and can be as much as two-thirds cheaper.

Or skip that highfalutin' stuff altogether. The late-night specials—a complete steak meal for just a few dollars—are also an important part of a good, decadent Vegas experience. And having complained about how prices are going up, we'll also tell you that you can still eat cheaply and decently (particularly if you are looking upon food only as fuel) all over town. The locals repeatedly say that they almost never cook, because in Vegas it is always cheaper to eat out. To locate budget fare, check local newspapers (especially Fri editions) and free magazines (such as *What's On in Las Vegas*), which are given away at hotel reception desks. Sometimes these sources also yield money-saving coupons.

Be on the lookout for weekday night specials as well. Many high-end restaurants offer prix-fixe menus on their off-nights for significantly less money. You may not be able to sample the truly extravagant dishes, but it'll get you a taste of the good life.

ABOUT PRICE CATEGORIES The restaurants in this chapter are arranged first by location, then by the following price categories (based on the average cost of a dinner entree): **Very Expensive,** more than $35; **Expensive,** $25 to $35; **Moderate,** $15 to $25; **Inexpensive,** under $15 (sometimes well under). In the expensive and very expensive restaurants, expect to spend no less than twice the price of the average entree for your entire meal, with a tip; you can usually get by on a bit less in moderate and inexpensive restaurants. Buffets and Sunday brunches are gathered in a separate section at the end of this chapter.

A FINAL WORD As welcome as the influx of designer chefs is, you can't help but notice that the majority are simply re-creating their best work (and sometimes not even that) from elsewhere rather than producing something new. So the Vegas food scene remains, like its architecture, a copy of something from somewhere else. And as happy as we are to encourage you to throw money at these guys, please don't forget the mom-and-pop places, which struggle not to disappear into the maw of the big hotel machines and which produce what comes the closest to true local quality. If you can, get in a car and check out some of the options listed below that are a bit off the beaten track. Show Vegas you aren't content—you want a meal you can brag about and afford, now!

RESTAURANTS BY CUISINE

Key to Abbreviations: $$$$ = Very Expensive $$$ = Expensive $$ = Moderate
$ = Inexpensive

AMERICAN
Carson Street Cafe ($, p. 198)
Dick's Last Resort ★★ ($$, p. 161)
Fix ★★ ($$$$, p. 167)
Hard Rock Cafe ★ ($$, p. 163)
Harley-Davidson Cafe ★ ($$, p. 163)
Hash House a Go Go ★★ ($$, p. 176)
Lagasse's Stadium ★ ($$, p. 177)
Magnolia's Veranda ($, p. 200)
Margaritaville ($$, p. 163)
Serendipity 3 ★ ($$, p. 178)
Table 10 ★★ ($$, p. 178)
Top of the World ($$$$, p. 171)

ASIAN
Grand Wok ★★ ($$, p. 161)
Red 8 ★★ ($$, p. 185)
Spago ★ ($$$$, p. 170)

BAGELS
Einstein Bros. Bagels ★ ($, p. 189)

BARBECUE
BB King's Blues Club ★ ($$, p. 175)
Gilley's ★★ ($$, p. 176)
Memphis Championship Barbecue ★★ ($$, p. 189)

BISTRO
Bouchon ★★★ ($$$, p. 172)
Daniel Boulud Brasserie ★ ($$$$, p. 182)
Mon Ami Gabi ★★ ($$, p. 177)
Payard Patisserie & Bistro ★★★ ($$, p. 178)
Pinot Brasserie ★★ ($$$, p. 174)

BUFFETS/BRUNCHES
Bellagio Buffet ★★ ($$$, p. 202)
The Buffet at Aria Las Vegas ★ ($$$, p. 201)
The Buffet at the Las Vegas Hilton ★ ($$, p. 205)
Circus Circus Buffet ($, p. 205)

Dishes, The Buffet at TI ★★ ($$, p. 204)

Excalibur's Roundtable Buffet ★ ($$, p. 202)

Flamingo Paradise Garden Buffet ★ ($$, p. 204)

Flavors at Harrah's ★ ($$, p. 204)

Fremont Paradise Buffet ★ ($, p. 206)

Gold Coast Ports O' Call ★ ($, p. 206)

Golden Nugget Buffet ★★ ($$, p. 206)

Le Village Buffet ★★★ ($$$, p. 203)

Main Street Station Garden Court ★★★ ($, p. 207)

Mandalay Bay's Bayside Buffet ★ ($$$, p. 201)

MGM Grand Buffet ($$$, p. 201)

Mirage Cravings Buffet ★ ($$$, p. 203)

Monte Carlo Buffet ★ ($$, p. 202)

MORE, The Buffet at Luxor ★★ ($$, p. 202)

Rio's Carnival World Buffet ★★ ($$$, p. 203)

Spice Market Buffet ★★ ($$, p. 205)

Wynn Las Vegas Buffet ★★★ ($$$$, p. 205)

CALIFORNIA

Spago ★ ($$$$, p. 170)

CHINESE

Cathay House ($$, p. 194)

Fin ★ ($$$$, p. 167)

Harbor Palace ★ ($$, p. 196)

CONTINENTAL

Alex ★★★ ($$$$, p. 180)

Red Square ★★ ($$$$, p. 158)

Top of the World ($$$$, p. 171)

CREOLE

Delmonico Steakhouse ★★ ($$$$, p. 166)

Emeril's New Orleans Fish House ★ ($$$$, p. 156)

DELI

Canter's Deli ★★ ($, p. 180)

Capriotti's ★★★ ($, p. 185)

Carnegie Deli ★★ ($, p. 180)

Jason's Deli ★ ($, p. 189)

Jody Maroni's Sausage Kingdom ★★★ ($, p. 164)

Pink's ★★★ ($, p. 179)

DINER

Bougainvillea ★★ ($, p. 189)

Burger Bar ★ ($$, p. 160)

Tiffany's ★★ ($, p. 186)

ECLECTIC

Sensi ★★ ($$$, p. 174)

FOOD COURT

Cypress Street Marketplace ★★ ($, p. 179)

FRENCH

Alizé ★★★ ($$$$, p. 165)

Andre's ★★ ($$$$, p. 154)

Brasserie Puck ★ ($$$, p. 154)

Eiffel Tower Restaurant ($$$$, p. 171)

Joël Robuchon at the Mansion ★★★ ($$$$, p. 156)

L'Atelier de Joël Robuchon ★★★ ($$$$, p. 157)

Le Cirque ★ ($$$$, p. 168)

Pamplemousse ★ ($$$$, p. 187)

Picasso ★★★ ($$$$, p. 170)

Switch ★ ($$$$, p. 182)

GERMAN

Cafe Heidelberg German Deli & Restaurant ★ ($$, p. 184)

INTERNATIONAL

Hugo's Cellar ★ ($$$$, p. 197)

Second Street Grill ★ ($$$, p. 198)

IRISH

Nine Fine Irishmen ★ ($$, p. 162)

ITALIAN

B&B Ristorante ★★ ($$$$, p. 165)

Bartolotta Ristorante di Mare ★★★ ($$$$, p. 181)

Canaletto ★★ ($$$, p. 173)

Carluccio's Tivoli Gardens ★★ ($$, p. 187)

Circo ★★ ($$$, p. 173)

Fellini's ★ ($$, p. 185)
Olives ★★ ($$$, p. 173)
Rao's ★ ($$$, p. 174)
Sinatra ★★★ ($$$$, p. 182)
Sirio ★★ ($$$, p. 159)
Stratta ★★ ($$$, p. 184)
Valentino ★ ($$$$, p. 172)

JAPANESE
Hyakumi ★ ($$$$, p. 168)
Raku Grill ★★★ ($$, p. 196)

MEDITERRANEAN
Olives ★★ ($$$, p. 173)
Paymon's Mediterranean Cafe &
Lounge ★ ($, p. 191)

MEXICAN
Border Grill ★★ ($$$, p. 159)
Cabo Wabo Cantina ★ ($$, p. 175)
Diablo's Cantina ★★ ($$, p. 160)
Dona Maria Tamales ★★ ($, p. 199)
El Sombrero Cafe ★★ ($, p. 200)
Hussong's Cantina ★ ($$, p. 161)
Isla ★★ ($$, p. 177)
Pink Taco ★ ($, p. 191)
Tacos & Tequila ★★ ($$, p. 162)
Toto's ★★ ($, p. 191)
Viva Mercado's ★★ ($$, p. 197)

NEW AMERICAN
Aureole ★★★ ($$$$, p. 154)
Mix ★★ ($$$$, p. 157)
Rosemary's Restaurant ★★★ ($$$,
p. 192)

PACIFIC RIM
Second Street Grill ★ ($$$, p. 198)

PUB FARE
Nine Fine Irishmen ★ ($$, p. 162)
Todd English P.U.B. ★★★ ($$, p. 161)

RUSSIAN
Red Square ★★ ($$$$, p. 158)

SANDWICHES
Earl of Sandwich ★★★ ($, p. 179)

SEAFOOD
Austin's Steakhouse ★★ ($$$, p.
192)
Bartolotta Ristorante di Mare ★★★
($$$$, p. 181)
Chart House ★ ($$$, p. 198)
Fin ★ ($$$$, p. 167)
Lawry's The Prime Rib ★★★ ($$$$,
p. 186)
Michael Mina ★ ($$$$, p. 169)
Morton's Steakhouse ★ ($$$$, p. 187)
The Palm ★★ ($$$$, p. 169)

SOUL FOOD
M&M Soul Food ★★ ($, p. 200)

SOUTHERN
House of Blues ★★ ($$$, p. 163)

SOUTHWESTERN
Mesa Grill ★★ ($$$$, p. 169)

SPANISH
Beso ★ ($$$, p. 158)
Julian Serrano ★★ ($$$, p. 159)

STEAK
Austin's Steakhouse ★★ ($$$, p.
192)
Charlie Palmer Steak ★★ ($$$$, p.
155)
Delmonico Steakhouse ★★ ($$$$,
p. 166)
Lawry's The Prime Rib ★★★ ($$$$,
p. 186)
Morton's Steakhouse ★ ($$$$, p. 187)
The Palm ★★ ($$$$, p. 169)
The Steakhouse ★ ($$$, p. 184)
Strip House ★★ ($$$$, p. 171)
Switch ★ ($$$$, p. 182)

SUSHI
Hyakumi ★ ($$$$, p. 168)

THAI
Komol ($, p. 190)
Lotus of Siam ★★★ ($, p. 190)
Thai Spice ($, p. 197)

SOUTH STRIP

Very Expensive

Andre's ★★ FRENCH The original and much-beloved Andre's, in Downtown Las Vegas, closed in 2008, but never fear—the branch at Monte Carlo is still going strong. While it may not have the ambience, it certainly has the menu, still overseen by owner/chef Andre, who brings over 40 years of experience to the table. Much of the waitstaff is also French, and they will happily lavish attention on you and guide you through the menu.

The food presentation is exquisite, and choices change seasonally. An example might be an appetizer of Northwest smoked salmon *mille-feuille* with cucumber salad and sevruga caviar, or a main course of grilled veal tournedos with chive sauce, accompanied by a mushroom and foie gras crepe. You get the idea. Desserts are similarly lovely, an exotic array of rich delights. An extensive wine list (more than 900 labels) is international in scope and includes many rare vintages; consult the sommelier.

In Monte Carlo, 3770 Las Vegas Blvd. S. ✆ **702/798-7151.** www.andrelv.com. Reservations required. Main courses $33–$68. AE, DC, MC, V. Tues–Sun 5:30–10:30pm.

Aureole ★★★ NEW AMERICAN This branch of a New York City fave (it's pronounced are-ree-*all*), run by Charlie Palmer, is noted for its glass wine tower. It's four stories of what is probably the finest wine collection in Vegas, made even more sensational thanks to catsuit-clad lovelies who are hoisted on wires to reach bottles requested from the uppermost heights. Amid this Vegas-show glitz is one of the better of the fine-dining experiences around. The menu is a three-course prix fixe, though if you are winsome enough, they might send out luxurious extras, such as pâté on brioche topped with shaved truffles, or an espresso cup of cold yellow-pepper soup with crab. Otherwise, expect such marvels as a tender roasted lamb loin and braised shoulder, or a rack of venison accompanied by sweet-potato purée and chestnut crisp. Everything demonstrates the hand of a true chef in the kitchen, someone paying close attention to his work and to his customers. Service is solicitous; on a recent visit, with one diner not feeling up to an actual meal, the concerned server presented special clear consommé and mild sorbets. Desserts are playful, including a bittersweet chocolate soufflé with blood-orange sorbet, and a Bartlett pear crisp with toasted cinnamon brioche and lemongrass foam. There is also an excellent cheese plate. Oh, and that wine tower? You can navigate it from your table with the innovative and highly engrossing handheld computer that not only helps you through the vast depths of the list but also makes suggestions for you, based on your meal choices.

In Mandalay Bay, 3950 Las Vegas Blvd. S. ✆ **877/632-1766.** www.aureolelv.com. Reservations required. Prix-fixe dinner $55; tasting menu $95. AE, DISC, MC, V. Daily 5:30–10:30pm.

Brasserie Puck ★ FRENCH You kind of have to squint to see the French on the menu at this latest restaurant from celebrity chef Puck. Yes there are words like *fromage* and *huitres,* but it is primarily an eclectic collection of everything from filet mignon au poivre and steak *tartine* to burgers and pizza. Hey, they have burgers and pizza in France! If you've got a group, start with *assiette de charcuterie,* essentially an antipasti plate with prosciutto, mild and hot salami, pâté, and more served with a crispy bread and three different dipping sauces. We loved the pizza done Alsatian style, with a paper-thin crust made with a pasta roller and topped with crème fraîche, roasted onions, and perfectly smoked, crumbly bacon. The

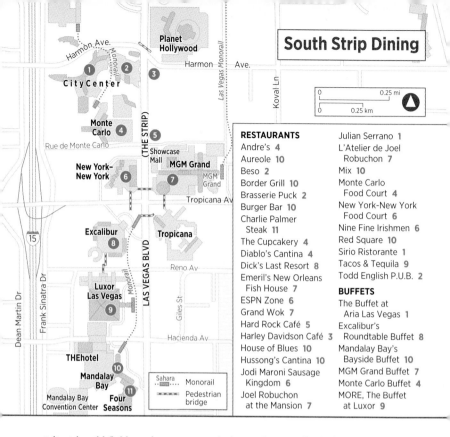

South Strip Dining

RESTAURANTS

Andre's **4**
Aureole **10**
Beso **2**
Border Grill **10**
Brasserie Puck **2**
Burger Bar **10**
Charlie Palmer
 Steak **11**
The Cupcakery **4**
Diablo's Cantina **4**
Dick's Last Resort **8**
Emeril's New Orleans
 Fish House **7**
ESPN Zone **6**
Grand Wok **7**
Hard Rock Café **5**
Harley Davidson Café **3**
House of Blues **10**
Hussong's Cantina **10**
Jodi Maroni Sausage
 Kingdom **6**
Joel Robuchon
 at the Mansion **7**

Julian Serrano **1**
L'Atelier de Joel
 Robuchon **7**
Mix **10**
Monte Carlo
 Food Court **4**
New York-New York
 Food Court **6**
Nine Fine Irishmen **6**
Red Square **10**
Sirio Ristorante **1**
Tacos & Tequila **9**
Todd English P.U.B. **2**

BUFFETS
The Buffet at
 Aria Las Vegas **1**
Excalibur's
 Roundtable Buffet **8**
Mandalay Bay's
 Bayside Buffet **10**
MGM Grand Buffet **7**
Monte Carlo Buffet **4**
MORE, The Buffet
 at Luxor **9**

ravioli with wild field mushrooms was a little too dense in flavor for our tastes, needing a hint of zest to give context to the 'shrooms, which overwhelmed the dish, but the Alaskan halibut, served on a bed of pureed potatoes drenched in butter was divine. There are lots of Puck restaurants in this town and your overall taste should guide you to which one is the best for you, but don't let the French words at this one scare you away from a fine dining experience.

At Crystals, 3720 Las Vegas Blvd. S., no. 240. © 702/238-1000. www.wolfgangpuck.com. Reservations recommended. Main courses $12–$27 lunch; $12–$46 dinner. AE, DC, DISC, MC, V. Sun-Thurs 11am–11pm; Fri-Sat 11am–midnight.

Charlie Palmer Steak ★★ STEAK There are many, many steakhouses in Vegas, as if there were some natural law stating that any hotel without one will suffer from entropy and eventually collapse into a black hole. Discerning palates know there can be a significant difference between steakhouses; discerning wallets might not care. If you find yourself among the former, do try Charlie Palmer's, probably the best of the costlier shrines to beef. Those with the latter can be reassured that with entrees weighing in at around 22 to 45 ounces *each*, diners can legitimately—and in the name of decency ought to—share portions, which makes this a much more affordable experience than it might appear at first glance. And why not? Those enormous slabs o' meat are as tender as anything because with the big bucks, you do get the best cuts. We prefer the flavorful ribeye to the other favorite, the Kansas City. Be sure to try the spinach salad topped with truffled fried egg and warm bacon vinaigrette as a starter (it gets a plus for presentation), and split sides, such as citrus-braised asparagus or a truffled potato purée (we are such suckers for what we call "gourmet baby food"). Desserts are stylish creations, and the entire place is set in a generic fancy space that can be a bit noisy and crowded, so if romance is on the agenda, ask for one of the two-person tables in the back. Charlie Palmer, by the way, is the chef mind behind Aureole, on the other side of Mandalay Bay; this makes two-for-two for this celeb chef.

In Four Seasons Hotel, 3960 Las Vegas Blvd. S. ✆ **702/632-5120.** www.charliepalmersteaklv.com. Reservations recommended. Main courses $30–$42. AE, DC, DISC, MC, V. Daily 5–10:30pm.

Emeril's New Orleans Fish House ★ CREOLE As with Wolfgang Puck, the ubiquitous Emeril Lagasse has probably spread himself too thin. Although we thoroughly enjoyed his shows on the Food Network and can attest that his flagship restaurant in New Orleans remains as good as ever, this Vegas outpost seems to have slipped. Part of that may be our prejudice about seafood restaurants in the desert—yes, we know about airplanes and refrigeration, but we rarely have good fish in Vegas, so there you go.

For that matter, at our last meal here, the most successful dish was the Creole-spiced, aged rib-eye, drizzled with a horseradish Worcestershire sauce (with Emeril's famous kick that is neatly tempered by the mashed potatoes). A salad of duck confit left us feeling the duck would be better on its own, but the sweet toasted-pecan vinaigrette was so good, it reconciled one diner toward eating previously loathed spinach. A signature dish remains the foie gras–topped ahi tuna, a combination that makes no more sense to us now than it did when we first tried it (because it tasted just fine with the side of spaghetti sauce). But the portions of foie gras can be generous, so you could just deconstruct it into a two-part appetizer. Still, you should try Emeril's famous lobster cheesecake appetizer, a savory delight like nothing you've tried before. The garlic-and-herb butter sauce that comes with the barbecued shrimp will have you mopping your plate with bread and asking for more of the petite rosemary biscuits that accompany it. And a slice of the banana-cream pie with banana crust and caramel drizzle is simple in its decadence.

In MGM Grand, 3799 Las Vegas Blvd. S. ✆ **702/891-7374.** www.emerils.com. Reservations required. Main courses $17–$30 lunch; $28–$45 dinner (more for lobster). AE, DC, DISC, MC, V. Daily 11:30am–2:30pm and 5–10:30pm.

Joël Robuchon at the Mansion ★★★ FRENCH This is listed under "Very Expensive" only because there is no category for "unbelievably, heart stoppingly, stratospherically expensive." But it's here because legendary chef Joël Robuchon—the first (and youngest) chef to win three consecutive Michelin stars—who closed his restaurants in France (where he was proclaimed "chef of the century") at the height of his fame, has proven that all the hype is justified. The *Los Angeles Times* gave Robuchon four stars (their highest rating)—only the second time they've done so—while the *New York Times* reviewer proclaimed this "some of the very best French food I've eaten on this continent." These are no pushovers. All exclaim over the perfect combination of gastronomic feats and culinary artistry. This is not food as fuel, food to bolt down greedily (even though you may want to), but to slowly savor. Pay attention as you chew, and notice how many layers of interest are revealed. Great care was taken in choosing and combining ingredients, to create not fuss but both surprise and a sense of rightness.

Exquisite, superb—name your superlative, and it's been levied toward this remarkable restaurant.

Chef Robuchon is not personally in the kitchen that often, but he has entrusted this kitchen to some of his top employees, and if they stay (no implied criticism, merely a reality of the restaurant world), so should the quality. The menu changes very frequently, with many key ingredients flown in daily from France. And the service reminds one that Michelin ratings take service into account, too. None of this comes cheap. Could it possibly be worth it? When restaurant critics claim they would spend their own money to dine here, quite very possibly, yes. Look at it this way: You can easily lose the cost of a meal here in 15 forgettable minutes at a blackjack table (not that we did just that, ahem), or you can spend 3 hours slowly enjoying a meal, storing up much more pleasurable (presumably) memories. And then there is always the somewhat less-expensive—that's relative, of course—neighbor **L'Atelier de Joël Robuchon,** where the focus is on counter seating, an intimate interactive experience between diner, server, and chef.

In MGM Grand, 3799 Las Vegas Blvd. S. © **702/891-7925.** Reservations strongly recommended. Jacket recommended. 6-course tasting menu $250; 16-course tasting menu $385. AE, DC, DISC, MC, V. Sun–Thurs 5:30-10pm; Fri–Sat 5:30-10:30pm.

L'Atelier de Joël Robuchon ★★★ FRENCH Despite the four-star L.A. and N.Y. *Times* reviews for the main establishment reviewed above, trustworthy foodies tipped this place as actually superior. Then it won the James Beard Foundation Award for best new restaurant in 2007, which only adds to the debate. You won't go wrong either way. Certainly, it's relatively cheaper here, but the casual, almost entirely counter seating (it's like an extremely high-style diner) might dismay those looking for a different sort of atmospheric experience. But food is supposed to be fun, and interacting with the charming (and often handsome and French) staff on the other side only adds to the great good pleasure.

Portions are small but exquisitely conceived and constructed. The tasting menu is probably your best way to go, but consider coming just to treat yourself to a couple of dishes, such as the wee, perfect burgers topped with foie gras, or the Maine lobster with curry scent and fennel foam, a dish that sent us into a fit of uncontrollable giggles of delight. *La Pied de Cochon* is pâté made of pigs' feet, a robust and yet unctuous pork topped with shaved truffle and Parmesan on toast. An *amuse-bouche* of foie gras parfait with port wine and Parmesan foam comes layered in a teeny parfait glass with all three flavors clear and distinct, and yet harmonizing into a powerful whole. The artistry only continues with dessert. A marvelous culinary experience.

In MGM Grand, 3799 Las Vegas Blvd. S. © **702/891-7358.** Reservations strongly recommended. Main courses $38–$70; 8-course discovery menu $135; small plates $16–$32. AE, DC, DISC, MC, V. Sun–Thurs 5:30-10:30pm; Fri–Sat 5-10:30pm.

Mix ★★ NEW AMERICAN This is highly revered French chef Alain Ducasse's first Vegas venture, and such a Big Deal needs a Big Deal setting, in this case, on the 64th (by their counting) floor of THEhotel at Mandalay Bay. It's yet another spectacular restaurant space in a hotel full of them, this one white on white on silver, a futuristic fantasy, including a set design sort of like a giant beaded curtain made of blown-glass balls, which envelopes a curving stairway plopped down in the middle. Some tables are set in silver "pods" that remind one of Woody Allen's *Sleeper.* It also has drama outside, thanks to top-of-the-tall-hotel Strip views.

The playful yet hip attitude is reflected in the food, which is a little self-conscious. Still, it's hard to resist a place that starts with bread flavors such as ketchup or bacon, with a side of homemade peanut butter. But it's the sort of meal that grows progressively less "wow" as the evening wears on; early courses of melting amberjack sashimi topped with osetra caviar and a little lemon and salt are superb, as are the lovely foie gras terrines with nifty accompaniments. The signature Ducasse pressed chicken with foie gras in black truffle sauce probably would be just that much better if Chef himself were making it. Fish dishes are solidly good but not transcendent, and by the time the meal gets to, say, the rack of lamb, you may be thinking, "Well, this is excellent, certainly, but not mind-blowingly so," which sounds like terrible nitpicking, but given the remarkable things going on in some other kitchens around town, and given the prices here, it's a fine line worth delineating. Still, the setting may make up for it.

In THEhotel, 3950 Las Vegas Blvd. S. ✆ **702/632-9500.** www.mandalaybay.com. Main courses $39–$60. AE, DISC, DC, MC, V. Daily 6–11pm.

Red Square ★★ CONTINENTAL/RUSSIAN The beheaded and pigeon-droppings-adorned statue of Lenin outside Red Square only hints at the near-profane delights on the interior. Inside you will find decayed posters that once glorified the Worker, cheek by jowl with a patchwork mix of remnants of Czarist trappings, as pillaged from toppled Bolsheviks and Stalinists. It is disconcerting to see the hammer and sickle so blithely and irreverently displayed, but then again, what better way to drain it of its power than to exploit it in a palace of capitalistic decadence? And then there's the ice-covered bar—all the better to keep your drinks nicely chilled. After all, they have 150 different kinds of vodka, perhaps the largest collection in the world. It's all just one big post-Communist party (sorry, we had to say it).

Anyway, if you can tear your eyes away from the theme run amok, you might notice that the menu is quite good, one of our favorites around. Blow your expense account on some caviar (we found we liked nutty osetra better than stronger beluga), properly chilled in ice, served with the correct pearl spoon. Or, more affordably, nosh on Siberian nachos—smoked salmon, citron caviar, and crème fraîche. The chef's special is a Roquefort-crusted tender filet mignon, with some soft caramelized garlic and a fine reduction sauce; it's a grand piece of meat, one of the best in town and more cheaply priced than similarly ranked places. We also very much liked the pan-seared halibut with a roasted beet vinaigrette and basil oil on a mushroom risotto. Try a silly themed drink, such as the Cuban Missile Crisis, which is Rain vodka, dark rum, sugar-cane syrup, and lime juice; or, better still, take advantage of that vodka menu and try a tasting flight of four kinds, joined by theme (in our case, the Ultimate Flight paired Polish, Russian, Scottish, and Estonian vodkas). Desserts are not so clever but are worth saving room for, especially the warm chocolate cake with a liquid center and the strawberries Romanoff.

In Mandalay Bay, 3950 Las Vegas Blvd. S. ✆ **702/632-7407.** Reservations recommended. Main courses $26–$40. AE, DC, MC, V. Sun–Thurs 5–10:30pm; Fri–Sat 5–11pm.

Expensive

Beso ★ SPANISH A partnership between a celebrity and a chef is certainly nothing new and often not noteworthy, but when the celeb in question is *Desperate Housewives* star Eva Longoria Parker and the guy behind the menu is none other than Todd English, the mastermind of two of our Vegas favorites in Olives and the Todd English P.U.B., the endeavor is worth paying attention to. Parker brings the style to the mostly black on black room, livened by huge windows flooding the space with light. English takes Parker's heritage to create a modern Latin steakhouse, heavy on the seafood and cuts of beef, many of which have a spicy kick to them. The tortilla soup with chicken, sour cream, and salsa verde is deliciously hot in more than one sense of the word and other starters bring on the guacamole (both regular and artichoke versions), grilled foie gras with tequila marinated mango, and a *taqueria* (taco) tasting that varies from day to day. The steaks are not quite as adventurous unless you go nuts with the sauces (tequila peppercorn anyone?), which you probably should. Be sure to throw in a side of the delectably creamy mac and cheese.

In Crystals at CityCenter, 3720 Las Vegas Blvd. S. ℭ 702/254-2376. www.besolasvegas.com. Reservations recommended. Main courses $28–$54. AE, DC, DISC, MC, V. Sun–Thurs 5:30–11pm; Fri–Sat 5:30pm–midnight.

Border Grill ★★ MEXICAN This big, cheerful space (like a Romper Room for adults) houses a branch of the much-lauded Los Angeles restaurant, conceived and run by Mary Sue Milliken and Susan Feniger, hosts of the 1990s' Food Network show *Two Hot Tamales*. This is truly authentic Mexican home cooking—the Tamales learned their craft south of the border—but with a *nuevo* twist. So don't expect precisely the same dishes you'd encounter in your favorite corner joint, but do expect fresh and fabulous food, sitting as brightly on the plates as the decor on the walls. Stay away from the occasionally bland fish and head right toward rich and cheesy dishes such as *chiles rellenos* (with perfect black beans) and chicken *chilaquiles* (a sister to the taco), or try new items such as mushroom empanadas. Don't miss the dense but fluffy Mexican chocolate-cream pie (with a meringue crust).

In Mandalay Bay, 3950 Las Vegas Blvd. S. ℭ **702/632-7403.** www.bordergrill.com. Reservations recommended. Main courses $15–$24 lunch, $21–34 dinner. AE, DC, DISC, MC, V. Mon–Fri 11:30am–10pm; Sat–Sun 11:30am–10pm.

Julian Serrano ★★ SPANISH Serrano is most famous in Vegas for his Picasso restaurant at Bellagio, a place that paved the way for all of the ultraexclusive, large-check restaurants that came after it. His eponymously named restaurant at Aria Las Vegas is much more accessible, both from a menu and price perspective. Tapas are the main draw here, allowing you to load up on small plates of often exquisite dishes, many with a Spanish flair to them. The *chorizo* was surprisingly mild but still playfully flavorful, and the lobster with a molecular pineapple gelatin will convert even nonseafood fans. Check out the "new" tapas section with funky combos such as ahi tuna with avocado and mango, and fried potatoes, eggs, and *chorizo* (breakfast on a stick!). If the small selections aren't doing it for you, go big with one of the signature paellas. The Valenciana has chicken and rabbit in a not-too-spicy Spanish rice, large enough to feed at least two people. The food, service, and ambience are all superb although it is worth noting that the bill can add up quickly if you go to crazy with tapas sampling.

In Aria Las Vegas, 3730 Las Vegas Blvd. S. ℭ **877/230-2742.** www.arialasvegas.com. Reservations recommended. Main courses $18–$35; tapas $8–$25. AE, DC, DISC, MC, V. Daily 11am–11pm.

Sirio Ristorante ★★ ITALIAN From the same family that brought us Le Cirque and Circo, Sirio serves decidedly upscale Italian fare with a heavy Tuscan influence, meaning simple concepts and ingredients often thrown together in revelatory ways. Start with a build-your-own antipasti platter and if you don't get the smoked rosemary ham as one of your choices, you only have yourself to blame. The three-meatball appetizer puts duck on a bed of wild mushrooms, veal on a tomato compote, and lamb over braised lentils. You'll have flavorful fun trying to decide which one you like best (we lean toward the duck). Hand-rolled spaghetti in a three-meat ragu is heavenly as is the pan-roasted tenderloin in garlic and Gorgonzola. Designer pizzas, salads, more pasta, seafood, and traditional favorites with words like *scallopini* and *Alfredo* in their title round out a very complete menu. Oh, and do not ignore the desserts. There are simply too many wonders to choose just one but if you must, go for the trio of tiramisu (traditional, strawberry, and caramel).

In Aria Las Vegas, 3730 Las Vegas Blvd. S. ☎ **877/230-2742.** www.arialasvegas.com. Reservations recommended. Main courses $18–$45. AE, DC, DISC, MC, V. Daily 5–10:30pm.

Moderate

Burger Bar ★ DINER See how Vegas is? They know you might be watching your budget or just wanting something simple but not boring, so they give you a place that specializes in hamburgers "your way," as the ads go. We love this concept, but we can't help but wince when we see how loading up a basic burger into a personalized creation turns a humble patty into a check for $15, and that's before we order fries and shakes. But we will eat at Burger Bar again because it starts with Ridgefield Farm (most recommended) and Black Angus beef, and all the toppings (the usuals, such as bacon and avocado, but also six kinds of cheese, prosciutto, chopped scallions, and even anchovies and lobster, for Pete's sake), plus a choice of bun. It adds up to a hilarious and, if you have a deft touch, delicious experience (though we have not yet gotten them to prepare the doneness of the burgers to our proper specifications, so we advise you to be very clear about your pink-to-gray meat-ratio preference).

Shakes are creamy, fries aren't bad (we like the skinny ones better than the fat ones), though if you haven't before, try the sweet-potato fries. One of the most clever desserts in town lurks on this menu, a "sweet burger"—a slab of really fine chocolate pâté "burger," on a warm donut "bun," topped with cunningly crafted strawberry "tomato" slices, mint "lettuce," and translucent passion-fruit "cheese." Note the weekend late hours. And skip the highfalutin' burger options—Kobe beef is too soft to use as burger meat, while foie gras is just wasted in this context. In other words, don't show off, but do have fun.

In Mandalay Place, 3930 Las Vegas Blvd. S. ☎ **702/632-9364.** Main courses $8–$24 (burgers start at $8, depending on kind of beef; toppings start at 65¢ and go way up). AE, DISC, MC, V. Sun–Thurs 11am–11pm; Fri–Sat 10am–1am.

Diablo's Cantina ★★ MEXICAN Located as it is in the southwestern part of the United States, you'd think Las Vegas would be able to do Mexican food better than it does. While there are a few standouts in town, the list of really good south-of-the-border eateries can be counted on one hand. Well, maybe two now with the addition of Diablo's Cantina.

Located right on the Strip with some fun people-watching views, Diablo's is a dark pueblo of a space serving up traditional Mexican fare at prices that will remind you that eating in Vegas doesn't need to be a bank-draining occasion. The menu, while not as mind-bogglingly expansive as similar restaurants, certainly covers all the basics with burritos, tacos, quesadillas, enchiladas, and fajitas, plus some sandwiches, burgers, and salads thrown in for those who need a little less spice in their life. Standouts include the Club Quesadilla, three layers of steak, pulled pork, and guacamole, and the tender steak fajitas, served sizzling—the way God intended them to be.

In Monte Carlo, 3770 Las Vegas Blvd. S. © **702/730-7979.** Main courses $10–$25. AE, MC, V. Daily 11am–11pm.

Dick's Last Resort ★★ AMERICAN Boy food for the boisterous. This is not the place to go for a relaxing or dainty meal. The gimmick is customer abuse— yes, you pay for the privilege of having waitstaff hurl napkins and cheerful invective at you. But they mean it with love. Sounds a bit strange, but it works, in a party-hearty way. Speaking of, the food itself is hearty indeed, with house specialties (barbecue ribs, honey-glazed chicken) arriving in buckets. Entrees are substantial, both in quantity and construction—look for chicken-fried steak, fried chicken, and meats or pastas covered in cream sauces. The most successful item could well be their burger, a juicy mammoth. Probably best for rowdy teenagers or stag parties, but both attitude and grub might be a relief after all those houses of reverent culinary worship.

In Excalibur, 3850 Las Vegas Blvd. S. © **702/597-7991.** Main courses $13–$24. AE, MC, V. Mon–Thurs 1pm–late; Fri–Sat 11am–late.

Grand Wok ★★ 🍴 ASIAN This place is no longer thoroughly Pan-Asian but still a solid choice for sushi and, more importantly, budget fare in the form of the combo soup full of noodles and different kinds of meat. It's particularly nice and more affordable than the usual hotel restaurant—and the primarily Asian clientele clearly agrees. Note that soup portions are most generous; four people could easily split one order and have a nice and very inexpensive lunch, an unexpected bargain option for the Strip.

In MGM Grand, 3799 Las Vegas Blvd. S. © **702/891-7777.** Reservations not accepted. Main courses $15–$38; sushi rolls and pieces $7–$30. AE, DC, DISC, MC, V. Restaurant Sun–Thurs 11am–10pm; Fri–Sat 11am–1am. Sushi bar Mon–Thurs 5–10pm; Fri–Sat 11am–1am; Sun 11am–10pm.

Hussong's Cantina ★ DINER The moderately priced Mexican joint seems to be a trend in Vegas these days. Where south-of-the-border used to be rare, it is now flourishing and Hussong's Cantina is an excellent example of the breed. It is based on the legendary Ensenada bar, in business since 1892, which claims to have been the site where the margarita was invented (a bartender reportedly concocted the mixture in 1941 for either the daughter of a Mexican ambassador or Rita Hayworth depending on who you ask—there was alcohol involved so the history is understandably fuzzy). Hussong's boldly proclaims to have "The Best Tacos in Town." Okay. Gauntlet thrown. You can build your own combo platter of three starting with steak, *carnitas*, chicken, lobster, or goat (no, really) and then add from over a dozen different toppings (cheeses, pico de gallo, onions, guacamole, and more) on a soft corn tortilla. We haven't sampled *every* taco in town but we can say without a doubt that these are worthy contenders for the "Best" title. The steak was the winner of the three, all smoky charbroiled goodness, but my-oh-my the *carnitas* (shredded, spiced pork) was pretty darned good too. Other options include burritos the size of a spare tire with a perfectly flaky crust, enchiladas, quesadillas, and all the other usual Mexican suspects. The margaritas are good, but perhaps floating a bit too much on their "we invented it!" reputation. You can get better just down the hall at Tacos and Tequila (p. 162). The only disappointment was the too-short and too-traditional dessert menu. Fried ice cream? Yawn.

At Mandalay Place, 3930 Las Vegas Blvd. S., no. 121B. ℭ **702/553-0123.** www.hussongslasvegas. com. Main courses $12–$18. AE, DISC, MC, V. Sun–Thurs 11am–11pm; Fri–Sat 11am–midnight.

Nine Fine Irishmen ★ IRISH/PUB FARE Travelin' foodies swear the once-maligned food in Ireland has improved enormously, so perhaps it's justified to have an Irish restaurant in the pantheon of new Vegas foodie destinations, though given our not-so-secret love of insta-decor, the interior of this one, mocked up to look like a rambling old Irish manor house, is enough for us. (Though once we start thinking about the complicated relationship the Irish have with New York City and vice versa, and the metaimplications of a faux-Irish restaurant set in a fantasy Irish house in the middle of a Vegas casino homage to NYC, our heads begin to hurt.) We will say that the caramelized apricot and pork sausage on a bed of potatoes was sweet and tangy and the Irish stew a right honest interpretation, complete with soda bread. Protestants and monarchists might want to try the beer-battered fish and chips, served as God and queen intended, in a newspaper cone. You'll find bacon rashers at breakfast and a large selection of Irish beer most of the time. Desserts are more silliness, including items such as the Dunbrody Kiss, fluffy chocolate mousse on a crunchy caramel base.

In New York–New York, 3790 Las Vegas Blvd. S. ℭ **702/740-6430.** www.ninefineirishmen.com. Reservations suggested. Main courses $18–$30; sandwiches $9–$12. AE, MC, V. Restaurant daily 11am–11pm. Bar daily 11am–3am.

Tacos & Tequila ★★ MEXICAN If you can get past the trendy trappings (bold colors, metal sculptures, a DJ!), the food and the drinks at this Mexican restaurant overlooking the Luxor lobby are about as good as you'll find anywhere in town, provided you like Mexican food, that is. Although there are more than a dozen varieties of tacos (Kobe beef, lobster, beer-battered Tilapia, and more) and more than 100 different tequilas, the menu goes beyond their namesake to include tostadas, enchiladas, burritos, quesadillas, seafood, soups, and salads, all done with an organic freshness that sets the dishes apart from the chain restaurants you're probably used to. A Sunday-only Mariachi Brunch adds a variety of breakfast items to the offerings including *huevos con tocino* or *chorizo,* burritos, and huevos rancheros. As good as the food is, you would be doing yourself a disservice if you don't try the margaritas, all made with hand-squeezed lime juice, organic agave nectar, and your choice of tequilas and flavors. We know people who are very picky about their margaritas and have declared these the best they have ever tasted. Prices are high for a Mexican joint but relatively affordable for a Strip restaurant.

In Luxor, 3900 Las Vegas Blvd. S. ℭ **702/262-5225.** www.tacosandtequilalv.com. Reservations suggested. Main courses $10–$23. AE, MC, V. Daily 11am–11pm.

Todd English P.U.B. ★★★ PUB FARE English's Olives restaurant up the street at Bellagio is one of our favorites so we had high hopes for his new pub concept at CityCenter. Hopes met and exceeded. A huge beer and wine list is enticing, as are the sun-dappled interiors with lots of TVs on which to catch your favorite game, but it is the menu that really seals the proverbial deal here. Want a sandwich? Make your own from The Carvery, with your choice of meat (prime

YOU GOTTA HAVE A theme

It shouldn't be too surprising to learn that a town devoted to gimmicks has just about every gimmick restaurant there is. Almost all have prominent celebrity co-owners and tons of "memorabilia" on the walls, which in virtually every case means throwaway items from blockbuster movies, or some article of clothing a celebrity wore once (if that) on stage or on the playing field. Almost all have virtually identical menus and have gift shops full of logo items.

This sounds cynical, and it is—but not without reason. Theme restaurants, for the most part, are noisy, cluttered, overpriced places that are strictly tourist traps, and, though some have their devotees, if you eat at one of these places, you've eaten at them all. We don't want to be total killjoys. Fans should have a good time checking out the stuff on the walls of the appropriate restaurant. And while the food won't be the most memorable ever, it probably won't be bad (and will be moderately priced). But that's not really what you go for.

The **House of Blues** ★★, in Mandalay Bay, 3950 Las Vegas Blvd. S. (© **702/632-7607;** www.hob.com; Sun–Thurs 7:30am–midnight, Fri–Sat 7:30am–1am), for our money, food- and themewise, is the best of the theme restaurants. The food is really pretty good (if a little more costly than it ought to be in a theme restaurant), and the mock Delta/New Orleans look works well, even if it is unavoidably commercial. You can dine here without committing to seeing whatever band is playing, as the dining room is separate from the club (note, though, that HOB gets very good bookings from nationally known acts). The gospel brunch might also be worth checking out (the food is good, though there's too much of it), but be warned: It's served inside the actual club, which can be unbelievably loud, so bring earplugs (we left with splitting headaches).

There are those who rave about the warm Tollhouse-cookie pie at the **Harley-Davidson Cafe** ★, 3725 Las Vegas Blvd. S., at Harmon Avenue (© **702/740-4555;** www.harley-davidsoncafe.com; Sun–Thurs 11am–midnight, Fri–Sat 11am–2am). But before you get to dessert, a full menu of southern staples (barbecue being chief among them) awaits.

The **Hard Rock Cafe** ★, 4475 Paradise Rd., at Harmon Avenue (© **702/733-8400;** www.hardrockcafe.com; Sun–Thurs 11am–11pm, Fri–Sat 11am–midnight; bar stays open an hour later than restaurant), has decent burgers. The serious hipster quotient at the adjacent hotel means that the people-watching opportunities are best here. *Note:* There is a second Hard Rock Cafe now open on the Strip (3771 Las Vegas Blvd. S.; © **702/733-7625**), a 42,000-square-foot, three-level behemoth with all sorts of high-tech gadgetry like interactive tables, a gigantic gift shop, a 1,000-seat concert venue, and more. Bigger, yes. Better? You decide.

Parrot Heads like to party it up at **Margaritaville,** singer Jimmy Buffet's tropical-themed cafe/bar/club, at the Flamingo ("Parrot Heads" is how his fans refer to themselves). The menu runs a range from Mexican to something sort of Caribbean themed to basic American, and it's not all that bad, considering. Partaking in lots of fruity tropical drinks doesn't hurt, either. It's in the Flamingo, 3555 Las Vegas Blvd. S. (© **702/733-3302;** www.margaritavillelasvegas.com; Mon–Thurs 8am–2am, Fri–Sun 7am–3am).

beef, roasted chicken, turkey, duck, salmon, and pastrami for starters), bread, and condiments. Be sure to accompany that with the spectacular prime rib chili, slathered in cheese and moderate on the spicy scale. Burgers, salads, bangers and mash, fish and chips, potpies, and a host of other sandwiches (the grilled cheese with brie and bacon is a winner) round out the menu. Best of all are the moderate prices. Forget the lunch buffets and come here instead.

In Crystals at CityCenter, 3720 Las Vegas Blvd. S. ✆ **702/489-8080.** www.toddenglishpub.com. Reservations recommended. Main courses $12–$24. AE, DC, DISC, MC, V. Sun–Thurs 11am–11pm; Fri–Sat 11am–midnight.

Inexpensive

Jody Maroni's Sausage Kingdom ★★★ DELI There are several worthy fast-food stands in the New York–New York food court, but this one deserves an individual mention. What began as a humble stand on the Venice boardwalk in Los Angeles has expanded into a sausage empire, and we are glad. You will be, too, especially if you take a chance on their menu and don't just stick with the basic hot dog (though they do offer three tempting varieties) and instead try something a little more adventurous, such as the tequila chicken sausage made with jalapeños, corn, and lime. (We wish that they offered samples and an even larger menu, as the original stand still does.) Or just vary your basic sweet Italian sausage with a hotter variety. Either way, you can top it with raw or grilled onions and peppers as it gets stuffed into a sesame-seed soft roll. Maybe some chili fries, too. This is our first choice for fast food in the immediate area.

In New York–New York, 3790 Las Vegas Blvd. S. ℂ **702/740-6969.** www.jodymaroni.com. Main courses $6–$11. AE, DC, MC, V. Sun–Thurs 10am–9:30pm; Fri–Sat 10am–11pm.

MID-STRIP
Very Expensive

Alizé ★★★ FRENCH Just a perfect restaurant, thanks to a combination of the most divine dining room and view in Vegas, not to mention one of the best chefs in Vegas. Situated at the top of the Palms Hotel, three sides of full-length windows allow a panoramic view of the night lights of Vegas; obviously, window-side tables are best, but even seats in the center of the room have a good view (though seats on the right are now bedeviled by the recent Palms tower addition). Many great chefs have restaurants locally but are rarely in their kitchens (we love Emeril and Wolfgang, but they can't be in 25 different places at once). This operation is carefully overseen by Andre, he of the eponymous (and excellent) restaurants Downtown and in the Monte Carlo. The menu changes seasonally, but anything you order will be heavenly.

We've rarely been disappointed in either the appetizer or main course departments. For the former, look for a shrimp and artichoke timbale trimmed with avocado and cucumber relish, or a tissue-thin Kobe beef carpaccio with dark pesto topping and tomato confit. The foie gras can come in a pink-grapefruit-and-citrus-honey reduction, a tangy combination. Fish can be a little dry here, so we suggest either the stunning New York steak with summer truffle jus and potato herb pancakes, or the meltingly tender lamb chops with some shredded lamb shank wrapped in a crispy fried crepe. Desserts are similarly outstanding and often of great frivolity, such as sorbet in a case of browned marshmallow, floating in raspberry soup. Yeah, we're going over the top on this one, but we bet you won't think we're wrong.

In Palms Casino Resort, 4321 W. Flamingo Rd. ℂ **702/951-7000.** Fax 702/951-7002. www. alizelv.com. Reservations strongly recommended. Main courses $34–$67; 5-course tasting menu $105; 7-course tasting menu $125. AE, DC, DISC, MC, V. Daily 5:30–10:30pm.

B&B Ristorante ★★ ITALIAN Long-time Food Network staple Mario Batali has a couple of Vegas outposts, and this is perhaps the most notable. It looks like an über-Italian trattoria, full of dark wood, quite inviting and unfortunately very loud. Naturally, the desirable room is in the wine cellar. The menu options are a little too casual for the price, and might be intimidating for those uninitiated in Batali, but there's probably no one in Vegas doing such interesting Italian food. To that end, you might be best served sticking with the *primi* (pasta selections), which are cheaper and arguably more interesting than the *secondi*, though portions are not hearty. Don't miss the beef-cheek ravioli with duck liver, but other notables are the mint love letters with lamb sausage, and the stinging nettle *pappardelle* with wild boar ragu. Or just do the rather reasonable $75 pasta tasting menu. Meanwhile, if you are lucky, Chef himself might be roaming the place in his famous clogs.

In The Venetian, 3355 Las Vegas Blvd. S. ℂ **702/266-9977.** Main courses $21–$49. AE, DISC, MC, V. Daily 5–11pm.

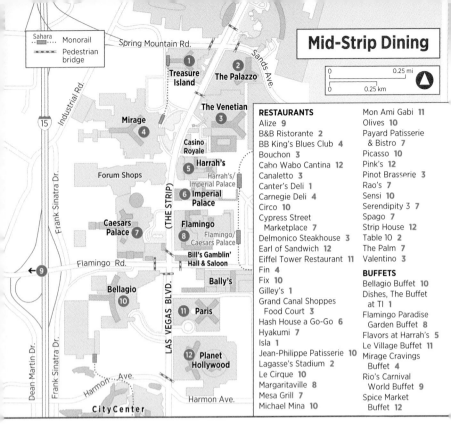

Delmonico Steakhouse ★★ CREOLE/STEAK You might well feel that Emeril Lagasse is omnipresent. This incarnation is a steakhouse version of his hard-core classic Creole restaurant; this ever-so-slight twist is just enough to make it a superior choice over the more disappointing New Orleans locale. It's set in two dining rooms; the left one is '70s den ugly—choose instead the Neutra/Schindler-influenced right side.

You can try Emeril's concoctions, plus fabulous cuts of red meat. You can't go wrong with most appetizers, especially the superbly rich smoked mushrooms with homemade tasso ham over pasta—it's enough for a meal in and of itself. The same advice holds for any of the specials, or the gumbo, particularly if it's the hearty, near-homemade country selection. If you want to experiment, definitely do it with the appetizers; you're better off steering clear of complex entrees, no matter how intriguing they sound (such as a 1-night special of foie gras–stuffed ahi tuna). We've found the entree specials to be generally disappointing; the deceptively simple choices are more successful. The bone-in rib-eye steak is rightly recommended (skip the gummy béarnaise sauce in favor of the fabulous home-made Worcestershire or A.O.K. sauce). The tableside-made Caesar was dubbed "transcendental" by one astute diner. Sides are hit or miss—the creamed spinach was too salty, but a sweet-potato purée (a special, but maybe they'll serve you a side if you ask sweetly) is most definitely a winner. Too full for dessert? No, you aren't. Have a bananas-Foster cream pie, butterscotch crème brûlée, or the lemon icebox pie, a chunk of curd that blasts tart lemon through your mouth.

In The Venetian, 3355 Las Vegas Blvd. S. ℂ **702/414-3737.** www.emerils.com. Reservations strongly recommended for dinner. Main courses $40–$50. AE, DC, DISC, MC, V. Sun–Thurs 11:30am–2pm and 5–10pm; Fri–Sat 1:30am–2pm and 5–10:30pm.

Fin ★ SEAFOOD/CHINESE Elegant and decorous, perhaps a little higher on style (love the glass ball curtains, evocative of bubbles rising in water) than on substance, though that may just be our reaction to the prices, especially when you see how cheap dim sum is in other (admittedly, much less convenient) parts of town. Still, the quiet flourish of ritual that accompanies course presentation makes for a peaceful break from casino madness. Highlights include the rice cooked in chicken fat, the crispy shiitake mushrooms in a sweet-and-sour sauce that ought to convert even a non–mushroom fan, and the deeply spicy seared black-pepper beef tenderloin.

In The Mirage, 3400 Las Vegas Blvd. S. ℂ **866/339-4566** or 702/791-7353. Reservations recommended. Main courses $19–$60. AE, DC, DISC, MC, V. Thurs–Mon 5–11pm.

Fix ★★ AMERICAN A just-right synthesis of gourmet dining, fun dining, and accessible dining, created by the people behind Bellagio's The Bank nightclub. Looking, as one visitor described it, like a "giant clam opening up toward the casino," Fix offers a menu that continues this playful vibe. Look for the silly presentation called Forks, appetizers of smoked salmon and caviar skewered on forks. Or desserts such as Shake and Cake (espresso shake and a brownie), a peanut butter and jelly crème brûlée (misconceived? Or an idea whose time has come? You decide!), and delightful banana sugared doughnuts with chocolate-and-peanut-butter dipping sauce.

But before those clever conclusions come particularly good (in a town not known for same) fish selections, including scallops stacked with a crust of potatoes on applewood-smoked bacon, and The Ultimate Shell, a selection of seafood (from clams to lobster) that comes in an XL size of dreamy decadence. Best of all are the steaks, which are grilled over cherrywood, giving the meat a smoky yet fruity flavor, reminding you that meat is supposed to have dimensions to its taste. From the

---

Great Meal Deals

We've already alluded to the rock-bottom budget meals and graveyard specials available at casino hotel restaurants. Quality not assured and Pepto-Bismol not provided. As prices and deals can change without notice, we don't want to list examples, but finding a full prime-rib dinner for around $5 is not rare (pun definitely intended).

Your best bet is to keep your eyes open as you travel through town, as hotels tend to advertise their specials on their marquees. Or you can go to **www.vegas. com** and click on **"Dining"** and then **"Dining Bargains,"** though the tips and prices may be somewhat out-of-date. Following are three examples of current options for late-night munchies: **Ellis Island** offers a $6.99 10-ounce steak (plus potato and other sides), and $7.99 gets you a porterhouse steak at **Arizona Charlie's Boulder.** At the Hard Rock Hotel, **Mr. Lucky's 24/7** is a particularly good diner, with particularly good people-watching. And then ask your server about the $7.77 steak, three barbecued shrimp, and sides; it's not on the menu, so you have to know about it.

trendy "small plates" to hamburgers, this is one complete menu. All in all, a good compromise for a special occasion or just a treat of a meal: not so froufrou that basic eaters will be dismayed, not so simplistic that foodies will feel cheated, and not in the least bit stodgy or intimidating. Given the late hours and the origins, though, expect a lively and young crowd, especially as the night wears on.

In Bellagio, 3600 Las Vegas Blvd. S. ✆ **702/693-7223.** Reservations recommended. Main courses $29–$75. AE, MC, V. Sun–Thurs 5pm–midnight; Fri–Sat 5pm–2am.

Hyakumi ★ JAPANESE/SUSHI Hyakumi (Yah-*koo*-me) is a quaint little oasis in the midst of a bustling casino. Tastefully decorated with hardwood floors in a tea-garden atmosphere, it is a relaxing respite from the madness of Vegas, as kimono-clad waitresses cater to your every need with a never-ending cup of particularly good green tea, plus hot towels, to put you in a Zen-like state.

But the setting, as serene and beautiful as it is, is not the reason for a visit to Hyakumi; it's the sushi. Supervised by Executive Chef Hiroji Obayashi, famed for his award-winning Hirozen Gourmet Restaurant in Los Angeles, Hyakumi offers some of the best sushi in town. It's not the cheapest, but it is well worth the extra cost. From the *toro* to the salmon roll, every bite melts in your mouth. The fish is shipped in daily and is prepared by friendly sushi chefs who obviously love what they do. If sushi isn't your thing, there is also a restaurant serving up traditional (but very expensive) Japanese fare in a lovely garden setting.

In Caesars Palace, 3570 Las Vegas Blvd. S. ✆ **877/346-4642.** Reservations recommended. Main courses $25–$60; sushi $6–$10 per roll or piece. AE, DC, DISC, MC, V. Daily 11am–3pm and 5–11pm.

Le Cirque ★ FRENCH The influx of haute-cuisine, high-profile restaurants in Vegas means there are ever so many places now where you may feel like you have to take out a bank loan in order to eat. Though generally we always feel free to spend your money for you, we actually are going to suggest that you hold on to it in the case of Le Cirque, unless someone else is doing the buying. It's not that the food is bad—quite the contrary—but it's not the very best in town, and it is among the most expensive. And remember what we said about most of Vegas being quite casual? Here, forget it. If you didn't bring your nicest black, you are going to feel very uncomfortable.

The surprisingly small dining room is decorated with murals of quaint bygone circus themes and a ceiling draped with gay fabric meant to evoke the Big Top. The busy decor adds to the cramped feeling. The menu changes seasonally, but you can expect genuine French cuisine—heavy, with lots of butter, though a recent visit brought a duo of cold cucumber and heirloom tomato soups that were immensely refreshing. The lobster salad is sweet and tender, with a perfect black-truffle dressing; risotto is French style, almost soupy, perfect with fresh morels (in season) and Parmesan. The filet mignon is, oddly, not as good a cut as served elsewhere, but it does come with a generous portion of foie gras. For dessert, we loved the white-chocolate cream (solid but not overwhelming), layered with banana and wrapped in phyllo, along with a milk-chocolate dome with crème brûlée espresso.

In Bellagio, 3600 Las Vegas Blvd. S. ✆ **702/693-7223.** Reservations required. Jacket preferred; no jeans, shorts, T-shirts, or sneakers. Prix-fixe dinner $98 and up. AE, DC, DISC, MC, V. Tues–Sun 5:30–10pm.

Mesa Grill ★★ SOUTHWESTERN Food Network darling Bobby Flay has his fans and his detractors, and we aren't going to mediate that argument here, especially since the man isn't cooking in the kitchen any more often than most celebrity chefs in this town. More significantly, regardless of where you fall in the debate, this is a worthy restaurant, if, like so much in Vegas, a bit overpriced. Just about every well-spiced entree is over $30, and sometimes well over.

Still, there is so much that is fun here: blue-corn pancakes with barbecue duck, or the chicken quesadilla (made in a special dedicated oven) that comes with garlic crème fraîche. Presentation is over the top—yes, this is playful food, we get it, now stop it—but those who are a bit on the wimpy side when it comes to spices will appreciate how each entree comes with its own cooling element (the aforementioned crème fraîche, for example). Desserts are equally frivolous, though not particularly theme intensive (unless you consider an exceptional raspberry and white-chocolate cheesecake "Southwestern"). Those wishing to try it without breaking the bank should either come at lunch or consider splitting appetizers as a light meal.

In Caesars Palace, 3570 Las Vegas Blvd. S. © **702/731-7731.** Main courses $12–$24 brunch and lunch, $23–$45 dinner. Mon–Fri 11am–2:30pm and 5–11pm; Sat–Sun 10:30am–3pm and 5–11pm.

Michael Mina ★ SEAFOOD What is it about Vegas and fish? Even this premier San Francisco piscine palace let us down. The signature lobster potpie is good, a splashy presentation that includes the wheeling of the pie to the table and the careful excising of the contents, including the broth and crusty top, which then fails to stay crusty thanks to the broth contact. The miso-glazed sea bass in mushroom consommé tasted like nothing more than seafood sukiyaki. Really good sukiyaki, but even so. Starters of langoustine and crab ravioli are mealy and dull, while the "tasting" of foie gras, instead of multiple presentations of same, was just one serving of seared liver, with a nice parsnip tarte tatin. Desserts, including an actual root-beer float and a chocolate tasting, are much more successful. Service is a bit too rushed, with bread and water delivered in the heedless manner of a coffee shop.

In Bellagio, 3600 Las Vegas Blvd. S. © **702/693-7223.** www.michaelmina.net. Reservations recommended. Main courses $36–$72 (lobster and whole foie gras higher). AE, DC, DISC, MC, V. Thurs–Tues 5:30–10:30pm.

The Palm ★★ STEAK/SEAFOOD A branch of the venerable New York eatery, which has been branching ever farther afield recently, this place attracts a star-studded clientele fond of the reliable and hearty, if not terribly exciting, bill of fare. (The famous may also be hoping to find their face among the many caricatures that cover the walls.) This is plain but filling food—at manly prices. Red-meat lovers will be happy with the high-quality steaks found here, though those on a budget will shudder in horror. The tendency is to give the meat a good charring, so if you don't like yours blackened, start with it less well done and send it back for more if necessary. If you've hit a jackpot, your money will be well spent on one of the Buick-size lobsters. They're utterly succulent and outrageously priced, but given their size—they start at 3 pounds—they can easily be shared. If you're worried that all this won't be enough, add one of the delicious appetizers (plump but high-priced shrimp cocktails or a perfect prosciutto with melon) or toss in a side of crispy deep-fried onions. Desserts are heavy and unspectacular.

In Caesars Palace Forum Shops, 3570 Las Vegas Blvd. S. ✆ **702/732-7256.** www.thepalm.com. Reservations recommended. Main courses $13–$22 lunch, $27–$83 dinner. AE, DC, MC, V. Daily 11:30am–11pm.

Picasso ★★★ FRENCH A Spanish chef who cooks French cuisine in an Italian-themed hotel in Vegas? Trust us, it works. This is one of the best restaurants in Vegas, and given the sudden serious competition for such a title, that says a lot. Steve Wynn spent months trying to talk Madrid-born chef Julian Serrano (whose Masa was considered the finest French restaurant in San Francisco) into coming to Bellagio. His bulldog tenacity paid off, and we should all thank him. This is an extraordinary dining experience that includes the thrill of having $30 million worth of Picassos gaze down over your shoulders while you eat. It's not like dining in a stuffy museum, however—the water fountains going off outside every 15 minutes (with staid diners rushing to the windows to check it out) pretty much takes care of that. Many of the furnishings were designed by one of Picasso's sons, and even the paintings themselves are challenged for beauty by the exceptional floral arrangements.

Serrano's cooking is a work of art that can proudly stand next to the masterpieces. The menu changes nightly and always offers a choice between a four- or five-course prix-fixe dinner or a tasting menu. The night we ate there, we were bowled over by roasted Maine lobster with a trio of corn—kernels, sauce, and a corn flan—that was like slightly solid sunshine. Hudson Valley foie gras was crusted in truffles and went down most smoothly. A filet of roasted sea bass came with a light saffron sauce and dots of cauliflower purée. And finally, pray that they're serving the lamb rôti—it was an outstanding piece of lamb, perfectly done, tender, and crusted with truffles. Portions are dainty but so rich that you'll have plenty to eat without groaning and feeling heavy when you leave. Desserts are powerful yet prettily constructed. A molten chocolate cake leaves any other you may have tried in the dust and comes with ice cream made with imported European chocolate. A crisp banana tart with coconut ice cream is a fine nonchocolate (foolish you) choice, while a passion-fruit flan in a citrus-soup sauce is perfect if you don't have much room left. Everything is delivered by attentive staff that makes you feel pampered. Can we go back soon and try it all again?

In Bellagio, 3600 Las Vegas Blvd. S. ✆ **866/259-7111.** Reservations recommended. Prix-fixe 4-course dinner $113; 5-course degustation $123. AE, DC, DISC, MC, V. Wed–Mon 6–9:30pm.

Spago ★ ✋ ASIAN/CALIFORNIA At this point in the game, Spago represents both the best and the worst of the celebrity chef phenomenon. If you eat at the Beverly Hills location, you might well have the very best meal of your life, and almost certainly something that demonstrates the reason why such a fuss is made about creative cooking. The problem is that Wolfgang Puck, the man who virtually invented the chef-as-household-name concept and certainly had as much to do as anyone with California cuisine becoming a viable food genre, has stretched himself too thin—seven restaurants in Vegas alone. No one can keep a personal watch on that many locations, and the result is that this one, the first sign that Vegas was becoming a viable restaurant destination, is now simply not our first, nor even our second, choice for you to spend your hard-won jackpot money.

The inside menu changes seasonally, but the signature dish is a Chinese-style duck, moist but with a perfectly crispy skin. It's about as good as duck gets, served with a doughy, steamed bun and Chinese vegetables. Our other suggestion is to come here for lunch, and that's still not the worst plan. Salads, sandwiches, and pastas are all generously portioned, and the signature Puck pizzas, like prosciutto and goat cheese and pear, are still quite good (ask for the off-the-menu and legendary "Jewish pizza," with salmon and crème fraîche). Nothing is all that innovative, however (braised leek and ham quiche with apple-smoked bacon—good, but you've seen it before), and nothing stands out. Desserts can actually be so poor—such as a dry chocolate cake—we won't even bother finishing them.

In Caesars Palace, 3570 Las Vegas Blvd. S. © **702/369-6300.** www.wolfgangpuck.com. Reservations recommended for the dining room, not accepted at the cafe. Main courses $28–$68 dining room, $15–$33 cafe. AE, DC, DISC, MC, V. Dining room daily 5:30–10pm. Cafe Sun–Thurs 11am–11pm; Fri–Sat 11am–midnight.

Strip House ★★ STEAK What turns a pedestrian steakhouse visit, admittedly a dime a dozen experience in Vegas, into something truly special? Here it comes down to the two prime ingredients: the atmosphere and the steaks.

Atmosphere first. The place is done in a cheeky bordello theme, with red-flocked walls adorned with black-and-white photos of peek-a-boo strippers from the bygone days when stripping seemed slightly naughty as opposed to today's raunchiness. These Bettie Page–like works of art are endlessly entertaining to look at, not for the titillation but for the kitsch factor. It is worth noting that while most of the photos are safe for young eyes, there are a few in the mix that are decidedly PG-13, so parents with children may want to scan the walls before sitting to make sure there are no uncomfortable questions during the appetizer course.

Speaking of appetizers, there are the traditional (shrimp cocktail, clams casino), but head directly for the warm garlic bread served in a bed of Gorgonzola fondue, cholesterol numbers be darned. Follow that up with any of the fine cuts of beef, all done in a black pepper rub that might be overwhelming to some with the first few bites, but go with it and you'll be rewarded with one of the best and most flavorful steaks on the Strip.

☉ A Dining Room, or Two, with a View

As we keep noting, the Strip at night is a dazzling sight, which is why hotel rooms with Strip views come at such a premium. Regardless of whether you were able to get the proverbial room with a view, consider dining at the chic **Eiffel Tower Restaurant,** in Paris Las Vegas, 3655 Las Vegas Blvd. S. (© **702/948-6937;** www.eiffeltower restaurant.com; Sun–Thurs 11:30am–2:30pm and 5–10:15pm, Fri–Sat 11:30am–2:30pm and 5–10:45pm), located on the 11th floor of said mid-Strip hotel. Or choose the Stratosphere's **Top of the World,** in Stratosphere Hotel & Casino, 2000 Las Vegas Blvd. S. (© **702/380-7711;** www.topoftheworldlv.com; daily 11am–3pm and 4:30–10pm), which is almost at the top of the north Strip's Stratosphere Tower, the tallest structure west of the Mississippi. Both offer fantastic views. The latter even revolves 360 degrees, while the former also looks down on the Bellagio fountains. Both, however, also match sky-high views with sky-high prices, and, unfortunately, neither has food worth the price. Go for a special night out, or see if you can get away with just ordering appetizers and dessert (which are both superior to the entrees anyway). You can also just have a drink at their respective bars, though each is set back far enough from the windows that drinkers have less-optimal views than diners.

In Planet Hollywood, 3667 Las Vegas Blvd. S. ☎ **702/737-5200.** Reservations recommended. Main courses $25–$60. AE, DC, MC, V. Sun–Thurs 5–11pm; Fri–Sat 5–midnight.

Valentino ★ ITALIAN Valentino was long considered the best Italian restaurant in Los Angeles, and even the best in America (per *Bon Appétit*, and we suppose they ought to know). But this branch (with generic nice restaurant decor) isn't quite as successful as its Southern California counterpart, with complicated offerings that too often just miss the mark. Quail stuffed with snails and served with white-and-yellow polenta, for example, or house-smoked shrimp with crispy veggies and an apple-balsamic sauce—they're all interesting, but the combinations don't quite work. Working entirely well, however, are the four-cheese ravioli with truffle-cream sauce and fresh truffle shavings—we shamelessly mopped our plate with our bread—and the wild-rabbit loin in rhubarb-encrusted prosciutto. The wine list is superb.

In The Venetian, 3355 Las Vegas Blvd. S. ☎ **702/414-3000.** www.pieroselvaggio.com. Reservations strongly recommended. Main courses $20–$49; tasting menus $90–$105, with wine pairing $110–$145. AE, DC, DISC, MC, V. Daily 11:30am–11pm.

Expensive

Bouchon ★★★ BISTRO Thomas Keller made his name with his Napa Valley restaurant French Laundry, considered by many to be the best restaurant in the United States. Bouchon is a version of his Napa Valley bistro. We had mixed expectations. On the one hand, he's a certifiably genius chef. On the other hand, he's not going to be in the kitchen that will be producing bistro (which is to say, not innovative) food and, what's more, based on the rather lackluster Napa Bouchon.

Our negative expectations were confounded by the right, left, and center of the menu—yeah, we've tried nearly all of it and can report that humble though these dishes sound, in nearly every case they are gold-standard versions of classics. Someone is certainly keeping a close eye on this kitchen, and that someone has learned the lessons well. Ever wondered why people get worked up over raw oysters? The sweet and supremely fresh (kept in water until the moment they are served to you) Snow Creek oysters will enlighten you, as they seem to melt on contact with your tongue. Fifty dollars seems like a lot for pâté, but here a complex multiday preparation produces a buttery whip that is so rich, it's an appropriate—and highly recommended—appetizer for four. Don't miss the bacon and poached-egg frisée salad, or the cleanly seared salmon over poached leeks, prepared to such perfection it doesn't need the accompanying sauce. Gnocchi is earthy and assertive, a peasant version of an Italian favorite, while beef Bourguignon is exactly as you expect it to be, in the divine perfection sense. Leg of lamb has all chewy bits excised before cooking, leaving it a garlic-permeated bit of tenderness. This is a superlative Vegas restaurant, and while it may be hard to reconcile the prices with the apparent simplicity of the food, recall that it takes serious skill to make even the most humble of dishes correctly, as your palate will reassure you.

In The Venetian, 3355 Las Vegas Blvd. S. ☎ **702/414-6200.** www.bouchonbistro.com. Reservations strongly recommended. Main courses $10–$20 breakfast, $22–$45 dinner, $21–$25 brunch. AE, DC, DISC, MC, V. Mon–Fri 7–10:30am and 5–10pm; Sat–Sun 8am–2pm (brunch). Oyster bar daily 3–10pm.

Canaletto ★★ ITALIAN Come here for solid, true Italian fare—and that means less sauce intensive than the red-checked-tablecloth establishments of our American youths. Here, the emphasis is on the pasta, not the accompaniments. This place is all the more enjoyable for being perched on the faux St. Mark's Square; in theory, you can pretend you are sitting on the edge of the real thing, a fantasy we don't mind admitting we briefly indulged in. A risotto of porcini, sausage, and white-truffle oil was full of strong flavors, while the wood-fired roast chicken was perfectly moist. A properly roasted chicken should be a much-celebrated thing, and that alone may be a reason to come here.

In The Venetian Grand Canal Shoppes, 3377 Las Vegas Blvd. S. ☏ **702/733-0070.** Reservations recommended for dinner. Main courses $14–$36. AE, DC, MC, V. Sun–Thurs 11:30am–11pm; Fri–Sat 11:30am–midnight.

Circo ★★ ITALIAN Yes, this is the less-expensive offering from the same family that brings you Le Cirque, but going to one does not excuse you from going to the other. (By the way, "less expensive" is a relative term.)

Le Cirque's gourmet French haute cuisine does not prepare you for what to expect from Circo, or, for that matter, vice versa. Ignore the bright primary-color scheme, meant to evoke the circus but instead sadly recalling outdated hotel buffets (albeit with expensive wood grain), in favor of watching the dancing fountains outside. And then order the *mista di campo,* a lovely little salad, both visually and in terms of taste; it's a creative construction of vegetables bound with cucumber and topped with a fab balsamic vinaigrette. Follow that with a perfect tagliatelle with rock shrimp—it comes loaded with various crustacean bits in a light sauce. Note that appetizer portions of pastas are plenty filling and cheaper than full-size servings. Entrees usually include more elaborate dishes, such as breast of Muscovy duck with dried organic fruit in port-wine sauce. Save room for desserts such as *panna cotta* (Italian cream–filled doughnuts) or *tutto ciocco-lato,* consisting of chocolate mousse, ice cream, and crumb cake.

In Bellagio, 3600 Las Vegas Blvd. S. ☏ **702/693-7223.** Reservations recommended. Main courses $16–$59. AE, DC, DISC, MC, V. Daily 5:30–10:30pm, last seating 10pm.

Olives ★★ ITALIAN/MEDITERRANEAN If there was an Olives in our neighborhood, we would eat there regularly. A branch of Todd English's original Boston-based restaurant, Olives is a strong choice for a light lunch that need not be as expensive as you might think. Here's how to enjoy a moderately priced meal here: Munch on the focaccia bread, olives, and excellent tapenade they give you at the start, have a lovely salad (maybe of bibb lettuce, Maytag bleu cheese, and walnut dressing), and then split a flatbread—think pizza with an ultrathin crust (like a slightly limp cracker), topped with delicious combinations such as the highly recommended Moroccan-spiced lamb, eggplant purée, and feta cheese, or our other favorite, fig, prosciutto, and Gorgonzola. They are rich and wonderful—split one between two people, and you have an affordable and terrific lunch. Or try pasta; we were steered toward the simple but marvelous spaghettini with roasted tomatoes, garlic, and Parmesan, and were happy with it. The constructed, but not too fussy, food gets more complicated and costly at night, adding an array of meats and chickens, plus pastas such as butternut squash with brown butter and sage.

In Bellagio, 3600 Las Vegas Blvd. S. ☏ **866/259-7111.** www.toddenglish.com. Reservations recommended. Main courses $17–$25 lunch, $24–$52 dinner. AE, DC, DISC, MC, V. Daily 11am–2:45pm and 5–10:30pm.

Pinot Brasserie ★★ BISTRO This is one incarnation of a series of well-regarded Los Angeles restaurants whose mother ship, Patina, regularly tops "Best of" lists among City of Angels foodies. While the more innovative cooking is going on back in Los Angeles, Pinot reliably delivers French and American favorites that are thoughtfully conceived and generally delicious. It's an excellent choice if you want a special meal that is neither stratospherically expensive nor too complex. And the space is highly attractive, with various props culled from French auctions and flea markets forming the archetypal, clubby bistro feel. We particularly like the small room off the bar to the right—just perfect for a tête-à-tête.

Salads are possibly fresher and more generous than other similar starters in town (thank that California influence), and they can come paired with various toppings for *crostini* (toasted slices of French bread) such as herbed goat cheese. The signature dish, beloved by many, is a roasted chicken accompanied by heaping mounds of garlic fries; but if you wish to get a little more elaborate (and yet rather light), thin slices of smoked salmon with celery rémoulade could be a way to go. Desserts are lovely, and the ice cream is homemade—the chocolate alone should make you wish you'd never eaten at 31 Flavors because it was wasted calories compared to this.

In The Venetian, 3355 Las Vegas Blvd. S. ✆ **702/414-8888.** www.patinagroup.com. Reservations recommended for dinner. Main courses $16–$31 lunch, $32–$46 dinner. AE, DISC, MC, V. Sun-Thurs 11:30am–3pm and 5:30–10pm; Fri-Sat 11:30am–3pm and 5:30–10:30pm.

Rao's ★ ITALIAN This is a meticulous re-creation of the famous 110-year-old East Harlem restaurant, which is notorious in equal measure for "Uncle Vincent's lemon chicken" and the near impossibility of getting a seat (there are only 10 tables, which are reserved a year in advance!). It was thoughtful of Vegas to replicate it at more than three times the original's size, allowing common folks to check it out (though keep an eye out for famous homesick New Yorkers holding court). On the other hand, because this isn't revelatory Italian cooking, you may justly wonder what all the fuss is about, especially since the "family portions" are smaller than that phrase implies. Expect comfort food—sweet Italian sausage, and ravioli with ricotta and brown-butter sage sauce. A safe and budget way to go is to try that lemon chicken, which really does live up to the hype, and split one of the "sides" of enormous meatballs (toss in some of the complimentary bread and you've got a meatball sandwich), along with expectation-fulfilling *pot au crème* and gelato. That is, assuming you can get in. Reservations here are at a premium, too!

In Caesars Palace, 3570 Las Vegas Blvd. S. ✆ **877/346-4642.** Reservations recommended. Main courses $18–$40. AE, DC, DISC, MC, V. Daily 5–11pm.

Sensi ★★ ECLECTIC It's usually a truism, as far as restaurants go, "jack of all trades, master of none." Sensi seems to be an exception, given that its menu is made up of Italian (fancy pizzas and pastas), wood-grilled American options (burgers, fish, chicken), and Asian-influenced dishes (and they mean "Pan-Asian," thus tandoori and sushi both). And yet, it does it all very well indeed. Best of all is the Sensi 41, a healthy take on the bento box, featuring such things as miso-glazed Chilean sea bass, some tender sashimi, piquant rice, and, disconcertingly, mozzarella salad. It finishes up with two small, cunning servings of fancy ice cream in wee cones. And do try that homemade ginger ale. A fun menu in a fun-looking space, laid out to surround one very busy and versatile kitchen.

In Bellagio, 3600 Las Vegas Blvd. S. ℂ **702/693-7223.** Main courses $22–$44 dinner. AE, DC, DISC, MC, V. Mon–Thurs 5–9:45pm; Fri–Sat 5–10:15pm.

Moderate

See also the listing for **Spago** (p. 170), an expensive restaurant fronted by a more moderately priced cafe.

BB King's Blues Club ★ BARBECUE As theme restaurants go, you can do a lot worse, especially in Las Vegas where every hotel seems to have at least one. But when the theme is "The Blues" from legendary guitarist King and his contemporaries, and the down-home cooking is a perfect companion, you really should take notice. The menu encompasses a range of deep-South styles including items such as pulled-pork barbecue, po' boys, fried chicken (even on a salad!), chicken and waffles, fried catfish, Delta shrimp, and a host of Cajun and Creole flavors. Everything has a zing or a zest—check out the Cajun carbonara pasta with blackened chicken—but there are a few milder options for those with sensitive palates. The place serves breakfast, lunch, and dinner and has a late-night menu to go with the blues bands that perform nightly.

In The Mirage, 3400 Las Vegas Blvd. S. ℂ **702/242-5464.** www.bbkingclubs.com. Main courses $10–$18 breakfast, $10–$36 lunch and dinner. AE, DC, DISC, MC, V. Sun–Fri 6:30am–2am; Sat 6:30am–3am.

Cabo Wabo Cantina ★ MEXICAN Should you really be taking culinary recommendations from Sammy Hagar? If it's at a place like his Cabo Wabo Cantina, then the answer is a resounding "why not?" Part restaurant and part party pit, this Vegas version of his famous (or is it infamous?) Cabo San Lucas joint definitely tries to bring a spring-break-in-Mexico vibe to the Strip with loud music, bright colors, and a waitstaff that may burst into the Cha Cha Slide at any moment.

😊 **FAMILY-FRIENDLY** restaurants

Buffets Cheap meals for the whole family. The kids can choose what they like, and there are sometimes make-your-own sundae machines. See "Buffets & Sunday Brunches," later in this chapter, for buffet reviews. Those with reduced prices for kids are noted.

Cypress Street Marketplace

(p. 179) Caesars Palace's food court (stylish enough to offer real plates and cloth napkins) offers a range of food (from very good hot dogs to wrap sandwiches to Vietnamese noodles) wide enough to ensure that bottomless-pit teenagers, picky grade schoolers, and

health-conscious parents will all find something that appeals, at affordable prices.

Fellini's (p. 185) With a menu that admittedly veers toward Italian-American rather than authentic food from the motherland, this is all the more appropriate for families, who probably want a good red-sauce pasta dish and some solid pizza rather than anything more elaborate.

Toto's (p. 191) This Mexican restaurant, featuring enormous portions served family style, is a casual place favored by locals.

The drink menu, featuring margaritas made with Hagar's Cabo Wabo Tequila of course, is bigger than the food menu but if you need something to soak up all that alcohol, the Mexican dishes are certainly up to the task. All the basics are covered—tacos, burritos, nachos (including a Cadillac variety where every chip is loaded separately), fajitas, and so forth—and it's all good, though not fantastic. Although if you have enough of the tequila, you'll probably be too busy doing the Cha Cha Slide with the waitresses to care.

In Planet Hollywood, 3663 Las Vegas Blvd. S. ✆ **702/385-2226.** www.cabowabocantinalv.com. Main courses $10–$24. AE, DISC, MC, V. Daily 11am–2am.

Gilley's ★★ BARBECUE When The Frontier closed in 2007, it took the beloved western honky-tonk Gilley's with it and cowboys everywhere had a little less bounce in their two-step. No more mechanical bull? Blasphemy! But their spurs are jangling once again now that the legendary country nightclub and restaurant has made a PBR Cup–worthy return to the Strip (at Treasure Island), and here's the great news: You don't have to be a cowboy to love this place. Located along the sidewalk with great people-watching and pirate-battle views, this bright and airy space is done like a roadhouse saloon, all rustic wood and metal, with two big bars. And, yes, the bull is back! His name is TIten (TI—Treasure Island—see what they did there?) and if you want to work off your lunch, you can ride him for $5 a pop. And you may just need to do that with the massive portions of down-home country cooking served here. Do not miss the award-winning pork-green chili, which is not green at all but filled with succulent, melt-in-your-mouth hunks of pork and not-too-spicy hatch and poblano chiles. The burgers are roughly the size of your head, made of deliciously smoky certified Black Angus beef and just waiting for one of the custom barbecue sauces (the roasted onion is our personal favorite). The pulled pork is as barbecue perfect as you're going to find west of the Mississippi and the rest of the menu is waistline expanding with hot links, fried chicken, chicken-fried steak, ribs, and more—most of it served with two sides, including such favorites as molasses baked beans, white cheddar and green chili grits, and corn on the cob It's all moderately priced, which is not to say exactly cheap ($14 for a burger!), but the combination of tasty food, friendly service, and a great location make it worth putting on your ten gallon and moseying on down.

At Treasure Island, 3300 Las Vegas Blvd. S. ✆ 702/894-7111. www.gilleyslasvegas.com. Main courses $13–$34. AE, DISC, MC, V. Daily 11am–10pm.

Hash House a Go Go ★★ AMERICAN Back when this place was located on the west side of town, we told you to go but we understood if it was too far to drive or cab. Now that there's a second, just as good location at the Imperial Palace on the Strip, you only have yourself to blame! Yes, you could go to a breakfast buffet and pay $15 for scrambled eggs warmed under a heat lamp but why not experience the "Twisted Farm Food" here instead? The brainchild of a couple of Midwest natives, breakfast (and dinner) go beyond the typical into realms of the almost unimaginable. Pancakes (traditional buttermilk to coconut mango) are the size of large pizzas, and waffles the size of checkerboards (and some come with bacon baked right inside). The signature hashes come in varieties from corned beef to meatloaf, and "scrambles" throw everything but the kitchen sink into a frying pan and serve it hot to your table that way. Been out partying too late? Try the O'Hare of the Dog special, a 24-ounce Budweiser served in a paper bag with a side of bacon.

Lunch and dinner add salads, sandwiches, burgers, fried chicken, potpie, and more, all with the same fun sensibility and a farm-fresh flavor that you can practically taste before you put it in your mouth. But it's breakfast that we dream about as we write this. *Note:* Another location is at 6800 W. Sahara Ave.

In Imperial Palace, 3535 Las Vegas Blvd. S. © **702/731-3311.** www.hashhouseagogo.com. Main courses $10–$24. AE, DC, DISC, MC, V. Sun–Thurs 7am–11pm; Fri–Sat 7am–2am.

Isla ★★ MEXICAN We tend to get a little snobby about Mexican restaurants, particularly those in casinos, because so often they seem careless. But you really should try this establishment specializing in "modern Mexican cuisine." This means dishes both traditional and with potentially dangerous twists; but because the place starts with handmade tortillas and heads right to guacamole made on demand, it's all trustworthy, even if some of that guac contains lobster and passion fruit (it's a sweet and curious take on tradition). Roast pork *pipián* with tamarind marinade and pumpkin-seed sauce is a lovely dish, as are the needlessly fried (though pleasantly crunchy) beef empanadas with dried cherries and chipotle tomato sauce—a mix of sweet and spiced. For the more timid, there is a nice assortment of particularly good tacos and burritos. There is also a charming dessert menu that includes a chocolate cactus stuck into a fudge hill and caramel cupcakes. The collection of 118 brands of tequila and a slightly modern nightclub interior remind you that dining in Vegas usually involves a gimmick.

In Treasure Island, 3300 Las Vegas Blvd. S. © **866/286-3809** or 702/894-7223. Main courses $10–$30. AE, DC, DISC, MC, V. Daily 4–10pm.

Lagasse's Stadium ★ AMERICAN This is what you get when you mix Emeril Lagasse's cooking with sports of every conceivable variety. Whether it's a good thing probably depends on which of those ingredients you care more about. Emeril fans will find a mix of some of his trademark New Orleans–style dishes (crab cakes, muffaletta pasta, Creole boiled shrimp) but mostly it's fairly standard pub grub: soups, salads, pizza, burgers, sandwiches, barbecue, and the like. While everything we sampled was certainly good, it may be disappointing to those looking for a true Lagasse experience. Sports fans will find more than 100 HDTVs showing everything from the NFL to girls' high school basketball and just about all of it can be bet on at the sports book conveniently located in the main dining room. They'll probably love it and not care a whit about the chef that designed the menu. Prices are affordable until you get to the table minimums ($25–$50 per person, depending on if you choose a table on the main floor, the upper mezzanine, or the big comfy couches in a stadium-like setting), and it's worth noting that sports fans and the games they watch are not terribly conducive to a quiet dining experience.

In Palazzo Las Vegas, 3325 Las Vegas Blvd. S. © **702/607-2665.** www.emerils.com. Reservations recommended. Main courses $12–$29. AE, DC, DISC, MC, V. Mon–Fri 11am–10pm; Sat 7:30am–10pm; Sun 8am–10pm.

Mon Ami Gabi ★★ BISTRO This charming bistro is one of our favorite local restaurants. It has it all: a delightful setting, better-than-average food, and affordable prices. Sure, it goes overboard in trying to replicate a classic Parisian bistro, but the results are less cheesy than most Vegas attempts at atmosphere, and the patio seating on the Strip (no reservations taken there—first-come, first-served, but a recent addition of 70 more seats probably helps matters) actually makes you feel like you're in a real, not a pre-fab, city. You can be budget-conscious and order just the very fine onion soup, or you can eat like a real French person and order classic steak (the filet mignon is probably the best cut, if not the cheapest) and *pommes frites* (french fries). There are plenty of less-expensive options (which is why we listed this place in the "Moderate" category, by the way). Yes, they have snails, and we loved 'em. Desserts, by the way, are massive and should be shared (another way to save). The baseball-size profiteroles (three or four to an order) filled with fine vanilla ice cream and the football-size bananas-Foster crepe are particularly recommended. And ooh-la-la—there is breakfast now. Omelet anyone?

In Paris Las Vegas, 3655 Las Vegas Blvd. S. ℂ **702/944-4224.** www.monamigabi.com. Reservations recommended. Main courses $18–$40. AE, DC, DISC, MC, V. Sun–Fri 7am–11pm; Sat 7am–midnight.

Payard Patisserie & Bistro ★★★ BISTRO Breakfast here offers one of the few real remaining bargains in Vegas, given quality-to-price ratio. Surely it can't last, considering the state of things in modern-day Vegas, but for now you can look forward to a continental breakfast like no other. Just $16 gets you cereals, fruits, yogurts, lox and bagels, and, most significantly, all the breakfast pastries you can eat. Because the chef has his roots in Paris, these buttery bits of brioche and croissant are as good as any you could consume by the Seine. One can easily spend that much on a breakfast buffet or a lunch entree elsewhere in town, but there is no comparison for quality. Lunch is light and of the French variety, while evening brings dessert tastings of inspired flights of sugary whimsy. Both are of particularly high quality and worth investigating, but it's the breakfast that has already earned the strong reputation.

In Caesars Palace, 3570 Las Vegas Blvd. S. ℂ **702/731-7110.** Breakfast $16; lunch main courses $16–$26. Daily 6:30–11:30am breakfast, 11am–2:30pm lunch. Pastry counter daily 6am–11pm.

Serendipity 3 ★ AMERICAN Yes, it has the famous foot-long hot dogs from the New York City original along with a full menu of quite good cafe food (including some very well-made hamburgers on freshly baked spiral buns), but it's really the frozen hot chocolate and other signature desserts that are bringing you here, right? That frozen hot chocolate, so beloved by generations of New Yorkers and tourists alike, is served in a giant overflowing glass with two straws. If that's not decadent enough for your sensibilities, perhaps you want to go for the Treasure Chest, made of chocolate and filled with cookies, cakes, ice cream, and more. It's $77, but it serves four! Still not hitting the over-the-top mark for you? How about the Golden Opulence dessert, recognized as the most expensive in the country? A cool $1,000 will get you a sundae made from rare ice creams and chocolate and topped with edible gold leaf. What else are you going to do with that slot-machine jackpot?

In Caesars Palace, 3570 Las Vegas Blvd. S. ℂ **877/346-4642.** www.caesarspalace.com. Reservations not accepted. Main courses $10–$20; desserts $10–$1,000. AE, DISC, MC, V. Mon–Thurs 7am–10:30am and 11am–11pm; Fri 7am–10:30am and 11am–midnight; Sat 7am–midnight; Sun 7am–11pm.

Table 10 ★★ AMERICAN Not a copy of another holding in the Emeril empire (as are the excellent Delmonico and the hit-and-miss Emeril's Seafood) but a new endeavor with its own personality—albeit one that clearly benefits from its Emeril origins. Named after a special seating spot in Emeril's flagship New

Orleans restaurant, this locale hits a high note with the food on a level with that standout eatery. While not cheap, meals here come off as a bargain in comparison to comparable fine-dining options in town. (As is often the case, you may want to consider dropping by for an even more affordable lunch.) Look for appetizers such as oyster fritters with Rockefeller sauce and bibb salad with housemade bacon, entrees such as tender roasted lamb with black truffle reduction, and sides that include a sumptuous lobster macaroni and cheese. Desserts are clever, while standout is the *malasada*, deep-fried dough balls filled with white chocolate.

In The Palazzo, 3328 Las Vegas Blvd. S. ℂ **702/607-6363.** www.emerils.com. Reservations recommended. Main courses $11–$29 lunch, $25–$38 dinner. AE, MC, V. Sun–Thurs 11am–10pm; Fri–Sat 11am–11pm.

Inexpensive

Cypress Street Marketplace ★★ ☺ FOOD COURT Often when we go to a Vegas buffet (and we are not alone in this), we sigh over all the choices, all those different kinds of pretty good, if not better, cuisines there for the taking, but, of course, we can't possibly try everything. And yet, in some of the higher-priced venues, we are charged as if we can. Here, in this modern version of the classic food court, it's sort of like being at a well-stocked buffet: There's darn fine barbecue (including North Carolina–influenced pulled pork), wrap sandwiches (grilled shrimp, for one example), Asian (including pot stickers and Vietnamese noodles), decent New York pizza, plump Chicago hot dogs, peel-and-eat shrimp and lobster chowder, a bargain-priced salad bar, plus pastries and even wine. And with the range of food, an entire family with very different tastes will all find something satisfactory.

In Caesars Palace, 3570 Las Vegas Blvd. S. ℂ **702/731-7110.** Most items under $15. AE, MC, V. Daily 11am–11pm.

Earl of Sandwich ★★★ SANDWICHES It seems credulity straining, but the sandwich was something that had to be invented, and thus someone got their simple yet ingenious idea named after them. At least, so the story goes, so sufficiently accepted as historical lore that it carries enough weight for the intrepid inventor's descendent, the 11th earl of Sandwich, to lend his name to a chain of sandwich shops. It's a gimmick, but a good one, and so is the food. The eponymous, and largely excellent, sandwiches are served warm (wraps are cold) on bread made for the shop and include varieties such as grilled Swiss, bleu and brie with applewood-smoked bacon, and roast beef with horseradish cream and cheddar cheese. There are also complex if unoriginal salads, smoothies, and breakfast sandwiches. Portions aren't huge, but it's not a problem if you are devoted to Vegas-size meals; the low prices make it possible to order two of everything if appetites demand.

In Planet Hollywood, 3667 Las Vegas Blvd. S. ℂ **702/463-0259.** www.earlofsandwichusa.com. All items under $6. AE, MC, V. Sun–Thurs 6am–midnight; Fri–Sat 6am–2am.

Pink's ★★★ DELI The hot dogs served by Pink's are legendary in Los Angeles, almost mythic in fact. In business at the same location for more than 70 years, the little shack draws hordes, with lines down the block turning peak dining times into waits of more than an hour. Why? Well, the all-beef dogs, cooked to "snapping" perfection, are certainly good, but it's the toppings that make it different: Chili, bacon, guacamole, mushroom and Swiss, sauerkraut, pastrami, nacho cheese—you name it and they probably put it on the bun. This Vegas location at Planet Hollywood is Pink's second full outlet and while the lines aren't as crazy, the dogs are just as good. All the traditional versions are on the menu—the bacon chili cheese, piled high with tomatoes and onions, is virtually impossible to pick up and a favorite of ours—but they also throw in some Vegas-only options like The Showgirl (relish, onions, bacon, tomato, sauerkraut, and sour cream), The Vegas Strip (two dogs in one bun with guacamole and jalapeños), and the Planet Hollywood (a Polish with grilled onions and mushrooms, bacon, and cheese). There are also burgers, burritos, and some nonbeef varieties, but that's just background noise as far as we are concerned. Nothing on the menu is over $9, which only adds to the allure.

At Planet Hollywood, 3663 Las Vegas Blvd. S. ✆ **702/785-5555.** www.pinkslv.com. Main courses $5–$9. AE, MC, V. Sun–Thurs 10:30am–midnight; Fri–Sat 10:30am–3am.

NORTH STRIP
Very Expensive

Alex ★★★ CONTINENTAL Alex Stratta (possibly familiar to you from his stint on the American television show *Iron Chef*) followed his boss Steve Wynn from The Mirage, closing his Renoir venue to open this eponymous one instead. A dramatic room, all swooping drapes and inlaid wood, it's about two fussy steps away from true elegance but still a place where grown-ups come to dine, while appreciating the venture as an "occasion." Stratta comes from a cosmopolitan and international background; add to that some years working under Alain Ducasse and a general sense of food as pleasure and art, and you have one of the most special dining experiences in Vegas. The menu changes regularly—Chef Alex is as exacting as a chef should be, and so the readiness of seasonal ingredients

---

Deli Delights

It's East Coast vs. West Coast in the battle of the famous delis, here in sister properties The Mirage and Treasure Island. The former has brought in New York's beloved **Carnegie Deli** ★★ (✆ 702/791-7310; daily 24 hr.), home of the towering sandwich, so large that no mere mortal can clamp his or her jaws around it. It's hardly the same joint New Yorkers are used to, given that this sleek and modern interpretation is crammed into a small corner of a casino. Bad puns still run amok on the menu (Tongues for the Memory, Nova on a Sunday, and The Egg and Oy!). We aren't happy that the famously huge sandwiches come with huge prices to match, along with a miserly $3 sharing fee. Treasure Island is home to the first offshoot of Los Angeles's **Canter's Deli** ★★ (✆ 702/894-7111; daily 11am–midnight), where many a musician has whiled away many an hour. As much as we admit that NYC is right to claim it has superior bagels, and the Carnegie definitely has better hours, the Canter's smells just like the one we spent much pleasurable time in during our formative years. Ah, just go do some pastrami taste-testing yourselves, youse.

dictates any particular evening's selection. If in Europe, the result would almost certainly earn a Michelin star.

Diners have their choice of two set tasting menus or a prix-fixe choice of appetizer, main course, and dessert. Expect starters such as carpaccio of Santa Barbara prawn topped with osetra caviar, or roasted scallop with basil purée, and don't neglect to ponder touches such as tiny vegetables ever so lightly cooked, the whole topped by translucent fried zucchini flower. Porcini gnocchi dissolves in the mouth, a terrine of foie gras is paired with the chef's interpretation of Waldorf salad, a main course of squab and sautéed foie gras, rhubarb, and spiced pineapple is deep, rich, and bold. Even the palate cleansers are serious, such as apricot gelée topped with coconut granita ringed by passion fruit, or strawberry gelée with lemongrass crème fraîche. As for wine, Master Sommelier Paolo Barbieri's thoughtful list includes over 1,000 labels, many of them French, with some 200 burgundies alone. Those on a budget should fear not, as the list includes such innovative treats as a "splash" of Chateau d'Yquem, which is plenty to accompany a foie gras starter and quite affordable. Desserts are of such gorgeous complexity that we cannot describe them adequately, but know that the construction is not served to the sacrifice of taste. You are in a master chef's hands; enjoy it.

In Wynn Las Vegas, 3131 Las Vegas Blvd. S. (© **888/352-3463** or 702/248-3463. Reservations strongly recommended. Jacket recommended. 3-course prix-fixe menu $125; 7-course tasting menu $195. AE, DC, DISC, MC, V. Wed–Sat 6–10pm.

Bartolotta Ristorante di Mare ★★★ ITALIAN/SEAFOOD This is the restaurant we are currently most likely to tout in Vegas. James Beard Foundation Award–winning chef Paul Bartolotta trained in Italy under master chefs before opening his highly acclaimed Spiaggia in Chicago. Now he's here, in this eponymous (and 2006 Best New Restaurant Beard finalist) kitchen, yet more proof that celebrity chefs are all very well and good, but it's not the same as having them on the premises. In this case, the result is as authentic Italian food as one can find outside Italy. Determined to produce just that, Bartolotta went to his boss, Steve Wynn, and insisted that his fish not just be ultrafresh but also be flown daily straight from the Mediterranean to his Vegas kitchen. Choices may include new-to-you (they were to us) possibilities such as orata and purple snapper, each topped with sweet Pachino tomatoes, arugula, garlic, and red onion.

Pastas are perfect, especially the delicate sheep's milk ricotta handkerchief-style ravioli, made both sweet and savory with a veal Marsala wine-reduction glaze. *Spaghetti allo Scoglio* comes with large chunks of lobster. Langoustines are grilled to charred smoky rightness, and seared scallops with porcini mushrooms in browned butter are what scallops should be.

Meanwhile, Sommelier Claudio Vilani, who honed his skills in his native Italy, created and oversees the (almost) all-Italian wine list. Leave yourself in his capable hands, as he pairs a regionally appropriate wine with the seafood cuisine. The space itself is perhaps the nicest in the hotel, a multilevel construction that gives a cafe feeling on the top level, a more elegant dining area down below (accessed by a dramatic curving, sweeping stairway), and, best of all, outdoor cabana seating by a small pond filled with reflecting balls, so fine for a long (as the Italians like to do it), sultry evening meal.

In Wynn Las Vegas, 3131 Las Vegas Blvd. S. (© **888/352-3463** or 702/248-3463. Reservations recommended. Main courses $20–$58. AE, DC, DISC, MC, V. Daily 5:30–10pm.

Daniel Boulud Brasserie ★ BISTRO Boulud is best known as the man who gave New York City the $29 hamburger (filled with foie gras, short rib meat, and truffles). This is classic French bistro food, and while Boulud himself is not in the house, he does have a superb French chef running the show, and he does it very well. Still, you can always tell when someone is cooking off another master chef's menu, as opposed to working their own magic.

The cuisine here is lovely; look at the beautifully composed salads, as roasted beets are laid out in precise order with endive and bleu cheese, or the stunning *tartine du tomato,* a whole reconstructed roasted tomato layered on goat cheese and puff pastry. The *foie gras chaud* is two fat lobes of liver on grilled pineapple, topped with a nearly see-through-thin pineapple chip. Lean toward the slow-cooked dishes, such as braised short ribs Bourguignon with *pomme mousseline* and spring ramps—earthy and hearty. Save some room for a cheese plate, and go through the evening's artisanal selections with your server. This restaurant is one of only two that allows viewing of the *Lake of Dreams* show at night. A way to get around some of the high-end price is to work with the appetizers—cheese and charcuterie (try the duck confit terrine) are filling—because the entree is a little too small to split.

In Wynn Las Vegas, 3131 Las Vegas Blvd. S. ℂ **888/352-3463** or 702/248-3463. Reservations recommended. Main courses $26–$44. AE, DC, DISC, MC, V. Daily 5:30–10pm.

Sinatra ★★★ ITALIAN Old Blue Eyes is the theme here, with memorabilia (including an Oscar and a Grammy), giant pictures of Frank, and even a few of his favorite menu items (*Ossobuco Milanese,* clams *Possilipo*) to choose from. But this swank restaurant is so much more than its gimmick. The dining room is one of the most gorgeous in town, with giant windows facing a garden patio and plush, eclectic, vaguely retro furnishings encouraging the kind of laid-back dining experience that is rare in this rush-to-get-the-check town. Chef Theo Schoenegger was born and raised in Italy, gaining fame in the U.S. during his stint as the executive chef at Los Angeles–based Patina, and his short but satisfying selection of northern Italian dishes is bursting with fresh flavors. Start with the prosciutto appetizer, almost sweet with a fire-roasted pepper accompaniment, then move on to the *agnolotti,* a handmade ravioli pasta stuffed with ricotta cheese and drenched in a buttery asparagus sauce. Or go crazy with the lasagna made with beef, veal, and pork. Seafood and meat options include Maine lobster and a delicious, herb-crusted rack of lamb served with a pepper stuffed with ratatouille. Desserts are equally satisfying as is the exceptional cocktail and wine list. Allow the expert sommelier to pair the perfect glass of vino with whatever you are having.

In Encore Las Vegas, 3121 Las Vegas Blvd. S. ℂ **702/248-3463.** www.encorelasvegas.com. Reservations required. Main courses $22–$49. AE, DISC, MC, V. Daily 5:30–10pm.

Switch ★ FRENCH/STEAK What will probably lure most people into this restaurant is the gimmick. Every 20 minutes or so the room literally switches (Get it?), with the exterior walls rolling up or down, the interior walls rotating, and the lighting and music morphing along with them. You may be enjoying your appetizer in the orange-hued glow of a countryside inn with bold floral paintings, French doors, and soft music, while your main course comes in the soft-white lighting of an estate, with stone walls and shelves of colorful bottles. As gimmicks go, it's a very effective one, turning the experience of dining into something like a ride at Disneyland.

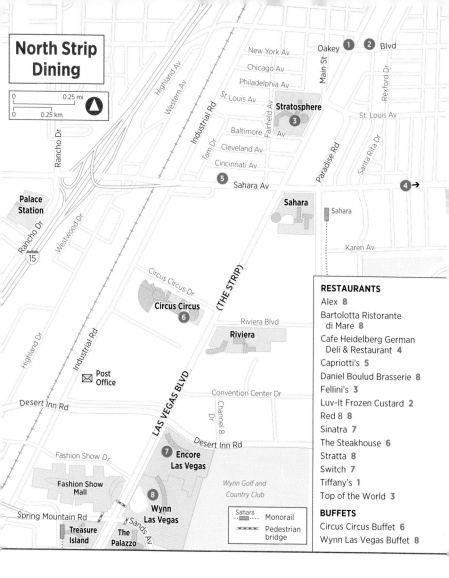

North Strip Dining

0   0.25 mi
0   0.25 km

RESTAURANTS

Alex **8**

Bartolotta Ristorante di Mare **8**

Cafe Heidelberg German Deli & Restaurant **4**

Capriotti's **5**

Daniel Boulud Brasserie **8**

Fellini's **3**

Luv-It Frozen Custard **2**

Red 8 **8**

Sinatra **7**

The Steakhouse **6**

Stratta **8**

Switch **7**

Tiffany's **1**

Top of the World **3**

BUFFETS

Circus Circus Buffet **6**

Wynn Las Vegas Buffet **8**

Sahara ▬▬ Monorail
▬▬ Pedestrian bridge

But it would all be for naught if the food didn't measure up to the experience. Luckily Chef Marc Poidevin's French-inspired menu is up to the challenge. French is more of a thought here than a theme. While you will find Burgundy snails in a garlic parsley butter and braised rabbit fricassee, most of the dishes are more steakhouse traditional with hints of Gallic influence. You can get your steak in a variety of cuts with a variety of sauces but follow our lead and get the side of grilled onions and jalapeños to really liven up your choice. A full wine list with a very knowledgeable sommelier completes the package.

In Encore Las Vegas, 3121 Las Vegas Blvd. S. ✆ **702/248-3463.** Reservations recommended. Main courses $22–$61. AE, DC, DISC, MC, V. Daily 5:30–10pm.

Expensive

The Steakhouse ★ STEAK Most of the steakhouses in Las Vegas have fallen prey to modernization, adding faux-elegant lounge-worthy design schemes, fancy extraneous dishes, cocktail menus, and prices that push into the stratosphere. What happened to the traditional meat and potatoes steakhouse? It's right here, my friends. In business for more than 2 decades, The Steakhouse at Circus Circus does things the old-fashioned way, with a dark cigar club–style design (think high-backed booths and faux animal heads on the wall), familial but professional service, classic cuts cooked over a wood flame, and prices that won't make you dip into your gambling budget. Regarding the latter, it may seem like $50 is not exactly cheap, but unlike most Strip steakhouses, the price is inclusive of soup or salad and a side dish, things that will cost you extra just about everywhere else. It's a retro delight in a town that currently seems ruthless about weeding out same.

In Circus Circus, 2880 Las Vegas Blvd. S. ✆ **702/794-3767.** Reservations recommended. Main courses $40–$50. AE, DC, DISC, MC, V. Daily 5–10pm.

Stratta ★★ ITALIAN If the creations from Chef Alex Stratta, at the restaurant that carries his first name, are a little too far out of your budget, try the more casual restaurant that carries his last name. Acting almost as a dress rehearsal space for the main event, Stratta has everything to love about its fancier brother, with a much more affordable bill at the end.

We didn't want to like Stratta, taking over the space of our much-beloved Corsa Cucina as it did, but we were immediately won over by the low-key, loungelike atmosphere, the convivial service, and the casual vibe that seems to encourage sitting and relaxing despite the fact that two of the four walls are open to the casino, thereby putting you under the microscope of gawking tourists.

What you will be eating is a simple yet effective menu of Italian- and Mediterranean-inspired dishes, starting with a basket of warm ciabatta bread and homemade pesto, and then graduating to bruschetta, beef carpaccio, and delicate prosciutto. Main courses include wood-fired pizzas, a variety of pastas, *osso buco*, veal Marsala, lasagna, and various cuts of meat and seafood. Check to see if the potato gnocchi is available as a starter; Chef won't put it on the menu unless the potatoes are perfect, and the results are creamy and delicately spiced. Pork chop fans would be remiss in not trying the superior thick cut stuffed with cheese and prosciutto. Yes, that's pork stuffed with pork. You got a problem with that?

In Wynn Las Vegas, 3131 Las Vegas Blvd. S. ✆ **702/770-3463.** Reservations strongly recommended. Main courses $24–$45. AE, DC, DISC, MC, V. Daily 5:30–10:30pm.

Moderate

Cafe Heidelberg German Deli & Restaurant ★ GERMAN Configured to look like a beer garden, this German cafe brings in locals and homesick Bavarians alike. It's a small, not typically Vegas place, and because it's close enough to the Strip, it's a good place for refuge, though it could be crowded when you go. The food is better than fine, though certainly not light fare, by any means. Recommended is the sausage sampler platter, so you can finally learn the difference between knockwurst and bratwurst, with sides such as potato pancakes, dumplings, excellent potato salad (choice of German or American style) and the like. Lunch brings sandwiches, such as perfect schnitzel, with the pork loin twice the size of the roll. Wash it down with an imported beer. There is live entertainment on the weekends in the early evening. This is also a full-service deli and German market, so it's a good place to pick up a picnic for sightseeing outside the city. On Sunday, dinner is served all day.

604 E. Sahara Ave. (at 6th St.). © **702/731-5310.** Reservations strongly recommended Fri-Sat nights. Main courses mostly under $13 lunch, $20–$26 dinner. AE, DC, DISC, MC, V. Daily 11am–8pm.

Fellini's ★ ☺ ITALIAN A Vegas institution (in its original, now-closed West Las Vegas location), much beloved by in-the-know locals, Fellini's is a classic Italian restaurant—you know, gloopy red sauce, garlicky cheesy bread—which isn't meant to be an insult at all. It might not be ambitious, but it is reliable and more than satisfying. Fellini's does a strong version of pasta (rigatoni, in this case) *amatriciana,* and they are generous with the pancetta. And while some Italian food purists would shudder at the gnocchi with tenderloin tips, topped with Gorgonzola and shallot cream sauce, they are just missing out, that's all. The well-proportioned menu offers a variety of options from *osso buco* to basic pizza, and, given the prices, that makes it a good option for families with a similar range of tastes and needs.

In Stratosphere Hotel & Casino, 2000 Las Vegas Blvd S. © **702/383-4859.** www.fellinislv.com. Main courses $11–$27. AE, DISC, MC, V. Mon–Thurs 5–11pm; Fri–Sat 5pm–midnight.

Red 8 ★★ ASIAN Such a relief, in the otherwise pricey Wynn, to find a dining spot that is both good and affordable. This visual standout is a small cafe—as you wander by, you think "Cool! Some of the tables overlook the casino!" Then you realize those are *all* of the tables—with a decor that screams the place's colorful name. It's probably going to be popular, given the location, size, and pricing—not to mention the quality of the food. Covering a sort of Pan-Asiatic (Southeast Asia, anyway) terrain, look for noodle dishes both wet (soup) and dry (pan-fried), rice (including porridge), dim sum, Korean barbecue, Mongolian beef, vegetarian options, and more. There are some "market price" specials that can quadruple a bill pretty fast, but otherwise, this is a pretty budget-friendly option.

In Wynn Las Vegas, 3131 Las Vegas Blvd. S. © **702/770-3380.** No reservations required. Main courses $12–$28. AE, DISC, MC, V. Sun–Thurs 11:30am–10:45pm; Fri–Sat 11:30am–12:45am.

Inexpensive

Capriotti's ★★★ 🏷 DELI It looks like a dump, but Capriotti's is one of the great deals in town, for quality and price. It roasts its own beef and turkey on the premises and stuffs them (or Italian cold cuts, or whatever) into sandwiches mislabeled "small," "medium," and "large"—the last clocks in at 20 inches, easily feeding two for under $10 total. And deliciously so. The Bobby (turkey, dressing, and cranberry sauce, like Thanksgiving dinner in sandwich form) would be our favorite sandwich in the world had we not tried the Slaw B Joe: roast beef, coleslaw, and Russian dressing. But other combos, such as the aforementioned Italian cold cuts, have their fans, too, and Capriotti's even has veggie varieties. There are outlets throughout the city, but this one is not only right off the Strip but also right by the freeway. We never leave town without a stop here, and you shouldn't either.

322 W. Sahara Ave. (at Las Vegas Blvd. S.). © **702/474-0229.** www.capriottis.com. Most sandwiches under $10. AE, MC, V. Mon–Sat 10am–8pm; Sun 11am–7pm.

Tiffany's ★★ 🍴 DINER Why bother with theme restaurants that pretend to be cheap diners when the real thing is just past the end of the Strip? This decidedly unflashy soda fountain/lunch counter was Las Vegas's first 24-hour restaurant, and it has been going strong for 60 years. Plunk down at the counter and watch the cooks go nuts trying to keep up with the orders. The menu is basic comfort food: standard items (meatloaf, ground round steak, chops, and so on), fluffy cream pies, and classic breakfasts served anytime—try the biscuits and cream gravy at 3am. But the best bet is a one-third-pound burger and "thick, creamy shake," both about as good as they get. At around $6, this is half what you would pay for a comparable meal at the Hard Rock Cafe. Places like this are a vanishing species—it's worth the short walk from the Stratosphere. Note, however, that the neighborhood remains stubbornly rough in appearance, and that can be a turnoff. Stay alert if you come here at night.

1700 Las Vegas Blvd. S. (at East Oakey Blvd.). © **702/444-4459.** Reservations not accepted. Most items under $8. No credit cards. Daily 24 hr.

EAST OF THE STRIP

In this section, we cover restaurants close to the Convention Center, along with those farther south on Paradise Road, Flamingo Road, and Tropicana Avenue.

Very Expensive

Lawry's The Prime Rib ★★★ STEAK/SEAFOOD Lawry's first opened in Los Angeles in 1938 and remains a popular tradition. Over the years, it has added three branches; the most recent landed in Las Vegas in 1997. Yes, you can get prime rib all over town for about $5. But, to mix a food metaphor, that's a tuna sandwich when you can have caviar at Lawry's.

Eating at Lawry's is a ceremony, with all the parts played the same way for the past 60 years. Waitresses in brown-and-white English-maid uniforms, complete with starched white cap, take your order—for side dishes, that is. The real decision, what cut of rib you are going to have, comes later. Actually, that's the only part of the tradition that has changed. Originally, all Lawry's offered was prime rib, which they did perfectly and with tremendous style. Now they have added fresh fish (halibut, salmon, or swordfish, depending on the evening) to the menu. Anyway, you tell the waitress what side dishes you might want (sublime creamed spinach, baked potato, and so on) for an extra price. Later, she returns with a spinning salad bowl. The bowl, resting on crushed ice, spins as she pours Lawry's special dressing in a stream from high over her head. Tomatoes garnish. Applause follows. Eventually, giant metal carving carts come to your table, bearing the meat. You name your cut (the regular Lawry's, the extra-large Diamond Jim Brady for serious carnivores, and the thin English cut) and specify how you'd like it cooked. It comes with terrific Yorkshire pudding, nicely browned and not soggy, and some creamed horseradish that is combined with fluffy whipped cream, simultaneously sweet and tart. Flavorful, tender, perfectly cooked, and lightly seasoned, this will be the best prime rib you will ever have.

4043 Howard Hughes Pkwy. (at Flamingo Rd., btw. Paradise Rd. and Koval Lane). © **702/893-2223.** www.lawrysonline.com. Reservations recommended. Main courses $32–$49. AE, DC, DISC, MC, V. Mon–Thurs 11:30am–2:30pm and 5–10pm; Fri 11:30am–2:30pm and 5–10:30pm; Sat 5–10:30pm; Sun 5–10pm.

Morton's Steakhouse ★ STEAK/SEAFOOD A venerable steakhouse with branches throughout the U.S.—in fact, Mr. Morton is the proud papa of Peter Morton, formerly of the Hard Rock Hotel over yonder. Like the **Palms** (p. 169), this place serves really good steaks, and we are not prepared to say which (The Palm or Morton's) has the better hunk o' red meat because, frankly, after a while, these subtle distinctions elude us. Anyway, this approximates an old-time Vegas hangout (most actual old-time Vegas hangouts have closed), even in its off-Strip location. In addition to your cut of beef, suggested sides include flavorfully fresh al dente asparagus served with hollandaise or hash browns. It's a good place to hang around postdinner, drink Scotch, and smoke.

400 E. Flamingo Rd. (at Paradise Rd.). ✆ **702/893-0703.** www.mortons.com. Reservations recommended. Main courses $28–$52. AE, DC, MC, V. Mon–Thurs 5–11pm; Fri–Sat 4–11pm; Sun 5–10pm.

Pamplemousse ★ FRENCH A little bit off the beaten path, Pamplemousse is a long-established Vegas restaurant that shouldn't be overlooked in the crush of new high-profile eateries. Evoking a cozy French-countryside inn (at least, on the interior), it's a catacomb of low-ceilinged rooms and intimate dining nooks with rough-hewn beams. It's all very charming and un-Vegasy. There's additional seating in a small garden sheltered by a striped tent. The restaurant's name, which means "grapefruit" in French, was suggested by the late singer Bobby Darin, one of the many celebrity pals of owner Georges La Forge.

Your waiter recites the menu, which changes nightly. The meal always begins with a large complimentary basket of crudités (about 10 different crisp, fresh vegetables), a big bowl of olives, and, in a nice country touch, a basket of hard-boiled eggs. Recent menu offerings have included out-of-this-world soups (French onion and cream of asparagus, to name a couple) and appetizers such as shrimp in cognac cream sauce, and Maryland crab cakes with macadamia nut crust. Recommended entrees include a sterling veal with mushrooms and Dijon sauce and an even-better rack of lamb with pistachio nut crust and rosemary cream sauce (all sauces, by the way, are made with whatever the chef has on hand that evening in the kitchen). Leave room for the fabulous desserts, such as homemade ice cream in a hard chocolate shell.

400 E. Sahara Ave. (btw. Santa Paula and Santa Rita drives, just east of Paradise Rd.). ✆ **702/733-2066.** www.pamplemousserestaurant.com. Reservations required. Main courses $12–$21 lunch, $27–$58 dinner. AE, DC, DISC, MC, V. Tues–Sun 5:30–10pm.

Moderate

Carluccio's Tivoli Gardens ★★ 🏚 ITALIAN A bit of a drive, but well worth it for those seeking an authentic Vegas experience. This joint used to be owned by none other than the Rhinestone King himself, Liberace. It was formerly Liberace's Tivoli Gardens, and he designed the interior himself, so you can guess what that looks like (it was reopened a few years after his death, and the owners kept the decor pretty much intact). This kind of history is more and more rare in this town with no memory, plus it's right next door to the Liberace Museum, so go pay your giggling respects in the late afternoon and then stop here for dinner. Expect traditional Italian food (pasta, pasta, pasta, and scampi), but done very, very well.

1775 E. Tropicana Blvd. (at Spencer St.). ✆ **702/795-3236.** Main courses $10–$18. AE, DC, DISC, MC, V. Tues–Sun 4:30–10pm.

Dining & Nightlife East of the Strip

| 0 | | 0.5 mi |
| 0 | 0.5 km | |

RESTAURANTS
Bougainvillea **10**
Carluccio's Tivoli
  Gardens **18**
Einstein Bros. Bagels **16**
Freed's Bakery **22**
Jason's Deli **6**
Komol **2**
Lawry's The Prime Rib **8**

Lotus of Siam **2**
Memphis Championship
  Barbecue **19**
Morton's Steakhouse **9**
Pamplemousse **1**
Paymon's Mediterranean
  Café and Lounge **7**
Pink Taco **11**
Toto's **20**

BUFFETS
The Buffet at the
  Las Vegas Hilton **3**

NIGHTLIFE
The Buffalo **15**
Champagne's Café **4**
Dispensary Lounge **21**
Double Down Saloon **15**
Free Zone **14**

Funhog Ranch **5**
Gipsy **12**
Good Times **17**
Piranha Las Vegas **13**
Vanity **11**

Memphis Championship Barbecue ★★ BARBECUE We simply refuse to get into the debate about Texas vs. Kansas City vs. Mississippi barbecue (and if you've got another place with the best dang barbecue, we really don't want to hear about it). But we can say that if you aren't physically in those places, you gotta take what you can get—and luckily for Vegas visitors, eating at Memphis Championship Barbecue is hardly settling. Its vinegar-based sauce is sweet but has a kick. Food is cooked over mesquite applewood, and the meat falls off the bone just the way you want it to. It offers hot links, baked beans, everything you would want and hope for. Standouts include a pulled-barbecue-chicken sandwich, onion straws, and delicious mac and cheese. *Note this special:* A $70 feast includes a rack of St. Louis ribs, a half-pound of pork, a half-pound of beef brisket, a half-pound of hot links, a whole chicken, baked beans, coleslaw, rolls, cream corn, and fries. It feeds four; we think even if two of those four are teenage boys, you might have leftovers.

2250 E. Warm Springs Rd. (near I-215). ✆ **702/260-6909.** www.memphis-bbq.com. Main courses $10–$20; special barbecue dinner for 4 $70. AE, MC, V. Mon–Fri 11am–10pm; Sat–Sun 8am–10pm.

Inexpensive

Bougainvillea ★★ 🍴 DINER Oh, how we love a Vegas coffee shop. You've got your all-day breakfasts, your graveyard-shift specials, your prime rib, and, of course, your full Chinese menu. And it's all hearty and well priced; we're talkin' build your own three-egg, three-ingredient omelet for around $5. You can get a full dinner entree or a nice light lunch of a large half sandwich and soup, also for around $5. And 24-hour specials—a slab of meat, potato or rice, veggies, soup or salad, and a 12-ounce draft beer—are an astounding $10. Yep. That's the ticket.

In Terrible's, 4100 Paradise Rd. ✆ **702/733-7000.** Main courses $5–$13. AE, MC, V. Daily 24 hr.

Einstein Bros. Bagels ★ BAGELS You may not like digging into an enormous buffet first thing in the morning, and the continental breakfast in most hotels is a rip-off. A welcome alternative is a fresh-baked bagel, of which there are 15 varieties here—everything from onion to wild blueberry. Cream cheeses also come in many flavors, anything from sun-dried tomato to vegetable and jalapeño. Einstein's is a pleasant place for a morning meal, with both indoor seating and outdoor tables cooled by misters. Service is friendly, and four special-blend coffees are available each day.

Note: Bagel buffs might also want to check out the nearby **Bagelmania,** at 855 E. Twain Ave. (✆ **702/369-3322**). The bagels are sometimes chilled for freshness, which is heresy, but you can avoid this problem by catching them early in the morning, when their extensive selection is hot and fresh.

In the University Gardens Shopping Center, 4626 S. Maryland Pkwy. (btw. Harmon and Tropicana aves.). ✆ **702/795-7800.** www.einsteinbros.com. All items under $6. MC, V. Daily 6:30am–3pm.

Jason's Deli ★ DELI A chain popular with locals, there are four Jason's in the area, but this one is convenient to those staying east of the Strip. It's a busy, bustling deli where all items are advertised as free of artificial trans fat, plus a selection of "slimwiches," so as multipurpose diner/delis go, this may be a fairly healthy option. Jason's also does a brisk take-out business, again useful for those staying in nearby chain hotels without much in the way of room service. There is the usual deli fare—at least a dozen soups, sandwiches, wraps, and junior meals. The wraps tip you off that this is not a Brooklyn-style pastrami deli but fancy California-influenced versions of sandwiches. A wild card is the New Orleans–inspired muffalettas. The sandwiches are piled with meat, and the chicken potpie is huge. Naturally, the salad bar contains pudding and vanilla wafers—wouldn't want to carry "healthy" too far.

3910 S. Maryland Pkwy. ℭ **702/893-9799.** www.jasonsdeli.com. All items under $10. AE, DISC, MC, V. Daily 10am–9pm.

Komol THAI This is a hole-in-the-wall dive, like most good ethnic places. The menu is pretty large, divided into different sections for poultry, beef, and pork, plus a separate section for vegetarian dishes, plus many rice and noodle selections. They'll spice the food to your specifications. Unless you know your spicy Asian food, it might be best to play it on the safe side. Although we don't want things bland, too much heat can overwhelm all other flavors. The mild to medium packs enough of a kick for most people.

Among the items tried during a recent visit were a vegetarian green curry and the *pad-kee-mao* (flat rice noodles stir-fried with ground chicken, mint, garlic, and hot peppers). *Nam sod* is ground pork with a hot-and-sour sauce, ginger, and peanuts, all of which you wrap up in lettuce leaves—sort of an Asian burrito. The Thai iced tea was particularly good—just the right amount of sweetness and tea taste for a drink that is often served overly sweet.

Worth noting: The Commercial Center also has a number of other ethnic (mostly Asian) restaurants, including Korean barbecue.

In the Commercial Center, 953 E. Sahara Ave. ℭ **702/731-6542.** www.komolrestaurant.com. Main courses $8–$13. AE, DISC, MC, V. Mon–Sat 11am–10pm; Sun noon–10pm.

Lotus of Siam ★★★ 🏆 THAI So we drag you out to a strip mall in the east end of nowhere and you wonder why? Because here is what critic Jonathan Gold of *Gourmet* magazine called no less than the best Thai restaurant in North America.

What makes this place so darn special? First of all, in addition to all the usual beloved Thai favorites, there is a separate menu featuring lesser-known dishes from northern Thailand—the staff doesn't routinely hand this one out (because most of the customers are there for the more pedestrian, if still excellent, $9 lunch buffet). Second, the owner drives at least twice a week back to Los Angeles to pick up the freshest herbs and other ingredients needed for his dishes' authenticity. That's dedication that should be rewarded with superlatives.

You might be best off letting them know you are interested in Northern food (with dried chilies and more pork; it's not un-Cajunlike, says the owner) and letting them guide you through, though you must assure them that you aren't of faint heart or palate (some customers complain the heat isn't enough, even with "well spiced" dishes, though others find even medium spice sufficient). Standouts include the Issan sausage (a grilled sour pork number), the *nam kao tod* (that same sausage, ground up with lime, green onion, fresh chili, and ginger, served with crispy rice), *nam sod* (ground pork mixed with ginger, green onion, and lime juice, served with sticky rice), jackfruit *larb* (spicy ground meat), and *sua rong hai* ("weeping tiger"), a dish of soft, sliced, and grilled marinated beef. If you insist on more conventional Thai, that's okay, in that it's unlikely you are going to have better *mee krob* noodles or *tom kah kai* (that beloved soup can also be served Northern style, if asked, which is without the coconut milk). If in season, finish with mango with sticky rice, or if not, coconut ice cream with sticky rice, something you would find at many a street stall in Thailand.

In the Commercial Center, 953 E. Sahara Ave. © **702/735-3033.** www.saipinchutima.com. Reservations strongly recommended for dinner, call at least a day in advance. Main courses $9–$20; lunch buffet $9. AE, MC, V. Mon–Thurs 11:30am–2:30pm and 5:30–9:30pm; Fri–Sun 5:30–10pm.

Paymon's Mediterranean Cafe & Lounge ★ MEDITERRANEAN The emphasis on safe, mainstream food for the masses, to say nothing of the basic economy involved in running a Vegas restaurant (take your pick, either pay costly rent to a Strip hotel or get less tourist traffic with an off-Strip site), means that the kind of eateries other big cities take for granted—you know, cheap holes-in-the-wall, or charming little quirky joints, or the kind of ethnic places the chowhound folks brag about discovering—are rare indeed. And when you do find them, they are always, but always, in a strip mall. Paymon's Mediterranean Cafe is no exception, and its main dining room has no decor worth mentioning. But it gets extra points for having a courtyard seating area full of Middle Eastern touches and an honest-to-goodness hookah lounge—it's a good break from an otherwise often stifled, insulating time in Sin City.

Plus, it's just so darn nice to find ethnic food in this town. As the menu warns, kabobs take 25 minutes, so order an appetizer plate with various dips to while away the time. The hummus here is too reminiscent of its chickpea origins, but the *baba ghanouj* is properly smoky, and the falafel has the right crunch. Gyros may not be the most adventurous thing to order, but who cares about that when you've got a well-stuffed pocket pita, gloopy with yogurt sauce. *Fesenjan* is a dish of falling-apart chicken swimming in a tangy pomegranate sauce; ask them to ensure that the ratio of sauce to chicken is greater than 10:1.

4147 S. Maryland Pkwy. (at Flamingo Rd., in the Tiffany Sq. strip mall). © **702/731-6030.** www.paymons.com. Reservations not accepted. Main courses $10–$19; most sandwiches under $8. AE, DISC, MC, V. Daily 11am–1am.

Pink Taco ★ MEXICAN A mega-hip Mexican cantina, this folk art–bedecked spot is a scene just waiting to happen. There are no surprises in terms of the food; you know the drill—tacos, burritos, quesadillas—but it's all tasty and filling, and some of it comes with some surprising accompaniments, such as tapenade, along with the usual guacamole and sour cream. This is hip Mexican as opposed to a mom-and-pop joint, and it's a good place to eat on this side of town.

In the Hard Rock Hotel & Casino, 4455 Paradise Rd. © **702/693-5525.** www.pinktaco.com. Reservations only accepted for groups of 10 or more. Main courses $7.50–$15. AE, DC, DISC, MC, V. Sun–Thurs 11am–10pm; Fri–Sun 11am–midnight. Bar stays open later.)

Toto's ★★ ☺ 🌶 MEXICAN A family-style Mexican restaurant favored by locals, with enormous portions and quick service, this is good value for your money. With all that food, you could probably split portions and still be satisfied. There are no surprises on the menu, though there are quite a few seafood dishes. Everything is quite tasty, and they don't skimp on the cheese. The nongreasy chips come with fresh salsa, and the nachos are terrific. Chicken tamales got a thumbs-up, while the veggie burrito was happily received by non–meat eaters (although it's not especially healthy, all the ingredients were fresh, with huge slices of zucchini and roasted bell peppers). The operative word here is *huge*; the burritos are almost the size of your arm. The generous portions continue with dessert—a piece of flan was practically pie size. The Sunday margarita brunch is quite fun, and the drinks are large (naturally) and yummy.

2055 E. Tropicana Ave. ☎ **702/895-7923.** Main courses $7–$15. AE, DISC, MC, V. Mon–Thurs 11am–10pm; Fri–Sat 11am–11pm; Sun 9:30am–10pm.

WEST OF THE STRIP
Expensive

Austin's Steakhouse ★★ 🎁 STEAK/SEAFOOD Now, understand that we don't send you out to nether regions such as Texas Station lightly. We do so here because, improbably, Austin's Steakhouse has gained a reputation for the best steak in town. Really. Even the snooty critics at the *Las Vegas Review-Journal* agree with the hubbub about this place. And here's what has everyone, including us, raving: a 24-ounce rib-eye—yes, we know, just split it—aged and marinated, cooked over mesquite applewood, then rubbed with peppercorns and pan seared in garlic, butter, and cilantro. A massive chunk of meat with a smoky, garlicky flavor like no other steak we can think of. The Maui onion soup is also a standout, as is, over in the desserts, the chocolate decadence cake, which actually has a molten center, sort of a semisoufflé. Note that a comparable meal on the Strip would cost $10 to $20 more per person—yet another reason to head out to the hinterlands.

In Texas Station, 2101 Texas Star Lane. ☎ **702/631-1033.** Reservations recommended. Main courses $15–$50. AE, DC, DISC, MC, V. Sun–Thurs 5–10pm; Fri–Sat 5–11pm.

Rosemary's Restaurant ★★★ 🎁 NEW AMERICAN No visitor would be blamed for never leaving the Vegas Strip—it's the raison d'être of any Vegas tourist—but a true foodie should make a point of finding the nearest moving vehicle that can get them to Rosemary's Restaurant. A 15-minute (or so) drive down Sahara (hardly anything) is all it takes to eat what may well be the best food in Las Vegas. (Certainly, it is consistently voted the best food in the *Las Vegas Review-Journal*'s annual poll, by food critics and readers alike.)

The brainchild of Michael and Wendy Jordan, both veterans of the New Orleans food scene (Michael opened Emeril's here in Vegas), Rosemary's Restaurant (named for Michael's mother) shows more than a few NOLA touches, from the food to the service, in a room that's warmer and more inviting than most others in Vegas. ***Note:*** You can get seats at the bar overlooking the open kitchen, great fun for foodie interaction and not a bad choice for singles, or for couples looking for an unusual romantic evening.

The cuisine covers most regions of the U.S., though Southern influences dominate. Seared foie gras with peach coulis, candied walnuts, and vanilla bean–scented arugula is like a quilt, with distinct flavors that all hang together nicely. Interesting sides include ultrarich blue-cheese slaw, slightly spicy crispy fried tortilla strips, and perfect cornmeal jalapeño hush puppies. A recent visit found the crispy striped bass fighting it out with the pan-seared honey-glazed salmon for "best fish dish we've ever had." Desserts are similarly Southern—lemon icebox pie!—and most pleasant.

There is a nice little wine list with a broad range, especially when it comes to half-price bottles. They also specialize, unusually, in beer suggestions to pair

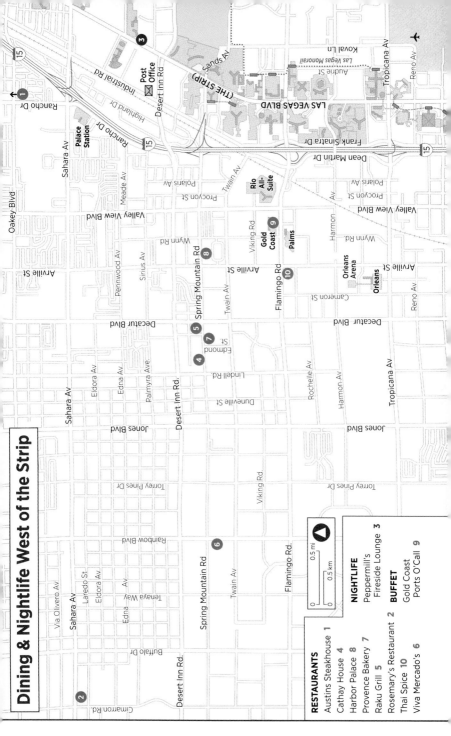

Dining & Nightlife West of the Strip

RESTAURANTS
Austins Steakhouse **1**
Cathay House **4**
Harbor Palace **8**
Provence Bakery **7**
Raku Grill **5**
Rosemary's Restaurant **2**
Thai Spice **10**
Viva Mercado's **6**

NIGHTLIFE
Peppermill's
Fireside Lounge **3**

BUFFET
Gold Coast
Ports O'Call **9**

with courses, including some fruity Belgian numbers; this is such a rare treat, if you drink beer, you must try some of their suggestions.

8125 W. Sahara. © **702/869-2251**. www.rosemarysrestaurant.com. Reservations strongly recommended. Main courses $14–$17 lunch; $27–$42 dinner. AE, DISC, MC, V. Mon–Fri 11:30am–2:15pm and 5:30–10:30pm; Sat–Sun 5:30–10:30pm.

Moderate

Cathay House CHINESE Las Vegas actually has a Chinatown—a very large strip mall (naturally) on Spring Mountain Road near Wynn Las Vegas. There are

---

sweet **SENSATIONS**

Plenty of opportunities exist in Vegas for satisfying your sweet tooth, but for the discriminating, here are six spots that you may have to make a detour for.

Jean-Philippe Patisserie (pictured at right), in Bellagio, 3600 Las Vegas Blvd. S. (© **702/693-8788**), makes us swoon, not just because it has the world's largest chocolate fountain (20 ft. high! Though only 11 ft. are on view, and they won't let us drink from it. Darn.), but perhaps, more to the point, it's the home of World Pastry champion Jean-Philippe Maury. (Yes, you can win gold medals for pastries.) Each visit causes us to spin around distractedly, trying to take in all the choices, both visually and gastronomically. From perfect gourmet chocolates to ice cream (diet-conscious folks will be relieved to learn the sorbets are excellent) to the eponymous pastries (each a little work of art), we hit greed overload. For us, this is true Vegas decadence—if only "what happens in Vegas, stays in Vegas" applied to calories. Our current favorites include a witty-looking version of lemon meringue pie to a chocolate hazelnut bombe with so many layers of interest we couldn't quite keep track, to brioches filled with either *dulce de leche* or Nutella. The patisserie also serves some solidly good sandwiches, and some adequate savory crepes. It is open daily from 7am to midnight.

A local favorite is **Freed's Bakery,** 4780 S. Eastern Ave., at Tropicana Boulevard (© **702/456-7762;** www.freedsbakery.com), open Monday through Saturday from 9am to 6:30pm and Sunday from 9am to 3pm. If you've got a serious sugar craving, this is worth the 15-minute drive from the Strip. Despite the minimalist setting, it's like walking into Grandma's kitchen (provided you had an old-fashioned granny who felt pastries should be gooey, chocolaty, and buttery). The chocolate coffeecake is especially good. There is also fresh bread, napoleons, strawberry cheesecake, cream puffs, sweet rolls, Danishes, and doughnuts, many of which are made with surprisingly fresh ingredients. Some may find the goodies too heavy and rich, but for those of us with a powerful sweet tooth, this place hits the spot.

We used to try to send you to Henderson to experience the delights of **The Cupcakery,** but now there's a branch open at Monte Carlo, 3770 Las Vegas Blvd. S. (© **702/207-2253;** www.thecupcakery.com). The delectable cakes here aren't large, but they pack a wallop of moist cake and creamy frosting.

---

several Asian restaurants there, but ask locals who look like they know, and they will send you instead farther up Spring Mountain Road to Cathay House (on the opposite side of the street). This only looks far from the Strip on a map; it's really about a 7-minute drive from Treasure Island.

Ordering dim sum, for those of you who haven't experienced it, is sort of like being at a Chinese sushi bar, in that you order many individual, tasty little dishes. Of course, dim sum itself is nothing like sushi. Rather, it's a range of pot stickers, pan-fried dumplings, *baos* (soft, doughy buns filled with such meat as barbecued pork), translucent rice noodles wrapped around shrimp, sticky rice in

Clever combinations include the Boston cream pie (filled with custardy cream), but even the basic chocolate-on-chocolate is a butter-cream pleasure. There are even sugar-free cupcakes for those with such dietary needs. The Cupcakery is open Monday to Friday 8am to 6pm, Saturday 10am to 8pm, and Sunday noon to 6pm.

Hot Vegas days call for cool desserts, and frozen custard (softer than regular ice cream, but harder than soft serve) is a fine way to go. Head for **Luv-It Frozen Custard,** 505 E. Oakey (*©* **702/384-6452;** www.luvitfrozen custard.com), open Tuesday through Thursday from 1 to 10pm and Friday and Saturday from 1 to 11pm. Because custard has less fat and sugar than premium ice cream, you can even fool yourself into thinking this is somewhat healthful (ha!). Made every few hours using fresh cream and eggs, the custard is available in basic flavors for cup or cone, but more exotic flavors (maple walnut, apple spice, and more) come in tubs.

Another Chinatown alternative for baked goods is the French/Asian **Provence Bakery ★**, 5115 Spring Mountain Rd., no. 225 (*©* **702/341-0168**). Try custard buns, sweet bread, and all manner of cookies, but definitely

grab one of the packages of little cream puffs, superior in many ways to the cream puffs made by chains popping up in other parts of the U.S. It all makes for good snack grabbing to and from Red Rock or as a post-Chinese meal dessert in the complex. There is also shaved ice and smoothies. It's open Monday through Saturday from 9:30am to 9pm and Sunday from 10am to 9pm.

lotus leaves, chicken feet, and so forth. Some of it is steamed; some is fried—for that extra-good grease! You can make your own dipping sauce by combining soy sauce, vinegar, and hot-pepper oil. The waitstaff pushes steam carts filled with little dishes; point, and they'll attempt to tell you what each one is. Better, just blindly order a bunch and dig in. Each dish ranges from approximately $1 to $3; each server makes a note of what you just received, and the total is tallied at the end. (For some reason, it almost always works out to about $9 per person.) Dim sum is usually available only until midafternoon.

5300 W. Spring Mountain Rd. © **702/876-3838.** Reservations recommended. Main courses $6.75–$19. AE, DC, DISC, MC, V. Daily 10:30am–10pm.

Harbor Palace ★ CHINESE Located in a mega–strip mall, with quite a few other Asian restaurants as competition, we point this out to you as another dim sum option. When you can get an order of commendable shrimp *hai gow* (little steamed rice noodle–wrapped balls of fresh shrimp) or pork *shiu mai* for $1.90, or pan-fried chive dumplings for $2.70, you might feel foolish eating dim sum on the Strip, where it will set you back five times as much. Harbor Palace also has a full menu of other Chinese dishes (as do the neighbors; you can pretty much head into whichever one looks the most popular and take a chance), and it does takeout. Since it's open till the wee hours, this is a good spot for postclubbing snacks, though the dim sum is usually not offered late.

4275 Spring Mountain Rd. © **702/253-1688.** Main courses $10–$20; dim sum $1.90–$6.50. AE, MC, V. Daily 10am–5am.

Raku Grill ★★★ JAPANESE At first glance, it's not the kind of place you'd expect to get rave notices in *GQ* and *New York*. It's also not the kind of place you'd expect master chefs like Paul Bartolotta to frequent. But get past the run-down Strip mall location on the west side of town and you'll find one of the most interesting, unique, and purely divine restaurants in all of Las Vegas. It's tiny, with seats for fewer than three dozen, and what with all the deserved attention it has gotten, those seats are hard to come by (make reservations at least a week if not more in advance). But if you get one, you'll be treated to a litany of taste-bud popping flavors from the Robata grill.

Everything is small plates, most served on skewers. It's the esoteric items that have gotten most of the press—pork ear, pork cheek, Kobe beef liver—but the long list includes perfectly moist chicken breast, Kobe with milder than expected wasabi, a miniature lamb chop, seared foie gras, grilled duck, asparagus or tomato wrapped in bacon (both joy inducing in their freshness), ground chicken, and much more. Daily specials include seafood flown in from Japan and there is also an *Odin* (broth pot) section and rice, noodle, and soup dishes. But it is that Robata grill that should dominate your choices—the smoky charcoal grill flavor brings everything to life but allows each dish to have its own distinct flavors. Even the somewhat less than mainstream options are heavenly, with the pork cheek tasting basically like a hunk of bacon lard, and we mean that in a good way. Although most of the selections are only a few bucks (most under $5), it is easy to wrack up a big bill here because after the first bite you'll be tempted to just have them bring you everything on the menu. And we would not blame you for doing so.

5030 W. Spring Mountain Rd., no. 2 (at Decatur). © **702/367-3511.** www.raku-grill.com. Reservations required. Robata grill items $2–$14. AE, MC, V. Daily 6pm–3am.

Viva Mercado's ★★ MEXICAN Ask any local about Mexican food in Vegas, and almost certainly they will point to Viva Mercado's as the best in town. That recommendation, plus the restaurant's health-conscious attitude, makes this worth the roughly 10-minute drive from the Strip.

Given all those warnings about Mexican food and its heart-attack-inducing properties, the approach at Viva Mercado's is nothing to be sniffed at. No dish is prepared with or cooked in any kind of animal fat. Nope, the lard so dear to Mexican cooking is not found here. The oil used is an artery-friendly canola. This makes the place particularly appealing to vegetarians, who will also be pleased by the regular veggie specials. Everything is quite fresh, and particularly amazing things are done with seafood. Try the *Maresco Vallarta,* which is orange roughy, shrimp, and scallops cooked in a coconut-tomato sauce, with capers and olives. There are all sorts of noteworthy shrimp dishes and 11 different salsas, ranked 1 to 10 for degree of spice. The staff is friendly (try to chat with owner Bobby Mercado) and the portions hearty.

3553 S. Rainbow Rd. (near Spring Mountain Rd.). © **702/871-8826.** www.vivamercadoslv.com. Reservations only accepted for large parties. Main courses $10–$20. AE, DISC, MC, V. Sun–Thurs 11am–9:30pm; Fri–Sat 11am–10pm.

Inexpensive

Thai Spice ✦ THAI Just off the Strip and across from the Rio, this modern-looking, nonglitzy Thai restaurant offers decent food at reasonable prices. The subdued ambience, quick service, and good food make it a local favorite. The menu is extensive and offers an array of Thai dishes and even some Chinese fare. For appetizers, the *tom kah kai* soup and pork or chicken satay (served on skewers, with a spicy peanut sauce) are excellent. Skip the terrible *moo goo gai pan* in favor of terrific *pad Thai* and tasty lemon chicken. Lunch specials are $6.95 and include spring rolls, salad, soup, and steamed rice. Make sure you tell the waitress how spicy you want your food.

4433 W. Flamingo Rd. (at Arville St.). © **702/362-5308.** Main courses $7 lunch, $9–$15 dinner. AE, DISC, MC, V. Sun–Thurs 11am–10pm; Fri–Sat 11am–10:30pm.

DOWNTOWN
Very Expensive

Hugo's Cellar ★ INTERNATIONAL Hugo's Cellar is indeed in a cellar, or at least below street level in the Four Queens hotel. No, they aren't ashamed of it—quite the opposite. This is their pride and joy, and it is highly regarded by the locals. This is Old School Vegas Classy Dining. Each female guest is given a red rose when she enters the restaurant—the first of a series of nice touches.

The meal is full of ceremony, perfectly delivered by a well-trained and cordial waitstaff. Salads, included in the price, are prepared at your table, from a cart full of choices. In Vegas style, though, most choices are on the calorie-intensive side, ranging from chopped egg and blue cheese to pine nuts and bay shrimp. Still, with a honey-orange-walnut vinaigrette, it's good enough to consider paying the $14 a la carte fee and just sticking with it. Unfortunately, the main courses are not all that novel (various cuts of meat, seafood, and chicken prepared in different ways), but on a recent visit, not one of six diners was anything less than delighted. The filet of beef stuffed with crabmeat and wrapped with bacon is over the top for us, but others loved it, while the roast duckling rubbed with anise and flambéed at the table is a guilty pleasure, just the right effect for this Old School Vegas dining experience. The T-bone steak was tender enough to cut with a fork. Vegetables and excellent starchy sides are included, as is a finish of chocolate-dipped fruits with cream.

The fact that salad and a small dessert are included makes an initially hefty-seeming price tag appear a bit more reasonable, especially compared to Strip establishments that aren't much better and can cost the same for just the entree. While it's not worth going out of your way for the food, perhaps it is worth it for the entire package.

In the Four Queens, 202 Fremont St. ✆ **702/385-4011.** www.hugoscellar.com. Reservations required. Main courses $36–$52. AE, DC, DISC, MC, V. Daily 5:30–11pm.

Expensive

The Chart House ★ SEAFOOD Downtown Las Vegas is a bit of a wasteland when it comes to fine dining experiences, so it was exciting when the Landry's restaurant chain took over the Golden Nugget. Among their additions is a branch of The Chart House, which is usually found overlooking some body of water to go along with a predominantly seafood menu. Because there are no bodies of water in Downtown Vegas, they built a 75,000-gallon aquarium as the focal point. It's beautiful, but may be a little unsettling if you choose a table right next to it and have a variety of colorful fish watching as you chow down on their brethren. If you can't decide between the lobster bisque, New England clam chowder, and gazpacho for your soup course, get all three in the Ménage sampler. The flounder stuffed with jumbo lump crab on a bed of Yukon gold potatoes was as close to perfect as you're going to get with fish in the Nevada desert. Although the menu is obviously seafood intensive, there are a few steak and chicken options available.

In Golden Nugget, 129 E. Fremont St. ✆ **702/386-8364.** www.chart-house.com. Reservations recommended. Main courses $16–$59. AE, DC, DISC, MC, V. Mon–Thurs 11:30am–11pm; Fri–Sat 11:30am–11:30pm; Sun 11:30am–10:30pm.

Second Street Grill ★ 🕎 INTERNATIONAL/PACIFIC RIM Our categorization notwithstanding, Second Street Grill calls itself "Continental American with Euro and Asian influences." And, yes, that translates to a bit of a muddle, but the portions are extremely generous, and it's hard to resist a place that plants two long potato chips in a pile of mashed potatoes, thereby creating a bunny rabbit. You are probably best off with grill dishes (various steaks and other cuts of meat), though here might be your best ratio of quality to price for lobster tail. Play around with the Hunan pork and beef lettuce wrap appetizers, and the Peking duck and shrimp tacos. The waist conscious will be very pleased with the bamboo-steamed snapper in a nice broth, while others may want to try the grilled salmon with goat cheese Parmesan crust. Desserts are disappointing, unfortunately. Overall, a nice place for a family event dinner Downtown, and certainly more affordable than fancy places on the Strip.

In Fremont Hotel & Casino, 200 E. Fremont St. ✆ **702/385-3232.** Reservations recommended. Main courses $17–$30. AE, DC, DISC, MC, V. Mon–Thurs 5–10pm; Fri–Sat 5–11pm.

Inexpensive

Carson Street Cafe AMERICAN Here's a slightly better-than-adequate hotel coffee shop, though it's a mixed bag in terms of quality of food. Sandwiches are

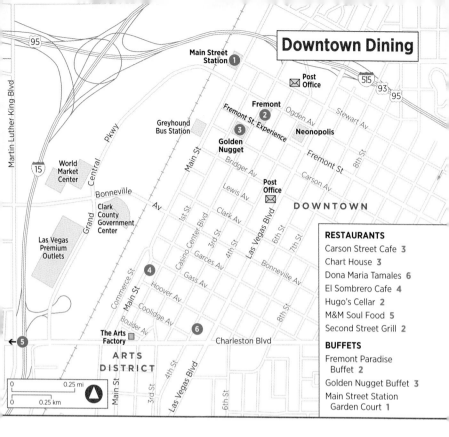

Downtown Dining

Main Street Station ①

Post Office

Fremont ②

Fremont St. Experience

Greyhound Bus Station

Golden Nugget ③

Neonopolis

Ogden Av

Stewart Av

Fremont St

Carson Av

Bridger Av

Lewis Av

Post Office

DOWNTOWN

World Market Center

Bonneville Av

Clark County Government Center

Las Vegas Premium Outlets

Clark Av

Garces Av

Gass Av

Bonneville Av

④

The Arts Factory

⑥

Charleston Blvd

ARTS DISTRICT

Martin Luther King Blvd

Grand Central Pkwy

Main St

Casino Center Blvd

1st St

3rd St

4th St

Las Vegas Blvd

6th St

7th St

8th St

Commerce St

Main St

Coolidge Av

Hoover Av

Boulder Av

4th St

3rd St

Las Vegas Blvd

6th St

← ⑤

0   0.25 mi
0   0.25 km

RESTAURANTS

Carson Street Cafe **3**
Chart House **3**
Dona Maria Tamales **6**
El Sombrero Cafe **4**
Hugo's Cellar **2**
M&M Soul Food **5**
Second Street Grill **2**

BUFFETS

Fremont Paradise Buffet **2**
Golden Nugget Buffet **3**
Main Street Station Garden Court **1**

better than ribs, burgers, and fries, all of which are merely just filling. On the other hand, the linguine with shrimp is surprisingly good, while desserts, especially pecan pie a la mode, more than earn their rep.

In Golden Nugget, 129 E. Fremont St. ℂ **702/385-7111.** Reservations not accepted. Main courses $6–$18. AE, DC, DISC, MC, V. Daily 24 hr.

Doña María Tamales ★★ MEXICAN Decorated with Tijuana-style quilt work and calendars, this quintessential Mexican diner is convenient to both the north end of the Strip and Downtown. The cooks use lots of lard, lots of cheese, and lots of sauce. As a result, the food is really good—and really fattening. Yep, the folks who did those health reports showing how bad Mexican food can be for your heart probably did some research here. The fat just makes it all the better, in our opinion. Locals apparently agree; even at lunchtime, the place is crowded.

You will start off with homemade chips and a spicy salsa served in a mortar. Meals are so large that it shouldn't be a problem getting full just ordering off the sides, which can make this even more of a budget option. Naturally, the specialty is the fantastic tamales, which come in red, green, cheese, or sweet. There are also excellent enchiladas, *chiles rellenos,* burritos, and fajitas. All dinners include rice, beans, tortillas, and soup or salad. Sauces are heavy but oh-so-good. For dessert, there is flan, fried ice cream, and Mexican-style pumpkin pie.

910 Las Vegas Blvd. S. (at Charleston Blvd.). ☎ **702/382-6538.** www.donamariatamales.com. Main courses $8-$12 breakfast and lunch, $12-$15 dinner. AE, MC, V. Sun–Thurs 8am–10pm; Fri–Sat 8am–11pm.

El Sombrero Cafe ★★ MEXICAN This kind of hole-in-the-wall Mexican joint can be found all over California but not always so readily elsewhere. It's also the kind of family-run (since 1950) place increasingly forced out of Vegas by giant hotel conglomerates, making it even more worth your time. Mexican-food fans, in particular, should seek out this friendly place, though it's not in an attractive part of town. Portions are generous and unexpectedly spicy. The staff also caters to special requests—changing the beef burrito to a chicken one (an option that comes highly recommended), for example, without batting an eyelash. The enchilada and taco combo also won raves.

807 S. Main St. (at Gass Ave.). ☎ **702/382-9234.** Main courses $8 lunch, $13 dinner. MC, V. Mon–Thurs 11am–4pm; Fri–Sat 11am–8:30pm.

M&M Soul Food ★★ 🏠 SOUL FOOD Though we've listed this in Downtown, it's really not too far from the Strip. At first glance, the neighborhood seems intimidating, but it's not actually threatening. Why come here? Because locals have voted this their favorite soul food place, and while the competition may not be all that high, the quality stands out regardless. Appropriately, it's a hole in the wall, with somewhat higher prices than one might expect, but the generous portions make up for it. Mini cornbread pancakes are served to every table. Smothered fried chicken is moist, slightly spicy, and topped with a robust gravy. The menu includes hot links, collard greens, and other typical options.

3923 W. Charleston. ☎ **702/453-7685.** Main courses $6-$17. AE, DISC, MC, V. Daily 7am–8pm.

Magnolia's Veranda AMERICAN So there you are, you can't possibly eat at another buffet and yet you don't want to spend $50 for a meal at a typical Vegas restaurant. Magnolia's Veranda seems to have been invented for folks just like you. This 24-hour cafe isn't going to win an epicurean award, but the food is better than coffee-shop average and is, without exception, affordable. With a menu that is more wide ranging than most buffets (soups, salads, sandwiches, burgers, pizza, pasta, breakfasts, steak, seafood), you'll be sure to find something here to please just about any taste. And meal-deal hunters should definitely pay attention to such things as the $8.95 prime rib dinners served nightly.

In the Four Queens, 202 E. Fremont St. ☎ **702/385-4011.** Main courses $6-19. MC, V. Daily 24 hr.

BUFFETS & SUNDAY BRUNCHES

Like so much else that was Vegas tradition, the buffets are evolving. The higher-end ones no longer put out heaping mounds o' stuff, which is probably for the best in terms of waste but is a departure from decadence that we are loath to see. And prices have been steadily creeping upward; the higher-end buffets are no longer a true bargain because it's unlikely you can (or should) eat enough to make you feel like you really got away with something. With the more expensive buffets, some of which have pretty good food, consider it this way: You would pay much more, per person, at one of the fancier restaurants in town, and you could order just one, potentially disappointing, item. Consider the higher-end recommended buffet as an alternative to a nice meal at a traditional restaurant.

More variety per person means less likelihood for disappointment. (Hate what you picked? Dump your plate and start all over.) Not nearly as atmospheric as a proper restaurant, but how else can you combine good barbecue with excellent Chinese and a cupcake or 10?

There is a lot of variety within the buffet genre. Some are just perfunctory steam-table displays and salad bars that are heavy on the iceberg lettuce, while others are unbelievably opulent spreads with caviar and free-flowing champagne. Some are quite beautifully presented as well. Some of the food is awful, some of it is decent, and some of it is memorable.

Buffets are extremely popular, and reservations are usually not taken (we've indicated when they are, and in all those cases, they are highly recommended). Arrive early (before opening) or late to avoid a long line, especially on weekends.

South Strip

EXPENSIVE

The Buffet at Aria ★ BUFFET While the food at Las Vegas's newest buffet may not be the pinnacle of all-you-can-eat delights, it is certainly a cut above standard buffet fare. Various regional and ethnic food stations (love the Tandoori oven!) serve up enough variety to keep your stomach confused for days (pizza, pot stickers, and hummus on one plate?) and the quality is evident with every bite, although very little of it is so good that it makes you want to go back for seconds. Well, maybe the full rack of bacon at the carving station during the weekend brunches is worth another helping. The room is bright, airy, modern, and totally forgettable, except for the very nice outdoor dining patio.

At Aria Las Vegas, 3730 Las Vegas Blvd. S. ✆ **877/230-2742.** www.arialasvegas.com. Breakfast $15; lunch $20; dinner $28-$36; Sat-Sun champagne brunch $29. AE, DC, DISC, MC, V. Daily 7am-10pm.

Mandalay Bay's Bayside Buffet ★ BUFFET This is a particularly pretty, not overly large buffet. Floor-to-ceiling windows overlooking the beach part of the elaborate pool area make it less stuffy and eliminate the closed-in feeling that so many of the other buffets in town have. The buffet itself is adequately arranged but features nothing particularly special, though there are some nice salads, hearty meats, and a larger and better-than-average dessert bar—they make their own desserts, and it shows.

In Mandalay Bay, 3950 Las Vegas Blvd. S. ✆ **702/632-7777.** Breakfast $17; lunch $21; dinner $27; Sun brunch $25. Reduced prices for children 5-11; free for children 4 and under. AE, DC, DISC, MC, V. Daily 7-11am breakfast, 11am-2:30pm lunch, 4:45-10pm dinner.

MGM Grand Buffet BUFFET This rather average buffet does feature a fresh Belgian waffle station at breakfast. Dinner also has an all-you-can-eat shrimp and prime-rib option. Also available: low-fat, sugar-free desserts! And at all meals, you get a full pot of coffee on your table. Still, those dinner prices do not justify a trip here.

In MGM Grand, 3799 Las Vegas Blvd. S. ✆ **702/891-7777.** Breakfast $14; lunch $17; dinner Sun-Thurs $26, Fri-Sat $28; Sat-Sun brunch $28. Reduced prices for children 4-11; free for children 3 and under. AE, DC, DISC, MC, V. Sun-Thurs 7am-2:30pm and 4:30-10pm; Fri-Sat 7am-2:30pm and 4:30-10:30pm.

MODERATE

Excalibur's Roundtable Buffet ★ BUFFET This one strikes the perfect balance of moderate prices, forgettable decor, and adequate food. It's what you want in a cheap Vegas buffet—except it's just not that cheap anymore. Then again, none are anymore, so this still qualifies and, thus, usually has long lines.

In Excalibur, 3850 Las Vegas Blvd. S. ✆ **702/597-7777.** Breakfast $15; lunch $16; dinner $20. All-day pass $27. Reduced prices for children 4–12; free for children 3 and under. AE, DC, DISC, MC, V. Daily 7am–10pm.

Monte Carlo Buffet ★ BUFFET A "courtyard" under a painted sky, the Monte Carlo's buffet room has a Moroccan market theme, with murals of Arab scenes, Moorish archways, Oriental carpets, and walls hung with photographs of and artifacts from Morocco. Dinner includes a rotisserie (for chicken and pork loin, or London broil), a Chinese food station, a taco/fajita bar, a baked potato bar, numerous salads, and more than a dozen desserts, plus frozen yogurt and ice-cream machines. Lunches are similar. At breakfast, the expected fare is supplemented by an omelet station, and choices include crepes, blintzes, and corned-beef hash. Fresh-baked bagels are a plus.

In Monte Carlo Resort & Casino, 3770 Las Vegas Blvd. S. ✆ **702/730-7777.** Breakfast $15; lunch $16; dinner $20; Sun brunch $21. Reduced prices for children 5–9; free for children 4 and under. AE, DC, DISC, MC, V. Daily 7am–3:30pm and 4–10pm.

MORE, The Buffet at Luxor ★★ BUFFET Once one of our favorite buffets not just for the excellent price-to-quality ratio, but also because of its Indiana Jones–invoking decor, the Luxor buffet has been redesigned and renamed as part of the ongoing de-Egypt-ing of the hotel. Dang. We are sick of neato modern classy already and want our mummies back. That said, the food is the best in its price range, and it is one of the top buffets in town. There's a Mexican station with some genuinely spicy food, a Chinese stir-fry station, and different Italian pastas. Desserts were disappointing, though they do offer a pretty large selection of diabetic-friendly options. The quality-to-price ratio is no secret, and, as a result, the lines are always enormous.

In Luxor, 3900 Las Vegas Blvd. S. ✆ **702/262-4000.** Breakfast $15; lunch $16; dinner $20; Sun brunch $20. All-day pass Mon–Fri $30, Sat–Sun $35. Reduced prices for children 4–10; free for children 3 and under. AE, DC, DISC, MC, V. Daily 7am–10pm.

Mid-Strip

EXPENSIVE

Bellagio Buffet ★★ BUFFET Though one of the priciest of the buffets, the Bellagio still gets high marks from visitors. The array of food is fabulous, with one ethnic cuisine after another (Japanese, Chinese that includes dim sum, build-it-yourself Mexican items, and so on). There are elaborate pastas and semitraditional Italian-style pizza from a wood-fired oven. The cold fish appetizers at each end of the line are not to be missed—scallops, smoked salmon, crab claws, shrimp, oysters, and assorted condiments. Other specialties include breast of duck and game hens. There is no carving station, but you can get the meat precarved. The salad bar is more ordinary, though prepared salads have some fine surprises, such as the eggplant-tofu salad and an exceptional Chinese chicken salad. Desserts, unfortunately, look better than they actually are.

In Bellagio, 3600 Las Vegas Blvd. S. ✆ **877/234-6358.** Mon–Thurs breakfast $16, lunch $20, dinner $28; Fri breakfast $16, lunch $20, dinner $36; Sat brunch $24–$29, dinner $36; Sun brunch $24–$29, dinner $28. Free for Children 2 and under. AE, DC, DISC, MC, V. Daily 7am–10pm.

Le Village Buffet ★★★ BUFFET One of the more ambitious buffets, with a price to match—still, you do get a fine assortment of food and more value for the dollar than you are likely to find anywhere else. The Paris buffet is housed in a Disneyland-esque replica of a French village that is either a charming respite from Vegas lights or sickening, depending on your perspective.

Buffet stations are grouped according to French regions, and though in theory entrees change daily, there do seem to be some constants: In Brittany, you'll find made-to-order crepes, surprisingly good roasted duck with green peppercorn and peaches, and steamed mussels with butter and shallots. In Normandy, there's quiche and some dry bay scallops with honey cider. The carving station shows up in Burgundy but distinguishes itself by adding options of chateaubriand sauce and cherry sauce Escoffier. Lamb stew is a possibility for Alsace, while Provence has pasta and a solidly good braised beef. You can skip the dessert station in favor of heading back to Brittany for some made-to-order crepes, but you might want to try the bananas Foster.

In Paris Las Vegas, 3655 Las Vegas Blvd. S. ✆ **888/266-5687.** Breakfast $15; lunch $18; dinner $25; Sun brunch $25. Reduced prices for children 4–10; free for children 3 and under. AE, DC, DISC, MC, V. Daily 7am–10pm.

Mirage Cravings Buffet ★ BUFFET This buffet features a gleaming, streamlined look, all shining steel and up-to-the-minute high-design concept. Gone are the heaping mounds of shrimp and other symbols of Vegas excess and bargain. In its place are plenty of live-action stations, but minimal offerings. This probably helps with waste, but if you are used to matters the other way, it does feel stingy. Seniors won't like the poor signage; kids may get tired long before completing the lengthy circuit. The line starts with excellent pizza. Look for pot stickers and Chinese barbecue pork, quite good barbecue, tangy Japanese cucumber salad, and slightly dry but flavorful Mexican slow-roasted pork. A trip to the made-to-order salad station is so pokey, you'll need to find the other salads that are hidden with the open-faced sandwiches (where you can also find the gefilte fish). The desserts are generally disappointing. Despite the drawbacks, this remains popular with buffet connoisseurs.

In The Mirage, 3400 Las Vegas Blvd. S. ✆ **702/791-7111.** Breakfast $14; lunch $18; dinner $25; Sat–Sun brunch $23. Reduced prices for children 5–10; free for children 4 and under. AE, DC, DISC, MC, V. Daily 7am–10pm.

Rio's Carnival World Buffet ★★ BUFFET This buffet has long been voted by locals as the best in Vegas. Qualitywise, it's probably as good as ever, and maybe even better. Decorwise, it's better still, as an overhaul was devoted mostly to improving the dining areas. Overall, this is simply more mainstream, an upscale food court with "South American" cooked-to-order stir-fries, Mexican taco fixings and accompaniments, Chinese fare, a Japanese sushi bar and *teppanyaki* grill, a Brazilian mixed grill, Italian pasta and antipasto, and fish and chips. There's even a diner setup for hot dogs, burgers, fries, and milkshakes. All this is in addition to the usual offerings of most Las Vegas buffets. Best of all, a brand-new dessert station features at least 70 kinds of pies, cakes, and pastries from an award-winning pastry chef, plus a large selection of gelatos and sorbets.

In Rio All-Suite Hotel & Casino, 3700 W. Flamingo Rd. ☏ **702/252-7777.** Breakfast $15; lunch $17; dinner $24; Sat-Sun champagne brunch $24. Reduced prices for children 4-7; free for children 3 and under. AE, DC, MC, V. Daily 8am–11pm.

MODERATE

Dishes, The Buffet at TI ★★ BUFFET Now easily the handsomest buffet space in town, sort of contemporary diner, all dark gleaming wood, mirrors, and geometric lines. We feel mixed on the food choices; this is a smaller buffet than one might expect for such a big hotel, and while there is a reasonable range of cuisines (Italian; Japanese, with sushi chefs who will make up fresh plates for you; Southern, including unexpected spoon bread; deli), there isn't the overwhelming bounty we've come to consider our right when it comes to Vegas buffets. However, there are some well-considered and fine-tasting deli sandwiches (brie and honey, roast beef with goat cheese), plus better-than-decent barbecue ribs and Chinese options. Some of the most charming dessert choices focus on such childhood tastes as cupcakes, fresh cotton candy, and quite good crème brûlée (yes, not exactly real kiddie fare, but, let's face it, it's just exceptionally good vanilla custard!). Best of all are the adorable minidoughnuts, fresh out of the fryer; we ate two dozen and we are not ashamed.

In Treasure Island, 3300 Las Vegas Blvd. S. ☏ **702/894-7111.** Breakfast $14; lunch $16; dinner Sun-Thurs $22, Fri-Sun $26; Sat-Sun champagne brunch $17-$22. Reduced prices for children 4-11; free for children 3 and under. AE, DC, DISC, MC, V. Daily 7am–10pm.

Flamingo Paradise Garden Buffet ★ BUFFET This buffet occupies a vast room, with floor-to-ceiling windows overlooking a verdant tropical landscape of cascading waterfalls and koi ponds. At dinner, there is an extensive international food station (which changes monthly), presenting French, Chinese, Mexican, German, or Italian specialties. A large salad bar, fresh salads, pastas, vegetables, potato dishes, and a vast dessert display round out the offerings. Lunch is similar, featuring international cuisines as well as a stir-fry station and a soup/salad/pasta bar. At breakfast, you'll find all the expected fare, including a made-to-order omelet station and fresh-baked breads. The seafood is dry and tough, and desserts are uninspired. Drinks are unlimited but are served in small glasses, so expect to call your server for many refills.

In Flamingo Las Vegas, 3555 Las Vegas Blvd. S. ☏ **702/733-3111.** Breakfast $15; lunch $17; dinner $22; Sat-Sun champagne brunch $20. Reduced prices for children 4-8; free for children 3 and under. AE, DC, DISC, MC, V. Breakfast Mon-Fri 7-11am; lunch daily 11am-3pm; dinner daily 4-10pm; brunch Sat-Sun 7am-3pm.

Flavors at Harrah's ★ BUFFET Not as bold a makeover as other recently refurbished buffets, but the redone room is certainly an improvement. Oddly, here it's the carving station that stands out, with simultaneous servings of turkey, ham, prime rib, chicken, game hen, sausage, roast vegetables, and lamb. The other stations are typical—Mexican, Italian, seafood, Chinese. A particularly good dessert area is heavy on the cookies, cakes, and little pastries, such as Oreo mousse tarts and mini crème brûlées. Best of all, there is a chocolate fountain with pound cake, fruit, brownies, and the like ready for dipping. It nearly overshadows the make-your-own root beer float station.

In Harrah's, 3475 Las Vegas Blvd. S. ☏ **702/369-5000.** Breakfast $16; lunch $17; dinner $22; brunch Sat-Sun $21. AE, MC, V. Daily 7am–10pm.

Spice Market Buffet ★★ BUFFET This is one of the better choices in the city, thanks to unexpected, and pretty good, Middle Eastern specialties, including the occasional Moroccan entrees. Look for tandoori chicken, hummus, couscous, stuffed tomatoes with ground lamb, and at dinner, lamb skewers. The Mexican station is particularly good as well, even if it confuses the palate to go from guacamole to hummus. The dim sum also gets a vote of confidence. There is cotton candy at lunch and a crepe-making station at dinner. We still wish it were a bit cheaper; at these prices, it's edging toward the high end.

3667 Las Vegas Blvd. S. ✆ **702/785-5555.** Breakfast $15; lunch $18; dinner $26. AE, DC, DISC, MC, V. Daily 7am–10pm.

North Strip
VERY EXPENSIVE

Wynn Las Vegas Buffet ★★★ BUFFET Goodness, we do love a nice buffet, and this one is particularly nice (if notably superexpensive). It's more thoughtful and artful than the average, starting with the *Alice in Wonderland*–evoking atrium styled with towers of fruit flowers and foliage and even some natural light. Don't worry if you don't score one of the few tables set there; it's a bit far from the food lines, and you want to be close to the action, after all. Look for such items as jerk chicken, wood-fired pizza, honey-glazed pork, nice little salmon rolls, five kinds of *ceviche,* sweet Kansas City–style barbecue, and tandoori chicken among the stations, which include Mexican, Southern, seafood, and Italian. Desserts are superior to those at probably all the other buffets, in construction and in taste, giving the impression that a pastry chef is active on the premises. Don't miss the mini floating islands, the unusual tiramisu, the excellent chocolate mousse and ice creams, and even a plate full of madeleines.

In Wynn Las Vegas, 3131 Las Vegas Blvd. S. ✆ **702/770-3463.** Breakfast $20; lunch $23; dinner $35–$39; Sat–Sun brunch $31–$39. AE, DC, DISC, MC, V. Sun–Thurs 8am–10pm; Fri–Sat 8am–10:30pm.

INEXPENSIVE

Circus Circus Buffet BUFFET Here's a trade-off: It's just about the cheapest buffet on the Strip but also what some consider the worst in town. Here you'll find 50 items of typical cafeteria fare, and none of them is all that good. If food is strictly fuel for you, you can't go wrong here. Otherwise, find another buffet.

2880 Las Vegas Blvd. S. ✆ **702/734-0410.** Breakfast $11; lunch $13; dinner $14. AE, DC, DISC, MC, V. Daily 7am–10pm.

East of the Strip
MODERATE

The Buffet at the Las Vegas Hilton ★ BUFFET A surprisingly stylish-looking room, with the usual suspects (salad bar, bagel bar, desserts) and a good selection of Chinese food (including Peking duck). The fare is fresh and delicious, with special mention going to the prime rib, the outstanding cream puffs, and the superior rice pudding. (It's hard to find good desserts at Vegas buffets.) There's plenty to eat here, but the place feels small compared to the newer lavish spreads on the Strip.

In Las Vegas Hilton, 3000 Paradise Rd. ✆ **702/732-5111.** Breakfast $13; lunch $14; dinner $18 (includes complimentary beer and wine); Sat–Sun brunch $18 (includes unlimited champagne). Half price for children 12 and under. DC, DISC, MC, V. Mon–Fri 7am-2:30pm and 5-10pm; Sat–Sun 8am-2:30pm and 5-10pm.

West of the Strip
INEXPENSIVE

Gold Coast Ports O' Call ★ BUFFET As formerly bargain buffet prices skyrocket—and we aren't helping matters by highly recommending $30-and-up places such as the Wynn buffet—it's getting harder and harder to find anything budget minded on the Strip. Well, anywhere worth eating, certainly. This isn't on the Strip, but it is nearby, and the prices are cheaper than at any buffet on the Strip. Plus, you are less likely to find tremendous lines here. Having said that, don't expect anything miraculous, though they get points for keeping the food at the correct temperature (many a buffet's hot food suffers from a cooling effect as it sits out). Options run the usual gamut: Asian (decent pot stickers), Mexican (fine beef fajitas), and a carving station (with full rotisserie chickens). There is an all-you-can-eat steak night and an all-you-can-eat seafood night.

In Gold Coast, 4400 West Flamingo Rd. ✆ **702/367-7111.** Breakfast $7; lunch $9; dinner $13-$17; Sun brunch $13. Reduced prices for children 4-9; free for children 3 and under. Mon–Sat 7-10:30am, 11am-3pm, and 4-9pm; Sun 8am-3pm and 4-9pm.

Downtown
MODERATE

Golden Nugget Buffet ★★ BUFFET This buffet has often been voted number one in Las Vegas and while we wouldn't go that far, it certainly is top quality. Most of the seating is in plush booths. The buffet tables are laden with an extensive salad bar (about 50 items), fresh fruit, and marvelous desserts. Fresh seafood is featured every night. Most lavish is the all-day Sunday champagne brunch, which adds such dishes as eggs Benedict, blintzes, pancakes, creamed herring, and smoked fish with bagels and cream cheese.

In Golden Nugget, 129 E. Fremont St. ✆ **702/385-7111.** Breakfast $10; lunch $11; dinner Mon–Thurs $18, Fri $30, Sat–Sun $21; Sat–Sun brunch $18. Half price for children 3-12; free for children 2 and under. AE, DC, DISC, MC, V. Mon–Fri 7am-10pm; Sat–Sun 8am-10pm.

INEXPENSIVE

Fremont Paradise Buffet ★ BUFFET Another buffet that makes us cross about rising Vegas prices; this was (at dinnertime) one of the cheapest buffets we could recommend, but now? Not so much (seems like every night's a theme night). However, lunchtime still brings a price that is a bargain. The selection isn't extensive (though with some surprises in the form of a "Southwestern" station and some Chinese), but the space is adequately attractive. Expect long lines.

In Fremont Hotel & Casino, 200 E. Fremont St. ✆ **702/385-3232.** Breakfast and lunch $8; dinner $10; Sun brunch $10; various theme (steak or seafood) nights $13-$16. Free for children 3 and under. AE, DC, DISC, MC, V. Mon–Fri 7-10:30am, 11am-3pm, and 4-10pm; Sat–Sun 7am-3pm and 4-10pm.

Main Street Station Garden Court ★★★ 🎁 BUFFET Set in what is truly one of the prettiest buffet spaces in town (and certainly in Downtown), with very high ceilings and tall windows bringing in much-needed natural light, the Main Street Station Garden Court buffet is one of the best in town, let alone Downtown. It features nine live-action stations where you can watch your food being prepared, including a wood-fired, brick-oven pizza (delicious); many fresh salsas at the Mexican station; a barbecue rotisserie; fresh sausage at the carving station; Chinese, Hawaiian, and Southern specialties (soul food and the like); and so many more we lost count. On Friday night, it has all this and nearly infinite varieties of seafood, all the way up to lobster. We ate ourselves into a stupor and didn't regret it.

At Main Street Station, 200 N. Main St. ⓒ **702/387-1896.** Breakfast $7; lunch $8; dinner $11–$16; Sat–Sun champagne brunch $11. Free for children 3 and under. AE, DC, DISC, MC, V. Daily 7–10:30am, 11am–3pm, and 4–10pm.

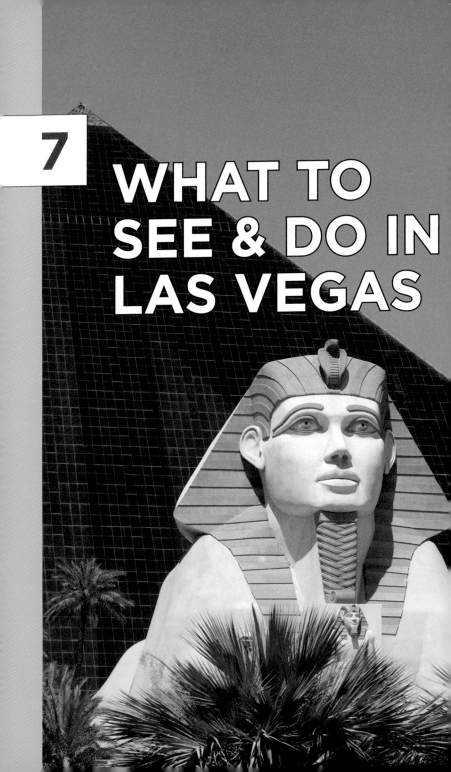

7

WHAT TO SEE & DO IN LAS VEGAS

Y ou aren't going to lack for things to do in Las Vegas. More than likely, you've come here for the gambling, which should keep you pretty busy. (We say that with some understatement.) But you can't sit at a slot machine forever. (Or maybe you can.) In any event, it shouldn't be too hard to find ways to fill your time between poker hands.

Just walking on the Strip and gazing at the gaudy, garish, absurd wonder of it all can occupy quite a lot of time. This is the number-one activity we recommend in Vegas; at night, it is a mind-boggling sight. And, of course, there are shows and plenty of other nighttime entertainment. Vegas is firmly set in such an "adult" entertainment direction that many attractions, particularly those with kid appeal, have closed, and though new, equally expensive options may come along to take their place, the emphasis right now seems to be on mature fun—drinking, gambling, nightclubbing, and the like.

Don't forget to check out the **free hotel attractions,** such as Bellagio's water-fountain ballet, The Mirage's volcano, the MGM lions, and the Show in the Sky at the Rio. Oh, yeah, and the utter piece of hooey that masquerades as the pirate show at Treasure Island. You can probably give that a miss.

You could also consider using a spa at a major hotel; they seem too pricey (as high as $30 a day) to fill in for your daily gym visit if you are just going to use a few machines, but spending a couple of hours working out, sweating out Vegas toxins in the steam room, and generally pampering yourself will leave you feeling relaxed, refreshed, and ready to go all night again.

There are also plenty of out-of-town sightseeing options, such as **Hoover Dam** (a major tourist destination), **Red Rock Canyon,** and excursions to the Grand Canyon. We've listed the best of these in chapter 11.

Suggested Las Vegas Itineraries

The itineraries outlined here are for adults. If you're traveling with kids, incorporate some of the suggestions from "Especially for Kids," listed later in this chapter. If you want itineraries that are more theme intensive, see chapter 3. The activities mentioned briefly here are described more fully later in this chapter.

IF YOU HAVE 1 DAY Spend most of the day **casino hopping.** These are buildings like no other (thank goodness). Each grandiose interior tops the last. You'll want to see as much as you can of CityCenter, a grandiose imagining of what Vegas may look like for the next few decades, complete with multiple hotels, a massive casino, shopping, and enough eye candy to last you for your entire trip. But also be sure to see Wynn Las Vegas, The Venetian, Bellagio, The Mirage, Treasure Island, Paris Las Vegas, Caesars Palace (including The Forum Shops and the talking statues), New York–New York, MGM Grand, and the exteriors of Excalibur and Luxor. Then at night, take

FACING PAGE: **A replica of the Sphinx guards entrance to the Luxor.**

FROM TOP: The Venetian, lit up at night, is one of the prettiest sights on the Strip; one of many colorful rock formations at Red Rock Canyon.

a drive (if you can) down **the Strip.** As amazing as all this is during the day, you just can't believe it at night. Aside from just the Strip itself, there are Bellagio's **water fountains,** which "perform" to various musical numbers, the dreadful (and even though it's free, still not worth the money) sexy **sirens vs. pirate battle** at Treasure Island, and the newly refurbished **volcano explosion** next door at The Mirage. Eat at a buffet (see chapter 6 for details and options) and have a drink at the top of the Stratosphere, goggling at the view from the tallest building west of the Mississippi (and leap off the top with **SkyJump** if you are so inclined and/or insane). Oh, and maybe you should gamble a little, too.

IF YOU HAVE 2 DAYS Do more of the above, as you may not have covered it all. Then head off to the Dolphin Habitat a the Mirage, which is worth a look in that it's unexpectedly not Las Vegas. At night, take in a show. We think *KÀ, O,* and *Mystère,* productions from the avant-garde **Cirque du Soleil,** are the finest in Vegas, but there are plenty to choose from, including a selection of Broadway babies, such as ***Phantom,*** and divas galore, including Cher and Céline Dion (who returns in March 2011). Though buffets are still the most Vegas-appropriate food experience, genuine haute cuisine by celebrity chefs has invaded the town and you should take advantage of it. **Bartolotta, Bouchon,** and **Picasso** are our top choices (not to mention

Joël Robuchon and **L'Atelier de Joël Robuchon** at the MGM Grand, if you can afford the supreme pleasure), but you can't go wrong with **Alex, Alizé,** or **Aureole,** plus there are branches of **Olives, Pinot Brasserie,** and the **Border Grill.** More affordable, yet still fantastic, choices include **Todd English P.U.B.** and **Hash House a Go-Go.** Be sure to leave some time to go Downtown to check out the much more affordable casinos in the classic Glitter Gulch and to visit the **Fremont Street Experience** light show.

IF YOU HAVE 3 DAYS By now you've spent 2 days gambling and gawking. So take a break and drive out to **Red Rock Canyon.** The panoramic 13-mile scenic loop drive is best seen early in the morning, when there's little traffic. If you're so inclined, spend some time hiking here. If you want to spend the entire day out, bring lunch from nearby **Red Rock Resort,** and then do a stop at nearby **Bonnie Springs Ranch,** where you can enjoy a guided trail ride into the desert wilderness or enjoy the silliness at **Old Nevada** (see chapter 11 for details).

IF YOU HAVE 4 DAYS OR MORE Plan a tour to **Hoover Dam.** Leave early in the morning, returning to Las Vegas after lunch via **Valley of Fire State Park,** stopping at the **Lost City Museum** in Overton en route (see chapter 11 for details). Alternatively, you can rest up by spending the day by the hotel pool or going to the hotel spa. At night, presumably refreshed and purged of toxins, hit the casinos and/or catch another show. There are lots of non-Cirque, nondiva shows that you haven't seen, such as the laugh-out-loud observations of **Rita Rudner,** or there is the arty weirdness of the **Blue Man Group** at The Venetian, or *Jubilee!* if your trip won't be complete without a topless revue. You can also feast at dinner, because you certainly haven't tried all there is. There is some great work being done by restaurants not associated with brand-name chefs, such as Raku Grill, Rosemary's, Alizé, and Andre's.

As you plan any additional days, consider excursions to other nearby attractions, such as **Lake Mead** and the **Grand Canyon.** Inquire about interesting possibilities at your hotel's tour desk.

THE TOP ATTRACTIONS

See also the listings for theme parks and other fun stuff in "Especially for Kids," later in this chapter.

The Arts Factory ★ 🏛 Believe it or not, Las Vegas has a burgeoning art scene (what some would consider soul crushing is what others consider inspirational), and this complex, located in the Gateway district, is the place to find proof. It features a few galleries and a number of work spaces for local artists. Several of the spaces are closed to the public. On the first Friday of each month, there is an evening party event ("First Friday") showcasing local artists and arts-oriented businesses, with live music, street performances, and other entertainment and activities.

107 E. Charleston Blvd. ✆ **702/383-3133.** www.theartsfactory.com. Free admission. Hours vary by gallery.

The Atomic Testing Museum ★★★ 🏛 From 1951 until 1992, the Nevada Test Site was this country's primary location for testing nuclear weapons. Aboveground blasts in the early days were visible to the tourists and residents of

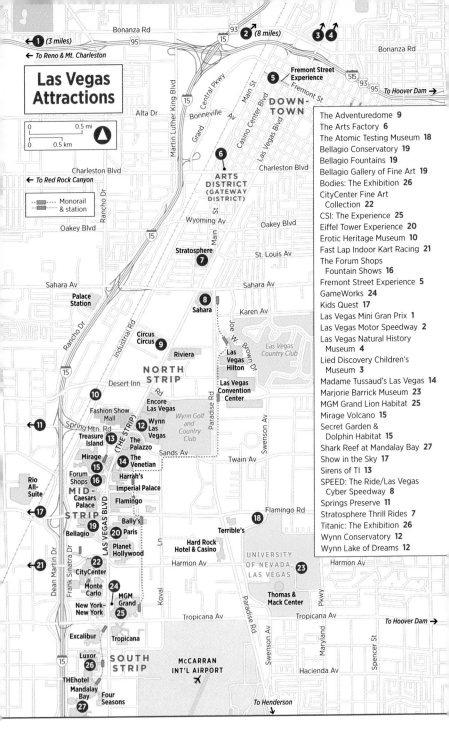

Las Vegas Attractions

To Reno & Mt. Charleston
← 1 (3 miles)
← To Red Rock Canyon
← To Hoover Dam →

2 (8 miles)

5 Fremont Street Experience

To Hoover Dam →

DOWN-TOWN

0   0.5 mi
0   0.5 km

Monorail & station

ARTS DISTRICT (GATEWAY DISTRICT) 6

7 Stratosphere

8 Sahara

9 Circus Circus

Riviera

Las Vegas Hilton

Las Vegas Country Club

NORTH STRIP

Las Vegas Convention Center

Wynn Golf and Country Club

10

Encore Las Vegas

11

Fashion Show Mall

12 Wynn Las Vegas

13 Treasure Island

The Palazzo

Mirage 15

14 The Venetian

16 Forum Shops

Harrah's

Imperial Palace

Flamingo

MID-Caesars Palace STRIP

Rio All-Suite

17

Bally's

19 Bellagio

20 Paris

Planet Hollywood

Terrible's

18

Hard Rock Hotel & Casino

21

22 CityCenter

Monte Carlo

24 MGM Grand

23

UNIVERSITY OF NEVADA, LAS VEGAS

Thomas & Mack Center

New York-New York 25

Excalibur

Tropicana

26 Luxor

SOUTH STRIP

McCARRAN INT'L AIRPORT ✈

THEhotel

27 Mandalay Bay

Four Seasons

To Hoover Dam →

To Henderson

First Friday event at The Arts Factory.

Las Vegas. This well-executed museum, library, and gallery space (a Smithsonian affiliate) offers visitors a fascinating glance at the test site from ancient days through modern times, with memorabilia, displays, official documents, videos, interactive displays, motion-simulator theaters (such as sitting in a bunker, watching a blast), and emotional testimony from the people who worked there. It respectfully treads that tricky line between honoring the work done at the site and understanding its terrible implications. Not to be missed, even if it's only because of the Albert Einstein action figure in the gift shop. Visitors should plan on spending at least an hour.

755 E. Flamingo Rd. (*C*) **702/794-5151.** www.atomictestingmuseum.org. Admission $12 adults; $9 seniors, military, students with ID, and Nevada residents; free for children 6 and under. Mon–Sat 9am–5pm; Sun noon–5pm. Closed Thanksgiving, Dec 25, and Jan 1.

Bellagio Gallery of Fine Art ★ Everyone scoffed when then–Bellagio owner Steve Wynn opened an art gallery on his fabulous property. Sure, Wynn's been a serious and respected fine-arts collector for years, and consequently there was good stuff on display (though there are no masterpieces, there certainly are serious works by masters), but who would go see *art* in Las Vegas? Tons of tourists, as it happens, so many that the gallery had to be relocated almost immediately to a larger space.

When MGM Resorts International bought Wynn's empire, the future of the gallery, which relied on his collection (he took most of it with him), was in doubt. The gallery is not only open again, but it's also getting written up by real art critics, thanks in part to such well-chosen shows as Warhol, Monet, Picasso ceramics, and Ansel Adams retrospectives, and an exhibit from the collection of none other than Steve Martin—yes, we mean the stand-up-comedian-turned-actor-turned-playwright/author.

FROM LEFT: The Atomic Testing Museum; the gift shop at the Bellagio Gallery of Fine Art.

Now, will there be as interesting a show when you go? Beats us. (When we wrote this, it was Figuratively Speaking, a collection of sculpture and paintings studying the human form.) Then there's that ticket price. Do let us point out that admission to the Louvre—needless to say, quite a bit larger and with, one can safely say, some notable works—is about $5 cheaper than the entry fee of this museum.

In Bellagio, 3600 Las Vegas Blvd. S. (℃) **702/693-7871.** www.bellagio.com. Reservations suggested, but walk-ins taken every 15 min. Admission $15 adults, $12 seniors and Nevada residents, $10 teachers and students with ID. Sun–Tues and Thurs 10am–6pm; Wed and Fri–Sat 10am–7pm. Last admission half-hour prior to closing.

Bodies . . . The Exhibition ★★ A stunning and controversial exhibit featuring what can be best described as real live dead bodies (13 of them and 260 organs!). Utilizing a patented freeze-dry operation, full bodies (donated by their former inhabitants, though that's where the controversy comes in), artfully dissected body parts, and stripped cadavers are on display not for sensationalism—though it is pretty sensational in nearly all senses of the word—but for visitors to fully appreciate the wonder and mechanics that go into our transient **flesh.** When a body is positioned in an athletic pose, you can see how the muscles work, and when a cross section of a lung afflicted with cancer is right in front of you, you may well be glad Vegas is increasingly a nonsmoking town. It's educational and bizarre and not something you are likely to forget soon. Surprisingly, not grotesque, but not for the ultrasqueamish.

In the Luxor, 3900 Las Vegas Blvd. S. (℃) **702/262-4400.** Admission $31 adults, $29 seniors 65 and over, $23 ages 4–12, free 3 and under, $28 Nevada residents. Tickets valid for 7 days from purchase. Daily 10am–10pm; last admission 9pm.

CityCenter Fine Art Collection ★ Previous attempts at displaying fine art have met with mixed success in Las Vegas. Of the four major galleries/museums to open over the last decade, only the one at Bellagio remains. But CityCenter has gone a different route, choosing to integrate its fine art collection throughout the resort, turning the entire place into one big gallery of sorts. There's a sculpture from Maya Lin, designer of the Vietnam War Memorial, over the check-in desk; the iconic *Reclining Connected Forms* sculpture by Henry Moore; a massive installation of canoes and rowboats in a valet area by Nancy Rubins; and a 250-foot-long LED display from street artist Jenny Holzer to name a few. You can pick up a brochure and map at the concierge desk at Aria Las Vegas that will guide you to the major works. Wear comfortable shoes; there is a lot of walking involved.

At CityCenter, 3730 Las Vegas Blvd. S. ⓒ **702/590-7111.** Free admission. Most artworks are outdoors or in 24-hour public spaces.

CSI: The Experience ★ Although spin-offs have moved the sleuthing to Miami and New York, the original *CSI* television show takes place in Las Vegas, so how apropos is this major attraction, which allows you to work a crime scene right here on the Strip. Three different crimes have occurred—a car has crashed into a house, a woman has been murdered behind a motel, and a skeleton has been found in the desert—and it's up to you to examine the crime scene, look for clues, take notes, and then run it all through an interactive lab of sorts with help from videos of various stars of the show and real-life CSI technicians. It's silly, gory and highly engrossing fun if you have an analytical mind (all but the most sullen of teenagers will love this!).

In MGM Grand, 3799 Las Vegas Blvd. S. ⓒ **877/660-0660.** Admission $30 for the first crime scene, $26 per experience after that. Daily 10am–10pm.

Eiffel Tower Experience ✋ Whether this is worth the dough depends on how much you like views. An elevator operator (we refuse to call them guides) delivers a few facts about this Eiffel Tower (this is a half-size exact replica, down to the paint color of the original) during the minute or so ride to the uppermost platform, where you are welcome to stand around and look out for as long as you want, which probably isn't 2 hours, the length of the average movie, which costs about what this does. Nice view, though.

Big Edge by Nancy Rubin, CityCenter Fine Art Collection.

Anatomical exhibit at Bodies . . . The Exhibition.

A "crime scene" at CSI: The Experience.

In Paris Las Vegas, 3655 Las Vegas Blvd. S. © **702/946-7000.** Admission $10 adults 9:30am–7:30pm, $12 7:30pm–close; $7 seniors 65 and over and children 6–12 9:30am–7:30pm, $10 7:30–close; free for children 5 and under. Daily 9:30am–12:30am, weather permitting.

Erotic Heritage Museum ★★★ It sounds like something you'd find next door to a strip club, and in fact it is, but this adjunct of the Institute for Advanced Study of Human Sexuality is not about cheap thrills. Instead, it's a totally engrossing (and sometimes simply gross) museum/art gallery devoted to the exploration of all things sex. Exhibits include artwork, sculpture, video, photographs, artifacts, interactive displays, and more that run the gamut from the ancient rituals of deflowerization to the peek-a-boo naughtiness of Bettie Page to the hard-core adult film industry, with stops at bondage, peep shows, the First Amendment, Tom of Finland, and Larry Flint along the way. It is at turns sobering (the AIDS panels on display are still moving), silly (a sculpture of a male, uh, "appendage" made of 100,000 pennies), and shocking (the mechanics of sadomasochism) and absolutely geared toward adults with an open mind. If you are one, this is one of the most original, informative, and entertaining museums anywhere in the world. A full erotic library, gift shop, performing arts/arts instruction venue, and even an erotic wedding chapel fill out the massive space.

3275 Industrial Rd. (at Desert Inn Rd.). © **702/369-6442.** Admission $15; discounts for college students. Not appropriate for children 17 and under. Wed–Thurs 6–10pm; Fri 3pm–midnight; Sat–Sun noon–midnight.

Fast Lap Indoor Kart Racing ★★ 🎁 When NASCAR pro Kurt Busch is in Las Vegas, this is the place he comes to play. Tucked away on a dead-end street in a mostly industrial part of town near the Strip, this is a no-frills go-kart experience, with a short track filling a former warehouse space that still looks like a warehouse. The gasoline-powered karts are equipped with 200cc Honda motors, allowing you to push the little monsters up to 50 mph (if you dare) as you battle in 10-minute-long races (as many laps as

The nighttime view from the Eiffel Tower Experience is superb if expensive.

Fast Lap Indoor Car Racing.

you can get) against other drivers. While bumping and other unsportsman-like contact is officially frowned upon, in reality this is a grown-up (mostly testosterone driven) sport. So put your foot on the gas and see if you can be first to the checkered flag! **Note:** You must be at least 5 feet tall to participate, and children 17 and under must be accompanied by a parent or guardian.

4288 Polaris Ave. © **702/736-8113.** www.fastlaplv.com. $25 per race or $62 for 3 races. Mon–Sat 11am–11pm; Sun 11am–9pm.

Fremont Street Experience ★★ The Fremont Street Experience is a 5-block open-air landscaped strip of outdoor snack shops, vendor carts, and colorful kiosks purveying food and merchandise. Overhead is a 90-foot-high steel-mesh "celestial vault." At night, it is the successfully revamped **Viva Vision,** a hightech light-and-laser show (the canopy is equipped with more than 12.5 million lights), enhanced by a concert hall–quality sound system, that takes place five times nightly. There are a number of different shows, and there's music between the light performances as well. Not only does the canopy provide shade, but it also cools the area through a misting system in summer and warms you with radiant heaters in winter. It's really cool, in that Vegas over-the-top way that we love so much. Go see for yourself; you will be pleased to see how a one-time ghost town of tacky, rapidly aging buildings, in an area with more undesirables than not, is now a bustling (at least at night), friendly, safe place (they have private security guards who hustle said undesirables away). It's a place where you can stroll, eat, or even dance to the music under the lights. The crowd it attracts is more upscale than in years past, and, of course, it's a lot less crowded than the hectic Strip. This helps give a second life to a deserving neighborhood. **Note:** A good place to view the Sky Parade light show is from the balcony at Fitzgerald's Casino & Hotel.

And in a further effort to retain as much of classic Las Vegas as possible, the **Neon Museum** has installed vintage hotel and casino signs along the promenade. The first installation was the horse and rider from the old Hacienda,

which presently rides the sky over the intersection of Fremont Street and Las Vegas Boulevard, while the lamp from the old Aladdin Hotel twinkles at the northwest corner. Eventually, the Neon Museum will have a complex at their Neon Boneyard, using the old La Concha Motel, itself a piece of classic Vegas architecture thankfully saved from the wrecking ball, as a centerpiece. It's supposed to open sometime in 2011 and will feature a park where you can wander amongst the restored signs.

Fremont St. (btw. Main St. and Las Vegas Blvd.), Downtown. www.vegasexperience.com. Free admission. Shows nightly.

FROM LEFT: "Vegas Vic," the most famous neon sign overlooking the Fremont Street Experience; GameWorks offers arcade fun for kids and adults.

GameWorks ★★ ☺ What do you get when Steven Spielberg and his DreamWorks team get in on the arcade video-game action? Grown-up, state-of-the-art fun. High-tech movie magic has taken over all sorts of traditional arcade games and turned them interactive, from a virtual-reality batting cage to a *Jurassic Park* game that lets you hunt dinosaurs. There are motion-simulator rides galore and even actual-motion activities, such as rock climbing. But classic games, from Pac-Man to pool tables, are here, too, though sometimes with surprising twists, such as air hockey where multiple pucks occasionally shoot out at once.

All this doesn't exactly come cheap. Prices for games start at $1. You can buy a dollar-value game card, or purchase time-play cards at the following prices: $20 for 1 hour, $25 for 2 hours, $30 for 3 hours, or an all-day pass for $35. Purchased points go on a debit card that you then insert into the various machines to activate them. Children probably should be 10 years old and up—any younger and parents will need to stand over them rather than go off and have considerable fun on their own. *Note:* If you don't like crowds, come here earlier rather than later, when it can get packed. There is a dress code (no excessively baggy clothes, no tattoos or clothing with profanity, no chains, and so on) that is enforced occasionally, and no one under 18 is allowed without parental supervision after 9pm.

In the Showcase Mall, 3785 Las Vegas Blvd. S. ☏ **702/432-4263.** www.gameworks.com. Game prices vary. Sun–Thurs 10am–midnight; Fri–Sat 10am–1am; Thanksgiving Day 10am–midnight; Dec 24–25, Dec 31, and Jan 1 10am–2am.

Las Vegas Mini Gran Prix ★★★ ☺ Finally, after all our yammering about how Vegas isn't for families and how most of the kid-friendly options are really overpriced tourist traps, we can wholeheartedly recommend an actual family-appropriate entertainment option. Part arcade, part go-kart racetrack, this is exactly what you want to help your kids (and maybe yourselves) work their ya-yas out. The arcade is well stocked, with a better quality of prizes than one often finds, but we suggest not spending too much time in there and instead hustling outside to the slide, the little roller coaster, and best of all, the four go-kart tracks. Each offers a different thrill, from the longest track in Vegas, full of twists and turns as you try to outrace other drivers (be a sport, let the little kids win occasionally), to a high-banked oval built just so you can try to make other drivers take spills onto the grass, to, best of all, a timed course. The last requires a driver's license, so it's for you rather than your kids (but the wee ones will find the fourth course is just for them), and here you can live out your Le Mans or police-chase fantasies as you blast through twisting runs one kart at a time, trying to beat your personal best. The staff is utterly friendly, and the pizzas at the food court are triple the size and half the price of those found in your hotel. The one drawback: It's far away from main Strip action, so you'll need that rental car. **Note:** Kids have to be at least 36 inches tall to ride any of the attractions.

1401 N. Rainbow Rd. (just off U.S. 95 N.). ☎ **702/259-7000.** www.lvmgp.com. Ride tickets $6.50 each, $6 for 5 or more; ride wristbands $18 per hour. Tickets good on all rides and at any time. Sun–Thurs 10am–10pm; Fri–Sat 10am–11pm.

Las Vegas Motor Speedway ★★ This 176,000-seat facility was the first new superspeedway to be built in the Southwest in over 2 decades. A $200-million state-of-the-art motorsports entertainment complex (with tens of millions more dumped into it since it opened), it includes a 1½-mile superspeedway, a 2½-mile FIA-approved road course, paved and dirt short-track ovals, and a 4,000-foot drag strip. Also on the property are facilities for go-kart, Legends Car, Sand Drag, and Motocross competition, as well as driving schools,

Las Vegas Mini Gran Prix.

Racing at the Las Vegas Motor Speedway.

and more. The place is so popular that condos are being built overlooking the track for those who apparently don't want to sleep on race days. Some major hotels have shuttles to the speedway during big events, so check with your hotel's front desk or concierge.

7000 Las Vegas Blvd. N. (directly across from Nellis Air Force Base). ⓒ **702/644-4443.** www.lvms.com. Tickets $10–$75 (higher for major events). Race days vary. Take I-15 North to Speedway, exit 54.

Madame Tussauds Las Vegas ★★

☺ Madame Tussauds's waxworks exhibition has been the top London attraction for nearly 2 centuries, so even if you aren't a fan of wax museums, this, its sole branch west of the Mississippi, is probably worth a stop—if you can stomach the admission price. Figures here are state-of-the-art, painstakingly constructed to perfectly match the real person. Truth be told, while some are nearly identical to their living counterparts—Brad Pitt gave us a start—others look about as much like the celebrity in question as a department-store mannequin. All the waxworks are free-standing, allowing, and indeed encouraging, guests to get up close and personal. Go ahead, lay

Get up close with Elvis and other wax celebrities at Madame Tussauds Las Vegas.

your cheek next to Elvis's or Sinatra's and have your photo taken. Or put on a wedding dress and get "married" to "George Clooney" (you know you want to). Or fondle J. Lo's butt (you know you want to). Live performers make the Haunted House section more stimulating than expected. There's also a behind-the-scenes look at the lengthy process involved in creating one of these figures.

In The Venetian, 3355 Las Vegas Blvd. S. ⓒ **702/862-7800.** www.mtvegas.com. Admission $25 adults, $18 seniors, $18 students, $15 children 7–12, free for children 6 and under. Discounts for booking online. Sun–Thurs 10am–9pm; Fri–Sat 10am–10pm; hours vary seasonally; may close early for private events and holidays.

Marjorie Barrick Museum ★

Formerly known as the Natural History Museum (as opposed to the Las Vegas Natural History Museum, which still exists), this is a cool place to beat the heat and noise of Vegas while examining some attractive, if not overly imaginative, displays on Native American craftwork and Las Vegas history. Crafts include 19th-century Mexican religious folk art, a variety of colorful dance masks from Mexico, and Native American pottery. The first part of the hall is often the highlight, with impressive traveling art exhibits. Children won't find much that's entertaining, other than some glass cases containing examples of local, usually poisonous, reptiles (who, if you are lucky—or unlucky, depending on your view—will be dining on mice when you drop by). Outside is a pretty garden that demonstrates how attractive desert-appropriate plants (in other words, those requiring little water) can be. You just wish the local casinos, with their lush and wasteful lawns, would take notice.

Marjorie Barrick Museum.

On the UNLV campus, 4505 Maryland Pkwy. © **702/895-3381.** http://barrickmuseum.unlv.edu. Suggested donation $5 adults, $2 seniors 62 and over. Mon–Fri 8am–4:45pm; Sat 10am–2pm. Closed on state and federal holidays.

MGM Grand Lion Habitat ★★ ☺ Hit this attraction at the right time, and it's one of the best freebies in town. It's a large, multilevel glass enclosure in which lions frolic during various times of day. In addition to regular viewing spots, you can walk through a glass tunnel and get a worm's-eye view of the underside of a lion (provided one is in position); note how very big Kitty's paws are. Multiple lions share show duties (about 6 hr. on and then 2 days off at a ranch for some free-range activity, so they're never cooped up here for long). You could see any combo, from one giant male to a pack of five females who have grown from cub to adult during their MGM time. Each comes with a trainer or three, who are there to keep the lions busy with play so they don't act like the big cats they are and sleep the entire time. But obviously, photo ops are more likely to occur as the more frisky youngsters tussle, so what you observe definitely depends on who is in residence when you drop by. ***Note:*** Hordes of tourists are often pressed against the glass, preventing you, not to mention your kids, from doing the same.

In MGM Grand, 3799 Las Vegas Blvd. S. © **702/891-7777.** Free admission. Daily 11am–10pm.

Secret Garden & Dolphin Habitat ★★★ ☺ Siegfried & Roy's white tigers went from famous to infamous when one of them either did what tigers all do eventually and attacked his owner/trainer, or—depending on whether you buy the following story—helped said owner/trainer when the latter was having a medical emergency. Either way this saga is played, it explains why the **Secret Garden** attraction is still up; no matter what, the tiger is not to blame. Here, white lions, Bengal tigers, an Asian elephant, a panther, and a snow leopard join the white tigers. (The culprit, Montecore, may sometimes be on exhibit.) It's really just a glorified zoo, featuring only the big-ticket animals; however, it is a very pretty

place, with plenty of foliage and some bits of Indian- and Asian-themed architecture. Zoo purists will be horrified at the small-ish spaces the animals occupy, but all the animals are rotated between here and their more lavish digs at the illusionist team's home. What this does allow you to do is get safely close to a tiger, which is quite a thrill—those paws are massive indeed.

The **Dolphin Habitat** is more satisfy-ing than the Secret Garden. It was designed to provide a nurturing environment and to educate the public about marine mammals and their role in the ecosystem. Specialists worldwide were consulted in creating the habitat. The pool is more than eight times larger than government regulations require,

FROM TOP: **MGM Grand Lion Habitat; a white tiger in The Secret Garden.**

and its 2.5 million gallons of human-made seawater are cycled and cleaned every 2 hours. The Mirage displays only dolphins already in captivity—no dolphins are taken from the wild. You can watch the dolphins frolic both above and below ground through viewing windows, in three different pools. The knowledgeable staff members, who surely have the best jobs in Vegas, will answer questions. If they aren't doing it already, ask them to play ball with the dolphins; they toss large beach balls into the pools, and the dolphins hit them out with their noses, leaping out of the water, cackling with dolphin glee. You catch the ball, getting nicely wet, and toss it back to them. If you have never played ball with a dolphin, shove that happy child next to you out of the way and go for it. You can stay as long as you like, which might just be hours.

Shark Reef at Mandalay Bay.

In The Mirage, 3400 Las Vegas Blvd. S. ✆ **702/791-7111.** www.mirage.com. Admission $15 adults, $10 children 4–10, free for children 3 and under if accompanied by an adult. Mon–Fri 11am–5:30pm; Sat–Sun and holidays 10am–5:30pm.

Shark Reef at Mandalay Bay ★ Given that watching fish can lower your blood pressure, it's practically a public service for Mandalay Bay to provide this facility in a city where craps tables and other gaming areas can bring your excitement level to dangerous heights. Although we admire the style (it's built to look like a sunken temple), and standing in the all-glass tunnel surrounded by sharks is cool, it's just a giant aquarium, which we like, but not at these prices. **Note:** It is *waaay* off in a remote part of Mandalay Bay, which might be a hassle for those with mobility problems.

In Mandalay Bay, 3950 Las Vegas Blvd. S. ✆ **702/632-4555.** www.mandalaybay.com. Admission $17 adults, $13 children 5–12, free for children 4 and under. Sun–Thurs 10am–8pm; Fri–Sat 10am–10pm. Last admission 1 hr. before closing.

SPEED: The Ride/Las Vegas Cyber Speedway ★★ Auto racing is the fastest-growing spectator sport in America, so it's no surprise that these two attractions at the Sahara are a popular stop. The first is an 8-minute, virtual-reality ride, **Cyber Speedway,** featuring a three-quarter-size replica of a NASCAR race car. Hop aboard for an animated, simulated ride—either the Las Vegas Motor Speedway or a race around the streets of Las Vegas (start with the Strip, with all the hotels flashing by, and then through The Forum Shops—whoops! There goes Versace!). Press the gas and you lean back and feel the rush of speed; hit a bump and you go flying. Should your car get in a crash, off you go to a pit stop. At the end, a computer-generated report tells you your average speed, how many laps you made, and how you did racing against the others next to you. It's a pretty remarkable experience.

free VEGAS

Vegas used to be the land of freebies—or at least, stuff so cheap it seemed free. Those days are an increasingly dim memory, but some hotels still offer free attractions designed to lure you into their casinos, where you might well then drop far more than the cost of a day ticket to Disney World. Here's a handy list of the best of the free bait, er, sights:

Bellagio Conservatory (in Bellagio) ★★★ A totally preposterous idea, a larger-than-life greenhouse atrium, filled with seasonal living foliage in riotous colors and styles, changed with meticulous regularity. From Easter to Chinese New Year, events are celebrated with carefully designed splashes of flowers, plants, and remarkable decorations— it's an incredible amount of labor for absolutely no immediate financial payoff. No wonder it's one of the most popular sights in Vegas. Open 24 hours.

Bellagio Fountains (outside Bellagio) ★★★ Giant spouts of water shoot up and down and sideways, and dance their little aquatic hearts out to music ranging from show tunes to Chopin. When we tell people about this, they roll their eyes when they think we aren't looking, and then they go see it for themselves . . . and end up staying for several numbers. Shows are daily every half-hour, starting early afternoon, then every 15 minutes 8pm to midnight. Closed when it's windy.

The Forum Shops Fountain Shows (in The Forum Shops at Caesars) ★ The first established of the free shows and easily the stupidest. We love it, in theory at least, as giant "marble" Greco-Roman statues come to creaky animatronic life and deliver a largely unintelligible speech, mostly exhorting the crowds to eat, drink, and get so merry they will think nothing of dropping a bundle at the slots. Not quite so bad it's good, but one day they are going to wise up and make the thing more high-tech, and a little something special will be lost. Daily every hour, starting at 10am.

Mirage Volcano (outside The Mirage) ★ The first curbside free attraction. One of the reasons Wynn designed it is so that you can't see his new mountain and lake show from the street (see "Wynn Lake of Dreams," below)—because that doesn't bring guests *into* the property. This paled in comparison to such things as dancing fountains and pirates, but a 2008 makeover amped up the fire, lights, sound, and effects to a much more entertaining level. Get up close to feel the heat of the "lava" blasts and the rumble of the sound system. Eruptions are daily on the hour after dark until midnight.

Show in the Sky (in the Rio-pictured at right) ★ Like TI's pirates, this formerly wholesome, if a bit weird, show has undergone a revamp to make it more sexy and adult oriented. It's still staged on floats that move above viewers' heads, but now those floats include "bedroom" and "spa" scenes peopled with what the

Wynn Conservatory (in Wynn Las Vegas) ★ Yes, remarkably like the one at Bellagio, this one is better placed, situated just inside the door and laid out so that you can stroll through it on your way to other parts of the hotel, as opposed to the tucked-in-a-corner Bellagio version. The floral displays change regularly, though they may reflect the striking floral mosaics on the floor below. We do hope it won't get as wacky as its Bellagio counterpart and will stick to the merely festive. Open 24 hours.

Wynn Lake of Dreams (in Wynn Las Vegas) ★ This is the most peculiar of the "free" shows in several ways: It's not easily defined (not dancing fountains, not a parade in the sky), and it's not easily seen. The 150-foot-tall mountain, complete with mature trees saved from the old Desert Inn golf course, plus several waterfalls, cannot be seen in its entirety from anywhere other than the hotel rooms facing west. The show itself can be watched only if you are dining in the Daniel Boulud Brasserie or SW Steakhouse, the Parasol or Chanel bars, or a small viewing platform set above those venues on the casino level. Nab a coveted spot there or else pay double (or more) digits to dine or drink while waiting for the shows. Should you bother? Maybe. Basically, twice an hour, the lake lights up with pretty colors, cued to tunes ranging from classical to Louis Armstrong for "interludes." At the top of the hour are bigger extravaganzas of weird hologram erotic-psychedelic images projected on the wall waterfall, while shapes and puppets pop out for even more weird action, with some rather adult imagery at times. Shows are every 20 minutes, from 7pm to midnight.

company calls "high energy performers of seduction." This gives you an idea of the kind of action contained therein. Prepare to try to distract your kids' attention elsewhere, though if you want a better view, grab a spot on the second floor of the village. Performed hourly from 7pm until midnight Thursday through Sunday.

Sirens of TI (outside Treasure Island; pictured left) ★ We gave it a star because it has such high production values, but man, it hurt us to do even that. See, this used to be a fun, hokey stunt show, where pirates attacked a British sailing vessel. Lusty men swashed and buckled, cannons exploded, ships sank, and the pirates always won. But Vegas is not for families anymore, and to prove it, the British were removed and now the pirates are lured by lingerie-clad lovelies. Stuff happens, but no one really cares; either you like the nekkid chicks, or you are so horrified by the whole spectacle because it's so appallingly bad that plot twists don't matter much. ***Parents, be warned:*** Between the gals and their undies and the 24-foot stark-raving-naked female figurehead on the ship right by the Strip entrance to Treasure Island, you may be in for an interesting conversation with your children. Shows are daily at 5:30, 7, 8:30, 10, and 11:30pm (summer only), weather permitting.

Speed junkies and race-car buffs will be in heaven here, though those with tender stomachs should consider shopping at the well-stocked theme gift shop instead or playing video games in the Pit Pass Arcade next door, which has 120 game stations.

SPEED: The Ride is a roller coaster that blasts riders out through a hole in the wall by the NASCAR Cafe, then through a loop, under the sidewalk, through the hotel's marquee, and finally straight up a 250-foot tower. At the peak, you feel a moment of weightlessness, and then you do the entire thing backward! Not for the faint of heart.

In the Sahara, 2535 Las Vegas Blvd. S. ✆ **702/737-2111.** www.nascarcafelasvegas.com. Cyber Speedway $10 for 1 ride; SPEED: The Ride $10 for 1 ride; $18 for 1 ride on each; $23 for unlimited rides on both. Mon–Thurs noon–8pm; Fri–Sun noon–10pm.

SPEED: The Ride.

Springs Preserve ★★★ By now, perhaps you've learned that *Las Vegas* is Spanish for "the meadows." This facility is set on the 180-acre site of the original springs that fed Las Vegas until it dried in the 1960s (told you that Hoover Dam comes in handy). These days, Las Vegas is an environmental nightmare, along with much of the rest of this planet, and this remarkable recreational attraction is here to educate us about the possibilities to reverse some of the damage.

Springs Preserve.

Set amid nature and hiking trails, plus man-made wetlands, which is an interesting concept, the focal point is a large interpretive center that gives the history of Las Vegas from a land- and water-use perspective. The displays are creative and interactive, including a room with a reproduction flash flood that uses 5,000 gallons of water and one with a simulation of the experience of working on Hoover Dam. The other buildings are all built according to standards that have the least environmental impact, using modern construction versions of adobe and other green concepts. Each building tackles an aspect of desert living and the environment, including one that instructs kids on the glories of recycling, complete with a compost tunnel to crawl through! Other displays focus on environmentally friendly kitchens and bathrooms while the gardens demonstrate environmentally friendly gardening, including a section instructing seniors and those with disabilities how to garden despite physical limitations.

The outdoor kids' play area is made from recycled materials and has big animals to climb on, in case the kiddies have grown tired of learning responsible stuff. The cafe menu is designed by Wolfgang Puck with further green emphasis. Given the care, knowledge, and urgency of the issues addressed, this is an extraordinary facility for any town but particularly for this one.

333 S. Valley View Blvd. ✆ **702/822-8344.** www.springspreserve.org. Admission $19 adults, $17 seniors and students with ID, $11 children 5–17, free for children under 5; $8.50 Nevada residents. Free admission to trails and gardens. Daily 10am–6pm.

Stratosphere Thrill Rides ★★ ☺ Atop the 1,149-foot Stratosphere Tower are four marvelous thrill rides that will test your mettle and perhaps how strong your stomach is. The **Big Shot** is a breathtaking free-fall ride that thrusts you 160 feet in the air along a 228-foot spire at the top of the tower and then plummets back down again. Sitting in an open car, you seem to be dangling in space over Las Vegas. We have one relative, a thrill-ride enthusiast, who said he never felt more scared than when he rode the Big Shot. After surviving, he promptly put his kids on it; they loved it. Amping up the terror factor is **X-Scream,** a

Insanity, Stratosphere.

SkyJump, Stratosphere.

Titanic: The Exhibition.

giant teeter-totter style device that propels you in an open car off the side of the 100-story tower and lets you dangle there weightlessly before returning you to relative safety. Then there's the aptly named **Insanity,** a spinning whirligig of a contraption that straps you into a seat and twirls you around 1,000 feet or so above terra firma. Insanity is right.

Finally, if whirling and twirling and spinning around at the top of the tower is just not good enough for you, there's **SkyJump,** in which you get to leap off the top of the thing. Although we kind of wish we were kidding, we're really not. Jumpers are put into flight suits and harnesses then taken up to the 108th floor where they get connected to a big cable/winch thing. Then, they jump. It's a "controlled" descent, meaning that you don't just drop the roughly 830 feet to the landing pad, but you are flying down at speeds of up to 40 mph with nothing but a couple of metal wires keeping you in place. There are lots of safety features that they tout and the three other SkyJumps around the world (in New Zealand, China, and South Korea) have sterling safety records. Nevertheless, they may call the other ride Insanity, but we think this one is the truly insane option. **Note:** The rides are shut down in inclement weather and high winds.

Atop Stratosphere Las Vegas, 2000 Las Vegas Blvd. S. ✆ **702/380-7777.** www.stratosphere hotel.com. Admission to Tower $16 adults; $12 seniors, Nevada residents and hotel guests; $10 children 4–12; free for children 3 and under. Big Shot $13, X-Scream $12, Insanity $12, SkyJump $99. Tower admission waived with SkyJump. Multiride and all-day packages available. Sun–Thurs 10am–1am; Fri–Sat 10am–2am. Hours vary seasonally. Minimum height 48 in. for Big Shot, 52 in. for X-Scream and Insanity. Maximum weight 275 lbs. for SkyJump.

Titanic: The Exhibition ★ It's too easy to say "you've seen the movie, now see the exhibit." But that is sort of the case; if you were captivated by the Oscar-winning epic, you will definitely want to take in this exhibit on the unsinkable luxury liner that sank on its maiden voyage. While it's a can't miss for buffs, it might still be of some interest for those with only marginal feelings about the massive 1912 disaster. It's a strangely somber subject for Vegas. It features displays explaining the ship's ill-fated maiden voyage; relics salvaged from the sunken liner; and even re-creations of sample cabins from first, second, and third class, including atmospheric conditions, giving you a sense of how it felt to travel aboard what was an incredible vessel. There is even a large chunk of real ice standing in for the culprit berg.

In the Luxor, 3900 Las Vegas Blvd. S. © **702/262-4400.** Admission $27 adults, $25 seniors 65 and over, $20 children 4–12, free for children 4 and under; $24 Nevada residents with ID. Daily 10am–10pm (last admission 9pm).

GETTING MARRIED

Getting hitched is one of the most popular things to do in Las Vegas. Just ask Britney Spears. As she rather infamously revealed, it's all too easy to get married here. See that total stranger/childhood friend standing next to you? Grab him or her and head down to the **Clark County Marriage License Bureau,** 201 Clark Ave. (© **702/761-0600;** daily, including holidays, 8am–midnight), to get your license. Find a wedding chapel (not hard, as there are about 50 of them in town; they line the north end of the Strip, and most hotels have them) and tie the knot. Just like that. No blood test, no waiting period—heck, not even an awkward dating period. Though you may have a potentially very awkward time explaining it afterward to your mother, your manager, and the press.

Even if you have actually known your intended for some time, Las Vegas is a great place to get married. The ease is the primary attraction, but there are a number of other appealing reasons. You can have any kind of wedding you want, from a big, traditional production number to a small, intimate affair; from a spur-of-the-moment "just-the-happy-couple-in-blue-jeans" kind of thing to an "Elvis-in-a-pink-Cadillac-at-a-drive-through-window" kind of thing (see the box "An Elvis Impersonator's Top 10 Reasons to Get Married in Las Vegas," below). The wedding chapels take care of everything; usually they'll even provide a limo to take you to the license bureau and back. Most offer all the accessories, from rings to flowers to a videotaped record of the event.

Clark County Marriage License Bureau.

We personally know several very happy couples who opted for the Vegas route. Motivations differed, with the ease factor heading the list (though the Vegas-ness of the whole thing came in a close second), but one and all reported having great fun. Is there a more romantic way to start off your life together than in gales of laughter?

In any event, the more than 100,000 couples who yearly take advantage of all this can't be wrong. If you want to follow in the footsteps of Elvis and Priscilla (at the first incarnation of the Aladdin Hotel), Michael Jordan, Jon Bon Jovi, Richard Gere and Cindy Crawford, Pamela Anderson and ill-fated husband no. 3, Angelina Jolie and Billy Bob, and, of course, Britney and What's-His-Name, you'll want to peruse the following list of the most notable wedding chapels on or near the Strip. There are many more in town, and almost all the major hotels offer chapels as well; though the latter are cleaner and less tacky than some of the Strip chapels, they do tend to be without any personality at all. One exception might be the chapel at the Excalibur, where you can dress in medieval costumes, and the lovely chapel at Bellagio, which has personal wedding coordinators and a high level of customer service, holding only 8 to 10 weddings a day—seems like a lot, but it's nothing compared to the volume on the Strip.

With regard to decor, there isn't a radical difference between the major places though some are decidedly spiffier and less sad than others. Attitude certainly makes a difference with several and varies radically, depending on who's working at any given time. Given how important your wedding is—or should be—we encourage you to give yourself time to comparison shop and spurn anyone who doesn't seem eager enough for your business.

You can also call **Las Vegas Weddings** (© **800/498-6285;** www.las vegasweddings.com), which offers one-stop shopping for wedding services. It will find a chapel or outdoor garden that suits your taste (not to mention such only-in-Vegas venues as the former mansions of Elvis Presley and Liberace); book you into a hotel for the honeymoon; arrange the ceremony; and provide flowers, a photographer (and/or videographer), a wedding cake, a limo, a rental car, music, champagne, balloons, and a garter for the bride. Theme weddings are a specialty. There is even a New Age minister on call who can perform a Native American ceremony. And yes, you can get married by an Elvis impersonator. Las Vegas Weddings can also arrange your honeymoon stay, complete with sightseeing tours, show tickets, and meals.

Weddings can be very inexpensive in Vegas: A license is $60 and a basic service not much more. Even a full-blown shebang package—photos, music, flowers, video, cake, and other doodads—will run only about $500 total. We haven't quoted any prices here because the ultimate cost depends entirely on how much you want to spend. Go cheap, and the whole thing will set you back maybe $100, including the license (maybe even somewhat less); go elaborate, and the price is still reasonable by today's wedding-price standards. Be sure to remember that there are often hidden charges, such as expected gratuities for the minister (about $25 should do; no real need to tip anyone else), and so forth. If you're penny-pinching, you'll want to keep those in mind.

Be aware that Valentine's Day is a very popular day to get married in Vegas. Some of the chapels perform as many as 80 services on February 14. But remember, you also don't have to plan ahead. Just show up, get your paperwork, close your eyes, and pick a chapel. And above all, have fun. Good luck and best wishes to you both.

Note: When we describe the following chapels and say "flowers," don't think fresh (unless it's part of a description of services provided); the permanent decorations are artificial and of varying levels of quality, though usually well dusted.

Chapel of the Bells Sporting perhaps the largest and gaudiest wedding chapel sign on the Strip, this is also one of the longest-running chapels, operating since 1957. This combination of classic Vegas "style" and "tradition" is most of what this place has going for it. The chapel is pretty, garnished with swaths of white material and light green accents, seating 25 to 35, but nothing dazzling. It's not particularly distinctive, but Kelly Ripa got married here, so there is that. The chapel prefers advance booking but can do same-day ceremonies.

2233 Las Vegas Blvd. S. (at Sahara Ave.). (℃ **800/233-2391** or 702/735-6803. www.chapelofthe bellslasvegas.com. Mon–Thurs 9am–10pm; Fri–Sat 9am–1am. Open as late as needed on holidays.

Chapel of the Flowers ★★ This chapel's claim to fame is that Dennis Rodman and Carmen Electra exchanged their deathless vows here but don't hold it against the place. A 2010 extreme makeover turned an already lovely facility into a truly stunning one, with gardens, updated decor in all three chapels, full services from photos to flowers, and more. The La Capella Chapel fits 50 and has a rustic Tuscan feel, with wood pews and frosted glass sconces. The Victorian chapel, which holds only 30, has white walls and dark-wood pews and doesn't look very Victorian at all—but as the plainest, it's also the nicest. The smallest is the Magnolia Chapel, done in simple white marble with a free-standing arch. If

> # AN ELVIS IMPERSONATOR'S TOP 10
> # REASONS TO get married IN LAS VEGAS
>
> Jesse Garon has appeared in numerous Las Vegas productions as "Young Elvis." He arrives at any special event in a 1955 pink, neon-lit Cadillac, and does weddings, receptions, birthdays, conventions, grand openings, and so on. For all your Elvis impersonator needs, call (℃ **702/741-4623,** or visit his website at **www.vegaselvis.com**.
>
> 1. It's the only place in the world where Elvis will marry you, at a drive-up window, in a pink Cadillac—24 hours a day.
>
> 2. Chances are, you'll never forget your anniversary.
>
> 3. Where else can you treat all your guests to a wedding buffet for only 99¢ a head?
>
> 4. Four words: One helluva bachelor party.
>
> 5. On your wedding night, show your spouse that new "watch me disappear" act you learned from Siegfried & Roy.
>
> 6. Show your parents who's boss—have your wedding your way.
>
> 7. Wedding bells ring for you everywhere you go. They just sound like slot machines.
>
> 8. You can throw dice instead of rice.
>
> 9. Easy to lie about age on the marriage certificate—just like Joan Collins did!
>
> 10. With all the money you save, it's dice clocks for everyone!

WHAT TO SEE & DO IN LAS VEGAS

Getting Married

7

231

you want an outdoor vow exchange, you might choose the gazebo by a running stream and waterfall that nearly drowns out Strip noise. There's also a medium-size reception room and live organ music upon request, plus Internet streaming of services is available for those of you who have second thoughts about not inviting the family to your vows. It's a pretty, friendly place (owned by the same family for more than 50 years) that seems to keep an eye on its bustling business. It does not allow rice or confetti throwing.

1717 Las Vegas Blvd. S. (at E. Oakey Blvd.). ☎ **800/843-2410** or 702/735-4331. www.littlechapel. com. Mon–Thurs 7am–8pm; Fri 7am–9pm; Sat 7am–9pm; Sun closed.

Graceland Wedding Chapel ★ Housed in a landmark building that's one of the oldest wedding chapels in Vegas, the Graceland bills itself as "the proverbial mom and pop outfit." No, Elvis never slept here, but one of the owners was friends with Elvis and asked his permission to use the name. This is a tiny New England church building with a small bridge and white picket fence out front. Inside is a 30-seat chapel; the walls are off-white, with a large, modern stained-glass window of doves and roses behind the pulpit. The pews are dark-blond wood. It's not the nicest of the chapels, but Jon Bon Jovi and Billy Ray Cyrus got married here, though not to each other. An Elvis package is available, and weddings are available for viewing online 45 minutes after the ceremony.

619 Las Vegas Blvd. S. (at E. Bonneville Ave.). ☎ **800/824-5732** or 702/382-0091. www. gracelandchapel.com. Daily 9am–11pm.

Little Church of the West ★★ Built in 1942 on the grounds of The Frontier, this gorgeous traditional chapel has been moved three times in its history and has hosted weddings for everyone from Judy Garland to Angelina Jolie. Elvis even got married here, at least on film—the building played the backdrop for his nuptials to Ann-Margret in *Viva Las Vegas*. There are rich wood walls, ceiling, and pews, stained-glass windows, and a traditional steeple amongst the well-landscaped grounds, making it a really lovely option for those looking to walk down the aisle.

4617 Las Vegas Blvd. S. (at Russell Rd.). ☎ **800/821-2452** or 702/739-7971. www.littlechurchlv. com. Daily 8am–midnight.

Little White Wedding Chapel This is arguably the most famous of the chapels on the Strip, maybe because there is a big sign saying Michael Jordan and Joan Collins were married here (again, not to each other), maybe because they were the first to do the drive-up window, or maybe because this is where Britney and that guy who isn't the guy from *Seinfeld* began their 51 hours of wedded bliss (no, we will never, ever get tired of mocking that bit of bad decision making). It is indeed little and white. However, it has a factory-line atmosphere, processing wedding after wedding all day. Move 'em in and move 'em out. No wonder they put in that drive-up window! The staff, dressed in no-nonsense black, is brusque, hasty, and has a bit of an attitude (though we know one couple who got married here and had no complaints). The chapel does offer full wedding ceremonies, complete with a candlelight service and traditional music. There are two chapels, the smaller of which has a large photo of a forest stream. There's also a gazebo for outdoor services, but because it's right on the Strip, it's not as nice as it sounds. If you want something special, there are probably better choices.

1301 Las Vegas Blvd. S. (btw. E. Oakey and Charleston blvds.). ☎ **800/545-8111** or 702/382-5943. www.alittlewhitechapel.com. Daily 8am–midnight.

Mon Bel Ami Wedding Chapel ★
Formerly the Silver Bells chapel, this got a spanking new redo a few years back that is holding up well; a pretty little churchlike building complete with a big gold- and flower-bedecked chapel room (maybe the taller peaked ceiling gives that effect) fitted with surround-sound speakers. The cupid bas-relief is a bit much. The chapel does frilly and fancy wedding receptions, as well as events where white doves are released. Perhaps because of this, the establishment seems to attract fewer walk-ins than prebooked weddings, so you should call in advance, or you might be stuck in the Strip-side gazebo. Along with Elvis, Tom Jones, Marilyn Monroe, and Elvira (!) impersonators are available.

607 Las Vegas Blvd. S. (at E. Bonneville Ave.). ✆ **866/503-4400** or 702/388-4445. www. monbelami.com. Sun–Fri 10am–8pm; Sat 10am–10pm.

FROM TOP: **Drive-up window at Little White Wedding Chapel; Mon Bel Ami Wedding Chapel.**

A Special Memory Wedding Chapel ★ This is a very nice wedding chapel, particularly compared to the rather tired facades of the classics on the Strip. This is absolutely the place to go if you want a traditional, big-production wedding; you won't feel it the least bit tacky. It's a New England church–style building,

A Special Memory Wedding Chapel.

complete with steeple. The interior looks like a proper church (well, a plain one—don't think ornate Gothic cathedral), with a peaked roof, pews with padded red seats, modern stained-glass windows of doves and flowers, and lots of dark wood. It's all very clean and new and seats about 87 comfortably. There is a short staircase leading to an actual bride's room; she can make an entrance coming down it or through the double doors at the back. The area outside the chapel is like a minimall of bridal paraphernalia stores. Should all this just be too darned nice and proper for you, they also offer a drive-up window (where they do about 300 weddings a month!). It'll cost you $25—just ring the buzzer for service. They have a photo studio on-site and will do receptions featuring a small cake, cold cuts, and champagne. There is a gazebo for outside weddings, and they sell T-shirts!

800 S. 4th St. (at Gass Ave.). ℰ **800/962-7798** or 702/384-2211. www.aspecialmemory.com. Sun–Thurs 8am–10pm; Fri–Sat 8am–midnight.

Viva Las Vegas Weddings ★★ Yes, you could come to Las Vegas and have a traditional wedding in a tasteful chapel where you walk down the aisle to a kindly minister. But wouldn't you rather literally ride into the chapel in the back of a pink Cadillac and get married by Elvis? Or wade in through dry ice fog while Dracula performs your ceremony? This is the mecca of the wacky themed Vegas wedding, complete with indoor and outdoor spaces, tux and costume rentals, florists, theme rooms for receptions, and a staff of former stage performers who love to put on a show. *THIS* is what a Vegas wedding should be like.

1205 Las Vegas Blvd. S. (btw. Charleston and Oakey blvds.). ℰ **800/574-4450** or 702/384-0771. www.vivalasvegasweddings.com. Mon–Thurs and Sun 9am–9pm; Fri–Sat 8am–10pm.

Wee Kirk O' the Heather ★ This is the oldest wedding chapel in Las Vegas (it's been here since 1940; ah, Vegas, and its mixed-up view of age) and the one at the very end of the Strip, right before Downtown (and thus close to the license

Theme wedding at Viva Las Vegas Weddings.

bureau). It was originally built as a house in 1925 for a local minister, but marriage bureau officials kept sending couples there to get married and they eventually just gave up and turned it into a chapel. The decor is entirely fresh, and while that means gold-satin-patterned wallpaper in the chapel, we like it a great deal. Just the right balance between kitsch and classic, and that's what you want in a Vegas wedding chapel. Plus, if there were a competition for the friendliest chapel in town, this one would win hands down.

231 Las Vegas Blvd. S. (btw. Bridger and Carson aves.). © **800/843-5266** or 702/382-9830. www.weekirk.com. Daily 10am–8pm.

ATTRACTIONS IN NEARBY HENDERSON

About 6 miles from the Strip in the town of Henderson are a couple of attractions that seem small-time in comparison with the glitz offered elsewhere. But if you need a break from all the high-tech, multimedia energy that buffets you in the city, you won't be alone. It's surprising how many people wander over this way for a bit more staid, though engaging, older-fashioned amusement.

To get to Henderson, drive east on Tropicana Avenue, make a right on Mountain Vista, then go 2 miles to Sunset Way; turn left into Green Valley Business Park. You will soon see Ethel M Chocolates, a good place to begin. Use the map in this section to find your way to the other facility.

Clark County Heritage Museum ★★ ☺ 🎁 Someday, one of these casino moguls (yeah, we're lookin' at you, Trump) is going to take just some of those megamillions they are pouring into yet another Strip hotel and put it into the museum that this bizarre town, and its ridiculously rich 100-year history, deserves. Until then, this dear little place will have to do its best—and that best is actually pretty good. With everything from dioramas of dinosaurs to a small street

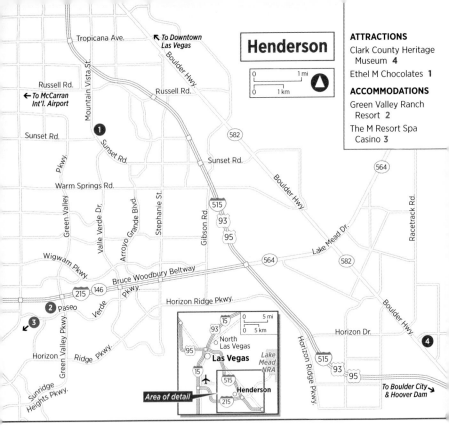

Henderson

0 1 mi
0 1 km

filled with original buildings, including the 1932 Boulder City train depot, this is a throwback to ghost towns and other low-tech diversions. Sweet, informative, and you can't beat the price. **Note:** Hot days will make the outdoor portions less than bearable.

1830 S. Boulder Hwy., Henderson. *702/455-7955.* www.accessclarkcounty.com. Admission $1.50 adults, $1 seniors and children 3–15, free for children 2 and under. Daily 9am–4:30pm. Closed Thanksgiving, Dec 25, and Jan 1.

Ethel M Chocolates ★ ☺ This tourist attraction draws about 2,000 visitors a day. Ethel Mars began making fine chocolates in a little candy kitchen in the early 20th century. Her small enterprise evolved to produce not only dozens of varieties of superb boxed chocolates, but also some of the world's most famous candies: M&Ms, Milky Way, 3 Musketeers, Snickers, and Mars bars.

Alas, the tour lasts only about 10 minutes and consists entirely of viewing stations with an audiotape explaining the chocolate-baking process. You learn very little. But the place does look like a bakery rather than a factory, which is nice, as no one wants to see their chocolates handled without love. Even more sadly, you get only one small chocolate as a sample—delicious, but hardly satisfying. Surely, this is by design; now overwhelmingly in the mood for sugar, you are more likely to buy some of their expensive chocolate. **Note:** Come before 2:30pm, which is when the workers start to pack up and go home.

Old Vegas memorabilia at the Clark County Heritage Museum.

Cactus garden at Ethel M Chocolates.

What's really worth seeing is outside: a lovely and extensive **2½-acre garden** ★ displaying 350 species of rare and exotic cacti with signs provided for self-guided tours. It's best appreciated in spring, when the cacti are in full bloom. There's a little gazebo in which to sit and enjoy the garden, which would be quite peaceful were it not for the busloads of tourists in the area. Behind the garden, also with a self-guided tour, is Ethel M's "Living Machine," a natural wastewater treatment and recycling plant that consists of aerated tanks, ecological fluid beds, constructed wetlands, reed beds, and a storage pond.

2 Cactus Garden Dr. (just off Mountain Vista and Sunset Way, in the Green Valley Business Park). ℂ **888/627-0990** or 702/433-2500 for recorded information. www.ethelschocolate.com. Free admission. Daily 8:30am–6pm. Self-guided chocolate factory tours daily 8:30am–4:30pm. Holiday hours may vary. Closed Dec 25.

ESPECIALLY FOR KIDS

Like much of the rest of the world, you may be under the impression that Las Vegas has evolved from an adults-only fantasyland into a vacation destination suitable for the entire family. The only explanation for this myth is that Las Vegas was referred to as "Disneyland for adults" by so many and for so long that the town became momentarily confused and decided it actually *was* Disneyland. Some of the gargantuan hotels then spent small fortunes on redecorating in an attempt to lure families, with vast quantities of junk food and a lot of hype. They now vehemently deny that any such notion ever crossed their collective minds, and, no, they don't know how that roller coaster got into the parking lot.

To put things simply, Las Vegas makes money—lots and lots of money—by promoting gambling, drinking, and sex. These are all fine pursuits if you happen to be an adult, but if you haven't reached the magical age of 21, you really don't count in this town. In any case, the casinos and even the Strip itself are simply too stimulating, noisy, and smoky for young kids.

Older progeny may have a tolerance for crowds and the incessant pinging of the slot machines, but they will be thoroughly annoyed with you when casino security chastises them if they so much as stop to tie their shoelaces anywhere near the gaming tables. Because you can't get from your hotel room to the parking lot without ambling through a casino, you can't reasonably expect a teenager to be in a good mood once you stagger outside. And those amusement parks and video halls that haven't yet been purged are very expensive places to park your kids for an afternoon or evening, assuming they are old enough to be left unsupervised.

Nevertheless, you may have a perfectly legitimate reason for bringing your children to Las Vegas (like Grandma was busy, or you were just stopping off on your way from somewhere else), so here are some places to take the children both on and off the Strip.

Circus Circus (p. 127) has ongoing circus acts throughout the day, a vast video-game-and-pinball arcade, and dozens of carnival games on its mezzanine level. Behind the hotel is the **Adventuredome,** detailed below.

Excalibur (p. 97) also offers video, carnival, and thrill cinemas.

At **Caesars Palace** (p. 104), animated talking statues in **The Forum Shops** are a kick, though smaller kids might be scared by them. Calm them down with a visit to the aquarium nearby, in the Atlantis wing of the shops.

The erupting volcano might divert kids, as the **Secret Garden** and **Dolphin Habitat** at The Mirage (p. 221) surely will; and the **Shark Reef** at Mandalay Bay (p. 223) is worth a look.

Consider carefully the attractions at Luxor Las Vegas: **Bodies: The Exhibition** may be too intense for kids, depending on their age, though will be happily grossed out and might even learn a thing or two, while only those with interest in the high seas, disasters, the *Titanic,* or the eponymous movie will want to browse through **Titanic: The Exhibition.**

Cyber Speedway and **Speed: The Ride** (p. 223) at the Sahara is the place for thrill-ride kids to get their kicks.

Children 10 and up will love the many options for play (from high-tech to low-tech, from video wonders to actual physical activity) offered at **GameWorks** (p. 218), as will their parents. Teens may enjoy the "ick" factor of **CSI: The Experience.**

Of moderate interest to youngsters is the **Ethel M Chocolates factory tour** in Henderson (see "Attractions in Nearby Henderson," above), not for the educational value but for the sweets at the end. More educational is the **Marjorie Barrick Museum,** at UNLV (p. 220), but only the reptile exhibit will really interest kids. The **Clark County Heritage Museum** (p. 235) is also a dear little throwback, and uncynical kids may enjoy wandering through the old buildings and checking out some of the dioramas.

Appropriate shows for kids include **Tournament of Kings** at Excalibur, **Mac King** at Harrah's, and Cirque du Soleil's *Mystère* at Treasure Island. As a general rule, early shows are less racy than late-night shows. All these productions are reviewed in detail in chapter 10, where you'll also find a few more suggestions for kid-friendly shows.

Beyond the city limits (see chapter 11 for details on all of these) is **Bonnie Springs Ranch/Old Nevada,** with trail and stagecoach rides, a petting zoo, old-fashioned melodramas, stunt shootouts, a Nevada-themed wax museum, crafts

Rollercoaster inside The Adventuredome.

demonstrations, and more. **Lake Mead** has great recreational facilities for family vacations. Finally, organized tours (see below) to the Grand Canyon and other interesting sights in southern Nevada and neighboring states can be fun family activities. Check with your hotel sightseeing desk. Kids should also be entertained by the personalized tours offered by **Creative Adventures** (✆ **702/893-2051;** www.creativeadventuresltd.net); see p. 242.

Specifically kid-pleasing attractions are described below.

The Adventuredome ★ ☺ This is an okay place to spend a hot afternoon, especially now that it's about all that remains of the great Vegas-Is-For-Kids-Too experiment. Plus, unlike most theme parks, it's indoors! The glass dome that towers overhead lets in natural light. Even so, the place is looking a little ragged, like it knows it's now an afterthought rather than a centerpiece. A double-loop roller coaster careens around the simulated Grand Canyon, and there's the requisite water flume, a laser-tag area, some bouncy/twirly/stomach-churning rides, and a modest number of other tamer rides for kids of all ages. Video games and a carnival-style arcade are separate from the attractions, though it all still feels pretty hectic. The SpongeBob SquarePants 4-D ride is disappointing, as the technology is about 10 years behind the times, and the story is hard to follow, thanks to bad acoustics. We suggest that you not leave kids here alone; they could easily get lost.

2880 Las Vegas Blvd. S. (behind Circus Circus). ✆ **702/794-3939.** www.adventuredome.com. Free admission; $4–$7 per ride; daily pass $25 adults, $15 children 33–47 in. tall. AE, DC, DISC, MC, V. Park hours vary seasonally but are usually Mon–Thurs 11am–6pm; Fri–Sat 10am–midnight; Sun 10am–9pm.

Kids Quest ★ ☺ This is part of a well-regarded chain of activity and babysitting centers, located in the Station Casino chain and the otherwise very adult Red Rock Resort. Given the loss of the MGM Grand's child-care facility, it's a boon to parents who have business or want a little quality adult time, and frankly to kids who might not be enjoying the Vegas experience as much as older folks.

The Red Rock facility is quite large, including a gym with a basketball court and a salon for the girlie minded. Kids can play dress up, scoot around a doll's house, or try out air hockey and video games. The ratio of staff to kids is 1 to 10, and 1 to 4 for babies and toddlers. The employees are all cute and earnest and have to pass certain qualifications to work here.

In the Palms, 4321 W. Flamingo Rd. *℃* **866/942-7777.** In Red Rock Resort, 11011 W. Charleston Blvd. *℃* **702/797-7646.** www.kidsquest.com. $6.75–$8/hr. Hours vary according to location; generally until 11pm Mon–Fri and 1am Sat–Sun.

Las Vegas Natural History Museum ★ ☺ Conveniently located across the street from the Lied Discovery Children's Museum (see below), this humble temple of taxidermy harkens back to elementary-school field trips, circa 1965, when stuffed elk and brown bears forever protecting their kill were as close as most of us got to exotic animals. Worn around the edges but very sweet and re-laxed, the museum is enlivened by a hands-on activity room and two life-size dinosaurs that roar at one another intermittently. A small boy was observed leaping toward his dad upon watching this display, so you might want to warn any sensitive little ones that the big tyrannosaurs aren't going anywhere. Surprisingly, the gift shop here is particularly well stocked with neat items you won't too terribly mind buying for the kids. When you are finished, you might as well scoot around the corner to the **Old Fort,** which isn't a strong enough attraction on its own but is a logical transition from this destination.

900 Las Vegas Blvd. N. (at Washington Ave.). *℃* **702/384-3466.** www.lvnhm.org. Admission $8 adults; $7 seniors, students, and military; $4 children 3–11; free for children 2 and under. Daily 9am–4pm. Closed Thanksgiving and Dec 25.

Dinosaur exhibit in the Las Vegas Natural History Museum.

Lied Discovery Children's Museum ★★ ☺ 🎁 A hands-on science museum designed for curious kids, the bright, airy, two-story Lied makes an ideal outing for toddlers and young children. With lots of interactive exhibits to examine, including a miniature grocery store, a tube for encasing oneself inside a soap bubble, a radio station where attendees can perform karaoke, and music and drawing areas, you'll soon forget your video/poker losses. Clever, thought-inducing exhibits are everywhere. Learn how it feels to be physically disabled by playing basketball from a wheelchair. Feed a wooden "sandwich" to a cutout of a snake and to a cutout of a human, and see how much nutrition each receives. See how much sunscreen the giant stuffed mascot needs to keep from burning. On Saturday afternoons, from 1 to 3pm, free drop-in art classes are offered, giving adults a bit of time to ramble around the gift store or read the fine print on the exhibit placards. The Lied also shares space with a city library branch, so after the kids run around, you can calm them back down with a story or two.

Lied Discovery Children's Museum.

833 Las Vegas Blvd. N. (½ block south of Washington, across from Cashman Field). ⓒ **702/382-5437.** www.ldcm.org. Admission $8.50 adults; $7.50 seniors, children 17 and under, and military. Tues–Fri 9am–4pm; Sat 10am–5pm; Sun noon–5pm. Closed Easter, Thanksgiving, Dec 24, Dec 25, and Jan 1.

ORGANIZED TOURS

Just about every hotel in town has a tour desk offering a seemingly infinite number of sightseeing opportunities in and around Las Vegas. You're sure to find a tour company that will take you where you want to go.

Gray Line (ⓒ **800/634-6579;** www.grayline.com) offers a rather comprehensive roster, including the following:

- A pair of 5- to 6-hour **city tours** (1 day, 1 night), with various itineraries, including visits to Ethel M Chocolates, and the Fremont Street Experience
- Half-day excursions to **Hoover Dam** and **Red Rock Canyon** (see chapter 11 for details)
- A half-day tour to **Lake Mead** and **Hoover Dam** (see chapter 11 for details)
- Several full-day **Grand Canyon excursions** (see chapter 11 for details) Call for details or inquire at your hotel's tour desk, where you'll also find free magazines with coupons for discounts on these tours.

Unique Desert Tours by Creative Adventures

A totally different type of tour is offered by Char Cruze of **Creative Adventures** ★★★ (🕾 **702/893-2051**; www.creativeadventuresltd.net). Char, a charming fourth-generation Las Vegan (she was at the opening of the Flamingo), spent her childhood riding horseback through the mesquite and cottonwoods of the Mojave Desert, discovering magical places you'd never find on your own or on a commercial tour. Char is a lecturer and storyteller as well as a tour guide. She has extensively studied southern Nevada's geology and desert wildlife, its regional history, and its Native American cultures. Her personalized tours are enhanced by fascinating stories about everything from miners to mobsters, visit haunted mines, sacred Paiute grounds, ghost towns, canyons, and ancient petroglyphs. She also has many things to entertain and educate children, and she carries a tote bag full of visual aids, such as a board covered in labeled rocks to better illustrate a lecture on local geology. Char has certain structured tours, but she loves to do individual tours tailored for a group. This is absolutely worth the money—you are definitely going to get something different than you would on a conventional tour, while Char herself is most accommodating, thoughtful, knowledgeable, and prompt. Char rents transport according to the size of the group and can accommodate clients with physical disabilities; foreign language translators are also available.

Each tour is customized based on your interests, so pricing varies dramatically, but figure at least $150 for the basics (which are much more than basic), with costs going up from there. It's a good idea to make arrangements with Char prior to leaving home.

FORE! GREAT DESERT GOLF

In addition to the listings below, there are dozens of local courses, including some very challenging ones that have hosted PGA tournaments. **Note:** Greens fees vary radically depending on time of day and year. Also, call for opening and

Angel Park Golf Club.

closing times, because these change frequently. Because of the heat, you will want to take advantage of the cart that in most cases is included in the greens fee.

Note also that the **Rio All-Suite Hotel** (p. 116) has an affiliated golf course. Also, **Wynn Las Vegas** (p. 123) has a state-of-the-art course, but we aren't including it for two reasons; at this writing, it is for guests only—and they mean it. If anyone in your party is not also staying at the hotel, they can't play. And the greens fees? A mere $500 a person. Call when you get to town to see whether they've come to their senses.

Angel Park Golf Club ★★ This 36-hole, par-70/71 public course is a local favorite. Arnold Palmer originally designed the Mountain and Palm courses (the Palm Course was redesigned several years later by Bob Cupp). Players call this a great escape from the casinos, claiming that no matter how many times they play it, they never get tired of it. The Palm Course has gently rolling fairways that offer golfers of all abilities a challenging yet forgiving layout. The Mountain Course has rolling natural terrain and gorgeous panoramic views. In addition to these two challenging 18-hole courses, Angel Park offers a night-lit Cloud 9 Course (12 holes for daylight play, 9 at night), where each hole is patterned after a famous par 3. You can reserve tee times up to 60 days in advance with a credit card guarantee.

Yardage: Palm Course 6,525 championship and 5,438 resort; Mountain Course 6,722 championship and 5,718 resort.

Facilities: Pro shop, night-lit driving range, 18-hole putting course, restaurant, cocktail bar, snack bar, and beverage cart.

100 S. Rampart Blvd. (btw. Summerlin Pkwy. and Alta St., 20 min. NW of the Strip). © **888/446-5358** or 702/254-4653. www.angelpark.com. Greens fees for 18-hole courses (includes cart, practice balls, and tax) $49–$99; short-course fees $25, excluding optional cart rental. Discounted twilight rates available for 18-hole course. Internet specials available.

Bali Hai Golf Club ★★★ One of the most exclusive golf addresses belongs to this multimillion-dollar course, built in 2000, on the Strip, just south of Mandalay Bay. Done in a wild South Seas theme, the par-72 course has over 7 acres of water features, including an island green, palm trees, and tropical foliage everywhere you look. Not impressed yet? How about the fact that all their golf carts are equipped with GPS? Or that celebrity chef Wolfgang Puck chose to open his newest Vegas eatery here? Okay, if that doesn't convince you of the upscale nature of the joint, check out the greens fees. Even at those prices, tee times are often booked 6 months in advance.

Yardage: 7,002 championship.

Facilities: Pro shop, putting green, gourmet restaurant, grill, and lounge.

5150 Las Vegas Blvd. S. © **702/479-6786.** www.balihaigolfclub.com. Greens fees (includes cart, range balls, and tax) $99–$395.

Black Mountain Golf & Country Club ★★ Two new greens have recently been added to this 27-hole, par-72 semiprivate course, which requires reservations 4 days in advance. It's considered a great old course, with lots of wildlife, including roadrunners. However, unpredictable winds may affect your game.

Yardage: 6,550 championship; 6,223 regular; and 5,518 ladies.

Facilities: Pro shop, driving range, putting green, restaurant, cocktail lounge, and snack bar.

500 Greenway Rd., Henderson. © **866/596-4833.** www.golfblackmountain.com. Greens fees (includes cart) $75–$95. Call for twilight rates.

Desert Rose Golf Club ★ 🏌 This is an 18-hole, par-71 public course built in 1963 and designed by Dick Wilson and Joe Lee. Narrow fairways feature Bermuda turf. You can reserve tee times up to 7 days in advance.

Yardage: 6,511 championship; 6,135 regular; and 5,458 ladies.

Facilities: Pro shop, driving range, putting and chipping greens, restaurant, cocktail lounge, and PGA teaching pro.

5483 Clubhouse Dr. (3 blocks west of Nellis Blvd., off Sahara Ave.). © **800/470-4622** or 702/431-4653. Greens fees (includes cart) $40–$59.

Las Vegas National Golf Club ★ This is an 18-hole (about 8 with water on them), par-71 public course, and a classic layout (not the desert layout you'd expect). If you play from the back tees, it can really be a challenge. The 1996 Las Vegas Invitational, won by Tiger Woods, was held here. Discounted tee times are often available. Reservations are taken up to 60 days in advance.

Yardage: 6,815 championship; 6,418 regular; and 5,741 ladies.

Facilities: Pro shop, driving range, restaurant, cocktail lounge, and golf school.

1911 Desert Inn Rd. (btw. Maryland Pkwy. and Eastern Ave.). © **702/734-1796.** www.lasvegas national.com. Greens fees (some include cart) $89–$119.

STAYING ACTIVE

You need not be a slot-hypnotized slug when you come to Vegas. The city and surrounding areas offer plenty of opportunities for active sports. In addition to many highly rated golf courses (described above), just about every hotel has a large swimming pool and health club, and tennis courts abound. All types of watersports are offered at Lake Mead National Recreation Area; there's rafting on the Colorado, horseback riding at Mount Charleston and Bonnie Springs, great

Bowling alley in The Orleans.

hiking in the canyons, and much, much more. Do plan to get out of those smoke-filled casinos and into the fresh air once in a while. It's good for your health and your finances.

For information on other recreational and outdoor activities, see chapter 11.

BOWLING Although the world's largest alley at the Showboat closed several years ago, serious bowlers still have some good options to choose from in Las Vegas. **Gold Coast Hotel,** 4000 W. Flamingo Rd. (at Valley View; © 702/367-7111), has a 70-lane bowling center open daily 24 hours. **The Orleans,** 4500 W. Tropicana Ave. (© 702/365-7400), has 70 lanes, a pro shop, lockers, meeting rooms, and more; it's also open daily 24 hours.

Out on the east side of town, you'll find 56 lanes at **Sam's Town,** 5111 Boulder Hwy. (© 702/456-7777), plus a snack shop, cocktail lounge, video arcade, day-care center, pro shop, and more. Open daily 24 hours.

Sunset Station, 1301 W. Sunset Rd., in Henderson (© 702/547-7467), has a high-tech 72-lane facility called Strike Zone. It's got all the latest automated scoring gizmos, giant video screens, a full bar, a snack shop, a pro shop, a video arcade, and more.

Up north at **Santa Fe Station,** 4949 N. Rancho Rd. (© 702/658-4995), you'll find a 60-lane alley with the most modern scoring equipment, new furnishings, a fun and funky bar, a small cafe, and much more. Just down the road is sister hotel **Texas Station,** 2101 Texas Star Lane (© 702/631-8128), with a 60-lane alley, video arcade, billiards, a snack bar and lounge, and more. Open 24 hours.

Suncoast, 9090 Alta Dr., in Summerlin (© 702/636-7111), offers 64 lanes divided by a unique center aisle. The high-tech center with touch-screen scoring has become a regular stop on the Pro Bowlers tours. Open daily 24 hours.

South Point, 9777 Las Vegas Blvd. (© **702/797-8080**), has a 64-lane facility with a similar divided layout to its sister at Suncoast. It has all the latest gee-whiz scoring and automation, plus the usual facilities. Open 24 hours.

ROCK CLIMBING **Red Rock Canyon** ★★★, just 19 miles west of Las Vegas, is one of the world's most popular rock-climbing areas. In addition to awe-inspiring natural beauty, it offers everything from boulders to big walls. If you'd like to join the bighorn sheep, Red Rock has more than 1,000 routes

---

DESERT hiking ADVICE

Except in summer, when temperatures can reach 120ºF (49ºC) in the shade, the Las Vegas area is great for hiking. The best hiking season is November through March. Great locales include the incredibly scenic Red Rock Canyon and Valley of Fire State Park (see chapter 11 for details on both).

Hiking in the desert is exceptionally rewarding, but it can be dangerous. Here are some safety tips:

1. Don't hike alone.

2. Carry plenty of water and drink it often. Don't assume that spring water is safe to drink. A gallon of water per person per day is recommended for hikers.

3. Be alert for signs of heat exhaustion (headache, nausea, dizziness, fatigue, and cool, damp, pale, or red skin).

4. Gauge your fitness accurately. Desert hiking may involve rough or steep terrain. Don't take on more than you can handle.

5. Check weather forecasts before starting out. Thunderstorms can turn into raging flash floods, which are extremely hazardous to hikers.

6. Dress properly. Wear sturdy walking shoes for rock scrambling, long pants (to protect yourself from rocks and cacti), a hat, and sunglasses.

7. Wear sunscreen and carry a small first-aid kit.

8. Be careful when climbing on sandstone, which can be surprisingly soft and crumbly.

9. Don't feed or play with animals, such as the wild burros in Red Rock Canyon. (It's actually illegal to approach them.)

10. Be alert for snakes and insects. Though they're rarely encountered, you'll want to look into a crevice before putting your hand into it.

11. Visit park or other information offices before you start out and acquaint yourself with rules and regulations and any possible hazards. It's also a good idea to tell the staff where you're going, when you'll return, how many are in your party, and so on. Some park offices offer hiker-registration programs.

12. Follow the hiker's creed: Take only photographs and leave only footprints.

Rock climbing in Red Rock Canyon.

Cosmo, the official mascot of the Las Vegas 51s.

to inaugurate beginners and challenge accomplished climbers. Experienced climbers can contact the **visitor center** (✆ **702/515-5350;** www.nv.blm. gov/redrockcanyon) for information. See chapter 11 for details about Red Rock.

TENNIS Tennis used to be a popular pastime in Vegas, but these days, buffs only have a couple of choices at hotels in town that have tennis courts.

Bally's ★★ (✆ **702/739-4111**) has eight night-lit hard courts. Fees start at $20 per hour for guests of Bally's or Paris Las Vegas and $25 per hour for nonguests, with rackets available for rental. Facilities include a pro shop. Hours vary seasonally. Reservations are advised.

Flamingo Las Vegas ★★ (✆ **702/733-3444**) has four outdoor night-lit hard courts and a pro shop. It's open to the public daily from 8am to 5pm. Rates are $20 per hour for guests of the Flamingo and $25 per hour for nonguests. Lessons are available. Reservations are required.

SPECTATOR SPORTS

Las Vegas isn't known for its sports teams. Except for minor-league baseball and hockey, the only consistent spectator sports are those at UNLV. For the pros, if watching Triple-A baseball (in this case, a Toronto Blue Jays farm team) in potentially triple-degree heat sounds like fun, the charmingly named and even-better merchandized **Las Vegas 51s** (as in Area 51, as in alien-themed gear!) is a hot ticket. The team's schedule and ticket info are available at **www.lv51. com**, or call ✆ **702/386-7200.** Ice hockey might be a better climate choice;

The MGM Grand's Garden Events Arena is a popular setting for major prize fights.

get info for the **Las Vegas Wranglers** at **www.lasvegaswranglers.com** or call ☏ **702/471-7825.**

The **Las Vegas Motor Speedway** (p. 219) is a main venue for car racing that draws major events to Las Vegas.

Because the city has several top-notch sporting arenas, important annual events take place in Las Vegas, details for which can be found in the "Las Vegas Calendar of Events" in chapter 3. The **Justin Timberlake Shriners Hospitals for Children Open** takes place in Las Vegas every October. The **National Finals Rodeo** is held in UNLV's Thomas & Mack Center in December. From time to time, you'll find NBA exhibition games, professional ice-skating competitions, or gymnastics exhibitions. Finally, Las Vegas is well known as a major location for **boxing matches.** These are held in several Strip hotels, most often at Caesars or the MGM Grand, but sometimes at The Mirage. Tickets are hard to come by and quite expensive.

Tickets to sporting events at hotels are available either through **Ticketmaster** (☏ **702/893-3000;** www.ticketmaster.com) or through the hotels themselves. (Why pay Ticketmaster's exorbitant service charges if you don't have to?)

Major Sports Venues in Hotels

The **MGM Grand's Garden Events Arena** (☏ **800/929-1111** or 702/891-7777) is a major venue for professional boxing matches, rodeos, tennis, ice-skating shows, World Figure Skating Championships, and more.

Mandalay Bay (☏ **877/632-7400**) has hosted a number of boxing matches in its 12,000-seat Events Center.

8

ABOUT CASINO GAMBLING

W hat? You didn't come to Las Vegas for the Atomic Testing Museum and Titanic: The Exhibition? Is the insanity that is SkyJump not enough to get your heart racing? We are shocked. *Shocked.* Yes, there are gambling opportunities in Vegas. We've noticed this. You will, too. The tip-off will be the slot machines in the airport as soon as you step off the plane. Or the slot machines in the convenience stores as soon as you drive across the state line. Let's not kid ourselves: Gambling is what Vegas is about. The bright lights, the shows, the showgirls, the food—it's all there just to lure you in and make you open your wallet. The free drinks certainly help ease the latter as well.

You can disappoint them if you want, but what would be the point? *This is Las Vegas.* You don't have to be a high roller. You would not believe how much fun you can have with a nickel slot machine. You won't get rich, but neither will most of those guys playing the $5 slots, either.

Of course, that's not going to stop anyone from trying. Almost everyone plays in Vegas with the hopes of winning The Big One. That only a few ever do win doesn't stop them from trying again and again and again. That's how the casinos make their money, by the way.

It's not that the odds are stacked so incredibly high in their favor—though the odds *are* in their favor, and don't ever think otherwise. Rather, it's that if there is one constant in this world, it's human greed. Look around in any casino, and you'll see countless souls who, having doubled their winnings, are now trying to quadruple them and are losing it all and then trying to recoup their initial bankroll and losing still more in the process.

Remember also that there is no system that's sure to help you win. Reading books and listening to others at the tables will help you pick up some tips, but if there were a surefire way to win, the casinos would have taken care of it (and we will leave you to imagine just what that might entail). Try to have the courage to walk away when your bankroll is up, not down. Remember, your children's college fund is just that, and not a gambling-budget supplement.

The first part of this chapter is a contribution from James Randi, a master magician, who looks at the four major fallacies people bring with them to the gaming tables in Las Vegas; it's fascinating, and we thank him for this contribution.

> ### Impressions
>
> *Stilled forever is the click of the roulette wheel, the rattle of dice, and the swish of cards.*
> —Shortsighted editorial in the *Nevada State Journal* after gambling was outlawed in 1910

The second part tells you the basics of betting. Knowing how to play the games not only improves your odds but also makes playing more enjoyable. In addition to the instructions here, you'll find dozens of books on how to gamble at all casino hotel gift shops, and many casinos offer free gaming lessons.

The third part of this chapter describes all the major casinos in town. Remember that gambling is supposed to be entertainment. Picking a gaming table where the other players are laughing, slapping each other on the back, and generally enjoying themselves tends to make for considerably more fun than a table where everyone is sitting around in stony silence, morosely staring at their cards. Unless you really need to concentrate, pick a table where all seem to be enjoying themselves, and you probably will, too, even if you don't win.

THE FOUR MOST PERVASIVE MYTHS ABOUT GAMBLING
by James Randi

Most of us know little, if anything, about statistics. It's a never-never land we can live without, something for those guys in white coats and thick glasses to mumble over. And because we don't bother to learn the basics of this rather interesting field of study, we sometimes find ourselves unable to deal with the realities that the gambling process produces.

I often present my audiences with a puzzle. Suppose that a mathematician, a gambler, and a magician are walking together on Broadway and come upon a small cluster of people who are observing a chap standing at a small table set up on the sidewalk. They are told that this fellow has just tossed a quarter into the air and allowed it to fall onto the table, nine times. And that has produced nine "tails" in a row. Now the crowd is being asked to bet on what the next toss of the coin will bring. The question: How will each of these three observers place their bets?

The mathematician will reason that each toss of the coin is independent of the last toss, so the chances are still exactly 50/50 for heads or tails. He'll say that either bet is okay and that it doesn't make any difference which decision is made.

The gambler will go one of two ways; either he'll reason that there's a "run" taking place here—and that a bet on another tail will be the better choice—or he'll opine that it's time for the head to come up, and he'll put his wager on that likelihood.

The magician? He has the best chance of winning because he knows that there is only one chance in 512 that a coin will come up tails nine times in a row—*unless there's something wrong with that coin!* He'll bet tails, and he'll win!

The reasoning of the mathematician is quite correct, that of the gambler is quite wrong (in either one of his scenarios), but just as long as that isn't a double-tailed coin. The point of view taken by the magician is highly specialized, but human nature being what it is, that view is probably the correct one.

In professional gambling centers such as Las Vegas, great care is taken to ensure that there are no two-tailed quarters or other purposeful anomalies that enable cheating to take place. The casinos make their percentages on the built-in mathematical advantage, which is clearly stated and available to any who ask, and though that is a very tiny "edge," it's enough to pay for the razzle-dazzle that lures in the customers. It's volume that supports the business. The scrutiny that is applied to each and every procedure in Vegas is evident everywhere.

So, **Fallacy Number One:** Cheating of some sort is necessary for an operation to prosper. It isn't.

Fallacy Number Two: Some people just have "hunches" and "visions" that enable them to win at the slots and tables. Sorry folks, it just ain't so. The science of parapsychology, which has studied such claims for many decades now, has never come up with evidence that any form of clairvoyance (clear seeing, the supposed ability to know hidden data, such as the next card to come up in a deal or the next face on the dice) or telepathy (mind reading) actually exists. It's remarkably easy for us to imagine that we have a hot streak going, or that the cards are falling our way, but the inexorable laws of chance prevail and always will.

Fallacy Number Three: There are folks who can give us systems for winning. Now, judicious bet placing is possible, and there are mathematical methods of minimizing losses, it's true. But the investment and base capital needed to follow through with these methods makes them a rather poor investment. The return percentage can be earned much more easily by almost any other form of endeavor, at less risk and less expenditure of boring hours following complicated charts and equations. The best observation we can make on the "systems" is this: Why would the inventors of the "systems" sell something that they themselves could use to get rich, which is what they say you can do with it? Think about that!

Of course, the simplest of all the systems is bet doubling. It sounds great in theory, but an hour spent tossing coins in your hotel room, or at the gaming tables, will convince you that theory and practice are quite different matters. Bet doubling, as applied to heads or tails (on a fair coin!), consists of placing a unit bet on the first coin toss, then pocketing the proceeds if you win but doubling your bet on the next toss if you lose. If you get a lose, lose, win sequence, that means you will have lost three units (one, plus two) and won four. You're up one unit. You start again. If you get a lose, lose, lose, win sequence, you've put out 15 units and brought in 16. Again, you're up only one unit. And no matter how long your sequences go, you'll always be up only one unit at the end of a sequence. It requires you to make that "unit" somewhat sizable if you want to have any significant winnings at all, and that may mean going bankrupt by simply running out of capital before a sequence ends—and if you hang on, you'll have been able to end up only one unit ahead, in any case. Not a good investment at all.

Fallacy Number Four: Studying the results of the roulette wheels will provide the bettor with useful data. We're peculiar animals, in that we constantly search for meaning in all sets of observations. That's how subjects of Rorschach tests find weird faces, figures, and creatures in inkblots that are actually random patterns with single symmetry. Similarly, any sets of roulette results are, essentially, random numbers; there are no patterns to be found there that can give indications of probable future spins of the wheels. Bearing in mind that those wheels are carefully monitored to detect any biases or defects, we should conclude that finding clues in past performances is futile.

The Amazing Randi

James Randi is a world-class magician (the Amazing Randi), now involved in examining supernatural, paranormal, and occult claims. He is the author of 11 books on these subjects and is the president of the James Randi Educational Foundation (JREF), in Fort Lauderdale, Florida. The JREF offers a prize of $1 million to any person who can produce a demonstration of any paranormal activity. His website is **www.randi.org**, where details of the offer can be found.

I recall that when I worked in Wiesbaden, Germany, just after World War II, I stuck around late one night after closing at the *spielbank* and watched as an elderly gentleman removed all the rotors of the 12 wheels they had in operation, wrote out the numbers 1 to 12 on separate scraps of paper, and reassembled the wheels according to the random order in which he drew each slip of paper from a bowl. He was ensuring that any inconsistencies in the wheels would be essentially nullified. Yet, as he told me, the front desk at the casino continued to sell booklets setting out the results of each of the wheels because patrons insisted on having them and persisted in believing that there just had to be a pattern there, if only it could be found.

We're only human. We can't escape certain defects in our thinking mechanism, but we can resist reacting to them. When we see Penn & Teller or Lance Burton doing their wonders, we smile smugly and assure ourselves that those miracles are only illusions. But if we haven't solved those illusions, and we haven't, how can we assume that we aren't being fooled by our own self-created delusions? Let's get a grip on reality and enjoy Las Vegas for what it really is: a grand illusion, a fairyland, a let's-pretend project, but not one in which the laws of nature are suspended or can be ignored.

THE GAMES

As you walk through the labyrinthine twists and turns of a casino floor, your attention will likely be dragged to the various games and, your interest piqued, your fingers may begin to twitch in anticipation of hitting it big. Before you put

your money on the line, it's imperative to know the rules of the game you want to play. Most casinos offer free gambling lessons at scheduled times on weekdays. This provides a risk-free environment for you to learn the games that tickle your fancy. Some casinos follow their lessons with low-stakes game play, enabling you to put your newfound knowledge to the test at small risk. During those instructional sessions, and even when playing on your own, dealers in most casinos will be more than happy to answer any questions you might have. Remember, the casino doesn't need to trick you into losing your money . . . the odds are already in their favor across the board; that's why it's called *gambling*. Another rule of thumb: Take a few minutes to watch a game being played in order to familiarize yourself with the motions and lingo. Then go back and reread this section—things will make a lot more sense at that point. Good luck!

A roulette wheel.

Baccarat

The ancient game of baccarat, or *chemin de fer*, is played with eight decks of cards. Firm rules apply, and there is no skill involved other than deciding whether to bet on the bank or the player. No, really—that's all you have to do. The dealer does all the other work. You can essentially stop reading here. Oh, all right, carry on.

Any beginner can play, but check the betting minimum before you sit down, as baccarat tends to be a high-stakes game. The cards are shuffled by the croupier and then placed in a box called the "shoe." Players may wager on "bank" or "player" at any time. Two cards are dealt from the shoe and given to the player who has the largest wager against the bank, and two cards are dealt to the croupier, acting as banker. If the rules call for a third card, the player or banker, or both, must take the third card. In the event of a tie, the hand is dealt over. **Note:** The guidelines that determine whether a third card must be drawn (by the player or banker) are provided at the baccarat table upon request.

The object of the game is to come as close as possible to the number 9. To score the hands, the cards of each hand are totaled and the *last digit* is used. All cards have face value. For example: 10 plus 5 equals 15 (score is 5); 10 plus 4 plus 9 equals 23 (score is 3); 4 plus 3 plus 3 equals 10 (score is 0); and 4 plus 2 plus 2 equals 9 (score is 9). The closest hand to 9 wins.

Each player has a chance to deal the cards. The shoe passes to the player on the right each time the bank loses. If the player wishes, he or she may pass the shoe at any time.

Note: When you bet on the bank and the bank wins, you are charged a 5% commission. This must be paid at the start of a new game or when you leave the table.

Big Six

Big Six provides pleasant recreation and involves no study or effort. The wheel has 56 positions on it, 54 of them marked by bills from $1 to $20. The other two spots are jokers, and each pays 40 to 1 if the wheel stops in that position. All other stops pay at face value. Those marked with $20 bills pay 20 to 1, the $5 bills pay 5 to 1, and so forth. The idea behind the game is to predict (or just blindly guess) what spot the wheel will stop at and place a bet accordingly.

Blackjack

In this popular game, the dealer starts by dealing each player two cards. In some casinos, they're dealt to the player face up, in others face down, but the dealer always gets one card up and one card down. Everybody plays against the dealer. The object is to get a total that is higher than that of the dealer without exceeding 21. All face cards count as 10; all other number cards, except aces, are counted at their face value. An ace may be counted as 1 or 11, whichever you choose it to be.

Starting at his or her left, the dealer gives additional cards to the players who wish to draw (be "hit") or none to a player who wishes to "stand" or "hold." If your count is nearer to 21 than the dealer's, you win. If it's under the dealer's, you lose. Ties are a "push" (standoff) and nobody wins. After all the players are satisfied with their counts, the dealer exposes his or her face-down card. If his or her two cards total 16 or less, the dealer must hit until reaching 17 or over. If the dealer's total exceeds 21, he or she must pay all the players whose hands have not gone "bust." It is important to note here that the blackjack dealer has no choice as to whether he or she should stay or draw. A dealer's decisions are predetermined and known to all the players at the table.

If you're a novice or just rusty, do yourself a favor and buy one of the small laminated cards available in shops all over town that illustrate proper play for every possible hand in blackjack. Even longtime players have been known to pull them out every now and then, and they can save you from making costly errors.

HOW TO PLAY

Here are eight "rules" for blackjack:

1. Place the number of chips that you want to bet on the betting space on your table.

2. Look at the first two cards the dealer gives you. If you wish to "stand," then wave your hand over your cards, palm down (watch your fellow players), indicating that you don't wish any additional cards. If you elect to draw an additional card, you tell the dealer to "hit" you by tapping the table with a finger. (Watch your fellow players.)

3. If your count goes over 21, you are "bust" and lose, even if the dealer also goes "bust" afterward.

4. If you make 21 in your first two cards (any picture card or 10 with an ace), you've got blackjack. In some casinos you will be paid 1½ times your bet, provided that the dealer does not have blackjack, too, in which case it's a "push," and nobody wins. (3:2 payouts are less common than in the past, with 6:5 the norm in many casinos.)

5. If you find a "pair" in your first two cards (say, two 8s or two aces), you may "split" the pair into two hands and treat each card as the first card dealt in two separate hands. You will need to place an additional bet, equal to your original bet, on the table. The dealer will then deal you a new *second* card to the first split card, and play commences as described above. This will be done for the second split card as well. ***Note:*** When you split aces, you will receive only one additional card per ace and must "stand."

6. After seeing your two starting cards, you have the option to "double down." You place an amount equal to your original bet on the table and you receive only one more card. Doubling down is a strategy to capitalize on a potentially strong hand against the dealer's weaker hand. ***Tip:*** You may double down for less than your original bet, but never for more.

7. Anytime the dealer deals himself or herself an ace for the "up" card, you may insure your hand against the possibility that the hole card is a 10 or face card, which would give him or her an automatic blackjack. To insure, you place an amount up to one-half of your bet on the "insurance" line. If the dealer does have a blackjack, you get paid 2 to 1 on the insurance money while losing your original bet: You break even. If the dealer does not have a blackjack, he or she takes your insurance money and play continues in the normal fashion.

8. The dealer must stand on 17 or more and must hit a hand of 16 or less.

PROFESSIONAL TIPS

Advice of the experts in playing blackjack is as follows:

1. *Do not* ask for an extra card if you have a count of 17 or higher, *ever*.

2. *Do not* ask for an extra card when you have a total of 12 or more if the dealer has a 2 through 6 showing in his or her "up" card.

3. *Ask* for an extra card or more when you have a count of 12 through 16 in your hand if the dealer's "up" card is a 7, 8, 9, 10, or ace.

There's a lot more to blackjack strategy than the above, of course. So consider this merely as the bare bones of the game. Blackjack is played with a single deck or with multiple decks; if you're looking for a single-deck game, your best bet is to head to a Downtown casino.

A final tip: Avoid insurance bets; they're sucker bait!

Craps

The most exciting casino action is usually found at the craps tables. Betting is frenetic, play fast-paced, and groups quickly bond while yelling and screaming in response to the action.

THE POSSIBLE BETS

The craps table is divided into marked areas (Pass, Come, Field, Big Six, Big Eight, and so on), where you place your chips to bet. The following are a few simple directions.

PASS LINE A "Pass Line" bet pays even money. If the first roll of the dice adds up to 7 or 11, you win your bet; if the first roll adds up to 2, 3, or 12, you lose your bet. If any other number comes up, it becomes your "point." If you roll your point again, you win, but if a 7 comes up again before your point is rolled, you lose.

DON'T PASS LINE Betting on the "Don't Pass Line" is the opposite of betting on the "Pass Line." This time, you lose if a 7 or an 11 is thrown on the first roll, and you win if a 2 or a 3 is thrown on the first roll.

If the first roll is 12, however, it's a "push" (standoff), and nobody wins. If none of these numbers is thrown and you have a point instead, in order to win, a 7 will have to be thrown before the point comes up again. A "Don't Pass" bet also pays even money.

Look, but Don't Touch!

1. **NEVER** touch your cards (or anyone else's), unless it's specifically stated at the table that you may. While you'll receive only a verbal slap on the wrist if you violate this rule, you *really* don't want to get one.

2. Players must use hand signals to indicate their wishes to the dealer. All verbal directions by players will be politely ignored by the dealer, who will remind players to use hand signals. The reason for this is the "eye in the sky," the casino's security system, which focuses an "eye" on every table and must record players' decisions to avoid accusations of misconduct or collusion.

COME Betting on "Come" is the same as betting on the Pass Line, but you must bet after the first roll or on any following roll. Again, you'll win on 7 or 11 and lose on 2, 3, or 12. Any other number is your point, and you win if your point comes up again before a 7.

DON'T COME This is the opposite of a Come bet. Again, you wait until after the first roll to bet. A 7 or an 11 means you lose; a 2 or a 3 means you win; 12 is a push, and nobody wins. You win if 7 comes up before the point. (The point, you'll recall, was the first number rolled if it was none of the above.)

FIELD This is a bet for one roll only. The "Field" consists of seven numbers: 2, 3, 4, 9, 10, 11, and 12. If any of these numbers is thrown on the next roll, you win even money, except on 2 and 12, which pay 2 to 1 (at some casinos 3 to 1).

BIG SIX AND EIGHT A "Big Six and Eight" bet pays even money. You win if either a 6 or an 8 is rolled before a 7. Mathematically, this is a sucker's bet.

ANY 7 An "Any 7" bet pays the winner 5 to 1. If a 7 is thrown on the first roll after you bet, you win.

"HARD WAY" BETS In the middle of a craps table are pictures of several possible dice combinations together with the odds the casino will pay you if you bet and win on any of those combinations being thrown. For example, if double 3s or 4s are rolled and you had bet on them, you will be paid 7 to 1. If double 2s or 5s are rolled and you had bet on them, you will be paid 9 to 1. If either a 7 is rolled or the number you bet on was rolled any way other than the "Hard Way," then the bet is lost. In-the-know gamblers tend to avoid "Hard Way" bets as it is an easy way to lose money.

ANY CRAPS Here you're lucky if the dice "crap out"—if they show 2, 3, or 12 on the first roll after you bet. If this happens, the bank pays 7 to 1. Any other number is a loser.

PLACE BETS You can make a "Place Bet" on any of the following numbers: 4, 5, 6, 8, 9, or 10. You're betting that the number you choose will be thrown before a 7 is thrown. If you win, the payoff is as follows: 4 or 10 pays at the rate of 9 to 5, 5 or 9 pays at the rate of 7 to 5, 6 or 8 pays at the rate of 7 to 6. "Place Bets" can be removed at any time before a roll.

Dice Probabilities

NUMBER	POSSIBLE COMBINATIONS	ACTUAL ODDS	PERCENTAGE PROBABILITY
2	1	35:1	2.8%
3	2	17:1	5.6%
4	3	11:1	8.3%
5	4	8:1	11.1%
6	5	6.2:1	13.9%
7	6	5:1	16.7%
8	5	6.2:1	13.9%
9	4	8:1	11.1%
10	3	11:1	8.3%
11	2	17:1	5.6%
12	1	35:1	2.8%

So 7 has an advantage over all other combinations, which, over the long run, is in favor of the casino. You can't beat the law of averages, but if you can't beat 'em, join 'em (that is, play the "Don't Pass" bet).

SOME PROBABILITIES

The probability of a certain number being rolled at the craps table is not a mystery. Because there are only 36 possible outcomes when the dice are rolled, the probability for each number being rolled is easily ascertained. See the "Dice Probabilities" chart below to help you, in case you decided it was fun to pass notes or sleep during math classes.

Keno

Originating in China, this is one of the oldest games of chance. Legend has it that funds acquired from the game were used to finance construction of the Great Wall of China.

Chinese railroad construction workers first introduced keno into the United States in the 1800s. Easy to play, and offering a chance to sit down and converse between bets, it is one of the most popular games in town—despite the fact that *the house percentage is greater than that of any other casino game!*

To play, you must first obtain a keno form, available at the counter in the keno lounge and in most Las Vegas coffee shops. In the latter, you'll usually find blank keno forms and thick black crayons on your table. Fill yours out, and a miniskirted keno runner will come and collect it. After the game is over, she'll return with your winning or losing ticket. If you've won, it's customary to offer a tip, depending on your winnings.

For those of you with state lotteries, this game will appear very familiar. You can select from 1 to 15 numbers (out of a total of 80), and if all of your numbers come up, you win. Depending on how many numbers you've selected, you can win smaller amounts if less than all of your numbers have come up. For example, if you bet a "3-spot" (selecting a total of three numbers) and two come up, you'll win something but not as much as if all three had shown up. A one-number mark is known as a 1-spot, a two-number selection is a 2-spot, and so on. After you have selected the number of spots you wish to play, write the amount you want to wager on the ticket, in the right-hand corner where indicated. The more you bet, the more you can win if your numbers come up. Before the game starts, you have to give the completed form to a keno runner, or hand it in at the keno lounge desk, and pay for your bet. You'll get back a duplicate form with the number of the game you're playing on it. Then the game begins. As numbers appear on the keno board, compare them to the numbers you've marked on your ticket. After 20 numbers have appeared on the board, the game is over; if you've won, turn in your ticket to collect your winnings.

The more numbers on the board matching the numbers on your ticket, the more you win (in some cases, you get paid if *none* of your numbers come up). If you want to keep playing the same numbers over and over, you can replay a ticket by handing in your duplicate to the keno runner; you don't have to keep rewriting it.

In addition to the straight bets described above, you can split your ticket, betting various amounts on two or more groups of numbers. It does get a little complex, as combination-betting options are almost infinite. Helpful casino personnel in the keno lounge can assist you with combination betting.

Poker

Poker is the game of the Old West (there seems to be at least one sequence in every Western where the hero faces off against the villain over a poker hand). In Las Vegas, poker is just about the biggest thing going, thanks to the popularity of celebrity poker TV shows, poker tours, books, and magazines. Just about every casino now has a poker room, and it's just a matter of time before the others catch up.

There are lots of variations on the basic game, but one of the most popular is **Hold 'Em.** Two cards are dealt, face down, to the players. After a betting round, five community cards (everyone can use them) are dealt face up on the table. Players make the best five-card hand, using their own cards and the "board" (the community cards), and the best hand wins. The house dealer takes care of the shuffling and the dealing, and moves a marker around the table to alternate the start of the deal. The house usually rakes around 10% (it depends on the casino) from each pot. Most casinos also provide tables for playing Seven-Card Stud, Omaha High, and Omaha Hi-Lo. A few even have Seven-Card Stud Hi-Lo split. To learn how these variations are played, either read a book or take lessons.

Warning: If you don't know how to play poker, don't attempt to learn at a table. Card sharks are not a rare species in Vegas; they will gladly feast on fresh meat (you!). Find a casino that provides free gaming lessons and learn, to quote Kenny Rogers, when to hold 'em and when to fold 'em.

PAI GOW

Pai Gow is a variation on poker that has become popular. The game is played with a traditional deck plus one joker. The joker is a wild card that can be used as an ace or to complete a straight, a flush, a straight flush, or a royal flush. Each player is dealt seven cards to arrange into two hands: a two-card hand and a five-card hand. As in standard poker, the highest two-card hand is two aces, and the highest five-card hand is a royal flush. The five-card hand *must* be higher than the two-card hand (if the two-card hand is a pair of 6s, for example, the five-card hand must be a pair of 7s or better). Any player's hand that is set incorrectly is an automatic loser. The object of the game is for both of the players' hands to rank higher than both of the banker's hands. Should one hand rank exactly the same as the banker's hand, this is a tie (called a "copy"), *and the banker wins all tie hands.* If the player wins one hand but loses the other, this is a "push," and no money changes hands. The house dealer or any player may be the banker. The bank is offered to each player, and each player may accept or pass. Winning hands are paid even money, less a 5% commission.

CARIBBEAN STUD

Caribbean Stud is yet another variation of poker that is gaining in popularity. Players put in a single ante bet and are dealt five cards, face down, from a single deck; they play solely against the dealer, who receives five cards, one of them face up. Players are then given the option of folding or calling, by making an additional bet that is double their original ante. After all player bets have been made, the dealer's cards are revealed. If the dealer doesn't qualify with *at least an ace/king combination,* players are paid even money on their ante, and their call bets are returned. If the dealer does qualify, each player's hand is compared to the dealer's. On winning hands, players receive even money on their ante bets, and call bets are paid out on a scale according to the value of their hands. The scale ranges from even money for a pair, to 100 to 1 on a royal flush, although there is usually a cap on the maximum payoff, which varies from casino to casino.

An additional feature of Caribbean Stud is the inclusion of a progressive jackpot. For an additional side bet of $1, a player may qualify for a payoff from a progressive jackpot. The jackpot bet pays off only on a flush or better, but you can win on this bet even if the dealer ends up with a better hand than you do. Dream all you want of getting that royal flush and taking home the jackpot, but the odds of it happening are astronomical, so don't be so quick to turn in your resignation letter. Most veteran gamblers will tell you this is a bad bet (from a strict mathematical standpoint, it is), but considering that Caribbean Stud already has a house advantage that is even larger than the one in roulette, if you're going to play, you might as well toss in the buck and pray.

LET IT RIDE

Let It Ride is another popular game that involves poker hands. You place three bets at the outset and are dealt three cards. The dealer is dealt two cards that act as community cards (you're not playing against the dealer). Once you've seen your cards, you can choose to pull the first of your three bets back or "let it ride." The object of this game is to get a pair of 10s or better by combining your cards with the community cards. If you're holding a pair of 10s or better in your first three cards (called a "no-brainer"), you want to let your bets ride the entire way through. Once you've decided whether or not to let your first bet ride, the dealer exposes one of his or her two cards. Once again, you must make a decision to take back your middle bet or keep on going. Then the dealer exposes the last of his or her cards; your third bet must stay. The dealer then turns over the hands of the players and determines whether you've won. Winning bets are paid on a scale, ranging from even money for a single pair up to 1,000 to 1 for a royal flush. These payouts are for each bet you have in play. Similar to Caribbean Stud, Let It Ride has a bonus that you can win for high hands if you cough up an additional $1 per hand, but be advised that the house advantage on that $1 is obscene. But hey, that's why it's called gambling.

THREE-CARD POKER

Three-Card Poker is rapidly gaining popularity, and now you'll find at least one table in most major Vegas casinos. It's actually more difficult to explain than to play. For this reason, we recommend watching a table for a while. You should grasp it pretty quickly.

Basically, players are dealt three cards with no draw and have to make the best poker hand out of those three cards. Possible combinations include a straight flush (three sequential cards of the same suit), three of a kind (three queens, for example), a straight (three sequential cards of any suit), a flush (three cards of the same suit), and a pair (two queens, for example). Even if you don't have one of the favored combinations, you can still win if you have cards higher than the dealer's.

On the table are three betting areas—Ante, Play, and Pair Plus. There are actually two games in one on a Three-Card Poker table—"Pair Plus" and "Ante and Play." You can play only Pair Plus or only Ante, or both. You place your chips in the areas in which you want to bet.

Impressions

If you aim to leave Las Vegas with a small fortune, go there with a large one.
—Anonymous

In Pair Plus, you are betting only on your hand, not competing against anyone else at the table or the dealer. If you get a pair or better, depending on your hand, the payoff can be pretty fab—straight flush: 40 to 1; three of a kind: 30 to 1; straight: 6 to 1; flush: 3 to 1; pair: 1 to 1.

In Ante and Play, you are betting that your hand will be better than the dealer's but you're not competing against anyone else at the table. You place an Ante bet, view your cards, and then, if you decide you like your hand, you place a bet in the Play area equal to your Ante bet. If you get lousy cards and don't want to go forward, you can fold, losing only your Ante bet and your Pair Plus bet, if you made one. Once all bets are made, the dealer's hand is revealed—he or she must have at least a single queen for the bet to count; if not, your Ante and Play bets are returned. If you beat the dealer's hand, you get a 1 to 1 payoff, but there is a bonus for a particularly good winning hand: straight flush, 5 to 1; three of a kind, 4 to 1; straight, 1 to 1.

Your three cards are dealt. If you play only Pair Plus, it doesn't matter what the dealer has—you get paid if you have a pair or better. If you don't, you lose your bet. If you play the Ante bet, you must then either fold and lose the Ante bet or match the Ante bet by placing the same amount on the Play area. The dealer's hand is revealed, and payouts happen accordingly. Each hand consists of one fresh 52-card deck.

Meanwhile, as if all this weren't enough, new variations on table games keep popping up. There's Crazy 4 Poker, similar to Three-Card Poker, only with five cards dealt, no draw, and make your best four-card poker hand out of it; a version of Texas Hold'em where you are not competing against other players; and more.

Roulette

Roulette is an extremely easy game to play, and it's really quite colorful and exciting to watch. The wheel spins, and the little ball bounces around, finally dropping into one of the slots, numbered 1 to 36, plus 0 and 00. You can place bets "Inside" the table and "Outside" the table. Inside bets are bets placed on a particular number or a set of numbers. Outside bets are those placed in the boxes surrounding the number table. If you bet on a specific number and it comes up, you are paid 35 to 1 on your bet. Bear in mind, however, that the odds of a particular number coming up are actually 38 to 1 (don't forget the 0 and 00!), so the house has an advantage the moment you place an inside bet. The methods of placing single-number bets, column bets, and others are fairly obvious. The dealer will be happy to show you how to make many interesting betting combinations, such as betting on six numbers at once. Each player is given different-colored chips so that it's easy to follow the numbers you've bet on.

Slots

You put the coin in the slot and pull the handle. What, you thought there was a trick to this?

Actually, there is a bit more to it. But first, some background. Old-timers will tell you slots were invented to give wives something to do while their husbands gambled. Slots used to be stuck at the edges of the casino and could be counted on one hand, maybe two. But now they *are* the casino. The casinos make more from slots than from craps, blackjack, and roulette combined. There are more than 150,000 slot machines (not including video poker) in the county. Some of these are at the airport, steps from you as you deplane. It's just a matter of time before the planes flying into Vegas feature slots that pop up as soon as you cross the state line.

But to keep up with the increasing competition, the plain old machine, where reels just spin, has become nearly obsolete. Now they are all computerized and have buttons to push so you can avoid getting carpal tunnel syndrome from yanking the handle all night (though the handles are still there on some of them). Many don't even have reels anymore but are entirely video screens, which offer a number of little bonus extras that have nothing to do with actual play. The idea is still simple: Get three (sometimes four) cherries (clowns, sevens, dinosaurs, whatever) in a row, and you win something. Each machine has its own combination. Some will pay you something with just one symbol showing; on most, the more combinations there are, the more opportunities for loot. Some will even pay if you get three blanks. Study each machine to learn what it does. *Note:* The **payback** goes up considerably if you bet the limit (from 2 to as many as 45 coins).

Progressive slots are groups of linked machines (sometimes spread over several casinos) where the jackpot gets bigger every few moments (just as lottery jackpots build up). Bigger and better games keep showing up; for example, there's Anchor Gaming's much-imitated **Wheel of Gold,** wherein if you get the right symbol, you get to spin a roulette wheel, which guarantees you a win of a serious number of coins. **Totem Pole** is the Godzilla of slot machines, a behemoth that allows you to spin up to three reels at once (provided you put in the limit).

Other gimmick machines include the popular **Wheel of Fortune** machines, slots that have a gorilla attempting to climb the Empire State Building, heading up as you win, and machines with such themes as Elvis or the Three Stooges. And, of course, there are always those **giant slot machines,** gimmicky devices that are becoming rare but are still found in some casinos. They may not win as often as regular slots (though there is no definite word on it one way or the other), but not only are they just plain fun to spin, they also often turn into audience-participation gambling, as watchers gather to cheer you on to victory.

Nickel slots, which for a long time had been overlooked, relegated to a lonely spot somewhere by a back wall because they were not as profitable for the casinos as quarter and dollar slots, have made a comeback. Many machines now offer a 45-nickel or more maximum (meaning a larger bet on those machines than on the five-quarter-maximum slots), and gamblers have been flocking to them. As a result, more cash is pocketed by the casino (which keeps a higher percentage of cash off of nickel slots than it does off of quarter slots), which is happy to accommodate this trend by offering up more and more nickel slots. See how this all works? Are you paying attention? Ultratightwads will be pleased by the increased presence of the humble penny slot, but few, if any, allow for only a penny bet—in fact, the minimum bet is $3 and sometimes higher!

Cashless machines are the standard in Vegas these days. Now when gambling, players insert their money, they play, and when they cash out, they get—instead of the clanging sound of coins cascading out into the tray—a little paper ticket with their total winnings on it. Those of us who find the sound of the coins pouring out a comfort are only slightly pleased to learn that the same noise plays, as a computer-generated audio effect, when the ticket is disgorged. Hand in your ticket at a cashier's window (or use the omnipresent ATM-style redemption machines), and you get your winnings. It's not nearly as viscerally satisfying, but the future is now. As a result of the cashless machine trend, the casinos are much quieter, as many of the formerly chatty machines have been largely silenced, and that famous Vegas clang-clang is somewhat dimmed.

The biggest revolution in gaming is the advent of server-based slots and video poker. This allows you or the casino to switch out themes and denominations on a single machine. Tired of playing the Double Diamond quarter machine? No problem! Hit a button and it can become a Lucky 7 dollar machine in an instant.

PLAYERS' clubs

If you play slots or video poker, or, indeed, just gamble quite a bit, or even just gamble, it definitely pays to join a players' club. These so-called clubs are designed to attract and keep customers in a given casino by providing incentives: meals, shows, discounts on rooms, gifts, tournament invitations, discounts at hotel shops, VIP treatment, and (more and more) cash rebates. Join a players' club (it doesn't cost a cent to sign up), and soon you, too, will be getting those great hotel-rate offers—$20-a-night rooms, affordable rooms at the luxury resorts, even free rooms. This is one way to beat the high hotel rates. Of course, your rewards are often greater

if you play just in one casino, but your mobility is limited.

When you join a players' club (inquire at the casino desk), you're given a card that looks like a credit card, which you must insert into an ATM-like device whenever you play. Yes, many casinos even have them for the tables as well as the machines. The device tracks your play and computes bonus points. Don't forget, as we sometimes do, to retrieve your card when you leave the machine—though that may work in your favor if someone comes along and plays the machine without removing it.

Which players' club should you join? Actually, you should join one at any casino where you play because even the act of joining usually entitles you to some benefits. It's convenient to concentrate play where you're staying; if you play a great deal, a casino-hotel's players' club benefits may be a factor in your accommodations choice. Consider, though, particularly if you aren't a high roller, the players' clubs Downtown. You get more bang for your buck, because you don't have to spend as much to start raking in the goodies.

Another advantage is to join a players' club that covers many hotels under the same corporate umbrella. Harrah's Entertainment operates the Total Rewards club, which is good at any of their casinos in Vegas (Harrah's, Rio, Caesars Palace, the Flamingo, Paris Las Vegas, Bally's, and Planet Hollywood; www.harrahs.com/total_rewards) or elsewhere around the world. The same goes for casinos in the MGM Resorts International stable (Aria Las Vegas, The Mirage, Bellagio, MGM Grand, Mandalay Bay, Luxor, Circus Circus, New York–New York, and Excalibur; www.playersclub. com), the locals' favorite Station Casinos (Palace, Sunset, Texas, and more; www. stationcasinos.com/gaming/boarding pass), and the other interlinked properties, which include Arizona Charlie's and the Stratosphere Casino Hotel & Tower.

Choosing the best club(s) for you can be a complex business. To get into it in-depth, see **www.lasvegasadvisor.com**. Also visit the sites for the individual casinos, many of which allow you to join their clubs online. Try it, and you might find yourself receiving discounts and freebies before you even set foot in Vegas.

Slot machine in the MGM Grand's casino.

These high-tech gadgets are also often integrated to a virtual version of the hosting hotel's concierge allowing you to find out restaurant and show information without ever getting up. You will have to get up to actually go see the show or eat at the restaurant, but we're sure they're working on a way around that, too.

Are there surefire ways to win on a slot machine? No. But you can lose more slowly. The slot machines use minicomputers known as random number generators (RNGs) to determine the winning combinations on a machine, and though each spin may indeed be random, individual machines are programmed to pay back different percentages over the long haul. As a result, a machine programmed to return a higher percentage might be "looser" than others. A bank of empty slots probably (but not certainly) means the machines are tight. Go find a line where lots of people are sitting around with trays full of money. A good rule of thumb is that if your slot doesn't hit something in four or five pulls, leave it and go find another. Also, each casino has a bank of slots that they advertise as more loose or with a bigger payback. Try these. It's what they want you to do, but what the heck.

Most slot machines no longer accept coins at all for bets. For these new machines, bets have to start with bills accepted into special slots. This makes all but extinct the famous change carts that used to roam the floors, helping people get rolls of quarters and the like.

Sports Books

Most of the larger hotels in Las Vegas have sports-book operations, which look a lot like commodities-futures trading boards. In some, almost as large as theaters, you can sit comfortably, occasionally in recliners, and sometimes with your own video screen, and watch ball games, fights, and, at some casinos, horse races on huge TV screens. To add to your enjoyment, there's usually a deli/bar nearby that serves sandwiches, hot dogs, soft drinks, and beer. As a matter of fact, some of the best sandwiches in Las Vegas are served next to the sports books. Sports books take bets on virtually every sport (and not just who'll win, but what the final score will be, who'll be first to hit a home run, who'll be MVP, who'll wear red shoes, you name it). They are best during important playoff games or big horse races, when everyone in the place is watching the same event—shrieking, shouting, and moaning, sometimes in unison. Joining in with a cheap bet (so you feel like you, too, have a personal stake in the matter) makes for bargain entertainment.

Video Poker

Rapidly gaining on slots in popularity, video poker works the same way as regular poker, except you play against the machine. You are dealt a hand, you pick which cards to keep and which to discard, and then you get your new hand. And, it is hoped, you collect your winnings. This is somewhat more of a challenge and more active than slots because you have some control (or at least the illusion of control) over your fate, and it's easier than playing actual poker with a table full of folks who probably take it very seriously.

There are a number of varieties of this machine, including **Jacks or Better, Deuces Wild,** and so forth. Be sure to study your machine before you play. (The best returns are offered on the **Bonus Poker** machines; the payback for a pair of jacks or better is two times your bet, and three times for three of a kind.) The Holy Grail of video-poker machines is the 9/6 (it pays nine coins for a full house, six coins for a flush), but you'll need to pray a lot before you find one in town. Some machines offer **double down:** After you have won, you get a chance to draw cards against the machine, with the higher card the winner. If you win, your money is doubled, and you are offered a chance to go again. Your money can increase nicely during this time, and you can also lose it all very quickly, which is most annoying.

Technology is catching up with video poker, too. Now they even have touch screens, which offer a variety of different poker games, blackjack, and video slots—just touch your screen and choose your poison.

THE CASINOS

Casino choice is a personal thing. Some like to find their lucky place and stick with it, while others love to take advantage of the nearly endless choices that Las Vegas offers. Everyone should casino-hop at least once to marvel (or get dizzy) at the decor/spectacle and the sheer excess of it all.

Virtually all casinos make sure they have no clocks or windows—they do not want you to interrupt your losing streak by realizing how much time has passed. Of course, we've all heard the legend that Las Vegas casinos pump in fresh oxygen to keep the players from getting tired and wanting to pack it in. The veracity of this is hard to confirm, but we can only hope it's true, especially when we think of that time we looked up after a long stretch of gambling and discovered it was Thursday.

Don't be a snob and don't be overly dazzled by the fancy casinos. Sometimes you can have a better time at one of the older places Downtown, where stakes are lower, pretensions are nonexistent, and the clientele is often friendlier. Frankly, real gamblers—and by that we don't necessarily mean high rollers, but those who play to win, regardless of the amount of said win—head straight for Downtown for these precise reasons, caring not a whit about glitz and glamour. Even if you don't take your gambling as seriously as that, you may well want to follow their example. After all, it's getting harder and harder to find cheap tables (where you can play a hand of blackjack, for example, for less than $10) on the Strip—so take your hard-earned money to where you can lose it more slowly!

We would also call your attention to less glamorous, less readily accessible casinos, such as local favorites Sunset Station, Texas Station, The Cannery, Fiesta Rancho, Fiesta Henderson, and Fiesta Santa Fe, where payoffs are often higher than on the Strip, and the limits are lower.

You can expect to find in every casino the usual and expected assortment of games—slot machines, of course, video poker, blackjack, table poker (making a big comeback after years of decline), a race and sports book, a keno lounge, a poker room, baccarat, minibaccarat, Caribbean Stud, Let It Ride, craps, roulette, Pai Gow, and more, more, more. If you want a particular game, and it's not one of the most obvious, you might want to call before heading over to a particular casino, just to make sure it's available there.

What follows is a description of most of the major casinos in Vegas, including their level of claustrophobia, and a completely arbitrary assessment based on whether we won there.

South Strip

Aria Las Vegas The newest casino in town is also one of the most dramatic from a visual perspective. Heavy use of wood, steel, glass, fabric, and stone accompanied by moody lighting give the expansive 150,000 square-foot room a look and feel that is dazzling and distinctly modern, although admittedly not to everyone's taste, especially the casino purists among us. "Why is there sunlight?!" The good news is that those architectural details break up the space to provide a more intimate feeling without increasing the claustrophobia quotient. Offerings include thousands of slots (traditional reel, video, and server based) of all denominations, dozens of table games, two high-limit lounges, a race and sports book, and a poker room. As a member of MGM Resorts International, Aria takes part in their M Life rewards program, which is also used at Bellagio, Mandalay Bay, New York–New York, and others (www.playersclub.com). 3730 Las Vegas Blvd. S. ✆ **702/590-7111.** www.arialasvegas.com.

Excalibur As you might expect, the Excalibur casino is replete with suits of armor, stained-glass panels, knights, dragons, and velvet and satin heraldic banners, with gaming action taking place beneath vast iron-and-gold chandeliers fit for a medieval castle fortress. This all makes it fine for kitsch seekers, but anyone who hates crowds or is sensitive to noise will hate it. The overall effect is less like a castle than like a dungeon. One of us won a lot of money here and refused to share it with the other, so our final judgment about the casino is, well, mixed. Excalibur is part of the MGM Resorts International M Life program, which is also used at MGM Grand, The Mirage, Bellagio, Luxor, Mandalay Bay, Circus Circus, and others (www.playersclub.com). 3850 Las Vegas Blvd. S. ✆ 702/597-7777. www.excalibur.com.

Impressions
Tip Number 3: Win a bunch of money. I can't recommend this too highly. If it hasn't occurred to you, win $1,200 and see for yourself. It's very energizing and really adds to your Vegas fun.
—Merrill Markoe, *Viva Las Wine Goddesses!*

memories **OF A LONGTIME DEALER**

Lou has been a part of the gaming industry for over 40 years, the first 20 of which he spent as a dealer in Las Vegas.

"My favorite places were the Flamingo, the Sands, and the Desert Inn. That's when the corporations weren't there. That's when the other folks were in. The mob guys—I never knew it, but that's what they were. I was just a kid. Bugsy had just gotten killed when I went to work at the Flamingo. The Sands was my very first favorite. That was the hotel of all hotels. They had the very best management team. They took care of their help. Their benefits were better than any union. It was the place.

"Years ago, you had great entertainment. You could go to a lounge and catch better acts than in the showroom. Major stars were in the lounges, or they would come in and sit in with the acts after the showroom closed. Don Rickles: Sinatra would get up with him once in a while. Sinatra gave me my first $100 tip. He was playing blackjack. Then he said, 'Do you want to play it or keep it?' I wanted to be polite, so I said, 'Bet it.' And he lost. In those days when the stars would appear on stage, between shows they would come out into the casinos. Sinatra and Sammy would deal. They would blow money, but the casinos didn't care. It was a fun, fun place.

"The casinos were run the way they were supposed to be run—for the customer, not so corporate-minded. In those days, you could go to Vegas, get your room very reasonable, your food was practically free, your shows were practically free, you would spend $500 in the casino, but you would come back and be happy because gaming was a form of entertainment. When they ran the casinos, you would have a ball, come home, and be happy. They were very happy if the restaurants and shows lost money—you still lost that $500. Now it would cost you $100 to stay at a hotel, and food is much more expensive, and to get a ticket to one of these shows is ridiculous. Now you gamble only $150 and you aren't as happy when you come home because you don't feel like you've been treated to anything. It all goes into the same pocket—what difference does it make? It gives the customer the same hours and more fun. They don't understand that. It's not the same industry as when the mob guys ran it. And it shows."

LOU THE DEALER'S GAMING TIPS

If you are a **craps** shooter, just look around at the tables where they have the most chips. Find the guy with the most chips, and do what he does. Follow him along.

For **blackjack,** everybody will tell you in all your books to try to play single and double decks. I don't agree with that, and I never will. The average player goes in to enjoy himself and to win a few dollars. So he is not a professional card counter. Play a shoe. If that shoe is going bad and you catch a run, you will make a lot more money than with a single deck.

Look at gaming as a form of entertainment. Look at that $100 that you might have spent on dinner or a club, where we laughed and had a few drinks and had a good time. Think of it that way.

If you double your money, quit. Not quit gambling, but quit that table. Go have a sandwich or watch a show. And *then* come back. The odds aren't that tremendously in favor of the casinos. How they make their money is through greed; gamblers doubling their money then trying to quadruple it and losing it all, and more.

Try to survive. Don't try to win the hotel. Just try to win a few dollars. Then stop and enjoy it.

Luxor Las Vegas The good news: It is more accessible than you might think, thanks to the air-conditioned people-mover from Excalibur and the monorail from Mandalay Bay. The bad news: Luxor has systematically stripped away anything Egypt about the place. The result—a casino that looks like all the other casinos in town. Bring back the talking camels and Tut! The casino did get a remodel that removed the space-wasting central area that used to contain the bathrooms, cashiers, and casino offices. This additional space gives the casino a much airier feel, which produces a low claustrophobia level—in parts of the place, you can see all the way up the inside of the pyramid. There is also a casino lounge called Aurora that is very nice. The MGM Resorts International M Life program offers rewards of cash, merchandise, meals, and special services to slot and table players. Sports action unfolds on both large screen and individual monitors in Luxor's race and sports book. We felt inclined to like this casino, thanks to a good run at blackjack, but we are most cranky about the de-Egypt-ification. 3900 Las Vegas Blvd. S. ℂ **702/262-4444.** www.luxor.com.

Mandalay Bay You'll find "elegant" gaming in a pre-fab, deliberate way, with a very high ceiling that produces a very low claustrophobia factor. This is definitely the right place to gamble if you're looking for less hectic, less gimmick-filled play. The layout makes it look airy, and it's marginally less confusing and certainly less overwhelming than many other casinos. Because it is so far down the Strip, there are fewer walk-in players, but the presence of the House of Blues, a happening center lounge, and the ongoing popularity of the **rumjungle nightclub** can mean a late-night influx of customers. There's a big, ultracomfortable sports-book area (complete with armchairs that could well encourage a relaxed gambler to fall asleep). Players can sign up for the M Life program (www.playersclub.com). 3950 Las Vegas Blvd. S. ℂ **702/632-7777.** www.mandalaybay.com.

MGM Grand Las Vegas's largest casino (171,500 sq. ft.)—we've been to countries that were smaller!—is divided into four areas, in a futile attempt to make it seem smaller. All of the *Wizard of Oz* decorations have been removed, but spend an hour in here, and you may feel like Dorothy after she was whisked away by the twister. You will get lost at least once. One section features a high-roller slot area with machines that operate on coins valued at $100 and $500! The sports casino houses a big poker room, a state-of-the-art race and sports book with private luxury sky boxes, and the Turf Bar. Carousels of progressive slots unique to the MGM Grand include the very popular Majestic Lions high-frequency $1 slot machines, which pay out more than $1 million daily. This hotel takes part in the M Life program (www.playersclub.com). 3799 Las Vegas Blvd. S. ℂ **702/891-7777.** www.mgmgrand.com.

Monte Carlo Resort & Casino A 2009 remodel turned this bland white room into a slightly less bland beige room. You wouldn't think beige would decrease the blandness but anytime you throw in new carpets, wall coverings, furnishings, and gaming tables, it's a definite improvement. Unfortunately they didn't do anything to change the fact that it is still essentially one big room so it leaves gamblers often feeling a bit exposed. There are plenty of slots and table games to distract you from that, of course, and the sports book and poker rooms offer some sanctuary. This casino takes part in the M Life program (www.playersclub.com). 3770 Las Vegas Blvd. S. ℂ **702/730-7777.** www.montecarlo.com.

New York–New York Just like sister casino Luxor, the theme-gone-mad here has been scaled way back, removing a lot of the wacky details that made this

Casino floor at New York–New York.

place fun. The Central Park effect has been replaced by smooth, modern lines (blech), generic styling, and an overall sense of "classy" that, while admittedly pretty, is certainly not as entertaining. Having said that, you can still get your game on here with a full array of slots, tables, sports betting, and more; and, if you feel the need to immerse yourself in the faux-Gotham glory, you can wander into the adjacent Greenwich Village shops and restaurant areas for a breather. New York–New York participates in the M Life program (www.playersclub.com). 3790 Las Vegas Blvd. S. © **702/740-6969.** www.nynyhotelcasino.com.

Tropicana After nearly a decade of promises (or was it threats?) to remodel this aging and somewhat dingy casino, the latest owners have finally come through and completely transformed the Trop into a modern, South Beach–themed showplace. White is the predominate color here in the marble floors, plantation shutter clad columns, and gaming table borders and chairs, all set off by vibrant splashes of orange, gold, and red. The famous Tiffany glass ceiling is gone, making Vegas history buffs weep on their collectible chips, but it's impossible to deny that the place looks a billion times better than it did. It's a relatively small space, at least in comparison to the behemoths nearby, but there are still plenty of slot, video poker, and table game options. 3801 Las Vegas Blvd. S. © **702/739-2222.** www. troplv.com.

Mid-Strip

Bally's Las Vegas Bally's casino is large (the size of a football field), with lots of colorful signage. The big ceiling makes for a low claustrophobia level although the open floor plan can leave gamblers who want a sense of privacy scuttling to the more secluded corners. The casino hosts frequent slot tournaments and offers free gaming lessons. Their players' club is valid at sister properties, such as Harrah's, Caesars, Paris Las Vegas, and others, offering members cash rebates, room discounts, free meals and show tickets, and invitations to special events, among other perks. 3645 Las Vegas Blvd. S. © **702/739-4111.** www.ballyslv.com.

Bellagio The slot machines here are mostly encased in marble and fine woods. How's that for upping the ante on classy? Bellagio comes the closest to re-creating the feel of gambling in Monte Carlo (the country, not the nearby casino), but its relentless good taste means that this is one pretty forgettable casino. After all, we are suckers for a wacky theme that screams "Vegas," and European class just doesn't cut it. Then again, we brought a pal of more refined sensibility, and she adored it, finding it the perfect antidote to New York–New York. Sure, there are good touches—we always like a high ceiling to reduce the claustrophobia index, and the place is laid out in an easy-to-navigate grid with ultrawide aisles, so walking through doesn't seem like such a crowded collision-course maze. And we won big here, so there's that. Anyway, the cozy sports book has individual TVs and entirely denlike leather chairs—quite, quite comfortable. Bellagio is part of the M Life program (www.playersclub.com). 3600 Las Vegas Blvd. S. ✆ **888/987-6667.** www.bellagio.com.

Bill's Gamblin' Hall & Saloon Bill's Gamblin' Hall & Saloon is an 1890s-style casino ornately decorated with $2 million worth of gorgeous stained-glass skylights and signs, as well as immense crystal-dangling globe chandeliers over the gaming tables. It's kind of small, dark, and cluttered, but it's also Old Las Vegas (and we mean "old" loosely, and certainly not true "Old" like Downtown Vegas), and small is rare on the Strip. Although the property is owned by Harrah's, it does not participate in their Total Rewards players' club. 3595 Las Vegas Blvd. S. ✆ **702/737-7111.** www.billslasvegas.com.

Caesars Palace The Caesars casino is simultaneously the ultimate in gambling luxury and the ultimate in Vegas kitsch. Where else can you gamble under the watchful gaze of faux-marble Roman statues? The very high ceiling in certain newer areas of the casino makes for a very low claustrophobia level but older areas still feel cramped. Although we love it, the casino has become somewhat confusing and unmanageable because of its size and meandering layout, like Caesars itself.

A notable facility is the state-of-the-art race and sports book, with huge electronic display boards and giant video screens. Caesars pioneered computer-generated wagering data that can be communicated in less than half a second, and it has sophisticated satellite equipment that can pick up the broadcast of virtually any sporting event in the world. It's quite comfortable, but is located right by the line of foot traffic. The domed VIP slot arena of The Forum Casino (minimum bet is $5, but you can wager up to $1,500 on a single pull!) is a plush, crystal-chandeliered precinct with seating in roomy, adjustable chairs. Gamblers can accumulate bonus points toward cash back, gifts, gratis show tickets, meals, and rooms by joining the Total Rewards players club. It's a gorgeous and elegant place to gamble, and we've actually won some money here so we love it. 3570 Las Vegas Blvd. S. ✆ **702/731-7110.** www.caesarspalace.com.

Flamingo Las Vegas If you've seen the movie *Bugsy,* you won't recognize this as Mr. Siegel's baby. We can't say for sure what the seemingly years-long casino renovation actually did. It all looks pretty much the same as it used to, but it might be marginally less confusing and tortuous a layout (trust us, anything is an improvement), with better, and most welcome, access to the street (before, you needed a trail of bread crumbs and a lot of stamina to find your way out). Still, the claustrophobia factor is moderately high, thanks to a still-low ceiling with electric bulbs and pink neon everywhere. It's old school and retro in the unintentional (that is to say, authentic) way, which means it looks tired compared to the fancy high-class operations across the street. But while it's uncoordinated and gaudy, it's also not threateningly chic or chilly or overrun with Paris Hilton wannabes. So there's something to be said for old school. We have to say that of all the casinos that qualify as older, this is the most pleasant one in which to play. Unfortunately, the gambler seems to be paying for it—no more daytime $3 blackjack. The Flamingo takes part in the Total Rewards players club. 3555 Las Vegas Blvd. S. ✆ **702/733-3111.** www.flamingolasvegas.com.

Gold Coast Adjacent to the Rio, this casino is not only well lit but also totally unique in Vegas: It has windows! It's a little thing, but it made us really excited. They also have a higher ratio of video-poker machines to slot machines, rather than the other way around. A remodeling made it much bigger, with high ceilings, and it's very bright overall. Nice job. The casino and the players' club (www.bconnectedonline.com) are tied to other Boyd Gaming properties, such as The Orleans and Sam's Town. 4000 W. Flamingo Rd. ✆ **702/367-7111.** www.goldcoastcasino.com.

Harrah's This is a mixed bag of a casino, one that is both dated (low ceilings, old lighting, stuffy) and fun (parts have high-enough ceilings and there are special attractions). It's also supercrowded, noisy, flashy, and claustrophobic. At night, the popular party pit (allegedly fun dealers, rowdy music) packs them in, but the entire place gets crowded by the end of the day. Slot and table-game players can earn bonus points toward complimentary rooms, meals, and show tickets by joining the Total Rewards players club in the casino. Free gaming lessons are offered on weekdays. 3475 Las Vegas Blvd. S. ✆ **702/369-5000.** www.harrahs.com.

The Mirage The Mirage is more inviting now than in its chaotic past, thanks to a design switch from heavy tropics to more soothing Asian wood accents. But it's still twisting and meandering, and the relatively low ceiling and black walls are still a medium claustrophobia issue. This remains one of our favorite places

Gold Coast casino.

to gamble. Facilities include a plush European-style *salon privé* for high rollers at baccarat, blackjack, and roulette; an elegant dining room serves catered meals to gamblers there. Slot and table players can join the M Life program and work toward bonus points for cash rebates, special room rates, complimentary meals and/or show tickets, and other benefits. The elaborate race and sports book offers theater stereo sound and a movie-theater-size screen. It's one of the most pleasant and popular casinos in town, so it's crowded more often than not. 3400 Las Vegas Blvd. S. ☎ **702/791-7111.** www.mirage.com.

The Palazzo This casino is so lacking in distinguishing features that when it came time to write it up, we couldn't remember if The Palazzo even *had* a casino. See the review below for the one at the adjoining Venetian and just lather, rinse, and repeat. Sure it's big and grand, but it's also beige and bland. Signage is just as confusing as over at The Venetian. Slots are almost all multipayline video screen rather than the traditional single-payline model, which is disappointing. The sports book is located on a different level, incorporated into an Emeril Lagasse restaurant, but it does offer in-line betting (wagers placed during the game instead of just on the game as a whole) and mobile gaming with hand-held devices that can be used in some (but not all) public spaces. 3335 Las Vegas Blvd St. ☎ **866/263-3001.** www.palazzolasvegas.com.

Palms Resort & Casino This desperately seeking-the-hip hotel has a bit of an identity crisis: It also wants to be a place where locals feel comfortable gambling. You know, like Palace and Texas Station. Huh? That's right, the Palms wants to mirror those hotels off the Strip that offer loose slots and other incentives to make the locals feel at home. This rarely makes for a chic playing area (because locals don't want to have to get glammed up to go out and play some slots). On the other hand, the area—especially on weekend nights—is ringed with the beautiful and aloof, desperate to get into ghostbar, Rain, Moon, and the Playboy Club. If they aren't inside, they are surly about it. It's actually a pretty fun place to play, so something works. The gaming area covers most of the ground floor and is replete with Miami tropical–inspired details. 4321 W. Flamingo Rd. ☎ **702/942-7777.** www.palms.com.

Paris Las Vegas Casino Surrounded by a rather Disney-esque one-third-scale replica of the streets of Paris, this 83,000-square-foot casino is a very pleasant place to gamble, in that Vegas gimmick kind of way. It's one of those kitschy places that "real" gamblers are appalled by. To heck with them, we say. A tall ceiling gives the illusion that you are trying to bust the bank while strolling outside and results in an airy effect. The place doesn't feel all that large, thanks to its layout. It has more than 2,000 slot machines and more than 100 table games. A state-of-the-art race and sports book features live satellite feeds of sporting events from around the world. The Paris is part of the Total Rewards players' club. 3655 Las Vegas Blvd. S. ☎ **702/946-7000.** www.parislasvegas.com.

Planet Hollywood A top-to-bottom remodel of the former Aladdin has classed up this place with nary a hint of its former identity. The interior is impressive, classic Hollywood glamour, with plenty of curving lines and dramatic folderol on columns and the like. In sharp contrast to the chaotic entrance, the interior is actually much calmer than it used to be. Check out the imaginative slot toppers, which usually proclaim "Double Diamond." All the usual casino suspects are still around, including thousands of slots, video-poker machines, plenty of table games, a high-limit salon, a poker room, and more. Now that the hotel is owned

Planet Hollywood Casino.

by Harrah's Entertainment, gambling here gets you points in the corporate Total Rewards club. 3667 Las Vegas Blvd. S. (*C*) **702/785-5555.** www.planethollywoodresort.com.

Rio All-Suite Hotel & Casino This Brazilian-themed resort's 85,000-square-foot casino is, despite the presence of plenty of glitter and neon, very dark. It has about the highest claustrophobia rating of the major casinos and seems very dated these days. Its sports book feels a little grimy. The waitresses wear scanty costumes (particularly in the back), probably in an effort to distract you and throw off your game (all the more so now that they have added "Bev-entertainment"—those poor drink-slingers are required to burst into song and/or dance in between beer deliveries). Why? Why not. The part of the casino in the Masquerade Village is considerably more pleasant (the very high ceilings help), though still crowded, and the loud live show here adds even more noise. In the high-end slot area ($5–$100 a pull), guests enjoy a private lounge and gratis champagne. The Rio participates in the Total Rewards players club. 3700 W. Flamingo Rd. (*C*) **702/252-7777.** www.riolasvegas.com.

Treasure Island We really loved it when this place was a casino set in Disneyland's Pirates of the Caribbean—or so it seemed. It doesn't seem like a big deal, the loss of those pirate chests dripping gold, jewels, and skulls with eye patches, but with the removal of the theme, this is now just a very nice casino. But it is that, so you should come here. There are nonsmoking gaming tables in each pit. A race and sports book boasts state-of-the-art electronic information boards and TV monitors at every seat, as well as numerous large-screen monitors. A new owner means this hotel is no longer part of the M Life program, but the casino has its own rewards program to try to keep you coming back. 3300 Las Vegas Blvd. S. (*C*) **702/894-7111.** www.treasureisland.com.

The Venetian *Tasteful* is the watchword in these days of classy Vegas gaming, and consequently, with the exception of more hand-painted Venetian art re-creations on parts of the ceiling, The Venetian's casino is interchangeable with those found at Mandalay Bay, the Monte Carlo, and, to a certain extent, Bellagio. All that gleaming marble, columns, and such are very nice, but after a while, they're also a bit ho-hum. Besides, this is Vegas, and we want our tacky theme elements, by gosh. The lack thereof, combined with poor signage, may be why this casino is so hard to get around—every part looks exactly the same as every other part. It's not exactly claustrophobic, but it can be confusing. On the other hand, we made a killing at blackjack, and one of our editors struck it rich at the slots, so we have to love the place for those reasons. Another (less personal) plus is that you can access the casino directly from the St. Mark's Square re-creation out front. The smoke-sensitive report that the ventilation system here is tops. Sports wagers should note that this is one of the few casinos in town that offers in-line betting and mobile gambling devices. 3355 Las Vegas Blvd. S. ✆ **702/414-1000.** www. venetian.com.

North Strip

Circus Circus This vast property has three full-size casinos that, combined, comprise one of the largest gaming operations in Nevada (more than 100,000 sq. ft.). More importantly, there is an entire circus midway set up throughout, so you are literally gambling with trapeze stunts going on over your head. The other great gimmick is the slot machine carousel—yep, it turns while you spin the reels. Unfortunately, the casino is crowded and noisy, and there are lots of children passing through (making it more crowded and noisy). That, plus some low ceilings (not in the Big Top, obviously), makes for a very high claustrophobia rating, though the current *Commedia dell'arte* clown motif (as opposed to the old garish circus motif) has upgraded the decor. Circus Circus participates in the M Life program. 2880 Las Vegas Blvd. S. ✆ **702/734-0410.** www.circuscircus.com.

Encore Las Vegas If you are looking for a unique casino experience, this should definitely be on your list. First, the room is smaller than most Strip casinos at only about 50,000 square feet, so it's much easier to navigate and you don't have to drop bread crumbs. The space is further broken up by lovely plantation shutters and heavy drapes that give the effect of a series of intimate gaming salons instead of one big room. Most notable though is the use of natural light, which floods the entire space from the atrium in front to the wall of windows facing the pool in the back. It's unlike any other casino in town—in a good way. Having said that, the smaller square-footage means less choice of machines and tables, the majority of which have higher denominations and limits (although there are a few penny, nickel, and quarter machines lurking around). Encore takes part in parent company Wynn Resorts Red Card players' reward program. 3121 Las Vegas Blvd. S. ✆ **800/320-7125.** www. encorelasvegas.com.

Circus acts above the crowds at the Circus Circus casino.

Riviera Riviera's 100,000-square-foot casino, once one of the largest in the world, offers plenty of opportunities to get lost and cranky. Especially if you, as one of us recently did, lose all your recent blackjack winnings at a table here. A wall of windows lets daylight stream in (most unusual), but as the hotel gets shabbier, every inch of the casino smells like smoke and age. The casino's players' clubs allow slot players to earn bonus points toward free meals, rooms, and show tickets. Nickeltown is just that— nothin' but nickel slots and video poker. The race and sports book here offers individual monitors at each of its 250 seats. 2901 Las Vegas Blvd. S. *©* **702/734-5110.** www.rivierahotel.com.

Sahara This is one place where there seems to be more tables than slots and video-poker machines. On a recent visit, the high ceilings and the unexpected *Arabian Nights* touches over the tables were nicer than we remembered from previous visits (maybe it all got dusted), and we made a killing at blackjack, so now we love this place again. Still, plans to morph the Sahara into something more like the Palms can only be a good move. The Sahara runs frequent slot tournaments and other events, and its slot club, Club Sahara, offers cash rebates and other perks. 2535 Las Vegas Blvd. S. *©* **702/737-2111.** www.saharavegas.com.

Stratosphere Casino Hotel & Tower Originally set up to evoke a world's fair but ending up more like a circus, Stratosphere redid its entire casino area to make it more appealing to the many adults who were staying away in droves. This should lure many of you, because it is a nicer, and less crowded, place to play. It heavily advertises its good odds: single-deck blackjack, single-zero roulette, and 10-times odds on craps. We can't say we noticed a difference, but other people around us were winning like crazy. The Ultimate Rewards Club sponsors frequent tournaments, and its members can earn points toward gifts, VIP perks, discounted room rates, meals, and cash rebates—just a bit of play here, and you may be getting more free-room offers than you know what to do with. 2000 Las Vegas Blvd. S. *©* **702/380-7777.** www.stratospherehotel.com.

Wynn Las Vegas Sprawling off the registration and conservatory/atrium/ garden walkway, this simply laid out but almost gaudily designed casino offers more than initially meets the eye. There are plenty of slots of all denominations (pennies to hundreds of dollars), more video poker than you'd expect in a major Strip casino, and dozens of table games with some surprisingly friendly dealers. It may not be the most memorable casino in town, but it's a place where you can gamble in a tastefully grown-up kind of way, although whether you actually want that is a question only you can answer. All the games you could want, plus a poker room and the rest, are here, though good luck trying to find a blackjack table under $15 a hand. The casino is tied to sister property Encore both physically and via the Wynn Red Card players' club. 3131 Las Vegas Blvd. S. *©* **702/770-7700.** www. wynnlasvegas.com.

East of the Strip

Hard Rock Hotel & Casino The Hard Rock certainly took casino decor to an entirely new level. The attention to detail and the resulting playfulness is admirable, if not incredible. Gaming tables have piano keyboards at one end, some slots have Fender guitar fret boards as arms, gaming chips have band names and/ or pictures on them, slot machines are similarly rock themed (check out the Jimi Hendrix machine!), and so it goes. Rock blares over the sound system, allowing boomers to boogie while they gamble—the noise level is above even that of a normal casino, and we just hated it. We are in the minority, though; most people love it, so assume you will be one of them. A 2009 expansion added more gaming

Sports book at the Las Vegas Hilton.

space in a much more luxe room (black walls, lots of crystal). The race and sports book here provides comfortable seating in leather-upholstered reclining armchairs. 4455 Paradise Rd. ℂ **702/693-5000.** www.hardrockhotel.com.

Las Vegas Hilton A makeover has given this place a much more modern and polished feel, although you'll be happy to note they kept the trademark Austrian-crystal chandeliers, which still add a strong touch of class. The casino is actually medium size, but it does have an enormous sports book—at 30,500 square feet, it's the world's largest race-and-sports-book facility. It, too, is a luxurious precinct equipped with the most advanced audio, video, and computer technology available, including 60 TV monitors, some as large as 15 feet across. In fact, its video wall is second in size only to NASA's. The casino is adjacent to the lobby but is neither especially loud nor frantic. Especially plush is the vast 6,900-square-foot baccarat room—with gorgeous crystal chandeliers, silk-covered walls, and velvet-upholstered furnishings—and the VIP slot area where personnel are attired in tuxedos. Both areas offer gracious service to players. 3000 Paradise Rd. ℂ **702/732-7111.** www.lvhilton.com.

Sam's Town On its two immense floors of gaming action (over 153,000 sq. ft., second only to the MGM Grand in size), Sam's Town maintains the friendly, just-folks ambience that characterizes the entire property. The casino is adorned with Old West paraphernalia (horseshoes, Winchester rifles, holsters, and saddlebags) and is looking a bit less dated, thanks to some recent sprucing up (it's subtle, but believe us, it's better). Sam's Town claims its friendliness extends to looser slots. The players' club card (www.bconnectedonline.com) gains you points at all Boyd Gaming casinos. Free gaming lessons are offered weekdays from 11am to 4pm, with poker lessons at other times. 5111 Boulder Hwy. (at Nellis Blvd.). ℂ **702/456-7777.** www.samstownlv.com.

West of the Strip

The Orleans This is not a particularly special gambling space, though it does have a low claustrophobia level. Another plus is that it sometimes plays Cajun and zydeco music over the sound system, so you can two-step while you gamble, which can make losing somewhat less painful. It has all the needed tables—blackjack, craps, and so forth—plus plenty of slots, including the popular Wheel of Fortune machine, which works like those other roulette-wheel slots, but in this case, actually plays the theme song from the TV show. It even applauds for you if you win. Because The Orleans is popular with locals, there are lots of video-poker options. And because it's not on the Strip, you'll find better odds for craps and cheaper table minimums. The players' club card (www.bconnected online.com) gains you points at all Boyd Gaming casinos, such as the Suncoast and Sam's Town. 4500 W. Tropicana Ave. © **702/365-7111.** www.orleanscasino.com.

Red Rock Resort A bit of a distance to travel just for gambling but perhaps worth it because this is one of the best-looking casinos in town. It utilizes natural woods, glass ornaments, and stone to provide a sense of texture to the space and as with the rest of the resort, it's a stunner. It's also a convivial place to play, but our good wins at blackjack probably had very little to do with that. Not only does Red Rock have traditional gaming tables, slots (from penny slots to high-roller $100 pulls!), a race and sports book, and a 24-hour Poker Room, it also has Bingo. Part of Station Casinos Players Club (www.stationcasinos.com), Red Rock offers points toward cash back and other rewards that can be redeemed here and at other casinos in the family, such as Palace Station and Boulder Station. 10973 W. Charleston Blvd. © **702/767-7773.** www.redrocklasvegas.com.

Henderson

Green Valley Ranch Resort It's probably too far for the average traveler to drive—after all, when there is a casino just steps (or floors) away from your hotel room (and between you and anywhere in the world apart from your hotel room), to say nothing of several dozen more within a few blocks of your hotel room, you may be disinclined to drive out to one that is isolated from many other decent casinos. But given that this is a swank resort (or at least, trying to be); that it's smallish and elegant; that it's got a happening, decadent bar with girls prancing in go-go boots right in the center; and that more bars attracting the young and beautiful and well-heeled are opening here, you might want to make a visit, just to see the scene. 2300 Paseo Verde Dr. (at I-215), Henderson. © **702/617-7777.** www. greenvalleyranchresort.com.

M Resort Although it has a Henderson address, M Resort is a straight shot down Las Vegas Boulevard about 10 miles from Mandalay Bay, the first casino people traveling in from Los Angeles see as they get to town. Done in similar tones to competitor Red Rock Resort, the heavy use of natural wood and stone mix well with lots of natural light to provide a lovely gaming space. Its 92,000 square-feet of gaming space offers up slots of all denominations, more than 60 table games, a poker room, and a sports book that is tied to The Venetian and The Palazzo and offers in-line betting (wagers on plays during the game). 12300 Las Vegas Blvd S. (at St. Rose Pkwy.), Henderson. © **702/797-1000.** www.themresort.com.

Downtown

Binion's 🎁 Binion's has had quite the ride lately. Here's the back story: Professionals in the know say that "for the serious player, the Binions are this town." Benny Binion could neither read nor write, but, boy, did he know how to run a casino. His venerable establishment has been eclipsed over the years, but it claims the highest betting limits in Las Vegas on all games (probably in the entire world, according to a spokesperson). Unfortunately, its last couple of years read like a Vegas soap opera—you know, in-family fighting, murder of one scion at the (alleged) hands of his stripper girlfriend, another taking out many of the elements that made Binion's famous, and the whole thing getting shuttered in early 2004, thanks to nonpayment of bills. To everyone's relief, after 3 months, the casino re-opened, thanks to the then dual owners, one of which was Harrah's, which managed it for a year before running off with the Horseshoe name (and rumors are running wild over what that might one day mean, including speculation that it will build a new "Harrah's Horseshoe" on the spot currently occupied by Bally's) and the rights to Binion's famous World Series of Poker, which was moved to the Rio in 2005. Binion's has since changed hands twice more and the drama continues with financial problems and the closure of the hotel rooms in 2009.

THE world series, LAS VEGAS–STYLE

Binion's was internationally known as the home of the **World Series of Poker.** "Nick the Greek" Dondolos first approached Benny Binion in 1949 with the idea for a high-stakes poker marathon between top players. Binion agreed, with the stipulation that the game be open to public viewing. The competition, between Dondolos and the legendary Johnny Moss, lasted 5 months, with breaks only for sleep. Moss ultimately won about $2 million. As Dondolos lost his last pot, he rose from his chair, bowed politely, and said, "Mr. Moss, I have to let you go."

In 1970, Binion decided to re-create the battle of poker giants, which evolved into the annual World Series of Poker. Johnny Moss won the first year and went on to snag the championship again in 1971 and 1974. Thomas "Amarillo Slim" Preston won the event in 1972 and popularized it on the talk-show circuit. In 2002, there were more than 7,595 entrants from over 22 countries, each ponying up the $10,000 entrance fee, and total winnings were in excess of $19 million (the tournament was also televised on ESPN). During one memorable year, the participants included actors Matt Damon and Edward Norton, fresh from *Rounders,* a movie in which they played a couple of card sharks. They decided to try out their newly acquired moves against the pros, who were unhappy that these kids were barging in on their action and so, rumor has it, offered a separate, large bounty to whichever player took them out. Both actors got knocked out on the first day but took it with good grace and apparently had a blast. Matt's buddy Ben Affleck, an experienced player, tried in 2003—the line on him to win (he didn't) was 400:1. **Note:** In 2005, the World Series of Poker moved to the Rio, under the auspices of Harrah's Entertainment, which bought the rights to the event in 2004. The 2010 top prize was $8.9 million.

Binion's has about 400 fewer slot machines than it used to, in an effort to improve flow, and some parts got painted, so it looks less dingy (but still like an Old West bordello), but otherwise it remains essentially the same. That includes the relatively high claustrophobia level. It offers single-deck blackjack and low minimums, 10-times odds on craps, and high progressive jackpots. Real gamblers still won't consider going anywhere else. 128 E. Fremont St. (btw. Casino Center Blvd. and 1st St.). ☏ **702/382-1600.** www.binions.com.

California Hotel & Casino The California is a festive place filled with Hawaiian shirts and balloons. This friendly facility actually provides sofas and armchairs in the casino area—an unheard-of luxury in this town. Players can join the BConnected club (which is also good at Main Street Station and the Fremont Hotel & Casino; www.bconnectedonline.com) and amass points toward gifts and cash prizes, or participate in daily slots tournaments. 12 Ogden Ave. (at 1st St.). ☏ **702/385-1222.** www.thecal.com.

El Cortez One of the last shreds of pre-1980s Las Vegas, this old gal just got a fantastic new face-lift, with a natural appeal based less on kitsch. By removing half the slot machines, the casino has been opened up and aired out. Plus, it has a more contemporary decor. Former owner and local legend Jackie Gaughin (who lives in the penthouse) still wanders through and dines in the restaurants from time to time. It features frequent big-prize drawings and special events designed to bring the locals in. It's also popular for low limits (10¢ roulette and 25¢ craps). 600 Fremont St. (btw. 6th and 7th sts.). ☏ **702/385-5200.** www.elcortezhotelcasino.com.

Fitzgeralds This casino is done up in greens and golds, and the overall effect is not quite as tacky as you might expect, though the now near-total absence of any overt Irish theme means it's rather forgettable. It's friendly and with a medium-to-low claustrophobia level, thanks in part to some windows to the outside Fremont Street. The casino actually has two levels; from the upstairs part, you can access a balcony from which you get an up-close view of the Fremont Street Experience.

Blackjack, craps, and keno tournaments are frequent events here. The Club Fitz card offers slots, video poker, and video keno players gifts, meals, and other perks for accumulated points. Several slot machines have cars as prizes, fun books provide two-for-one gaming coupons, and, if you're lucky, you might find a blackjack table with something less than a $10 per-hand minimum. 301 Fremont St. (at 3rd St.). ☏ **702/388-2400.** www.fitzgeraldslasvegas.com.

Four Queens The Four Queens is New Orleans themed, with late-19th-century-style globe chandeliers, which make for good lighting and a low claustrophobia level. It's small, but the dealers are helpful, which is one of the pluses of gambling in the more manageably sized casinos. Slots tournaments are frequent events, and there are major poker tournaments throughout the year. The casino also offers exciting multiple-action blackjack (it's like playing three hands at once, with separate wagers on each). The Royal Players Club offers players bonus points toward cash rebates. 202 Fremont St. (at Casino Center Blvd.). ☏ **702/385-4011.** www.fourqueens.com.

Fremont Hotel & Casino This 32,000-square-foot casino—it's much bigger than it initially looks—offers a relaxed atmosphere. In some ways, it's more comfortable gambling here than on the Strip, possibly in part because the beautiful people don't bother with places like this. But lots of other people do, and so it can be more crowded than other Downtown casinos, even during the day. Low

Main Street Station is the best place to gamble Downtown.

gambling limits ($5 blackjack, 25¢ roulette, though not as many tables with these as we would like) help. It's also surprisingly open and bright for a Downtown casino. Casino guests can accumulate bonus points redeemable for cash by joining the BConnected club (which is also good at Main Street Station and the California Hotel & Casino; www.bconnected online.com). Guests can also take part in frequent slots and keno tournaments. No giant slot machine, though. 200 E. Fremont St. (btw. Casino Center Blvd. and 3rd St.). ℭ **702/385-3232.** www.fremont casino.com.

The Golden Gate This is one of the oldest casinos in Downtown, and though its age is showing, it's still fun to go there. As you might expect from the name, old San Francisco artifacts and decor abound (think earthquake time). At one end of the narrow casino is the bar, where a piano player performs ragtime jazz, which is better than the homogenized pop offered in most casino lounges. Unfortunately, the low ceiling, dark period wallpaper, and small dimensions give this a high claustrophobia level. 1 Fremont St. ℭ **702/382-3510.** www.goldengate casino.net.

Golden Nugget While this is not the standout among casino properties developed by Steve Wynn (now owned by Landry's Restaurants), it's still one of the nicest places to gamble, looks-wise, in Downtown. We prefer Main Street Station, but you might prefer the more obvious attempts at class that this place exudes. The new owners gave it a gorgeous makeover, all rich tones with splashes of color, and it's now even nicer (and bigger) than ever. Some tables are only $5 minimum, at least during the day. And compared to most other Downtown properties, this is the most like the Strip. Of course, it has a players' club. 129 E. Fremont St. (at Casino Center Blvd.). ℭ **702/385-7111.** www.goldennugget.com.

Main Street Station 🎁 This is the best of the Downtown casinos, at least in terms of comfort and a pleasant environment. Even the Golden Nugget, nice as it is, has more noise and distractions. The decor here is, again, classic Vegas/old-timey (Victorian-era) San Francisco, but with extra touches (check out the old-fashioned fans above the truly beautiful bar) that make it work much better than other attempts at the same decor. Strangely, it seems just about smoke free, perhaps thanks in part to a very high ceiling. The claustrophobia level is zero. Players can join the BConnected club (www.bconnectedonline.com), which is also good at Fremont Hotel & Casino and the California Hotel & Casino. 200 N. Main St. (btw. Fremont St. and U.S. 95). ℭ **702/387-1896.** www.mainstreetcasino.com.

9

SHOPPING

S hopping in Vegas—Nirvana or an endless Sisyphean repetition of every mall you've ever been to? Depends on your viewpoint. If you are looking for quaint, clever, unique stores, this isn't the town for you (with a few notable exceptions, most of which will require you to drive some blocks off the Strip). But if you are looking for general shop-till-you-drop fun, this is your kind of town. In addition to some extensive malls, many hotels have comprehensive, and sometimes highly themed, shopping arcades. The most notable of the arcades are in Caesars Palace, Planet Hollywood, and The Venetian (details below). Thankfully, catering to the weird schedules kept by many Vegas visitors, most shops in the major hotel malls stay open until 11pm or midnight, so your spending isn't curtailed by limited retail hours. However, given the unstable Vegas landscape, to save you a potential inconvenience, if you are interested in a particular shop listed at a specific mall, shopping arcade, or especially an outlet, you probably should call first to ensure that the establishment in question is still there.

In addition to exploring the malls, outlets, and shops listed below, you might consider driving **Maryland Parkway,** which runs parallel to the Strip on the east and has just about one of everything: Target, Toys "R" Us, several major department stores, major drugstores (in case you forgot your shampoo and don't want to spend $8 on a new bottle in your hotel's sundry shop), some alternative-culture stores (tattoo parlors and hip clothing stores), and so forth. It goes on for blocks.

THE MALLS

The Boulevard ★ The Boulevard is the second-largest mall in Las Vegas—Fashion Show on the Strip has it beat. Its 140-plus stores and restaurants are arranged in arcade fashion on a single floor occupying 1.2 million square feet. Geared to the average consumer, it has anchors such as Sears, JCPenney, Macy's, Dillard's, and Marshalls. There's a wide variety of shops offering all sorts of items—moderately priced shoes and clothing for the entire family, books and gifts, jewelry, and home furnishings. There are also more than a dozen fast-food eateries. In short, you can find just about anything you need here. The mall is open Monday through Saturday from 10am to 9pm and Sunday from 11am to 6pm. 3528 S. Maryland Pkwy. (btw. Twain Ave. and Desert Inn Rd.). ✆ **702/735-8268.** www. boulevardmall.com.

PREVIOUS PAGE: **Tiffany's, in Crystals, is a great place to blow your winnings.**

One of several cool art installations inside Crystals.

Crystals ★ Architecturally speaking, Crystals is as evocative a building as you'll find in Vegas. All sharp angles jutting into the sky, the shape is meant to evoke a pile of crystals (get it?), and it is nothing if not dramatic. Inside, the soaring ceilings and plenty of windows give an airy feeling, but too much white space makes it a little bland once you get past the way the place was built. We're willing to forgive it since it is part of an extended environmental building plan that includes radiant heating in the floors and recycled construction materials. Stores are all almost exclusively the highest of high-end, including a 10,000-square-foot Tiffany & Co., Tom Ford, Louis Vuitton, Prada, and Porsche Design in case you can't actually afford to own the vehicle but want to look like you do. Restaurants include actress Eva Longoria Parker's Beso (p. 158), the fantastic Todd English P.U.B. (p. 162), a couple of Wolfgang Puck eateries, Mastro's Ocean Club, and the return of the much-beloved sushi restaurant/nightclub Social House. Don't miss the two water features by the same folks who did the Bellagio Fountains. These are smaller and not as "wow" but still cool. The mall is open daily 10am to midnight but individual store and restaurant hours may vary. 3720 Las Vegas Blvd. S. (at CityCenter). © 702/590-9299. www.crystalsatcitycenter.com.

The Fashion Show is an architectural wonder . . . and a good place to shop.

Fashion Show ★★ What was a nondescript, if large, mall has been revamped with a *yowsa!* exterior much more fitting of Las Vegas. It's capped by a giant . . . well . . . they call it a "cloud," but we call it "that weird thingy that looks like a spaceport for UFOs." Inside, it's still, more or less, a basic mall, including Nevada's only Nordstrom, a Bloomingdale's Home store, Saks Fifth Avenue, a Neiman Marcus, and other high-end retailers. The mall hosts more than 250 shops, restaurants, and services. And the cloud/alien spaceport thingy has giant LED screens, music, and other distractions—again, much more fitting for Vegas, where even the malls have to light up. Valet parking is available, and you can even arrange to have your car hand washed while you shop. The Fashion Show is open Monday through Saturday from 10am to 9pm and Sunday from 11am to 7pm. 3200 Las Vegas Blvd. S. (at the corner of Spring Mountain Rd.). ☏ **702/784-7000.** www.thefashionshow.com.

The Galleria at Sunset ★ This is the farthest-away mall of the bunch (9 miles southeast of Downtown Las Vegas, in Henderson) but the most aesthetically pleasing, a 1-million-square-foot Southwestern-themed shopping center, with topiary animals adding a sweet touch to the food court. Anchored by Dillard's, JCPenney, and Macy's, the Galleria's 140 emporia include branches of American Eagle Outfitters, Vans, Abercrombie & Fitch, bebe, Caché, Lane Bryant, Victoria's Secret, The Body Shop, Hot Topic, and Dick's Sporting Goods. In addition to shoes and clothing for the entire family, you'll find electronics, eyewear, gifts, books, home furnishings, jewelry, and luggage here. Dining facilities include an extensive food court and several restaurants. It's open Monday through Saturday from 10am to 9pm and Sunday from 11am to 6pm. 1300 W. Sunset Rd. (at Stephanie St., just off I-15), Henderson. ☏ **702/434-0202.** www.galleriaatsunset.com.

Meadows Mall ★ Another immense mall, this one has more than 140 shops, services, and eateries, anchored by four department stores: Macy's, Dillard's, Sears, and JCPenney. In addition, there are more than a dozen shoe stores, a full array of apparel for the entire family (including maternity wear, petites, and large sizes), an extensive food court, and shops purveying toys, books, music, luggage, gifts, jewelry, home furnishings, accessories, and so on. Fountains and trees enhance Meadows Mall's ultramodern, high-ceilinged interior, and there are a few

When the weather's good, it's a pleasure to stroll the shops that line Town Square.

comfortable seating areas for resting your feet a moment. The Meadows Mall is open Monday through Saturday from 10am to 9pm and Sunday from 10am to 6pm. 4300 Meadows Lane (at the intersection of Valley View and U.S. 95). © **702/878-3331.** www.meadowsmall.com.

Showcase Mall ★ Less a traditional mall than an entertainment center, this place has plenty of shopping and fun—we rarely miss a chance to drop by M&M's World (p. 296). Other occupants include GameWorks, the World of Coca-Cola store, Grand Canyon Experience, United Artists theaters—the only regular movie theater complex on the Strip—a few fast-food eateries, and the Strip's first Hard Rock Cafe. Hours vary by store. 3785 S. Las Vegas Blvd. (right next to the MGM Grand). © **702/597-3122.**

Town Square ★ Instead of an enclosed mall or boring box store shopping center, Town Square is designed to look like, well, a town. Tree-lined streets bisect the 117-acre property, and if you're lucky, you can grab a parking space right in front of whatever store you're visiting (or park in one of the huge lots or garages nearby). The facades of the buildings resemble small-town America, only cleaner and more crowded than most. It's a great place to stroll and window-shop, at least on the roughly 27 days a year when it isn't either insanely hot or blustery and chilly. More than 150 shops and boutiques include plenty of typical mall favorites, such as GAP, American Eagle, Old Navy, J. Crew, and Banana Republic—plus some unique outlets, such as H&M, an Apple store, Sephora, Borders, and even a Whole Foods market. More than a dozen restaurants (Claim Jumper, California Pizza Kitchen, Texas de Brazil) provide sustenance, and bars, movie theaters, parks, and playgrounds offer entertainment. Hours vary by store. 6605 Las Vegas Blvd. S. (at I-215). © **702/269-5000.** www.townsquarelasvegas.com.

FACTORY OUTLETS

Fashion Outlets Las Vegas ★★★ Dedicated bargain hunters (we stop here every time we drive by) may want to make the roughly 40-minute drive along I-15 to this big outlet complex in Primm, Nevada, right on the border of California. There's also a shuttle from the MGM Grand, The Fashion Show Mall, and The Miracle Mile Shops at Planet Hollywood. Round-trip fare is $15 and includes a savings book for discounts at the outlets. Also, check the website for a shuttle discount coupon. This large factory outlet has some designer names prominent enough to make the trip worthwhile—Kenneth Cole, Juicy Couture, Coach, Gap, Banana Republic, Old Navy, even a rare Williams-Sonoma, among several others. Why so far out of town? Our guess is that some of these companies have full-price boutiques in various hotels and malls, and they don't want you ignoring those in favor of discounted items. Fashion Outlets is open daily from 10am to 8pm. 32100 Las Vegas Blvd. S. © **888/424-6898** or 702/874-1400. www.fashionoutlet lasvegas.com.

Las Vegas Outlet Center ★ This massive complex houses 130 air-conditioned outlets, including a few dozen clothing stores and shoe stores. It offers a range of merchandise, but even with our understanding of the hit-and-miss nature of outlets, we never buy anything here and feel nothing but apathy for the center. Among other stores (which you will perhaps find less disappointing than we have), you'll find Liz Claiborne, Perry Ellis, Converse, Levi's, Nike, Lane Bryant, Reebok, Jockey, Van Heusen, Tommy Hilfiger, Burlington, Royal Doulton, Corningware/Corelle, and Calvin Klein. There is also a carousel and a

Las Vegas Premium Outlets.

food court. The mall is open Monday through Saturday from 10am to 9pm and Sunday from 10am to 8pm. 7400 Las Vegas Blvd. S. (at Warm Springs Rd.). ℂ **702/896-5599.** www.premiumoutlets.com.

Las Vegas Premium Outlets We had such high hopes for this, the most conveniently located, and largest outlet mall in Las Vegas. We can say that it looks nice, in that pretty outdoor mall kind of way. But the key here is "outdoor." It's fine on a regular day, but on a hot Vegas day—and there are plenty of those—this is an open oven of misery. They should put a roof over the thing or at least install a lot more misters. You'll roast away while shopping among disappointingly dull stores, some of which are "outlets" only because they aren't in regular malls. Maybe we are just feeling bitter about that pair of Bass shoes that were half a size too small. Or that we can't quite fit into the Dolce & Gabbana sample sizes. Still, bring a lot of water if you go during the summer. **Warning:** Parking here is often a nightmare. Consider taking a cab. Stores include Brooks Brothers, Armani, Dolce & Gabbana, Lacoste, Bose, Kenneth Cole, Wilson's Leather, Calvin Klein, Coach, Nike, Perry Ellis, Crabtree & Evelyn, Quicksilver, Samsonite, Timberland, Tommy Hilfiger, and Zales. The mall is open Monday through Saturday from 10am to 9pm and Sunday from 10am to 8pm. 875 S. Grand Central Pkwy. (at I-15). ℂ **702/474-7500.** www.premiumoutlets.com.

HOTEL SHOPPING ARCADES

Just about every Las Vegas hotel offers some shopping opportunities. The following have the most extensive arcades. The physical spaces of these shopping arcades are always open, but individual stores keep unpredictable hours. For addresses and telephone numbers, see the hotels' listings in chapter 5.

Note: The Forum Shops at Caesars, the Grand Canal Shoppes at The Venetian, and the Miracle Mile Shops at Planet Hollywood—as much sightseeing attractions as shopping arcades—are in the must-see category.

Bally's Bally's **Avenue Shoppes** consist of around 20 emporia offering, you know, stuff (kitschy card-shop knickknacks and the like). In addition, there are several gift shops, a Marshall Rousso clothing store, and a Harley Davidson accessories emporium (no motorcycles, sorry). There are blackjack and slots tournaments right in the mall. You can dispatch the kids to a video arcade here while you shop (or gamble).

Bellagio ★★ The **Via Bellagio** collection of stores isn't as big as some of the other megahotel shopping arcades, but here it's definitely quality over quantity. It's a veritable roll call of glossy magazine ads: Armani, Prada, Chanel, Tiffany, Fred Leighton, Gucci, Dior, Fendi, and Yves Saint Laurent. That's about it. You need anything else? Well, yes—money. If you can afford this stuff, good for you, you lucky dog. (Actually, we've discovered affordable, good-taste items in every store here, from Tiffany's $30 silver key chains to $100 Prada business-card holders.) A nice touch is a parking lot by the far entrance to Via Bellagio, so you need not navigate the great distance from Bellagio's main parking structure; instead, you can simply pop in and pick up a little something.

Caesars Palace ★★★ Since 1978, Caesars has had an impressive arcade of shops called the **Appian Way,** highlighted by an immense white Carrara-marble replica of Michelangelo's *David* standing more than 18 feet high. All in all, a respectable grouping of hotel shops. But in the hotel's tradition of constantly surpassing itself, in 1992 Caesars inaugurated the fabulous **Forum Shops,** an independently operated 375,000-square-foot Rodeo-Drive-meets-the-Roman-Empire affair, complete with a 48-foot triumphal arch entranceway, a painted Mediterranean sky that changes as the day progresses from rosy-tinted dawn to twinkling evening stars, acres of marble, lofty Corinthian columns with gold capitals, and a welcoming goddess of fortune under a central dome. The architecture and sculpture span from 300 B.C. to A.D. 1700, so you've got all your ancient Italian cityscape clichés. Then there is the Festival Fountain, where some

Caesars Forum Shops.

seemingly immovable "marble" animatronic statues of Bacchus (slightly in his cups), a lyre-playing Apollo, Plutus, and Venus come to life for a 7-minute revel with dancing waters and high-tech laser-light effects. The shows take place every hour on the hour. The entire thing is pretty incredible, but also very Vegas—particularly the Bacchus show, which is truly frightening and bizarre. Even if you don't like shopping, it's worth the stroll just to giggle.

Additions over the years have added a 50,000-gallon aquarium with another fountain show involving fire (don't stand to close, it gets really hot) and a circular escalator (said to be one of only two in the world), and a lot more stores.

Oh right, the stores. With all the gawking opportunities, it may be easy to forget that you can shop and buy things here (so much so that Caesars claims this is the most profitable mall in America). Tenants are mostly of the exclusive variety, although there are a few more "Average Joe" kind of stores (yes, of course there's a Gap). Some examples: Louis Vuitton, bebe, Christian Dior, Agent Provocateur, A/X Armani Exchange, Nanette Lapore (drop-dead cute clothing with only a handful of stores worldwide), Gucci, Gianni Versace, Harry Winston jewelers, Brooks Brothers, Juicy Couture, a Playboy store, Kiehl's cosmetics (worth a trip just for that), M.A.C., and especially Vosges Haut Chocolate—makeup and sweets, that sounds like shopping heaven to us!

The majority of the Caesars Palace shops are open Sunday through Thursday from 10am to 11pm and Friday and Saturday from 10am to midnight.

Circus Circus There are about a dozen shops between the casino and the Adventuredome (p. 239), offering a selection of gifts and sundries, logo items, toys and games, jewelry, liquor, resort apparel for the entire family, T-shirts, homemade fudge/candy/soft ice cream, and, fittingly, clown dolls and puppets. Adjacent to the Adventuredome, there's a shopping arcade (with the usual souvenir stores and such) themed as a European village, with cobblestone walkways, fake woods, and so forth, decorated with replicas of vintage circus posters.

Encore Lining the walkway from sister hotel Wynn Las Vegas are about a dozen boutiques, mostly of the upscale (read: expensive) variety. Hermès and Chanel are the most recognizable names, but take a peek at the Rock and Republic boutique, an edgy clothing and "lifestyle" store that is designed to bring out your inner *American Idol* wannabe. Hey, Posh Spice had a line of jeans with them for a while, so that's pop-culture cred! If you're a fan of the surroundings at Encore or Wynn Las Vegas, stop at the Homestore, which is filled with furnishings from the hotel that you can take home with you.

Excalibur For the most part, the shops of the **Castle Walk** reflect the hotel's medieval theme. Dragon's Lair, for example, features items ranging from pewter swords and shields to full suits of armor, plus crystal balls and the like. Other shops carry more conventional wares—gifts, candy, jewelry, women's clothing, and Excalibur logo items. And most importantly, they have a branch of that medieval staple—Krispy Kreme Doughnuts!

Flamingo Las Vegas The **Crystal Court** shopping promenade here accommodates men's and women's clothing/accessories stores, gift shops, and a variety of other emporia selling jewelry, beachwear, fresh-baked goods, logo items, children's gifts, toys, and games.

Harrah's ★ Carnaval Court is a small outdoor shopping promenade, a concept unique to the Strip. It consists mostly of little stalls selling bits and bobs, such as hippie-inspired floaty dresses and tops, saucy underwear with catchy

SHOPPING | Hotel Shopping Arcades

phrases on it, jewelry, and knock-off purses. A store highlight is a Ghirardelli chocolate shop, a branch of the famous San Francisco–based chocolate company. It's a smaller version of the one in San Francisco (alas, without the vats of liquid chocolate being mixed up), and in addition to candy, you can get a variety of delicious sundaes and other ice-cream treats.

Luxor A 20,000-square-foot shopping arcade with more than 20 full shops. Most of the stores emphasize clothing, jewelry, and sundry items but if you want to get your Mindfreak on, there is an official Criss Angel store here selling everything from DVDs to motorcycles.

Mandalay Place ★ In appearance, more like an actual indoor mall than a hotel shopping arcade, but in content it has neither the rarified atmosphere of Via Bellagio or the Wynn Promenade, nor does it have the collection of The Forum Shops. But there is a men's shop called the Art of Shaving, a great wine store, and a Frederick's of Hollywood if you're feeling the need to make your husband happy.

MGM Grand The hotel's **Star Lane Shops** include more than a dozen mostly pedestrian emporia lining the corridors en route from the monorail entrance. **Studio Walk** is another shopping area adjacent to the main casino, featuring some upscale boutiques and several restaurants.

Miracle Mile Shops at Planet Hollywood ★★ Though not without some

eye-catching details, these shops aren't all that glamorous: It's pretty much a new-Vegas, whiz-bang version of every nice upper-end mall in America, a generic letdown all the worse because the original version was so charming.

At least the shops somewhat stand out, including several listed separately below, plus Frederick's of Hollywood, Crocs, Two Lips Shoes (affordable, stylish, and comfortable shoes), Steve Madden, Ann Taylor, Urban Outfitters, bebe, BCBG, Sephora, and a branch of the insanely popular H&M clothing store. The shops are open Sunday through Thursday from 10am to 11pm and Friday and Saturday from 10am to midnight.

Monte Carlo A cobblestone arcade of retail shops, the **Street of Dreams** includes several upscale clothing, timepiece, eyewear, and gift boutiques, plus a Harley Davidson clothing and accessories store and, most importantly, a branch of The Cupcakery, which serves up some of the best cakes in a cup in the entire world as far as we're concerned.

Miracle Mile Shops at Planet Hollywood.

The Palazzo ★★ The sister hotel to The Venetian couldn't hold its resort head up without its own luxury shopping area. As with the super high-end experience at Bellagio and Wynn, this brings all kinds of names to town, names sure to thrill the souls—and diminish the wallets—of dedicated fashionistas. A branch of Barneys New York is the star of the retail show, but Christian Louboutin, Bottega Veneta, Chloe, Diane von Furstenberg, Michael Kors, and Van Cleef & Arpels are hardly second string. It's like the pages of *Vogue* come to life!

Rio The **Masquerade Village** is an adequately executed shopping arcade at Rio. It's done as a European village and is two stories tall, featuring a few shops, mostly selling clothes, jewelry, and gifts. One notable outlet is Nawlins, which includes "authentic" voodoo items, Mardi Gras masks, and so forth.

Riviera Though nothing like the higher-end shopping galleries, the Riviera's fairly extensive shopping arcade comprises art galleries, jewelers, shops specializing in women's shoes and handbags, clothing for the entire family, furs, gifts, logo items, toys, phones and electronic gadgets, and chocolates.

Stratosphere The internationally themed (though in a high-school production kind of way, compared to what's over at Planet Hollywood and The Venetian) second-floor **Tower Shops** promenade, housing more than 40 stores, is entered via an escalator from the casino. Some shops are in "Paris," along the Rue Lafayette and Avenue de l'Opéra (there are replicas of the Eiffel Tower and the Arc de Triomphe in this section). Others occupy Hong Kong and New York City streetscapes.

Treasure Island TI's shopping promenade is nowhere near as interesting since they took out all the pirate-themed bits. Emporia here include the TI Store (your basic hotel gift/sundry shop, also offering much pirate-themed merchandise) plus the *Sirens of TI*–themed lingerie shop. Cirque du Soleil and *Mystère* logo wares are also sold in a shop near the ticket office in the hotel.

The Venetian ★★ After you've shopped Ancient Rome at Caesars, come to **The Grand Canal Shoppes** and see if shopping in Renaissance-era (more or less) Venice is any different. Certainly the production values stay high: This is a re-created Italian village, complete with a painted, cloud-studded blue sky over-head, and a canal right down the center on which gondoliers float and sing. Pay them ($16), and you can take a lazy float down and back, serenaded by your boatman (actors hired especially for this purpose and with accents perfect enough to fool Roberto Benigni). As you pass by, under, and over bridges, flower girls will serenade you and courtesans will flirt with you, and you may have an encounter with a famous Venetian or two, as Marco Polo discusses his travels and Casanova exerts his famous charm. The stroll (or float) ends at a miniature (though not by all that much) version of St. Mark's Square, the central landmark of Venice. Here, you'll find opera singers, strolling musicians, glass blowers, and other bustling marketplace activity. It's all most ambitious and beats the heck out of animatronic statues.

The Shoppes are accessible directly from outside (so you don't have to navigate miles of casino and other clutter) via a grand staircase whose ceiling features more of those impressive hand-painted art re-creations. It's quite smashing.

Oh, the shops themselves? The usual high- and medium-end brand names: Movado, Davidoff, Kenneth Cole, Ann Taylor, BCBG, bebe, Banana Republic, Rockport, and more, plus Venetian glass and paper shops. Madame Tussauds Celebrity Encounter (p. 220) is also located here, and so is the Canyon Ranch

Esplanade at Wynn Las Vegas.

Spa Club. The Shoppes are open Sunday through Thursday from 10am to 11pm and Friday and Saturday from 10am to midnight.

Wynn Las Vegas ★★ The **Esplanade** is along the same rarified lines of the Bellagio shopping area, in that it's a Euro-style-esque (love those Vegas qualifiers!) shopping street lined with pricey places with famous names—Oscar de la Renta (his only store outside of NYC), Manolo Blahnik, Chanel, Cartier, Dior, Alexander McQueen, and Jo Malone. We prefer it to the one at Bellagio because it seems like it has just enough shops that nearly reach an average person's budget.

FASHION & BEAUTY

There are a number of clothing shops in Vegas, though most are of the name-brand chain variety, from high to low end. Here are a couple of more interesting standouts. In addition to those listed below, Miracle Mile has an **H&M,** where the clothes are cheap and fashionable and the lines to try them on are very long. Go as soon they open to avoid the crowds.

Agent Provocateur ★★★ Vegas doesn't lack for lingerie stores (including Frederick's of Hollywood and Playboy), but if you can only make time for one, it has to be this British import. The designs are clever and witty, in addition to being drop-dead sexy and ultracool. Kate Moss has long been the face and body of the line and even starred in a short movie ad for the line directed by Mike Figgis. Seduction should start someplace special. Agent Provocateur is open Sunday through Thursday from 10am to 11pm and Friday and Saturday from 10am to midnight. In The Forum Shops at Caesars Palace, 3500 Las Vegas Blvd. S. ℂ **702/696-7174.**

Ben Sherman ★ British designer Ben Sherman started during the mod era, but now his clean-lined clothes seem more Sloane Ranger–conservative than cutting-edge London irony. Given that there are only seven outposts in the world, Anglo fashionphiles will still need to make a pilgrimage. This location is open Sunday through Thursday from 10am to 11pm and Friday and Saturday from 10am to midnight. In Miracle Mile, 3663 Las Vegas Blvd. S. © **702/688-4227.**

Bettie Page Boutique ★★ It's the old story. Needing a job, curvaceous gal poses for naughty photos, and her cheery good humor in all kinds of bondage photos, not to mention a gleaming black pageboy hairdo, makes her an icon. The next thing you know, there's a store dedicated to all things Bettie. Dress like a pin-up thanks to a line of Page-inspired '50s-style dresses, corsets, hosiery, and more. You can't have a venture like this without a wink, and so the shop, all done up in leopard, is a hoot. There is also plenty of Bettie artwork by renowned pin-up artist Olivia de Berardinis for sale. The boutique is open Sunday through Thursday from 10am to 11pm and Friday and Saturday from 10am to midnight. In Miracle Mile, 3663 Las Vegas Blvd. S. © **702/636-1100.** www.bettiepageclothing.com.

VINTAGE CLOTHING

The Attic ★ The Attic, former star of a Visa commercial, is the sort of place where they make poodle skirts in all sizes, in addition to the usual vintage and vintage-influenced wares stuffed on the crowded racks. Not so much of a scenester hangout as it used to be, but still worth a browse. The Attic is open Tuesday through Saturday 10am to 6pm. 1018 S. Main St. © **702/388-4088.** www.attic vintage.com.

Buffalo Exchange ★ This is actually a branch of a chain of stores spread out across the United States. If the chain part worries you, don't let it—this merchandise doesn't feel processed. Staffed by plenty of incredibly hip alt-culture kids (ask them what's happening in town during your visit), it is stuffed with dresses, shirts, pants, and so forth. You can easily go in and come out with 12 fabulous new outfits, but you can just as easily go in and come up dry. But it's still probably the most reliable of the local vintage shops. The store is open Monday through Saturday from 10am to 8pm and Sunday from 11am to 7pm. 4110 S. Maryland Pkwy. (at Flamingo Rd.). © **702/791-3960.** www.buffaloexchange.com.

The Attic.

Gift shop at the Atomic Museum.

SOUVENIRS

The **Arts Factory Complex ★★★**, 107 E. Charleston Blvd. (✆ 702/383-3133), is full of galleries of local artists working in a variety of different mediums, and one of their works would make for an original souvenir.

If you prefer your souvenirs to be a little less class and a little more kitsch, head over to the **Bonanza Gift and Souvenir Shop ★★**, 2460 Las Vegas Blvd. S. (✆ 702/385-7539). It's the self-proclaimed "World's Largest Gift Shop," and it certainly is big. T-shirts; Native American "handicrafts;" all kinds of playing cards, both new and used (casinos have to change decks frequently, so this is where used packs go); dice; things covered in rhinestones; snow globes—in short, something for everyone, provided "everyone" has a certain sensibility. We looked, and we felt the tackiest item available was the pair of earrings made out of poker chips. The coolest? Some inexpensive, old-fashioned-style dice.

For mixed emotions, little can beat items emblazoned with vintage images of bomb tests and other glories to the good old days of atomic blasts, at the **Atomic Testing Museum gift store ★★**, 755 E. Flamingo Rd. (✆ 702/794-5161).

READING MATERIAL & MUSIC
Used Books

Dead Poet Bookstore ★★ 🎁 The dead poet in question was the man from whose estate the owners bought their start-up stock. He had such good taste in books that they "fell in love with him" and wanted to name the store in his memory. Just one problem—they never did get his name. So they just called him "the dead poet." His legacy continues at this book-lover's haven. It's open Monday through Saturday from 10am to 6pm. 937 S. Rainbow Blvd. ✆ **702/227-4070.**

Mural on the exterior of the Gamblers General Store.

Las Vegas Specialty Bookstores

Gambler's Book Shop ★ Here you can buy a book on any system ever devised to beat casino odds. Owner Edna Luckman carries more than 4,000 gambling-related titles, including many out-of-print books, computer software, and video-tapes. She describes her store as a place where "gamblers, writers, researchers, statisticians, and computer specialists can meet and exchange information." On request, knowledgeable clerks provide on-the-spot expert advice on handicapping the ponies and other aspects of sports betting. The store's motto is "knowledge is protection." The shop is open Monday through Friday from 9am to 5pm. 1550 E. Tropicana Ave., no. 4. ℂ **800/522-1777** or 702/382-7555. www.gamblersbook.com.

Gamblers General Store ★ This is a gambler's paradise stocked with a massive book collection, antique and modern slot machines, gaming tables (black-jack, craps, and so on), roulette wheels, collectible chips, casino dice, classic Vegas photos, and a ton of gaming-related souvenirs. The store is open daily from 9am to 6pm. 800 S. Main St. (Downtown). ℂ **800/322-2447** or 702/382-9903. www. gamblersgeneralstore.com.

Comic Books

Alternate Reality Comics ★ This is the best place in Vegas for all your comic-book needs. It has a nearly comprehensive selection, with a heavy emphasis on underground comics. But don't worry—the superheroes are here, too. It's open Sunday through Tuesday from noon to 6pm and Wednesday through Saturday from 11am to 7pm. 4800 S. Maryland Pkwy., Ste. D. ℂ **702/736-3673.** www.alternate realitycomics.net.

Music

Zia Record Exchange ★★ A sign that individual Vegas culture might not be dead after all, this fairly large shop mixes new and used records. The emphasis is on CDs, but there is a big vinyl section, and both show a varied selection of music styles (rock, punk, jazz, soundtracks, and so on). Cleverly, the store spotlights bands coming to Vegas, both large and small, with special displays, plus there are always bins of music from local acts. On Friday and Saturday, local acts play live in the shop. Please note the signs cautioning against slam dancing! Zia's is open daily from 10am to midnight. 4225 S. Eastern Ave., no. 17. *©* **702/735-4942.** www.ziarecords.com.

CANDY & FOOD

The Chocolate Swan and Jean Phillipe Patisserie, which also sell chocolates in addition to pastries and more, are listed in chapter 6.

British Foods, Inc. ★★ Here's a wild card even for this city: an import shop dedicated to all things U.K. Mostly edibles, though there are some Union Jack and other national imagery–inspired trinkets, and not just from Blighty—they also import from Australia and other parts of the Commonwealth. Come here for your Cadbury fix; there's a wide range of that favorite candy line, including items not regularly found on these shores. Stock up on teas, biscuits, bangers, jams, Ambrosia custards and puddings, British bacon, pasties, and even haggis. No lager, though. Sorry. The shop is open daily from 10am to 6pm. 3375 S. Decatur Blvd., no. 11. *©* **702/579-7777.** www.britishgrocer.com.

Ethel's Chocolate Lounge ★ A creation of local confectioner Ethel M that is part cafe, part lounge. "You love chocolate. We are here to help." is the shop's motto. This location isn't as large or as immediately fun as others around the country, but it's still a fun blood-sugar pick-me-up. Choose fancy chocolates from

9

SHOPPING | Candy & Food

M&M's World.

the carefully designed ones on display, such as pomegranate, champagne cocktail, and even margarita flavor, or savor a fondue or other appropriate nosh. Because it keeps mall hours—Monday through Saturday from 10am to 9pm and Sunday from 11am to 7pm—Ethel's is more of a midafternoon snack spot than a postdinner wind-down option. In Fashion Show Mall, 3200 Las Vegas Blvd. S. © **702/796-6662.**

M&M's World ★★ ☺ What can one do when faced with a wall of M&Ms in colors never before seen by man or woman (purple! teal! lime green!)? Overpriced? Yeah! Who cares? There are doodads galore, replete with the M&M's logo, and a surprisingly enjoyable short film and comedy routine, ostensibly about the "history" of the candy but really just a cute little adventure with a decent budget behind it. It's open Sunday through Thursday from 9am until 11pm and Friday and Saturday from 9am until midnight. In the Showcase Mall, 3785 Las Vegas Blvd. S. (just north of the MGM Grand Hotel). © **702/736-7611.**

ANTIQUES

Antiques in Vegas? You mean really old slot machines, or the people playing the really old slot machines?

Actually, Vegas has quite a few antiques stores—nearly two dozen—of consistent quality and price, mostly located within a few blocks of each other. We have one friend, someone who takes interior design very seriously, who says most of her best finds were in Vegas. You should see her antique chandelier collection!

To get to this antiquing mecca, start in the middle of the **1600 block of East Charleston Boulevard** and keep driving east. The little stores, nearly all in old houses dating from the '30s, line each side of the street.

Antiques at the Market ★ This is an antiques minimall (for lack of a better phrase) with a number of individuals operating stalls under one roof. It's open Monday through Saturday from 10am to 6pm and Sunday from noon to 5pm. 6665 S. Eastern Ave. (btw. Sunset and Warm Springs roads). © **702/307-3960.**

Antique Square ★ It's a cruddy-looking collection of stores in several remodeled houses arranged in a square, but every good antiques shopper knows that these kinds of crammed junk stores are the places to find real treasures and to do real antiques hunting (because once the merchandise has been really picked through and prettily displayed by pros, you can kiss bargains and real finds goodbye). Individual store hours vary, but most are closed on Sunday and Monday. 2014–2034 E. Charleston Blvd. (at Eastern Ave.). © **702/471-6500.**

Red Rooster Antique Mall ★ The Red Rooster is a minimall of sorts, only with "antiques" instead of a 7-Eleven and a nail salon. The place is old and battered and features individual stalls selling all categories of stuff, from junk to treasures. Individual store hours vary, but most are open Monday through Saturday 10am to 6pm and Sunday from 11am to 4pm. 1109 Western Ave. (at Charleston and I-15). © **702/382-5253.**

LAS VEGAS AFTER DARK

AFTER

DARK

You will not lack for things to do at night in Vegas. This is a town that truly comes alive only after dark. Don't believe us? Just look at the difference between the Strip during the day, when it's kind of dingy and nothing special, and at night, when the lights hit and the place glows in all its glory. Night is when it's happening in this 24-hour town. In fact, most bars and clubs don't even get going until close to midnight. That's because it's only around then that all the restaurant workers and people connected with the shows get off the clock and can go out and play themselves. It's extraordinary. Just sit down in a bar at 11pm; it's empty. You might well conclude it's dead. Return in 2 hours, and you'll find it completely full and jumping.

But you also won't lack for things to do before 11pm. There are shows all over town, though traditional variety and magic shows have largely given way to Cirque du Soleil. The showgirls remain, topless and otherwise, but the current trend is toward big-name headliners and big Broadway productions. Every hotel has at least one lounge, usually offering live music. But the days of fabulous Vegas lounge entertainment, when the lounge acts were sometimes of better quality than the headliners (and headliners, such as Sinatra, would join the lounge acts on stage between their own sets), are gone. Most of what remains is homogeneous and bland and serves best as a brief respite or background noise. On the other hand, finding the most awful lounge act in town can be a rewarding pursuit of its own. Many lounges and bars have replaced live music with DJs and go-go dancers.

Vegas still attracts some dazzling headliner entertainment in its showrooms and arenas. Madonna's 2006 shows commanded the top prices on her tour; Bruce Springsteen played his first Vegas show ever in 2000; U2 started their PopMart tour at UNLV's stadium; the Rolling Stones played both the MGM Grand and the Hard Rock Hotel's The Joint; Pavarotti inaugurated Mandalay Bay's Arena, and Bob Dylan did the same for the House of Blues; Cher opened up The Venetian, and Sting got a reported $1 million to open Red Rock Resort with a 60-minute set. The Red Hot Chili Peppers gave a free concert to celebrate the city's centennial. It is still a badge of honor for comedians to play Vegas, and there is almost always someone of marquee value playing one showroom or the other.

Admission to shows runs the gamut, from about $25 for Mac King (comedy magic show at Harrah's) to $250 and more for top headliners. Prices occasionally include two drinks.

To find out who's performing during your stay and for up-to-date listings of shows (prices change, shows close), you can call the various hotels, using their

PREVIOUS PAGE: **Cirque du Soleil's** *Mystère.*

toll-free numbers. Or call the **Las Vegas Convention and Visitors Authority** (✆ **877/847-4858** or 702/892-0711), and ask them to send you a free copy of *Showguide* or *What's On in Las Vegas* (one or both of which will probably be in your hotel room). You can also check out what's playing at **www.visitlasvegas.com**. It's best to plan well ahead if you have your heart set on seeing one of the most popular shows or catching a major headliner.

The hotel entertainment options described in this chapter include information on ticket prices, what's included in that price (drinks, dinner, taxes, and/or gratuities), showroom policies (whether it's preassigned or maitre d' seating), and how to make reservations. Whenever possible, reserve in advance, especially on weekends and holidays. Although it's almost extinct, if the showroom has **maitre d' seating** (as opposed to preassigned seats), you may want to tip him to upgrade your seat. A tip of $15 to $20 per couple will usually do the trick at a major show, less at a small showroom. Whatever you tip, the proper etiquette is to do it rather subtly—a kind of palm-to-palm action. There's really no reason for this, because everyone knows what's going on, but being blatant is in poor taste. Arrive early at maitre d' shows to get the best choice of seats.

If you buy tickets for an assigned-seat show in person, you can look over a seating chart. Avoid sitting right up by the stage, if possible, especially for big-production shows. Dance numbers are better viewed from the middle of the theater. With headliners, you might like to sit up close. All these caveats and instructions aside, most casino-hotel showrooms offer good visibility from just about every seat in the house.

If you prefer alternative or real rock music, your choices used to be limited, but that's all changed. Most touring rock bands make at least one stop in the city.

LOUNGE LIZARD supreme

All those faux-hipster artists doing woeful lounge-act characters in Hollywood and New York only wish they could be **Mr. Cook E. Jarr,** whose sincerity and obvious drive to entertain puts mere performance artists to shame. With George Hamilton's tan, Cher's first shag haircut (it's certainly not his factory-original coif), and a bottomless, borderless catalog of rock, pop, soul, swing, and standard favorites, he's more Vegas than Wayne Newton.

Cook has a cult following of blue-collar casino denizens and the youthful cocktail set, who listen enraptured as he plays human jukebox, complete with karaoke-style backing recordings, terrible jokes, an array of disco-era lights, and (his favorite) a smoke machine. He's actually a solid, throaty singer, with a gift for vocal mimicry as he moves from Ben E. King to Bee Gees to Tony Bennett turf. And his tribute the night Sinatra died—a version of "My Way" in which he voiced, alternately, Sammy, Dino, and Elvis welcoming Ol' Blue Eyes to heaven—was priceless.

He moves around a lot, but you can often catch him on Friday and Saturday nights, 6 to 8pm, at **Harrah's Carnaval Court Lounge,** at 3475 Las Vegas Blvd. S. (✆ **702/369-5222;** www.cookejarr.com). Don't miss him! (And if he has left there by the time you read this, try to track him down.)

But otherwise, the alternative club scene in town is no great shakes. If you want to know what's playing during your stay, consult the local free alternative papers: the **Las Vegas Weekly** (biweekly, with great club and bar descriptions in its listings; www.lasvegasweekly.com), and **City Life** (weekly, with no descriptions but comprehensive listings of what's playing where all over town; www.lasvegascity life.com). Both can be picked up at restaurants, bars, record and music stores, and hip retail stores. If you're looking for good alt-culture tips, try asking the cool staff at **Zia Records** (✆ **702/735-4942**); not only does it have bins dedicated to local artists but local acts also play live in stores on the weekend.

In addition to the listings in this chapter, consider the **Fremont Street Experience,** described on p. 217.

Be aware that there is a curfew law in Vegas: Anyone under 18 is forbidden from being on the Strip without a parent after 9pm on weekends and holidays. In the rest of the county, minors cannot be out without parents after 10pm on school nights and midnight on weekends.

WHAT'S PLAYING WHERE

It used to be that seeing a show was an essential part of the Vegas experience. Back in those days, a show was pretty simple: A bunch of scantily (and we mean scantily) clad showgirls paraded around while a comedian engaged in some raunchy patter. The showgirls are still here and still scantily clad (though not as often topless; guess cable TV has taken some of that thrill away), but the productions around them have gotten impossibly elaborate. And they have to be, because they have to compete with a free dancing-water-fountains show held several times nightly right on the Strip. Not to mention a volcano, a Mardi Gras parade in the sky, lounge acts galore, and the occasional imploding building—all free.

The big resort hotels, in keeping with their general over-the-top tendencies, are pouring mountains of money into high-spectacle extravaganzas, luring big-name acts into decades-long residencies and surrounding them with special effects that would put some Hollywood movies to shame. Which is not to say the results are Broadway quality—they're big, cheesy fun. Still, with the exception of the astonishing work done by the Cirque du Soleil productions, most of what passes for a "show" in Vegas is just a flashy revue, with a predictable lineup of production number/magic act/production number/acrobatics/production number.

Unfortunately, along with big budgets and big goals come big-ticket prices. Sure, you can still take the entire family of four to a show for under $200, but

---

Our Favorites

Our vote for **best show?** It's a toss-up between *KÀ* at the MGM Grand, *O* at Bellagio, and *Mystère* at Treasure Island, all by Cirque du Soleil. Each has to be seen to be believed—and even then you may not believe it, but you won't be forgetting the experience anytime soon. The **most intelligent show** is put on by Penn & Teller, and we are grateful. The **best headliner** is Garth Brooks, by a country mile. The **best classic Vegas topless revue** is *Jubilee!* at Bally's, even though it wins by default because it's the last true example of the breed.

you're not going to get the same production values that you'd get by splurging on a Cirque du Soleil show. Which is not to say you always get what you pay for: There are some reasonably priced shows that are considerably better values than their more expensive counterparts.

Note: Although every effort has been made to keep up with the volatile Las Vegas show scene, keep in mind that the following reviews may not be indicative of the actual show you'll see, but the basic concept and idea will be the same. What's more, the show itself may have closed, so it's a good idea to always call the venue and check.

The following section describes the major production shows currently playing in Las Vegas, arranged alphabetically by the title of the production. But first, here's a handy list arranged alphabetically by hotel:

- **Aria Las Vegas:** *Viva Elvis* by Cirque du Soleil (Cirque meets The King)
- **Bally's:** *Jubilee!* (Las Vegas–style revue), *The Price is Right*
- **Bellagio:** Cirque du Soleil's *O* (unique circus-meets-performance-art theatrical experience)
- **Caesars Palace:** Céline Dion (music and variety)
- **Encore Las Vegas:** Garth Brooks (music)
- **Excalibur:** Tournament of Kings (medieval-themed revue)
- **The Flamingo Las Vegas:** Donny and Marie (music and variety); Nathan Burton (comedy and magic)
- **Harrah's:** Mac King (comedy and magic); Rita Rudner (comedy); *Legends in Concert* (celebrity impersonators)
- **Imperial Palace:** *Human Nature* (tribute to Motown); *Divas Las Vegas* (female impersonators)
- **Luxor:** *Believe* (illusionist Criss Angel and Cirque du Soleil collaborate)
- **Mandalay Bay:** Disney's *The Lion King* (award-winning Broadway musical)
- **MGM Grand:** Cirque du Soleil's *KÀ* (astounding martial arts and acrobatics); *Crazy Horse Paris* (adults-only topless dancing)
- **The Mirage:** Cirque du Soleil's *Love* (featuring the music of the Beatles); Terry Fator (impressions and ventriloquism)
- **New York–New York:** Cirque du Soleil's *Zumanity* (adults-only provocative revue)
- **Paris Las Vegas:** *Barry Manilow* (he writes the songs)
- **Rio All-Suite Hotel & Casino:** Penn & Teller (illusions); Chippendales
- **The Riviera:** *Crazy Girls* (sexy Las Vegas–style revue); *ICE*
- **Stratosphere Hotel & Casino:** *American Superstars* (an impression-filled production show)
- **Treasure Island:** Cirque du Soleil's *Mystère* (unique circus performance)
- **The Venetian:** Blue Man Group (hilarious performance art), *Phantom* (Andrew Lloyd Webber's most popular musical), *Jersey Boys* (award-winning Broadway musical)
- **Wynn Las Vegas:** *Le Rêve* (water-themed production show)

THE MAJOR PRODUCTION SHOWS

This category covers all the major Las Vegas production shows and a few of the minor ones as well. In addition to the following we also recommend **Louie Anderson**'s comic stylings at Excalibur, **Wayne Brady**'s music and comedy improv show at The Venetian, and, believe it or not, **Carrot Top**'s prop-fueled riffs at Luxor that are so random and rapid fire that they nearly become a philosophical exercise. No, really.

There is also a new trend of major headliners doing semipermanent but irregular stints in the big showrooms. **Beyoncé** did a stand at Encore Las Vegas and **Jerry Seinfeld** calls the Colosseum at Caesars Palace his domain when he is in town.

Shows can close without warning, even ones that have been running just shy of forever, so please call first. You might also want to double-check on days and times of performances; schedules can change without notice. **Note:** Some ticket prices may not include tax or drinks, so you might also check for those potential hidden costs.

American Superstars ★ ☺ One of a number of celebrity-impersonator shows (well, it's cheaper than getting the real headliners), *American Superstars* is one of the few shows where the impersonators actually sing live. Five performers do their thing; the celebs impersonated vary depending on the evening.

A typical Friday night features Christina Aguilera, Britney Spears, Tim McGraw, Michael Jackson, and Elvis. The performers aren't bad. Actually, they were closer in voice than in looks to the celebs in question (half the black performers were played by white actors), which is an unusual switch for Vegas impersonators. The action is also shown on two large, and completely unnecessary, video screens flanking the stage, so you don't have to miss a moment. Shows are offered Sunday through Tuesday at 7pm and Wednesday, Friday, and Saturday at 6:30 and 8:30pm. In the Stratosphere Casino Hotel & Tower, 2000 Las Vegas Blvd. S. ✆ **800/998-6937** or 702/380-7711. www.stratospherehotel.com. Tickets $40 adults, $39 children 5–12; show and dinner package $45 (restaurants vary).

Hot Tip!

Tix4Tonight (✆ **877/849-4868;** www.tix4tonight.com) is a service that puts any unsold seats for that evening on sale, starting at 2pm, for—get this!—*half price.* Hot diggity! Of course, there are some drawbacks. It's downright unlikely that really ultra-super-duper shows are ever going to have unsold seats (because the hotel will just sell them to the always-waiting-and-happy-to-pay-full-price standby line), but you'd be shocked at the range otherwise, from basic crap to stuff that we would recommend even at full price (they aren't allowed to say on the record which shows' tickets often come up for sale). Alas, the very nature of the service means you can't plan; you have to stand in line and take your chances starting at about noon (we advise getting in line even earlier than that). So if you have your heart set on ambiguously gendered contortionists, don't rely on Tix4Tonight, but, if like a good gambler, you like taking chances, head for 3785 Las Vegas Blvd. S. (in the giant Coke bottle, at the Showcase Mall).

Barry Manilow.

Barry Manilow ★★ Moving from the Las Vegas Hilton to Paris Las Vegas has only further magnified how great a performer Mr. Manilow still is. Sure, to many his songs represent a bland era of '70s cheese but with the benefit of 30 some-odd years of hindsight, it's easier to see them for what they are: perfectly crafted pop that almost defies you to not sing along. From the happy, skippy "Daybreak" to the still powerful "Weekend in New England" with stops along the way at "Mandy," "I Write the Songs," and (of course) "Copacabana," the show is a retro wonder made all the more enjoyable by Manilow's clear, powerful voice and natural charm. That's right, Barry is not just for Fanilows anymore. The show is not scheduled every weekend, but when it is, it runs Friday through Sunday at 7:30pm. In Paris Las Vegas, 3655 Las Vegas Blvd. S. ℂ **800/745-3000.** www. manilowparis.com. Tickets $95–$250.

Blue Man Group ★★ Are they blue? Indeed they are—three hairless, non-speaking men dipped in azure paint (you may have seen them in a commercial or two and wondered what in the heck they were all about), doing decidedly odd stunts with marshmallows, art supplies, audience members, tons of paper, and an amazing array of percussion instruments fashioned fancifully from PVC piping. If that doesn't sound very Vegas, well, it's not. It's a franchise of a New York–born

Blue Man Group.

performance-art troupe that seems to have slipped into town through a side door opened by Cirque du Soleil's groundbreaking successes. Don't get the wrong idea: This is no Cirque clone. There are no acrobatics or flowing choreography, no attempt to create an alternate universe—just a series of surreal, unconnected bits. It's funny in the weirdest and most unexpected ways, and the crowd is usually roaring by the end. Fans of typical Vegas shows may leave scratching their heads, but we are glad there is another color in the Vegas entertainment spectrum. The Blue Man Group theater at The Venetian is not quite as comfy as its former home at Luxor, but most folks are so amused by the onstage antics that they forget about elbow room. The show is held nightly at 7 and 10pm. At The Venetian, 3355 Las Vegas Blvd. S. ☎ 866/641-7469 or 702/414-9000. www.venetian.com. Tickets $54–$143 (includes tax and service fees).

Cirque du Soleil's *KÀ* ★★★ ☺ *KÀ* subverts expectations by largely eschewing the usual Cirque format—wide-eyed innocent is taken on surreal adventure, beautiful but aimless, complete with acrobats and clowns and lots of weird floaty things—in favor of an actual plot, as a brother and sister from some mythical Asian kingdom are separated by enemy raiders and have to endure various trials and tribulations before being reunited. Gleefully borrowing imagery from magical realist martial arts movies, such as *Crouching Tiger, Hidden Dragon,* the production makes use of a technically extraordinary set that shifts the stage not just horizontally but vertically, as the action moves from under the sea to the side of a steep cliff and beyond. The circus elements—acrobats, clowns—are for once incorporated into the show in a way that makes some loose narrative sense, though this does mean that the physical stunts are mostly pretty much in service to the story rather than random feats of derring-do.

The story is by turns funny, tragic, and whimsical. There are at least two moments that are nothing but simple stagecraft and yet are exquisite, among the most memorable of any current Vegas show. The theater is cavernous, but extensive catwalks and other staging tricks mean that those in the back won't feel far from the action. It might be too long and intense for younger children, but older ones will be enthralled—and so will you. Performances are held Tuesday through Saturday at 7 and 9:30pm. In the MGM Grand, 3799 Las Vegas Blvd. S. ☎ 866/774-7117. www.cirquedusoleil.com. Tickets $69–$150 (plus tax).

Cirque du Soleil's *LOVE* ★ ☺ A collaboration between the Beatles (by way of Sir George Martin's son, who remixed and reconfigured the music with a free hand that may distress purists) and Cirque du Soleil, this is the usual Cirque triumph of imaginative design, but it also feels surprisingly hollow. In one sense, it's an inspired pairing, in that the Beatles' music provides an apt vehicle for Cirque's joyous spectacle. But while Cirque shows have never been big on plot, the particular aimlessness of this production means that the show too quickly dissolves into simply the introduction of one novel staging element after another. In other words, its visual fabulousness ends up repetitious rather than thrilling. Beatles fans will still have a good time, but others may wish to spend their Cirque money on one of the other options. Shows are held Thursday through Monday at 7 and 9:30pm. At The Mirage, 3400 Las Vegas Blvd. S. ☎ 800/963-9637 or 702/792-7777. www.beatles.com. Tickets $94–$150 (plus tax).

Cirque du Soleil's *Mystère* ★★★ ☺ The in-house ads for *Mystère* (Miss-tair) once said "Words don't do it justice," and for once, that's not just hype. Simply calling it a circus is like calling the Hope Diamond a gem or the Taj Mahal a building. It's accurate but, as the ad says, doesn't begin to do it justice.

CIRQUE DU thriller

For years there had been rumors of a possible collaboration between Cirque du Soleil and Michael Jackson, but it took the singer's untimely death in 2009 to make the dream a reality. A new Cirque production featuring Jackson's music will debut in a permanent home in Las Vegas sometime in 2012. At press time, details of where, when, and exactly what were not being released, but it will most likely be at one of the MGM Resorts International hotels and will be accompanied by a Michael Jackson-themed nightclub. For updates, visit **www.cirquedusoleil.com**.

Cirque du Soleil began in Montréal as a unique circus experience, not only shunning traditional animal acts in favor of gorgeous feats of human strength and agility, but also adding elements of the surreal and the absurd. The result seems like a collaboration by Salvador Dalí and Luis Buñuel, with a few touches by Magritte and choreography by Twyla Tharp. MGM Resorts International has built the troupe its own theater, an incredible space with an enormous dome and superhydraulics that allow the Cirque performers to fly in space. Or so it seems.

While part of the fun of the early Cirque was seeing what amazing stuff they could do on a shoestring, seeing what they can do with virtually unlimited funds is spectacular. Cirque took full advantage of MGM Resorts International's largesse, and their art only rose with their budget. The show features one simply unbelievable act after another (seemingly boneless contortionists and acrobats, breathtakingly beautiful aerial maneuvers), interspersed with Dadaist/commedia dell'arte clowns, and everyone clad in costumes like nothing you've ever seen before. All this and a giant snail!

The show is dreamlike, suspenseful, funny, erotic, mesmerizing, and just lovely. At times, you might even find yourself moved to tears. For some children, however, it might be a bit too sophisticated and arty. Even if you've seen Cirque before, this show is worth checking out, thanks to the large production values. It's a world-class show, no matter where it's playing. That this arty and intellectual show is playing in Vegas is astonishing. Catch it Saturday through Wednesday at 7 and 9:30pm. In Treasure Island, 3300 Las Vegas Blvd. S. © **800/392-1999** or 702/894-7772. www.cirquedusoleil.com. Tickets $60–$95 (plus tax and service fee).

Cirque du Soleil's O ★★★ How to describe the seemingly indescribable wonder and artistry of Cirque du Soleil's still utterly dazzling display? An Esther Williams–Busby Berkeley spectacular on peyote? A Salvador Dalí painting come to life? A stage show by Fellini? The French-Canadian troupe has topped itself with this production—and not simply because it's situated its breathtaking acrobatics in, on, around, and above a 1.5-million-gallon pool (*eau*—pronounced O—is French for "water"). Even without those impossible feats, this might be worth the price just to see the presentation, a constantly shifting dreamscape that's a marvel of imagination and staging. If you've seen *Mystère* at Treasure Island, or other Cirque productions, you'll be amazed that they've once again raised the bar to new heights without losing any of the humor or stylistic trademarks, including the sensuous music.

We know—those ticket prices, especially when we keep pointing you in the direction of other Cirque shows—*ouch!* We want to say that we can guarantee it's

Appropriate shows for kids, all described in this chapter, include the following:

worth it, but that's a decision only you can make. (No one we've personally sent has come back with regrets.) Performances are held Wednesday through Sunday at 7:30 and 10pm. In Bellagio, 3600 Las Vegas Blvd. S. ✆ **888/488-7111** or 702/693-7722. www.cirquedusoleil.com. Tickets $94–$150 (plus tax).

Cirque du Soleil's Viva Elvis ★ ☺ It's logical, really: Marry the biggest Vegas icon with the biggest producer of Vegas shows. It's Elvis Presley meets Cirque du Soleil, and we're actually a little surprised it took this long. Unlike the underwhelming *Love,* which is more Beatles and not enough Cirque, this production is a solid partnership that takes The King's music, life, and legacy and reinterprets them through the Cirque lens with multimedia displays, bit set pieces, dancers, acrobats, gymnasts, aerialists, and more than a few Elvis impersonators. *Viva Elvis* is by far the most accessible and downright fun of the Cirque shows, and it is Presley's music that keeps propelling it forward whether it's a gospel rave-up version of "All Shook Up" or a rumba remix of "It's Now or Never." Highlights include an Alicia Keys–esque singer/pianist doing "One Night With You" while twin aerialists representing Elvis and his twin Jesse (who died during childbirth) swing on a giant guitar above the stage and a thrilling lyrical dance number to "Caught in a Trap" meant to symbolize the end of Elvis' relationship with Priscilla. There are a few stumbles—we don't need the Colonel Tom Parker narration and the Elvis/Priscilla

Cirque du Soleil's *Viva Elvis.*

wedding segment with a giant cake and performers on roller skates is strange at best—but overall it is an entertaining, and at times downright joyous, way to celebrate the King being back in the building. Shows are held Friday through Tuesday at 7 and 9:30pm. At Aria Las Vegas, 3720 Las Vegas Blvd. S. ✆ **877/25-ELVIS (253-5847).** www.vivaelvis.com. Tickets $99–$175 (plus tax).

Cirque du Soleil's _Zumanity_ ✋ We really need to tell you one more time, Las Vegas is not for kids. And here is the final proof: Cirque du Soleil, long considered the smartest family entertainment around, now produces this, an adult show dedicated to celebrating human sexuality.

A bevy of acts are all meant to be lewd or alluring or both, if you pay attention. They are mostly just basic Cirque acts (and worse, just basic striptease acts, which you can see anywhere in town for a great deal less money), though instead of giving the illusion of near nakedness, they give the illusion of total nakedness (an illusion that works better the farther you sit from the stage). As they contort and writhe and feign pleasure or apathy, we feel sympathy for all the parents who spent money on gymnastics and ballet lessons over the years, only to have their poor kids end up in this. See, Cirque is naturally sexy and erotic, so all this is gilding the lily until it chokes from lack of oxygen and dies. There are some visually stunning moments (two women splashing about in a large glass, a woman performing with a dozen hula hoops), but overall this is an endeavor of such cynicism that it makes our own look faint-hearted. Save your money for MGM Grand's _Crazy Horse Paris_ across the street, or just go to Sapphire and tip the best dancer there. Shows are held Tuesday, Wednesday, and Friday through Sunday at 7:30 and 10:30pm. In New York–New York, 3790 Las Vegas Blvd. S. ✆ **866/606-7111** or 702/740-6815. www.zumanity.com. Tickets $69–$142. Only ages 18 and over admitted.

Crazy Girls _Crazy Girls,_ presented in an intimate theater, is probably the raciest revue on the Strip. It features sexy showgirls with perfect bodies in erotic song-and-dance numbers enhanced by innovative lighting effects. Think of _Penthouse_ poses coming to life. Perhaps it was best summed up by one older man from Kentucky: "It's okay if you like boobs and butt. But most of the girls can't even dance." The show is held nightly at 9:30pm. In the Riviera Hotel & Casino, 2901 Las Vegas Blvd. S. ✆ **877/892-7469** or 702/794-9433. www.rivierahotel.com. Tickets $45–$60 (plus tax). Only ages 18 and over admitted.

Criss Angel: Believe with Cirque _du Soleil_ The reviews on illusionist Criss Angel's union with Cirque du Soleil have been savage at best, including the much publicized in-theater feud with a Tweeting Perez Hilton. But the good news is that it really isn't quite as bad as all of that. The bad news is that it certainly isn't good. The show has evolved since its early, disastrously reviewed incarnation (a lot of the Cirque elements were being stripped out at press time) and continues to morph, so who knows; by the time you read this it might actually be mediocre.

The set up is strange, but simple, starting as a traditional Criss Angel magic show (think loud music and lots of jewelry), but then something goes horribly awry and Angel is "injured" doing one of his own stunts. This sends our intrepid rock-'n'-roll illusionist on a journey of sorts as he hovers between life and death, accompanied along the way by plenty of Cirque-style set pieces interspersed with the occasional large-scale magic trick. The avant-garde theater portions done by Cirque are visually stunning, including one almost breathtaking sequence that changes the stage from a wintery wonderland into a blazing red springtime scene in what seems like the blink of an eye. And some of Angel's illusions are interesting in a "how'd they do that?" kind of way. But while the pieces may be worthy, they don't add up to a cohesive whole, meaning that the show ultimately fails. Fans of Angel will likely be disappointed that there aren't more illusions, fans of Cirque will likely be annoyed that there are so many, and casual observers will most likely just shake their heads and wonder why they paid so much for a ticket. Shows are held Tuesday through Saturday at 7 and 9:30pm. In the Luxor, 3900 Las Vegas Blvd. S. ☎ **800/557-7428.** Tickets $70–$181.

Disney's The Lion King ★★ ☺ Broadway hits have met with mixed success in Vegas. *Hairspray* closed after 3 months but *Mamma Mia!* played for over 5 years in the very theater in which a new production of *The Lion King* is now treading the boards. Unlike many Broadway-to-Vegas transfers, this is a nearly complete version of the show, with only minor trims to the traditional two-act with an intermission structure, resulting in a 2½-hour-long affair. The staging, by certified theatrical genius Julie Taymor, is the true star here, with puppetry, dramatic set pieces (including a harrowing stampede scene), costumes, and special effects that magnificently distract from the slight story and mostly forgettable music. It's a surprisingly dark piece, especially for something that purports to be kid friendly—there are some truly scary moments that may be too intense for younger viewers, until the second act gets some much needed comic relief from sidekicks Timon and Pumba. Elton John and Tim Rice's songs include the hits "Circle of Life" and "Can You Feel the Love Tonight," but most of the rest of the score is not exactly hummable, although the African roots are a nice change of pace from generic Vegas. Performances are held Monday through Thursday at 7:30pm and Saturday and Sunday at 4pm and 8pm. At Mandalay Bay, 3950 Las Vegas Blvd. S. ☎ **877/623-7400** or 702/632-7777. www.mandalaybay.com. Tickets $53–$169 (includes tax and service fees).

Divas Las Vegas ★ Star impersonator Frank Marino hosted the similar *La Cage* for more than 2 decades up the street at the Riviera. His new show at the Imperial Palace isn't really all that new in that it still features Marino as Joan Rivers in a series of Bob Mackie–esque gowns telling groan-worthy jokes and introducing a lineup of female impersonators. The "ladies" vary in quality and illusion: "Beyoncé" is done more for laughs and "Madonna" and "Dolly" are good, but "Céline Dion" is dead-on and "Lady Gaga" is frighteningly accurate (but hey, she kind of looks like a drag queen anyway). They lip-synch their way through hits often accompanied

HER HEART WILL COME BACK: Céline RETURNS TO VEGAS

The Colosseum at Caesars Palace was built for Céline Dion and after 5 years of performing there, she left for other pastures, turning the keys over to the likes of Elton John, Cher, and Bette Midler. But Dion is coming back, kicking off a new 3-year residency scheduled to begin in March 2011. Meant to "capture the romance of classic Hollywood movies," she will be backed by a full orchestra and the production will feature big-scale sets and visuals effects. Dion will perform roughly 70 shows per year and tickets, which range from $55 to $250, are available now by phone ☎ 877/423-5463 and online at www.ticketmaster.com (keyword "Celine").

by scantily clad male dancers, which gives you something to look at if the imper-sonator isn't up to snuff. Shows are held Saturday through Thursday at 10pm. In Imperial Palace, 3535 Las Vegas Blvd. S. © **702/731-3311.** Tickets $69–$79.

Donny and Marie ★ Yes, proving that a good fainting spell on *Dancing with the Stars* is worth a lot more than you'd expect, the wholesome brother-sister duo of Donny and Marie has made a comeback on the stages of Las Vegas, performing their personal blend of music, comedy, and variety at the Flamingo. The show is a lot more fun than it has any right to be as long as you go in with your tongue placed firmly in cheek. But really, $255? Really? Shows are held Tuesday through Saturday at 7:30pm. In the Flamingo, 3555 Las Vegas Blvd. S. © **702/733-3333.** Tickets $90–$255.

Garth Brooks ★★★ Back before Garth Brooks retired, his concerts regularly broke box office records with tens of thousands lured to the stadium-size spec-tacles he put on around the world. Now, Brooks has been lured out of retirement for a series of weekend shows at Encore Las Vegas and his return to the stage is both triumphant and completely unexpected. The spectacle is gone; instead what you get is a guy and a guitar. No sets, no band, no special effects, just a laser focus on what made this man and his music. Brooks comes across as every-man—your very funny best friend who wants to tell stories and play a few songs on his guitar. Although it is acoustic, what he does is electrifying, taking the au-dience on a journey through his life and the music that formed him. He doesn't actually play that many of his own songs, instead covering classics by everyone from Merle Haggard to Elton John, then uses those tunes to showcase the influ-ences in his music. For instance, an exploration of a dark Bob Seger song ("the chords paint a picture") leads to his own "Thunder Rolls." He even responds to shouted out requests, in one instance pulling an entire catalog of Jim Croce songs out of his trucker cap without breaking a sweat. You may not like country music—heck, you may not even like Garth Brooks's music—you just need to like music, period. The show is performed on select Fridays and Sundays at 8pm and Saturdays at 8pm and 10:30pm. In the Encore Las Vegas, 3121 Las Vegas Blvd. S. © **702/770-7469.** Tickets $125.

Human Nature ★ Who would've believed that the Vegas show with the most soul would come from a group of four white guys from Australia? *Human Nature* is one of that country's biggest singing groups and this revue, presented by no less than Smokey Robinson, is a nostalgic and high-energy trip back through the greatest hits of Motown. The classics like "Baby I Need Your Lovin'" and "You Can't Hurry Love" with a crack six-piece band are fun, but it is when they go a cappella on songs like "Just My Imagination" and "People Get Ready" that they really shine. Too bad the traditional showroom (narrow tables, high-backed booths) is so painfully uncomfortable that it distracts from how much fun the show is. Performances are held Saturday through Thursday at 7:30pm. In Imperial Palace, 3535 Las Vegas Blvd. S. © **702/731-3311.** Tickets $50–$60.

Jersey Boys Vegas ★★ Between 1962 and 1975, Frankie Valli and the Four Seasons racked up an astonishingly long string of catchy, well-crafted pop hits that are as beloved as any in pop music. These time-tested songs are the central draw of the massively popular, Tony Award–winning (for Best Musical) *Jersey Boys*. But this is far more than a rote musical revue, or just another re-creation of a popular oldies act. It's a real musical play, with a compelling street-to-suite storyline, a fair share of drama, and enough humor and uplift to satisfy both the theater veteran and the vacationing family (with a mild warning for some salty, Jersey-esque language). A dazzlingly visual production that crackles with energy and shines with precision stagecraft, *Jersey Boys* has already had an enthusiastic post-Broadway life. With its visual wow factor and an excitingly faithful recreation of the Four Seasons' music, it just may be the perfect vehicle to break the theatrical Vegas jinx (which has seen other Tony winners such as *Hairspray, The Producers,* and *Spamalot* slink off in defeat) and settle in for a long run. Performances are Monday, Thursday, Friday, and Sunday at 7pm and Tuesday and Saturday at 6:30 and 9:30pm. In The Palazzo, 3325 Las Vegas Blvd. © **866/641-7469.** Tickets $64–$235.

Jubilee! ★★ A classic Vegas spectacular, crammed with singing, dancing, magic, acrobats, elaborate costumes and sets, and, of course, bare breasts. And now that *Folies Bergere* has closed, *Jubilee!* is the only showgirl spectacular left in town. It's a basic revue, with production numbers featuring homogenized versions of standards (Gershwin, Cole Porter, some Fred Astaire numbers) sometimes sung live, sometimes lip-synced, and always accompanied by lavishly costumed and frequently topless showgirls. Humorous set pieces about Samson and Delilah, and the sinking of the *Titanic* show off some pretty awesome sets. They were doing the *Titanic* long before a certain movie, and recent attendees claimed the ship-sinking effect on stage here was better than the one in the movie. The finale features aerodynamically impossible feathered and bejeweled costumes and headpieces designed by Bob Mackie. So what if the dancers are occasionally out of step, and the action sometimes veers into the dubious (a Vegas-style revue about a disaster that took more than 1,000 lives?) or even the inexplicable (a finale praising beautiful and bare-breasted girls suddenly stops for three lines of "Somewhere Over the Rainbow"?). Note that *Jubilee!* offers a marvelous backstage walking tour Monday, Wednesday, and Saturday at 11am. Shows are held Saturday through Thursday at 7:30 and 10:30pm. In Bally's Las Vegas, 3645 Las Vegas

Jubilee!

An Elton John impersonator performs in *Legends in Concert.*

Blvd. S. ✆ **800/237-7469** or 702/946-4567. www.ballys.com. Tickets $53–$113 (plus tax). Only ages 18 and over admitted.

Legends in Concert ★ It's hard to have staying power in Las Vegas, a town that delights in the concept of bigger, newer, better. So the fact that this celebrity impersonator show has been running in various forms at various hotels for more than 25 years is noteworthy. After spending the bulk of those years at Imperial Palace, the production moved next door to Harrah's in 2008, giving it a nicer showroom and slightly improved production values. But the real stars of the show are the faux celebrities who do their best to make you believe they are the real thing (with varying results). Performers will vary depending on when you see the show; you may catch "Janet Jackson" and "Diana Ross" or you could get "Dolly Parton" and "Cher," but you will almost always get "Elvis." Unlike other impersonator shows, the singing is live (no lip-syncing, even when "Britney" is performing), which can enhance the illusion or destroy it. Some performers succeed more in appearance and others do better with vocal mimicry, and while most are at least passable, there are a few that will leave you wondering if he or she is the real thing playing a joke on the audience. Don't scoff; Ellen Degeneres did that very thing during at 2008 show and captured the audience reactions ("didn't look anything like her") for her daytime talkfest. Shows are held Sunday through Friday at 7:30 and 10pm (with select days at 6:30pm). In Harrah's Las Vegas, 3475 Las Vegas Blvd. ✆ **702/396-5111.** Tickets $48–$58.

Le Rêve ★ Challenged from the get-go, thanks to a decision to base this Cirque-like show around a stage of water, thus prompting inevitable comparisons with O down the street, this production has received major revamps, both in staging and choreography. By and large, the choices—particularly to get revered avant-garde choreographer and MOMIX-genius Moses Pendleton to take over the choreography (thus increasing the presence of dance)—have been good ones, and this production now stands on its own as a visual spectacle and emotionally satisfying entertainment.

Le Rêve, named for the most significant of the paintings owned by Steve Wynn, is an extravaganza featuring all the usual elements: gorgeously sculpted athletic performers who twist, contort, and mostly pose in filmy tattered outfits before and after diving in and splashing out of a giant pool. Intermittently funny clowns do their thing. Magritte figures float by. Fountains rise out of the stage. The result is pure spectacle, with a slight narrative suggesting the proceedings are the dreams of a woman dealing with a turbulent romantic issue. It's like the biggest, most impressive Esther Williams production you can imagine. Speaking of which, you may wish to avoid sitting in the front rows, unless you don't mind spending 90 minutes huddling under the provided towels—not only does the in-the-round staging mean the performers routinely splash water, but also that long, filmy costumes, when hauled out of said water and lifted high in the air, drip most impressively and most wetly on the first couple of rows. Because no seat is that far from the stage, stay back and stay dry.

One advantage this production has over *O* is the top-end seats: placed in the back row, in cushy armchairs, equipped with video screens that show the off-stage action (when a performer plunges into the pool, patrons can see where they go when they disappear from regular view), plus a bottle of champagne and some chocolate-dipped strawberries. A nice gimmick. Shows are held Friday through Tuesday at 7 and 9:30pm. In Wynn Las Vegas, 3131 Las Vegas Blvd. S. ℂ **888/320-7110.** www.wynnlasvegas.com. Tickets $99–$179. Only ages 13 and over admitted.

Mac King ★★★ ☺ 🍸 One of the best entertainment values in Vegas, this is an afternoon comedy-magic show—and note the order of precedence in that introduction. King does magic, thankfully, emphasizing the only kind that's really mind-blowing these days—those close-up tricks that defy your eyes and mind. But he surrounds his tricks with whimsy and wit, and sometimes gut-busting guffaws, which all serve to make you wonder how someone else can still perform stunts with a straight face. Check out how he takes a $100 bill and—wait, we don't want to give it away, but suffice it to say it involves an old shoe, a Fig Newton, and several other unexpected props. Perfect for the kids, perfect for the budget, perfect timing if you need something in the afternoon before an evening of gambling, dining, and cavorting. Then again, we are rather surprised he's still just an afternoon gig. One day, someone is going to wise up and move him to the big time, and his ticket prices will move up, too. So catch him while he's still a bargain. Shows are held Tuesday through Saturday at 1 and 3pm. In Harrah's, 3475 Las Vegas Blvd. S. ℂ **800/427-7247** or 702/369-5222. www.harrahslasvegas.com. Tickets $25 (plus tax and service fees).

MGM Grand's *Crazy Horse Paris* ★★ Further proof that Vegas is trying to distance itself from the "Vegas Is for Families" image, "Classy Adult Entertainment" are the new watchwords in several hotels, with *Crazy Horse Paris* leading the pack. Allegedly the same show that has been running for years in a famous racy French nightclub, this show is just a bunch of pretty girls taking their clothes off. Except that the girls are smashingly pretty, with the kind of bodies just not found on real live human beings, and they take their clothes off in curious and, yes, artistic ways, gyrating *en pointe* while holding on to ropes or hoops, falling over sofas while lip-syncing to French torch songs—in short, it's what striptease ought to be, and by gosh, if strip clubs were this well

MGM Grand's *Crazy Horse Paris*.

staged, we'd go to them all the time. But $50 a ticket is a great deal to pay for arty nudie fun, especially when the routines, no matter how clever or how naked (the girls get down to a postage-stamp-size triangle soul patch covering the naughtiest of their bits, so they aren't "nude," but talk about a technicality), start to seem alike after a while. Shows are held Wednesday through Monday at 8 and 10:30pm. In the MGM Grand, 3799 Las Vegas Blvd. S. © **877/880-0880** or 702/891-7777. www.mgmgrand.com. Tickets $50–$60 (including tax and fees). Only ages

Penn & Teller ★★★  The most intelligent show in Vegas, as these two—magicians? illusionists? truth-tellers? BS artists? geniuses?—put on 90 minutes of, yes, magic and juggling, but also acerbic comedy, mean stunts, and quiet beauty. Looking like two characters out of Dr. Seuss, big, loud Penn and smaller, silent Teller (to reduce them to their basic characteristics) perform magic, reveal the secrets behind a few major magic tricks, discuss why magic is nothing but a bunch of lies, and then turn around and show why magic is as lovely an art form as any other. We won't tell you much about the various tricks and acts for fear of ruining punch lines, but watching Teller fish money out of an empty glass aquarium or play with shadows is to belie Penn's earlier caveats about learning how tricks are done—it doesn't ruin the wonder of it, not at all, nor the serenity that settles in your Vegas-sensory-overloaded brain. Shows are held Saturday through Wednesday at 9pm. In the Rio Hotel, 3700 W. Flamingo. © **888/746-7784.** www. riolasvegas.com. Tickets $75–$85 (plus tax). Only ages 5 and over admitted.

Phantom This is a 90-minute, intermission-free, heavy-on-the-special-effects, costly staging of Andrew Lloyd Webber's ubiquitous musical, *The Phantom of the Opera.* The show's fans (and they are legion) will either yowl or not care because it's still *Phantom,* but they survived the movie adaptation, while the rest of us might be a little happier with some of the fat trimmed away, though somewhat

Penn & Teller.

PENN & TELLER'S TOP 10 THINGS ONE SHOULD NEVER DO IN A VEGAS magic show

Penn & Teller have been exercising their acerbic wit and magical talents in numerous forums together for more than 25 years, and their show at the Rio is one of Vegas's best and most intelligent. We must confess that we couldn't get the quieter half of the duo, Teller, to cough up a few words, but the more verbose Penn Jillette was happy to share.

1. Costume yourself in gray business suits totally lacking in rhinestones, animal patterns, Mylar, capes, bell-bottoms, shoulder pads, and top hats.

2. Wear your hair in any style that could *not* be described as "feathered" or "spiked."

3. Use really good live jazz music instead of canned sound-alike cheesy rip-off fake pop "music."

4. Cruelly (but truthfully) make fun of your siblings in the magic brotherhood.

5. Do the dangerous tricks on each other instead of anonymous show women with aftermarket breasts and/or endangered species.

6. Toss a cute little magic bunny into a cute little chipper-shredder.

7. Open your show by explaining *and* demonstrating how other magicians on the Strip do their most amazing tricks, and then do that venerable classic of magic "The Cups and Balls," with transparent plastic cups.

8. Treat the audience as if they had a brain in their collective head.

9. Allow audience members to sign real bullets, load them into real guns, and fire those bullets into your face.

10. Bleed.

(You will find many of these "don'ts" in the *Penn & Teller* show at the Rio All-Suite Hotel & Casino.)

befuddled by the plot. The lowdown: There's a guy in a mask, and he loves a girl who sings, and she loves him, but she also loves another boy, and there are caverns and canals and romance and tragedy and mystery and murder and light opera. Staged on the former site of the failed Guggenheim Museum (transformed into a $40-million theater), the musical is even more high-tech than the original Broadway staging, with increased special effects and whatnot (like anything can top that chandelier crash). *Phantom* is over the top, but then, so is Vegas, and this seems like a good fit. Shows are held Monday through Saturday at 7pm; Monday and Saturday also have a 9:30pm show. At The Venetian, 3355 Las Vegas Blvd. S. ✆ **866/641-7469** or 702/414-7469. www.venetian.com. Tickets $69–$165 (plus tax).

Rita Rudner ★★ She stands in front of an audience for about an hour and tells the truth. It's that simple. It's also funny as heck, and oddly endearing, as Rudner's successful shtick is to present herself as Every Woman, not to mention the audience's Best Friend Forever. She wryly and dryly tosses out one-liners about gender relationships in an attempt to explain that age-old problem—What Do Women Want? And Why Don't Men Understand It's Shoes? Shows are held

Monday through Saturday at 8:30pm. At Harrah's, 3475 Las Vegas Blvd. S. ✆ **702/369-5222.** Tickets $54–$90.

Terry Fator ★ *America's Got Talent* winner Fator is no Susan Boyle, that's for sure, but his shtick—ventriloquism meets impersonation—is downright entertaining. The format of the 80-minute show is fairly standard: A series of puppets joins Fator on stage, and proceeds to do a song or three impersonating a famous voice. Winston the Turtle does a serviceable Roy Orbison and an eerily familiar James Blunt, while Walter the Cowboy kills on a Brooks and Dunn song—or rather Fator does, of course. Even the less than perfect impressions are still impressive considering the fact that he's doing it all with his mouth closed. Fator's overall demeanor is a little too laconic, especially when he doesn't have a piece of felt on his hand, but the show mostly hits its middle-of-the-road target on the bull's eye, offering up some decent chuckles and a nice night of music. Try to get a seat in the center section, otherwise you'll spend most of your time watching the giant TV screens instead of the guy (and his friends) on stage. Shows are Tuesday through Saturday at 7:30pm. At The Mirage, 3400 Las Vegas Blvd. S. ✆ **800/963-9634** or 702/792-7777. www.mirage.com. Tickets $59–$129 (plus tax and service fees).

Tournament of Kings ★ ☺ Lords and Ladies, Wizards and Wenches, hasten thee to thy throne for the battle is about to commence. Yes, that's how they talk at this dinner show—like a Renaissance fair only with better production values. If you're familiar with the Medieval Times chain, this will look familiar. For a fixed price, you get a dinner that's better than you might expect (Cornish game hen, very fine baked potato, and more), which you eat with your hands (in keeping with the theme), while Merlin (or someone like him) spends too much time trying to work the crowd up with a singalong. This gives way to a competition among the kings of various medieval countries, competing for titles in knightly contests (jousting, horse races, and such) that are every bit as unrehearsed and spontaneous as a professional wrestling match. Eventually, good triumphs over evil and all that.

Each section of the arena is given a king to be the subject of and to root for, and the audience is encouraged to hoot, holler, and pound on the tables, which kids love but teens will be too jaded for (though we know some from whom a spontaneous "way cool" slipped out, unchecked, a few times). Many adults might find it tiresome, particularly when they insist you shout "huzzah!" and other supposedly period slang. Acrobatics are terrific, and certain buff performers make for a different sort of enjoyment. Shows are Monday through Thursday at 6pm and Friday through Sunday at 6 and 8:30pm. In Excalibur, 3850 Las Vegas Blvd. S. ✆ **800/933-1334** or 702/597-7600. www.excalibur.com. Tickets $55 (plus tax).

HEADLINER SHOWROOMS

Vegas entertainment made its name with its showrooms, though its glory days are somewhat behind it, gone with the Rat Pack themselves. For a long time, Vegas headliners were something of a joke; only those on the downhill side of fame were thought to play here. But with all the new performance spaces—and high fees—offered by the new hotels, Vegas suddenly has respect again, especially, on (of all things) the rock scene. Both the Hard Rock Hotel's The Joint and the House of Blues attract very current and very popular acts who find it hip, rather than humiliating, to play Sin City. However, the classic Vegas showroom itself does seem headed the way of the dinosaurs; many of the hotels have shuttered theirs. As for

afternoon DELIGHT?

By now, it will not have escaped your attention that most of the nighttime shows in Vegas, at least the ones of any quality, cost a lot. Except for the ones that cost a whole heck of a lot. And that we tend to prefer the latter. "Isn't there *any* cheap entertainment in this town?" you may have begun to wonder, and trust us, even if we are awfully liberal with the contents of your wallets, we feel your pain.

So, barring the possibility that you might be the kind of gambler we wish to be—the sort who gets comped free tickets to expensive shows (that you could probably afford anyway, in typical Vegas irony)—there are some alternatives. Several Vegas hotels offer afternoon shows, at much more reasonable prices—that, of course, being a relative term. Most are probably not worth your time and effort (Pet comedy? Really?), but we did find some satisfying illusions and humor in the afternoon show by **Nathan Burton** ★ (in the Flamingo, 3355 Las Vegas Blvd. S.; ✆ **702/733-3333;** www.flamingolv.com; Sun–Fri

4pm; tickets $34–$44). A winner of NBC's *America's Got Talent,* Burton is a genial host who infuses magic tricks both big and small with a good-natured comedy spin that may not break any new ground but adds up to an enjoyable afternoon distraction.

(**Note:** The best afternoon show, Mac King, gets his own full review above.)

Discount coupons for afternoon shows are often found in those free magazines in hotel rooms. Sometimes the discount gets you in with just the price of a drink.

the remainder, one is pretty much like the other, with the exception of the Hard Rock and House of Blues (hence their detailed descriptions), and in any case, audiences go based on the performer rather than the space. Check with your hotel, or those free magazines in your room, to see who is in town when you are.

Major headliner showrooms in Vegas include the following:

- o **Center for the Performing Arts** In the Planet Hollywood Hotel & Casino, 3667 Las Vegas Blvd. S. (✆ **877/333-9474** or 702/785-5555)
- o **Las Vegas Hilton Showroom** In the Las Vegas Hilton, 3000 Paradise Rd. (✆ **800/222-5361** or 702/732-5755)
- o **Mandalay Bay Events Center** In Mandalay Bay, 3950 Las Vegas Blvd. S. (✆ **877/632-7400** or 702/632-7580)
- o **MGM Grand Garden Events Arena** In the MGM Grand Hotel & Casino, 3799 Las Vegas Blvd. S. (✆ **800/929-1111** or 702/891-7777)
- o **MGM Grand Hollywood Theatre** In the MGM Grand Hotel & Casino, 3799 Las Vegas Blvd. S. (✆ **800/929-1111** or 702/891-7777)
- o **The Orleans Showroom** In The Orleans, 4500 W. Tropicana Ave. (✆ **800/675-3267**)

Hard Rock Hotel's The Joint Despite the renowned rock acts who played there (the Rolling Stones, Coldplay, Nine Inch Nails), the original Joint venue was basically an oversized ballroom with uncomfortable folding chairs and limited sight lines to the stage from everywhere but the primo seats. Odd then that when they decided to build a new Joint they pretty much kept everything the same, only bigger. The 4,000-seat barn of a space has two balconies overlooking the floor and a series of VIP boxes at the back, which are undeniably luxurious, but the main seating section is a concrete bore with thinly padded folding chairs on a flat floor that leads to sore backs and great views of the hairstyle of whomever is sitting in front of you. Concerts that allow for the seats to be removed entirely with the crowd standing, dancing, rocking, moshing, or whatever else they are inclined to do are probably better suited for the space.

Showroom Policies: Smoking is not permitted; seating is either preassigned or general, depending on the performer. **Prices:** $20 to $250, depending on the performer (tax and drinks extra). **Showtimes:** Times and nights of performance vary. **Reservations:** You can reserve up to 30 days in advance. In the Hard Rock Hotel & Casino, 4455 Paradise Rd. ✆ **800/693-7625** or 702/693-5000. www. hardrockhotel.com.

House of Blues ★★ The House of Blues goes head-to-head with The Joint at the Hard Rock Hotel, and it does seem as though acts looking to do spontaneous shows pick HOB over The Joint. On its own merits, the House of Blues is an intimate room with a cozy floor surrounded by a bar area, and an upstairs balcony area that has actual theater seating. (The balcony might be a better place to see a show, as the sightlines are unobscured, unlike down below, where posts and such can get in the way.) It's probably the most comfortable and user-friendly place to see a rock show in Vegas.

The heavy theme decor (a constant evocation of the Delta region and New Orleans) is a bit too Disneyland-meets-Hearst-Castle, with corrugated-tin this and weathered-wood that, plus walls covered in outsider/primitive/folk art from various Southern artists. But it annoys us less in Vegas than it does in New Orleans; here it's sort of a welcome touch of the genuine amid the artificial, while in the actual Big Easy, it comes off as prefab.

Showroom Policies: Smoking is not permitted; seating is either preassigned or general, depending on the performer. (Some shows are all general admission, with everyone standing.) **Prices:** $18 to $250, depending on the performer. **Showtimes:** Vary, but usually 8pm. **Reservations:** You can buy tickets as soon as shows are announced; lead time varies with each artist. In Mandalay Bay, 3950 Las Vegas Blvd. S. ✆ **877/632-7400** or 702/632-7600. www.hob.com.

Headliner Stadiums

Sam Boyd Stadium, the outdoor stadium for the University of Nevada, Las Vegas (UNLV), has been host to such major acts as Paul McCartney, the Eagles, and Metallica. Still, both it and the **Thomas & Mack Center,** the university's indoor arena, have been losing headliners to the MGM Grand Garden and the Mandalay Bay Center (which have recently welcomed such acts as the Police reunion, Lady Gaga, the Black Eyed Peas, and the annual CMA Awards) and are more likely to host sporting events these days. Sam Boyd is located at Boulder Highway and Russell Road while Thomas & Mack is on the UNLV campus at Swenson and Tropicana (✆ **800/745-3000**). **Ticketmaster** (✆ **702/474-4000;** www.ticketmaster.com) handles ticketing for both arenas.

> # WAYNE NEWTON'S TOP 10 FAVORITE
> ## lounge SONGS
>
> Wayne Newton is the consummate entertainer. He has performed more than 25,000 concerts in Las Vegas alone, and in front of more than 25 million people worldwide. Wayne has received more standing ovations than any other entertainer in history. Along with his singing credits, his acting credits are soaring—one of his most fun credits is *Vegas Vacation*.
>
> 1. "You're Nobody, 'Til Somebody Loves You" (You don't have a body unless somebody loves you!)
>
> 2. "Up a Lazy River" (or "Up Your Lazy River!")
>
> 3. "Don't Go Changing (Just the Way You Are)" (The clothes will last another week!)
>
> 4. "Having My Baby" (Oh, God!)
>
> 5. "The Windmills of My Mind" (A mind is a terrible thing to waste!)
>
> 6. "The Wind Beneath My Wings" (Soft and Dry usually helps!)
>
> 7. "Copacabana"
>
> 8. "When the Saints Go Marching In"
>
> 9. "I Am, I Said" (Huh?!)
>
> 10. "The Theme from *The Love Boat*" (or "Would a Dinghy Do?")

COMEDY CLUBS

Comedy Club The Riviera's comedy club, on the second floor of the Mardi Gras Plaza, showcases several comedians nightly. They are usually nobody you've ever heard of, and the place tends to draw a breed of comic that goes for the gross-out, insult-every-minority brand of "humor" instead of actual humor. Shows are daily at 8:30 and 10:30pm. In the Riviera Hotel & Casino, 2901 Las Vegas Blvd. S. ☏ **800/634-6753** or 702/794-9433. Tickets $25 (plus tax and fees).

The Improv ★★ This offshoot of Budd Friedman's famed comedy club (the first one opened in 1963 in New York City) presents about four comedians per show in a 400-seat showroom. These are talented performers—the top comics on the circuit, ones you're likely to see on Leno and Letterman. You can be sure of an entertaining evening. Shows are Tuesday through Sunday at 8:30 and 10:30pm. In Harrah's Las Vegas, 3475 Las Vegas Blvd. S. ☏ **800/392-9002** or 702/369-5000. Tickets $40 (includes taxes and fees).

BARS

In addition to the venues listed below, consider hanging out, as the locals quickly began doing, at **Aureole** ★★, **Red Square** ★★, and the **House of Blues** ★★, all in Mandalay Bay. There's a separate bar at Aureole (p. 154), facing the wine tower, where your wish for wine sends comely lasses flying up four stories, courtesy of *Peter Pan*–style harnesses, to fetch your desired bottle. At

Red Square (p. 158), keep your drink nicely chilled all night long on the ice bar, created by water that's freshly poured and frozen daily. Or hang out and feel the blues at the small bottle-cap-bedecked bar in the corner of the House of Blues restaurant (see "You Gotta Have a Theme," p. 163), which gets quite lively with off-duty locals after midnight.

You might also check out the incredible nighttime view at the bars atop the **Stratosphere Casino Hotel & Tower** (p. 126)—nothing beats it.

There's also the **Viva Las Vegas Lounge** at the Hard Rock Hotel (p. 130), which every rock-connected person in Vegas will eventually pass through.

Caramel ★★ It's small, but worlds away from the Bellagio-business-as-usual just outside its doors. How happy the 20-somethings are that there is this hip-hop spinning, nonthreatening, scene-intensive hangout with caramel-and-choc-olate-coated drink glasses and glowing bar in the middle of Bellagio. How much does this prove Bellagio is trying to lure the ghostbar crowd away from the Palms? Not that this will do it, but if you are here and young, it's where you should be. Caramel is open daily 5pm to 5am. In Bellagio, 3600 Las Vegas Blvd. S. ℭ **702/693-7111.**

Champagnes Cafe ★★ Wonder where Old Vegas went? It ossified right here. Red- and gold-flocked wallpaper and other such trappings of "glamour" never die—in fact, with this ultralow lighting, they will never even fade. It's a seedy old bar with seedy old men leering away. They even serve ice-cream shakes spiked with booze—two indulgences wrapped into one frothy package, and quite a double addiction delight. Some might run screaming from the place, while others will think they've died and gone to heaven. It's the kind of place that refuses to serve food any more because that would mean it would have to ban smoking. So cool it's going to keep going from passé to hot and back again in the course of an evening. Karaoke is offered Friday through Saturday from 10pm to 2am. The cafe is open daily 24 hours. 3557 S. Maryland Pkwy. (btw. Twain Ave. and Desert Inn Rd.). ℭ **702/737-1699.**

Coyote Ugly ★ You've seen the movie, now go have some of that prepackaged fun for yourself. Oh, come on—you don't think those bartender girls really dance on the bar and hose down the crowd just because they are so full of spontane-ous rowdy high spirits, now do you? Not when the original locale built a reputa-tion (and inspired a bad movie) on just such behavior, creating a success strong enough to start an entire chain of such frat-boy fun places? By the way, sarcastic and cynical as we are, can we say it's a totally fun place? It's open Sunday through Thursday from 6pm until 2am and Friday and Saturday from 6pm until 3am. In New York–New York, 3790 Las Vegas Blvd. S. (at Tropicana Ave.). ℭ **702/740-6969.** www.coyoteuglysaloon.com. Cover varies, usually $10 and up after 9pm.

Dispensary Lounge ★ Stuck in a '70s time warp (the water wheel and the ferns are the tip-off, though the Muzak songs confirm it), this is a fine place for a nice, long drink. One that lasts decades, perhaps. It's very quiet, low-key, and often on the empty side. Things pick up on weekends, but it still isn't the sort of place that attracts raucous drunks. (Of course, if it were on the Strip instead of being tucked away, it probably would.) "We leave you alone if you don't want to be bothered," says the proprietor. If you are a hep cat, but one on the mild side, you'll love it. The Lounge is open daily 24 hours. 2451 E. Tropicana Ave. (at Eastern Ave.). ℭ **702/458-6343.**

Double Down Saloon ★★★ 🎁 "House rule: You puke, you clean." Okay, that about sums up the Double Down. Well, no, it doesn't really do the place justice. This is a big local hangout, with management quoting an old *Scope* magazine description of its clientele: "Hipsters, blue collars, the well-heeled lunatic fringe." Rumored to have been spotted here: director Tim Burton and the late Dr. Timothy Leary. Need to know more? Okay, trippy hallucinogenic graffiti covers the walls, the ceiling, the tables, and possibly you, if you sit there long enough. Decor includes thrift-store battered armchairs and sofa, a couple of pool tables, and a jukebox that holds everything from the Germs to Link Wray, Dick Dale, and Reverend Horton Heat. Oddly, the Double Down swears it invented the bacon martini here. On Wednesday night, there is a live blues band, while other nights you might find local alternative, punk, or ska groups performing. On the last Sunday of every month, the Blue Man Group plays, but under another name, as a percussion band. Call about that, for sure. There's no cover unless an out-of-town band is playing that actually has a label. The Double Down is open daily 24 hours. 4640 Paradise Rd. (at Naples Dr.). © **702/791-5775.** www.doubledownsaloon.com.

Downtown Cocktail Lounge ★★ One of three (and counting) friendly and individualistic bars just a couple blocks from the Fremont Street Experience, this is the place to go for true modern Vegas cool, as opposed to the prefab (not to mention costly) Strip-side hotel bars. Once you find the door (it's hidden behind an industrial metal sheet on the left), you enter an Asian *moderne* space, complete with lounges that invite posing. It feels a little more young-executive friendly than its neighbor, the gothic Griffin (see below). The cocktail menu is as substantial as it ought to be. It's open Monday through Friday from 4pm until 2am and Saturday from 7pm until 2am. 111 Las Vegas Blvd. © **702/880-3696.**

Drop Bar ★ Smack in the middle of the Green Valley Ranch Resort, with '60s-inspired go-go girls dancing away. It's open daily 24 hours. In Green Valley Ranch Resort, 2300 Paseo Verde Pkwy., Henderson. © **702/221-6560.**

Eiffel Tower Bar ★ From this chic and elegant room, in the restaurant on the 11th floor of the Eiffel Tower, you can look down on everyone, just like a real Parisian! (Just kidding, Francophiles.) But really, this is a date-impressing bar, and, because there's no cover or minimum, it's a cost-effective alternative to the overly inflated food prices at the restaurant. Drop by for a drink, but try to look sophisticated. And then you can cop an attitude and dismiss everything as gauche—or droit, depending on which way you are seated. A business-attire dress code is enforced after 4:30pm. It's open daily 11:30am to 11pm. In Paris Las Vegas, 3655 Las Vegas Blvd. S. © **702/948-6937.**

NO smoking!

Long the last best hope for smokers, Vegas is considerably less smoky these days. A recent ban forbids smoking in any place that serves food, such as a restaurant, supermarket, or bar with a pub menu. Stand-alone bars and casinos are exempt, which, in theory, means you can't smoke in a hotel lobby, but you can a few feet away in a casino. It's an interesting evolution for a town so dedicated to hedonistic pursuits.

ghostbar has some of the best views in Vegas.

ghostbar ★★ Probably the most interesting aspect of this desperate-to-get-into-the-gossip-pages-as-the-trendy-bar-of-the-moment place (decorated with a '60s mod/futuristic silver-gleam look) is that, though much is made of the fact that it's on the 55th floor, it's really on the 42nd. Something about the number four being bad luck in Asian cultures. Whatever. The view still is fabulous, which is the main reason to come here, that and to peer at those tousled-hair beauties copping an attitude on the couches. This may be the hot bar of the moment by the time you get here (dress up), or everyone may have moved on. Who knows? ghostbar is open daily 8pm until dawn. In the Palms Resort & Casino, 4321 W. Flamingo Rd. (just west of the Strip). ☎ **702/942-6832.** Cover varies, usually $10 and up.

Griffin ★★ Part of a promising trend to revitalize the Fremont East District (just a couple of blocks from the Fremont Street Experience), the fun starts with the old stone facade and eponymous sign and continues inside with the stone pillars, arched cave ceiling, and two fire pits. Just what you want in a stylish bar that revels in its history but at the same time doesn't try too hard. Given its proximity to other top-notch downtown hangouts, such as Downtown Cocktail Lounge, this is a must stop on the anti-Strip and hotel bar tour. There are DJs on the weekends. It's open Monday through Friday from 5pm until close and Saturday and Sunday 8pm until close. 511 E. Fremont St. ☎ **702/382-0577.**

Hogs & Heifers Saloon ★ While there is a chain of Coyote Ugly nightclubs (including one here in Vegas), the movie of the same name was based on the high jinks that happened at the New York version of this rowdy roadhouse saloon. In Sin City since 2005, the hogs here are of the motorcycle variety, and the place definitely draws a crowd that can look intimidating but is usually a friendly (and boisterous) bunch. Saucy bar maidens and outdoor barbecues on select weekends make this one of the few good options for nightlife in the Downtown area. It's open daily, usually 1pm to 6am (call to check, as hours vary by month). 201 N. 3rd St. (btw. Ogden and Stewart aves., 1 block from the Fremont Street Experience). ☎ **702/676-1457.**

Peppermill's Fireside Lounge.

Peppermill's Fireside Lounge ★ 🎁 Walk through the classic Peppermill's coffee shop (not a bad place to eat, by the way) on the Strip, and you land in this fabulously dated bar. It has low, circular banquette seats, fake floral foliage, a whole bunch of pink neon, and electric candles. But best of all is the water and fire pit as the room's centerpiece—a piece of kitsch thought to be long vanished from Earth and attracting nostalgia buffs like moths to a flame. Recently added neon detracts somewhat from the fire-pit centerpiece, but it's still wonderfully retro for unwinding a bit after some time spent on the hectic Strip. You might well be joined by entertainers and others winding down after a late night. The enormous, froufrou tropical drinks (including the signature bathtub-size margaritas) will ensure that you sink into a comfortable stupor. Peppermill's is open daily 24 hours. 2985 Las Vegas Blvd. S. ☏ **702/735-4177.**

Petrossian ★★★ Those despairing of a grown-up place to drink, a place for people who want a real cocktail made by people who know that martinis really do require vermouth (none of this "just wave the bottle in the general direction of the glass" nonsense and that "shaken not stirred" is a silly debate), rejoice and come here. Located just off the Bellagio lobby, this is one of the prettiest places to imbibe in the city as the glorious Dale Chihuly glass flowers "bloom" near your head. The bartenders are required to attend ongoing cocktail education, so they really know their stuff. Said stuff is made with the finest ingredients, which means none of the drinks come cheap. But the extra is worth it if you want it done right. They also have a good selection of high-end snacks. A little beluga with your booze? Open daily 24 hours. In Bellagio, 3600 Las Vegas Blvd. S. ☏ **702/693-7111.**

Playboy Club ★ A generation mourned when the last of the Playboy Clubs closed. Once the sine non qua of naughty, sexy, mature fun, it somehow lost its mojo. This new incarnation doesn't capture the vibe of exclusive adult cool, but its presence is still a happy thing for swingers, ironically retro and deadly serious alike. Positioned so that attendees can move between it and the Moon nightclub, there's expensive gambling and vintage magazine covers rotating on video screens. Although it's not nearly the bastion of cool that it once was, it's still kind of swell to see the Bunnies again, even if they do make lousy dealers. It's open daily 9pm until dawn. In the Palms, 4321 W. Flamingo Rd. ☎ **702/942-6832.** Cover varies, includes admission to Moon nightclub.

Revolution ★ This place is tied to the Beatles-themed Cirque *LOVE* show, so think White Album, not Chairman Mao. While we dig the Union Jack–miniskirt-clad greeters, we wish the somewhat sterile interior was more shagadelic. Apart from some random Beatles-esque elements, the furnishings are pretty much beanbag chairs, silver mirrors, and a whiff of Austin Powers. Plus, the music relates not at all to the '60s. Having said that, lots of oddballs show up to spin records; in one week, Tommy Lee and Kevin Federline both headlined. The Abbey Road Bar, which fronts the place, is a good hangout, especially if you can kick out a go-go dancer and nab one of the seats in the REVOLUTION letters. The bar is open daily noon to 4am, and the club is open daily 10pm to 4am. In The Mirage, 3400 Las Vegas Blvd. S. ☎ **702/791-1111.**

Triple 7 Brew Pub ★ 🎁 Yet another of the many things the Main Street Station hotel has done right. Stepping into its microbrew pub feels like stepping out of Vegas. Well, except for the dueling-piano entertainment. The place has a partially modern warehouse look (exposed pipes, microbrew fixtures visible through exposed glass at the back, and a very high ceiling), but a hammered-tin ceiling continues the hotel's Victorian decor; the overall effect seems straight out of San Francisco's North Beach. It's a bit yuppified but escapes being pretentious. And frankly, it's a much-needed modern space for the Downtown area. This place has its own brew master and a number of microbrews ready to try, and if you want a quick bite, there's also an oyster-and-sushi bar, plus fancy burgers and pizzas.

Triple 7 Brew Pub.

It can get noisy during the aforementioned piano-duel act, but
otherwise casino noise stays out.
Because all of Downtown is too
heavy on Old Las Vegas (which is
fine, but not *all* the time), this is
good for a suitable breather. Triple
7 is open daily 11am to 7am. In
Main Street Station, 200 N. Main St.
© **702/387-1896.**

> ### 📎 Bathroom Break
>
> **When you gotta go, you gotta go, particu-
> larly if you've tried drinking at every bar
> listed here. So when you do, try to do so in
> the unisex, free-standing Space Age pods at
> Mandalay Bay's China Grill.**

Zuri ★ This is the best of the casino-hotel free bars (free as in no cover), probably because it is a semicurtained enclave just off the elevators (as opposed to a
space just plunked down right in the middle of a casino). With swooping wood
and red-velvet couches, the drinks are expensive, but at least you can hear your
partner's whispered sweet nothings (a rare thing in a Vegas hotel). Zuri is open 24
hours. In the MGM Grand, 3799 Las Vegas Blvd. S. © **702/891-7777.**

PIANO BARS

The Bar at Times Square ★ If you're looking for a quiet piano bar, this is not
the place for you. It's smack in the middle of the Central Park part of the New
York–New York casino. Two pianos are going strong every night, and the cigar-
smoking crowd overflows out the doors. It always seems to be packed with a
singing, swaying throng full of camaraderie and good cheer—or at least, full of
booze. Hugely fun, provided you can get a foot in the door. Shows are daily from
8pm to 2:15am. In New York–New York, 3790 Las Vegas Blvd. S. © **702/740-6969.** Cover
$10 after 7pm.

Napoleon's ★★ A once sedate space in the Paris Las Vegas shopping gallery has been transformed into a rollicking good-time venue with the addition of

Dueling pianos at The Bar at Times Square.

dueling piano performances. The bar is a mixture of French old-world charm and Las Vegas showmanship, with lots of comfy seating scattered about. The pianists play daily 9pm to 1am. In Paris Las Vegas, 3570 Las Vegas Blvd. S. © **702/946-7000.**

GAY BARS

Hip and happening Vegas locals know that some of the best scenes and dance action can be found in the city's gay bars. And no, they don't ask for sexuality ID at the door. All are welcome at any of the following establishments—as long as you don't have a problem with the people inside, they aren't going to have a problem with you. For women, this can be a fun way to dance and not get hassled by overeager Lotharios.

If you want to know what's going on in gay Las Vegas during your visit, pick up a copy of *Q Vegas,* which is also available at any of the places described below. You can also call © **702/650-0636** or check out the online edition at **www.qvegas.com**. Gay nightlife listings can also be found on the Web at **www. gayvegas.com**.

The Buffalo ★ Close to Gipsy and several other gay establishments, this is a leather/Levi's bar popular with motorcycle clubs. It features beer busts (all the beer you can drink for a small cover) and other drink specials throughout the week. There are pool tables and darts, and music videos play in this not-striking environment. It's very cheap, with longnecks going for a few bucks, and it gets very, very busy, very late (3 or 4am). The Buffalo is open daily 24 hours. 4640 Paradise Rd. (at Naples Dr.). © **702/733-8355.**

Free Zone ★ One of several bars within a few steps of each other on the corner of Paradise Road and Naples Drive, Free Zone plays the role of friendly neighborhood club (as opposed to the nearby swank lounges or leather bars) with a variety of theme nights (everything from country to karaoke), lots of comfortable sitting areas, chatty bartenders, video poker, and inexpensive drinks. A moderately sized dance floor gets busy on weekend nights but for the most part this is a place to sit and drink with friends. Free Zone is open 24 hours. 610 E. Naples Dr. (at Paradise Rd.). © **702/794-2300.** www.freezonelv.com. Cover varies.

Funhog Ranch You know those trendy nightclubs where you stand in line for hours, pay outrageously high cover charges and drink prices, and are surrounded by opulence and beauty everywhere you turn once you finally get inside? This isn't one of them. As down-home as it gets, Funhog Ranch is just a bar, a few booths, some video poker, a jukebox, and an electronic dartboard. Drinks are rock-bottom cheap and the clientele, which skews a bit older and is more of the leather/Levi's crowd, is enormously friendly. There is no standing and posing allowed and nobody is going to care what you are wearing unless you go out of your way to try to make them. Funhog is open daily 24 hours. 495 E. Twain Ave. (just east of Paradise Rd.). © **702/791-7001.**

Gipsy ★ For years, Gipsy reigned supreme as the best gay dance place in the city due to its great location (Paradise Rd., near the Hard Rock) and excellent layout (sunken dance floor and two bars). A few years ago, some fierce competition stole some of its spotlight, along with a good portion of the clientele, so the Gipsy fought back with a $750,000 renovation that recaptured past glories. Drink specials, along with theme nights, shows, and male dancers make this a good party

Krave.

bar. These days it is only open Friday and Saturday from 10pm to dawn, but the party goes all week at sister club Piranha right next door. 4605 Paradise Rd. (at Naples Dr.). ✆ **702/731-1919.** Cover varies but is usually $5 and up.

Good Times ★ This quiet neighborhood bar is located a few miles east of the MGM Grand. There's a small dance floor, but on a recent Friday night, nobody was using it, the crowd preferring instead to take advantage of the cozy bar area. A small conversation pit is a perfect spot for an intimate chat. There's the omnipresent pool and video poker if you're not interested in witty repartee. We remember this place as being a lot more crowded than it was during our most recent visit (but perhaps we were there on an off night). Good Times is open daily 24 hours. In the Liberace Plaza, 1775 E. Tropicana Ave. (at Spencer St.). ✆ **702/736-9494.** www.goodtimeslv.com.

Krave ★★ The first gay club on the Strip, not that anyone's admitting it's a gay club anymore, using "alternative" as the winking buzzword. The result is a more mixed crowd than you might get at other, openly gay clubs. The interior is a well-crafted Gothic explosion, with a dance floor and some go-go platforms that can feature dancers of either gender. The Strip access is important, as most other local gay bars take some doing to get to. *Note:* If you don't pay the club valet, you have to park in the regular hotel parking, and that calls for a long jog through the Desert Passage shopping mall, which might be uncomfortable in club togs. Krave is open daily except Monday from 8pm until late (after hours until dawn Fri–Sat). At Planet Hollywood Hotel & Casino, 3667 Las Vegas Blvd. S. (entrance on Harmon). ✆ **702/836-0830.** www.kravelasvegas.com. Cover varies.

Piranha Las Vegas/8½ Ultra Lounge ★★ Although they are connected, these two gay hot spots operate as distinct bars. Piranha is the dance club, a high-energy space done in lush colors and fabrics complete with a VIP area (that has reportedly drawn everyone from Janet to Britney) and several skyboxes that overlook the always-packed dance floor. Of note here is the outdoor patio, complete with fireplaces, and comfortable seating. The aquariums that used to hold the signature piranhas are empty, a victim of city regulations that apparently govern things like killer fish in a gay bar. The 8½ is cool and groovy, with lots of space

crowd **CONTROL**

Huge lines outside are a point of pride for Vegas clubs. So if you're into dancing, you may spend a good chunk of the night single file, double file, or in an enormous, unwieldy cluster out in front of a club—particularly on Friday or Saturday. We're not kidding: Lines can be hours long (see below), and once you get to the front, you'll find that there's no actual order. You're at the mercy of a power-wielding, eye-contact-avoiding "executive doorman"—bouncer—who gives attractive women priority.

To minimize your time in line, try the following strategies:

Call ahead. Many clubs will put you on the guest list at no cost if you merely call and request it. But be on time. Reservations are quickly canceled if you're late.

Arrive before 11pm. You'll have a harder time getting in if you show up between 12:30 and 1am, the busiest period at clubs.

Group yourself smartly. The larger the group, the longer the wait—especially a large group of mostly (or all) guys. Split up if you have to, but always keep some women with each part of your group (it's much harder for unaccompanied men to get into the clubs).

If you're trying to tip your way in, don't make it obvious. It's a negotiation. Don't wave cash above your head (the IRS has recently been clamping down on unreported tip income, so that tactic will make you *very* unpopular). Discreetly and respectfully hand the doorman $20 and ask if he can take care of you.

DON'T buy a VIP Pass. Can you say "scam"? Many passes require you get there before midnight (a time when there'd normally be no line) and with others you're paying big bucks just to have someone make the call ahead that you could have made yourself. Again: *Don't* fall for this scam.

Dress to impress. For women: Antediluvian but true—showing more cleavage is a line-skipping tactic. If that's not an option, stick with a little black dress or nice jeans and a sexy or club-wear-style top. For men: Look good. Avoid baggy jeans, shorts, tennis shoes, or work boots. Nice jeans or pants and a collared shirt work well.

Look confident. While cockiness never helps, assertiveness never hurts.

10

LAS VEGAS AFTER DARK   Gay Bars

to relax, video screens to keep you entertained, and lots of comfy seating. This is one of the most popular gay clubs in town; as a consequence, lines are often long, and cover and drink prices are both high. Dress to impress. Both are open nightly 9pm to dawn. 4633 Paradise Rd. (at Naples Dr.). ℂ **702/791-0100.** www.piranha vegas.com. Cover varies, usually $20.

DANCE CLUBS

In addition to the pop/dance clubs in this section, country-music fans might want to mosey on in to **Gilley's** (listed below) or **Toby Keith's I Love This Bar & Grill,** in Harrah's, 3475 Las Vegas Blvd. S. (ℂ **702/369-5084**), not for the grill part—the food is definitely on the overpriced and unexceptional side—but for the bar portion of the program, with live entertainment Sunday through Thursday 9pm to 2am and Friday and Saturday until 3am. The eponymous owner has been known to drop in and play from time to time.

Note about cover fees: Many of the following have absurdly high door charges, prices that go up—way, way, way up—if you either encounter one of those doormen who will accept discrete (and significant) tips to let you bypass the inevitable line, or if you reserve one of the obnoxious "bottle service tables." Many of the clubs reserve all tables (and thus, chairs) for "bottle service," which requires the purchase of a bottle or two of booze, usually running triple digits and way up. By the time you factor in the inflated cost of the bottle (which is often smaller than usual), taxes, and other fees, not to mention the original door charge, your evening out has hit mid–three figures or more. Unless your wallets are heavy, skip this racket and resign yourself to maneuvering for a place to stand on the floor.

One bright note—women are often charged less for admission than men (sometimes even allowed in free), and any guest can get a comped ticket to even the hottest clubs, if you play it right. If there is a sign advertising the club (or even just the hotel) as you walk around the ground floor, and there is a person from the hotel standing by it (who will be in a suit with a nametag), go talk to them. Odds are good they will offer you comps to the club for that night. If you are gambling for any length of time, ask the pit boss for comps.

As far as a dress code is concerned, you are going to go farther with more obviously expensive clothes, but you may not have the budget or fashion sense for that (and who travels with really good clothes, anyway?). When in doubt, all black should do it, and showing skin helps. Otherwise, just dress as nicely as you can and hope they don't notice your sneakers. But do avoid sports team–affiliated jerseys and baseball hats, baggy pants, and other things that might fall under the heading "gangsta" because that's one sure way of not getting past the velvet rope.

The Bank ★★ Because Vegas can never sit still, the otherwise alluring Light nightclub had to be demolished while it was still new-ish to make room for yet another hot spot. The entrance, lined with 500 bottles of Cristal champagne, with crystal hanging from the ceiling, and the bar lined with gold crocodile skin, puts a guest on notice: This is high-end clubbing. Look for hefty cover charges (though ladies are often free), and as a result, it attracts the deep-pocket crowd. Top-of-the-line everything nearly justifies prices; the lights respond to the music, 10 machines pump snow effects over the hot crowd, and the staff is in couture suits. They may or may not let you in if you aren't dressed to the nines. The Bank is open Thursday through Sunday from 10:30pm to 4am. In Bellagio, 3600 Las Vegas Blvd. S. ℂ **702/693-8300.** Cover usually $50, ladies free.

The Bank.

Cleopatra's Barge ★ This is a small, unique nightclub set in part on a floating barge—you can feel it rocking. The bandstand, a small dance floor, and a few (usually reserved) tables are here, while others are set around the boat on "land." It's a gimmick (in fact, it was the first themed nightclub in America), but one that makes this far more fun than other, more pedestrian, hotel bars. Plenty of dark makes for romance, but blaring volume levels mean you will have to scream those sweet nothings. Cleopatra's is open nightly 10:30pm to 3am. In Caesars Palace, 3570 Las Vegas Blvd. S. ☎ **702/731-7110.** 2-drink minimum.

Eve ★ Above her Latin-themed steakhouse Beso (p. 158), *Desperate Housewives* star Eva Longoria Parker brings a club that Gabby would certainly like but Bree would probably find distasteful (but not for any real reason). There's a multimedia display above the big center dance floor, and windows offer a nice change of pace from the typical nightclub darkness. Perhaps it's the restaurant affiliation, but this place has less of that Las Vegas nightclub insanity and more of a grown-up feeling. A nice change of pace. Maybe Bree would approve after all. Eve is open Wednesday, Friday, and Saturday from 10:30pm until 4am. In Crystals, 3720 Las Vegas Blvd. S. ☎ **702/227-3838.** www.evethenightclub.com. Cover varies, usually $20 and up.

Gilley's ★★ Yeehaw! When Gilley's former location at The Frontier closed, it was a sad day for the boot-scootin' boogie crowd in Las Vegas, but this institution, made famous in the movie *Urban Cowboy*, is back at Treasure Island and significantly upgraded. The dance floor is small, but there is still room for line dancing (with lessons on select nights) and the mechanical bull is ready to embarrass all of you tenderfoots. DJs or live bands provide the country music accompaniment, and there is even Cowboy Karaoke if you feel like emulating Garth or Gretchen. Gilley's is open nightly from 8pm until 2am, later on weekends. In Treasure Island, 3300 Las Vegas Blvd. S. ☎ **702/894-7111.** www.gilleyslasvegas.com.

Haze ★ The latest from the Light Group (Bank at Bellagio, Jet at The Mirage), this place has all the ingredients that seem to make Las Vegas nightclubs popular these days. It is crowded, dark, insanely expensive, loud, attitudinal, at times downright obnoxious, and yet somehow it all works. If you manage to make it past the crazy long lines, the dimly lit interior of the club features multiple levels, several bars, a big dance floor, lots of VIP bottle service booths and tables, and a killer light and sound system, plus strange little exhibition rooms where costumed models pose in various states of repose. Are those wood nymphs? Okay. It's like a fever dream with a bass beat. Haze! Got it. It's open Thursday through Saturday from 10:30pm until 4am. In Aria Las Vegas, 3730 Las Vegas Blvd. S. 🕾 **702/693-8300.** Cover varies, usually $40 and up.

Jet ★★ Done by the same folks who do Bank and Haze, this club at The Mirage takes everything they have done right in other venues and throws more money, more space, and more everything at it. The club is stunning, with three dance floors, each with its own vibe and musical style, and four bars on multiple levels to keep you entertained and give you something to look at. Wildly successful if you are of a certain age, but the combination of higher-than-average cover charges and the "club of the moment" vibe can be a bit exhausting for anyone looking for a slightly less competitive experience. Jet is open Thursday through Saturday and Monday 10:30pm to 4am. In The Mirage, 3400 Las Vegas Blvd. S. 🕾 **702/693-8300.** Cover varies, usually $30.

LAX ★ Pop diva Christina Aguilera is one of the celebrity investors in this hugely popular nightclub. Dimly lit to the point of needing a flashlight at times, the decor (when you can see it) is swank supper club gone mad; deep red padded vinyl walls, richly textured curtains in red and purple, and plenty of high-gloss black marble lend an air of sophistication that the aggressively young and trendy clientele probably don't appreciate as much as the multiple bars and

Jet.

L.A. INVASION

Los Angeles is the closest major metropolitan area to Las Vegas, but its influence is felt in more than just the number of people that drive to Sin City on the weekends. Many of the major nightclubs in Vegas are based on originals located in Hollywood and that trend is set to continue with two major venues scheduled to be open by the time you read this book.

The Skybar, perched at the top of the Mondrian hotel in Los Angeles, has long been one of the city's most in-demand hot spots with celebrity sightings a nightly occurrence. Vegas's version of Skybar, at the **Hard Rock Hotel,** 4455 Paradise Rd. (📞 **702/693-5243;** www.hardrockhotel.com), won't be quite as high, but it will have a commanding view of the Hard Rock's beach club area and will feature its own pool, private cabanas, and DJs and will offer both daytime and nighttime socializing and schmoozing opportunities.

Going for a distinctly different, harder-edged vibe, will be **The Crown Theater and Nightclub,** at the Rio, 3700 W. Flamingo Rd. (📞 **866/746-7671;** www.playrio.com). The space is being created by Darin Feinstein, owner of the legendary Viper Room on the Sunset Strip, and will feature indie rock and alternative bands in concert and then morph into a nightclub venue.

ultra-high-tech dance floor. LAX is open Friday through Monday 10pm until dawn. In Luxor Las Vegas, 3900 Las Vegas Blvd. S. 📞 **702/242-4529.** www.laxthenightclub.com. Cover varies.

Moon ★ This is another basic trendy nightclub—dance floor, smoke machines, house music—not nearly as inviting as Jet or Rain, its closest competitors, and certainly not a design stunner like Tao. You go one night, and it's raging; you go another night, and the DJ has misread the crowd and the dance floor is empty. Of course there is the retractable roof, which gives you a view of the club's namesake if the weather is cooperating. That's kind of cool. You can quickly take it in after a brief tour of the Playboy Club just above it, as one (pricey) admission gets you into both. Moon is open Thursday through Sunday and Tuesday at 11pm and closes at 4am. In the Palms Resort & Casino, 4321 W. Flamingo Rd. 📞 **702/942-6832.** Cover varies.

PURE ★★ The biggest club on the Strip, PURE is everything a big, loud nightclub ought to be. People line up hours before opening for the chance to share in the mayhem. (This is the place where Britney passed out on New Year's instead of completing her hostess duties, while Christina Aguilera held an after-show party here.) The theme is reflected in the decor—or lack of it, because just about everything is as white as Ivory Soap (get the name?). The noise and lack of cushy corners means this is a definite get-your-booty-in-motion kind of place, though there is ample space (seriously, there are airline hangars that are smaller) for just standing around watching other booties in motion. There is also a rooftop club, itself bigger than most regular Vegas clubs, with views of the Strip. PURE is open Thursday through Sunday and Tuesday 10pm to dawn. In Caesars Palace, 3570 Las Vegas Blvd. S. 📞 **702/731-7873.** Cover varies.

Rain Nightclub.

Rain Nightclub ★★ Despite considerable competition, this is still one of the hottest nightclubs in Vegas. Which means you probably will spend most of your time trying to convince someone, anyone, to let you in—you and a couple thousand 20-somethings who feel they will simply cease to exist if they don't get inside. We smirk and snicker at their desperation because it makes us feel superior. But we also have to be honest; if you can brave the wait, the crowds, and the attitude, you will be inside a club that has done everything right, from the multilevel layout that allows it to pack the crowds in and allows those crowds to peer up and down at their brethren, to DJs who play the right house and techno cuts (at a pulse-thumping tempo, so don't expect your good pickup lines to be heard), to the scaffolding that holds pyrotechnics and other mood-revvers, to the go-go girls dressed like strippers. If this is your choice, then note that people start lining up way before the opening time. Rain is open Friday and Saturday 10pm to 5am. In the Palms, 4321 W. Flamingo Rd. ✆ **702/942-6832.** Cover usually $25.

Studio 54 👋 The legendary Studio 54 has been resurrected here in Las Vegas, but with all the bad elements and none of the good ones. Forget Truman, Halston, and Liza doing illegal (or at least immoral) things in the bathroom stalls; that part of Studio 54 remains but a fond memory. The snooty, exclusive door attitude has been retained, however. Oddly, this doesn't lead to a high-class clientele; of all the new clubs, this is the trashiest (though apparently the hot night for locals is Tues). The large dance floor has a balcony overlooking it, the decor is industrial (exposed piping and the like), the music is hip-hop and electronic, and there is nothing to do other than dance. If the real Studio 54 were this boring, no one would remember it today. Studio 54 is open Tuesday through Saturday 10pm until dawn. In the MGM Grand, 3799 Las Vegas Blvd. S. ✆ **702/891-1111.** www.studio54lv.com. Cover usually $10–$20.

Tabú ★ This place is a little by the numbers for a nightclub, but less stripper saucy than the other new "ultralounges," and consequently more grown-up (though just as loud). With an interior of high-tech/industrial meets '80s bachelor's den, it's nothing aesthetically special, though there are some nice spots for canoodling. But do find a wall or the circular couch if you want to hear yourself think. Tabú is open Friday and Saturday from 10pm until 5am and Sunday and Monday from 10pm until 4am. At MGM Grand, 3799 Las Vegas Blvd. S. ✆ **702/891-7183.** www.tabulv.com. Cover usually $10–$20; ladies free.

Tao Nightclub ★ As of this writing, this is one of the hottest of the Vegas hotspots. Done as a Buddhist temple run amok, this multilevel club is drawing the party faithful and the celebrity entourages in droves, so expect long lines and high cover charges. Some may find the wall-to-wall crowds, flashing lights, pounding music, and general chaos overwhelming, but Tao is obviously doing something right. It's open Thursday and Friday from 10pm until dawn and Saturday from 9:30pm until dawn. In The Venetian, 3355 Las Vegas Blvd. S. ✆ **702/388-8588.** Cover varies.

Tryst ★ Wynn's first stab at a nightclub, La Bête, tanked, and mere months after it opened with the hotel in April 2005, he shut it down, brought in new management, revamped the place, and tried again. The result is much more subtle than the beast-themed original, although the dance floor opens up onto a 90-foot waterfall, so it's all relative. Expect a slightly more refined crowd than you usually find at such places, which may be a good or bad thing, depending on your viewpoint. Then again, this was briefly Britney and Paris's Vegas nightspot of choice, so "refined" is definitely open to interpretation. Tryst is open Thursday through Saturday 10pm to 4am. In Wynn Las Vegas, 3131 Las Vegas Blvd. S. ✆ **702/770-3375.** Cover varies.

Vanity ★★ The Hard Rock knows how to do nightclubs with the near-legendary Baby's and Body English once ruling the party scene in Vegas. Those clubs are gone now, replaced by this multilevel indoor/outdoor space, which includes lots of cozy banquettes (a few of which are even open to the general public, not just bottle service buyers), fireplaces, cabanas, and a slamming dance floor. Hanging above the latter is the club's centerpiece, a "chandelier" made up of more than 20,000 crystal LED lights, allowing shapes, patterns, and images to be broadcast above the booty-shaking crowd. It should come as no surprise that lines are long and attitude is high, so bring your A game. Vanity is open Thursday through Saturday 10pm to 4am. In the Hard Rock Hotel, 4455 Paradise Rd. ✆ **702/693-5555.** www.vanitylv.com. Cover varies.

VooDoo Lounge ★ Occupying, along with the VooDoo Cafe, two floors in the newer addition to the Rio, the VooDoo Lounge almost successfully combines Haitian voodoo and New Orleans Creole in its decor and theme. There are two main rooms: one with a large dance floor and stage for live music, and a disco room, which is filled with large video screens and serious light action. Big club chairs in groups form conversation pits, where you might actually be able to have a conversation. The big seller? The bartenders put on a show, à la Tom Cruise in *Cocktail.* They shake, jiggle, and light stuff on fire. Supposedly, the live music includes Cajun acts, but when it comes down to it, rock seems to rule the day. And if you don't suffer from paralyzing vertigo, be sure to check out the dramatic outdoor, multilevel patio, which offers some amazing views of the Strip. The mid- to

XS.

late-20s crowd is more heavily local than you might expect. It's open nightly 5pm to 3am. In the Rio All-Suite Hotel & Casino, 3700 Las Vegas Blvd. S. ☎ **702/252-7777.** Cover $10 and up.

XS ★★ If you've been to the other Wynn club, Tryst, you'll definitely recognize the relationship when you walk into sister property Encore's version. The aptly named XS has the same basic floor plan as Tryst only bigger and, well, more of just about everything. Done in an eye-catching gold, pink, and purple color scheme, the semicircular rings of booths and tables cascade down to a center dance floor that opens up onto a giant outdoor patio complete with its own pool, fireplaces, and lounge spaces. More grown-up than most Vegas nightclubs, XS offers the same kind of high-energy vibe with a bit more sophistication and lighting—you can actually see who you're bumping into as you try to navigate the crowds. XS is open Friday through Monday 10pm to 4am. In Encore Las Vegas, 3121 Las Vegas Blvd. S. ☎ **702/770-0097.** www.xslasvegas.com. Cover varies.

STRIP CLUBS

No, we don't mean entertainment establishments on Las Vegas Boulevard South. We mean the other kind of "strip." Yes, people come to town for the gambling and the wedding chapels, but the lure of Vegas doesn't stop there. Though prostitution is not legal within the city, the sex industry is an active and obvious force in town. Every other cab carries a placard for a strip club, and a walk down the Strip at night will have dozens of men thrusting fliers at you for clubs, escort services, phone-sex lines, and more. And some of you are going to want to check it out.

And why not? An essential part of the Vegas allure is decadence, and naked flesh would certainly qualify, as does the thrill of trying something new and daring. Of course, by and large, the nicer bars aren't particularly daring, and if you go to more than one in an evening, the thrill wears off, and the breasts don't look quite so bare.

In the finest of Vegas traditions, the "something for everyone" mentality extends to strip clubs. Here is a guide to the most prominent and heavily advertised; there are plenty more, of increasing seediness, out there. You don't have to look too hard. The most crowded and zoolike times are after midnight, especially on Friday and Saturday nights. Should you want a "meaningful" experience, you might wish to avoid the rush and choose an off-hour for a visit.

Cheetah's ★ This is the strip club used as the set in the movie *Showgirls,* but thanks to renovations by the club, only the main stage will look vaguely familiar to those looking for Nomi Malone. There's also a smaller stage, plus three tiny "tip stages" so that you can really get close to (and give much money to) the woman of your choice. Eight TVs line the walls; the club does a brisk business during major sporting events. The management believes, "if you treat people right, they will keep coming back," so the atmosphere is friendlier than at other clubs. They encourage couples to come here, though on a crowded Saturday night, some unescorted women were turned away, despite policy. Lap dances are $20. Cheetah's is open daily 24 hours. 2112 Western Ave. ✆ **702/384-0074.** Topless. Cover $30 8pm–5am.

Club Paradise ★ Until the new behemoths moved into town, this was the nicest of the strip clubs. Which isn't to say it isn't still nice; it's just got competition. The outside looks a lot like the Golden Nugget; the interior and atmosphere are rather like that of a hot nightclub where most of the women happen to be topless. The glitzy stage looks like something from a miniature showroom. The lights flash and the dance music pounds. There are two big video screens (one featuring soft porn, the other showing sports), and the chairs are plush and comfortable. The place is relatively bright by strip-club standards, and it offers champagne and cigars. Not too surprisingly, the crowd is very white collar here.

The women ("actual centerfolds") are heavy (and we do mean heavy) on the silicone. They don't so much dance as pose and prance, after which they don skimpy evening dresses and come down to solicit lap dances, which eventually fills the place up with writhing females in thongs. The club says it is "women friendly," and indeed there were a few couples, including one woman who was receiving a lap dance herself. Occasionally, the action stops for a mini-revue, which ends up being more like seminaked cheerleading than a show. Lap dances are $20. Club Paradise is open Monday through Friday 5pm to 8am and Saturday and Sunday 6pm to 8am. 4416 Paradise Rd. ✆ **702/734-7990.** Topless. Cover $30. Unescorted women allowed.

Déjà Vu Showgirls ★★ This place both deeply perturbs us and amuses the heck out of us. The latter because it's one of the rare strip clubs where the women actually perform numbers. Instead of just coming out and taking off an article or two of clothing and then parading around in a desultory manner before collecting a few tips and running off to solicit lap dances, each stripper comes out and does an actual routine—well, okay, maybe not so much, but she does remove her clothes to personally chosen music, shedding an outfit tailored to her music selection. And so it happened that we have now seen a punk-rock chick strip to "Anarchy in the UK" and a Ramones tune. But it also distresses us because it's the kind

For Men Only?

Many of the strip clubs will not allow women in unless they're escorted by a man—presumably to protect ogling husbands from suspicious wives. If you're looking for a ladies' night out and want to check out the topless action, be sure and call ahead to find out what each individual club allows.

of place where guys bring their buds the night before their wedding to make sure they get photographed with a naked girl (yes, the girls get totally naked here) performing something raunchy with a sex toy—that's the kind of fun that leaves a bad taste in the mouth. "Shower" and "couch" dances are $20, "theme" dances $30. **Déjà Vu** is open Monday through Saturday 11am to 6am and Sunday 6pm to 4am. 3247 Industrial Rd. © **702/894-4167.** Totally nude. No alcohol. Cover charge $15. Unescorted women allowed. Only ages 18 and over admitted.

Glitter Gulch ★ Right there in the middle of the Fremont Street Experience, Glitter Gulch is either an eyesore or the last bastion of Old Las Vegas, depending on your point of view. One of the most venerable strip clubs in town, it has undergone a $3.5-million renovation, which just shows you what kind of money there is in nearly nekkid girls. Gone are the old burlesque gaudy trappings and fixtures, and in their place is an interior that rivals some of the midlevel Strip ultralounges. It's still a little cramped and naturally dark. The location is the most convenient of all of the strip clubs—right on Fremont Street—but it's also the most conspicuous—given that you have to exit right on Fremont Street. Not so good for the bashful or discrete. Still, it means customers include groups of women and even a 90-year-old couple. Given its convenient location, this is the perfect place for the merely curious—you can easily pop in, check things out, goggle and ogle, and then hit the road. Table dances are $35. Glitter Gulch is open daily 1pm to 4am. 20 Fremont St. © **702/385-4774.** Topless. Cover $20 (includes 1 drink) after 8pm; 2-drink minimum (drinks $7 and up) before 8pm.

Olympic Gardens Topless Cabaret ★ Once the largest of the strip clubs, this almost feels like a family operation, thanks to the middle-age women often handling the door—maybe they're the reason for the equal-opportunity male strippers on most nights. It also has a boutique that sells lingerie and naughty outfits. (They get a lot of couples coming in, so perhaps this is in case someone gets inspired and wants to try out what they learned here at home.) There are two rooms: one with large padded tables for the women to dance on, the other featuring a more classic strip runway. The girls were all really cute—perhaps the best looking of the major clubs. The crowd is a mix of 20s to 30s geeks and blue-collar guys. As the place fills up and the chairs are crammed in next to each other, it's hard to see how enjoyable, or intimate, a lap dance can be when the guy next to you is getting one as well. That didn't seem to stop all the guys there, who seemed appropriately blissed out.

Oh, and by the way, there are also male strippers most nights of the week, so you ladies won't feel left out. Lap dances are $20, more in the VIP room. Olympic Gardens is open daily 24 hours. 1531 Las Vegas Blvd. S. © **702/385-8987.** Topless. Cover $30 after 6pm. Unescorted women allowed.

The Palomino ★ This one-time classically elegant nudie bar—you know, red flocked wallpaper and the like—became pretty rundown over the years, as places like that

Question Your Cabbie
If there's a particular strip club that you want to visit, don't let your cab driver talk you out of it. Clubs give cab drivers kickbacks for delivering customers. So be leery of drivers who suggest one club over another. They may be making $20 for delivering you there. And don't accept a higher cover charge than we've listed here; the clubs are trying to get you to cover the kickback they just gave the cabbie.

generally do. Even the offer of total nudity was not quite enough to lure visitors to this seedy part of town. The owners then came up with an ingenious make-over. In addition to updating the downstairs (gone, sadly, is the aforementioned vintage look in favor of a flashy runway, neon, flatscreen TVs, and other modern gizmos; it's new, but it's also generic), they had the inspiration to introduce male stripping—yes, still totally nude—upstairs on the weekends. This something-for-everyone equality approach results in a bustling crowd, packed with women, with an atmosphere that can be a little intense rather than bachelorette ribald. Expect a largely urban crowd and a lot of couples. And in case you were wondering, the guys do lap dances too. Topless lap dances are $20; totally nude dances are $40. The Palomino is open daily 4pm to 5am. 1848 Las Vegas Blvd. N. © **702/642-2984.** Totally nude. Cover $20.

Sapphire Gentleman's Club ★★★ Ladies and gentlemen (particularly the latter), Las Vegas, home of the largest everything else, now brings you—drum roll—the largest strip club *in the world!* That's right, 71,000 square feet of nakedity. Of course, you have to see it—and, of course, that's what they are counting on. But let's say this: While really it's nothing you haven't seen before strip-club-wise, if you haven't seen a strip club, this is the place to start because it's modern and clean, and, frankly, it's not all that different, looks-wise, from Rain, the superhot nightclub over at the Rio, except that here you can actually hear yourself think, and the girls sometimes wear more clothes than at Rain. It's also more friendly and less attitudinal.

Expect three stages in a bridge shape (including one where gawkers who paid for the privilege can watch the action from below, thanks to a glass floor), and a fourth in a separate—and still large—room, with several poles and strippers all working it at the same time. Giant video screens occasionally act as a JumboTron for the action on the other side of the cavernous room. Upstairs are incredibly posh and incredibly expensive rooms for wealthy sports and movie figures to utilize. Oh, and ladies are not only allowed to visit, but they'll also have their very own male strippers to leer at. Lap dances start at $20. Sapphire is open daily 24 hours. 3025 S. Industrial. © **702/796-6000.** Topless. Cover $30 6pm–6am. Unescorted women allowed.

Spearmint Rhino ★ Did you know that even strip bars come in chains? They do, and this is a familiar brand to those in the know, or to those who read bill-boards close to airports. The runway (where some of the dancers get a little personal with each other) is actually in a separate back area, so it is possible to have a drink at the front (where there are many TVs) and never see a naked girl (save for the smaller stage and pole nearby). On a busy night, it's crammed with grown-up frat boys enjoying a clubby space. There can be a veritable assembly line of lap dances during these busy periods, which frankly, seems the opposite of a turn-on to us. Unescorted women should also note that while normally they are permitted, lately it seems that they might be taken for hookers and turned away from the door (lest they come inside and lure customers away). Lap dances are $20. Spearmint Rhino is open daily 24 hours. 3344 S. Highland Dr. © **702/796-3600.** Topless. Cover $30. Unescorted women allowed.

Tommy Rocker's Mojave Beach Longtime bar owner and local musician Tommy Rocker decided to revamp his frat-boy fave and turn it into a strip club, gleefully saying his new place's motto is "Fun for the whole family, except for your wife and kids." A dark but warm den of a space, the club features the prerequisite poles (and the girls to swing on them) but also provides other distractions, including a full menu, video poker, and TVs showing various sporting events. Tommy, of course, still plays on Saturday nights. Lap dances are $30 and up. Tommy Rocker's is open 24 hours. 4275 Dean Martin Dr. ℂ **702/261-6688.** Topless. Cover $20; locals free.

Treasures.

Treasures ★★★ Right now, along with Sapphire, this is our favorite of the strip clubs, for several reasons. From the outside, this looks like one of the new fancy casino-hotels (if considerably smaller), but inside it's straight out of a Victorian sporting house (that's a brothel, by the way), down to replicas of 19th-century girlie pictures on the walls. On stage, the performers actually perform; anyone who has witnessed the desultory swaying of the hips and vacant stare of a bored stripper will appreciate not just the bump-and-grind (some of which gets on the raunchy side) dance routines but also the special effects, from hair-blowing fans to smoke machines to a neon pole. We are suckers for this combination of period-inspired style and contemporary approach to the business at hand. This is an excellent and comfortable venue for couples and first timers. **Note:** The entrance to the parking lot can be hard to spot after dark. Go down Highland and keep your eyes peeled. Lap dances are $30 and up. Treasures is open daily 4pm to 6am. 2801 Westwood Dr. ℂ **702/257-3030.** Topless. Cover $30. No unescorted women.

Velvet Lion ★★ Formerly Strip Tease Cabaret, and after that Eden, this club has been redone to eliminate the rather disturbing "fantasy rooms" (where lap dances could occur in private), replacing them with a generic "classy" gentlemen's-club look, all shiny runways and stages (three total, plus the "shower" stage, where periodically two girls will soap each other up). One of the bouncers was in the film *Ocean's Eleven* as a thug menacing George Clooney. With live DJs and girls far more interested in working the lap-dance angle than dancing, it's a fine, safe, first-time strip-bar experience, but not one to make you see what all the fuss is about. Lap dances are $20 and up. The Velvet Lion is open daily 1pm to 5am. 3750 S. Valley View Blvd. ℂ **702/253-1555.** Topless. Cover $30. Unescorted women allowed; couples encouraged.

11

SIDE TRIPS FROM LAS VEGAS

Though Vegas is designed to make you forget that there is an outside world, it might do you and your pocketbook some good to reacquaint yourself with the non-Vegas realm. Actually, if you're spending more than 3 days in Vegas, this may become a necessity; 2 days with kids, and it absolutely will.

Plus, there is such a startling contrast between the artificial wonders of Sin City and the natural wonders that, in some cases, lie just a few miles away. Few places are as developed and modern as Vegas; few places are as untouched as some of the canyons, desert, and mountains that surround it. The electrical and design marvel that is the Strip couldn't exist without the extraordinary structural feat that is Hoover Dam. Need some fresh air? There are plenty of opportunities for outdoor recreation, all in a landscape all the more jarring for the contrast it has with the city.

With the exception of the Grand Canyon, the excursions covered in this chapter will take you from 20 to 60 miles out of town. Every one of them offers a memorable travel experience.

HOOVER DAM, LAKE MEAD & LAKE LAS VEGAS

30 miles SE of Las Vegas

This is one of the most popular excursions from Las Vegas. Hoover Dam is visited by as many as 3,000 people daily. Why should you join them? Because Hoover Dam is an engineering and architectural marvel, and it changed the Southwest forever. Without it, you wouldn't even be going to Vegas. Kids may be bored, unless they like machinery or just plain big things, but expose them to it anyway, for their own good. Buy them ice cream and a Hoover Dam snow globe as a bribe. If you are staying at Lake Mead, it's a must.

The tour itself is a bit cursory, but you do get up close and personal with the dam. Wear comfortable shoes; the tour involves a bit of walking. Try to take the tour in the morning to beat the desert heat and the really big crowds. You can have lunch out in Boulder City and then drive back through the **Valley of Fire State Park** (a landscape of wind- and water-hewn formations of red sandstone; described later in this chapter), which is about 60 magnificently scenic miles from Lake Mead (purchase gas before you start!). Or you can spend the afternoon on Lake Mead–centered pursuits, such as hiking, boating, scuba diving (in season), or rafting down the Colorado River.

Getting There

Drive east on Flamingo Road or Tropicana Avenue to U.S. 515 South, which automatically turns into I-93 South and takes you right to the dam. This involves

PREVIOUS PAGE: **Hoover Dam.**

| 0 | | | | 20 mi |
| 0 | | 20 km | | |

NELLIS AFB

Arrow Canyon Wilderness

Moapa
Glendale

Desert National
Wildlife Range

MOAPA RIVER
INDIAN
RESERVATION

Logandale
Moapa Valley

Indian Springs

NELLIS AFB

Overton

Dry Lake

Valley of Fire
State Park **3**

Spring Mountains

National

Recreation

LAS VEGAS COLONY
INDIAN RESERVATION

Area

NELLIS AFB

Muddy Mountains Wilderness

Echo Wash

Mt. Charleston Wilderness

La Madre Mountain Wilderness

Red Rock Canyon

North Las Vegas

NELLIS AFB

Lake Mead

LAS VEGAS

Rainbow Mountain Wilderness

Nat'l.
Conservation Area

East Las Vegas

4

National

Recreation

Blue Diamond

HENDERSON

Hoover Dam

Mount Wilson Wilderness

Area

Arden

5

Sloan

Boulder City

North McCullough Wilderness

Goodsprings

CALIFORNIA

Jean

Eldorado Wilderness

Colorado River

ARIZONA

Nelson

South McCullough Wilderness

Ireteba Wilderness

Bonnie Springs Ranch	**1**
Hoover Dam	**5**
Lake Mead	**4**
Red Rock Canyon	**2**
Valley of Fire State Park	**3**

Wee Thump Joshua Tree Wilderness

Nipton

Searchlight

a dramatic drive as you go through Boulder City and come over a rise, and Lake Mead suddenly appears spread out before you. It's a beautiful sight. At about this point, the road narrows to two lanes, and traffic can slow considerably. On normal busy tourist days, this drive would take about an hour. But between construction and security measures that call for most trucks and many other vehicles to be stopped and searched during peak hours (particularly Sun and Mon of holiday weekends, when visitors are returning through Arizona), the drive takes longer than ever. Plan accordingly.

Go past the turnoff to Lake Mead. As you near the dam, you'll see a five-story parking structure tucked into the canyon wall on your left. Park here ($5 charge) and take the elevators or stairs to the walkway leading to the new visitor center.

If you would rather go on an **organized tour,** check out **Gray Line** (*①* **800/634-6579;** www.grayline.com), which offers a half-day tour of the dam for $60 or a day-long tour that includes a paddleboat cruise of Lake Mead and a tour of the Ethel M Chocolate factory for $92.

Hoover Dam ★★★

There would be no Las Vegas as we know it without Hoover Dam. Certainly, the neon and glitz that we know and love would not exist. In fact, the growth of the entire Southwest can be tied directly to the electricity created by the dam.

Until Hoover Dam was built, much of the southwestern United States was plagued by two natural problems: parched, sandy terrain that lacked irrigation for most of the year and extensive flooding in spring and early summer, when the mighty Colorado River, fed by melting snow from its source in the Rocky Mountains, overflowed its banks and destroyed crops, lives, and property. On the positive side, raging unchecked over eons, the river's turbulent, rushing waters carved the Grand Canyon.

In 1928, prodded by the seven states through which the river runs during the course of its 1,400-mile journey to the Gulf of California, Congress authorized construction of a dam at Boulder Canyon (later moved to Black Canyon). The Senate's declaration of intention states, "A mighty river, now a source of destruction, is to be curbed and put to work in the interests of society." Construction began in 1931. Because of its vast scope and the unprecedented problems posed in its realization, the project generated significant advances in many areas of machinery production, engineering, and construction. An army of more than 5,200 laborers was assembled, and work proceeded 24 hours a day. Completed in 1936,

Winged Figures of the Republic, Hoover Dam.

2 years ahead of schedule and $15 million under budget (it is, no doubt, a Wonder of the Modern Fiscal World), the dam stopped the annual floods and conserved water for irrigation, industry, and domestic uses. Equally important, it became one of the world's major electrical-generating plants, providing low-cost, pollution-free hydroelectric power to a score of surrounding communities. Hoover Dam's $165-million cost has been repaid with interest by the sale of inexpensive power to a number of California cities and the states of Arizona and Nevada. The dam is a government project that paid for itself—a feat almost as awe-inspiring as its engineering.

The dam itself is a massive curved wall, 660 feet thick at the bottom, tapering to 45 feet where a road crosses it at the top. It towers 726 feet above bedrock (about

Hoover Dam installations at Lake Mead.

the height of a 60-story skyscraper) and acts as a plug between the canyon walls to hold back up to 9.2 trillion gallons of water in Lake Mead, the reservoir created by its construction. Four concrete intake towers on the lake side drop the water down about 600 feet to drive turbines and create power, after which the water spills out into the river and continues south.

All the architecture is on a grand scale, and the design has beautiful Art Deco elements, unusual in an engineering project. Note, for instance, the monumental 30-foot bronze sculpture, *Winged Figures of the Republic,* flanking a 142-foot flagpole at the Nevada entrance. According to its creator, Oskar Hansen, the sculpture symbolizes "the immutable calm of intellectual resolution, and the enormous power of trained physical strength, equally enthroned in placid triumph of scientific achievement."

The dam has become a major sightseeing attraction, along with Lake Mead, America's largest artificial reservoir and a major Nevada recreation area.

Seven miles northwest of the dam on U.S. 93, you'll pass through **Boulder City,** which was built to house managerial and construction workers. Sweltering summer heat (many days it is 125°F/52°C) ruled out a campsite by the dam. The higher elevation of Boulder City offered lower temperatures. The city emerged within a single year, turning a desert wasteland into a community of 6,000. By 1934, it was Nevada's third-largest town.

TOURING THE DAM

The very nice **Hoover Dam Visitor Center,** a vast three-level circular concrete structure with a rooftop overlook, opened in 1995. You'll enter the Reception Lobby (bags have not been allowed inside since the September 11, 2001, terrorist attacks, but ask about current security measures, as they may have changed), where you can buy tour tickets; peruse informational exhibits, photographs, and memorabilia; and view three 12-minute video presentations about the importance of water to life, the events leading up to the construction of Hoover Dam, and the construction itself. Exhibits on the Plaza Level include interactive displays on the environment, habitation, the development of the Southwest, the people who built the dam, and related topics.

Yet another floor up, galleries on the Overlook Level demonstrate, via sculpted bronze panels, the benefits of Hoover Dam and Lake Mead to the states of Arizona, Nevada, and California. The Overlook Level additionally provides an unobstructed view of Lake Mead, the dam, the power plant, the Colorado River, and Black Canyon. There are multiple photo opportunities throughout this trip.

You can visit an exhibit center across the street where a 10-minute presentation in a small theater focuses on a topographical map of the 1,400-mile Colorado River. It also has a cafeteria. It costs $8 to visit just this portion, but for an extra $3 you can get the Powerplant tour as well (see below). The center closes at 6pm, and 5:15pm is the last admission time, though hours vary seasonally.

There are two tours available, the Powerplant Tour and the Hoover Dam Tour. The cost of the former is $11 for adults; $9 for seniors, children 4 to 16, and military personnel and their dependents; and free for children 3 and under and military in uniform. It is self-guided and takes about two hours if you really stop to look at and read everything (less if you're a skimmer). The more extensive Hoover Dam Tour includes the self-guided portion but adds an hour-long guided tour into the deeper recesses of the facility. It is $30 per person; no children under 8 years old are allowed. Tickets for the Hoover Dam Tour must be purchased at the Visitor Center, while admission to the Visitors Center and tickets for the Powerplant Tour are available online. Parking is $7 no matter which tour you take, and the lot takes cash only. There is no need to call ahead to reserve a place, but for more information, call © **866/730-9097** or 702/494-2517.

At this writing, because of post–September 11 security measures, tours of the dam are somewhat restricted. It's no longer the nifty, and lengthy, experience it once was because access is so limited. On the Powerplant Tour, visitors go to the center, see a movie, and walk on top of the dam. While both tours include a 530-foot descent via elevator into the dam to view the massive generators, the Powerplant Tour is a self-guided tour aided by the occasional information kiosk or guide/docent stationed at intervals along the way; the pricier Hoover Dam Tour offers the same attractions and viewing opportunities, but it is guided, lasts an hour, and is limited to 20 people. If you plan on taking that tour, be aware that it covers over a mile and a half of walking on concrete and gravel, with no handicapped access. The Hoover Dam Tour is offered every half-hour, with the last tour at 3:30pm, while the final Powerplant admission is at 5:15pm.

There is talk of more extensive tours becoming available in 2011 after the Highway 93 Hoover Dam Bypass project is complete. This will reroute all of the traffic that currently needs to pass over the dam to a bridge just south of it, which will not only make it easier from a traffic standpoint but also from a security one as well. Check the website or call to see if there are any changes in the tour offerings.

Some fun facts you might hear on the tour: It took 6½ years to fill the lake. Though 96 workers were killed during construction, contrary to popular myth, none were accidentally buried as the concrete was poured (it was poured only at a level of 8 in. at a time). Look for a monument outside dedicated to the workers who were killed—"they died to make the desert bloom"—along with a tombstone for their doggy mascot who was also killed, albeit after the dam was completed. Compare their wages of 50¢ an hour to those of their Depression-era peers, who made 5¢ to 30¢. For more information on the dam, and sometimes discount coupons, visit **www.usbr.gov/lc/hooverdam**.

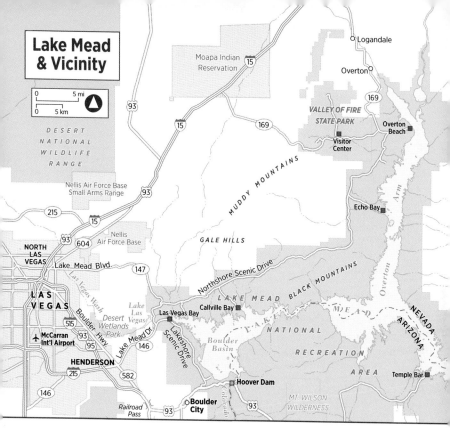

Lake Mead National Recreation Area ★★

Under the auspices of the National Park Service, 1.5-million-acre Lake Mead National Recreation Area was created in 1936 around Lake Mead (the reservoir lake that is the result of the construction of Hoover Dam) and later Lake Mohave to the south (formed by the construction of Davis Dam). Before the lakes emerged, this desert region was brutally hot, dry, and rugged—unfit for human habitation. Today, it's one of the nation's most popular playgrounds, attracting about 9 million visitors annually. The two lakes comprise 291 square miles. At an elevation of 1,221 feet, Lake Mead itself extends some 110 miles upstream toward the Grand Canyon. Its 550-mile shoreline, backed by spectacular cliff and canyon scenery, forms a perfect setting for a wide variety of watersports and desert hiking.

Having said all that, Lake Mead is in the beginning stages of a crisis so large that if unchecked, it would spell the end for Vegas entirely. The nation's largest reservoir has experienced a severe drop-off in levels since 2000, a combination of drought, global warming, and increased use. Whole portions of the lake's edges are now dry, in the process exposing the remains of some of the small towns that were flooded to build the thing in the first place. These have become tourist spots themselves. There is a 50% chance the lake will go dry by 2021 and because it supplies water to Las Vegas (not to mention hydroelectric power), that has grave implications for that city. Let's encourage those fancy new hotels to put in drought-tolerant plants instead of more grass. And don't ask for your towels to be changed every day.

Keep in mind that if the lake water shortage continues, many of the following activities will probably be affected in one way or another, if they aren't already.

The **Alan Bible Visitor Center,** also known as the Lake Mead Visitor Center, 4 miles northeast of Boulder City on U.S. 93, at NV 166 (© **702/293-8990**), can provide information on all area activities and services. You can pick up trail maps and brochures here, view informative films, and find out about scenic drives, accommodations, ranger-guided hikes, naturalist programs and lectures, bird-watching, canoeing, camping, lakeside RV parks, and picnic facilities. The center has some sweet exhibits about the area and is staffed by friendly folks full of local pride. It's open daily from 8:30am to 4:30pm except Thanksgiving, Christmas, and New Year's Day.

For information on camping, boat rentals, fishing, tours, and more, visit the National Parks Service website at **www.nps.gov/lame**.

The **entry fee** for the area is $5 per vehicle, which covers all passengers, or $3 per person if you're walking, motorcycling, or biking in.

Outdoor Activities

This is a lovely area for scenic drives amid the dramatic desert landscape. One popular route follows the Lakeshore and Northshore scenic drives along the edge of Lake Mead. From these roads, there are panoramic views of the blue lake, set against a backdrop of the browns, blacks, reds, and grays that make up the desert mountains. Northshore Scenic Drive also leads through areas of brilliant red boulders and rock formations, and you'll find a picnic area along the way.

Boating on Lake Mead.

BOATING & FISHING The **Las Vegas Boat Harbor** (© 702/293-1191; www. boatinglakemead.com) rents power boats, pontoon boats, personal watercraft, and water sports equipment. It also carries groceries, clothing, marine supplies, sporting goods, water-skiing gear, fishing equipment, and bait and tackle. Similar services are offered at the **Callville Bay Resort & Marina** (© 800/255-5561 or 702/565-8958; www.callvillebay.com), which is usually less crowded. Nonresidents can get a fishing license here ($69 for a year or $18 for 1 day plus $7 for each additional day; discounts for children 14 and under are available; additional fees apply for special fishing classifications, including trout, which require a $10 stamp for taking or possessing that fish). Largemouth bass, striped bass, channel catfish, crappie, and bluegill are found in Lake Mead; rainbow trout, largemouth bass, and striped bass in Lake Mohave. You can also arrange here to rent a fully equipped houseboat at **Echo Bay,** 40 miles north.

CAMPING Lake Mead's shoreline is dotted with campsites, all of them equipped with running water, picnic tables, and grills. Available on a first-come, first-served basis, they are administered by the **National Park Service** (© 702/293-8990; www.nps.gov/lame). There's a charge of $10 per night at each campsite.

CANOEING The **Alan Bible Visitor Center** (see above) can provide a list of outfitters that rent canoes for trips on the Colorado River. A canoeing permit ($10 per person) is required in advance for certain areas near the dam and is available from the **Bureau of Reclamation** (Attn.: Canoe Launch Permits), Box 60400, Boulder City, NV 89006-0400 (© 702/293-8204; www.usbr.gov/lc). You can apply for and receive the permit on the same day that you plan to canoe.

HIKING The best season for hiking is November through March (it's too hot the rest of the year). Some ranger-guided hikes are offered via the **Alan Bible Visitor Center** (see above), which also stocks detailed trail maps. Three trails, ranging in length from .75 mile to 6 miles, originate at the visitor center. The 6-mile trail goes past remains of the railroad built for the dam project. Be sure to take all necessary desert-hiking precautions. (See "Desert Hiking Advice" on p. 246.)

LAKE CRUISES A delightful way to enjoy Lake Mead is on a cruise aboard the **Lake Mead Cruises** boat *Desert Princess* ★ (© 702/293-6180; www. lakemeadcruises.com), a Mississippi-style paddle-wheeler. Cruises depart year-round. It's a relaxing, scenic trip (enjoyed from an open promenade deck or one of two fully enclosed, climate-controlled decks) through Black Canyon and past colorful rock formations known as the Arizona Paint Pots en route to Hoover Dam, which is lit at night. Options include narrated midday cruises ($24 adults, $12 children), brunch cruises ($39 adults, $18 children), and dinner cruises ($49 adults, $25 children). Dinner is served in a pleasant, windowed, air-conditioned dining room. There's a full onboard bar. Brunch and dinner cruises run April through October. Call for departure times.

SCUBA DIVING October through April, there's good visibility, lessened in summer months when algae flourishes. A list of good dive locations, authorized instructors, and nearby dive shops is available at the **Alan Bible Visitor Center** (see above). There's a designated underwater-diving area near Lake Mead Marina.

Boulder City

You might want to consider poking around Boulder City on your way back to Vegas. Literally the company town for those building Hoover Dam, it was created by the wives who came with their husbands and turned a temporary site into a real community, since aided by the recreational attractions and attendant businesses of Lake Mead. It doesn't look like much as you first approach it, but once you are in the heart, you'll discover that it's quite charming, an old-fashioned town all the more preserved and quiet due to its status as the only city in Nevada where gambling is illegal. It's worth getting out and taking a little stroll. There are some antiques and curio shops, and a number of burger and Mexican-food joints and family-style restaurants, including the **Coffee Cup Diner,** 512 Nevada Hwy. (✆ **702/294-0517;** www.worldfamouscoffeecup.com), which is right on the road to and from the dam. A '50s diner in looks and menu, it has the usual burgers, shakes, and fries, plus complete breakfasts, and is inexpensive, friendly, and a good place to take the kids. *Note:* The restaurant is only open for breakfast and lunch, from 6am until 2pm.

WHERE TO STAY

There are no hotels on Lake Mead proper anymore, so if you want to do an overnight visit that doesn't involve a tent, your closest options include the resorts at Lake Las Vegas (covered separately in this chapter) or nearby Boulder City. The latter offers several small no-frills motels, RV parks, and a couple of noteworthy

---

LEAVING (lake) LAS VEGAS

Originally created as a playground for the rich and famous (Céline Dion has a house here), Lake Las Vegas is a man-made reservoir created in a formerly dry, dusty valley about 20 miles east of the city on the way to Lake Mead. Surrounded by multimillion-dollar houses and rambling upscale condominium complexes, the bulk of the area is privately owned; but curving gracefully around the western lip of the lake is MonteLago Village, an homage to an Italian seaside community that featured accommodations, dining, shopping, entertainment, and recreation options for those with a taste (and a budget) for the finer things in life.

But the area has been hit hard by the global economic recession and many of the reasons to visit have vanished. The fantastic Ritz-Carlton hotel, the casino, and two of the three golf courses have all closed.

There are still several shops and restaurants at **MonteLago Village,** 75 Strada Nathan, Henderson (✆ **866/752-9558;** www.montelagovillage.com), and the **Loews Lake Las Vegas,** 101 MonteLago Blvd. (✆ **702/567-7000;** www.loewslakelasvegas.com) is still

up and running. The latter is a true resort facility that may look familiar if you remember the Julia Roberts/John Cusack movie *America's Sweethearts,* which was largely filmed here. The entire property has a subtle Moroccan design scheme that flows from the public areas to the more than 500 rooms. With a spa, several pools, restaurants, recreation programs, kids programs, and more, you won't be lacking in things to do here or in ways to be pampered.

accommodations, including the historic **Boulder Dam Hotel,** 1305 Arizona St. (𝄞 **702/293-3510;** www.boulderdamhotel.com), which was built in 1933 as a place for high-level government supervisors to stay during construction of the dam; and the **Best Western Lighthouse Inn and Resort,** 110 Ville Dr. (𝄞 **800/934-8282**), which offers a host of up-to-date amenities and some pretty good views of the lake.

For more information on Boulder City accommodations, call the **Las Vegas Convention and Visitors Authority** at 𝄞 **877/847-4858.**

VALLEY OF FIRE STATE PARK ★★

60 miles NE of Las Vegas

Most people visualize the desert as a vast expanse of undulating sands punctuated by the occasional cactus or palm-fringed oasis. But the desert of America's Southwest bears little relation to this Lawrence of Arabia image. Stretching for hundreds of miles around Las Vegas in every direction is a seemingly lifeless tundra of vivid reddish earth, shaped by time, climate, and subterranean upheavals into majestic canyons, cliffs, and ridges.

The 36,000-acre Valley of Fire State Park typifies the mountainous, red Mojave Desert. It derives its name from the brilliant sandstone formations that were created 150 million years ago by a great shifting of sand and that continue to be shaped by the geologic processes of wind and water erosion. These are rock formations like you'll never see anywhere else. There is nothing green, just fiery red rocks swirling unrelieved as far as the eye can see. No wonder various sci-fi movies have used this place as a stand-in for another planet—it has a most otherworldly look. The entire place is very mysterious, loaded with petroglyphs, and totally inhospitable. It's not hard to believe that for the Indians it was a sacred place, where men came as a test of their manhood. It is a natural wonder that must be seen to be appreciated.

Although it's hard to imagine in the sweltering Nevada heat, for billions of years, these rocks were under hundreds of feet of ocean. This ocean floor began to rise some 200 million years ago, and the waters became more and more shallow. Eventually, the sea made a complete retreat, leaving a muddy terrain traversed by ever-diminishing streams. A great sandy desert covered much of the southwestern part of the American continent until about 140 million years ago. Over eons, winds, massive fault action, and water erosion

One of the Seven Sisters rock formations at Valley of Fire State Park.

sculpted fantastic formations of sand and limestone. Oxidation of iron in the sands and mud—and the effect of groundwater leaching the oxidized iron—turned the rocks the many hues of red, pink, russet, lavender, and white that can be seen today. Logs of ancient forests washed down from faraway highlands and became petrified fossils, which can be seen along two interpretive trails.

Human beings occupied the region as far back as 4,000 years ago. They didn't live in the Valley of Fire, but during the Gypsum period (2000 B.C.–300 B.C.), men hunted bighorn sheep (a source of food, clothing, blankets, and hut coverings) here with notched sticks called *atlatls* that are depicted in the park's petroglyphs. Women and children caught rabbits, tortoises, and other small game. In the next phase, from 300 B.C. to A.D. 700, the climate became warmer and drier. Bows and arrows replaced *atlatls,* and the hunters and gatherers discovered farming. The ancestral Puebloan people began cultivating corn, squash, and beans, and communities began replacing small nomadic family groups. These ancient people wove watertight baskets, mats, hunting nets, and clothing. Around A.D. 300, they learned how to make sun-dried ceramic pottery. Other tribes, notably the Paiute, migrated to the area. By A.D. 1150, they had become the dominant group. Unlike the ancestral Puebloans, they were still nomadic and used the Valley of Fire region seasonally. These were the inhabitants whom white settlers found when they entered the area in the early to mid-1800s. The newcomers diverted river and spring waters to irrigate their farmlands, destroying the nature-based Paiute way of life. About 300 descendants of those Paiute tribespeople still live on the Moapa Indian Reservation (about 20 miles northwest) that was established along the Muddy River in 1872.

Getting There

From Las Vegas, take I-15 north to exit 75 (Valley of Fire turnoff). However, the more scenic route is I-15 north to Lake Mead Boulevard east to Northshore Road (NV 167) and then proceed north to the Valley of Fire exit. The first route takes about an hour, the second 1½ hours.

There is a $5-per-vehicle admission charge to the park, regardless of how many people you cram inside.

Plan on spending a minimum of an hour in the park, though you can spend a great deal more time. It can get very hot in there (there is nothing to relieve the sun beating down on and reflecting off of all that red), and there is no water, so be certain to bring a liter, maybe two, per person in the summer. Without a guide, you must stay on paved roads, but don't worry if they end; you can always turn around and go back to the main road. You can see a great deal from the car, and there are also hiking trails.

Numerous **sightseeing tours** go to the Valley of Fire; inquire at your hotel tour desk. Char Cruze of **Creative Adventures** (p. 242) also offers a fantastic tour.

The Valley of Fire can also be visited in conjunction with Lake Mead. Take NV 166 (Lakeshore Rd.) north, make a right turn on NV 167 (Northshore Rd.), turn left on NV 169 (Moapa Valley Blvd.) West—a spectacularly scenic drive—and follow the signs. Valley of Fire is about 65 miles from Hoover Dam.

Lost City Museum.

What to See & Do

There are no food concessions or gas stations in the park; however, you can obtain meals or gas on NV 167 or in nearby **Overton** (15 miles northwest on NV 169). Overton is a fertile valley town replete with trees, agricultural crops, horses, and herds of cattle—quite a change in scenery. On your way in or out of the teeming metropolis, do stop off at **Inside Scoop ★**, 395 S. Moapa Valley Blvd. (② 702/397-2055), open Monday through Saturday from 10am to 8pm and Sunday from 11am to 7pm. It's a sweet, old-fashioned ice-cream parlor run by extremely friendly people, with a proper menu that, in addition to classic sandwiches and the like, features some surprising options—a vegetarian sandwich and a fish salad with crab and shrimp, for example. Everything is quite tasty and fresh. Inside Scoop also does box lunches, perfect for picnicking inside the park.

At the southern edge of town is the **Lost City Museum ★**, 721 S. Moapa Valley Blvd. (② 702/397-2193), a sweet little museum, very nicely done, commemorating an ancient ancestral Puebloan village that was discovered in the region in 1924. Artifacts dating back 12,000 years are on display, as are clay jars, dried corn and beans, arrowheads, seashell necklaces, and willow baskets from the ancient Pueblo culture that inhabited this region between A.D. 300 and 1150. Other exhibits document the Mormon farmers who settled the valley in the 1860s. A large collection of local rocks—petrified wood, fern fossils, iron pyrite, green copper, and red iron oxide, along with manganese blown bottles turned purple by the ultraviolet rays of the sun—are also displayed here. The museum is surrounded by reconstructed wattle-and-daub pueblos. Admission is $5 for adults, free for children 17 and under. It's open Thursday through Sunday 8:30am to 4:30pm, but closed Thanksgiving, December 25, and January 1.

Information headquarters for Valley of Fire is the **Visitor Center** on NV 169, 6 miles west of Northshore Road (② 702/397-2088). It's open daily 8:30am to 4:30pm and is worth a quick stop for information and a bit of history before entering the park. Exhibits on the premises explain the origin and geologic history of the park's colorful sandstone formations, describe the ancient peoples who carved their rock art on canyon walls, and identify the plants and wildlife you're likely to see. Postcards, books, slides, and films are for sale here, and you

A hiker in Valley of Fire State Park.

can pick up hiking maps and brochures. Rangers can answer your park-related questions. For online information about the park, which is open sunrise to sunset, go to **www.parks.nv.gov/vf.htm.**

There are **hiking trails, shaded picnic sites,** and **two campgrounds** in the park. Most sites are equipped with tables, grills, water, and restrooms. A $20-per-vehicle, per-night camping fee is charged for use of the campground (plus $10 for utility hook-ups); if you're not camping, it costs $10 per vehicle to enter the park.

Some of the notable formations in the park have been named for the shapes they vaguely resemble—a duck, an elephant, seven sisters, domes, beehives, and so on. Mouse's Tank is a natural basin that collects rainwater, so named for a fugitive Paiute called Mouse, who hid there in the late 1890s. **Native American petroglyphs** etched into the rock walls and boulders—some dating from 3,000 years ago—can be observed on self-guided trails. Petroglyphs at Atlatl Rock and Petroglyph Canyon are both easily accessible. In summer, when temperatures are usually over 100°F (38°C), you may have to settle for driving through the park in an air-conditioned car.

RED ROCK CANYON ★★★

19 miles W of Las Vegas

If you need a break from the casinos of Vegas, Red Rock Canyon is balm for your overstimulated soul. Less than 20 miles away—but a world apart—this is a magnificent unspoiled vista that should cleanse and refresh you (and if you must, a morning visit should leave you enough time for an afternoon's gambling). You can drive the panoramic 13-mile **Scenic Drive** (daily 6am–dusk) or explore more in-depth on foot, making it perfect for athletes and armchair types alike. There are many interesting sights and trail heads along the drive itself. The **National Conservation Area** (www.nv.blm.gov/redrockcanyon) offers hiking trails and internationally acclaimed rock-climbing opportunities. Especially notable is 7,068-foot Mount Wilson, the highest sandstone peak among the bluffs; for information on climbing, contact the **Red Rock Canyon Visitor Center** at *©* **702/515-5350.** There are picnic areas along the drive and in nearby **Spring Mountain Ranch State Park** (www.parks.nv.gov/smr.htm), 5 miles south, which also offers plays in an outdoor theater during the summer. Because Bonnie Springs Ranch (see below) is just a few miles away, it makes a great base for exploring Red Rock Canyon. The entrance fee is $9 per vehicle.

Getting There

Just drive west on Charleston Boulevard, which becomes NV 159. As soon as you leave the city, the red rocks will begin to loom around you. The visitor center will appear on your right, though the sign is not the best, so keep a sharp eye out.

You can also go on an **organized tour. Gray Line** (*©* **800/634-6579;** www.grayline.com), among other companies, runs bus tours to Red Rock Canyon. Inquire at your hotel tour desk.

Finally, you can go **by bike.** Not very far out of town (at Rainbow Blvd.), Charleston Boulevard is flanked by a bike path that continues for about 11 miles to the visitor center/scenic drive. The path is hilly but not difficult, if you're in reasonable shape. However, exploring Red Rock Canyon by bike should be attempted only by exceptionally fit and experienced bikers.

Just off NV 159, you'll see the turnoff for the **Red Rock Canyon Visitor Center** (*©* **702/515-5350;** www.nv.blm.gov/redrockcanyon), which marks the actual entrance to the park. Redesigned and revamped in 2010, the center now

features outdoor exhibits on the flora and fauna found in the canyon. There, you can also pick up information on trails and the driving route. The center is open daily from 8am to 4:30pm.

About Red Rock Canyon

The geological history of these ancient stones goes back some 600 million years. Over eons, the forces of nature have formed Red Rock's sandstone monoliths into arches, natural bridges, and massive sculptures painted in a stunning palette of gray-white limestone and dolomite, black mineral deposits, and oxidized minerals in earth-toned sienna hues ranging from pink to crimson and burgundy. Orange and green lichens add further contrast, as do spring-fed areas of lush foliage. And formations, such as **Calico Hill,** are brilliantly white where groundwater has leached out oxidized iron. Cliffs cut by deep canyons tower 2,000 feet above the valley floor.

Calico Basino, Red Rock Canyon.

During most of its history, Red Rock Canyon was below a warm, shallow sea. Massive fault action and volcanic eruptions caused this seabed to begin rising some 225 million years ago. As the waters receded, sea creatures died, and the calcium in their bodies combined with sea minerals to form limestone cliffs studded with ancient fossils. Some 45 million years later, the region was buried beneath thousands of feet of windblown sand. As time progressed, iron oxide and calcium carbonate infiltrated the sand, consolidating it into cross-bedded rock.

Shallow streams began carving the Red Rock landscape, and logs that washed down from ancient highland forests fossilized, their molecules gradually replaced by quartz and other minerals. These petrified stone logs, which the Paiute Indians believed were weapons of the wolf god Shinarav, can be viewed in the **Chinle Formation** at the base of the Red Rock Cliffs. About 100 million years ago, massive fault action began dramatically shifting the rock landscape here, forming spectacular limestone and sandstone cliffs and rugged canyons punctuated by waterfalls, shallow streams, and serene oasis pools. Especially notable is the **Keystone Thrust Fault,** dating back about 65 million years, when two of the earth's crustal plates collided, forcing older limestone and dolomite plates from the ancient seas over younger red and white sandstones. Over the years, water and wind have been ever-creative sculptors, continuing to redefine this strikingly beautiful landscape.

Red Rock's valley is home to more than 45 species of mammals, about 100 species of birds, 30 reptiles and amphibians, and an abundance of plant life. Ascending the slopes from the valley, you'll see cactus and creosote bushes, aromatic purple sage, yellow-flowering blackbrush, yucca and Joshua trees, and, at higher elevations, clusters of forest-green pinyon, juniper, and ponderosa pines. In spring, the desert blooms with extraordinary wildflowers.

Archaeological studies of Red Rock have turned up pottery fragments, stone tools, pictographs (rock drawings), and petroglyphs (rock etchings), along with other ancient artifacts. They show that humans have been in this region since about 3000 B.C. (some experts say as early as 10,000 B.C.). You can still see remains of early inhabitants on hiking expeditions in the park. As for habitation of Red Rock, the same ancient Puebloan-to-Paiute-to-white-settlers progression that occurred in the Valley of Fire (see above) occurred here.

In the latter part of the 19th century, Red Rock was a mining site and later a sandstone quarry that provided materials for many buildings in Los Angeles, San Francisco, and early Las Vegas. By the end of World War II, as Las Vegas developed, many people became aware of the importance of preserving the canyon. In 1967, the secretary of the interior designated 62,000 acres as Red Rock Canyon Recreation Lands, under the auspices of the Bureau of Land Management, and later legislation banned all development except hiking trails and limited recreational facilities. In 1990, Red Rock Canyon became a National Conservation Area, further elevating its protected status. Its current acreage is 197,000.

What to See & Do

Begin with a stop at the **Visitor Center;** while there is a $9 per-vehicle fee for entering the park, you also can pick up a variety of helpful literature: history, guides, hiking trail maps, and lists of local flora and fauna. You can also view exhibits that tell the history of the canyon and depict its plant and animal life. You'll see a fascinating video here about Nevada's thousands of wild horses and burros, protected by an act of Congress since 1971. Call ahead to find out about ranger-guided tours as well as informative guided hikes offered by such groups as the Sierra Club and the Audubon Society. And if you're traveling with children, ask about the free *Junior Ranger Discovery Book,* filled with fun family activities. Books and videotapes are for sale here, including a guidebook that identifies more than 100 top-rated climbing sites.

The easiest thing to do is to **drive the 13-mile scenic loop** ★★★ (or you can bike it, if you wish). It really is a loop, and it only goes one way, so once you start, you are committed to driving the entire thing. You can stop the car to admire a number of fabulous views and sights along the way, or have a picnic, or take a walk or hike. As you drive, observe how dramatically the milky-white limestone alternates with iron-rich red rocks. Farther along, the mountains become solid limestone, with canyons running between them, which lead to an evergreen forest—a surprising sight in the desert.

Biking the scenic loop at Red Rock Canyon.

If you're up to it, however, we can't stress enough that the way to really see the canyon is by **hiking.** Every trail is incredible—glance over your options and decide what you might be looking for. You can begin from the Visitor Center or drive into the loop, park your car, and start from points therein. Hiking trails range from a .7-mile-loop stroll to a waterfall (its flow varying seasonally) at Lost Creek to much longer and more strenuous treks. Actually, all the hikes involve a certain amount of effort, as you have to scramble over rocks on even the shortest hikes. Unfit or undexterous people should beware. Be sure to wear good shoes, as the rocks can be slippery. You must have a map; you won't get lost forever (there usually are other hikers around to help you out, eventually), but you can still get lost. Once deep into the rocks, everything looks the same, even with the map, so give yourself extra time for each hike (at least an additional hour), regardless of its billed length.

A popular 2-mile round-trip hike leads to **Pine Creek Canyon** and the creekside ruins of a historic home site surrounded by ponderosa pine trees. Our hiking trail of choice is the **Calico Basin,** which is accessed along the loop. After an hour walk up the rocks (which is not that well marked), you end up at an oasis surrounded by sheer walls of limestone (which makes the oasis itself inaccessible, alas). In the summer, flowers and deciduous trees grow out of the walls.

As you hike, keep your eyes peeled for lizards, the occasional desert tortoise, herds of bighorn sheep, birds, and other critters. But the rocks themselves are the most fun, with small caves to explore and rock formations to climb on. On trails along Calico Hills and the escarpment, look for "Indian marbles," a local name for small, rounded sandstone rocks that have eroded off larger sandstone formations. Petroglyphs are also tucked away in various locales.

Biking is a tremendous way to travel the loop. There are also terrific off-road mountain-biking trails, with levels from amateur to expert.

The gleaming luxury **Red Rock Resort,** 10973 W. Charleston Rd. (© **866/767-7773;** www.redrocklasvegas.com), gives day-trippers a new, highly desirable refueling point on a trip to the canyon. It's a gorgeous facility and a good place for celebrity spotting. There's a casino, if you are getting the jitters, and a set of movie theaters if you realize it's really, really hot and you don't want to take a hike after all but are too ashamed to come back without having done *something*. Best of all, the food court contains a **Capriotti's,** the economical submarine sandwich shop (p. 185). The subs are ideal for takeout for picnics in the park (buy a cheap Styrofoam ice chest at a convenience store) or for in-room dining as you rest up in your hotel posthike.

BONNIE SPRINGS RANCH/OLD NEVADA ★★

About 24 miles W of Las Vegas, 5 miles past Red Rock Canyon

Bonnie Springs Ranch/Old Nevada is a kind of Wild West theme park with accommodations and a restaurant. If you're traveling with kids, a day trip to Bonnie Springs is recommended, but it is appealing for adults, too. It could even be a romantic getaway, as it offers horseback riding, gorgeous mountain vistas, proximity to Red Rock Canyon, and temperatures 5° to 10° cooler than on the Strip.

For additional information, you can call **Bonnie Springs Ranch/Old Nevada** at © **702/875-4191,** or visit them on the Web at **www.bonniesprings. com**.

If you're **driving,** a trip to Bonnie Springs Ranch can be combined easily with a day trip to Red Rock Canyon; it is about 5 miles farther. But you can also stay overnight.

Jeep tours to and from Las Vegas are available through **Action Tours.** Call © **888/288-5200** or 702/566-7400 or visit www.actiontours.com for details.

What to See & Do in Old Nevada

Old Nevada ★★ (© **702/875-4191;** www.bonniesprings.com) is a re-creation of an 1880s frontier town, built on the site of a very old ranch. As tourist sights go, this is a classic one, if a bit worn around the edges; it's a bit cheesy, but knowingly, perhaps even deliberately, so. It's terrific for kids up to about the age of 12 or so (before teenage cynicism kicks in) but not all that bad for adults fondly remembering similar places from their own childhoods. Many go expecting a tourist trap, only to come away saying that it really was rather cute and charming. Still others find it old in the bad way.

Old Nevada looks authentic, with rustic buildings made entirely of weathered wood. And the setting, right in front of beautiful mountains with layered red rock, couldn't be more perfect for a Western. You can wander the town (it's only about a block long), taking peeps into places of business, such as a blacksmith shop, a working mill, a saloon, and an old-fashioned general store (cum gift shop)

FROM TOP: **Old Nevada; Bonnie Springs is full of hokey but fun tourist options.**

and museum that has a potpourri of items from the Old West and Old Las Vegas: antique gaming tables and slot machines, typewriters, and a great display of old shoes, including lace-up boots. There is also a rather lame wax museum; the less said about it, the better.

Country music is played in the saloon during the day, except when **stage melodramas** take place (at frequent intervals 11:30am–5pm). These are entirely tongue-in-cheek— the actors are goofy and know it, and the plot is hokey and fully intended to be that way. Somehow, it just heightens the fun factor. It's interactive with the audience, which, in response to cue cards held up by the players, boos and hisses the mustache-twirling villain, sobs in sympathy with the distressed heroine, and laughs, cheers, and applauds. Kids love it, though younger ones might be scared by the occasional gunshot.

Following each melodrama, a **Western drama** is presented outside the saloon, involving a bank robbery, a shootout, and the trial of the bad guy. A judge, a prosecuting attorney, and a defense attorney are chosen from the audience, and the remainder acts as the jury. The action always culminates in a hanging. None of this is particularly polished act, but the dialogue is quite funny, and the entire thing is performed with enthusiasm and affection.

Throughout the area, cowboys continually interact with visiting kids, who, on the weekends, are given badges so that they can join a posse hunting for bad guys. There are also **stunt shootouts** (maybe not at the level found at, say, Universal Studios) in this wild frontier town, and some rather unsavory characters occasionally languish in the town jail.

In the **Old Nevada Photograph Shoppe** you can have a tintype picture taken in 1890s Wild West costume (there is a fairly large selection) with a

120-year-old camera. There are replicas of a turn-of-the-20th-century church and stamp mill; the latter, which has original 1902 machinery, was used to extract gold and silver. You can tour the remains of the **old Comstock lode silver mine,** though there isn't much to see there. There is also a nicely maintained **chapel** that would be a hoot to get married in. You can also shop for a variety of "Western" souvenirs (though to us, that's when the tourist-trap part kicks in). Eateries in Old Nevada are discussed below. There's plenty of parking; on weekends and holidays, a free shuttle train takes visitors from the parking lot to the entrance.

Admission is $20 per car (for up to six people), or $3 per person for those who arrive by bus. From November through April, Old Nevada is open Wednesday through Friday from 11am until 5pm and Saturday and Sunday from 10:30am until 5pm (closed Mon–Tues). The rest of the year it is open from 10:30am until 6pm Wednesday through Sunday.

What to See & Do at Bonnie Springs Ranch

There are several things to do here free of charge, and it's right next door to Old Nevada. It's quite a pretty place, in a funky, ramshackle kind of way, and in season, there are tons of flowers everywhere, including honeysuckle and roses. The main attraction is the small **zoo** ★ on the premises. Now, when we say "zoo," unfortunately we mean that in addition to a petting zoo with the usual suspects (deer, sheep, goats, and rabbits) and some unusual animals (potbelly pigs and snooty llamas) to caress and feed, there is also a mazelike enclosure with wire-mesh pens that contain a variety of livestock, some of which should not be penned up (though they are well taken care of), including wolves and bobcats. Still, it's more than diverting for kids.

Less politically and ecologically distressing is the aviary, which houses peacocks, Polish chickens, peachface and blackmask lovebirds, finches, parakeets,

Trail ride at Bonnie Springs ranch.

ravens, ducks, pheasants, and geese. Keep your eyes peeled for the peacocks roaming free; with luck, they will spread their tails for a photo op. With greater luck, some of the angelic, rare white peacocks will do the same. It may be worth dropping by just in the hopes of spotting one in full fan-tailed glory.

Riding stables offer guided hour-long trail rides into the mountain area on a continuous basis throughout the day (spring–fall 10:30am–5pm, summer until 6pm). Children must be at least 6 years old to participate. Cost is $55 per person. There are also breakfast, lunch, and dinner rides, which cost from $120 to $140 per person. For more information, call ✆ **702/875-4191.**

Where to Stay & Dine

In Old Nevada, the **Miner's Restaurant** is a snack bar that looks great thanks to Western-motif accessories. Inexpensive fare is served (sandwiches, decent burgers, pizza, and hot dogs), along with fresh-baked desserts. There are tables out on the porch. In summer, you can also get beer and soft drinks in a similarly old-fashioned **Beer Parlor.**

Bonnie Springs Motel ★ This is a funky, friendly little place in the middle of nowhere—except that nowhere is a gorgeous setting. The motel is in two two-story buildings and offers regular rooms, "Western" rooms, specialty theme rooms, and kitchen suites.

Each theme is expressed mostly through the use of fabrics, personally decorated by the owner, who did a pretty nice job. The "gay 1890s" room is done in black and pink, with a lace canopy over the bed, an old-fashioned commode, and liberal use of velvet. The American Indian room uses skins and feathers and has a bearskin-covered burl-wood chair. The "Western" rooms have more burl-wood furniture and electric-log fireplaces that blow heat into the rooms.

All special theme rooms (also known as fantasy suites) have mirrors over the beds and big whirlpool tubs in the middle of the rooms (not in the bathrooms), and come with bottles of champagne (the empties of which you can see littering the road on your way out). All the rooms are quite large and have private balconies or patios, and mountain views. There are also large family suites with fully equipped kitchens, bedrooms, living rooms (with convertible sofas), and dressing areas; these are equipped with two phones and two TVs, and are available for long-term rentals (many of the people who work at Old Nevada rent these as apartments). There is even a tiny train that takes you around the grounds and on a short tour of the desert.

The **Bonnie Springs Ranch Restaurant** has a lot of character and is a perfect family place. It's heavily rustic, with stone floors, log beams, chairs made from tree branches, a roaring fire in winter, and plenty of dead animals adorning the walls. The food is basic—steak, ribs, chicken, burgers, and potato skins; pancakes and eggs for breakfast; it's all greasy but good. There is a cozy bar attached to the restaurant, its walls covered with thousands of dollar bills with messages on them—a classic neighborhood bar, if it were actually in a neighborhood.

1 Gunfighter Lane, Old Nevada, NV 89004. ✆ **702/875-4400.** Fax 702/875-4424. www. bonniesprings.com/motel.html. 50 units. Sun–Thurs $85–$95 double, $125 family suite, $150 fantasy suite; Fri–Sat and holidays $100–$110 double, $140 family suite, $165 fantasy suite; weekly rates available. Family suite rates based on 4 people. Extra person $5. Refundable deposit of $50–$100 required. AE, MC, V. Amenities: Restaurant; pool; smoke-free rooms. *In room:* A/C, TV, dial-up Internet.

THE GRAND CANYON

About 270 miles E of Las Vegas

The geographically challenged among us believe that the Grand Canyon is just a hop, skip, and a jump from Las Vegas and therefore a great idea for a side trip while visiting Sin City. While this may be true from a strictly comparative basis—the canyon is closer to Vegas than it is to, say, London—it is not exactly what you might call "close." The South Rim is about 270 miles from Las Vegas via two- and four-lane highways. This equates to a solid 5-hour drive on a good day and an hour or two more than that during peak traffic times. In other words, if you want to take a quick day trip to the Grand Canyon from Las Vegas, you better accept the fact that it's going to be a very long day and you won't have much time at the park. An overnight visit or taking advantage of an air tour is probably a better bet.

But if you have the time and the energy, visiting the Grand Canyon is a breathtaking experience. There's a reason why it is considered one of the seven natural wonders of the world.

Open year-round, the South Rim is the most popular area of the park and the one that you should visit if you have never been, as it offers the most options in terms of lodging, tours, activities, restaurants, and more. Keep in mind, however, that there are other areas of the park worth visiting. For more information on the North Rim and other Grand Canyon National Park destinations, visit **www.frommers.com**.

Getting There

If you're taking your own car, head east on Flamingo Road or Tropicana Boulevard to I-515 South. This becomes NV 93, which crosses over Hoover Dam into Arizona and will lead to I-40 at Kingman. Take the interstate east to NV 64 at Williams, Arizona, and follow the signs north. Drivers should be advised that much of the route to the Grand Canyon from Las Vegas is along narrow, twisty roads that can be a challenge and are often jammed with traffic.

Lipan Point, the Grand Canyon's South Rim.

FAST FACTS

[FastFACTS] LAS VEGAS

Area Codes The local area code is 702.

Business Hours Casinos and most bars are open 24 hours a day; nightclubs are usually open only late at night into the early morning hours, and restaurant and attraction hours vary.

Cellphones (Mobile Phones) See "Staying Connected," p. 54.

Drinking Laws The legal age for purchase and consumption of alcoholic beverages is 21; proof of age is required and often requested at bars, nightclubs, and restaurants, so it's always a good idea to bring ID when you go out.

Beer, wine, and liquor are sold in all kinds of stores pretty much around the clock in Vegas; trust us, you won't have a hard time finding a drink in this town.

Do not carry open containers of alcohol in your car or any public area that isn't zoned for alcohol consumption, which includes the Strip and the Fremont Street Experience downtown. The police can fine you on the spot. And nothing will ruin your trip faster than getting a citation for DUI (driving under the influence), so don't even think about driving while intoxicated.

Driving Rules See "Getting There & Getting Around," p. 40.

Electricity Like Canada, the United States uses 110 to 120 volts AC (60 cycles), compared to 220 to 240 volts AC (50 cycles) in most of Europe, Australia, and New Zealand. Downward converters that change 220–240 volts to 110–120 volts are difficult to find in the United States, so bring one with you.

Embassies & Consulates All embassies are in the nation's capital, Washington, D.C. Some consulates are in major U.S. cities, and most nations have a mission to the United Nations in New York City. If your country isn't listed below, call for directory information in Washington, D.C. (☎ **202/555-1212**) or check **www.embassy.org/embassies**.

The embassy of **Australia** is at 1601 Massachusetts Ave. NW, Washington, DC 20036 (☎ **202/797-3000;** http://australia.visahq.com). Consulates are in New York, Honolulu, Houston, Los Angeles, and San Francisco.

The embassy of **Canada** is at 501 Pennsylvania Ave. NW, Washington, DC 20001 (☏ **202/682-1740;** www.canadainternational.gc.ca/washington). Other Canadian consulates are in Buffalo (New York), Detroit, Los Angeles, New York, and Seattle.

The embassy of **Ireland** is at 2234 Massachusetts Ave. NW, Washington, DC 20008 (☏ **202/462-3939;** www.embassyofireland.org). Irish consulates are in Boston, Chicago, New York, San Francisco, and other cities. See the website for a complete listing.

The embassy of **New Zealand** is at 37 Observatory Circle NW, Washington, DC 20008 (☏ **202/328-4800;** www.nzembassy.com). New Zealand consulates are in Los Angeles, Salt Lake City, San Francisco, and Seattle.

The embassy of the **United Kingdom** is at 3100 Massachusetts Ave. NW, Washington, DC 20008 (☏ **202/588-6500;** http://ukinusa.fco.gov.uk). Other British consulates are in Atlanta, Boston, Chicago, Cleveland, Houston, Los Angeles, New York, San Francisco, and Seattle.

Emergencies   Dial ☏ **911** to contact the police or fire department, or to call an ambulance.

Gasoline (Petrol)   At press time, in the U.S., the cost of gasoline (also known as gas, but never petrol), is around $3 per gallon and tends to vary unpredictably. Taxes are already included in the printed price. One U.S. gallon equals 3.8 liters or .85 imperial gallons. Fill-up locations are known as gas or service stations. Las Vegas prices typically fall near the nationwide average. You can also check **www.vegasgasprices. com** for recent costs.

Holidays   Banks, government offices, post offices, and many stores, restaurants, and museums are closed on the following legal national holidays: January 1 (New Year's Day), the third Monday in January (Martin Luther King Day), the third Monday in February (Presidents' Day), the last Monday in May (Memorial Day), July 4 (Independence Day), the first Monday in September (Labor Day), the second Monday in October (Columbus Day), November 11 (Veterans Day/Armistice Day), the fourth Thursday in November (Thanksgiving Day), and December 25 (Christmas). The Tuesday after the first Monday in November is Election Day, a federal government holiday in presidential-election years (held every 4 years, and next in 2012).

For more information on holidays see "Las Vegas Calendar of Events," in chapter 3.

Hospitals   Emergency services are available 24 hours a day at **University Medical Center,** 1800 W. Charleston Blvd., at Shadow Lane (☏ **702/383-2000;** www. umc-cares.org); the emergency-room entrance is on the corner of Hastings and Rose streets. **Sunrise Hospital and Medical Center,** 3186 Maryland Pkwy., between Desert Inn Road and Sahara Avenue (☏ **702/731-8080;** www.sunrisehospital.com), also has a 24-hour emergency room.

For more minor problems, try the **Harmon Medical Urgent Care Center,** the closest urgent care center to the Strip, with doctors and X-ray machines; it's located at 105 E. Harmon at Koval, near the MGM Grand (☏ **702/796-1116;** www.harmonmedicalcenter. com). It's open 24 hours, and there is a pharmacy on-site.

Hotels usually have lists of doctors, should you need one. In addition, doctors are listed in the Yellow Pages. For physician referrals, call the **Desert Springs Hospital** (☏ **702/388-4888;** www.desertspringshospital.net). Hours are Monday to Friday from 8am to 8pm and Saturday from 9am to 3pm.

Insurance   Traveler's insurance is not required for visiting Las Vegas and whether or not it's right for you depends on your circumstances. For example, most Las Vegas travel arrangements that include hotels are refundable or cancelable up to the last moment, so insurance is probably not necessary. If, however, you have prepaid a non-refundable package, then it could be worth considering insurance. For information on traveler's insurance, trip cancellation insurance, and medical insurance while traveling, please visit www.frommers.com/tips.

Internet Access See "Staying Connected," p. 54.

Legal Aid If you are "pulled over" for a minor infraction (such as speeding), never attempt to pay the fine directly to a police officer; this could be construed as attempted bribery, a much more serious crime. Pay fines by mail, or directly into the hands of the clerk of the court. If accused of a more serious offense, say and do nothing before consulting a lawyer. Here the burden is on the state to prove a person's guilt beyond a reasonable doubt, and everyone has the right to remain silent, whether he or she is suspected of a crime or actually arrested. Once arrested, a person can make one telephone call to a party of his or her choice. An international visitor should call his or her embassy or consulate.

Mail As of press time, domestic postage rates are 28¢ for a postcard and 44¢ for a letter. For international mail, a first-class letter of up to 1 ounce costs 98¢ (75¢ to Canada and 79¢ to Mexico); a first-class postcard costs the same as a letter. For more information go to **www.usps.com**.

If you aren't sure what your address will be in the United States, mail can be sent to you, in your name, c/o General Delivery at the main post office in Las Vegas, which is located Downtown at 200 S. Main St., near the Fremont Street casinos and hotels. (Call ✆ **800/275-8777** for information on the nearest post office for other locations.) The addressee must pick up mail in person and must produce proof of identity (such as a driver's license or passport). The main Las Vegas post office is open Monday through Friday from 8:30am until 5pm.

Always include a zip code when mailing items in the U.S. If you don't know a zip code, visit www.usps.com/zip4.

The most convenient post office to the Strip is immediately behind Circus Circus at 3100 S. Industrial Rd., between Sahara and Spring Mountain Road (✆ **800/275-8777**). It's open Monday through Friday from 8:30am to 5pm. You can also mail letters and packages at your hotel, and there's a drop-off box in The Forum Shops at Caesars Palace.

Newspapers & Magazines See "Staying Connected," p. 55.

Passports See "Embassies & Consulates," above, for whom to contact if you lose your passport while traveling in the U.S. For other information, contact the following agencies:

For Residents of Australia Contact the Australian Passport Information Service at ✆ 131-232, or visit www.passports.gov.au.

For Residents of Canada Contact the central **Passport Office,** Department of Foreign Affairs and International Trade, Ottawa, ON K1A 0G3 (✆ **800/567-6868;** www.ppt.gc.ca).

For Residents of Ireland Contact the **Passport Office,** Setanta Centre, Molesworth Street, Dublin 2 (✆ **01/671-1633;** www.foreignaffairs.gov.ie).

For Residents of New Zealand Contact the **Passports Office,** Department of Internal Affairs, 47 Boulcott St., Wellington, 6011 (✆ **0800/225-050** in New Zealand or 04/474-8100; www.passports.govt.nz).

For Residents of the United Kingdom Visit your nearest passport office, major post office, or travel agency in the U.K. or contact the **Identity and Passport Service (IPS),** 89 Eccleston Square, London, SW1V 1PN (✆ **0300/222-0000;** www.ips.gov.uk).

For Residents of the United States To find your regional passport office, check the U.S. State Department website (www.travel.state.gov/passport) or call the **National Passport Information Center** (📞 877/487-2778) for automated information.

Police For nonemergencies, call 📞 **702/795-3111.** For emergencies, call 📞 **911.**

Smoking Vegas is decidedly no longer a smoker's haven. Increasingly strict smoking laws prohibit puffing virtually everywhere indoors except in designated hotel rooms, bars that don't serve food, and on the casino floor itself. Because it's frequently hard to tell where a casino ends and basic public area begins, don't fret too much about stepping across some invisible line. Hotels still dedicate floors for smokers and non-smokers. There is a significant charge, approximately $300, for smoking *anything* in a nonsmoking room.

Taxes The United States has no value-added tax (VAT) or other indirect tax at the national level. Every state, county, and city may levy its own local tax on all purchases, including hotel and restaurant checks and airline tickets. These taxes will not appear on price tags.

The sales tax in Las Vegas is 8.1% and is added to food and drink bills. Hotel rooms on the Strip come with a 12% tax while those in the Downtown area carry 13%. Taxes are also added to show tickets.

Telephones See "Staying Connected," p. 56.

Time The continental United States is divided into **four time zones:** Eastern Standard Time (EST), Central Standard Time (CST), Mountain Standard Time (MST), and Pacific Standard Time (PST). Alaska and Hawaii have their own zones. Las Vegas is in the Pacific Time zone, 8 hours behind Greenwich Mean Time (GMT), 3 hours behind the East Coast and 2 behind the Midwest. For example, when it's 9am in Las Vegas (PST), it's 7am in Honolulu (Hawaii Standard Time), 10am in Denver (MST), 11am in Chicago (CST), noon in New York City (EST), 5pm in London (GMT), and 2am the next day in Sydney.

Daylight saving time (summer time) is in effect from 1am on the second Sunday in March to 1am on the first Sunday in November, except in Arizona, Hawaii, the U.S. Virgin Islands, and Puerto Rico. Daylight saving time moves the clock 1 hour ahead of standard time.

Tipping In hotels, tip **bellhops** at least $1 per bag ($2–$3 if you have a lot of luggage) and tip the **chamber staff** $3 to $5 per day (more if you've left a big mess for him or her to clean up). Tip the **doorman** or **concierge** only if he or she has provided you with some specific service (for example obtaining difficult-to-get theater tickets). Tip the **valet-parking attendant** $2 to $3 every time you get your car.

In restaurants, bars, and nightclubs, tip **service staff** and **bartenders** 15% to 20% of the check and tip **checkroom attendants** $1 per garment. In the casinos, tip **cocktail waitresses** $1 per drink and tipping **dealers** 5% of any big wins is nice but not mandatory.

As for other service personnel, tip **cab drivers** 15% of the fare; tip **skycaps** at airports at least $1 per bag ($2–$3 if you have a lot of luggage); and tip **hairdressers** and **barbers** 15% to 20%.

Toilets You won't find public toilets or "restrooms" on the streets in most U.S. cities but they can be found in hotel lobbies, bars, restaurants, museums, department stores, railway and bus stations, and service stations. In Las Vegas, you are almost always near a bathroom as long as you are in one of the tourist areas, with the casinos being the most obvious example. All have multiple facilities and they are usually among the cleanest you'll find in any public location. One small annoyance is that many hotel restaurants do not have their own restrooms, meaning you may need to go into the casino to find the nearest one.

Visas For information about U.S. visas go to **www.travel.state.gov** and click on "Visas." Or go to one of the following websites:

Australian citizens can obtain up-to-date visa information from the **U.S. Embassy Canberra,** Moonah Place, Yarralumla, ACT 2600 (✆ **02/6214-5600**) or by checking the U.S. Diplomatic Mission's website at **http://canberra.usembassy.gov/visas.html**.

British subjects can obtain up-to-date visa information by calling the **U.S. Embassy Visa Information Line** (✆ **0891/200-290**) or by visiting the "Visas to the U.S." section of the American Embassy London's website at **www.usembassy.org.uk**.

Irish citizens can obtain up-to-date visa information through the **U.S. Embassy Dublin,** 42 Elgin Rd., Ballsbridge, Dublin 4 (✆ **353/1-668-8777; http://dublin.usembassy.gov**.

Citizens of **New Zealand** can obtain up-to-date visa information by contacting the **U.S. Embassy New Zealand,** 29 Fitzherbert Terrace, Thorndon, Wellington (✆ **644/472-2068; http://newzealand.usembassy.gov**).

Visitor Information The **Las Vegas Convention and Visitors Authority** (✆ **877/847-4858** or 702/892-7575; www.visitlasvegas.com) provides information, hotel reservation assistance, show guides, convention calendars, and more.

Wi-Fi See "Staying Connected," p. 54.

AIRLINE WEBSITES

MAJOR AIRLINES

Aeroméxico
www.aeromexico.com

Air Canada
www.aircanada.ca

Alaska Airlines/Horizon Air
www.alaskaair.com

American Airlines
www.aa.com

Aviacsa (Mexico & Southern U.S.)
www.aviacsa.com.mx

British Airways
www.british-airways.com

Continental Airlines
www.continental.com

Delta Air Lines
www.delta.com

Frontier Airlines
www.frontierairlines.com

Hawaiian Airlines
www.hawaiianair.com

JetBlue Airways
www.jetblue.com

Korean Air
www.koreanair.com

Midwest Airlines
www.midwestairlines.com

Philippine Airlines
www.philippineairlines.com

United Airlines
www.united.com

US Airways
www.usairways.com

Virgin America
www.virginamerica.com

Virgin Atlantic Airways
www.virgin-atlantic.com

BUDGET AIRLINES

AirTran Airways
www.airtran.com

Allegiant Air
www.allegiantair.com

Frontier Airlines
www.frontierairlines.com

JetBlue Airways
www.jetblue.com

Southwest Airlines
www.southwest.com

Spirit Airlines
www.spiritair.com

Sun Country Airlines
www.suncountry.com

WestJet
www.westjet.com

INDEX

PHOTO CREDITS

p. i: © Richard Cummins/SuperStock; p. iii: © Eric Parsons; p. 1: © Eric Parsons; p. 2: © Eric Parsons; p. 5: © Eric Parsons; p. 6: © Eric Parsons; p. 7: © James Glover II; p. 8: © Eric Parsons; p. 9: © Eric Parsons; p. 10: © Eric Parsons; p. 11: © Eric Parsons; p. 12: © Eric Parsons; p. 13: © Eric Parsons; p. 14: © Eric Parsons; p. 15: © Eric Parsons; p. 16: © Sean DuFrene; p. 17: Courtesy Pure Nightclub; p. 18: © Sean DuFrene; p. 19: © Michael Ochs Archives/Getty Images; p. 20: © Bettmann/Corbis; p. 21: © Photri/SuperStock ; p. 22: © Bob Willoughby/Getty Images; p. 23: © American Stock Archive/Getty Images; p. 24: © Eric Parsons; p. 25: © Eric Parsons; p. 26: © Eric Parsons; p. 27: © James Glover II; p. 28: © Eric Parsons; p. 30: © Warner Bros/Photofest; p. 32: © Eric Parsons; p. 57: © James Glover II; p. 59: © James Glover II; p. 61: © James Glover II; p. 64: © Eric Parsons; p. 65: Courtesy of Caesars Palace; p. 67: Courtesy of Bali Hai Golf Course; p. 68: © Eric Parsons; p. 69, left: © Eric Parsons; p. 69, right: © Eric Parsons; p. 70: © Eric Parsons; p. 71: © James Glover II; p. 73: Courtesy of the Venetian Hotel; p. 82: Courtesy of Four Seasons; p. 84: Courtesy of City Center Las Vegas; p. 85: Courtesy of City Center Las Vegas; p. 87: © Sean DuFrene; p. 89: © Eric Parsons; p. 90: © Eric Parsons; p. 92: © Sean DuFrene; p. 93: © Eric Parsons; p. 95: © Eric Parsons; p. 96: Courtesy of City Center Las Vegas; p. 97: © Eric Parsons; p. 98: © Eric Parsons; p. 99: © Darren Carroll/Sports Illustrated/Getty Images; p. 102: © Eric Parsons; p. 103: Courtesy MGM Resorts; p. 104, left: © Eric Parsons; p. 104, right: © Eric Parsons; p. 106: Courtesy of Palazzo Las Vegas; p. 107: © Eric Parsons; p. 109, left: © Naomi Kraus; p. 109, right: © Eric Parsons; p. 110: © James Glover II; p. 112, left: © Eric Parsons; p. 112, right: © Sean DuFrene; p. 115: Courtesy Planet Hollywood Resort & Casino; p. 116: © Eric Parsons; p. 117: © Eric Parsons; p. 119, left: © Eric Parsons; p. 119, right: © James Glover II; p. 122: © Naomi Kraus; p. 123: © Eric Parsons; p. 125: © Eric Parsons; p. 126: © Sean DuFrene; p. 127: © James Glover II; p. 128: © James Glover II; p. 130: © James Glover II; p. 134: © Sean DuFrene; p. 137: © Eric Parsons; p. 139: © Eric Parsons; p. 140, left: © James Glover II; p. 140, right: © Eric Parsons; p. 143: © Eric Parsons; p. 144: © Demetrio Carrasco/Rough Guides/Newscom; p. 145: © Eric Parsons; p. 146: © Sean DuFrene; p. 147: © Eric Parsons; p. 148: © Sean DuFrene; p. 195: © James Glover II; p. 208: © Eric Parsons; p. 210, top: © Naomi Kraus; p. 210, bottom: © James Glover II; p. 213: © Eric Parsons; p. 214, left: © Eric Parsons; p. 214, right: © Eric Parsons; p. 215, left: © Sean DuFrene; p. 215, right: © Sean DuFrene; p. 216, top: © Sean DuFrene; p. 216, bottom: © Naomi Kraus; p. 217: © Eric Parsons; p. 218, left: © Richard Cummins/Lonely Planet Images; p. 218, right: © James Glover II; p. 219, left: © Sean DuFrene; p. 219, right: © Sean DuFrene; p. 220: © Sean DuFrene; p. 221: © Sean DuFrene; p. 222, top: © Eric Parsons; p. 222, bottom: © Eric Parsons; p. 223: © Eric Parsons; p. 224: © Sean DuFrene; p. 225: © Sean DuFrene; p. 226, top: © James Glover II; p. 226, bottom: © James Glover II; p. 227: © James Glover II; p. 228, left: © James Glover II; p. 228, right: © Sean DuFrene; p. 229: © Paul Cichocki/FremontStock; p. 233, top: © James Glover II; p. 233, bottom: © Eric Parsons; p. 234: © Eric Parsons; p. 235: © Eric Parsons; p. 237, left: © Zuma/Newscom; p. 237, right: © Sean DuFrene; p. 239: © James Glover II; p. 240: © Sean DuFrene; p. 241: © Sean DuFrene; p. 242: © Sean DuFrene; p. 245: © Eric Parsons; p. 247, left: © Eric Parsons; p. 247, right: © Sean DuFrene; p. 248: © Ethan Miller/Getty Images; p. 249: © Sean DuFrene; p. 253: © Sean DuFrene; p. 264: © Gerhard Zwerger-Schoner/Imagebroker/Alamy; p. 269: © Sean DuFrene; p. 271: © Sean DuFrene; p. 273: © Sean DuFrene; p. 274: © James Glover II; p. 276: © Roger Williams/UPI Photos/Newscom; p. 280: © James Glover II; p. 281: © Sean DuFrene; p. 283, top: © James Glover II; p. 283, bottom: © Eric Parsons; p. 284: © Eric Parsons; p. 286: © James Glover II; p. 287: © Eric Parsons; p. 289: © James Glover II; p. 291: © Eric Parsons; p. 292: © Eric Parsons; p. 293: © Eric Parsons; p. 294: © Sean DuFrene; p. 295: © James Glover II; p. 297: Courtesy of Cirque Du Soleil, photo by Richard Termine; p. 303, top: Courtesy of Kirvin Doak Communications, photo by Denise Truscello; p. 303, bottom: Courtesy of BMP, photo by Ken Howard; p. 306: Courtesy of Cirque Du Soleil, photo by Julie Aucoin; p. 310: © Sean DuFrene; p. 311: © Sean DuFrene; p. 312: © Sean DuFrene; p. 313: © Sean DuFrene; p. 321: © Sean DuFrene; p. 322: © Eric Parsons; p. 323: © Sean DuFrene; p. 324: © Sean DuFrene; p. 326: © Sean DuFrene; p. 327: © Eric Parsons; p. 329: © Sean DuFrene; p. 330: © Sean DuFrene; p. 332: © Sean DuFrene; p. 334: Courtesy of XS the Nightclub at Encore, photo by Barbara Kraft; p. 338: © Sean DuFrene; p. 339: © Scott Warren/Aurora Photos/Alamy; p. 342: © Eric Parsons; p. 343: © Eric Parsons; p. 346: © Eric Parsons; p. 349: © James Glover II; p. 351: © James Glover II; p. 352: © James Glover II; p. 353: © Eric Parsons; p. 355: © Eric Parsons; p. 357, top: © Eric Parsons; p. 357, bottom: © Eric Parsons; p. 358: © Eric Parsons; p. 360: © Josh Biggs